COVID-19

This comprehensive book looks at COVID-19, along with other recent infectious disease outbreaks, with the broad aim of providing constructive lessons and critical reflections from across a wide range of perspectives and disciplinary interests within the risk analysis field.

The chapters in this edited volume probe the roles of risk communication, risk perception, and risk science in helping to manage the ever-growing pandemic that was declared a public health emergency of international concern in the beginning of 2020. A few chapters in the book also include relevant content discussing past disease outbreaks, such as Zika, Ebola, and MERS-CoV. This book distils past and present knowledge, appraises current responses, introduces new ideas and data, and offers key recommendations, which will help illuminate different aspects of the global health crisis. It also explores how different constructive insights offered from a 'risk perspective' might inform decisions on how best to proceed in response as the pandemic continues.

The chapters in this book were originally published as a special issue of the *Journal of Risk Research*.

Jamie K. Wardman is Assistant Professor of Risk Management at Nottingham University Business School, UK. His research is primarily focussed on the sociology of risk and the theory and practice of risk communication as this relates to such issues as organisational operations, science and technology controversies, emergency preparedness, crisis response, public policy, and health and safety. He is particularly interested in how sociocultural perspectives on risk and its representation can help inform risk management policy design, operations, and evaluation.

Ragnar E. Löfstedt is Professor of Risk Management and the Director of King's Centre for Risk Management, UK, where he teaches and conducts research on risk communication and management. Ragnar has conducted research in risk communication and management in such areas as renewable energy policy, transboundary environmental issues (acid rain and nuclear power), health and safety, telecommunications, biosafety, pharmaceuticals, and the siting of the building of incinerators, fuel policy, nuclear waste installations, and railways.

COVID-19

Confronting a New World Risk

Edited by
Jamie K. Wardman and Ragnar E. Löfstedt

Routledge
Taylor & Francis Group

LONDON AND NEW YORK

First published 2023
by Routledge
4 Park Square, Milton Park, Abingdon, Oxon OX14 4RN

and by Routledge
605 Third Avenue, New York, NY 10158

Routledge is an imprint of the Taylor & Francis Group, an informa business

Introduction, Chapters 1, 3–13, 15, 16, and 18–25 © 2023 Taylor & Francis
Chapter 2 © 2020 Terje Aven and Frederic Bouder. Originally published as Open Access.
Chapter 14 © 2020 Sarah Dryhurst, Claudia R. Schneider, John Kerr, Alexandra L. J. Freeman,
Gabriel Recchia, Anne Marthe van der Bles, David Spiegelhalter and Sander van der Linden.
Originally published as Open Access.
Chapter 17 © 2020 Katarina Giritli Nygrena and Anna Olofsson. Originally published as Open
Access.

British Library Cataloguing in Publication Data
A catalogue record for this book is available from the British Library

ISBN13: 978-1-032-32674-0 (hbk)
ISBN13: 978-1-032-32676-4 (pbk)
ISBN13: 978-1-003-31616-9 (ebk)

DOI: 10.4324/9781003316169

Typeset in Myriad Pro
by Newgen Publishing UK

Publisher's Note
The publisher accepts responsibility for any inconsistencies that may have arisen during the
conversion of this book from journal articles to book chapters, namely the inclusion of journal
terminology.

Disclaimer
Every effort has been made to contact copyright holders for their permission to reprint
material in this book. The publishers would be grateful to hear from any copyright holder
who is not here acknowledged and will undertake to rectify any errors or omissions in future
editions of this book.

Contents

Citation Information

The chapters in this book were originally published in the *Journal of Risk Research*, volume 23, issue 7–8 (2020). When citing this material, please use the original page numbering for each article, as follows:

For any permission-related enquiries please visit:
www.tandfonline.com/page/help/permissions

Notes on Contributors

The following affiliations are from the time the journal articles were originally published:

David Abramson, Program on Population Impact Recovery and Resilience, New York University College of Global Public Health, New York, NY, USA.

Jisoo Ahn, Health and New Media Research Institute, Hallym University, Chuncheon, KR, South Korea.

S. Ashby, Vlerick Business School, Brussel, Belgium.

Terje Aven, University of Stavanger, Stavanger, Norway.

Dominic H. P. Balog-Way, Department of Communication, Cornell University, Ithaca, NY, USA.

Becca Beets, Department of Life Sciences Communication, University of Wisconsin-Madison, Madison, WI, USA.

Fabiola Bertolotti, Department of Sciences and Methods for Engineering, University of Modena and Reggio Emilia, Reggio Emilia, Italy.

Otto Bodi-Fernandez, Institute for Sociology, University of Graz, Graz, Austria.

Gisela Böhm, Department of Psychosocial Science, University of Bergen, Bergen, Norway.

Ann Bostrom, Daniel J. Evans School of Public Policy & Governance, University of Washington, Seattle, Washington, USA.

Frederic Bouder, University of Stavanger, Stavanger, Norway.

Dominique Brossard, Life Sciences Communication, University of Wisconsin Madison, Madison, WI, USA.

C. Bryce, Cass Business School, City, University of London, London, UK.

M. Selim Cakir, Rights Lab and Business School, University of Nottingham, Nottingham, UK.

Doo-Hun Choi, Department of Media and Communication, Sejong University, Gwangjin-gu, Seoul, South Korea.

Aengus Collins, EPFL International Risk Governance Center (IRGC), Lausanne, Switzerland.

Wolfgang Dorl, Freelancer, Jena, Germany.

Sarah Dryhurst, Winton Centre for Risk and Evidence Communication, University of Cambridge, Cambridge, UK.

Norman E. Fenton, School of Electronic Engineering and Computer Science, Queen Mary University of London, London, UK.

Marie-Valentine Florin, EPFL International Risk Governance Center (IRGC), Lausanne, Switzerland.

Alexandra L. J. Freeman, Winton Centre for Risk and Evidence Communication, University of Cambridge, Cambridge, UK.

Isabelle Freiling, Department of Communication, University of Vienna, Vienna, Austria.

King-wa Fu, Journalism and Media Studies Centre, The University of Hong Kong, Hong Kong.

Stefan Gold, Faculty of Economics and Management, University of Kassel, Kassel, Germany.

Pradipta Halder, Business School, University of Eastern Finland, Joensuu, Finland.

Daniel Hanss, Department of Social Sciences, Hochschule Darmstadt – University of Applied Sciences, Darmstadt, Germany.

Olivia Jensen, Institute for the Public Understanding of Risk, National University of Singapore, Singapore.

Lee Ann Kahlor, Stan Richards School of Advertising and Public Relations, The University of Texas at Austin, Austin, TX, USA.

John Kerr, Winton Centre for Risk and Evidence Communication, University of Cambridge, Cambridge, UK.

Yushim Kim, School of Public Affairs, Arizona State University, Phoenix, AZ, USA.

Nicole M. Krause, Department of Life Sciences Communication, University of Wisconsin-Madison, Madison, WI, USA.

Minyoung Ku, Department of Public Management, John Jay College, CUNY, New York, NY, USA.

Todd Landman, School of Politics and International Relations, University of Nottingham, Nottingham, UK.

Ragnar E. Löfstedt, King's Centre for Risk Management, King's College London, UK.

Katherine A. McComas, Department of Communication, Cornell University, Ithaca, NY, USA.

Scott McLachlan, School of Electronic Engineering and Computer Science, Queen Mary University of London, London, UK.

Martin Neil, School of Electronic Engineering and Computer Science, Queen Mary University of London, London, UK.

Ghee-Young Noh, School of Media, Hallym University, Chuncheon, KR, South Korea.

Katarina Giritli Nygren, Forum for Gender Studies, Mid Sweden University, Sundsvall, Sweden.

Robert E. O'Connor, Division of Social and Economic Sciences, National Science Foundation, Arlington, VA, USA.

Seong Soo Oh, Department of Public Administration, Hanyang University, Seongdong-gu, South Korea.

Anna Olofsson, Risk & Crisis Research Centre, Mid Sweden University, €Ostersund, Sweden.

Magda Osman, School of Biological and Chemical Sciences, Queen Mary University of London, London, UK.

Rachael Piltch-Loeb, Emergency Preparedness Research Evaluation & Practice Program, Division of Policy Translation and Leadership Development, Harvard T.H. Chan School of Public Health, Boston, MA, USA.

Gabriel Recchia, Winton Centre for Risk and Evidence Communication, University of Cambridge, Cambridge, UK.

Ortwin Renn, Institute for Advanced Sustainability Studies (IASS), Potsdam, Germany.

P. Ring, Caledonian Business School, Glasgow Caledonian University, Glasgow, UK.

Maria Laura Ruiu, Social Sciences, Northumbria University, Newcastle upon Tyne, UK.

Martin C. Schleper, Department of Management, University of Sussex Business School, Brighton, UK.

Claudia R. Schneider, Winton Centre for Risk and Evidence Communication, University of Cambridge, Cambridge, UK.

Arkadiusz Sieroń, Faculty of Law, Administration and Economics, Uniwersytet Wroclawski, Wroclaw, Poland.

David Spiegelhalter, Winton Centre for Risk and Evidence Communication, University of Cambridge, Cambridge, UK.

Luca Di Gennaro Splendore, Institute for Tourism Studies, Ħal Luqa, Malta.

Esi E. Thompson, The Media School, Franklin Hall, Indiana University, Bloomington, IN, USA.

Alexander Trautrims, Rights Lab and Business School, University of Nottingham, Nottingham, UK.

Paula Ungureanu, Department of Sciences and Methods for Engineering, University of Modena and Reggio Emilia, Reggio Emilia, Italy.

Anne Marthe van der Bles, Department of Psychology, University of Groningen, Groningen, Netherlands.

Sander van der Linden, Winton Centre for Risk and Evidence Communication, University of Cambridge, Cambridge, UK.

Jamie K. Wardman, Nottingham University Business School, University of Nottingham, UK.

Peter M. Wiedemann, Social Sciences, University of Wollongong, Wollongong, Australia.

Catherine Mei Ling Wong, Institute for the Public Understanding of Risk, National University of Singapore, Singapore.

Woohyun Yoo, Department of Mass Communication & Institute of Social Sciences, Incheon National University, Incheon, South Korea.

Yuner Zhu, Journalism and Media Studies Centre, The University of Hong Kong, Hong Kong.

Jens O. Zinn, School of Social and Political Sciences, University of Melbourne, Melbourne, Australia.

Introduction – COVID-19: confronting a new world risk

Jamie K. Wardman and Ragnar E. Löfstedt

On 30th January 2020, the Director-General of the World Health Organisation (WHO) announced a public health emergency of international concern (PHEIC) regarding the outbreak of the novel coronavirus SARS-CoV-2 and resulting disease that soon became widely known as 'COVID-19'. The sounding of this 'highest level of alarm' followed from the emergence of COVID-19 in the city of Wuhan, in Hubei Province, China, along with being identified in 18 other countries. At that point, there was early evidence of human-to-human transmission in at least four other countries, but outside China there had been no known deaths and only 98 confirmed cases. Within a matter of weeks, however, total infections increased to more than 100,000, and on 11th March 2020 COVID-19 was declared a 'pandemic emergency' following the 'alarming levels of spread and severity' associated with this new global disease (WHO 2020a). Confirmed cases of COVID-19 subsequently passed 1 million by the first week of April, a more than tenfold increase in the space of less than a month (WHO 2020b). At the time of writing, estimates indicate that the total number of recorded COVID-19 infections is fast approaching 42 million, with the virus having claimed more than 1.1 million lives across 218 countries or regions, allowing for reporting differences (John Hopkins University Coronavirus Resource Center 2020).

While the cause of Covid-19 is still being determined, it is known to be part of a family of coronaviruses which stem from zoonotic sources (WHO 2020c). It is also highly transmissible with infections spreading through pathways primarily thought to include respiratory droplets transferred by interpersonal contact, airborne routes particularly within confined spaces, and picked up from infected surfaces (WHO 2020a). Mortality risk is strongly associated with age with young people and particularly children of 10 years and under rarely found to succumb to the worst effects of the virus, whereas those over 70 years of age in particular are most likely to suffer the most adverse reactions (Spiegelhalter 2020). The highest mortality rates are also found amongst persons of any age with underlying health conditions (e.g. diabetes) or taking treatments which impact on their immunity and thereby exacerbate the effects of the virus. Studies also indicate that background factors such as ethnicity, being male, obese, and poor are associated with an increased risk of death (Pareek et al. 2020). However, while youth, strong immunity, and good health are key to warding off the virus, people have nonetheless fallen ill and died from COVID-19 irrespective of exhibiting underlying risk factors. As understandings of the impacts of the virus have grown, it has also become apparent that people can suffer from prolonged symptoms – termed 'long COVID' – and there are lasting health effects for many of those recovering from serious infection, including long term or irreversible lung and kidney damage amongst others (Carfi, Bernabei, and Landi 2020).

At present there are very few medical treatments available to fight the disease, though there are currently more than 170 vaccines at various stages of development and testing that are exploring a wide range of viral mechanisms to encourage immunity and ward off the disease. The aim is to fast-track successful vaccines for approved use, and so many trials have been combining different testing stages to shorten the normal trial timeframe in a bid to 'steal a march' on the virus. Nonetheless, even at this 'breakneck' speed, while a vaccine might be produced by the end of this year, it could be up to a further two to four years before demonstrably safe and effective COVID-19 vaccines can not only be produced, but crucially also be administered to populations worldwide at the scale required to bring the pandemic under control.

Suffice to say, the spread of COVID-19 relies on human interaction and so emergency response plans in the interim must necessarily incorporate behavioural, biomedical, epidemio-logical, and logistical considerations when devising measures to bring the pandemic under con-trol (Michie et al. 2020; Smith and Gibson 2020). Many of the procedures for dealing with infectious diseases are well established in public health following lessons learned from past out-breaks. At the same time, the pandemic has been accompanied by an 'infodemic' of superabun-dant information and misinformation about COVID-19 exacerbating the high uncertainties surrounding what for many is already a difficult and disputed science policy terrain (Krause et al. 2020; Roozenbeek et al. 2020; Slovic 2020). The shifting facts, broken narratives, and disinte-grated understandings enveloping people's experiential encounters with the virus now all form part of the blurred reality of COVID-19 pandemic discourse (Krause et al. 2020; Wardman 2017). It should come as no surprise then if official assessments and proposed measures to combat the 'real' and 'anticipated' threats posed by the virus are followed by some and ignored by others, while becoming hotly contested and reformulated as points of contention and provocation to buttress ongoing 'culture wars' that nowadays underpin public discourse in the so called 'post-truth' era (Hsiehchen, Espinoza, and Slovic 2020; Roozenbeek et al. 2020; van der Linden and Löfstedt 2019).

Viewed through a macrosocial lens, current projections of the cross-cutting exposures to harm, common institutional failures at all levels, parallel explosion of media coverage, and plummeting public trust in expert systems observed might be considered to make COVID-19 emblematic of Beck's (1992) 'World Risk Society' writ large (Nygren and Olofsson 2020). COVID-19 has certainly foregrounded the limited abilities of nation states to stave off global threats and highlighted how the transnational contours and broader constitutive dynamics of globalisation and modernisation have been key to the rapid spread of the virus (Aven and Zio 2021; Burgess, Wardman, and Mythen 2018). That the physical explosion of COVID-19 has also been accompanied by a parallel explosion of pandemic media coverage obsessively reporting on all aspects of the virus outbreak has no doubt also helped to accelerate and amplify contemporary feelings of precariousness and anxiety and the search for security (Krause et al. 2020; Mythen, Burgess, and Wardman 2018).

Yet, while the high uncertainty and contested knowledge claims surrounding COVID-19 undoubtedly add significant complications to dealing with the problem, it can also be said that consideration of such issues is not new to the risk field (Kasperson 2014; Wardman and Mythen 2016). In particular, the global health crisis carries all of the hallmarks of long identified 'post-normal' risk and science problems notably discussed in the first pages of this journal insofar as 'the facts are uncertain, values are in dispute, stakes are high, and decisions are urgent' (Rosa 1998; Ravetz and Funtowicz 1998). All of which adds to the difficulty of putting the risk of COVID-19 into perspective while people may not in any case agree on the levels of harm they might accept or indeed what measures to take in response even if they did so (Hsiehchen, Espinoza, and Slovic 2020; Lofstedt et al. 2011; Slovic 2020; Wardman 2014).

However, a growing body of research has suggested that depending on how risk communica-tion and governance is handled, underlying assumptions about the inabilities of societies and citizens to handle uncertainty and ambiguity may in some cases be overstated and need not necessarily have as detrimental an impact as is typically believed provided that institutions behave credibly (Van Der Bles et al. 2019; Fischhoff 2013; Fischhoff 2020a; Wardman and Löfstedt 2018). COVID-19 has undoubtedly had a profound global impact leading both to obvi-ous and untold effects that will be felt for years to come. The crisis is far from over and it will take extensive efforts to completely understand and unravel its impacts, let alone fully appraise how institutions at both national and international levels have performed in response to COVID-

19 and its many challenges (Fischhoff 2020a). Indications in the interim do, however, point to significant problems experienced worldwide (Abbey et al. 2020). In particular, the difficulties encountered in fighting COVID-19 have shone a spotlight on widespread weaknesses in global health systems and infrastructure, along with science policy and institutional shortcomings that are apparent across many areas and levels of national and international risk governance (Aven and Zio 2021; Scally et al. 2020).

While this is not quite a universal picture, and certainly some nations have by all means responded admirably and in good faith to the viral threat (Abbey et al. 2020), the manner and extent of these problems may prompt introspection and wider critical questions for risk scholars concerning not only the effectiveness of current risk tools, technologies, and techniques for confronting risks such as COVID-19, but also the adequacy of current policy frameworks for ensuring their appropriate use and application . Orthodoxies within the risk field speak to the idea that agency and uncertainty are inherent components of risk (Aven and Renn 2019; Fischhoff 1995). This means that probable and potential harm can often be identified, assessed, managed, offset, or displaced, but not always located or abolished completely (Beck 1992; Wardman and Mythen 2016). As a case in point, the eradication of smallpox stands as a testament to human ingenuity and endeavour to protect people from infectious diseases, but also as an exception to the general success of disease eradication efforts historically. Trade-offs will inevitably be required when attempting to control risk, and unintended consequences and counter-veiling harms associated with doing so can be difficult to avoid (Fischhoff 2020b; Lofstedt et al. 2011). Contextualising and finding an acceptable level of risk can prove challenging because risk assessment can be complex, assumptions can be questioned, risk perception has many components, and people bring different value judgments and multiple perspectives to bear on such decisions (Fischhoff 2005; Kasperson 2014; Wardman 2014). Differentiating people's needs and respectively supporting them where required can however bolster resilience and pay dividends for public safety and confidence (Crouse Quinn 2008; Finucane et al. 2020). The interests and views of those at risk should therefore be represented and form part of pandemic decision-making processes that support policy recommendations and solutions (Fischhoff 2005).

It is with these many issues and concerns in mind that this Journal of Risk Research Special Issue brings together a timely collection of 'rapid-response' viewpoints and full research papers on the theme of COVID-19, along with other recent infectious disease outbreaks, with the broad aim of providing constructive lessons and critical reflections from across a wide range of perspectives and disciplinary interests within the risk analysis field. These contributions have commendably met the call to distil past and present knowledge, appraise current responses, introduce new ideas and data, and offer key recommendations, which we hope readers will find help illuminate different aspects of the global health crisis, and how different constructive insights offered from a 'risk perspective' might inform decisions on how best to proceed in response as the pandemic continues.

References

Abbey, E. J., B. A. Khalifa, M. O. Oduwole, S. K. Ayeh, R. D. Nudotor, E. L. Salia, O. Lasisi, et al. 2020. "The Global Health Security Index Is Not Predictive of Coronavirus Pandemic Responses among Organization for Economic Cooperation and Development Countries." *PLoS One* 15 (10): e0239398. doi:10.1371/journal.pone.0239398.

Aven, T., and O. Renn. 2019. "Some Foundational Issues Related to Risk Governance and Different Types of Risks." *Journal of Risk Research*, 205:1–14.

Aven, T., and E. Zio. 2021. "Globalization and Global Risk: How Risk Analysis Needs to Be Enhanced to Be Effective in Confronting Current Threats." *Reliability Engineering & System Safety* 205: 107270.

Beck, Ulrich. 1992. *Risk Society: Towards a New Modernity*. London: Sage Publications.

Burgess, A., J. Wardman, and G. Mythen. 2018. "Considering Risk: Placing the Work of Ulrich Beck in Context." *Journal of Risk Research* 21 (1): 1–5.

Carfi, A., R. Bernabei, and F. Landi. 2020. "Persistent Symptoms in Patients after Acute COVID-19." *JAMA* 324 (6): 603–605. doi:10.1001/jama.2020.12603.

Crouse Quinn, S. 2008. "Crisis and Emergency Risk Communication in a Pandemic: A Model for Building Capacity and Resilience of Minority Communities." *Health Promotion Practice* 9 (4 Suppl): 18S–25S. doi:10.1177/1524839908324022.

Finucane, M. L., M. J. Blum, R. Ramchand, A. M. Parker, S. Nataraj, N. Clancy, G. Cecchine, et al. 2020. "Advancing Community Resilience Research and Practice: Moving from "Me" to "we" to "3D." *Journal of Risk Research* 23 (1): 1–10.

Fischhoff, B. 1995. "Risk Perception and Communication Unplugged: twenty Years of Process." *Risk Analysis* 15 (2): 137–145. doi:10.1111/j.1539-6924.1995.tb00308.x.

Fischhoff, B. 2005. "Scientifically Sound Pandemic Risk Communication." US House Science Committee Briefing: Gaps in the National Flu Preparedness Plan, Social Science Planning and Response 14.

Fischhoff, B. 2013. "Non-Persuasive Communication about Matters of Greatest Urgency." *Risk Analysis and Human Behavior*, 223.

Fischhoff, B. 2020a. "The Importance of Testing Messages." *World Health Organization. Bulletin of the World Health Organization* 98 (8): 516–517.

Fischhoff, B. 2020b. "Making Decisions in a COVID-19 World." JAMA. Published online June 04, 2020. doi:10.1001/jama.2020.10178.[]

Hsiehchen, D., M. Espinoza, and P. Slovic. 2020. "Political Partisanship and Mobility Restriction during the COVID-19 Pandemic." *Public Health* 187: 111–114. doi:10.1016/j.puhe.2020.08.009.

John Hopkins University Coronavirus Resource Center. 2020. "Coronavirus COVID-19 Global Cases." https://coronavirus.jhu.edu/map.html

Kasperson, R. 2014. "Four Questions for Risk Communication." *Journal of Risk Research* 17 (10): 1233–1239.

Krause, N. M., I. Freiling, B. Beets, and D. Brossard. 2020. "Fact-Checking as Risk Communication: The Multi-Layered Risk of Misinformation in Times of COVID-19." *Journal of Risk Research*, This Issue.

Löfstedt, R. 2005. *Risk Management in Post-Trust Societies*. New York: Palgrave Macmillan.

Lofstedt, R., F. Bouder, J. Wardman, and S. Chakraborty. 2011. "The Changing Nature of Communication and Regulation of Risk in Europe." *Journal of Risk Research* 14 (4): 409–429.

Michie, S., R. West, M. B. Rogers, C. Bonell, G. J. Rubin, and R. Amlôt. 2020. "Reducing SARS-CoV-2 Transmission in the UK: A Behavioural Science Approach to Identifying Options for Increasing Adherence to Social Distancing and Shielding Vulnerable People." *British Journal of Health Psychology*. 25 (4): 945–956.

Mythen, G., A. Burgess, and J. K. Wardman. 2018. "The Prophecy of Ulrich Beck: Signposts for the Social Sciences." *Journal of Risk Research* 21 (1): 96–100.

Nygren, K. G., and A. Olofsson. 2020. "Managing the Covid-19 Pandemic through Individual Responsibility: The Consequences of a World Risk Society and Enhanced Ethopolitics." *Journal of Risk Research*. doi:10.1080/13669877.2020.1756382.

Pareek, M., M. N. Bangash, N. Pareek, D. Pan, S. Sze, J. S. Minhas, W. Hanif, and K. Khunti. 2020. "Ethnicity and COVID-19: An Urgent Public Health Research Priority." *The Lancet* 395 (10234): 1421–1422.

Ravetz, Jerry, and, Silvio Funtowicz. 1998. "Commentary." *Journal of Risk Research* 1 (1): 45–48. doi:10.1080/136698798377312.

Roozenbeek, J., C. R. Schneider, S. Dryhurst, J. Kerr, A. L. Freeman, G. Recchia, A. M. van der Bles, and S. van der Linden. 2020. "Susceptibility to Misinformation about COVID-19 around the World." *Royal Society Open Science* 7 (10): 201199.

Rosa, Eugene A. 1998. "Metatheoretical Foundations for Post-Normal Risk." *Journal of Risk Research* 1 (1): 15–44. doi:10.1080/136698798377303.

Scally, G., Jacobson, B. and Abbasi, K., 2020. The UK's public health response to covid-19. BMJ (Clinical Research ed.), 369, pp.m1932–m1932.

Spiegelhalter, D. 2020. "Use of "Normal" Risk to Improve Understanding of Dangers of Covid-19." *BMJ* 370.

Van Der Bles, Anne Marthe, Sander Van Der Linden, AlexandraL. J Freeman, James Mitchell, Ana B Galvao, Lisa Zaval, and David J Spiegelhalter. 2019. "Communicating Uncertainty about Facts, Numbers and Science." *Royal Society Open Science* 6 (5): 181870 doi:10.1098/rsos.181870.

Slovic, P. 2020. "Risk Perception and Risk Analysis in a Hyperpartisan and Virtuously Violent World." *Risk Analysis*. In press.

Smith, LauraG. E, and Stephen Gibson. 2020. "Social Psychological Theory and Research on the Novel Coronavirus Disease (COVID-19) Pandemic: Introduction to the Rapid Response Special Section." *British Journal of Social Psychology* 59 (3): 571–583. doi:10.1111/bjso.12402.

van der Linden, S. and R. E. Löfstedt, eds., 2019. *Risk and Uncertainty in a Post-Truth Society*. New York: Routledge.

Wardman, J. K. 2014. "Sociocultural Vectors of Effective Risk Communication." *Journal of Risk Research* 17 (10): 1251–1257.

Wardman, J. K. 2017. "Nothing to Fear but Fear Itself? Liquid Provocations for New Media and Fear of Crime." In *The Routledge International Handbook on Fear of Crime*, edited by M. Lee and G. Mythen, 121–134. New York: Routledge.

Wardman, J. K., and R. Löfstedt. 2018. "Anticipating or Accommodating to Public Concern? Risk Amplification and the Politics of Precaution Reexamined." *Risk Analysis* 38 (9): 1802–1819. doi:10.1111/risa.12997.

Wardman, J. K., and G. Mythen. 2016. "Risk Communication: Against the Gods or against All Odds? Problems and Prospects of Accounting for Black Swans." *Journal of Risk Research* 19 (10): 1220–1230.

WHO. 2020a. "WHO Director-General's Opening Remarks at the Media Briefing on COVID-19 – 11 March." https://www.who.int/dg/speeches/detail/who-director-general-s-opening-remarks-at-the-media-briefing-on-covid-19

WHO. 2020b. "Coronavirus Disease 2019 (COVID-19): Situation Report – 84." Accessed 13 April 2020. https://www.who.int/docs/default-source/coronaviruse/situation-reports/20200413-sitrep-84-covid-19.pdf?sfvrsn=44f511ab_2

Jamie K. Wardman

Ragnar Lofstedt

COVID-19: Reflections on trust, tradeoffs, and preparedness

Dominic H. P. Balog-Way 🆔 and Katherine A. McComas

ABSTRACT
The global coronavirus disease (COVID-19) pandemic has already had an enormous impact and will surely have profound consequences for many years to come. The authors reflect on three risk communication themes related to the pandemic: trust, tradeoffs, and preparedness. Trust is critically important during such a rapidly evolving event characterized by scientific uncertainty. Reflections focus on uncertainty communication, transparency, and long-term implications for trust in government and science. On tradeoffs, the positive and unintended negative effects of three key risk communication messages are considered (1) stay at home, (2) some groups are at higher risk, and (3) daily infections and deaths. The authors argue that greater attention to message 'tradeoffs' over 'effectiveness' and 'evaluation' over 'intuition' would help guide risk communicators under pressure. On preparedness, past infectious disease outbreak recommendations are examined. Although COVID-19 was inevitably 'unexpected', important preparedness actions were largely overlooked such as building key risk communication capacities.

1. Introduction

On March 11, 2020, exactly one month after naming the coronavirus disease 'COVID-19'[1], the World Health Organization (WHO) officially declared a global pandemic (WHO 2020b). At the time of writing, over 100,000 deaths have been reported globally with almost every country in the world having at least one laboratory confirmed case (WHO 2020c). Despite continuing uncertainties (Adam 2020), the virus is known to be highly transmissible and healthcare systems can quickly become overwhelmed (WHO 2020c). Those at highest risk of severe disease and death include adults aged 60 years old and over and individuals with underlying health conditions (e.g. hypertension, diabetes, cancer) (WHO 2020c; Verity et al. forthcoming). Infectious disease modelers predict larger deaths tolls unless unprecedented action is taken early and maintained (Ferguson et al. 2020; Adam 2020; Davies et al. forthcoming).

The authors reflect on three risk communication themes related to the pandemic: trust, tradeoffs, and preparedness. While many other risk communication themes are important, these three were considered particularly relevant and striking. The pandemic will inevitably have an enormous impact on almost every country, discipline, and segment of society and there is much still to unfold. Examples are mostly from the United States (US) and United Kingdom (UK). The authors also are cognizant that reflections should avoid being ephemeral during such a rapidly evolving event with limited empirical data available. Thus, observations are tied to extant theory and risk communication research to increase the paper's longevity and relevance.

2. Trust

Trust is critically important during infectious disease outbreaks, evidenced by research on events such as SARS (2002–2003), swine flu (2009–2010), and Ebola (2014–2016) (Smith 2006; Cairns, Andrade, and MacDonald 2013; National Academy of Sciences 2016; Fischhoff et al. 2018). Trust can influence perceived severity and transmissibility, willingness to adopt interventions such as physical distancing, and information seeking behavior (Blair, Morse, and Tsai 2017; Vinck et al. 2019). As Baruch Fischhoff commented in a National Academy of Sciences (2016, 15) workshop on infectious disease threats, " … trust building activities can enable organizations to get out in front and stay ahead of problems".

Several COVID-19 pandemic characteristics pose particularly challenging problems for building trust; specific among them is uncertainty. COVID-19 is a new, invisible, and unfamiliar threat, which, as Paul Slovic comments, 'hits all the hot buttons that lead to heightened risk perception' (Fisher 2020). Anxiety is fuelled by highly emotional messages, upsetting images, and widely reported daily death tolls (Peters 2020). The rapidly evolving nature of the outbreak combined with persistent uncertainties create remarkable complications. Uncertainties include questions over the incubation period, infectivity before symptoms, seasonal dimensions, specificity of the disease for certain population groups, re-infection rates, and, perhaps most importantly, the mortality rate (Ioannidis 2020). No one currently knows for sure which disease model will prove most accurate, or the effectiveness of various physical distancing measures such as closing schools and other 'non-essential' businesses (Couzin-Frankel 2020; Adam 2020).

A striking feature of the pandemic has been the pace at which leading risk communicators have changed their messages. A month after the US Surgeon General tweeted that face masks "are NOT effective" for the general public (Jingnan 2020), new evidence on asymptomatic infections convinced the US Centers for Disease Control and Prevention (CDC) to recommend wearing "cloth face coverings" in public (CDC 2020a). The British government almost immediately announced stringent new physical distancing interventions after being updated on a new COVID-19 model (Ferguson et al. 2020), which indicated the UK healthcare system would soon be overwhelmed (Adam 2020). In just over a month, US President Donald Trump characterized COVID-19 as being 'like the flu' (February 26), only to later say: "This is not the flu. It is vicious" (March 31); and declared a medical war (March 19), five days before suggesting the outbreak would be over by Easter (two weeks later) (March 24) (Watson 2020; Bennett and Berenson, 2020).

This 'fog of pandemic', punctuated by rapidly evolving knowledge and mixed messages, raises important trust-related questions (Warzel 2020; Fuller 2020): How transparent should risk communicators be about scientific and policy uncertainties? Does transparency build or erode trust in risk communicators?

Some argue that transparency is essential for maintaining and strengthening trust. If risk communicators are not transparent, they may be perceived as misleading or misinforming the public (MacDonald 2006). As one bioethicist commented, "Public health depends a lot on public trust. […]. If the public feels as though they are being misled or misinformed, their willingness to make sacrifices — in this case social distancing — is reduced" (Fuller 2020). Better informed citizens are expected to have more trust while being well-placed to judge the trustworthiness of risk communicators (Hood 2006). Transparency is often seen as the inverse of secrecy and dishonesty (Black 1997; Birchall 2011). Despite defending its response as 'open and transparent', China has been criticized for covering-up the initial outbreak and concealing the extent of diagnoses and deaths (Barnes 2020; Bloomberg 2020).

However, transparency also can have severe unintended and unwanted effects that can erode public trust. *Effective* transparency requires that outsiders can receive, process, digest, and use information made available (Heald, 2006). Yet, an avalanche of media reporting, government briefings, and interpersonal discussions have bombarded the public with mixed messages.

Should we wear face masks or not? How long will the pandemic last? Which disease model should we believe? A key issue is that *ineffective* transparency results in audiences, and especially those less adept at filtering, becoming less informed and more confused (O'Neill, 2006). Put differently, effective transparency and trust-building requires well-communicated information (Way 2017). Unfettered transparency can break public trust by undervaluing the merits of confidentiality, privacy, and anonymity (Zarsky 2015). Such 'full disclosure' about COVID-19 can fuel stigmatization of specific populations and groups. For example, publishing data on positive COVID-19 tests with a "census tract or a city name […] has the risk of stigmatizing areas and regions of the country in a way that does not help" (Fuller 2020).

Albeit brief, these reflections highlight the key distinction between effective and ineffective transparency (Heald, 2006). Effective transparency requires thoughtful risk communication (*see* Way 2017, 207-208) that helps audiences understand the uncertainties alongside the information having a strong scientific consensus. Without careful communication, there is no real transparency: data and risk information will continue to be hidden in plain sight. A recent experimental study (van Der Bles et al. 2020), and follow-up results on COVID-19 (Roberts 2020), found that communicating uncertainty may cause only a small decrease in trust while enabling important factual and scientific information to be conveyed. Such *well-communicated* uncertainty in risk information therefore may be able to achieve important risk communication goals with only limited effects on trust.

Two COVID-19 examples of effective, trust-building transparency strategies are particularly noteworthy. First, several risk communicators have built trust by sharing personal stories and 'making messages personal.' For example, Andrew Cuomo, New York State's Governor, has particularly benefitted from his "articulate and consistent" messages and, perhaps most notably, empathetic and personal style (McKinley and Goldmacher 2020). Cuomo has built trust by sharing personal stories, inviting his daughter to press conferences, and allowing his CNN reporter brother, Chris Cuomo, to interview him live (Smith 2020). Other communicators have hesitated to add such personal touches, including British Prime Minister Boris Johnson who was indecisive when asked if he would visit his (elderly) mother on Mother's Day. Risk communication research emphasizes that narratives, storytelling, and empathy can go a long way toward enhancing transparency and maintaining trust, especially during such a turbulent event (Siegrist, Cvetkovich, and Gutscher 2001); such stories also can communicate the extent to which a communicator shares an audience's values and would act in a manner similar to them in a similar circumstance.

Second, leading government communicators have built trust by aligning with trusted scientific experts. In the UK, Chief Medical Officer, Professor Chris Whitty, and Chief Scientific Advisor, Sir Patrick Vallance, have added scientific credibility and legitimacy to daily briefings, while fielding challenging technical questions. A similar approach in the US, with experts such as Dr. Anthony Fauci, Director of the US National Institute of Allergy and Infectious Diseases, and Dr. Deborah Birx, the Coronavirus Response Coordinator for the White House Coronavirus Task Force, has proven equally effective. Aligning with scientific and public health experts publicly signals a strategic affirmation of trust between politicians, one of the least trusted professions, and scientists, one of the most trusted professions.

COVID-19 will surely have trust-related consequences for many years to come. Major trust-eroding events, notably the BSE-crisis in the UK, demonstrate how poor risk communication can have profound long-lasting effects (Powell and Leiss 1997; Löfstedt 2005). Yet, despite sharp criticisms, recent polls suggest relatively high support for the US and UK governments' COVID-19 responses. In late March, 72% of the British public thought the UK government was "handling the outbreak well" (YouGov 2020). Meanwhile, President Trump's approval ratings reached the highest of his presidency (49%) (Montanaro 2020). At the time of writing, the pandemic is far from over though, with neither country having set out clear strategies for easing physical distancing interventions. Other important questions abound including the impacts of public trust on vaccines and seasonal flu communication. Although several 'anti-vaxx' politicians have come under fire (Thompson et al. 2020), a rise in COVID-19 anti-vaccination conspiracy theories pose refreshed challenges for health authorities (Butler 2020; Pransky 2020). Ultimately, only time will tell what long-term impacts the pandemic will have on trust in government and science.

3. Tradeoffs

Even the most well-intentioned messages from highly competent sources have both positive and negative effects (Byrne and Hart 2009; Hart 2014; Salmon, Byrne, and Fernandez 2014; Way 2017). COVID-19 messages are not simply effective or ineffective but have the potential to promote harm and damaging risk-taking behavior. Here, the authors discuss the intended positive and unintended negative effects of three key risk communication messages: (1) stay at home, (2) some groups are at higher risk, and (3) daily infections and deaths. To be clear, the authors do not debate the intent of these messages. For example, physical distancing measures seek to slow the virus spreading and protect vulnerable groups (i.e. the intent), but they also have enormous risk-risk tradeoffs, not addressed here, including surges in unemployment, domestic violence, and loneliness, to name a few.

Many key pandemic messages center on physical/social distancing interventions, which seek to "deliberately increase the physical space between people to avoid spreading illness" (Maragakis 2020). Mobile phone tracking and transport use change data suggest high compliance in many populations and countries (Fowler 2020; Public Health England 2020a). However, even with the threat of stringent enforcement, compliance has not been absolute and physical distancing messages have resulted in unintended negative consequences, including boomerang effects, where messages have generated "the opposite effects of what [was] intended" (Hart 2014, 304).

One issue is that well-intended 'stay-at-home' messages can distract people from the real issue (Salmon, Byrne, and Fernandez 2014), in this case, of protecting and 'shielding' vulnerable groups. Some parents have enlisted elderly relatives to watch their children after schools closed (Winfield 2020). Many younger adults have moved into their parental homes after university closures (Mervosh and Swales 2020), or to get more space, avoid loneliness, and seek emotional support (Rodkey and Graber-Mitchell, 2020; Goodman and Bubola 2020). High case fatality rates in Italy and Spain may very well be due to older and younger adults coinhabiting and socializing at home (Stancati 2020).

Messages requesting individuals refrain from one behavior also can cause the same individuals to turn their attention to different outlets (Salmon, Byrne, and Fernandez 2014). Closing every 'non-essential' business such as bars, theatres, and restaurants has undeniably significantly increased physical distancing. However, with few places to go, many have turned to other outlets resulting, most visibly, in large outdoor congregations. For example, in both the UK and US, media outlets have captured images of packed beaches and parks (e.g. Fry [2020])

A second key message centers on which population groups are at highest risk. Adults aged over 60 and individuals with serious underlying medical conditions are currently considered at highest risk of severe disease (CDC 2020b). Such information is vital for targeting interventions. In the UK, for instance, around 1.5 million high risk individuals were sent letters providing additional protective guidance information (Public Health England 2020b). As a side effect, less vulnerable populations, including children and parents, may become less anxious and worried.

Yet, messages identifying specific high-risk populations can cause others to determine they are not part of that population and hence "discontinue feeling concerned" (Salmon, Byrne, and Fernandez 2014, 296). This is problematic as anyone, regardless of their risk profile or whether they become infected or not, can spread the virus (CDC 2020b). Many individuals congregating outdoors were younger adults seemingly ignoring government requests. In March 2020, for example, spring-breakers and Mardi Gras revelers flocked to US beaches. One young spring-breaker, Brady Sluder, has since apologized for commenting: "If I get corona, I get corona. At the end of the day, I'm not going to let it stop me from partying" (Reinstein 2020). Such widely reported comments can cause others to do the same and disregard recommended behavior (Salmon, Byrne, and Fernandez 2014).

Those at highest risk also are likely to become more concerned and anxious. Anxiety is not trivial, especially during a health pandemic. Vulnerable populations may choose to smoke more, exercise less, drink more alcohol, and get less sleep, all of which can weaken the immune system. Similarly, emphasizing the importance of 'reducing density' may have inadvertently sent the message that those living in less dense areas are safe. This may explain why rural populations have been less compliant (Morris 2020). Such unintended messages also may have contributed to the exodus of urbanities to rural areas, setting-up conflict when 'summer residents' are perceived as spreading the virus to lower capacity rural healthcare systems (Bogel-Burrougs 2020).

A third key pandemic message has been the daily reporting of new infections and deaths. Headlines such as 'Deaths in X country rise for a second consecutive day', or 'Global coronavirus cases reach a new high' are commonplace. In the authors' local newspaper, *The Ithaca Times*, charts tracking local COVID-19 cases are frequently updated including pending, negative, and positive test results. Knowing how many people have become infected or died is vitally important for strategic pandemic responses. 'Hot-spots', for example, can be identified enabling authorities to re-prioritize limited resources such as personal protective equipment and ventilators. The public have a right-to-know and many consider such data necessary for staying informed.

Publishing infection rates and death tolls, however, can unintentionally cause confusion (Schraer 2020). Confirmed COVID-19 cases often reflect testing capabilities rather than the true number of infections. Daily spikes and dips in death tolls, often reported as signs of worsening or improving conditions, can be caused by reporting irregularities (Schraer 2020). Hospitals, for example, report at inconsistent times, sometimes with multi-week lag times between deaths and national reporting.

Reading such data obsessively can create unnecessary anxiety and worry. Peters (2020) reported results from a recent US COVID-19 survey (N = 1,279). The study found that so-called 'statistics stalkers', those who read statistical information on COVID-19 every day over the previous week, were much more anxious. Statistics stalkers were more likely to believe they would get COVID-19, agree that it was important to stock-up, and buy surgical masks (Peters 2020). New deaths are also much more widely reported than the ~98% or so that recover often with mild symptoms (Fisher 2020). Worried individuals can put unnecessary demands on already limited support systems (Salmon, Byrne, and Fernandez 2014, 294). For example, even when testing was severely restricted and prioritized, over 90% of all individuals tested in the US and UK were found negative.

Identifying both positive and negative risk communication message effects does not necessarily mean the original message was ineffective or inappropriate. Telling people to stay at home, conveying who is most at risk, and releasing daily statistics all communicate essential information. However, the COVID-19 pandemic shows how even the most effectively designed messages have unintended negative effects. As Salmon, Byrne, and Fernandez (2014, 298) note: "all risk messages disseminated broadly will engender some unintended effects on some audience members under some circumstances". For this reason, risk communicators would benefit from paying greater attention to message 'tradeoffs' over 'effectiveness' and 'evaluation' over 'intuition' (Fischhoff 2019). Focusing on tradeoffs and evaluation allows risk communicators to identify unintended negative effects, respond quickly, and stay ahead. Strategically targeting additional messages at younger and rural populations, for example, may help limit unwanted behavior. Crucially, pre-testing risk communication messages among target populations do not have to be expensive or time-consuming, and extensive advice already exists (e.g., Downs 2011; National Academy of Sciences 2016).

4. Preparedness

Numerous guidance materials, academic papers, and strategic documents stress the importance of preparing for infectious disease threats (Rickard et al. 2013; National Academy of Sciences 2016; UK Government 2018). The 2018 *UK Biological Security Strategy*, for instance, includes details on understanding, preventing, detecting, and responding to significant outbreaks in the UK. Specific risk communication guidance on infectious disease threats also has been explored for pre-crisis, crisis, and post-crisis event stages (Rickard et al. 2013). Many recommendations, however, have not been widely implemented that could have improved the current situation. For instance, Sir Ian Boyd, former Chief Scientific Advisor at the UK Department for Environment, Food and Rural Affairs (DEFRA), recently commented: " ... getting sufficient resource just to write a decent biosecurity strategy was tough. Getting resource to properly underpin implementation of what it said was impossible" (Carrington 2020). In seeking to take advantage of the currently heightened attention to pandemics, the authors outline three recommendations particularly relevant to COVID-19.

4.1. Develop long-term trusted relationships

Risk communicators, such as public health authorities, would greatly benefit from proactively developing and maintaining long-term relationships with key actors including other agencies and journalists. Such relationships are important not only when an unprecedented pandemic emerges, but also for addressing more familiar and regular threats (e.g. seasonal flu or a safety recall). 'Pre-accumulated' interagency trust can enable authorities to speak with one voice, coordinate activities together, and share information quickly (Rickard et al. 2013). During the COVID-19 pandemic, for example, the strength of ties between state, federal, and local health agencies has proven particularly important in the US. Authorities can make journalists partners rather than enemies with long-term trusted relationships (Löfstedt 2003, 425). For example, misinformation and inaccuracies about the severity or transmissibility of COVID-19 can be corrected more quickly. Continually developing relationships as regular practice also allows organizations to exchange risk communication knowledge, such as best practices on uncertainty communication and effective transparency, during less pressurized times (Boholm, 2019).

4.2. Build baseline and surge capacities

Effective risk communication and response requires diverse forms of expertise and trusted relationships to be readily available (National Academy of Sciences 2016). Building baseline capacities include, for example, hiring permanent and trained risk communicators and involving them at the strategic level of decision-making. Regularly gathering baseline data, such as on public trust, can be particularly useful during acute events (Balog-Way et al. 2020). Risk communication surge capacity complements baseline capacities by providing scalability and flexibility. This might involve building ties with experts who are "not on the front lines at all times" but can be called upon during an acute event (National Academy of Sciences 2016, 15). Regular risk communication advisory committee meetings provide one way of building surge capacity (Bouder et al. 2015; Way et al. 2016). The Food and Drug Administration (FDA), for instance, can draw on a wealth of risk communication knowledge and known experts from its Risk Communication Advisory Committee, or quickly convene a special pandemic event. Other sources of expertise include colleges, universities, and scientific organizations, like the Society for Risk Analysis.

4.3. Design clearly structured systems

Well-designed and structured risk communication systems are needed to, for example, coordinate aforementioned activities, connect professionals within and outside their own knowledge domains, and coordinate interactions with public audiences (National Academy of Sciences 2016). Structured systems allow for appropriate risk communication tactics to be strategically deployed at different stages of the risk event (Rickard et al. 2013). Disbanding the US National Security Council unit responsible for pandemic preparedness in 2018, for example, has been criticized for significantly weakening the US government's COVID-19 pandemic response. Creating clear structures can enable organizations to 'speak with one voice', especially if individuals know their roles and key points of contact. Moreover, well-designed systems enable quick organizational responses at the first sign of outbreak, when, as has been the case with COVID-19, the opportunity for control is largest. For example, organizations can communicate proactively and before other people with different agendas start "grabbing the microphone" and conveying misinformation (National Academy of Sciences 2016, 15). Furthermore, organizations can become more strategic and evidence-informed by making risk communication evaluations a standard operating procedure (National Academy of Sciences 2016; Fischhoff 2019).

5. Conclusion

In this rapid response, reflections were given on three risk communication themes – trust, trade-offs, and preparedness – all of which struck the authors as particularly relevant to the rapidly evolving COVID-19 pandemic. As stressed from the outset, other risk communication themes are highly relevant to such a large-scale and unprecedented event. One centers on how risk communication has led to group stigmatization, prejudice, and discrimination. For instance, younger adults have been labeled as vectors of disease, and ethnic Asian people in predominately White countries have suffered verbal and physical attacks because of the virus's association with China (Nature Editorial 2020). Another theme is national variation, culture, and country-specific issues that are less salient in the US and UK. For example, Sweden, a country known for its high levels of public trust, stands out as taking a remarkably different approach to the pandemic. Developing nations are facing their own extraordinary challenges as well. For example, while the US currently has around 160,000 ventilators, Sierra Leone has thirteen and the Central African Republic has three (NYT Editorial Board 2020). Such marked healthcare system differences alone highlight unprecedented global challenges, and, of course, not just for risk communication. Even so, the authors argue that key themes highlighted in this rapid response are highly relevant to other countries and contexts, though understandably in locally-specific ways, and propose that future interdisciplinary and multinational research is needed.

Note

1. On February 11, 2020, the International Committee on Taxonomy of Viruses (ICTV) officially names the *virus* SARS-CoV-2 (severe acute respiratory syndrome coronavirus 2), while WHO labelled the *disease* COVID-19 (coronavirus disease) (WHO, 2020a).

Disclosure statement

No potential conflict of interest was reported by the authors.

ORCID

Dominic H. P. Balog-Way 🔟 http://orcid.org/0000-0002-0581-640X

References

Adam, D. 2020. "Special Report: The Simulations Driving the World's Response to COVID-19." *Nature* 580 (7803): 316–318. doi:10.1038/d41586-020-01003-6.

Balog-Way, D. H. P., D. Evensen, R. E. Löfstedt, and F. Bouder. 2020. Effects of public trust on behavioural intentions in the pharmaceutical sector: data from six European countries. *Journal of Risk Research*, 1–28 doi: 10.1080/13669877.2019.1694962

Barnes, J. E. 2020. "C.I.A. Hunts for Authentic Virus Totals in China, Dismissing Government Tallies." *The New York Times* April 7, 2020. Accessed 13 April 2020: https://www.nytimes.com/2020/04/02/us/politics/cia-coronavirus-china.html.

Bennett, B., and T. Berenson. "Our Big War.' as Coronavirus Spreads, Trump Refashions Himself as a Wartime President." *Time*, March 19. Accessed 13 April 2020: https://time.com/5806657/donald-trump-coronavirus-war-china/.

Birchall, C. 2011. "Introduction to 'Secrecy and Transparency' the Politics of Opacity and Openness." *Theory, Culture & Society* 28 (7-8): 7–25. doi:10.1177/0263276411427744.

Black, J. 1997. "Transparent Policy Measures." *Oxford Dictionary of Economics*. Oxford, UK: Oxford University Press.

Blair, R. A., B. S. Morse, and L. L. Tsai. 2017. "Public Health and Public Trust: Survey Evidence from the Ebola Virus Disease Epidemic in Liberia." *Social Science & Medicine* 172: 89–97. doi:10.1016/j.socscimed.2016.11.016.

Bloomberg 2020. China Hits Back at Report That It Hid Coronavirus Numbers. Time, April 2, 2020. Accessed 13 April 2020: https://time.com/5814313/china-denies-hiding-coronavirus/

Bogel-Burrougs, N. 2020. "Rhode Island Pulls over New Yorkers to Keep the Virus at Bay." *The New York Times* March 28, 2020. Accessed 13 April. https://www.nytimes.com/2020/03/28/us/coronavirus-rhode-island-checkpoint.html.

Boholm, Åsa. 2019. "Risk Communication as Government Agency Organizational Practice." *Risk Analysis* 39 (8): 1695–1707. doi:10.1111/risa.13302.

Bouder, F., D. H. P. Way, R. Löfstedt, and D. Evensen. 2015. "Transparency in Europe: A Quantitative Study." *Risk Analysis* 35 (7): 1210–1229. doi:10.1111/risa.12386.

Butler, K. 2020. "A Fake Pandemic": anti-Vaxxers Are Spreading Coronavirus Conspiracy Theories." *Mother Jones* March 24, 2020. Accessed 13 April 2020: https://www.motherjones.com/politics/2020/03/a-fake-pandemic-anti-vaxxers-are-spreading-coronavirus-conspiracy-theories/.

Byrne, S., and P. S. Hart. 2009. The 'Boomerang' Effect: A Synthesis of Findings and a Preliminary Theoretical Framework. In *Communication Yearbook 33*, edited by C. Beck, 3–37. Mahawah, NJ: Lawrence Erlbaum. doi:10.1080/23808985.2009.11679083.

Cairns, G., M. Andrade, and L. MacDonald. 2013. "Reputation, Relationships, Risk Communication, and the Role of Trust in the Prevention and Control of Communicable Disease: A Review." *Journal of Health Communication* 18 (12): 1550–1565. doi:10.1080/10810730.2013.840696.

Carrington, D. 2020. "UK Strategy to Address Pandemic Threat 'Not Properly Implemented." *The Guardian* March 29, 2020. Accessed 13 April. https://www.theguardian.com/politics/2020/mar/29/uk-strategy-to-address-pandemic-threat-not-properly-implemented.

CDC 2020a. Recommendation Regarding the Use of Cloth Face Coverings, Especially in Areas of Significant Community-Based Transmission. Accessed 13 April 2020. https://www.cdc.gov/coronavirus/2019-ncov/prevent-getting-sick/cloth-face-cover.html#studies

CDC 2020b. People Who Are at Higher Risk for Severe Illness. Accessed 13 April. https://www.cdc.gov/coronavirus/2019-ncov/need-extra-precautions/people-at-higher-risk.html

Couzin-Frankel, J. 2020. "Does Closing Schools Slow the Spread of Coronavirus? Past Outbreaks Provide Clues." *Science* doi:10.1126/science.abb6686.

Davies, N. G., A. J. Kuckarski, R. M. Eggo, and A. Gimma. Forthcoming. "The Effect of Non-Pharmaceutical Interventions on COVID-19 Cases, Deaths and Demand for Hospital Services in the UK: A Modelling Study." Accessed 13 April 2020. https://www.medrxiv.org/content/10.1101/2020.04.01.20049908v1.

Downs, J. S. 2011. "Chapter 3: Evaluation." In: *Communicating risks and benefits: An evidence-based user's guide*, edited by B. Fischhoff, N. T. Brewer, and J. S. Downs. Silver Spring: FDA.

Ferguson, N. M., D. Laydon, G. Nedjati-Gilani, N. Imai, K. Ainslie, M. Baguelin, S. Bhatia, et al. "Impact of Non-Pharmaceutical Interventions (NPIs) to Reduce COVID19 Mortality and Healthcare Demand." *Imperial College COVID-19 Response Team* Accessed 13 April 2020: https://www.imperial.ac.uk/media/imperial-college/medicine/sph/ide/gida-fellowships/Imperial-College-COVID19-NPI-modelling-16-03-2020.pdf.

Fischhoff, B. 2019. "Evaluating Science Communication." *Proceedings of the National Academy of Sciences* 116 (16): 7670–7675. doi:10.1073/pnas.1805863115.

Fischhoff, B., Wong, G. -Parodi, D. R. Garfin, E. A. Holman, and R. Cohen Silver. 2018. "Public Understanding of Ebola Risks: Mastering an Unfamiliar Threat." *Risk Analysis* 38 (1): 71–83. doi:10.1111/risa.12794.

Fisher, M. 2020. " Coronavirus 'Hits All the Hot Buttons' for How We Misjudge Risk." *The New York Times* February 13. Accessed April 13. https://www.nytimes.com/2020/02/13/world/asia/coronavirus-risk-interpreter.html.

Fowler, G. 2020. "Smartphone Data Reveal Which Americans Are Social Distancing (and Not)." *Washington Post*, March 24. https://www.washingtonpost.com/technology/2020/03/24/social-distancing-maps-cellphone-location/.

Fry, H. 2020. "Manhattan Beach Issues 129 Citations for Coronavirus Social-Distancing Violations." *LA Times*, April 7. Accessed April 13. https://www.latimes.com/california/story/2020-04-07/manhattan-beach-citations-coronavirus-social-distancing-violations.

Fuller, T. 2020. "How Much Should the Public Know about Who Has Coronavirus?" *The New York Times* March 30, 2020. Accessed April 13. https://www.nytimes.com/2020/03/28/us/coronavirus-data-privacy.html?referringSource=articleShare.

Goodman, P. S., and E. Bubola. 2020. "Are Adults Living with Parents Making the Pandemic More Deadly?" *The New York Times* April 8, 2020. Accessed April 13. https://www.nytimes.com/2020/04/08/world/europe/adults-parents-home-coronavirus.html.

Hart, S. 2014. "Boomerang Effects in Risk Communication." In *Effective risk communication*, edited by J. Arvai and L. Rivers III, 304–332. Routledge: Oxon, UK.

Heald, D. 2006. "Transparency as an Instrumental Value." In *Transparency: The key to better governance?*, edited by C. Hood and D. Heald, 59-74. Oxford, UK: Oxford University Press.

Hood, C. 2006. "Beyond Exchanging First Principles? Some Closing Comments." In *Transparency: The Key to Better Governance?, edited by* C. Hood and D. Heald, 211-226. Oxford, UK: Oxford University Press.

Ioannidis, J. P. A. 2020. "A Fiasco in the Making? as the Coronavirus Pandemic Takes Hold, we Are Making Decisions without Reliable Data." *STAT*. Accessed 13 April. https://www.statnews.com/2020/03/17/a-fiasco-in-the-making-as-the-coronavirus-pandemic-takes-hold-we-are-making-decisions-without-reliable-data/.

Jingnan, H. 2020. "Why There Are so Many Different Guidelines for Face Masks for the Public." *NPR* April 10. Accessed April 13. https://www.npr.org/sections/goatsandsoda/2020/04/10/829890635/why-there-so-many-different-guidelines-for-face-masks-for-the-public.

Löfstedt, R. E. 2003. "Science Communication and the Swedish Acrylamide Alarm." *Journal of Health Communication* 8 (5): 407–432. doi:10.1080/713852123.

Löfstedt, R. E. 2005. *Risk Management in Post-Trust Societies*. New York: Palgrave Macmillan.

MacDonald, A. 2006. "What Hope for Freedom of Information in the UK?." In: C. Hood and D. Heald (eds) *Transparency: The Key to Better Governance?* Oxford: Oxford University Press.

Maragakis, L. L. 2020. Coronavirus, Social and Physical Distancing and Self-Quarantine. *John Hopkins Health* April 11, 2020. Accessed 22 April 2020: https://www.hopkinsmedicine.org/health/conditions-and-diseases/coronavirus/coronavirus-social-distancing-and-self-quarantine

McKinley, J., and S. Goldmacher. 2020. "How Cuomo, Once on Sidelines, Became the Politician of the Moment." *The New York Times* April 9, 2020. Accessed April 13. https://www.nytimes.com/2020/03/24/nyregion/governor-andrew-cuomo-coronavirus.html.

Mervosh, S., and V. Swales. 2020. "Colleges and Universities Cancel Classes and Move Online amid Coronavirus Fears." *The New York Times* March 12, 2020. Accessed April 13. https://www.nytimes.com/2020/03/10/us/coronavirus-closings.html.

Montanaro, D. 2020. "Trump's Approval Hits New High, but a Rally-Around-the-Flag Effect is Small." *NPR*, March 27. Accessed April 13. https://www.npr.org/2020/03/27/822043781/trumps-approval-hits-new-high-but-a-rally-around-the-flag-effect-is-small.

Morris, F. 2020. "Rural Towns Insulated from Coronavirus Now May Take a Harder Hit Later." *NPR*, March 13. Accessed April 13. https://www.npr.org/2020/03/13/814917520/rural-towns-insulated-from-coronavirus-now-may-take-a-harder-hit-later.

National Academy of Sciences. 2016. *Building Communication Capacity to Counter Infectious Disease Threats: Proceedings of a Workshop*. Washington, DC: National Academies Press.

Nature Editorial 2020. "Stop the Coronavirus Stigma Now." *Nature* (165): 580. doi:10.1038/d41586-020-01009-0.

NYT Editorial Board. 2020. "The Global Coronavirus Crisis is Poised to Get Much, Much Worse." *The New York Times*, 13 April 2020. Accessed April 14. https://www.nytimes.com/2020/04/13/opinion/coronavirus-cases.html.

O'Neill, O., 2006. "Transparency and the Ethics of Communication." In *Transparency: The Key to Better Governance?*, edited by C. Hood and D. Heald, 211–226. Oxford: Oxford University Press.

Peters, E. 2020. "Is Obsessing over Daily Coronavirus Statistics Counterproductive?" *The New York Times*, March 12. Accessed 13 April. https://www.nytimes.com/2020/03/12/opinion/sunday/coronavirus-statistics.html.

Public Health England. 2020a. *"UK Cabinet Office Briefing Room (COBR): Final Press Conference Slides."* Accessed April 13. https://assets.publishing.service.gov.uk/government/uploads/system/uploads/attachment_data/file/876889/FINAL_Press_Conference_Slides_20200330.pdf.

Public Health England. 2020b. "Guidance on Shielding and Protecting People Defined on Medical Grounds as Extremely Vulnerable from COVID-19." Accessed 13 April. https://www.gov.uk/government/publications/guidance-on-shielding-and-protecting-extremely-vulnerable-persons-from-covid-19.

Powell, D., and W. Leiss. 1997. *Mad Cows and Mother's Milk: The Perils of Poor Risk Communication*. Canada: McGill-Queen's Press-MQUP.

Pransky, N. 2020. "Poll: Less than a Third of America Will Rush to Get Coronavirus Vaccine." *NBC San Diego*, April 2. Accessed April 1. https://www.nbcsandiego.com/news/coronavirus/poll-less-than-a-third-of-america-will-rush-to-get-coronavirus-vaccine/2298088/.

Reinstein, J. 2020. "The Spring Breaker Who Was IDGAF about Coronavirus Has Apologized." *Buzzfeed News*, March 24. Accessed April 13. https://www.buzzfeednews.com/article/juliareinstein/coronavirus-spring-break-instagram-apology-miami-video-viral.

Rickard, L. N., K. A. McComas, C. E. Clarke, R. C. Stedman, and D. J. Decker. 2013. "Exploring Risk Attenuation and Crisis Communication after a Plague Death in Grand Canyon." *Journal of Risk Research* 16 (2): 145–167. doi:10.1080/13669877.2012.725673.

Roberts, S. 2020. "Embracing the Uncertainties." *The New York Times*, April 7. Accessed 13 April 2020: https://www.nytimes.com/2020/04/07/science/coronavirus-uncertainty-scientific-trust.html.

Rodkey, R., and C. Graber-Mitchell. 2020. "Why Shutting down Colleges Only Shifts the Coronavirus Burden onto Others." *The Washington Post*, March 11. Accessed 13 April. https://www.washingtonpost.com/opinions/2020/03/11/they-shut-down-our-college-because-coronavirus-will-that-help/.

Salmon, C. T., S. Byrne, and L. Fernandez. 2014. "Exploring Unintended Consequences of Risk Communication Messages." In *Effective Risk Communication*, edited by J. Arvai and L. Rivers III. Routledge: Oxon, UK, 292–303.

Schraer, R. 2020. "Coronavirus: Warning Over Daily Death Figures." *BBC News*, April 7. Accessed 13 April: https://www.bbc.com/news/health-52167016

Siegrist, M., G. T. Cvetkovich, and H. Gutscher. 2001. "Shared Values, Social Trust, and the Perception of Geographic Cancer Clusters." *Risk Analysis* 21 (6): 1047–1054. doi:10.1111/0272-4332.216173.

Smith, B. 2020. "Americans Don't Trust the Media Anymore. So Why Do They Trust the Cuomos?", *The New York Times*, April 5. Accessed 13 April. https://www.nytimes.com/2020/04/05/business/media/brothers-cuomo-andrew-chris.html

Smith, Richard D. 2006. "Responding to Global Infectious Disease Outbreaks: lessons from SARS on the Role of Risk Perception, Communication and Management." *Social Science & Medicine* 63 (12): 3113–3123. doi:10.1016/j.socscimed.2006.08.004.

Stancati, M. 2020. "Family is Italy's Great Strength. Coronavirus Made It Deadly." *Wall Street Journal*, March 24. Accessed 13 April: https://www.wsj.com/articles/family-is-italys-great-strength-coronavirus-made-it-deadly-11585058566.

Thompson, A., H. Otterbein, and A. M. Ollstein. 2020. *Politico*, March 21. Accessed 13 April . https://www.politico.com/news/2020/03/21/anti-vaccine-coronavirus-137446

van Der Bles, A. M., S. van der Linden, A. L. J. Freeman, and D. J. Spiegelhalter. 2020. "The Effects of Communicating Uncertainty on Public Trust in Facts and Numbers." *Proceedings of the National Academy of Sciences* 117 (14): 7672–7683. doi:10.1073/pnas.1913678117.

UK Government 2018. *UK Biological Security Strategy*. London: HM Government.

Verity, R., L. C. Okell, I. Dorigatti, P. Winskill, C. Whittaker, N. Imai, G. Cuomo-Dannenburg, et al. "Forthcoming. Estimates of the Severity of Coronavirus Disease 2019: A Model-Based Analysis." *The Lancet Infectious Diseases* Accessed 13 April 2020: https://www.thelancet.com/journals/laninf/article/PIIS1473-3099(20)30243-7/fulltext.

Vinck, P., P. N. Pham, K. K. Bindu, J. Bedford, and E. J. Nilles. 2019. "Institutional Trust and Misinformation in the Response to the 2018–19 Ebola Outbreak in North Kivu, DR Congo: A Population-Based Survey." *The Lancet Infectious Diseases* 19 (5): 529–536. doi:10.1016/S1473-3099(19)30063-5.

Warzel, C. 2020. "The Coronavirus Misinformation War." *The New York Times* (print edition), April 5, p. 4.

Watson, K. 2020. A timeline of what Trump has said on coronavirus. *CBS News*, April 3. Accessed 13 April. https://www.cbsnews.com/news/timeline-president-donald-trump-changing-statements-on-coronavirus/

Way, D. 2017. "Transparency in Risk Regulation: The Case of the European Medicines Agency." PhD diss., King's College London.

Way, D. H. P., F. Bouder, R. E. Löfstedt, and D. Evensen. 2016. "Medicines Transparency at the European Medicines Agency (EMA) in the New Information Age: The Perspectives of Patients." *Journal of Risk Research* 19 (9): 1185–1215. doi:10.1080/13669877.2016.1200652.

WHO 2020a. "Naming the Coronavirus Disease (COVID-19) and the Virus that Causes It." Accessed 13 April 2020. https://www.who.int/emergencies/diseases/novel-coronavirus-2019/technical-guidance/naming-the-coronavirus-disease-(covid-2019)-and-the-virus-that-causes-it

WHO 2020b. "WHO Director-General's Opening Remarks at the Media Briefing on COVID-19 – 11 March." Accessed 13 April 2020. https://www.who.int/dg/speeches/detail/who-director-general-s-opening-remarks-at-the-media-briefing-on-covid-19

WHO 2020c. "Coronavirus Disease 2019 (COVID-19): Situation Report – 84." Accessed 13 April 2020. https://www.who.int/docs/default-source/coronaviruse/situation-reports/20200413-sitrep-84-covid-19.pdf?sfvrsn=44f511ab_2

Winfield, N. 2020. Virus, What Virus? Italy's "nonni" Step in as Schools Close." *The San Diego Union Tribune*, March 5. Accessed 13 April. https://www.sandiegouniontribune.com/news/nation-world/story/2020-03-05/virus-what-virus-italys-nonni-step-in-as-schools-close

YouGov 2020. "YouGov Survey Results. Sample: 2105 GB Adults. Fieldwork: 26–27 March 2020." Accessed 13 April 2020. https://docs.cdn.yougov.com/fxydtk8mdw/Results%20for%20Coronavirus%20Tracker%20GB%20-%20Wave%203_27.03.2020_w.pdf

Zarsky, T. 2015. "The Privacy–Innovation Conundrum." *Lewis & Clark Law Review* 19 (1): 115–168

The COVID-19 pandemic: how can risk science help?

Terje Aven and Frederic Bouder

ABSTRACT

This paper reflects on how risk science, with its concepts, principles, approaches, methods and models, can support the actual assessments, communication and handling of the vulnerabilities and risks related to the Coronavirus (Covid-19) pandemic. We highlight the importance of acknowledging uncertainty as a main component of risk, in order to properly characterize and communicate risk, as well as to understand the difference between professional risk judgements and risk perception. We challenge the use of the commonly referred to phrase that the policies adopted are science-based, in a situation like this characterized by fundamental uncertainties about the underlying phenomena and the effects of possible interventions. Arguments are provided for a 'balanced' use of precaution, combined with adaptive management and learning.

1. Introduction

The current situation related to the Coronavirus pandemic triggers many issues concerning risk and risk science, including how to characterize and communicate the risks, as well as how to handle them. We hear experts and politicians making numerous statements on a daily basis about the magnitude of the risks, using different formats and terms but all highlighting the large uncertainties and the difficulties of being able to make accurate predictions. We experience different countries adopting different policies, from severe lockdown to non-binding public health advice to follow social distancing, all claiming to be science-based and often referring to the precautionary principle but ending up with different strategies to confront the virus. A balance clearly has to be struck between different concerns. Societies are faced with a health crisis, but the implications of societal shutdowns are huge, and, when considering what to do next, the risks related to the Coronavirus pandemic obviously have to be seen in relation to all the relevant aspects – and risks – involved.

The politicians are guided by health experts, physicians, immunologists and others with extensive knowledge on the topic. Other experts provide input on economic and societal impacts. In times of crisis, the balance between these different inputs, however, varies. For instance, we observe that the Coronavirus crisis has brought epidemiological models to the fore. With little time to engage in a lengthy peer-reviewed process, early results have been shared with the policy level. A flow of messages often perceived as contradictory (Van Elsland and O'Hare 2020; Lourenço et al. 2020) is challenging the scientific process. 'Scientific consensus' is difficult to reach, and communication becomes particularly challenging to articulate. In this paper, we offer some reflections on how risk science and risk scientists can support the handling of this pandemic and related situations. Previous attempts have shown that pandemic response can benefit from risk studies (Fischhoff et al. 2018). This science provides the current most justified knowledge – represented by concepts, principles, approaches, methods and models for assessing, communicating and handling risk – produced by the risk field. There are a number of issues that can be discussed in relation to risk science and this case; we highlight some of these, selected on the basis of our competencies and what we consider important for improving today's situation.

First, we reflect on how Coronavirus-related risks are currently described and communicated. We point to several areas where enhancements can be made. Then we look into the differences between professional risk judgements and risk perception. We argue that it is essential for the risk communication to understand that laypersons' risk perceptions may capture not only feelings like fear and dread but also conscious judgements of uncertainties, which are not always incorporated in professional characterizations of risk. Finally, we discuss issues related to the relationship between science, policy and politics, as introduced above. We argue that i) current policies based on applications of the precautionary principle are justified as far as they remain proportionate and prudent (Health Council of the Netherlands 2008); and ii) it is critical to public communication that the message is put forward that the role of science is to inform policy and politicians. Science cannot and should not prescribe what decisions to make in the case of risks subject to large uncertainties.

2. Improving the way risk is described and communicated

Literature, both scientific and popular, is rapidly emerging on risk issues associated with the Coronavirus and related matters. In this huge corpus, risk is commonly referred to, described and measured, although it is seldom precisely defined. It is, however, often clear from the context that the authors have in mind a thinking about risk that reflects probabilities and proportions of people with some specific features (e.g. sickness, death). Readers will intuitively get a feel for the message that is being presented. However, from a science point of view, this is not satisfactory. Fundamental concepts need to be precisely defined and interpreted. Failure to do so can seriously hamper the risk communication and the risk handling. Risk science can provide essential help in this regard (e.g. SRA 2015, 2017a, 2017b; Aven 2018a, 2020). To understand risk, we need to clarify the role of uncertainty and knowledge (Lofstedt and Bouder 2017). It is not enough to talk about probabilities and historical data. Think about a study, performed in early March 2020, of the risk related to the number of deaths in the coming months as a result of Coronavirus. The way risk is conceptualized and described could be very important for how the authorities judge the magnitude of the risk, communicate the risk to the public and conclude what to do. With large uncertainties, as in this case, it is clear that accurate predictions cannot be made. Yet such predictions are made, usually based on models of the phenomena studied. However, as the knowledge is weak, the models are based on strong assumptions, which could turn out to be far from reality (Adam 2020). Models to express risk thus need to be used with care, to avoid extreme scenarios being given stronger authority than is justified.

The number of deaths due to the Coronavirus in the coming month is not risk. It is an unknown quantity. To talk about risk, we also have to include uncertainty – we do not know today what this number will be. We assess these uncertainties in risk assessments using all relevant knowledge, founded on data, information, models, tests, analysis and argumentation. Probabilities are used to express these uncertainties, but probability is just a tool and has limitations. For example, in the case above, when considering risk related to deaths in early March, analysts could perform a risk assessment establishing a probability for a maximum number of deaths, given the implementation of a specific policy. However, such a probability should be communicated with care, as the knowledge supporting it is rather weak. It is a fundamental risk science insight today that probabilities should always be accompanied by judgements of the knowledge supporting these probabilities. In line with this, the communication of risk could be formulated as follows:

The result of the risk assessment is that the number of deaths is unlikely (less than 5%) to exceed x in the coming month, given the implementation of policy y. This assessment is based on current knowledge on the topic using the best models and data available. There are, however, considerable uncertainties about the underlying phenomena and how the epidemic will develop – many of the assumptions of the models used are subject to large uncertainties. Overall, the knowledge supporting the risk assessment is considered rather weak.

As another example, think about the message that the authorities would like to convey, that you stay safe when following the guidance on how to protect yourself against getting the Coronavirus (washing your hands frequently, maintaining social distancing, etc.). However, understanding what 'safe' here means is not straightforward. Clearly, we would still face some risks. The point is that the probability of you getting the virus when following these guidelines is judged to be very low, and this conclusion is supported by strong knowledge/evidence. We have not yet heard any politician or expert using such words, but, in our view, this type of explanation would strengthen the risk communication. Departing from the 'safe'/'unsafe' approach will also ease communication on fluctuating public health advice, such as whether or not to wear protective face masks.

3. The difference between professional risk judgements and risk perception

Today many people are experiencing stress from the risks related to the Coronavirus. People's risk perception is strongly influenced by repeatedly hearing about cases and deaths. Media stories, death counts and public campaigns that amplify danger may stir emotions and exaggerate the feeling of risk (Slovic 2010), while increasing the availability of negative events (Tversky and Kahneman 1973). Risk science has developed considerable knowledge about how and why this happens (e.g. Slovic 1987; Kahneman 2011). As we easily retrieve from memory a vast number of 'alarms', the conclusion is that the risk is high. The representativeness is not reflected. The Coronavirus hits all the hot buttons: unknown, new and delays in effects, lack of control, and catastrophic potential, often summarized by the two dimensions, newness and dread. The result is that the risk is amplified, and there is a potential for overreaction, which may in turn induce reckless behaviour and harm (e.g. mental health issues and suicides, car accidents when escaping 'danger zones', domestic violence, neglect of other health issues).

Risk science also explains that lay people's risk perception is not only about feelings. It can also capture conscious judgements of uncertainties (Aven 2015, 2018b). History has shown many examples of this, where highly relevant uncertainties were ignored by the professional risk judgements but included in lay people's risk appraisals (for example, in relation to nuclear risk). It is well-documented that traditional, professional perspectives on risk, which are built on probability, historical data and models, have failed to properly reflect the important uncertainty aspects of risk (e.g. Fischhoff 1995; Aven 2011). Contemporary risk science provides clarity on these issues, by showing the importance of knowledge and lack of knowledge when characterizing risk (SRA 2015, 2017a; Aven 2020). The concept of risk includes uncertainties, and people may have good reasons in many cases for questioning issues linked to these uncertainties. If the experts build their risk assessments on a 'narrow' perspective on risk, they may be tempted to downplay such questioning, considering it to be influenced by affects and not the result of conscious judgements of uncertainties and risk.

It is essential for the quality of the analysis that the risk assessments are placed in a 'broad' risk framework (Renn 2008), which gives due attention to all aspects of uncertainties and knowledge. Traditional probabilistic risk assessments are not sufficient for adequately studying risk in the case of large uncertainties. Using such a broad framework makes us better able to understand and value lay-people's risk perception.

4. Science and the precautionary principle

Our basic idea of the precautionary principle is this: if the consequences of an activity could be serious and subject to scientific uncertainties, then precautionary measures should be taken, or the activity should not be carried out (SRA 2015). In this Corona case, we are faced with the potential for serious consequences and there are scientific uncertainties – the principle applies. As most countries have referred to this principle in their policies for confronting the Coronavirus, they have found the principle relevant and meaningful. Nonetheless, the principle has been subject to considerable discussion and critique over the years (e.g. Löfstedt and Vogel 2001; Majone 2002; Sandin et al. 2002; Sunstein 2005; Boyer-Kassem 2017; Stefánsson 2019; Aven 2019). The current situation represents an excellent illustration of why this principle makes sense when faced with high risk for which the uncertainties are large and scientific. Accurate models providing accurate predictions are not available. The precautionary principle should be interpreted as a guiding perspective for prudent risk handling, when faced with such uncertainties (Renn 2008; Aven 2020). There is not really an alternative. Because of the uncertainties, science alone cannot lead us to the right decisions. Yet, it is also our view that the principle should be used 'prudently' and with care and that it should be embedded in a scientific approach. There should not be a conflict between the precautionary principle and science. The precautionary principle should be used to stimulate and justify research aiming at reducing the scientific uncertainties, and this is exactly what happens in the Coronavirus case. While we are on lockdown, new knowledge about the virus and pandemic is gained, theoretical as well as empirical. An adaptive risk handling is adopted all over the world, combining precautionary measures and scientific analysis. We cannot see how it is possible to argue that a policy is purely science-based when the consequences are subject to scientific uncertainties. What can be said is that the policy is informed by science. The fact that different countries have come to different policies demonstrates this.

   At this stage of the development of the pandemic (early April 2020), there is a discussion in many countries as to when and how to open up key functions of society again. Experts indicate that the risks in relation to the negative effects of shutdown are as least at large as the risks related to the Coronavirus. These types of statements lack, however, a strong rationale. The uncertainties are too large to make accurate estimates and predictions, yet the elected officials have to make decisions (Van Eeten and Bouder 2012). Then, it is important to acknowledge that there is not a scientifically correct answer. Different weights on the uncertainties would lead to different conclusions. Different 'schools' (e.g. economists, health scientists, health bureaucrats) will provide different perspectives, but in the end it is our politicians that need to balance all the different concerns and views and make the difficult decisions. This is a well-known principle of risk management and governance (Renn 2008; SRA 2017a; Aven 2020), which cannot be repeated too often. How we confront the Coronavirus is mainly politics, not science. It is popular to state that we need to base these decisions on data and data analytics. These are buzzwords today. Without reducing the importance of data, information and knowledge, the present authors are glad that the important decisions that politicians must make in the coming months are not mechanized or automatized. They are too complicated to be prescribed by some algorithms. What are needed are broad deliberations of all relevant input, supported by experts, and that is exactly what our politicians have been elected to do.

5. Conclusions

We conclude that risk science represents an important knowledge basis for guiding the use of concepts, principles, approaches, methods and models for assessing, communicating and handling the Coronavirus risk and related situations. We have here looked into some issues and examples. This science is developing, and its societal impact is still rather limited. As discussed in Aven (2020), efforts are needed to strengthen the foundation and practice of this science. The Society for Risk Analysis (SRA) has formulated general goals and strategies to this end (SRA 2018), which we strongly support. The Coronavirus pandemic demonstrates the relevancy of the risk science in many ways, from risk understanding to risk assessment and communication, and risk handling. Risk is a key concept. Then, it is essential that there is a strong science supporting the analyses and management. The opposite is a situation where different application areas start basically from scratch, developing their own concepts, principles, approaches, methods and models. However, risk is a generic term, and all types of applications would benefit from having a generic, fundamental knowledge basis that integrates the insights from all domains and is able to transform this knowledge back to the different applications.

Disclosure statement

No potential conflict of interest was reported by the authors.

References

Adam, D. 2020. "How Epidemiologists Rushed to Model the Coronavirus Pandemic." Nature Special Report: The Simulations Driving the World's Response to COVID-19. April 3. Accessed April 6, 2020. https://www.nature.com/articles/d41586-020-01003-6.
Aven, T. 2011. "Selective Critique of Risk Assessments with Recommendations for Improving Methodology and Practice." *Reliability Engineering & System Safety* 96 (5): 509–514. doi:10.1016/j.ress.2010.12.021.
Aven, T. 2015. "On the Allegations That Small Risks Are Treated out of Proportion to Their Importance." *Reliability Engineering & System Safety* 140: 116–121. doi:10.1016/j.ress.2015.04.001.
Aven, T. 2018a. "An Emerging New Risk Analysis Science: Foundations and Implications." *Risk Analysis* 38 (5): 876–888. doi:10.1111/risa.12899.
Aven, T. 2018b. "How the Integration of System 1-System 2 Thinking and Recent Risk Perspectives Can Improve Risk Assessment and Management." *Reliability Engineering & System Safety* 180: 237–244. doi:10.1016/j.ress.2018.07.031.
Aven, T. 2019. "Comments to Orri Stefánsson's Paper on the Precautionary Principle." *Risk Analysis* 39 (6): 1223–1224. doi:10.1111/risa.13270.
Aven, T. 2020. *The Science of Risk Analysis*. New York: Routledge.
Boyer-Kassem, T. 2017. "Is the Precautionary Principle Really Incoherent?" *Risk Analysis* 37 (11): 2026–2043. doi:10.1111/risa.12774.
Fischhoff, B. 1995. "Risk Perception and Communication Unplugged: Twenty Years of Process." *Risk Analysis* 15 (2): 137–145. doi:10.1111/j.1539-6924.1995.tb00308.x.
Fischhoff, B., G. Wong-Parodi, D. R. Garfin, E. A. Holman, and R. Cohen Silver. 2018. "Public Understanding of Ebola Risks: Mastering an Unfamiliar Threat." *Risk Analysis* 38 (1): 71–83. doi:10.1111/risa.12794.
Health Council of the Netherlands. 2008. *Advisory Report Prudent Precaution*. September 26. Accessed April 6, 2020. https://www.healthcouncil.nl/documents/advisory-reports/2008/09/26/prudent-precaution.
Kahneman, D. 2011. *Thinking, Fast and Slow*. New York: Farrar, Straus and Giroux.
Lofstedt, R., and F. Bouder. 2017. "Evidence-Based Uncertainty Analysis: What Should We Now Do in Europe? A View Point." *Journal of Risk Research*: 1–20. doi:10.1080/13669877.2017.1316763.
Löfstedt, R. E., and D. Vogel. 2001. "The Changing Character of Regulation: A Comparison of Europe and the United States." *Risk Analysis* 21 (3): 399–410. doi:10.1111/0272-4332.213121.
Lourenço, J., R. Paton, M. Ghafari, M. Kraemer, C. Thompson, R. Simmonds, P. Klenerman, and S. Gupta. 2020. "Fundamental Principles of Epidemic Spread Highlight the Immediate Need for Large-Scale." *Serological Surveys to Assess the Stage of the SARS-CoV-2 Epidemic*. doi: . doi:10.1101/2020.03.24.20042291..
Majone, G. 2002. "What Price Safety? The Precautionary Principle and Its Policy Implications." *Journal of Common Market Studies* 40 (1): 89–106. doi:10.1111/1468-5965.00345.
Renn, O. 2008. *Risk Governance: Coping with Uncertainty in a Complex World*. London: Earthscan.
Sandin, P., M. Peterson, S. O. Hansson, C. Rudén, and A. Juthe. 2002. "Five Charges against the Precautionary Principle." *Journal of Risk Research* 5 (4): 287–299. doi:10.1080/13669870110073729.
Slovic, P. 1987. "Perception of Risk." *Science* 236 (4799): 280–285. doi:10.1126/science.3563507.
Slovic, P. 2010. *The Feeling of Risk: New Perspectives on Risk Perception*. Abingdon, UK: Earthscan.

SRA. 2015. "Glossary Society for Risk Analysis." Accessed March 29, 2020. https://www.sra.org/resources.
SRA. 2017a. "Risk Analysis: Fundamental Principles." Accessed March 29, 2020. https://www.sra.org/resources.
SRA. 2017b. "Core Subjects of Risk Analysis." Accessed March 29, 2020. https://www.sra.org/resources.
SRA. 2018. "Society for Risk Analysis strategic plan." Accessed March 29, 2020. https://www.sra.org/strategic-plan.
Stefánsson, O. 2019. "On the Limits of the Precautionary Principle." *Risk Analysis* 39 (6): 1204–1222. With Replay: 1227–1228.
Sunstein, C. R. 2005. *Laws of Fear. Beyond the Precautionary Principle*. Cambridge: Cambridge University Press.
Tversky, A., and D. Kahneman. 1973. "Availability: A Heuristic for Judging Frequency and Probability." *Cognitive Psychology* 5 (2): 207–232. doi:10.1016/0010-0285(73)90033-9.
Van Eeten, M., and F. Bouder. 2012. "The Diva and Destiny: Can the Voter Be Appeased with Fatalism?" *European Journal of Risk Regulation* 3 (3): 293–303. doi:10.1017/S1867299X00002208.
Van Elsland, S., and R. O'Hare. 2020. "COVID-19: Imperial Researchers Model Likely Impact of Public Health Measures." Accessed April 6, 2020. https://www.imperial.ac.uk/news/196234/covid-19-imperial-researchers-model-likely-impact/.

Does the COVID-19 pandemic refute probability neglect?

Arkadiusz Sieroń

ABSTRACT
Cass Sunstein coined the term 'probability neglect' to characterize the
cognitive bias of disregarding probability when assessing low-probability but high-impact threats. He also related this cognitive bias to terrorism risk, andapplied the concept to the COVID-19 pandemic. In this
article, I show that such claims are not justified. I argue that an alternative hypothesis could be that people who downplay the epidemiological
threat and do not take precautionary measures suffer from exponential-
growth bias. I also show that probability theory, and thus the concept
of probability neglect, cannot be easily applied to real-world problems,
such as terrorist attacks or pandemics, occurring in a non-ergodic,
uncertain environment.

1. Introduction

In a *Bloomberg* opinion piece titled 'The Cognitive Bias That Makes Us Panic About Coronavirus',
published on February 28, 2020, just before the outbreak of the COVID-19 pandemic in the
United States, Cass Sunstein suggests that fear of coronavirus was resulting from probability neglect—that is, a cognitive bias that makes people tend to focus on the consequences of an event
while neglecting its likelihood (Sunstein 2020a). Similar claims that worries about the COVID-19
pandemic demonstrate people's irrationality were made by DeSteno (2020) and Gigerenzer
(2020).[1] But long before the COVID-19 pandemic, Sunstein (2002, 2003) argued that probability
neglect can partially explain excessive reactions to low-probability but high-impact hazards. In
particular, Sunstein (2003) asserts that people are far more concerned about the risks of terrorism
than about statistically larger risks, which leads to significant private and public costs such as the
increase in traffic fatalities resulted from the substitution of car journeys for air travels in the
aftermath of the terrorist attack.

The fact that many households, companies, and governments underestimated their exposure
to pandemic risk and reacted too slowly rather than excessively to the threat of COVID-19
(Karnitschnig 2020; Schoenfeld 2020) creates a perfect opportunity to critically examine the concept of probability neglect and the general claim of behavioral economics that people behave
irrationally because they miscalculate probability.

Section 2 analyzes the COVID-19 pandemic, arguing that one might claim that a part of the
public suffered from exponential-growth bias rather than probability neglect. Sections 3 and 4
examine the adequacy of the concept of probability neglect in a non-ergodic and uncertain
world, respectively. Section 5 concludes.

2. Reactions to COVID-19 pandemic: probability neglect or exponential-growth bias?

Sunstein (2020a) argues that because COVID-19 is a new disease that can be lethal for some individuals, it evokes strong emotions that obscure rational probability analysis. As a consequence, people neglect the low probability of death and take exaggerated actions.

However, the application of the probability neglect to the COVID-19 pandemic is an oversimplification, as the details of susceptibility and severity of a new disease were initially simply not known, and our knowledge about the new coronavirus and related disease is still limited.[2] But with the benefit of hindsight, we know that people were justifiably worried about their health, especially given the uncertainty about the course of the pandemic and governments' response. Although the case fatality rate of the COVID-19 remains low, it is estimated to be significantly higher than that of influenza (Baud et al. 2020; Spychalski, Błażyńska-Spychalska, and Kobiela 2020; Verity et al. 2020).

Actually, given the neglect of the pandemic threat and the inappropriate comparisons of COVID-19 to influenza (Faust 2020; Resnick and Animashaun 2020), one might argue that a part of the public, including the experts who warned against probability neglect or fearing dread risks, suffered from exponential-growth bias rather than probability neglect (Levy and Tasoff 2017). According to Stango and Zinman (2009, 2807), exponential-growth bias is 'the pervasive tendency to linearize exponential functions when assessing them intuitively'. In other words, people underestimate exponential growth due to neglecting compound interest. Goda et al. (2015) cite a large body of literature suggesting that the exponential-growth bias is widespread and robust. As people are accustomed to thinking in linear terms, the specifics of exponential growth are difficult to grasp, which explains such things as some stylized facts in household finance like undersaving for retirement, understating the pace of technical progress, and—as most epidemics initially grow approximately exponentially (Ma 2020)[3]—underestimating epidemiological risk.

The problem is that the power of exponential growth manifests only after some time; it begins slowly and steadily, which makes it difficult to distinguish from linear growth. This deceptive feature prompts some people, including DeSteno (2020), Gigerenzer (2020), and Sunstein (2020a), to erroneously compare COVID-19 with the seasonal flu, despite the difference in their basic reproduction number and their pace of transmission.[4] Although initially the number of COVID-19 infections was small, it grew to considerable size over time because of its exponential dynamics.

3. Do people neglect probability in a non-ergodic world?

The difficulties with assessing nonlinear trends, which can make people downplay a threat rather than exaggerate it, are not the only problems with probability neglect. The main issue is the use of probability theory in a non-ergodic environment full of uncertainty.

Both neoclassical and behavioral economists incorrectly assume that the world is ergodic—that is, one in which the time average of the process (the average of outcomes over time) is the same as its average over probability space. According to Horst (2008, 30), 'a stochastic system is called ergodic if it tends in probability to a limiting form that is independent of the initial conditions'. The ergodicity, thus, implies that the long-term equilibrium is practically independent of the initial conditions, and that extrapolation of the past is a reliable indication of the future, which means. It can be thus represented by mathematical formulas and econometrically tested, replacing historical time with logical time. As Davidson (1987, 148) notes, in such a world 'knowledge about the future involves the relating of statistical averages based on past and/or current realizations to forthcoming events'.

But the world is non-ergodic, so the past data cannot provide a statistically reliable estimate, and the probabilistic risk is replaced by the uncertainty. The non-ergodicity also means that the time average differs from the average for the population at a given time. It implies that the risk for a single person is different from the risk for the whole community.

Let's assume that the case fatality rate of COVID-19 is 1 percent. It implies that 1 percent of people who are infected by the coronavirus will die. But none of those infected know who will die. To put it differently, the probability of death of 1 percent means that if one person was somehow infected one million times (maybe via cloning), she would die, on average, in just ten thousand cases. However, people have only one life to live, and the bad outcome may happen at the very beginning, which ends the whole game. Just as there is no guarantee that the number of heads and tails will be even roughly equal in a small sample, there is no guarantee that a person will not die from COVID-19, although the statistical probability of death might be low.

Similarly, to demonstrate probability neglect, Sunstein (2002, 2003) cites the results of Rottenstreich and Hsee (2001), who investigated how much money people are willing to pay to avoid 'short, painful, but not dangerous electric shock' as part of a hypothetical experiment.[5] It turned out that the participants were ready to pay $10 to avoid a 99 percent chance of the electric shock and $7 (only 30 percent less) to avoid a 1 percent chance of the shock, although the chances of being shocked were significantly lower. Sunstein's interpretation was that when strong emotions are involved, people ignore probability.

But is it really surprising that people do not want to be electrocuted, no matter what the odds are? The fact that the chance of being subjected to electric shock is 1 percent is irrelevant for a single event. When a person tosses a coin and gets a head, it does not mean that a tail will fall next. The fact that the electrical machine statistically shocks one in a hundred cases does not mean that it is very unlikely that it will hurt a given person.

Another example of apparently neglecting low probabilities is a refusal to play Russian roulette. As one-sixth is not low probability, let's assume that one refuses to play a special version of the game with a gun with one hundred chambers and only one bullet. That refusal does not prove irrationality or probability neglect; it is a manifestation of common sense and an elementary desire to survive. Although the expected payout could be large, when played for money, anyone who continues to play long enough will eventually end up in the cemetery (Taleb 2018).

What is important is that the payoff trajectory for one person is something completely different from the average payoff from all parallel universes.[6] Although only in 1 percent of parallel universes would a person get an electric shock, die from a fire, or die from COVID-19, the situation looks different from the dynamic point of view, as she can get shocked, fired, or seriously ill at the very beginning of her life's trajectory. In other words, when the choice can never be presented again, as it could end with death, there will be no large number of subsequent events to which probability theory could be applied (Weckstein 1952). As Mises (1981[1957], 11) notes:

> When we speak of the 'probability of death', the exact meaning of this expression can be defined in the following way only. We must not think of an individual, but of a certain class as a whole, e.g., 'all insured men forty-one years old living in a given country and not engaged in certain dangerous occupations'. A probability of death is attached to the class of men or to another class that can be defined in a similar way. We can say nothing about the probability of death of an individual even if we know his condition of life and health in detail. The phrase 'probability of death', when it refers to a single person, has no meaning for us at all.[7]

Hence, the insensitivity to significant variations within the category of low-probability events documented by Sunstein (2003) is not necessarily an anomaly that results from cognitive bias. It rather shows the uselessness of using concepts from probability theory in real, non-ergodic life. If probability theory does not strictly apply to daily life, why should people treat the arithmetically expressed probabilities in any other way than as rough indicators or just metaphors, and why should they react to changes within the low range of chances, especially when they have only limited time and cognitive resources (Simon 1956)?

4. Do people neglect probability in an uncertain world?

Moreover, while ergodicity means that the future is risky in a probabilistic sense, non-ergodicity implies that the future is truly uncertain. Neither past nor current developments can be the guide to the future (Davidson 1987). Hence, the problem is not how to compute the probability, but how to live in an uncertain world without knowing what we don't know. Probability theory is helpful in a casino, but it is not sufficient in an uncertain world where there are many unknown unknowns. As Keynes (1937, 214) writes, there are significant differences between a roulette game and the possibilities of new inventions, the prospect of war, or the outlook for asset prices: 'About these matters there is no scientific basis on which to form any calculable probability whatever. We simply do not know'.

In other words, Sunstein and other behavioral researchers (for example, Kahneman 2011) confuse risk with uncertainty (Knight 1921), or class probability with case probability (Mises 1998). The problem is that risk, or class probability, refers to homogeneous, repetitive events whose probability we can estimate, such as a specific result of a roll of the dice. But it does not apply to activities whose probability is not known—that is, to the vast majority of events in business and everyday life, including terrorist attacks or pandemics. Statistics (about the past) say nothing about future threats that are fundamentally uncertain.

For example, flying into the twin towers of the World Trade Center was a unique event. How were people to assess the danger of the next terrorist attack and determine the risk of traveling by airplane in the United States in a world of new threats? After the 9/11 attack, Americans could reasonably assume that their world had changed and instead of inserting new information into the old algorithm, they simply discarded the algorithm saying that planes are safer than cars. A world in which planes are hijacked and flown into skyscrapers is qualitatively different from a world in which planes are not hijacked. In other words, the 9/11 attack reformulated the decision situation, changing not only probabilities but also the possible outcomes (Meder, Le Lec, and Osman 2013).

Similarly, the COVID-19 pandemic is a unique one. Surely, there have been pandemics before. But the sample is very small, and the pandemics have all been different. COVID-19 is caused by a new, not yet fully understood coronavirus, and we still do not have authoritative data about the nature of the pathogen and the illness—just estimates.[8] The concept of risk here is thus useless, as probability statements refer to large classes of events. Instead, we operate in a dynamic, environment full of uncertainty. No wonder that people have been cautious. Under risk, the outcomes and probabilities are known, while under uncertainty the probabilities, or even both probabilities and outcomes, are unknown.[9] Facing threats whose probability we cannot estimate, it is simply more rational from the evolutionary point of view to err on the safe side and to overestimate rather than underestimate the possibility of danger.

Moreover, COVID-19 is an infectious disease, which means that the risk is multiplicative. It implies that actions that seem irrational or exaggerated at an individual level are precisely the actions we need from the systemic point of view (Taleb and Norman 2020). In other words, society can overcome the epidemic only when some people react excessively and take aggressive precautionary measures to limit contagion. Some individuals may, therefore, underestimate the danger and write about exaggerated reactions of other people only because these other people 'overestimate' the threat, acting to limit it for themselves and the whole society.

The thesis that people overestimate or neglect the very low risk of terrorist attacks or epidemics is therefore misguided because the concept of risk does not apply here at all; the chances cannot be estimated. It is therefore difficult to claim that people neglected probability or behaved irrationally in opting (in the case of terrorist attacks) for a form of transport that was more under their control and minimized a new, undefined threat, even if it could ultimately prove more dangerous. Since we cannot determine the likelihood of the threat, no criteria are showing whether our response is exaggerated. In other words, without known odds, there is no single optimizing solution. As (Arthur 1992, 6) notes, 'Where a problem is ill-defined, optimizing behavior is also ill-defined'.

5. Conclusions

I have shown that claims that probability neglect applies to terrorist attacks and the COVID-19 pandemic are not justified. The fact that some people take precautionary steps to avoid infection from COVID-19 does not necessarily imply neglect of probability. An alternative hypothesis could be that people who downplay the epidemiological threat and do not take precautionary measures suffer from exponential-growth bias. To be clear, although there is some evidence that people think in linear rather than exponential terms (Stango and Zinman 2009; Levy and Tasoff 2017; Goda et al. 2015), I do not argue that such a tendency necessarily constitutes a cognitive bias. My point is to demonstrate how one can easily come up with a cognitive bias people admittedly suffer from. Gigerenzer (2018) calls such a tendency to spot systematic biases even if there are none the 'bias bias'.[10] However, although it is still too early for a thorough assessment, the later development of the COVID-19 pandemic seems to confirm the exponential-growth-bias hypothesis rather than the probability-neglect hypothesis. Even Sunstein himself changed his mind in an article with the telling title 'This Time the Numbers Show We Can't Be Too Careful' (Sunstein 2020b).[11]

Importantly, my critique of the concept of probability neglect is not restricted to the case of pandemics, which are very specific events of exponential and multiplicative nature. It also applies to the risk of terrorism. Although it is true that generally the number of deaths due to terrorist attacks remains low, the 9/11 attack was a unique, unprecedented event, and Americans could reasonably change their paradigm instead of merely adjusting the probabilities slightly. Thus, people's reactions did not show that they neglected *probability*, but rather that they had to cope somehow with the newly generated *uncertainty*. As King (2016, 131–134) notes:

> In a world of radical uncertainty, where it is not possible to compute the 'expected utility' of an action, there is no such thing as optimizing behavior … humans do not optimise; they cope. They respond and adapt to new surroundings, new stimuli and new challenges. The concept of coping behaviour does not, however, mean that people are irrational. On the contrary, coping is an entirely rational response to the recognition that the world is uncertain.

More generally, this article argues that the very concept of probability neglect as a cognitive bias is dubious, as observations that in certain settings people demonstrate insensitivity to changes within the range of low statistical probabilities do not prove cognitive bias.[12] They can rather mean that probability theory cannot be easily applied to human actions occurring in a world of non-ergodicity and uncertainty.

In other words, pandemics and other real-world problems highlight limitations in the way judgment and decision-making is often conceptualized in the behavioral economics (Meder, Le Lec, and Osman 2013). The conditions for the correct application of probability theory are simply not present in the situation in which people are coping with a new coronavirus of unknown nature. So what appears to be irrational under risk is not always irrational under uncertainty. If there is no comparative standard, the whole idea of deviations from the benchmark fails. If the probability cannot be applied and estimated, it cannot be overestimated or neglected.[13]

Notes

1. To be precise, Gigerenzer (2020) refers to people's tendency to fear dread risks (Slovic 1987; Gigerenzer 2004; Gigerenzer 2006). However, as they are defined as low-probability, high-consequence events, the tendency to avoid them is conceptually similar to Sunstain's probability neglect, i.e. disregarding the likelihood when assessing low-probability but high-impact threats.
2. I thank the anonymous reviewer for pointing this out to me.
3. The word 'initially' is crucial here, as an epidemiological curve is logistic.
4. The seasonal flu and COVID-19 differ also in other aspects, such as the incubation time, hospitalization rate, and case fatality rate, in such a way that the latter is potentially more dangerous (Resnick and Animashaun 2020). Ioannidis et al. (2020) compare the mortality risk of COVID-19 with that of car accidents, which makes

even less sense, as car accidents are not infectious diseases of exponential nature, and their mortality risk is not multiplicative.

5. Please note that participants were only asked to imagine that they were required to participate in such a psychological experiment. Hence, generalizations from people's response to such study into a real terrorist attack or pandemic seem to be questionable, if not an example of hasty generalization fallacy.

6. Similarly, the risk of investing into a single entrepreneurial project – such as shares of one company or one oil drill – is higher than the risk of investing in a diversified portfolio of shares of one hundred companies or one hundred of oil drills.

7. One could argue that our critique of probability neglect relies on the frequentist theory of probability. However, if the subjective theory of probability is true, and probability measures only the degree of belief, then it is questionable to argue that people miscalculate or neglect the probability. De gustibus non est disputandum. A more detailed discussion of different theories of probabilities is beyond the scope of this article.

8. The emergence of a novel coronavirus with limited data about it should evoke epistemic humility among scientists, especially from non-epidemiologists (Angner 2020). Instead, we have rather seen overconfidence among the above-cited behavioral researchers.

9. The former kind of uncertainty is Knightian uncertainty, while the latter is radical uncertainty (Mader et al. 2013).

10. However, Gigerenzer (2020) seems to explain the fear of COVID-19 by reference to risk illiteracy or the tendency to fear of dread risk.

11. Sunstein (2020b) makes no reference to Sunstein (2020a). I am aware that a popular article is not a scientific paper, but in some sense that makes the matter even worse, as more people read popular than scientific articles. Intellectual honesty would require a reference, especially since all opinions about the threat of COVID-19 can potentially affect people's behavior and thus their health.

12. To be clear, people sometimes neglect probability, just as they sometimes focus too much on it, but occasional behavior does not prove cognitive bias.

13. Sunstein (2020a) notices that it is impossible to determine the exact danger from the COVID-19 pandemic, but he nevertheless claims that people feel excessive fear: 'At this stage, no one can specify the magnitude of the threat from the coronavirus. But one thing is clear: A lot of people are more scared than they have any reason to be. They have an exaggerated sense of their own personal risk'.

Disclosure statement

No potential conflict of interest was reported by the authors.

References

Angner, E. 2020. "Epistemic Humility—Knowing Your Limits in a Pandemic." *Behavioral Scientist*, April 13. Accessed April 21, 2020. https://behavioralscientist.org/epistemic-humility-coronavirus-knowing-your-limits-in-a-pandemic/

Arthur, W. B. 1992. "On Learning and Adaptation in the Economy," Queen's Economics Department Working Paper, No. 854, Department of Economics Queen's University.

Baud, D., X. Qi, K. Nielsen-Saines, D. Musso, L. Pomar, and G. Favre. 2020. "Real Estimates of Mortality following COVID-19 Infection." *Lancet Infectious Diseases*. Correspondence. https://www.thelancet.com/journals/laninf/article/PIIS1473-3099(20)30195-X/fulltext#articleInformation

Davidson, P. 1987. "Sensible Expectations and the Long-Run Non-Neutrality of Money." *Journal of Post Keynesian Economics* 10 (1): 146–153. doi:10.1080/01603477.1987.11489666.

DeSteno, D. 2020. "How Fear Distorts Our Thinking About the Coronavirus." *The New York Times*, February 11. Accessed April 21, 2020. https://www.nytimes.com/2020/02/11/opinion/international-world/coronavirus-fear.html

Faust, J. S. 2020. "Comparing COVID-19 Deaths to Flu Deaths Is like Comparing Apples to Oranges." *Scientific American*, April 28. Accessed May 7, 2020. https://blogs.scientificamerican.com/observations/comparing-covid-19-deaths-to-flu-deaths-is-like-comparing-apples-to-oranges/

Gigerenzer, G. 2004. "Dread Risk, September 11, and Fatal Traffic Accidents." *Psychological Science* 15 (4): 286–287. doi:10.1111/j.0956-7976.2004.00668.x.

Gigerenzer, G. 2006. "Out of the Frying Pan into the Fire: Behavioral Reactions to Terrorist Attacks." *Risk Analysis: An Official Publication of the Society for Risk Analysis* 26 (2): 347–351. doi:10.1111/j.1539-6924.2006.00753.x.

Gigerenzer, G. 2018. "The Bias Bias in Behavioral Economics." *Review of Behavioral Economics* 5 (3-4): 303–336. doi: http://dx.doi.org/10.1561/105.00000092.

Gigerenzer, G. 2020. "Why What Does Not Kill Us Makes Us Panic." *Project Syndicate*, March 12. Accessed April 21, 2020. https://www.project-syndicate.org/commentary/greater-risk-literacy-can-reduce-coronavirus-fear-by-gerd-gigerenzer-2020–03

Goda, G. S., M. R. Levy, C. F. Manchester, A. Sojourner, and J. Tasoff. 2015. "The Role of Time Preferences and Exponential-Growth Bias in Retirement Savings." NBER Working Papers No. 21482. doi: 10.3386/w21482.

Horst, U. 2008. "Ergodicity and Nonergodicity in Economics." In *The New Palgrave Dictionary of Economics*, edited by S. N. Durlauf and L. E. Blume, vol. 3, 2 ed., 30–33. London: Palgrave Macmillan.

Ioannidis, J. P. A., C. Axfors, and D. G. Contopoulos-Ioannidis. 2020. "Population-Level COVID-19 Mortality Risk for Non-Elderly Individuals Overall and for Non-Elderly Individuals Without Underlying Diseases in Pandemic Epicenters." medRxiv 2020.04.05.20054361. doi:https://doi.org/10.1101/2020.04.05.20054361.

Kahneman, D. 2011. *Thinking, Fast and Slow*. New York: Farrar, Straus and Giroux.

Karnitschnig, M. 2020. "The Incompetence Pandemic." *Politico*, March 16. Accessed April 20, 2020. https://www.politico.com/news/2020/03/16/coronavirus-pandemic-leadership-13154

Keynes, J. M. 1937. "The General Theory of Employment." *The Quarterly Journal of Economics* 51 (2): 209–222. doi: 10.2307/1882087.

King, M. 2016. *The End of Alchemy: Money, Banking and the Future of the Global Economy*. London: Little, Brown, kindle edition.

Knight, F. H. 1921. *Risk, Uncertainty, and Profit*. Boston, MA: Hart, Schaffner & Marx; Houghton Mifflin Company.

Levy, M. R., and J. Tasoff. 2017. "Exponential-Growth Bias and Overconfidence." *Journal of Economic Psychology* 58: 1–14. doi:http://dx.doi.org/10.1016/j.joep.2016.11.001.

Ma, J. 2020. "Estimating Epidemic Exponential Growth Rate and Basic Reproduction Number." *Infectious Disease Modelling* 5: 129–141. doi:10.1016/j.idm.2019.12.009.

Meder, B., F. Le Lec, and M. Osman. 2013. "Decision Making in Uncertain Times: What Can Cognitive and Decision Sciences Say about or Learn from Economic Crises?" *Trends in Cognitive Sciences* 17 (6): 257–260. doi:10.1016/j.tics.2013.04.008.

Mises, L. 1998. *Human Action: A Treatise on Economics*. The Scholar's ed. Auburn: Ludwig von Mises Institute.

Mises, R. 1981. *Probability, Statistics and Truth*. 2nd revised ed. New York: Dover.

Resnick, B., and Ch Animashaun. 2020. "Why Covid-19 Is Worse that the Flu, in One Chart." *VOX*, March 18. Accessed April 21, 2020. https://www.vox.com/science-and-health/2020/3/18/21184992/coronavirus-covid-19-flu-comparison-chart

Rottenstreich, Y., and C. Hsee. 2001. "Money, Kisses, and Electric Shocks: On the Affective Psychology of Risk." *Psychological Science* 12 (3): 185–190. doi:10.1111/1467-9280.00334.

Schoenfeld, J. 2020. "The Invisible Risk: Pandemics and the Financial Markets." *COVID Economics. Vetted and Real-Time Papers*, CEPR Press, Centre for Economic Policy Research, 119–136. Issue 6, April 17.

Simon, H. A. 1956. "Rational Choice and the Structure of the Environment." *Psychological Review* 63 (2): 129–138. doi:10.1037/h0042769.

Slovic, P. 1987. "Perception of Risk." *Science (New York, N.Y.)* 236 (4799): 280–285. doi:10.1126/science.3563507.

Spychalski, P., A. Błażyńska-Spychalska, and J. Kobiela. 2020. "Estimating Case Fatality Rates of COVID-19." *The Lancet Infectious Diseases*. Correspondence. doi:10.1016/S1473-3099(20)30246-2.

Stango, V., and J. Zinman. 2009. "Exponential Growth Bias and Household Finance." *The Journal of Finance* 64 (6): 2807–2849. doi:10.1111/j.1540-6261.2009.01518.x.

Sunstein, C. R. 2002. "Probability Neglect: Emotions, Worst Cases, and Law." *The Yale Law Journal* 112 (1): 61. doi:10.2307/1562234.

Sunstein, C. R. 2003. "Terrorism and Probability Neglect." *Journal of Risk and Uncertainty* 26 (2-3): 121–136. doi:10.1023/A:1024111006336.

Sunstein, C. R. 2020a. "The Cognitive Bias That Makes Us Panic About Coronavirus." *Bloomberg*, February 28. Accessed April 21, 2020. https://www.bloomberg.com/opinion/articles/2020–02–28/coronavirus-panic-caused-by-probability-neglect

Sunstein, C. R. 2020b. "This Time the Numbers Show We Can't Be Too Careful." *Bloomberg*, March 26. Accessed April 21, 2020. https://www.bloomberg.com/opinion/articles/2020–03–26/coronavirus-lockdowns-look-smart-under-cost-benefit-scrutiny

Taleb, N. N. 2018. *Skin in the Game: Hidden Asymmetries in Daily Life*. New York: Random House.

Taleb, N. N., and J. Norman. 2020. "Ethics of Precaution: Individual and Systemic Risk." Accessed April 21, 2020. https://www.academia.edu/42223846/Ethics_of_Precaution_Individual_and_Systemic_Risk

Weckstein, R. S. 1952. "On the Use of the Theory of Probability in Economics." *The Review of Economic Studies* 20 (3): 191–198. doi:10.2307/2295889.

Verity, R, L. C. Okell, I. Dorigatti, P. Winskill, C. Whittaker, N. Imai, G. Cuomo-Dannenburg, et al. 2020. "Estimates of the Severity of Coronavirus Disease 2019: A Model-Based Analysis." *The Lancet Infectious Disease*. doi:https://doi.org/10.1016/S1473–3099(20)30243–7.

COVID-19 infection and death rates: the need to incorporate causal explanations for the data and avoid bias in testing

Norman E. Fenton, Martin Neil (iD), Magda Osman (iD) and Scott McLachlan

ABSTRACT

COVID-19 testing strategies are primarily driven by medical need - focusing on people already hospitalized with significant symptoms or on people most at risk. However, such testing is highly biased because it fails to identify the extent to which COVID-19 is present in people with mild or no symptoms. If we wish to understand the true rate of COVID-19 infection and death, we need to take full account of the causal explanations for the resulting data to avoid highly misleading conclusions about infection and death rates. We describe how causal (Bayesian network) models can provide such explanations and the need to combine these with more random testing in order to achieve reliable data and predictions for the both policy makers and the public.

Misleading death rates

Suppose we wanted to estimate how many car owners there are in the UK and how many of those own a Ford Fiesta, but we only have sampled data on those people who visited Ford Car Showrooms in the last year. If 9% of the showroom visitors owned a Fiesta then, because of this selection bias in the sampled data, this would certainly overestimate the proportion of Ford Fiesta owners in the country. Estimating death rates for people with COVID-19 is currently under-taken largely along the same lines.

Take the UK as an example, where at the time of writing almost all testing of COVID-19 is performed on people already hospitalized with COVID-19 symptoms. At the time of writing,[1] there were – according to the official NHS reporting figures – 33,722 confirmed COVID-19 cases (analogous to car owners visiting a showroom) of whom 2,921 have died (Ford Fiesta owners who visited a showroom). Concluding that the death rate from COVID-19 is on average 9% (2,921 out of 33,722) ignores the many people with COVID-19 who are not hospitalized and have not died (analogous to car owners who did not visit a Ford showroom and who do not own a Ford Fiesta). It is therefore equivalent to making the mistake of concluding that 9% of all car owners own a Ford Fiesta.

There are many prominent examples of this sort of erroneous conclusion. The Oxford COVID-19 Evidence Service (Oke and Heneghan 2020) have undertaken a thorough statistical analysis. They acknowledge potential selection bias, but for them 'uncertainty' takes the form of

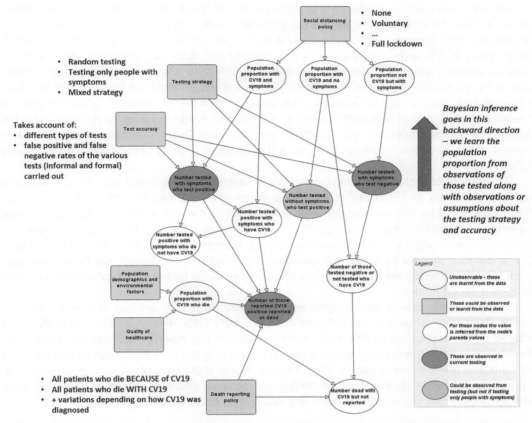

Figure 1. Causal Bayesian network model for learning population COVID-19 infected and death rates. This is a single time slice. It is can be updated daily and so enables us also to learn the true rate of spread of the infection. 'With symptoms' means serious symptoms.

confidence bounds around the (potentially highly misleading) proportion of deaths among confirmed COVID-19 patients. They also note various factors that can result in wide national differences, such as different demographic factors and differences in the way deaths are reported. The latter clearly may be a critical factor in explaining why a country like the UK's 9% (mean) 'death rate' is so high compared to Germany's 0.74%. We know that in the UK currently everybody who dies *with* COVID-19 is recorded as a COVID-19 death, even if the disease was not the actual cause of death; but it is also possible that people may die from the virus without actually having been diagnosed with COVID-19 (Henriques 2020).

The fact that all the uncertainty around the death rates remains I anchored around one statistic, reported deaths per confirmed cases, is awkward. It fails to incorporate explicit causal explanations that might enable us to make more meaningful inferences from the available data, including data on virus testing. To do this we need explicit causal/graphical models (Pearl and Mackenzie 2018).

The need for a causal model

Figure 1 is an example of a causal model, represented by a graph (called a Bayesian network), that might be applicable to any given country and its population. It shows that the COVID-19 death rate is as much a function of sampling methods, testing and reporting, as it is determined by the underlying rate of infection in a vulnerable population.

The links between the variables in the model (nodes in graph) show how they are dependent on each other. For example, the 'population proportion with COVID-19 who die' is dependent on 'population demographics and environmental factors' as well as 'Quality of healthcare' (which might cover factors such as intensive care unit capacity etc). Note that the model carefully distinguishes between whether or not a person really has COVID-19 and whether the person is *classified* as having COVID-19 (i.e. the model takes account of the potential for false positive and false negative test results). So, for example, the variable 'Number of reported COVID-19 positive reported as died' (which is the official figure of 'COVID-19 deaths reported) is dependent on the actual 'Population proportion with COVID-19 who die', the 'Death Reporting Policy' as well as several other variables including 'Number tested positive with symptoms who do not have COVID-19'.

The strength of each dependency, as well as the uncertainty associated with these is captured using probabilities and statistical distributions. When observed data is entered into the model for specific variables that are subsequently observed all of the probabilities for, as yet, unknown variable are updated using an AI algorithm called Bayesian inference. The model in Figure 1 is more accurately called a (causal) Bayesian network (Fenton and Neil 2018), because it explains the underlying process by which the observed data might be generated. We have developed such models for many similar problems and are currently gathering the data needed to determine this causal model.

Therefore, while clinical, demographic and environmental factors can lead to genuine differences in death rates shown across different countries, very large differences may be likely to be caused by the application of different sampling strategies and reporting policies (Binnicker 2020; FindX 2020) and not necessarily because they are managing the virus any better or that the virus has infected fewer or more people. With a causal model that explains the data generating process we might better account for these differences between countries and more accurately learn the underlying true population infection and death rates from the observed data.

The need for more random testing

In the absence of community-wide testing, only random testing, applied throughout the population, will help us learn the number of people with COVID-19 who are asymptomatic or have already recovered, and hence also estimate the underlying infection and death rates. It will also help us learn the accuracy of the testing undertaken (false positive and false negative rates). Random testing remains the most effective strategy to avoid selection bias and reduce the distortions in reported statistics, but it also needs to be combined with a causal model in order to better determine the prevalence, severity, and ultimately societal impact of COVID-19.

Currently it seems there are no state-wide protocols in place in any country for randomised community testing of citizens for COVID-19. Spain did attempt it, but that involved purchasing large volumes of rapid COVID-19 tests, and they soon discovered that some Chinese-sourced tests had poor validity and reliability delivering only 30% accuracy – resulting in high numbers of false positives. Countries like Norway have proposed introducing such tests, but there is uncertainty around how to legislatively compel citizens to test – and what might constitute an appropriate randomisation protocol. In Iceland, they have voluntary sampling which has covered 3% of the population, but this isn't random. Some countries with large scale testing, like South Korea, might get closer to being random.

The reason it is so hard to achieve random testing is that you have to account for several practical and psychological factors. How does one collect samples randomly? Gathering samples from volunteers may not be sufficient as it does not prevent self-selection bias.

During the H1N1 influenza pandemic of 2009–2010, there was a lot of anxiety about the disease that created 'mass psychogenic illness' (Wheaton et al. 2012). This is when hypersensitivity to particular symptoms leads to healthy people self-diagnosing as having a virus – meaning they would be highly incentivised to get tested. This could, in part, further contribute to false positive rates if the sensitivity and specificity of the tests are not fully understood.

While self-selection bias is not going to be eliminated, it could be reduced by running field tests. This could involve asking the public to volunteer samples in locations where, even in a lockdown state, they might be expected to attend and also from those in self-imposed isolation or quarantine. In any event, when statistics are communicated at press conferences or in the media, their limitations should be explained and any relevance to the individual or population should be properly delineated. It is this which we contend is lacking in the current crisis.

Note

1. https://experience.arcgis.com/experience/685d0ace521648f8a5beeeee1b9125cd

Disclosure statement

Norman Fenton and Martin Neil are Directors of Agena Ltd.

Funding

This work was supported in part by EPSRC under project EP/P009964/1: PAMBAYESIAN: Patient Managed decision-support using Bayesian Networks.

ORCID

Martin Neil http://orcid.org/0000-0002-4922-0843
Magda Osman http://orcid.org/0000-0003-1480-6657

References

Binnicker, M. 2020. "Emergence of a Novel Coronavirus Disease (COVID-19) and Importance of Diagnostic Testing: Why Partnership between Clinical Laboratories, Public Health Agencies and Industry is Essential to Control the Outbreak." *Clinical Chemistry*. 12 March https://academic.oup.com/clinchem/article/doi/10.1093/clinchem/hvaa071/5741389
Fenton, N. E., and M. Neil. 2018. *Risk Assessment and Decision Analysis with Bayesian Networks*. 2nd ed. Boca Raton: CRC Press.
FindX. 2020. "COVID-19 Diagnostics." 7 April. https://www.finddx.org/covid-19/
Henriques, M. 2020. "Coronavirus: Why Death and Mortality Rates Differ." BBC Future website. 7 April. https://www.bbc.com/future/article/20200401-coronavirus-why-death-and-mortality-rates-differ
Oke, J., and C. Heneghan. 2020. "Oxford COVID-19 Evidence Service." 7 April. https://www.cebm.net/covid-19/global-covid-19-case-fatality-rates/
Pearl, J., and D. Mackenzie. 2018. *The Book of Why: The New Science of Cause and Effect*. New York: Basic Books.
Wheaton, M. G., J. S. Abramowitz, N. C. Berman, L. E. Fabricant, and B. O. Olatunji. 2012. "Psychological Predictors of Anxiety in Response to the H1N1 (Swine Flu) Pandemic." *Cognitive Therapy and Research* 36 (3): 210–218. doi: 10.1007/s10608-011-9353-3.

Bayesian network analysis of Covid-19 data reveals higher infection prevalence rates and lower fatality rates than widely reported

Martin Neil (iD), Norman E. Fenton (iD), Magda Osman (iD) and Scott McLachlan

ABSTRACT

Widely reported statistics on Covid-19 across the globe fail to take account of both the uncertainty of the data and possible explanations for this uncertainty. In this article, we use a Bayesian Network (BN) model to estimate the Covid-19 *infection prevalence rate* (*IPR*) and *infection fatality rate* (*IFR*) for different countries and regions, where relevant data are available. This combines multiple sources of data in a single model. The results show that Chelsea Mass. USA and Gangelt Germany have relatively higher *IPR*s than Santa Clara USA, Kobe, Japan, and England and Wales. In all cases the infection prevalence is significantly higher than what has been widely reported, with much higher community infection rates in all locations. For Santa Clara and Chelsea, both in the USA, the most likely *IFR* values are 0.3–0.4%. Kobe, Japan is very unusual in comparison with the others with values an order of magnitude less than the others at, 0.001%. The *IFR* for Spain is centred around 1%. England and Wales lie between Spain and the USA/German values with an *IFR* around 0.8%. There remains some uncertainty around these estimates but an *IFR* greater than 1% looks remote for all regions/countries. We use a Bayesian technique called 'virtual evidence' to test the sensitivity of the *IFR* to two significant sources of uncertainty: survey quality and uncertainty about Covid-19 death counts. In response the adjusted estimates for *IFR* are most likely to be in the range 0.3–0.5%.

1. Introduction

Widely reported statistics on Covid-19 across the globe fail to take account of both the uncertainty of the data and possible explanations for this uncertainty (Fenton et al. 2020a, 2020b). In this article, we use a Bayesian Network (BN) model to estimate the Covid-19 *infection prevalence rate* (*IPR*) and *infection fatality rate* (*IFR*) for different countries and regions, where relevant data are available. Unlike other statistical techniques that have been used to interpret Covid-19 data, BNs combine multiple sources of data in a single model that provides statistical estimates that better reflect the uncertainty regarding mechanisms that generate the data, and the amount and type of data that is available.

The article examines results from recent serological antibody surveys carried out globally. Plainly, any uncertainty about the accuracy of serological testing will influence the estimate of the size of community infected with Covid-19 and this will in turn influence any estimate of the *IFR*. A serological test with low accuracy will tend to poorly estimate the size of the community infected and this, in turn, will lead to a poor estimate of the fatality rate. Also, if the fatality count is itself unreliable the fatality rate will suffer again, because if we do not know how many had the disease and how many have died, we cannot estimate the fatality rate with confidence.

The Bayesian approach is generally recognised as more advanced than classical statistical approaches that are typically applied and can therefore address more complex questions (Pearl 1986, Fenton and Neil. 2018). Unfortunately, while it may seem like there has been a deluge of Covid-19 data, there is a dearth of publicly available data of the type necessary for conducting an unbiased analysis of true infection and death rates. Typically, there is also a lack of transparency surrounding the analysis and use of data, with much of the detail and data remaining secret. Hence, we have gathered data from academic papers (mainly pre-prints), press interviews, and other sources including state archives and the mass media.

The BN model (which is implemented in a commercial, state of the art, probabilistic modelling software application – AgenaRisk; Agena Ltd 2020) provides answers to these questions, even in the presence of such basic uncertainties. Specifically:

- What is the accuracy of serological antibody testing under development and how well does it estimate population infection prevalence?
- What serological testing surveys have been done and what does the data tell us about the prevalence of community infection in different locations.
- If the serological testing surveys are imperfect what effect does this have on our estimated *IPR* s?
- Given our prevalence estimates, how does this compare to the case infection numbers? (those who test positive for Covid-19) that is, how much higher is actual community infection compared to reported infection?
- From reported fatality statistics what is the *IFR*? How does serological test quality affect the reliability of these estimates? Likewise, how does uncertainty about fatality counts affect these estimates?
- How do our estimates of covid-19 *IFR* compare to influenza *IFR*?

The article is structured as follows: In Section 2, we discuss Covid-19 testing with a particular focus on serological tests and their accuracy (sensitivity and specificity). In Section 3, we present the data and assumptions used in our analysis. In Section 4, we present the single BN model that provides answers to a series of epidemiological questions about the disease, prevalence and infection, simultaneously, and in such a way that uncertainties about the answers to one question will influence our uncertainties about the other and vice versa. The results are presented in Section 5. Our conclusions are presented in Section 6.

2. Covid-19 serological testing

What is the accuracy of serological antibody tests under development how well does it estimate population infection prevalence?

The Covid-19 *IPR* rate can be deduced from serological antibody testing, which identifies those in the tested population whose body retains an immune response arising from prior infection with Covid-19. As the disease spreads through the population, the proportion of people who develop antibodies increases and the proportion with antibodies depends on exposure and time since the disease was introduced into the community. Hence, different countries and regions will be at different points in this process and will exhibit different *IPR* rates.

The Covid-19 *IPR* rate will also be crucially dependant on our ability to accurately measure whether an individual has antibodies. Typically, serological tests of blood or other body fluids are used to detect antibody levels and hence determine either infection (IgM antibodies) or potential immunity (IgG antibodies). Presence of the latter identifies whether patients have previously had the disease, independent of whether they exhibited symptoms. Leaving aside concerns about whether immunity is temporary or indeed absent, our uncertainty about whether a patient has had Covid-19 depends on the accuracy of the serological testing process. A patient who has tested positive using a Covid-19 serological test can do so for two reasons—they genuinely have antibodies at detectable levels (these are called 'true positives'), or the testing process falsely identifies them as antibody positive (these are called 'false positives'). Hence, accuracy of the test is determined by its sensitivity[1] and specificity, where:

$$Sensitivity = True\ positive\ rate = 1 - (False\ negative\ rate)$$
$$Specificity = 1 - (False\ positive\ rate)$$

As false positive and false negative rates rise, the greater our uncertainty will be about any diagnosis of Covid-19 for an individual and across a population.

Serological testing processes, kits and machines are presently being assessed for accuracy using samples drawn from patients who are known to have the disease or are disease free. Pharmaceutical companies and academic researchers use these known samples to determine the sensitivity and specificity. At the time of writing a number of pharmaceutical serological tests have been made available in the marketplace and indeed some have received FDA emergency authorised approval for use (FDA 2020). Accuracy for many of these tests is presently being debated.

The Covid-19 *IFR* rate is simply the number of fatalities up to some point in time divided by the size of the community infected with the virus. The number of infected will include those who test positive for antibodies, which includes those who tested positive (IgM antibodies) and those who currently test negative, but show an immune response (IgG antibodies) identifying that they were infected with Covid-19 sometime in the past. Likewise, the number of community infected cases will include those who are asymptomatic and symptomatic, whether hospitalized or not, those who finally die with (or of) the disease, and those who were infected but have fully recovered. We can estimate the number of community infected from the serological testing, and as we have said, this depends on the accuracy of the testing process. If the serological tests are inaccurate estimates of the number of infected will be more uncertain, leading to less reliable estimates for *IFR*. Similarly, the number of fatalities, and any uncertainty about the true number of fatalities, also influences the *IFR*. For example, overestimation of causalities by certifying Covid-19 deaths where patients died as a result of some pre-existing condition while infected with Covid-19, rather than only those where Covid-19 was the direct cause of their death (Fenton et al. 2020a) will lead to greater uncertainty about the fatality rate.

3. Data and assumptions

What serological testing surveys have been done and what does the data tell us about the prevalence of community infection in different locations?

We use serological antibody survey data from these sources:

- Santa Clara County, California, USA (Bendavid et al. 2020)
- Kobe, Japan (Doi 2020)
- Gangelt, Germany (Streeck et al. 2020)
- Chelsea, Massachusetts, USA (Saltzman 2020)

- NHS England and Wales serological survey, UK (Blanchard 2020)
- Spain (Carlos 2020)

We have also gathered and used publicly available data on serological antibody test accuracy for each of these test sources from the FDA (2020), manufacturer websites and research papers:

- Roche, as hypothetical for England and Wales UK (FDA 2020)
- Kurabo Inc, for Kobe, Japan (Karubo Ltd 2020)
- Premier Biotech, for Santa Clara, California, USA (Bendavid et al. 2020)
- EUROIMMUN for Gangelt (FDA 2020)
- BioMedomics for Chelsea, Massachusetts, USA (BioMedomics 2020)
- Orient Gene Biotech, for Spain (Carlos 2020)

It is important note that the sensitivity and specificity values are normally calculated using simply arithmetic ratios; so if the sample tested had zero false positives or false negatives then the sensitivity and specificity would be reported to be perfect (100%), no matter how many were tested. However, if you run one, and only one, test and confirm it positive, would you believe the test to be perfect on such a small experiment? This issue is addressed by the BN model. Some tests identify early or existing infection through detection of IgM antibodies. Other tests can identify patients who at some point in the past were infected with and successfully fought off the disease through detection of IgG antibodies. Many antibody tests are developed that can detect both, and where a test has this capability the regulated clinical trial and test validation process generally identifies different sensitivity and specificity values for that test for each antibody. Many of the Covid-19 antibody tests receiving emergency clearance can detect two or three antibodies but are only reporting one sensitivity and specificity value. More often this is for IgM antibodies, creating further uncertainty when we use that test to identify those who previously had the disease.

To illustrate our uncertainties about the results of serological testing we look at the false positive and false negative rates for the various serological test sources, used to estimate population infection prevalence, as shown in Table 1.

UK fatality data and Covid-19 infection rates were collected from the UK Office for National Statistics (ONS) (ONS 2020a) and from the worldometers website (Worldometers 2020).

All available data are taken from the mid-April to early May 2020 snapshot. Thus, different countries and regions within countries will have different *IPRs* as these will be a determined by when the virus was first introduced and the time elapsed. For data we assume the time from infection to recovery (or fatality) is sufficient to ensure that any anyone infected will have detectable traces of antibodies in their blood.

4. The Bayesian network (BN) model

A BN is a graphical model consisting of nodes and arcs where the nodes represent variables and an arc between two variables represents a dependency. The strength of each dependency, as

Table 1. Sensitivity and specificity tests.

Test source	Number of FP tests	False positives	Specificity (%)	Number of FN tests	False negatives	Sensitivity (%)
Roche	5272	10	99.8	29	0	100.0
Kurabo[a]	521	0	100.0	500	100	80.0
Premier Biotech	371	2	99.5	160	7	95.6
EUROIMMUN	80	0	100.0	30	3	90.0
BioMedomics	128	12	90.6	397	45	88.7
Orient Gene Biotech[a]	500	0	100.0	500	75	85.0

a Note the Karubo and Orient Biotech test sources are inferred from published sensitivity and specificity statics and total sample sizes.

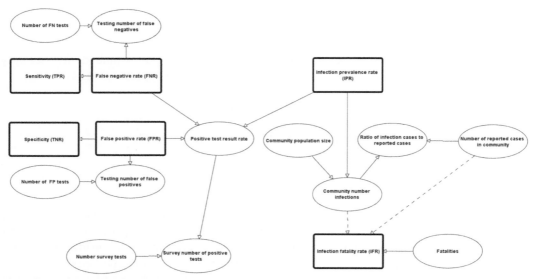

Figure 1. Bayesian Network Model to estimate Covid-19 *IPR* and *IFR*.

well as the uncertainty associated with these, is captured using probabilities and statistical distributions. When observed data are entered into the model for specific variables all the probabilities for, as yet unknown, unobserved or latent variables, are updated by Bayesian inference.

The BN model used for our analysis is shown in Figure 1 for the joint probability density function below:

$$f(TPR, FNR, \ldots, IFR) = f(TPR|FNR)f(FN|n_{FN}, FNR) \times$$
$$f(TNR|FPR)f(FP|n_{FP}, FPR)f(P|IPR, FNR, FPR) \times$$
$$f(PS|n_S, P)f(C|Z, P)f(R|C, RCC)f(IFR|F, C) \; f(IPR)f(Z)f(RCC)$$

This represents the conditonal and prior probability functions for these variables, as shown in Table 2. The statistical distributions and conditional probability densities are given in the Appendix.

Bayesian inference is performed in AgenaRisk (Agena Ltd 2020) which uses the dynamic discretization algorithm (Neil, Tailor, and Marquez 2007).

The goal of a mass serological antibody survey is to estimate the *IPR* of the virus in the population. If we knew the *IPR*, the false negative rate (*FNR*), and false positive rate (*FPR*) then we can determine the probability, *P*, of a positive test result as:

$$P = IPR(1 - FNR) + (1 - IPR)FPR$$

This is because there are two ways to test positive. The first is where someone is infected (probability *IPR*) and correctly test positive (probability $(1 - FNR)$), giving $(1 - FNR) \times IPR$. The second is where someone is *not* infected, $(1 - IPR)$, but they falsely test positive, *FPR* and this gives us $(1 - IPR)FPR$.

Here we use the BN to solve the 'inverse problem', where we estimate the *IPR* given information about *FNR*, *FPR*, and *P*, that is, the test accuracy (sensitivity and specificity) and the number of positive tests from a given serological survey. Again, poor test accuracy will lead to poorer estimates of the *IPR* and, again, the size of the survey, in terms of samples taken, will determine the confidence in our estimates, with bigger samples translating to better information.

Once the BN model estimates the distribution for *IPR* this is used to estimate community infections, *C*, and ultimately the infection fatality rate, *IFR*.

Table 2. Variables in Bayesian Network model.

TPR	True positive rate (sensitivity)	IPR	Infection Prevalance Rate
TNR	True negative rate (specificity)	PS	Survey number of positive tests
FN	False negatives in testing	n_S	Number of survey tests
FP	False positives in testing	IFR	Infection fatality rate
n_{FN}	Number of false negative tests	C	Community number of infections
n_{FP}	Number of false positive tests	Z	Community population size
FPR	False positive rate	R	Ratio of infection cases to reported cases
FNR	False negatve rate	RCC	Number of reported cases in community
P	Positive test result rate	F	Number of fatalilites

5. Results using available data

5.1. Infection prevalence rates

If the serological testing surveys are imperfect what effect does this have on our estimated IPR s?

To date very few serological surveys have been carried out and where they have been, some results have been difficult to obtain given the secrecy involved. The survey data and sources are listed below in Table 3. Note that here we are using raw data unadjusted for demographic or other population features.

*Note that the positive test results for England and Wales is inferred from public announcements made by the UK Government's Chief Medical Officer (Blanchard 2020) about the UK ONS antibody survey (ONS 2020b).

We have the serological test results from the Santa Clara County, California USA, study (Biomedomics 2020) and Gangelt, Germany (FDA 2020). However, for the Kobe, Japan, study we only had specificity and sensitivity point values and total sample sizes from Kurano (Karubo Ltd 2020) and had to infer the likely values. Also, we do not know what serological tests were applied in England and Wales. The UK government have, however, announced they were choosing Roche as one of their serological antibody test suppliers, and so we assume a test with equivalent accuracy was used (FDA 2020).

The full probability distributions that the BN model computes IPR for all cases are shown in Figure 2 and the associated summary statistics are listed in Table 4.

From Figure 2 and Table 4 we can see that Chelsea Mass. USA and Gangelt Germany have relatively higher IPRs than Santa Clara USA, Kobe, Japan and England and Wales.

5.2. Estimates of community infections

Given our prevalence estimates, how does this compare to the case infection numbers? (those who test positive for Covid-19) that is, how much higher is actual community infection compared to reported infection?

Now we have an estimate of the IPR we can use this to estimate the number of community infections, C, in a region or country, given the relevant community population size. We can also compare this estimate with the number of reported cases of Covid-19 in the community, to determine the extent to which Covid-19 is more or less widespread than thought and also to determine proportion of cases likely to be symptomatic/asymptomatic and severe/slight.

Source data on the actual number of Covid-19 infection cases have been taken from the relevant research papers or other sources, and in the case of the UK from worldometers, for mid-April, where it reported to be circa. 100,000 (Worldometers 2020). The summary statistics form the distributions calculated from the BN of the number of community infections are given in Table 5.

Table 5 shows that the estimated community prevalence is much higher than reported prevalence. Figure 3 and Table 6 show the results from the model of the ratio of estimated to

Table 3. Serological surveys.

Test source	Samples	Positive tests
Santa Clara	3330	50
Kobe	521	22
Gangelt	500	75
Chelsea	200	64
England and Wales	1000	50*
Spain	50983	3049

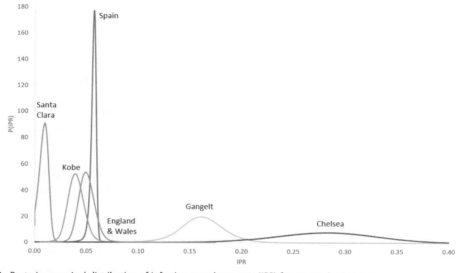

Figure 2. Posterior marginal distribution of Infection prevalence rate (*IPR*) for country/region cases.

Table 4. Summary statistics for *IPR*.

Case	Test source	Assumption	Mean	95% CI
Santa Clara	Premier Biotech	Actual source	0.00879 (0.88%)	(0.0009, 0.0165)
Kobe	Kurabo	Actual source	0.040 (0.4%)	(0.0254, 0.0562)
Gangelt	EUROIMMUN	Actual source	0.162 (16.2%)	(0.1162, 0.0208)
Chelsea Mass.	BioMedomics	Actual source	0.28 (28.1%)	(0.1795, 0.3780)
England and Wales	Roche	Hypothesised source	0.0506 (0.51%)	(0.0368, 0.0670)
Spain	Orient Gene Biotech	Actual source	0.05663 (0.56%)	(0.0496, 0.0617)

reported cases and the effect that unreliability in survey testing has on the result. Clearly in all cases the extent of community prevalence is much higher than reported. There is however considerable uncertainty about the ratio distribution for Kobe and Santa Clara, given their confidence interval is so wide.

5.3. Infection fatality rates

From reported fatality statistics what is the Covid-19 *IFR*?

The final piece of the jigsaw puzzle is our estimation of *IFR*, for each of the countries and regions where we have data available, and here this includes, England and Wales and Chelsea Mass. USA, Santa Clara USA, Kobe Japan, Spain, and Gangelt, Germany.

The reported fatalities up to mid-April in the UK is 23,554 (ONS 2020b). The reported fatality count for Chelsea, Massachusetts is 39 (Saltzman 2020) and for Santa Clara, California is 94 (Ioannidis 2020). For Gangelt, Germany it is 7 (Streeck et al. 2020). For Spain, the fatality count is

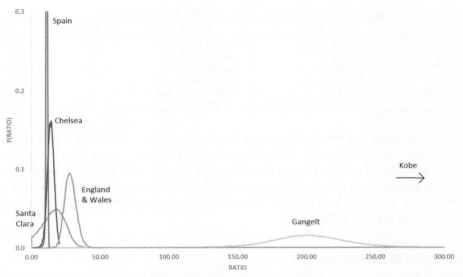

Figure 3. Posterior marginal distribution of Ratio of estimated community infections (*R*) to cases to reported cases by country/region cases (excluding Kobe, Japan).

Table 5. Summary statistics for Community number infections, *C*.

Case	Test source	Assumption	Mean	95% CI	Reported cases
Santa Clara	Premier Biotech	Actual source	15,668	(1617, 29529)	956
Kobe	Kurabo	Actual source	60,839	(38428, 85499)	69
Gangelt	EUROIMMUN	Actual source	2,015	(1443, 2595)	10
Chelsea Mass.	BioMedomics	Actual source	16,131	(12821 19637)	803
England and Wales	Roche	Hypothesised source	2,839,500	(2057300, 3753600)	100,000
Spain	Orient Gene Biotech	Actual source	2,600,100	(2274700, 2804900)	230,000

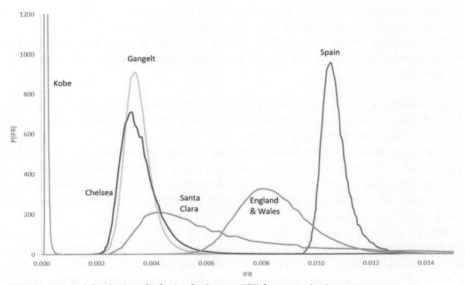

Figure 4. Posterior marginal distribution of Infection fatality rate (*IFR*) for country/region cases.

27,888 (Worldometers 2020) and for Kobe Japan it is 10 (Ioannidis 2020). Figure 4 shows the predicted distributions from the BN model for each *IFR*, while Table 7 shows the summary statistics.

The most likely (modal) *IFR* values are grouped for Santa Clara and Chelsea, both in the USA, with mode values of 0.3–0.4%. However, for Santa Clara there is higher uncertainty giving a long

Table 6. Summary statistics for ratio of estimated community infections, R, to reported cases.

Case	Test source	Assumption	Mean	95% CI
Santa Clara	Premier Biotech	Actual source	16	(1.68, 30.98)
Kobe	Kurabo	Actual source	881	(556.93, 1240.5)
Gangelt	EUROIMMUN	Actual source	201	(144.24, 259.7)
Chelsea Mass.	BioMedomics	Actual source	14	(8.95, 18.92)
England and Wales	Roche	Hypothesised source	28	(20.3, 37.5)
Spain	Orient Gene Biotech	Actual source	11	(9.88, 12.19)

tail in the data hence the mean value is significantly higher at 1.02%. This shows the estimate for Santa Clara is less informative. Kobe, Japan is very unusual in comparison with the others with values an order of magnitude less at 0.001%. The *IFR* for Spain has a low variance, which is unsurprising given the very large survey conducted, with a mean and mode rate close to each other centred around 1%. England and Wales lie between Spain and the USA/German values with a mode and mean of 0.8%.

5.5. Sensitivity to uncertainty

How does serological test quality affect the reliability of the above estimates of the *IFR*? Likewise, how does uncertainty about fatality counts affect these estimates?

The preceding analysis has simply used the available 'raw' data without any adjustment for demographics or to take account of differences between countries and regions. In this section, we choose two sources of uncertainty that have not been covered by other researchers and which strongly determine the sensitivity of results, especially for *IFR*. These concern fatality counts and the quality of the serological surveys themselves.

There is some controversy over UK fatality counts (Fenton et al. 2020a) and there appear to be many reasons not to trust the fatality count, including:

- Ambiguity and confusion about diagnostic criteria for Covid-19
- Care home deaths not certified by a qualified medical practitioner
- Hospital and other deaths signed off as 'caused by' Covid-19 when they are 'with' Covid-19
- The number of excess deaths could be much higher because of cases that remain undiagnosed

Similar concerns apply to Spain and potentially elsewhere. Given that these uncertainties work in both directions we must be careful to include under and over-estimates and not chose one to suit our prejudices or political outlook.

The Santa Clara study has been heavily criticised by some statisticians in a popular blog (Stats Blog 2020), mainly because subjects were recruited using Facebook and perceived issues with sample sizes and other aspects of the analysis undertaken. Similar observations and comments have been made about the Chelsea study because subjects were chosen for convenience and availability rather than at random.

Typically, experimenters would design their study to address the sensitivity of the results to uncertainties, using relevant and, potentially, causal classifications such as demographic stratification of the relevant population. However, given that we have observational rather than experimental data we can only perform a post hoc evaluation of the sensitivity of the results. Hence, in this section we address these major uncertainties, using our BN model. The lack of controls in these observational studies translates into less informative estimates and more variability.

We use the notion of 'virtual' evidence to assess how different observations might affect our results. In this way we view the observations not as 'facts' but as random variables, bounded by possible ranges of value. This enables us to ask hypothetical questions such as: What would the

Table 7. Summary statistics for the *IFR* rate.

Case	Test source	Fatality count	Mode	Mean	95% CI
Santa Clara	Premier Biotech	94	0.004 (0.4%)	0.0102 (1.02%)	(0.0031, 0.0595)
Kobe, Japan	Kurabo	10	0.00015 (0.001%)	$1.7271E-4$ (0.0002%)	$(1.16E-4, 2.60E-4)$
Chelsea Mass.	BioMedomics	39	0.003 (0.3%)	0.0029 (0.29%)	(0.0025, 0.0054)
Gangelt, Germany	EUROIMMUN	7	0.003 (0.3%)	0.0036 (0.36%)	(0.0026, 0.0048)
England and Wales	Roche	23,554	0.008 (0.8%)	0.0085 (0.85%)	(0.0062, 0.0114)
Spain	Orient Gene Biotech	27,888	0.010 (1.0%)	0.0107 (0.107%)	(0.0099, 0.0122)

Table 8. Virtual evidence scenarios.

Case	Virtual evidence
Santa Clara	Observed positives $PS_{obs} \sim Uniform(1, 50)$
Chelsea Mass.	Observed positives $PS_{obs} \sim Uniform(1, 64)$
England and Wales	Fatalities $F_{obs} \sim Triangular(5000, 10000, 30000)$
Spain	Fatalities $F_{obs} \sim Triangular(6000, 12000, 35000)$

results have been had fatalities been exaggerated or the number of positives from a study been fewer?

For the Santa Clara $PS_{obs} = Binomial(n_S, P) = 50$, meaning we have 50 positive results from the binomial model. Virtual evidence allows us to place a likelihood over the distribution for PS_{obs} that reflects our uncertainty about the study design. Here we use $PS_{obs} \sim Uniform(1, 50)$ representing a sceptical belief that any value between one and fifty is equally likely from this study because the study design was such that it made it more likely that prior infected subjects would volunteer. Once we enter this virtual evidence into the BN it will compute the posterior probability distribution using this likelihood instead of a single point observation. Bayesian inference then computes the posterior distribution using this 'sceptical' likelihood along with other evidence in the model. Clearly, the resulting posterior will not necessarily match the likelihood provided, and indeed may contradict it, perhaps demonstrating the scepticism was unwarranted. We can apply the same process to the fatality counts and apply 'virtual evidence' that reflects deeper uncertainties about whether people 'died because of' Covid-19 as opposed to 'with' Covid-19.

We applied virtual evidence in four cases, as shown in Table 8. Uncertainties about the study design are represented for Santa Carla and Chelsea, Mass., USA. Uncertainties about the true fatality count are represented for England & Wales and Spain.

The sensitivity of *IFR* to these changes to the evidence is shown with the full distributions in Figure 5 and summary statistics in Table 9.

The effect of virtual evidence is to increase the variability of the results, as one would expect. For the Santa Clara and Chelsea studies where we adjusted the observed survey positives the mean fatality rate estimates increase. However, the modal values do not change much at all, remaining around 0.3–0.5%, suggesting that the BN model is balancing the sceptical explanations against other evidence in the model and discounting any virtual evidence that is perhaps too sceptical. Figure 6 shows the posterior marginal distributions that result from the application of virtual evidence on the number of positive tests for these studies. Clearly any strong scepticism that the number of genuine positives must be close to zero is not warranted and in the case of Chelsea observations less than 30 are difficult to justify. The model clearly 'believes' the survey results are credible.

After the adjustment, distributions of the *IFR* across the USA, Spain and the UK look very similar; the most likely range for *IFR* is between 0.2 and 1%, with values beyond this looking less likely.

5.6. Comparison with influenza

How do our estimates of covid-19 *IFR* compare to influenza *IFR*?

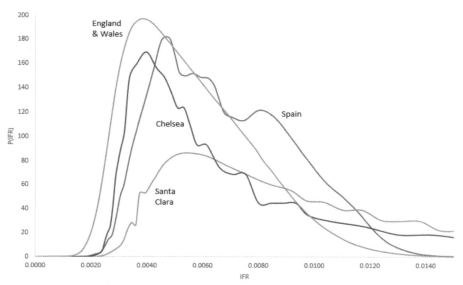

Figure 5. Posterior marginal distribution of Infection fatality rate (*IFR*) for country/region cases in virtual evidence scenarios.

Table 9. Summary statistics for *IFR* in virtual evidence scenarios.

Case	Test source	Fatality count	Mode	Mean	95% CI
Santa Clara	Premier Biotech	94	0.005 (0.5%)	0.0217 (2.17%)	(0.0038, 0.0968)
Chelsea Mass.	BioMedomics	39	0.003 (0.3%)	0.0124 (1.24%)	(0.0030, 0.0485)
England and Wales	Roche	23,554	0.004 (0.4%)	0.0056 (0.56%)	(0.0024, 0.0106)
Spain	Orient Gene Biotech	27,888	0.004 (0.4%)	0.0107 (1.07%)	(0.0032, 0.0118)

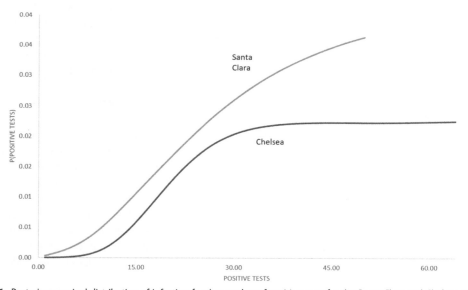

Figure 6. Posterior marginal distribution of Infection for the number of positive tests for the Santa Clara and Chelsea cases.

For comparison, the fatalities in England and Wales for the 'higher than seasonal average' in the year 1999/2000 were 21,290 excess deaths attributed to influenza like illness (Crofts et al. 2004), from an infected population of 440,440 (influenza like illness reports) (ONS 2015). With a population of approximately 52 m this is an *IPR* of just over 0.8% and a case fatality rate *CFR* of

4.8%. However, it should be noted that the equivalent of population level serological antibody testing is not routinely performed for influenza hence the *IPR* is likely to be underestimated and the *IFR* significantly less than the *CFR*.

6. Conclusion

Widely reported statistics on Covid-19 across the globe fail to take account of both the uncertainty of the data and possible explanations for this uncertainty. In this article, we have used a BN model to estimate the Covid-19 *IPR* and *IFR* for different countries and regions, where relevant data are available. This combines multiple sources of data in a single model.

We used this model, and available data on serological surveys, fatality counts and test accuracy, to answer the following questions: What is the accuracy of serological antibody tests under development and will it be sufficient to estimate population infection prevalence? What serological testing surveys have been done and what does the data tell us about the prevalence of community infection in different locations? If the serological testing surveys are imperfect what effect does this have on our estimated *IPR* s? Given, our prevalence estimates, how does this compare to the case infection numbers? From reported fatality statistics what is the *IFR*? How does serological test quality affect the reliability of these estimates? Likewise, how does uncertainty about fatality counts affect these estimates? How do our estimates of Covid-19 *IFR* compare to influenza *IFR*?

The results show that Chelsea Mass. USA and Gangelt Germany have relatively higher *IPRs* than Santa Clara USA, Kobe, Japan and England and Wales. In all cases the infection prevalence is significantly higher than has been widely reported, with much higher community infection rates in all locations. For Santa Clara and Chelsea, both in the USA, with most likely *IFR* values of 0.3–0.4%. Kobe, Japan is very unusual in comparison with the others with values an order of magnitude less than the others at, 0.001%. The *IFR* for Spain has a low variance, which is unsurprising given the large survey conducted, with an *IFR* centred around 1%. England and Wales lie between Spain and the USA/German values with an *IFR* around 0.8%. There remains some uncertainty around these estimates but an *IFR* greater than 1% looks remote. We used a Bayesian technique called 'virtual evidence' to test the sensitivity of the *IFR* to two significant sources of uncertainty: survey quality and uncertainty about death rates. In response the adjusted estimates for *IFR* that are most likely to be in the range 0.3–0.5%. The unadjusted and adjusted Covid-19 *IFR* s calculated may be significantly less than that from the 1999/2000 UK influenza season, which had an *IPR* of just over 0.8% and a case fatality rate *CFR* of 4.8%. However, the influenza *IPR* is likely to be underestimated and the *IFR* significantly less than the *CFR* due to the absence of routine serological surveillance.

It is worth emphasising the significant problems facing any researcher with objectives like ours. There is a severe lack of transparency and important data sets are inaccessible. To support open debate these should be treated as a public good and shared openly throughout the scientific community in a timely manner.

Note

1. Note that these rates can either be presented as percentages (ranging from 0 to 100%) or as probabilities (ranging from 0 to 1) as done in the formulas here.

Acknowledgements

We are grateful to Elma Neil for producing the template for the statistical graphs.

Disclosure statement

No potential conflict of interest was reported by the author(s).

Funding

This work was supported in part by the EPSRC under project EP/P009964/1: PAMBAYESIAN: Patient Managed decision-support using Bayesian Networks.

ORCID

Martin Neil ⓘD http://orcid.org/0000-0002-4922-0843
Norman Fenton ⓘD http://orcid.org/0000-0003-2924-0510
Magda Osman ⓘD http://orcid.org/0000-0003-1480-6657

References

Agena Ltd. 2020. "AgenaRisk". http://www.agenarisk.com.

Bendavid, E., B. Mulaney, N. Sood, S. Shah, E. Ling, R. Bromley-Dulfano, C. Lai, et al. 2020. COVID-19 Antibody Seroprevalence in Santa Clara County, California. *medRxiv*. https://www.medrxiv.org/content/ doi:10.1101/2020.04.14.20062463v2..2020. doi:10.1101/2020.04.14.20062463.

Biomedomics. 2020. COVID-19 IgM/IgG Rapid Test. Biomedics Inc. https://www.biomedomics.com/products/infectious-disease/covid-19-rt/

Blanchard, S. 2020. Comments made in press report by Whitty, C., Chief Medical Officer, UK Government. How many people in London have REALLY had coronavirus? *Daily Mail newspaper*. Accessed 24 April 2020. https://www.dailymail.co.uk/news/article-8250371/How-people-REALLY-caught-coronavirus.html.

Carlos. 2020. Instituto de Salud, Carlos III. Estudio ENE-Covid-19: Estudio nacional de seor-epidemiologia de la infection por SARS-Cov-2 en Espana. May 2020. https://portalcne.isciii.es/enecovid19/documentos/ene_covid19_res.pdf

Crofts, J. P., C. A. Joseph, M. Zambon, J. Ellis, D. M. Fleming, and J. M. Watson. 2004. "Influenza Surveillance in the United Kingdom: October 2002 to May 2003." *Communicable Disease Report. CDR Supplement* 14: 1–9.

Doi, A., K. Iwata, H. Kuroda, T. Hasuike, S. Nasu, A. Kanda, T. Nagao, et al. Seroprevalence of novel coronavirus disease (COVID-19) in Kobe, Japan. *medRxiv* https://www.medrxiv.org/content/10.1101/2020.04.26.20079822v2.

FDA. 2020. U.S. Food and Drug Administration. EUA Authorized Serology Test Performance. Accessed 22 April 2020. https://www.fda.gov/medical-devices/emergency-situations-medical-devices/eua-authorized-serology-test-performance.

Fenton, N., and M. Neil. 2018. *Risk Assessment and Decision Analysis with Bayesian Networks*. Boca Raton, FL: CRC Press.

Fenton, N. E., M. Neil, M. Osman, and S. McLachlan. 2020a. "COVID-19 Infection and Death Rates: The Need to Incorporate Causal Explanations for the Data and Avoid Bias in Testing." *Journal of Risk Research* 1–4. doi:10.1080/13669877.2020.1756381.

Fenton, N., M. Osman, M. Neil, and S. McLachlan. 2020b. Coronavirus: Country comparisons are pointless unless we account for these biases in testing. *The Conversation*. https://theconversation.com/coronavirus-country-comparisons-are-pointless-unless-we-account-for-these-biases-in-testing-135464

Ioannidis, J. 2020. The infection fatality rate of COVID-19 inferred from seroprevalence data. *medRxiv*. https://www.medrxiv.org/content/10.1101/2020.05.13.20101253v1. doi:10.1101/2020.05.13.20101253.

Karubo Ltd. 2020. *Products and Technology*. https://www.kurabo.co.jp/bio/English/index.html.

Neil, M., M. Tailor, and D. Marquez. 2007. "Inference in Hybrid Bayesian Networks Using Dynamic Discretization." *Statistics and Computing* 17 (3): 219–233. doi:10.1007/s11222-007-9018-y.

ONS. 2015. UK Office for National Statistics. Highest number of excess winter deaths since 1999/2000. Accessed 25 November 2015. https://www.ons.gov.uk/peoplepopulationandcommunity/birthsdeathsandmarriages/deaths/articles/highestnumberofexcesswinterdeathssince19992000/2015-11-25

ONS. 2020a. Deaths involving COVID-19, England and Wales. *UK Office for National Statistics*. https://www.ons.gov.uk/peoplepopulationandcommunity/birthsdeathsandmarriages/deaths/datasets/deathsinvolvingcovid19englandandwales.

ONS. 2020b. ONS jointly leading government's large-scale virus infection and antibody test study. *UK Office for National Statistics*. Accessed 22 April 2020. https://www.ons.gov.uk/news/news/onsjointlyleadinggovernmentslargescalevirusinfectionandantibodyteststudy

Pearl, J. 1986. "Fusion, Propagation, and Structuring in Belief Networks." *Artificial Intelligence* 29 (3): 241–288. doi:10.1016/0004-3702(86)90072-X.

Saltzman, J. 2020. Nearly a third of 200 blood samples taken in Chelsea show exposure to coronavirus, *Boston Globe*. Accessed 17 April 2020. https://www.bostonglobe.com/2020/04/17/business/nearly-third-200-blood-samples-taken-chelsea-show-exposure-coronavirus/

Stats Blog. 2020. Concerns with that Stanford study of coronavirus prevalence. Statistical modelling, causal inference and social science blog. 2020. https://statmodeling.stat.columbia.edu/2020/04/19/fatal-flaws-in-stanford-study-of-coronavirus-prevalence/

Streeck, H., B. Schulte, B. Kuemmerer, E. Richter, T. Höller, C. Fuhrmann, E. Bartok, et al. 2020. Infection fatality rate of SARS-CoV-2 infection in a German community with a super-spreading event. *medRxiv.* https://www.ukbonn.de/C12582D3002FD21D/vwLookupDownloads/Streeck_et_al_Infection_fatality_rate_of_SARS_CoV_2_infection2.pdf/$FILE/Streeck_et_al_Infection_fatality_rate_of_SARS_CoV_2_infection2.pdf.

Worldometers. 2020. *COVID-19 Coronavirus Pandemic.* https://www.worldometers.info/coronavirus/.

Appendix: Bayesian network model

$$f(TPR, FNR, \ldots, IFR) = f(TPRFNR)f(FNn_{FN}, FNR) \times$$
$$f(TNRFPR)f(FP|n_{FP}, FPR)f(P|IPR, FNR, FPR) \times$$
$$f(PS|n_S, P)f(CZ, P)f(R|C, RCC)f(IFR|F, C) \ f(IPR)f(Z)f(RCC)$$

False Positive Rate : $FPR \sim Uniform(0, 1)$

False Negative Rate : $FNR \sim Uniform(0, 1)$

Specificity $(FPR) = 1 - FPR$

Sensitivity $(TPR) = 1 - FNR$

Testing number of false positives : $FP \sim Binomial(n_{FP}, FPR)$

Number of FP tests : n_{FP}

Testing number of false negatives : $FN \sim Binomial(n_{FN}, FNR)$

Number of FN tests : n_{FN}

Infection prevalence rate : $IPR \sim Uniform(0, 1)$

Positive test result rate : $P = IPR(1 - FNR) + (1 - IPR)FPR$

Number of survey tests : n_S

Survey number of positive tests : $PS \sim Binomial(n_S, P)$

Community population size : $Z \sim Uniform(1, 1E10)$

Number of reported Covid19 cases in the community : RCC

Community number of infections : $C \sim max(RCC, Binomial(Z, IPR))$

Ratio of infected cases to reported cases : $R = \dfrac{C}{RCC}$

Fatalities : F

Infection Fatality Rate : $IFR = F/C$

Virtual evidence for England and Wales: *Fatalities* : $F_{obs} \sim Triangular(5000, 10000, 30000)$
Virtual evidence for Spain: *Fatalities* : $F_{obs} \sim Triangular(6000, 12000, 35000)$
Virtual evidence for Santa Clara, USA study: $PS_{obs} \sim Uniform(1, 50)$
Virtual evidence for Chelsea, USA study: $PS_{obs} \sim Uniform(1, 64)$

Resilience in the face of uncertainty: early lessons from the COVID-19 pandemic

C. Bryce, P. Ring, S. Ashby and Jamine. K. Wardman

ABSTRACT

The transboundary dynamics of COVID-19 present an unprecedented test of organisational resilience. In the UK, the National Health Service (NHS), a talisman of collective fortitude against disease and illness, has struggled to cope with inadequate provision of virus tests, ventilators, and personal protective equipment needed to fight the pandemic. In this paper, we reflect on the historic dynamics and strategic priorities that have undermined the NHS's attempts to navigate these troubled times. We invoke the organisational resilience literature to address 'the good, the bad and the ugly' of preparedness in readiness and response to the current pandemic. In particular, we draw on Meyer's (1982) seminal work on 'adaptation to jolts', excavating current preparedness failings. We argue an overreliance on perceived efficiency benefits of 'lean production' and 'just in time' continuity planning superseded strategic redundancy and slack in the system. This strategic focus was not simply the result of a failure in foresight, but rather a failure to act adaptively on knowledge of the known threats and weaknesses spotlighted by earlier projections of an inevitable pandemic threat. In conclusion, we consider how the UK Government and NHS must now undergo a phase of 'readjustment' in Meyer's terms, in light of these failings. We suggest that independent responsibility for national future preparedness should be handed to the NHS free from political interference. This would operate under the umbrella of a national emergency preparedness, resilience and response public body, enshrined in law, and similar in governance to the current Bank of England. This will help ensure that foresight is accompanied by durability and fortitude in safeguarding the UK against future pandemic threats.

1. Introduction

Nothing has changed, yet everything is different

Jean-Paul Sartre

In the past few decades, businesses have maintained the continuity of their operations in the face of AIDS, SARS, Avian Flu, Zika, and Ebola amongst other health crises,[1] and for the most part they have recovered quickly. A month after the outbreak of COVID-19 being reported by the World Health Organisation (WHO) on 31st January 2020, some commentators were already predicting a similar outcome, suggesting that worries were overblown and that we should carry on as normal (Sunstein 2020). Some world leaders including Donald Trump mistakenly suggested that Covid-19 was *'not as bad a seasonal flu'* (Trump 2020). Boris Johnson, the UK Prime Minister, in turn suggested that the UK could strike a balance somewhere between *'taking it on the chin'* and *'extra precautions'*, all while assuring that UK health workers 'have all preparations, all the kit that they need for us to get through' (ITV 2020). Now such optimism is in short supply.

Though COVID-19 was previously unknown to science, its behaviour is typical of other coronaviruses. It is part of a large family of respiratory tract diseases that includes the common cold and its closest predecessor SARS (Severe Acute Respiratory Syndrome). Usually the symptoms of COVID-19 are mild to moderate, but for some, especially those with pre-existing health conditions, they can be fatal. While global epidemics aren't new, COVID-19 inhabits a world of growing complexity, technological advancement and interconnections, where relatively small risk events can develop in unexpected ways. It is a transboundary crisis with a current localised exponential growth rate of 2.5 (Boin 2019).

These transboundary crises present a significant challenge for organisations, including businesses and public institutions. Established crisis management responses can be ineffective and business continuity can be severely disrupted as problems occur over multiple domains and manifest in unfamiliar ways. Often escalating and migrating risk quickly across political and social boundaries to affect society, businesses, and global financial markets (Grabowski and Roberts 1997).

More challenging still, transboundary crises involve multiple actors and conflicting responsibilities (Burgess, Wardman, and Mythen 2018). There are no easy solutions. As we have seen with COVID-19 a common early government response is to enforce social distancing through 'lockdowns', where non-essential leisure and work activities are banned in an attempt to limit transmission. However, the effects of these measures on consumer spending and business operations have been devastating, with multiple household names such as 'Flybe' filing for, or on the brink of, bankruptcy (Hollinger et al. 2020).

How then should organisations navigate transboundary crises and what does the COVID-19 pandemic teach us about the effectiveness of their response? Can organisations adapt and survive, maintaining the continuity of their operations in the face of an escalating global pandemic and equally threatening public policy responses to limiting its spread? In this paper we invoke the literature on organisational resilience to explore the good, the bad and the ugly in terms of preparedness and initial response.

2. The good, the bad and the ugly

'Unexpected events often audit our resilience' (Weick and Sutcliffe 2007). Put another way, resilience is not an outcome, but rather a process (Weick, Sutcliffe, and Obstfeld 1999) by which organisations continuously work to anticipate, and respond, to external threats on a continuous basis. In his seminal paper, Meyer (1982) suggests that 'adaptations to jolts' can be understood as having an 'anticipatory', 'responsive', and a 'readjustment' phase. Subsequent literature on resilience has, generally, fallen into one of these three areas (Bhamra, Dani, and Burnard 2011). Sutcliffe and Vogus (2003) also examine adaptability of organisations in the face of both severe and less severe challenging conditions, noting that this adds *'both to the strength of the current entity and also to the strength of the future entity, in that resilience is the continuing ability to use internal and external resources successfully to resolve issues'* (2003, 96).

The hindsight of past incidents undoubtedly provides a window of foresight for those prepared to look into what their organisational resilience (or lack of) could be (Meyer 1982). Take the case of H-E-B supermarkets in Texas, which had been developing and refining their emergency preparedness plans for over 15 years (Solomon and Forbes 2020). The H1N1 swine flu virus in 2009 provided them with a 'window into the future' by which to learn key insights about ensuring product supply chains and employees were resilient to the challenges COVID-19. As early as the second week in January organisational personnel were establishing what worked and what didn't across the supply chains of all the major countries affected by the pandemic, making sure their local Texan communities were resourced correctly. This proactive approach stands in stark contrast to what we have seen in the UK, with mounting criticism that the difficulties confronting the NHS represent a fundamental failure of preparedness by the national government. Most stern criticism relates to NHS staff not being adequately tested or properly resourced with Personal Protective Equipment (PPE), and the poor provision of ventilators (along with trained staff able to operate them) for severely ill patients.

If a supermarket chain in Texas can react as quickly as it did, why has NHS preparedness for those on the frontline of the crisis been so wanting? To help address this question, it is instructive to examine the adaptive response and resilience of the NHS to the COVID-19 crisis so far.

For Meyer (1982), the anticipatory element of resilience is based upon 'foresight'. His examination of San Francisco hospitals found that foresight derives from organisations adopting entrepreneurial and outward looking strategies. An appreciation of the world around them (opportunities and threats), and an openness to new ideas (see also De Geus 1999; Ashby, Bryce, and Ring 2018) are clear. The importance of anticipation is also underscored by Weick and Sutcliffe (2007) examination of High Reliability Organisations (HROs). They argue that organisations exhibiting high reliability are able to sense weak signals that may presage significant unexpected events, in so far as 'sense' means appreciating the meaning and implications of those signals (as opposed to perceiving those signals more rapidly). That said, anticipation will also include what Walker, Nilakant, and Baird (2014) refer to as 'planned resilience'; that is, business continuity and risk management plans that set out how to avoid or minimise the effect of a crisis.

In the case of the NHS and COVID-19, a lack of foresight into the possibility of a major pandemic outbreak does not appear to have been the main issue. Pandemic influenza is, and was, regarded as one of the highest risks faced by the UK. For instance, within the six year old national pandemic influenza response plan the CEO of Public Health England (PHE) states that *'Ensuring the country is fully prepared and able to respond quickly and effectively is a top priority for Public Health England and, of course, for the government'* (PHE 2014a, 5). Moreover, in 2016, the NHS in collaboration with PHE conducted reasonable worst-case scenario stress test of its influenza preparedness called 'Exercise Cygnus' (NHS 2017b). Whilst the results of this exercise have not been made public, the then Chief Medical Officer indicated afterwards that Britain faced the threat of 'inadequate ventilation' (Lambert 2020). Given that emergency preparedness, resilience, and response are statutory requirements of the NHS in the Civil Contingencies Act (2004), the onus was on the NHS and the government to tackle these clearly anticipated weaknesses.

The findings of 'Exercise Cygnus' and other such exercises in anticipation were clearly never acted upon in a meaningful way. Which is to say, responsibility for managing the stockpiles of PPE used by frontline health and social care staff as outlined by PHE (2014b) appears to have constituted little more than preparedness on paper only. Normally, redundancy in any system means that there is duplication and backups (Landau 1969; Lerner 1986; Husted 1993). This technical redundancy within system critical processes is fundamental to their functioning under extreme environmental stressors (Grabowski and Roberts 1997). Whereas in this case, the NHS (2017a) framework for managing a response to a pandemic influenza outbreak indicates that stockpiles of PPE and other such equipment are also made up of 'just in time' contracts for supplies (2017a, 21). This then relied upon an assumption that supply chains would always remain resilient to failures (Grabowski and Roberts 1997). In the event, what we have seen in the last few weeks is the current Health Secretary pleading in a reactionary way for companies to come forward who could build ventilators at scale and speed. Necessity is the mother of invention, and those manufacturers, and Formula 1 – University partnerships that have risen to the challenge to provide 'bounce back' should be commended (UCL 2020). However, the reality is that the systemic threat posed by the pandemic has proven disruptive to the very supply lines of health equipment we are dependent upon to stop its spread and help those in most dire need of assistance. Had the warnings of 'Exercise Cygnus' been acted upon 4 years ago, such efforts would not be so fraught or needed in the first place.

Lean production methods, such as just-in-time supply chains, are not limited to the NHS in the UK. Global businesses and public institutions use them to reduce costs and improve responsiveness to consumer needs. While such methods can improve economic efficiency and production flexibility, helping to manage a range of strategic risks (e.g. fluctuating consumer demand) they are vulnerable to extreme operational stress. As Richardson (1994, 73) observes *'strategic management is not only the inventor of strategies for the management of chaos it is also the propeller of chaos itself'*. That is not to say that operational stresses cannot be managed through collaboration with supply chain partners, as in the case of Toyota and the Aisin fire (e.g. Brüning, Hartono, and Bendul 2015). However, when all of the available partners are simultaneously shut down, collaboration is no longer feasible.

The COVID-19 pandemic has revealed the weaknesses of lean production and just-in-time delivery. The effective closure of Chinese manufacturing from late January through much of February, with a tentative recovery in March has caused global disruption (McMorrow and Mitchel 2020). China is the major global supplier of the personal protective equipment much needed in the fight against the virus. It also supplies components for a range of products found in local supermarkets, a fundamental reason why H-E-B was so alert to the pandemic in the first place. H-E-B understood the importance of constantly monitoring this region given its business model's sensitivity to it. In the US, 94% of Fortune 500 companies experienced disruptions to their supply chains (Sherman 2020). To make matters worse, restrictions on international travel, imposed to prevent the spread of the virus, have impacted on shipping and logistics activities, meaning that even when PPE was available it could not be delivered (Edgecliffe-Johnson 2020; Peel 2020). Nevertheless, lean supply chains do not explain the lack of urgency by the UK government and its agencies to ramp up their preparedness and systemic resilience in the face of early mounting evidence and warnings from mid-January (Huang et al. 2020; Wu, Leung, and Leung 2020).

History is littered with similar failings in organisational resilience and disaster preparedness (Perrow, 2011). Warnings by scientists about back-up diesel generators to water pumps being stored below sea level at the Fukushima Daiichi nuclear power station were also ignored (Srinivasan and Rethinaraj 2013; Synolakis and Kânoğlu 2015). The subsequent inability to cool the nuclear reactors with water after the tsunami knocked out power led to their eventual meltdown - the comparison is not lost in this current context.

An argument could be made that had the consequences of the H1N1 pandemic in 2009 not been 'mild' in the UK (PHE 2014a), and therefore tested the resilience of the UK's response plans more thoroughly, the need for stockpiling of PPE and ventilators to develop redundancy would have been taken more seriously.

Instead, the immediate aftermath of the H1N1 epidemic in the UK actually marked the beginning of the incubation period for this current crisis (Turner 1976; Turner and Pidgeon 1997; Roux-Dufort 2009). It is perhaps no coincidence that countries such as South Korea, which learned concrete lessons from its severe experience of SARS in 2002–2003, have been better at both anticipating and containing COVID-19. Their sensitivity to ensure 'anomalies' do not become 'vulnerabilities' (Roux-Dufort 2009) was well placed, an example in the practice of 'foresight' leading to effective responsiveness.

As the unexpected 'jolt' hopefully subsides, 'readjustment', Meyer's (1982) third phase of resilience then draws our attention to the potential for adaptation in response to the crisis. In essence, he considers whether the event is regarded as a problem-solving exercise to be framed within existing institutional frameworks and strategies, or whether it raises more fundamental issues concerning core values and assumptions.

What then is the answer? Our current understanding of the situation is that the latter should dominate future preparedness for transboundary crises. Though nothing has changed, in the sense that future crises, including pandemics, are inevitable, the nature of these crises will be very different, requiring a rethink in anticipation and response.

We suggest that in a world of unfamiliar transboundary crises, the old solutions can prove best. This means redundancy, inventory and shortening the supply chain to ensure that products are close to where they are needed. Where the unexpected happens, resilience involves the ability to continue functioning and, if degraded, to 'bounce back' (Wildavsky 1988; Weick and Sutcliffe 2007) – the 'response' in Meyer's trifurcation. 'Planned resilience' may become more, or less, redundant as the organisation attempts to develop new capacities in response to unknown emergent situations. In Wildavsky's terms, it requires organisations 'to investigate, to learn, and to act without knowing in advance what one will be called to act upon', (1988, 77), and in so doing avoid rigid, narrowing and maladaptive responses (Staw, Sandelands, and Dutton 1981). The strategic business model can be important here, where innovation, diversity, flexibility and the ability to work across boundaries may encourage new and adaptive approaches in the face of adversity (Meyer 1982; Hamel and Valikangas 2003). Likewise, the ability to deploy slack resources, both tangible and intangible, can act as a shock absorber to dampen the impact of events as well as fuel adaptive responses (Gittell et al. 2006; Meyer 1982; Weick and Roberts 1993). One example of this is Switzerland (Jones 2020), which maintains one of the largest strategic stockpiles of essential goods in the world (3–6 months of basic foods, animal feed, and medicines). The Swiss Government increased these stockpiles in 2016, having become concerned about the fragility of modern supply chains (Switzerland's history of self-reliance and land-locked geography were key elements in this). As a result of these stockpiles, businesses and hospitals have been able to continue operating and consumer hording has been kept in check. Interestingly, one of the unintended consequences of the threat of a 'no-deal' Brexit has meant that some UK car manufacturers who had attended to the outcomes of reasonable worst case scenarios appear more operationally resilient to factory shutdowns (Campbell 2020).

3. Conclusions and future research

In a world of growing complexity, technological advancement and interconnections, it's very easy to get blinded by the idea that the advances we have seen in every facet of our lives will ultimately protect us. The harsh reality today indicates that planning and preparedness will always trump technological reaction and adaptation. That is not to say that the ability to flex and remain malleable that technology provides is not to be appreciated - it is. However, a reliance on a reactionary approach to any crisis, not least a transboundary one, will be sub-optimal. There can be no substitute for actionable and feasible emergency preparedness and resilience plans, devoid of short term politicisation. Ultimately, it doesn't matter if you're a national health provider or a Texan supermarket chain. If you don't invest in developing resilience through financial resources and strategic direction, your likelihood of success is reduced. To paraphrase the Chinese proverb, without rice, even the cleverest cannot cook.

The relationship between the Civil Contingencies Act (2010) and the Health and Safety at Work Act (1974) will never be more strained than it is now. The risks employees are expected to face on a daily basis, due to the inadequacy of their government's approach to preparation for a key national risk, is unprecedented. This should never be repeated.

This is not to say that making fundamental changes to core institutional arrangements would be without its challenges, but this is not without precedent, and instructive lessons and inspiration can be drawn from changes introduced to another key UK sector. The stability of the UK's financial system is based on the Bank of England remaining free from day-to-day political influence, having specific statutory responsibilities for regulation across multiple domains. It is time that national emergency preparedness, resilience, and response to transboundary risks follows suit via a public body with governance arrangements similar to those of the Bank of England. This public body would be enshrined in law, with the NHS pandemic preparedness and resilience responsibilities falling under its umbrella. It is not the first time this idea of operational independence has been proposed for the NHS, albeit not specific to emergency preparedness, residence and response (Vaithianathan and Lewis 2008). The Department of Health, acting as the lead agency in pandemic preparedness, has been found wanting. No matter how low the probabilities are, when societal stakes are so high there can be no room for complacency, posturing, political ideology, or underlap.

Given the current timeline and fluid nature of this virus our research agenda has been primarily focused on the ability to anticipate and respond to COVID-19 within the UK. We call for equal appreciation and credence to be given to the national and international 'readjustment' that follows, it will no doubt be critical to future resilience.

Note

1. For a complete list of recent disease outbreaks see: www.who.int/emergencies/diseases/en/

Acknowledgments

We would like to thank everyone who has taken a swift personal response to this situation by staying at home. Given everything that is outlined above it is clear that we all must play our part in the responsive phase of this pandemic. Finally, we feel a special thank you is required for every health/social scare employee, every delivery driver, every supermarket assistant, and all those other service providers who have inadvertently become first responders. Putting your own lives in danger will be remembered as one of the greatest and largest peacetime feats of bravery humankind will ever display. Our paper is not intended to demean your efforts, by shining a light on the current situation we hope in some small way to ensure you are never placed in this situation again.

Disclosure statement

No potential conflict of interest was reported by the authors.

References

Ashby, S., C. Bryce, and P. Ring. 2018. *Risk and the Strategic Role of Leadership*. London: ACCA.
Bhamra, R., S. Dani, and K. Burnard. 2011. "Resilience: The Concept, a Literature Review and Future Directions." *International Journal of Production Research* 49 (18): 5375–5393. doi:10.1080/00207543.2011.563826.
Boin, A. 2019. "The Transboundary Crisis: Why We Are Unprepared and the Road Ahead." *Journal of Contingencies and Crisis Management* 27 (1): 94–99. doi:10.1111/1468-5973.12241.
Brüning, M., N. T. P. Hartono, and J. Bendul. 2015. "Collaborative Recovery from Supply Chain Disruptions: Characteristics and Enablers." *Research in Logistics & Production* 5: 225–237.
Burgess, A., J. Wardman, and G. Mythen. 2018. "Considering Risk: Placing the Work of Ulrich Beck in Context." *Journal of Risk Research* 21 (1): 1–5. doi:10.1080/13669877.2017.1383075.
Campbell, P. 2020. "Carmakers Dust Off Brexit Plans to Deal with Factory Shutdowns." *Financial Times*, March 22, 2020. Accessed 25 March 2020. www.ft.com/content/d179ec0c-6ac9-11ea-800d-da70cff6e4d3
Edgecliffe-Johnson, A. 2020. "US Supply Chains and Ports under Stress from the Coronavirus." *Financial Times*, March 2, 2020. www.ft.com/content/5b5b8990-5a98-11ea-a528-dd0f971febbc
De Geus, A. 1999. *The Living Company: Growth Learning and Longevity in Business*. Boston. Nicholas Brealey Publishing.

Gittell, J. H., K. Cameron, S. Lim, and V. Rivas. 2006. "Relationships, Layoffs, and Organizational Resilience: Airline Industry Responses to September 11." *The Journal of Applied Behavioral Science* 42 (3): 300–329. doi:10.1177/0021886306286466.

Grabowski, M., and K. Roberts. 1997. "Risk Mitigation in Large-Scale Systems: Lessons from High Reliability Organizations." *California Management Review* 39 (4): 152–161. doi:10.2307/41165914.

Hamel, G., and L. Valikangas. 2003. "The Quest for Resilience." *Harvard Business Review* 81 (9): 52–65.

Hollinger, P., and M. McCormick. 2020. "Most Airlines Face Bankruptcy by End of May, Industry Body Warns." *Financial Times*, March 16, 2020. Accessed 20 March 2020. https://www.ft.com/content/30a3a26e-674f-11ea-800d-da70cff6e4d3

Huang, C., Y. Wang, X. Li, L. Ren, J. Zhao, Y. Hu, L. Zhang, et al. 2020. "Clinical Features of Patients Infected with 2019 Novel Coronavirus in Wuhan, China." *The Lancet* 395 (10223): 497–506. doi:10.1016/S0140-6736(20)30183-5.

Husted, B. W. 1993. "Reliability and the Design or Ethical Organizations." *Journal of Business Ethics* 12 (10): 761–769.

ITV. 2020. "This Morning – Interview with Boris Johnson." *ITV*. March 5, 10:00.

Jones, S. 2020. "Swiss Keep Calm and Rest on Their Months of Stockpiles." *Financial Times*, March 21 2020. Accessed 23 March 2020. www.ft.com/content/b6ca9ded-00d5-4eed-a9b7-ed76a5df818a

Lambert, H. 2020. "Government Documents Show No Planning for Ventilators in the Event of a Pandemic." *New Statesmen*, March 16, 2020. https://www.newstatesman.com/politics/health/2020/03/government-documents-show-no-planning-ventilators-event-pandemic

Landau, M. 1969. "Redundancy, Rationality, and the Problem of Duplication and Overlap." *Public Administration Review* 29 (4): 346–358.

Lerner, A. W. 1986. "There Is More than One Way to Be Redundant. A Comparison of Alternatives for the Design and Use of Redundancy in Organizations." *Administration & Society* 18 (3): 334–359.

McMorrow, R., and T. Mitchel. 2020. "China Manufacturing Index Rebounds in March." *Financial Times*, March 31, 2020. Accessed 1 April 2020. https://www.ft.com/content/c0eddc35-9bab-44ff-9974-ebfdd8edee6f

Meyer, A. D. 1982. "Adapting to Environmental Jolts." *Administrative Science Quarterly* 27 (4): 515–537. doi:10.2307/2392528.

NHS. 2017a. "Operating Framework for Managing the Response to Pandemic Influenza." Accessed 20 March 2020. https://www.england.nhs.uk/wp-content/uploads/2017/12/nhs-england-pandmic-influenza-operating-framework-v2.pdf

NHS. 2017b. "Emergency Preparedness, Resilience and Response (EPRR) Board Papers." Accessed 20 March 2020. https://www.england.nhs.uk/wp-content/uploads/2017/03/board-paper-300317-item-10.pdf

Peel, E. 2020. "Air Freight Shortage Limits Europe's Access to Coronavirus Drugs." *Financial Times*, March 25, 2020. Accessed 1 April 2020. www.ft.com/content/79a02264-6edc-11ea-89df-41bea055720b

Perrow, Charles. 2011. "Fukushima and the Inevitability of Accidents." *Bulletin of the Atomic Scientists* 67 (6): 44–52. doi:10.1177/0096340211426395.

PHE. 2014a. "Pandemic Influenza Strategic Framework." Accessed 20 March 2020. https://assets.publishing.service.gov.uk/government/uploads/system/uploads/attachment_data/file/344696/PI_Strategic_Framework_13_Aug.pdf

PHE. 2014b. "Pandemic Influenza Response Plan." Accessed 20 March 2020. https://assets.publishing.service.gov.uk/government/uploads/system/uploads/attachment_data/file/344695/PI_Response_Plan_13_Aug.pdf

Richardson, B. 1994. "Crisis Management and Management Strategy-Time to "Loop the Loop"?" *Disaster Prevention and Management: An International Journal* 3 (3): 59–80. doi:10.1108/09653569410795632.

Roux-Dufort. C. 2009. "The Devil Lies in Details! How Crises Build up within Organizations." *Journal of Contingencies and Crisis Management* 17 (1): 4–11.

Sherman, E. 2020. "94% of the Fortune 1000 Are Seeing Coronavirus Supply Chain Disruptions: Report." *Forbes*, February 21, 2020. Accessed 20 March 2020. https://fortune.com/2020/02/21/fortune-1000-coronavirus-china-supply-chain-impact/

Srinivasan, T. N., and T. G. Rethinaraj. 2013. "Fukushima and Thereafter: Reassessment of Risks of Nuclear Power." *Energy Policy* 52: 726–736. doi:10.1016/j.enpol.2012.10.036.

Staw, B. M., L. E. Sandelands, and J. E. Dutton. 1981. "Threat Rigidity Effects in Organizational Behavior: A Multilevel Analysis." *Administrative Science Quarterly* 26 (4): 501–524. doi:10.2307/2392337.

Sunstein, C. 2020. "The Cognitive Bias That Makes Us Panic About Coronavirus." *Bloomberg Opinion*, February 28, 2020. Accessed 17 March 2020. https://www.bloomberg.com/opinion/articles/2020-02-28/coronavirus-panic-caused-by-probability-neglect

Sutcliffe, K. M., and T. J. Vogus. 2003. "Organizing for Resilience." In *Positive Organizational Scholarship: Foundations of a New Discipline*, edited by K. S. Cameron, J. E. Dutton, and R. E. Quinn, 1-20. San Francisco: Berrett-Koehler.

Synolakis, C., and U. Kânoğlu. 2015. "The Fukushima Accident Was Preventable." *Philosophical Transactions of the Royal Society A: Mathematical, Physical and Engineering Sciences* 373 (2053): 20140379. doi:10.1098/rsta.2014.0379.

Solomon, D., and P. Forbes. 2020. "Inside the Story of How H-E-B Planned for the Pandemic." *Texas Monthly*, March 26, 2020.

Trump, D. 2020. "@realdonaldtrump." March 9, 2020. https://twitter.com/realdonaldtrump/status/1237027356314869761

Turner, B. 1976. "The Organizational and Interorganizational Development of Disasters." *Administrative Science Quarterly* 21 (3): 378–397. doi:10.2307/2391850.

Turner, B., and N. F. Pidgeon. 1997. *Man-Made Disasters*. 2nd ed. Oxford, UK: Butterworth-Heinemann.

UCL. 2020. "UCL, UCLH and Formula One Develop Life-Saving Breathing Aids for the NHS." Accessed 1 April 2020. https://www.ucl.ac.uk/news/2020/mar/ucl-uclh-and-formula-one-develop-life-saving-breathing-aids-nhs

Vaithianathan, R., and G. Lewis. 2008. "Operational Independence for the NHS." *BMJ* 337 (jul22 3): a497. doi:10.1136/bmj.a497.

Walker, B., V. Nilakant, and R. Baird. 2014. "Promoting Organisational Resilience through Sustaining Engagement in a Disruptive Environment: What Are the Implications for HRM?" *Research Forum*, 1–20.

Weick, K. E., and K. H. Roberts. 1993. "Collective Mind in Organizations: Heedful Interrelating on Flight Decks." *Administrative Science Quarterly* 38 (3): 357–381. doi:10.2307/2393372.

Weick, K. E., and K. M. Sutcliffe. 2007. *Managing the Unexpected: Resilient Performance in an Age of Uncertainty*. San Francisco: Jossey-Bass.

Weick, K. E., K. M. Sutcliffe, and D. Obstfeld. 1999. "Organizing for High Reliability: Processes of Collective Mindfulness." *Research in Organizational Behavior* 21: 81–124.

Wildavsky, A. B. 1988. *Searching for Safety*. Piscataway, NJ: Transaction Publishers.

Wu, J. T., K. Leung, and G. M. Leung. 2020. "Nowcasting and Forecasting the Potential Domestic and International Spread of the 2019-nCoV Outbreak Originating in Wuhan, China: A Modelling Study." *The Lancet* 395 (10225): 689–697. doi:10.1016/S0140-6736(20)30260-9.

Backing up emergency teams in healthcare and law enforcement organizations: strategies to socialize newcomers in the time of COVID-19

Paula Ungureanu and Fabiola Bertolotti

ABSTRACT

The COVID-19 pandemic is putting significant pressure on emergency teams in healthcare and law enforcement organizations. In order to provide rapid backup, new workers must be socialized rapidly and effectively. In addition to considering the pros and cons of various new-comer socialization strategies and tools, healthcare and law enforcement organizations may need to design hybrid socialization strategies at the light of four essential processes of emergency teams: roles, knowledge, interpersonal relations and emotion management. We suggest that emergency teams based on the combined resources of old-timers and newcomers where the more experienced team members contribute actively to the socialization of new members can have unexpected positive effects on the team.

Introduction

The COVID-19 outbreak is imposing an unprecedented burden on healthcare and law enforcement workers across the world. The rise in the number of reported cases of COVID-19 is accompanied by the need for rapid responses to requests for medical assessment and medical treatment, and enforcement of social distancing and quarantine to try to reduce the spread of the disease. However, these measures are disrupting healthcare and law enforcement processes and increasing these organizations' vulnerability while limiting their ability to provide timely and efficient responses to the epidemic. A major concern is that COVID-19 requires teams of health-care workers, police, military and immigration officers across the world to reorganize their work. For example, in Northern Italy one of the first places in Europe to be affected by the pandemic, entire hospitals have been dedicated to COVID-19 cases while medical departments dealing with other pathologies have been reorganized at the regional level to offer just a few essential medical services. In addition, new temporary hospitals have been established in military facilities and spaces used normally for international expositions (Al-Arshani 2020). These changes together with the need to quarantine and replace the increasing number of medical staff infected with COVID-19, led the Italian Government to issue decree *Cura Italia* (Italian-Government-D-L-17.03.20). This decree legalizes the hiring of 20,000 additional public healthcare system workers based on a simplified procedure. Two weeks after publication of the decree, 8,000 new workers had been identified: new graduates and retired professionals, and army and non-profit organiza-tion (NGO) medical staff and paramedics were mobilized to work in hospitals across Italy. Alongside this effort, officers from various law-enforcement organizations were forming teams to enforce the lockdown.

In our modern, globalized society where social, economic, environmental and health risks are often interconnected (Aven and Bouder 2020, Beck 1992, Nygren and Olofsson 2020) such situ-ation of organizational frailty has spread with an unprecedented speed across the globe, from China to Italy, Spain, U.S., France, Sweden, Russia and the Middle East, just to name a few, and awaits responsible management of risk and uncertainty at all levels, from policymakers to organi-zations and single individuals (Aven and Bouder 2020, Bao, Liao, and Hine 2019, Bouder, Slavin, and Löfstedt 2007, Fu and Zhu 2020, Nygren and Olofsson 2020). The rapid socialization of newly hired staff or staff transferred from other organizations to support emergency teams already in place, represents one of the pressing needs for crisis management. It is well-known that organi-zations which favor the accelerated transition of newcomers into their new roles can start bene-fiting sooner from the new workforce (Chao et al. 1994, Cooper-Thomas and Anderson 2006). We know also that different organizations favor different newcomer socialization strategies and that their choices can affect the performance of the individuals and their organizations (Bauer et al. 1996, Saks and Ashforth 1997) . However, less is known about whether these strategies are suc-cessful in the context of emergency teams that might include professionals with diverse expert-ise and little mutual knowledge but need to perform immediately, reliably and effectively. In this work, we offer some recommendations related to real time building of effective emergency teams that include newcomers. Given that we are dealing with a risk subject to large uncertain-ties, we take the view that the role of science is to inform policy and organizations about pos-sible courses of action, thus encouraging a balanced evaluation of available choices and related consequences, and not to prescribe the specific decisions to be made (Aven and Bouder 2020). Specifically, we suggest that in the current emergency of COVID-19, it may not be enough that organizations examine the pros and cons of available socialization tools and strategies and decide which to adopt. A deep understanding of different socialization approaches should enable organizations to design their own hybrid approach, as to maximize the performance of emergency teams in four essential aspects: roles, knowledge, interpersonal relations and emotion management. As a general rule, if existing emergency team members contribute actively to the socialization of newcomers this can have many positive consequences. It helps to consolidate team roles, facilitate exchange of knowledge, allow rapid development of trust and contribute to the management of emotions.

Approaches to the socialization of newcomers in organizations: institutionalization or individualization

To understand risk for newcomer socialization in emergency teams dealing with COVID-19, we need to clarify the role of uncertainty and knowledge in how emergency teams operate (Argote 1982, Bouder, Slavin, and Löfstedt 2007, Lofstedt et al. 2011, Milburn and Billings 1976). Organizational socialization includes newcomers learning about and adjusting to the work con-text and making the transition from organizational outsider to insider (Ashforth, Sluss, and Saks 2007, Bauer et al. 1996, Saks and Ashforth 1997). Both seminal work on socialization dating back to the 1970s (Feldman 1981, Van Maanen and Schein 1977) and some very recent studies (Bauer et al. 2007, Saks and Gruman 2018) agree that to perform well, newcomers to an organization must be familiarized with the requirements (knowledge) of the job and their role in the organiza-tion. This requires a period of socialization. Van Maanen and Schein (1977) identify a spectrum of six socialization strategies. The organization can subject all newcomers to a set of common expe-riences or introduce individual newcomers to particular experiences (collective vs. individual socializing). They may define a certain socialization period during which the newcomer is isolated from old-timers or they may encourage newcomers to learn on the job (formal vs. informal socialization). Roles may be "learned" according to a fixed sequence of steps (sequential vs. random) or according to a specific timetable (fixed vs. variable). The organization may identify old-timer experts to socialize newcomers (serial vs. disjunctive) and integrate their existing characteristics or provide guidance about how they should change (investiture vs. divestiture). Building on these ideas, Jones (1986) proposed that these strategies reflected a broader choice between a structured approach or 'institutionalization' vs. an unstructured approach or 'individualization'. In institutionalized socialization (i.e. collective, formal, sequential, fixed, serial and investiture-based), newcomers are guided by the organization; during individualized socialization (i.e. individual, informal, random, variable, disjunctive and divestiture) newcomers are encouraged by the organization to develop their own approach to their work role (Ashforth, Sluss, and Saks 2007, Saks and Gruman 2018).

In terms of outcomes, the research suggests that newcomers who experience institutionalized socialization have greater job satisfaction, are more committed to and identify more with the organization and are less likely to quit. In contrast, it has been shown that newcomers who experience socialization are more independent and innovative at work but are more confused and conflicted about their roles, experience more stress and likely perform less optimally (Bauer et al. 2007, Haueter, Macan, and Winter 2003).

However, we are interested in whether these research findings apply to emergency teams which are time-pressed and face high levels of abrupt change including frequent changes to team composition (Blomqvist and Cook 2018, Dietz et al. 2017, Driskell, Salas, and Driskell 2018). Because teams fighting to contain emergencies such as pandemics have limited time and resources, it is essential for newcomers to be immediately operative but to also avoid making fatal errors. In this context, we propose that a hybrid strategy that we call 'swift socialization' may be the most effective. We examine the strategies and tools related to swift socialization in relation to team member's role, knowledge, interpersonal relations and emotions.

Importantly, we take the context of the COVID-19 outbreak as an opportunity to discuss about what it means to provide rapid and concomitant inclusion for different types of newcomers such as graduates, veterans and transfers from other organizations.

Support for swift role crafting

Roles refer to the patterns that guide people's expectations and behaviors in the workplace and allow stable and predictable interactions (Ashforth, Sluss, and Saks 2007, Stryker and Statham 1985). In emergency contexts, roles provide guidance and protect team members against uncertainty and panic. However, overly rigid roles can constrain prompt reactions to the unexpected. Since emergencies involve both iron rules and flexibility, healthcare and law enforcement organizations may prefer the hybrid strategy of 'swift role crafting'. This involves use of guidelines such as pre-entry job training and role mentoring to establish an unambiguous role learning frame for the newcomer combined with incentives to act independently during emergencies while negotiating their role with those of old-timers. Several tools are available for swift role crafting.

Negotiating roles through boundary objects

When joining a law enforcement or medical organization, diagnostic equipment, standardized reports, emergency protocols, medical databases and workflow charts are the first 'working tools' the newcomer encounters and learns to master. While it might be tempting for organizations to use pre-entry training as an occasion to hand these tools to newcomers, for instance, by teaching newcomers how to use an X-ray machine, offering tutorials on criminal records databases or simulating emergency situations to test life-saving protocols, it has been shown role socialization is more successful if these tools are mastered as 'boundary objects' during day-to-day practice. That is, tools that are sufficiently concrete to maintain a line of conduct throughout the team/ organization but flexible enough to adapt to workers' local needs (Bechky 2003, Star and Griesemer 1989). To transform workplace tools into boundary objects requires the organization to provide clear but broad instructions about their use and importance and requires both new-comers and old-timers to have the opportunity to explore them together as quickly and as much as possible. This renders a fertile terrain for negotiating roles (Barley 1986, Bechky 2003, Ungureanu and Bertolotti 2016, 2018). To enable this, boundary objects must be placed at the center of the relationship between old-timers and newcomers. For instance, old-timers may dir-ect newcomers' attention to how an internal database or protocol for using CT scanners reflect the organization's role structure. This will allow dynamic learning of roles (tools can serve as win-dows through which newcomers view an organization's whole role structure) and alignment with personal abilities (newcomers can negotiate roles with old timers to suit them best). Old timers can use this as an opportunity to update their role understanding and reflect on how the roles within the team have changed as a result of COVID-19. A new person in the team could also serve as a boundary (i.e., mediation) object for old-timers with different backgrounds and interests, by becoming 'neutral' communication ground for emergencies, and by resolving old role conflicts that otherwise could damage the team performance (Langley et al. 2019).

Performing vigilant role crafting

As highlighted above, the strategy of role crafting implies that newcomers learn the basics of their organizational roles by engaging in creative work practices aided by old-timers. This relieves the organization of some of its training burden and enables flexibility to respond to crises. However, although fast response is important for emergency teams, a leader or expert member must act as coordinator to avoid conflict over roles and responsibilities, and consequent team vulnerability. Media stories, death counts, public campaigns and patient misinformation may stir negative emotions and attitudes in workers dealing with the COVID-19 emergency and may even lead them to exaggerate the feeling of risk (Aven and Bouder 2020, Krause et al. 2020). In Italy, for instance, the mass media frequently highlighted newcomers' exposure to extreme adversity such as contamination of a new graduate with COVID-19 after just two work shifts and the deaths of several veterans who had reenrolled to help fight virus. As both newcomers and old-timers are risking their and their families' health, they may be tempted to use role crafting opportunistically, for instance as an excuse to shirk responsibilities and avoid dangerous tasks (e.g. old-timers assigning newcomers to complex triage activities or newcomers refusing tasks due to lack of training or equipment). Yet, also the opposite risk may verify, wherein over-enthu-siastic but little experienced new graduates underestimate safety protocols and expose the entire team to the risk of contamination. To avoid these risks, organizations dealing with emergencies may need to engage in vigilant crafting by appointing mentors to control how and which roles newcomers perform. Knowing that a mentor is checking their activities can provide newcomers with the psychological reassurance to engage in risky behaviors such as treating their first COVID-19 patients and to avoid irresponsible behavior (Colquitt, Scott, and LePine 2007, Perrot et al. 2014). This generally implies that mentors, team leaders and organizational leaders need to work together to streamline old-timers' and newcomers' roles: identify the most important tasks and responsibilities and postpone or cancel irrelevant tasks, to prevent overburdening.

Endorsing differentiated role crafting

Since the COVID-19 emergency is requiring organizations to socialize new graduates, veterans and transfers, it may be decided to give these professionals different discretion over crafting their roles. The aim is that newcomers may monitor and energize each other, relieving this way the pressure on old-timers. For instance, newcomers and transfers tend to approach role learning positively because they associate roles with career promotion and life evolutions (Ashforth, Sluss, and Saks 2007, Saks and Gruman 2018). However, in the context of a pandemic where new-comers usually enter teams to replace staff infected with COVID-19, this motivation may come short. On the other hand, veterans might be more motivated to lead by example in difficult sit-uations; if they have more discretion to craft their roles, they may serve as exemplars for new graduates, and energize transfers from other organizations (Hong, Park, and Cameron 2020). However, since veterans may be less respectful of the team's leadership and try to forge their own way by comparing expertise with old-timers, ranking them similarly to transfers and new graduates could help temper potential power battles in the team. In sum, organizations encour-aging differentiated role crafting and providing role training and guidance in groups that include old-timers, veterans, new graduates and transfers might achieve swifter, and more resourceful and effective role negotiation within the team.

Supporting situated transactional knowledge management

Coronavirus hits all the hot buttons that may disrupt a team's ability to exchange knowledge: Not only it is new, unknown, and has delayed effects, but it also deprives medical staff of the planning and control functions afforded by previously accumulated knowledge (Argote 1982). Research shows that institutionalized socialization provides newcomers with more opportunities to learn and process information. In contrast, individualized strategies are more effective if time is too short to teach new-comers how to manage the range of knowledge and expertise available in the organization. However, individualized strategies can reduce the accuracy of knowledge transfer inside the organiza-tion (Cooper-Thomas and Anderson 2002). The following tools can serve to mitigate these trade-offs.

Cross team training for boundary use of knowledge repositories

Protocols, guidebooks, wikis and digital databases allow organizations to store, retrieve and share knowledge. We have described how machines, procedures and protocols can become boundary objects for emergency teams and facilitate role negotiation and learning (see previous section). Here we want to highlight the importance of considering information and communication technologies (ICTs) as boundary objects for cross team training -i.e., teach team members to shift gears and sup-port each other as needed (Constantinides, Kouroubali, and Barrett 2008, Constantinides and Barrett 2012, Levina and Vaast 2005). ICTs allow the tracking and transmission of real time information on the status of emergency incidents and the actions being taken by each team member, which allows both established and new members of teams to feel more in control of the information they are add-ing to the system, and better able to understand each other (Cooke et al. 2003). In this process, new-comers may become precious brokers. For instance, the hospitals in Brescia and Bergamo, Northern Italy, are experimenting with a new way of monitoring COVID-19 patients from their homes using electronic bracelets proposed by transfers from the international NGO Doctors without Borders based on their experience with the Ebola crisis in Africa. The devices require the organization to update its ICT system, and consequently, its roles and work culture, while also reinforcing the relationship between patients, old-timers and newcomers.

Integrating transactive memory systems and team situation models

Teams required to react quickly need to form what researchers call a 'single information process-ing system' allowing rapid encoding, storage and retrieval of information and identification of where the knowledge is stored in the system (Langan-Fox, Anglim, and Wilson 2004, Pramanik

2015, Rico et al. 2008). When this happens, it is typically said that a team developed a transactive memory system. Since stress is a major disruptor of the team's ability to exchange knowledge, transactive memory allows retention of 'the big picture' and a continued focus on patients and teammates (Dietz et al. 2017, Driskell, Salas, and Driskell 2018, Ellis 2006). However, the rigidity of transactive memory systems can constrain the ability to adapt to urgencies. For example, doctors, nurses, and technicians working in intensive care develop mental models based on their experience (doctors have a mental model of the evolution of a disease and the related medical protocols, technicians have a mental model of how diagnostic devices function, etc.). However, these mental models may fail in the context of emergencies such as COVID-19. With lack of time, resources and operating space, also a team's transactive memory, and members' ability to act coordinately face the risk of breakdown. The inclusion in the team of newcomers can exacerbate this situation. In Northern Italy, gynecologists, plastic surgeons, dermatologists and urologists have become transfers in COVID-19 emergency teams. Although these experts are familiar with the hospital environment, they will need some help to translate and update their mental models to suit the situation of the intensive care unit. Veterans unfamiliar with intensive care may also find it difficult to adjust whereas recent graduates who are less conditioned by pre-existing mental models may serve as examples of flexibility for the more experienced teammates.

Such situations require training and support to develop team situation models (TSMs) which are agile, tacit, 'context-driven', shared mental models which team members update continuously and in a coordinated way in order to avoid being off the pace (Bao, Liao, and Hine 2019, Cooke et al. 2003, Rico et al. 2008). Unfortunately, developing a well-functioning TSM can be a lengthy process, especially for team members who come from different organizations (Rico et al. 2008, Ungureanu, Bertolotti, et al. 2018). However, the organization can accelerate it through regular team briefings (i.e. a team organizes 15-20-minute team briefings on current issues before and during shifts), and leader debriefings (i.e. the team receives information updates and feedback from team leaders as often as necessary). Closed-loop communication (CLC) is another technique used by emergency teams to update TSMs. It involves an initial message sender, and a receiver who acknowledges and interprets the message. The sender will make every effort to have the message answered (e.g. repeating the question, addressing the receiver by name, physically nudging the receiver, etc.) or ensure the message was interpreted correction (reformulating the question several times) (Fernandez et al. 2008).

Support interpersonal relations: towards support for swift trust development

Mutual trust is essential for members of emergency teams to disclose their knowledge and negotiate roles during emergencies. However, interpersonal trust is difficult for most COVID-19 emergency teams which often are formed on a temporary basis and which experience frequent changes of personnel (Balog-Way and McComas 2020). For instance, Pramanik (2015) has analyzed situations of collaboration between multiple civil agencies and the military in recent disasters such as the hurricane Katrina, the Indian Ocean tsunami and the earthquake in Haiti, showing how a lack of knowledge of each other's working procedures and identities resulted in stereotyping and prejudices, which are root obstacles to coordination. One big issue in such contexts is not only that team members do not have enough information about where the others are coming from, and how good they are on their job, but also that opportunities to demonstrate that you are as good as your word and are reliable are particularly scant. Team members then must rely on the phenomenon of 'swift trust' whereby they come to trust each other almost immediately if the organization clearly defines roles and reputation cues, tasks and deadlines in order to facilitate trusting (see institutionalization strategy) (Blomqvist and Cook 2018, Meyerson, Weick, and Kramer 1996). We have discussed the importance of clear roles and tasks; here, we highlight some complementary mechanisms:

Signaling reputation cues and proactive behaviors

For swift trust to develop, old-timers must be given information on the reputation of newcomers. Knowing that these newcomers come from a limited pool of 'talent' or belong to the 'right' networks (Meyerson, Weick, and Kramer 1996) promotes trust among old-timers based on their reputation which serves to guarantee trustworthiness. However, in a pandemic context, recruitment may not be based on merit. For instance, the Italian government appealed to anyone with medical training in Italy or from abroad, and simplified recruitment of new graduates by canceling the requirement for national certification to allow them to work in a hospital (Italian-Government-D-L-17.03.20). When reputation cues are not available, the team relies on the authority of mentors and team leaders to signal the reputation of newcomers. Also, newcomers need to understand that they need to be proactive to demonstrate their trustworthiness to old-timers, e.g. by showing ability to perform assigned tasks and displaying integrity (Ashforth, Sluss, and Saks 2007, Moreland and Levine 2002). It would seem that newcomers are more likely to engage in such proactive behaviors if they have experienced a structured socialization where proactivity is encouraged compared to individualized socialization which focuses more on informal relationships (Jesús Bravo et al. 2003). Organizations may thus promote interpersonal socialization in COVID-19 emergency teams using two stages: First, in the institutionalized socialization stage leaders attribute clear roles and tasks to newcomers and provide reputation cues to the rest of the team; second, the stage of individualized socialization encourages both newcomers and old-timers to be proactive and responsive in their jobs (Ashforth, Sluss, and Saks 2007, Meyerson, Weick, and Kramer 1996). In this second stage, several tools may be employed. The CLC technique can engender trust in emergency teams by encouraging constant feedback and proactive communication (Fernandez et al. 2008). Inciting team members to use instant communication technologies and team ware even when they are physically located in the same building (or room) can also further help newcomers to demonstrate reliability and responsiveness to teammates' needs (Driskell, Salas, and Driskell 2018, Moreland and Levine 2002).

Leveraging newcomers for team (re)orientation

It is suggested that teams are likely to worsen or even exasperate interpersonal relations in the prolonged battle against an imminent threat. Once the emergency becomes the 'new normality'(Zinn 2020), irritability, hostility, and personality conflicts may emerge. Collins (2003) cites an instance when cosmonauts aboard the Salyut space station became so frustrated with the ground personnel that they cut off communication for two days. Also, Smith-Jentsch and colleagues (Smith-Jentsch et al. 2015) who studied NASA missions suggest that organizations rarely train emergency teams to maintain a collective orientation during critical incidents and this is a major cause of mission failure. We suggest that adding newcomers to the team can help to 'declutter' relations among the old-timers in the team. Communication is an essential issue in developing a long-trusted relationship in the time of COVID-19 (Balog-Way and McComas 2020). The need to be examples for new graduates and to communicate competence to veterans and transfers can redirect old-timers' emotions and smooth conflicts. To support this process, organizations must design the interactions between newcomers and old timers, including their working spaces, having in mind team (re)orientation. Defining shared spaces for training and leisure activities and private spaces that allow separation can help to balance the socialization needs of old-timers' and newcomers dealing with a prolonged crisis (Driskell, Salas, and Driskell 2018, Ungureanu, Rietti, et al. 2018). Also, Mearns, Flin, and O'Connor (2001) suggested that a type of training called Crew Resource Management (CRM), first developed in the aviation industry and now expanded to other domains, may be used to emphasize essential skills in emergency teams such as communication, leadership, trust-building and decision making, breaking down the barriers that exist between organizational work subcultures such as newcomers and old-timers, or old-timers with different expertise, goals and/or orientations.

Emotional support based on cultural toolkits

Emergency teams may seem to be driven mainly by rational rules and procedures rather than members' emotional interactions. However, affect is important for emergency team resilience -i.e. their capacity to respond to and recover from crises (Saks and Gruman 2018, Tasic et al. 2019, Wright, Zammuto, and Liesch 2017). Research shows that effective performance under stress requires individuals to maintain emotional control (Blomqvist and Cook 2018, Dietz et al. 2017, Driskell, Salas, and Driskell 2018). If working in intensive care can be an emotional rollercoaster, doing it in the middle of the COVID-19 emergency may equivalate to being pushed in an emotional vortex. Huge workloads, long shifts, worsening work conditions, and patient deaths can trigger negative feelings such as anger, annoyance, tension, and frustration whereas seeing patients recover and experiencing moments of team solidarity can engender excessive self-worth and enthusiasm. Also, continuous amendments by policymakers, mass media catastrophic reports, the rapid diffusion of fake news and the continuous change of regulations at the organizational level, may amplify workers' perception of risk, increase their level of stress and the potential for overreactions (Aven and Bouder 2020, Balog-Way and McComas 2020, Krause et al. 2020). Below we discuss various tools to help emergency teams cope with these emotions as they socialize newcomers.

Cultural toolkits

Healthcare and law enforcement organizations usually have well defined missions and strong work cultures which guide newcomers through their emotional socialization. The stories, narratives, and metaphors used by emergency team members at work are cultural tools which exorcise fear of failing (Katz 1990, Scott and Myers 2005, Wright, Zammuto, and Liesch 2017). Cultural toolkits are used especially by experienced old-timers to 'acculturate' new employees. For instance, firefighters learn to deal with danger and anxiety by retelling the myths and stories circulating in the workplace, and by roleplay and positive self-talk (modeling) (Scott and Myers 2005). For the newcomer, joining a COVID-19 emergency team can be akin to stepping in the trenches, and their morale will depend on whether the other team members tell them stories of victory or defeat. At the same time, newcomers can contribute to recalibrating emotional work in emergency teams. For instance, pictures of military forces directing 70 trucks loaded with coffins from the city of Bergamo which was dubbed 'Italian Wuhan' to crematoria in other parts of Italy, and emotional clips of doctors working in Bergamo's public hospital highlighted the fine line between repressing and embracing emotions during the fight against COVID-19. The recent study by Wright and colleagues (Wright, Zammuto, and Liesch 2017) shows that moral emotions -i.e. emotions linked to others' interests, play a key role in maintaining this delicate balance between repressing, condemning, and justifying emotions in emergency units. While old-timers might be tempted initially to view newcomers with some level of doubt, suspicion or fear that they will not respect organizational norms (which could be fatal for the team in a COVID-19 work environment), by contributing to their socialization they will begin to experience positive feelings and be motivated to act as role models and show their pride in being able to work together for the common good. The different backgrounds and experience of newcomers can contribute balance to the emergency team's emotions. The new perspectives brought in by veterans and transfers may promote emotional labor among new graduates and old-timers. Vice versa, new graduates and transfers may help to reduce the emotional loads of old timers (Scott and Myers 2005). For example, medical staff transferred to hospitals in northern Italy from

Doctors Without Borders are providing valuable epidemic expertise and emotions management. In a recent press release from the organization (Lodesani 2020), the director of the Italian NGO working in a hospital in Lodi, Lombardy at the epicenter of the COVID-19 outbreak in Italy, discussed the power of narratives in emotional labor and team building: *"With our hospital colleagues we started having an immediate feeling. As we entered the team, we immediately started listening because we know from experience that doctors dealing with epidemics have an extreme need to talk, to tell stories about what they saw in the emergency unit all day. We listened to the incredible stories of these extraordinary doctors and nurses and we saw their tears. By listening, we became a real team in only few hours, and we started working side by side as if we had known each other for ages"*.

Emotional labor through ICTs

ICTs can be used to manage emotions in emergency units. Constantinides, Kouroubali, and Barrett (2008) show how ICT systems can mediate emotions about critical incidents. By codifying and storing information in ICTs ambulance operators and dispatchers manage to rationalize "blinding emotional states" experienced during field interventions, while specialist doctors can offer them advice on self-protection during future interventions. Learning to use ICTs thus also means becoming more aware of one's emotions (Constantinides and Barrett 2012).

Complementary emotional cross team training

On the institutionalization-individualization continuum, strategies related to emotional labor are closer to individualization because the stories, myths and confessions circulating in the workplace are spontaneously leveraged by team members in times of hardship, and not the result of an organization's ad hoc training. However, if the organization does decide to provide specialized stress training or psychological support to emergency teams, these tools must be considered complementary (and secondary) and as not substituting for the spontaneous emotional labor which emerges on the job (Driskell et al. 2008, Pratt and Barnett 1997, Ungureanu, Bertolotti, and Pilati 2019). For instance, in Rome's largest hospital, medical staff receives psychological counseling to deal with their isolation from family and friends, and patient deaths (Florentino 2020). However, one member of staff in a press communication stated that: *"I am sure that psychological support will be very useful once this whole thing is over. But now, we are supporting one another through the fact that we must give all we have to save as many lives as we can. For now, this is our therapy"*.

Discussion and conclusions

In this paper, we have summarized, integrated and analyzed several socialization strategies and tools available to law enforcement and healthcare organizations that need to introduce different typologies of newcomers in emergency teams dealing with the COVID-19 emergency. Drawing on the idea of the precautionary principle in applying science indications for risk management, we suggest that it is essential that risk assessments regarding each of the strategies here described are placed in a 'broad' risk framework that considers not only the most efficient solutions, but also their potential trade-offs (Balog-Way and McComas 2020, Bouder, Slavin, and Löfstedt 2007). Table 1 summarizes the strategies and tools available to organizations to support newcomer socialization in emergency teams. They are classified along the institutionalization-individualization continuum, according to the extent of the support they provide to the four aspects of role crafting, knowledge management, interpersonal relations and emotional labor. In sum, most of the socialization strategies and tools identified require institutionalized strategies

Table 1. Summary of socialization approaches, strategies and tools available to organizations backing up emergency teams dealing with COVID-19.

Org. approach to socialization	Specific socialization tools/strategies	Significant team processes being leveraged			
		Roles	Knowledge	Interpersonal relations	Emotions
Institutionalization					
	Performing vigilant role crafting	•			
	Endorsing differentiated role crafting	•			
	Cross team training for boundary use of knowledge repositories	•	•		
	Complementary emotional cross team training				•
	Signaling reputation cues and proactive behaviors	•		•	
	Integrating transactive memory systems and team situation models	•	•	•	
	Negotiating roles through boundary objects	•	•	•	•
	Leveraging newcomer arrival in team (re)orientation	•		•	•
	Emotional labor through ICTs		•		•
	Mobilizing cultural toolkits				•
Individualization					

which means that despite the overwhelming problems related to dealing with COVID-19, organizations cannot leave newcomer socialization unattended. However, whether a strategy will be effective or ineffective depends on the context of use and the synergy with other adopted strategies.

Given thus a precautionary approach, it appears important to highlight that there is no one best strategies for all organizations, and that organizations will often need to design hybrid socialization strategies which combine multiple strategies presented in Table 1.

Table 1 shows that strategies positioned in the middle of the institutionalization-individualization continuum may shape team processes more deeply by acting simultaneously on roles, knowledge, relations, and emotions. For instance, integrating transactive memory systems and TSMs using boundary objects to perform role negotiation, and leveraging the arrival of newcomers to reorient the whole team are hybrid strategies involving the two-step process discussed above. In contrast, institutionalization strategies based on cross team training are usually more specific, which is why organizations may need to come up with additional strategies to update other team dimensions (e.g. if cross team training targets mainly role or knowledge interventions, organizations may need to organize other cross team training initiatives related to emotions and interpersonal relations). This applies also to the other end of the continuum where the organization intervenes only minimally (e.g. use of cultural toolkits for emotional labor). Therefore, a hybrid approach positioned midway between individualization and institutionalization might be the best response to emergency teams' need for rigor and fast-paced change. Thus, despite common beliefs, the most precious support that organizations can offer to newcomers is not so much the investment in well-structured programs of pre-entry training, as the constant guidance and coordination of the teams in which they are inserted. Providing coordination and support implies investing team leaders and experts with the trust and authority needed to facilitate dynamic exchanges between old-timers and newcomers, and joint monitoring of critical team incidents to avoid the escalation of stress, information chaos, and interpersonal conflict.

Summarizing, organizations that a) establish a clear but 'light' support structure for newcomer socialization, b) strengthen a team's leadership to help them deal with newcomers while also c) allowing newcomers and old-timers to 'fine tune' their work relationships through work boundary objects, might achieve a complete updating of team processes. Investigating these processes along a time dimension could also allow the organization to develop new simulation tools and platforms for designing emergency scenarios, and training newcomers and assessing their performance in the team (Fernandez et al. 2008, Langan-Fox, Anglim, and Wilson 2004, Tasic et al. 2019). While simulation models can be useful to respond to emergency teams' changing needs, they are not a crisis response because they depend on the organization's long-term commitment to a team process analysis.

Disclosure statement

No potential conflict of interest was reported by the author(s).

References

Al-Arshani, Sarah. 2020. "The Healthcare System in Italy's Lombardy Region is so Strained from the New Coronavirus That Officials Are Asking Doctors to Come out of Retirement and Nursing Students Are Being Fast-Tracked to Graduation." *Business Insider*, March, 3. https://www.businessinsider.com/italys-lombardy-regions-healthcare-system-is-crumbling-to-covid-19-2020-3?IR=T

Argote, Linda. 1982. "Input Uncertainty and Organizational Coordination in Hospital Emergency Units." *Administrative Science Quarterly* 27 (3): 420–434. [Mismatch] doi:10.2307/2392320.

Ashforth, Blake E., David M. Sluss, and Alan M. Saks. 2007. "Socialization Tactics, Proactive Behavior, and Newcomer Learning: Integrating Socialization Models." *Journal of Vocational Behavior* 70 (3): 447–462. doi:10.1016/j.jvb.2007.02.001.

Aven, Terje, and Frederic Bouder. 2020. "The COVID-19 Pandemic: how Can Risk Science Help?" *Journal of Risk Research* : 1–6. doi:10.1080/13669877.2020.1756383.

Balog-Way, Dominic H. P., and Katherine A. McComas. 2020. "COVID-19: Reflections on Trust, Tradeoffs, and Preparedness." *Journal of Risk Research* : 1–11. doi:10.1080/13669877.2020.1758192.

Bao, Gongmin, Zhongju Liao, and Damian Hine. 2019. "Managerial Cognition, Emergency Preparedness and Firm's Emergency Response Performance." *Journal of Risk Research* 22 (12): 1490–1502. doi:10.1080/13669877.2018.1485171.

Barley, S. R. 1986. "Technology as an Occasion for Structuring: Evidence from Observations of CT Scanners and the Social Order of Radiology Departments." *Administrative Science Quarterly* 31 (1): 78–108. [Mismatch] doi:10.2307/2392767.

Bauer, Talya N., Todd Bodner, Berrin Erdogan, Donald M. Truxillo, and Jennifer S. Tucker. 2007. "Newcomer Adjustment during Organizational Socialization: A Meta-Analytic Review of Antecedents, Outcomes, and Methods." *Journal of Applied Psychology* 92 (3): 707–721. doi:10.1037/0021-9010.92.3.707.

Bauer, Talya Niehaus, Elizabeth'Wolfe Morrison, and Ronda Roberts Callister. 1996. "Organizational Socialization." *APA Handbook of I/O Psychology* 3: 51–64.

Bechky, Beth A. 2003. "Sharing Meaning across Occupational Communities: The Transformation of Understanding on a Production Floor." *Organization Science* 14 (3): 312–330. doi:10.1287/orsc.14.3.312.15162.

Beck, Ulrich. 1992. *Risk Society: Towards a New Modernity*. 17 Vols. London: Sage Publications Limited.

Blomqvist, Kirsimarja, and Karen S. Cook. 2018. "Swift Trust: State-of-the-Art and Future Research Directions." In *The Routledge Companion to Trust*, 29–49. New York: Routledge.

Bouder, Frédéric, David Slavin, and Ragnar Löfstedt. 2007. *The Tolerability of Risk: A New Framework for Risk Management*. London: Earthscan.

Chao, Georgia T., Anne M. O'Leary-Kelly, Samantha Wolf, Howard J. Klein, and Philip D. Gardner. 1994. "Organizational Socialization: Its Content and Consequences." *Journal of Applied Psychology* 79 (5): 730–743. doi:10.1037/0021-9010.79.5.730.

Collins, Daniel L. 2003. "Psychological Issues Relevant to Astronaut Selection for Long-Duration Space Flight: A Review of the Literature." *Journal of Human Performance in Extreme Environments* 7 (1): 1. doi:10.7771/2327-2937.1021.

Colquitt, Jason A., Brent A. Scott, and Jeffery A. LePine. 2007. "Trust, Trustworthiness, and Trust Propensity: A Meta-Analytic Test of Their Unique Relationships with Risk Taking and Job Performance." *Journal of Applied Psychology* 92 (4): 909–927. doi:10.1037/0021-9010.92.4.909.

Constantinides, Panos, and Michael Barrett. 2012. "A Narrative Networks Approach to Understanding Coordination Practices in Emergency Response." *Information and Organization* 22 (4): 273–294. [Mismatch] doi:10.1016/j.infoandorg.2012.07.001.

Constantinides, Panos, Angelina Kouroubali, and Michael Barrett. 2008. "Transacting Expertise in Emergency Management and Response." ICIS 2008 Proceedings:15.

Cooke, Nancy J., Preston A. Kiekel, Eduardo Salas, Renée Stout, Clint Bowers, and Janis Cannon-Bowers. 2003. "Measuring Team Knowledge: A Window to the Cognitive Underpinnings of Team Performance." *Group Dynamics: Theory, Research, and Practice* 7 (3): 179–199. doi:10.1037/1089-2699.7.3.179.

Cooper-Thomas, Helena, and Neil Anderson. 2002. "Newcomer Adjustment: The Relationship between Organizational Socialization Tactics, Information Acquisition and Attitudes." *Journal of Occupational and Organizational Psychology* 75 (4): 423–437. doi:10.1348/096317902321119583.

Cooper-Thomas, Helena D., and Neil Anderson. 2006. "Organizational Socialization." *Journal of Managerial Psychology* 21 (5): 492–516. doi:10.1108/02683940610673997.

Dietz, AaronS, JamesE. Driskell, MaryJane Sierra, SallieJ. Weaver, Tripp Driskell, and Salas Eduardo. 2017. "Teamwork under Stress." In *The Wiley Blackwell Handbook of the Psychology of Team Working and Collaborative Processes*, 297–315, Croydon: John Wiley & Sons.

Driskell, James E., Eduardo Salas, Joan H. Johnston, and Terry N. Wollert. 2008. "Stress Exposure Training: An Event-Based Approach." In *Performance under Stress, edited by* Peter A. Hancock and James L. Szalma, 271–286. Aldershot: Ashgate LTD..

Driskell, Tripp, Eduardo Salas, and James E. Driskell. 2018. "Teams in Extreme Environments: Alterations in Team Development and Teamwork." *Human Resource Management Review* 28 (4): 434–449. doi:10.1016/j.hrmr.2017.01.002.

Ellis, Aleksander P. J. 2006. "System Breakdown: The Role of Mental Models and Transactive Memory in the Relationship between Acute Stress and Team Performance." *Academy of Management Journal* 49 (3): 576–589. doi:10.5465/amj.2006.21794674.

Feldman, Daniel Charles. 1981. "The Multiple Socialization of Organization Members." *Academy of Management Review* 6 (2): 309–318. doi:10.5465/amr.1981.4287859.

Fernandez, Rosemarie, Steve W. J. Kozlowski, Marc J. Shapiro, and Eduardo Salas. 2008. "Toward a Definition of Teamwork in Emergency Medicine." *Academic Emergency Medicine* 15 (11): 1104–1112. doi:10.1111/j.1553-2712.2008.00250.x.

Florentino, Flavia. 2020. "Al Gemelli Supporto Psicologico per Medici e Infermieri." Corriere Della Sera, March 26. https://roma.corriere.it/notizie/cronaca/20_marzo_26/sostegno-psicologico-dottori-70d3ebbe-6eb1-11ea-925b-a0c3cdbe1130.shtml.

Fu, King-wa, and Yuner Zhu. 2020. "Did the World Overlook the Media's Early Warning of COVID-19?" *Journal of Risk Research* : 1–5. doi:10.1080/13669877.2020.1756380.

Nygren, Giritli Katarina, and Anna Olofsson. 2020. "Managing the Covid-19 Pandemic through Individual Responsibility: The Consequences of a World Risk Society and Enhanced Ethopolitics." *Journal of Risk Research* : 1–5. doi:10.1080/13669877.2020.1756382.

Haueter, Jill A., Therese Hoff Macan, and Joel Winter. 2003. "Measurement of Newcomer Socialization: Construct Validation of a Multidimensional Scale." *Journal of Vocational Behavior* 63 (1): 20–39. doi:10.1016/S0001-8791(02)00017-9.

Hong, Seoyeon, Eun Hae Park, and Glen Cameron. 2020. "Look Who is Warning: individual Differences in Motivation Activation Influence Behaviors during Disasters." *Journal of Risk Research* 23 (3): 398–410. doi:10.1080/13669877.2019.1569100.

Italian-Government-D-L-17.03.20. 2020. DECRETO-LEGGE 17 marzo 2020, n. 18 Misure di potenziamento del Servizio sanitario nazionale e di sostegno economico per famiglie, lavoratori e imprese connesse all'emergenza epidemiologica da COVID-19. In *(20G00034) (GU Serie Generale n.70 del 17-03*

Jesús Bravo, Maria, José Maria Peiró, Isabel Rodriguez, and William T. Whitely. 2003. "Social Antecedents of the Role Stress and Career-Enhancing Strategies of Newcomers to Organizations: A Longitudinal Study." *Work & Stress* 17 (3): 195–217. doi:10.1080/02678370310001625658.

Jones, Gareth R. 1986. "Socialization Tactics, Self-Efficacy, and Newcomers' Adjustments to Organizations." *Academy of Management Journal* 29 (2): 262–279. doi:10.5465/256188.

Katz, Pearl. 1990. "Emotional Metaphors, Socialization, and Roles of Drill Sergeants." *Ethos* 18 (4): 457–480. doi:10.1525/eth.1990.18.4.02a00060.

Krause, Nicole M., Isabelle Freiling, Becca Beets, and Dominique Brossard. 2020. "Fact-Checking as Risk Communication: The Multi-Layered Risk of Misinformation in Times of COVID-19." *Journal of Risk Research* : 1–8. doi:10.1080/13669877.2020.1756385.

Langan-Fox, Janice, Jeromy Anglim, and John R. Wilson. 2004. "Mental Models, Team Mental Models, and Performance: Process, Development, and Future Directions." *Human Factors and Ergonomics in Manufacturing* 14 (4): 331–352. doi:10.1002/hfm.20004.

Langley, Ann, Kajsa Lindberg, Bjørn Erik Mørk, Davide Nicolini, Elena Raviola, and Lars Walter. 2019. "Boundary Work among Groups, Occupations, and Organizations: From Cartography to Process." *Academy of Management Annals* 13 (2): 704–736. doi:10.5465/annals.2017.0089.

Levina, Natalia, and Emmanuelle Vaast. 2005. "The Emergence of Boundary Spanning Competence in Practice: Implications for Implementation and Use of Information Systems." *MIS Quarterly* 29 (2): 335–363.

Lodesani, Claudia. 2020. "Coronavirus in Italia. Con i Medici Del Lodigiano Un'unica Squadra." *MSF Press Release*

Lofstedt, Ragnar, Frederic Bouder, Jamie Wardman, and Sweta Chakraborty. 2011. "The Changing Nature of Communication and Regulation of Risk in Europe." *Journal of Risk Research* 14 (4): 409–429. doi:10.1080/13669877.2011.557479.

Mearns, Kathryn, Rhona Flin, and Paul O'Connor. 2001. "Sharing 'Worlds of Risk'; Improving Communication with Crew Resource Management." *Journal of Risk Research* 4 (4): 377–392. doi:10.1080/13669870110063225.

Meyerson, Debra, Karl E. Weick, and Roderick M. Kramer. 1996. "Swift Trust and Temporary Groups." *Trust in Organizations: Frontiers of Theory and Research* 166: 195.

Milburn, Thomas W., and Robert S. Billings. 1976. "Decision-Making Perspectives from Psychology: Dealing with Risk and Uncertainty." *American Behavioral Scientist* 20 (1): 111–126. doi:10.1177/000276427602000107.

Moreland, Richard L., and John M. Levine. 2002. "Socialization and Trust in Work Groups." *Group Processes & Intergroup Relations* 5 (3): 185–201. doi:10.1177/1368430202005003001.

Perrot, Serge, Talya N. Bauer, David Abonneau, Eric Campoy, Berrin Erdogan, and Robert C. Liden. 2014. "Organizational Socialization Tactics and Newcomer Adjustment: The Moderating Role of Perceived Organizational Support." *Group & Organization Management* 39 (3): 247–273. doi:10.1177/1059601114535469.

Pramanik, Roshni. 2015. "Challenges in Coordination: differences in Perception of Civil and Military Organizations by Comparing International Scientific Literature and Field Experiences." *Journal of Risk Research* 18 (7): 989–1007. doi:10.1080/13669877.2015.1043566.

Pratt, Michael G., and Carole K. Barnett. 1997. "Emotions and Unlearning in Amway Recruiting Techniques: Promoting Change through Safe' Ambivalence." *Management Learning* 28 (1): 65–88. doi:10.1177/1350507697281005.

Rico, Ramón, Miriam Sánchez-Manzanares, Francisco Gil, and Cristina Gibson. 2008. "Team Implicit Coordination Processes: A Team Knowledge–Based Approach." *Academy of Management Review* 33 (1): 163–184. doi:10.5465/amr.2008.27751276.

Saks, Alan M., and Blake E. Ashforth. 1997. "Organizational Socialization: Making Sense of the past and Present as a Prologue for the Future." *Journal of Vocational Behavior* 51 (2): 234–279. doi:10.1006/jvbe.1997.1614.

Saks, Alan M., and Jamie A. Gruman. 2018. "Socialization Resources Theory and Newcomers' Work Engagement." *Career Development International* 23 (1): 12–32. doi:10.1108/CDI-12-2016-0214.

Scott, Clifton, and Karen Kroman Myers. 2005. "The Socialization of Emotion: Learning Emotion Management at the Fire Station." *Journal of Applied Communication Research* 33 (1): 67–92. doi:10.1080/0090988042000318521.

Smith-Jentsch, Kimberly A, Mary J. Sierra, Sallie J. Weaver, Wendy L. Bedwell, Aaron S. Dietz, Dorothy Carter-Berenson, James Oglesby, Steven M. Fiore and Eduardo Sala.. 2015. "Training'the Right Stuff': An Assessment of Team Training Needs for Long-Duration Spaceflight Crews." (Report No. NASA-TM-2015-218589). Houston, TX: National Aeronautics and Space Administration.

Star, S. L., and J. R. Griesemer. 1989. "Institutional Ecology, Translations' and Boundary Objects: Amateurs and Professionals in Berkeley's Museum of Vertebrate Zoology." *Social Studies of Science* 19 (3): 387–420. doi:10.1177/030631289019003001.

Stryker, Sheldon, and Anne Statham. 1985. "Symbolic Interaction and Role Theory." *Handbook of Social Psychology* 1: 311–378.

Tasic, Justyna, Sulfikar Amir, Jethro Tan, and Majeed Khader. 2019. "A Multilevel Framework to Enhance Organizational Resilience." *Journal of Risk Research* : 1–20. doi:10.1080/13669877.2019.1617340.

Ungureanu, Paula, and Fabiola Bertolotti. 2016. "The Role of Executive Programs in Bridging Conversations between Academics and Practitioners." *Academy of Management Proceedings* 2016 (1): 15623. [Mismatch] doi:10.5465/ambpp.2016.110.

Ungureanu, Paula, and Fabiola Bertolotti. 2018. "Building and Breaching Boundaries at Once: An Exploration of How Management Academics and Practitioners Perform Boundary Work in Executive Classrooms." *Academy of Management Learning & Education* 17 (4): 425–452. doi:10.5465/amle.2016.0095.

Ungureanu, Paula, Fabiola Bertolotti, and Diego Macri. 2018. "Brokers or Platforms? a Longitudinal Study of How Hybrid Interorganizational Partnerships for Regional Innovation Deal with VUCA Environments." *European Journal of Innovation Management* 21 (4): 636–671. doi:10.1108/EJIM-01-2018-0015.

Ungureanu, Paula, Fabiola Bertolotti, and Massimo Pilati. 2019. "What Drives Alignment between Offered and Perceived Well-Being Initiatives in Organizations? a Cross-Case Analysis of Employer–Employee Shared Strategic Intentionality." *European Management Journal* 37 (6): 742–759. doi:10.1016/j.emj.2019.03.005.

Ungureanu, Paula, Deborah Rietti, and Luca Giustiniano. 2018. "How Does Organizational Space Help Organizations Cope with the Challenges of Ambidexterity and Continue to Innovate? a Space Reorganization Experiment in a Transitioning Organization." *CERN IdeaSquare Journal of Experimental Innovation* 2 (1): 38–45.

Van Maanen, John Eastin, and Edgar Henry Schein. 1977. "Toward a theory of organizational socialization."

Wright, April L., Raymond F. Zammuto, and Peter W. Liesch. 2017. "Maintaining the Values of a Profession: Institutional Work and Moral Emotions in the Emergency Department." *Academy of Management Journal* 60 (1): 200–237. doi:10.5465/amj.2013.0870.

Zinn, Jens O. 2020. "A Monstrous Threat': how a State of Exception Turns into a 'New Normal." *Journal of Risk Research*: 1–9. doi:10.1080/13669877.2020.1758194.

Comparative risk science for the coronavirus pandemic

Ann Bostrom (iD), Gisela Böhm (iD), Robert E. O'Connor, Daniel Hanss (iD),
Otto Bodi-Fernandez and Pradipta Halder

ABSTRACT
Judgment, decision making, and risk researchers have learned a great
deal over the years about how people prepare for and react to global
risks. In recent years, risk scholars have increasingly focused their ener-
gies on climate change, and as pandemic coronavirus has swept the
globe many of these scholars are comparing the coronavirus pandemic
with climate change to inform risk management. Risk communication
research and the best practices developed from it are predicated on
findings from the 1970's to the present showing that there are structural similarities in how people think about widely divergent risks.
Consequently, these lessons from risk communication of climate change
(and from the canon of best practices) apply to the coronavirus pandemic. In the empirical comparison of student perceptions reported
here, we replicate these structural similarity findings, but also find that
moral concerns in particular deserve attention as a potentially distinct
dimension of risk perception, on which different risks may also differ, as
pandemic risks appear to evoke less moral concern than climate
change. The need for communications to be timely, honest, credible,
empathetic, and informative for useful individual actions is fundamental
and essential for communicating effectively about the coronavirus epidemic. Some countries have heeded risk sciences, and are coping more
successfully with pandemic coronavirus. Others have failed to implement these old lessons, which our data suggest still apply. While these
failures may reinforce cynicism about political and public enthusiasm for
accepting science, comparisons between the coronavirus pandemic and
climate change may also foster greater aspirations for collective action.

Risk researchers are no strangers to pandemic disease and the climate crisis, which have been topics of research and comparison for many decades (e.g. Fischhoff and Furby 1983; Fischhoff, Slovic, and Lichtenstein 1982; Kates and Kasperson 1983; Slovic, Fischhoff, and Lichtenstein 1984). These early efforts were exceptionally fruitful. Together with advances in understanding judgment and decision making, these have led to risk management insights and approaches, which governments have begun—if in a limited way—to assess and adopt (e.g. Fischhoff,

Brewer, and Downs 2011; Samson 2019; WHO 2017). Judgment, decision making, and risk researchers have long called for these lessons to be applied broadly, and mere weeks into the pandemic are pointing with new urgency to how comparisons between pandemic coronavirus and climate change can inform risk management (e.g. Edelman 2020; Kunreuther and Slovic 2020; Van Bavel et al. 2020; Zarnett 2020). As evident from this burst of recent pandemic coronavirus–climate change comparisons, comparing these two global risks to inform risk management is irresistible. Far be it from us to resist this temptation. To the small numbers of these recent comparisons that highlight public perceptions (e.g. Kunreuther and Slovic 2020), we add our perspective based on empirical comparison.

Comparisons and analogies are to learning as information is to democracy; essential, wildly influential, and potentially hugely misleading. It is in this spirit that we anchor our perspective on coronavirus in a previously unpublished comparison of the psychometrics of pandemics and climate change. Our purpose is to explore whether people are using the same constructs to make sense of climate change and pandemic risks and suggest that, if they are thinking about these two seemingly quite different phenomena in the same way, then lessons from risk communication of climate change apply to the coronavirus pandemic. After briefly reporting our findings we discuss lessons for—and from—the coronavirus pandemic.

Methods and materials

Participants

During the 2009–2010 academic year, 664 undergraduate students from six countries, majoring in either economics or business administration participated in a survey. The survey was conducted at universities in six countries: Austria, Bangladesh, Finland, Germany, Norway, and the USA. A detailed account of the recruitment and data collection is given in Bostrom et al. (2012).

Measures and methods

The questionnaire focused on climate change and comprised measures of perceived risk, causal beliefs, and policy support with respect to climate change. The climate change related results are published in (Bostrom et al. 2012). In addition, the questionnaire contained an as-yet unpublished measure of perceived risk concerning pandemic influenza as a comparison case for climate change. This measure consisted of the 12 psychometric scales listed in Table 1. We conducted a series of factor analytic procedures. All are based on exploratory principal component analysis (PCA) with varimax rotation. Following common psychometric analysis procedures (e.g. Fischhoff et al. 1978), we report methods of dimension reduction followed by mean profiles of climate change and pandemics across the psychometric scales.

Results

Risk dimensions

From analysis of pandemic influenzas and climate change conducted on the combined data set we extract four factors, shown in Table 1.[1] The loading pattern suggests the following interpretations of these factors: Threat/Dread, Moral responsibility, Known risk, and Benefits.

The Threat/Dread dimension shows high loadings for perceived threat for the three targets: humankind, personal threat, and threat to plants and animals. Feelings of dread also load highly on this factor. Moral concern shows a cross-loading on this factor, indicating that judgments of threat and morality are not entirely independent.

Table 1. Principal component analysis of psychometric scales, mutual analysis of pandemic influenzas and climate change.

Psychometric scale	PCA factor loading			
	Threat/Dread	Moral responsibility	Known risk	Benefits
How serious a threat < are pandemic influenzas / is climate change > to humankind? *(1: No threat, 7: Very serious threat)*	**.88**	.14	.01	.02
How serious a threat < are pandemic influenzas / is climate change > to you personally? *(1: No threat, 7: Very serious threat)*	**.83**	−.08	.03	−.12
How serious a threat < are pandemic influenzas / is climate change > to plants and animals? *(1: No threat, 7: Very serious threat)*	**.74**	.19	−.01	.30
How much does the idea of < pandemic influenzas / climate change > fill you with dread? *(1: Not at all dreadful, 7: Very dreadful)*	**.73**	.20	−.04	−.21
To what extent do you have moral concerns about < pandemic influenzas / climate change>? *(1: No moral concern, 7: Very strong moral concern)*	**.58**	**.51**	.10	.09
How much can you personally contribute to mitigating (reducing or stopping) <pandemic influenzas / climate change>? *(1: Can do nothing personally, 7: Can do a great deal personally)*	.20	**.73**	.08	−.05
Are the risks and benefits of < pandemic influenzas / climate change > equitably distributed among humans *(1: Very equitably distributed, 7: Very inequitably distributed)*	.05	**.66**	−.01	−.03
How well < are pandemic influenzas / is climate change > understood by science? *(1: Not at all understood, 7: Very well understood)*	.13	−.16	**.84**	−.09
How well informed do you feel about < pandemic influenzas / climate change>? *(1: Not informed at all, 7: Very well informed)*	−.09	.33	**.74**	.04
How much do humans benefit from < pandemic influenzas / climate change>? *(1: Not at all, 7: A great deal)*	−.04	.12	.08	**.70**
How soon will the consequences of < pandemic influenzas / climate change > be experienced? *(1: Immediate, 7: Far in the future)*	−.17	−.24	.00	**.57**
To what extent are the consequences of < pandemic influenzas / climate change > controllable? *(1: Not at all controllable, 7: Completely controllable)*	−.20	.02	.24	**−.48**
% of variance explained (after rotation; 59% of the total variance is explained by these four factors):	25%	13%	11%	10%

Note. $N = 644$. These were the first questions in the questionnaire. Wording: 'Please circle the number that corresponds to your best judgment for each of the following. Questions about climate change are followed by questions about pandemic influenzas'. The response scale ranged from 1 to 7 with endpoints labeled as indicated for each item. The analysis was conducted across both risk domains (climate change and pandemic influenzas) and all countries, with equal weighting for each country. Factor loadings are derived from principal components factor analysis, with varimax rotation. Factor loadings with absolute values above .40 are in bold.

Variables with high loadings on the Moral Responsibility factor are moral concern, personal contribution to mitigation, and equitable distribution of risks and benefits.

The Known Risk factor very clearly comprises judgments of how well the risk issue is understood by science and how well informed the respondent feels about the risk issue.

The Benefits factor shows high loadings for human benefits, delay of consequences, and the extent to which consequences are uncontrollable (negative loading of controllability of consequences).

This factor structure is clear, with only a few aspects deserving extra comments. One is the cross-loading of moral concern on the Threat/Dread factor. Previous research has found that threat and moral judgments are related (Bassarak, Pfister, and Böhm 2017). However, this

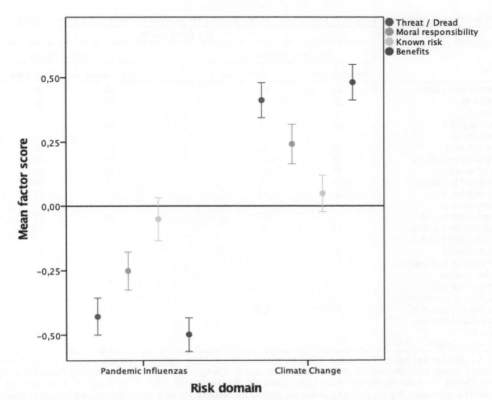

Figure 1. Plot of mean PCA factor scores by risk domain (pandemic influenzas vs. climate change).

research also showed that these two kinds of judgment are far from being redundant; they contribute independently to explaining, for example, overall perceived risk. Our interpretation is that threat and moral judgments are based on different features of a risk issue but that a certain amount of risk is necessary to elicit moral concerns (Böhm and Pfister 2017). Another aspect is that personal contribution to mitigation might be expected to be related to perceived controllability. The fact that personal contribution to mitigation loads on Moral Responsibility suggests that the implications of personal contribution for the assignment of responsibility and blame are particularly salient in the context of these two risk issues, more so than the causal implications of personal contributions. A somewhat puzzling finding is that perceived human benefits go together with the perception that consequences are delayed and uncontrollable. This might reflect a cognitive appeasement strategy in the sense that risks are downplayed as being delayed and, anyway, uncontrollable if high benefits are involved; the affect heuristic (Finucane et al. 2000) explains this mechanism by postulating that perceived benefits and perceived risks shape each other via the affect that they arouse, resulting in a negative correlation between the two.

Figure 1 shows the means of pandemic influenza and climate change on the four factors (factore scores, aggregated across respondents for the two risk domains). As can be seen, climate change is perceived as more threatening, raising more moral responsibility concerns, and bringing more benefits for humans than pandemics; the two risk issues do not differ with respect to how much they appear as known. We will consider in the discussion section to what extent differences can be expected compared to the current Corona crisis.

In the psychometrics of risk literature, two factors are commonly extracted: Dread and Unknown/Known Risk (Slovic, 1987). To facilitate comparisons with this approach, we also conducted separate analyses for pandemics and climate change, extracting two factors in each of these analyses. The results are included in Table 2. The two factors are reproduced for both risk

Table 2. Principal component analyses of psychometric scales, separate for pandemic influenzas and climate change.

Psychometric scale	PCA factor loading			
	Pandemic influenzas		Climate change	
	Threat/ dread	Known risk	Threat/ dread	Known risk
Threat to humankind	.85	−.05	.88	.02
Personal threat	.80	−.12	.72	.01
Dread	.77	.01	.76	.11
Threat to plants and animals	.66	−.29	.76	.07
Moral concerns	.59	.32	.63	.33
Delay of consequences	−.08	−.02	−.55	−.26
Well informed	−.18	.67	−.10	.86
Understood by science	−.05	.63	.13	.50
Controllability of consequences	.00	.53	.00	.14
Personal contribution	.25	.47	.43	.37
Inequitable distribution of risks and benefits	.12	.39	.20	.43
Human benefits	−.02	.10	−.29	−.01
% of variance explained (after rotation; 38% of the total variance is explained by the two factors for pandemic influenzas, 42% for climate change):	24%	14%	29%	13%

Note. $N = 632$ for pandemic influenzas, $N = 656$ for climate change. These were the first questions in the questionnaire. Wording: 'Please circle the number that corresponds to your best judgment for each of the following. Questions about climate change are followed by questions about pandemic influenzas'. See Table 1 for complete item wordings. The response scale ranged from 1 to 7 with endpoints labeled as indicated for each item. Separate analyses were conducted for the two risk domains (pandemic influenzas and climate change). Both analyses are across all countries and are based on equal weighting for each country. Factor loadings are derived from principal components factor analysis, with varimax rotation. PCA factors with eigenvalues greater than 1 were extracted. Factor loadings with absolute values above .40 are in bold.

domains, in that the core variables load on the respective factors (the threat and dread variables on the Dread factor and known to science and well informed on the Known Risk factor). It is also apparent, though, that several variables are not as well represented in the two-factor solutions. These are: delay of consequences, human benefits, and equitable distribution of risks and benefits in the solution for pandemics, and controllability in the solution for climate change.

There are strong commonalities in the factor structures emerging from the two-factor analyses of pandemics and climate change, reminiscent of the large body of work revealing Dread and Known/Unknown as important in people's thinking about risks. Differences in the two-factor solutions—regarding individual control, equitable distribution of risk, and moral responsibility, on the one hand, and immediacy, controllability, and benefits on the other—come into focus in the four-factor solution for the combined data. The four-factor solution explains almost twice as much variance, by accounting separately for moral responsibility, and benefits (uncontrollability). In sum, the four factors compared to the two factors add a substantial increase in explained variance and provide a clearer and more nuanced description of the dimensions underlying perceived risks of pandemics and climate change.

Risk profiles

Overall, the picture that emerged from the dimensional analyses is one of similarity between perceived risks of pandemic disease and global climate change. In order to take a more detailed

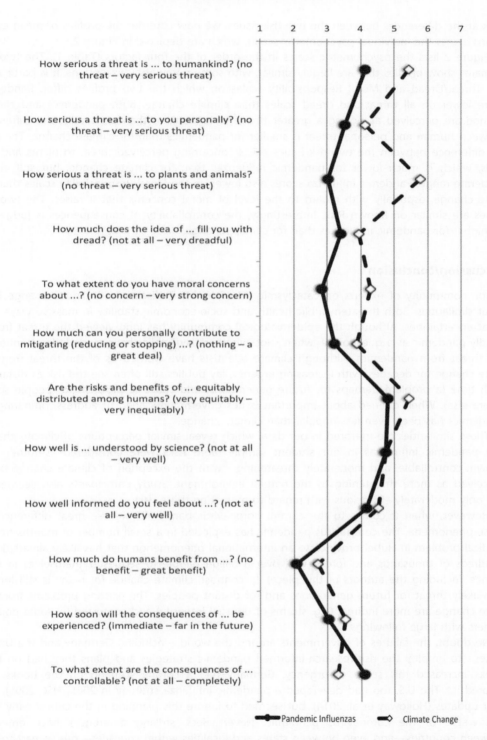

Figure 2. Profiles of mean ratings on psychometric scales for climate change and pandemic influenzas. Means are aggregated across countries, with equal weighting for each country.

look at the differences between the two risk issues, we now consider the profiles of mean evalu-ations across the individual psychometric scales, which are depicted in Figure 2.

Figure 2 lists the psychometric scales in the order of the four factors (Table 1). The two risk domains show profiles that are largely similar, with some noteworthy exceptions. It is particularly the Threat/Dread and Moral Responsibility scales on which the two profiles differ. Pandemics score lower on all threat and dread scales than climate change. Both pandemics and climate change are perceived as posing a greater threat to humankind than personally; this difference between human and personal threat is smaller for pandemics than for climate change. The larg-est difference between the two risk issues exists concerning perceived threat to plants and ani-mals, which is much lower for pandemic influenzas than for climate change, but still in the moderate range. Pandemic influenza scores also lower on the Moral Responsibility scales than cli-mate change, especially with regard to the level of moral concerns that it raises. The two risk issues are similar on Known Risk. Interestingly, the controllability of consequences is judged to be higher for pandemic influenzas than for climate change.

Discussion/conclusion

In the community of experts on cataclysmic risks, pandemic disease and climate change have great similarities. Both threaten public health and socio-economic stability in massive ways with great uncertainties. Although the epidemiological community has long viewed the threat from a deadly pandemic as a question of 'when', not 'whether', lay publics have given little attention to the threat from pandemics. Although climate scientists have warned us of the threat from cli-mate change for decades, with increasing urgency, lay publics still often see the risk as distant in both time (a problem perhaps for future generations) and space (a problem for people some-where else). When queried about important issues governments need to address, preparing for pandemics has been even less popular than climate change.

These similarities are mirrored in our data, which reveal similar perceptions of climate change and pandemic influenzas in our student sample. Both risks were considered as rather well known, controllable, and moderately threatening - with the exception of climate change being perceived as more threatening to the natural environment. Study participants also seemed to feel only moderately efficacious with regard to mitigating these risks.

However, when it comes to the current coronavirus pandemic, we see great differences in these phenomena. The coronavirus pandemic has exploded in a small number of months from a medical problem in Hubei province to an international phenomenon that has likely already killed hundreds of thousands and forced well over a billion people to sequester themselves in their homes (including the authors of this piece). In contrast, climate change for many is still lurking as a likely threat for future generations and for distant peoples. The existing problems from cli-mate change are more indirect (e.g. storms of unusual intensity) and contested by some political leaders with large followings.

No doubt, the failures of governments around the world—including Germany and the United States—to employ the risk research-informed pandemic strategies and plans they had on their books increased this sense of urgency. Germany had a corona scenario on the books, but ignored it.[2] The U.S. too had developed a pandemic influenza strategy in 2005 (HSC 2005), and later updates (Holloway et al. 2014), but seemed to ignore this planning in the critical early days and weeks of the coronavirus pandemic. Nevertheless, striking differences have emerged between countries—and even between states and localities within countries—due in part to var-iations in the quality of public health care in each place, but also to the level of attention leader-ship has paid to risk sciences – including risk communication research (CDC 2018; WHO 2017). Case-fatality ratios remain low in Germany. Surveys show that Germans support current lock-down measures and have trust in the competence of both science and politics.[3] The Norwegian

Citizen Panel Survey shows similar results for Norway. In contrast, surveys in the U.S.[4] show increasing distrust in the president (ABC News/Ipsos 2020),[5] as concerns grow about the crisis.

Our results throw light on the question of whether people think of different potentially catastrophic risks in the same way or instead formulate their thinking in different ways tied to the specific dangers associated with the risk. The answer matters to risk communicators who want to know if risk communication research results generalize, and are germane to the coronavirus situation, or if different practices are in order. Our findings reaffirm that the best practices of risk communication apply to the coronavirus crisis. As Lunn et al. (2020) put it, 'Effective crisis communication involves speed, honesty, credibility, empathy, and promoting useful individual actions'. This aligns with the WHO (2017) Guideline for communicating risk in health emergences, which summarizes a suite of systematic reviews. Ignoring this science is costly.

Among the young, climate change appears to evoke more dread than pandemics. As we are beginning to collect and analyze new data, some from students similar to those represented in the U.S. sample included above, this difference—that climate change is the more dreaded—persists, despite the exponentially increasing coronavirus cases and deaths in parts of the United States. How well known these risks are, however, shows evidence of change. In the data presented here both risks are perceived as similarly known—respondents feel moderately well informed about them, and report that science understands both of them somewhat more. Our analysis in progress of coronavirus perceptions suggest that climate change may be perceived as better known than pandemic coronavirus. Anecdotally, doctors protest that 'we know nothing' about coronavirus. In contrast, after decades of research, IPCC reports, and risk communication efforts, the balance finally appears to be shifting on climate change (Leiserowitz et al. 2019). In light of this, it is perhaps not surprising that the lessons our students draw from coronavirus-climate change comparisons include that governments can act, and that collective action can work, and so it must be possible to flatten the curve on climate change.

Our findings also show that pandemic influenzas raise less moral concern than climate change does. A prerequisite of moral concern is perceived human causation (Böhm and Pfister 2017). The difference that we find between the two risk issues may thus suggest that pandemic influenzas are seen as a more 'natural' risk than is climate change. One might speculate whether this is different now for the current pandemic, although analyses in progress with new data suggest that it is not. The 2009-10 survey took place in the aftermath of the swine flu, which remained, at least for Europe and North America, a much more remote problem than COVID-19 is now. People's conception of a pandemic may then have focused on the biological mechanism of a virus. The current pandemic, in contrast, is hugely affecting people's everyday life, with the 'Stay Home—Stay Safe' measures taken by most governments drawing attention to the social behaviors that contribute to causing the problem. Disaster researchers have long highlighted that disasters are 'by design' (Mileti 1999), and pandemics are no exception. The roots of disasters lie in the societal choices we make (Oliver-Smith et al. 2017; Tierney 2014, 2019), the inequitable risk protections afforded to vulnerable populations (Howell and Elliott 2019), and the risk management strategies we fail to assess or adopt (Kunreuther 2016).

Notes

1. When analyzing climate change and pandemics separately, the solutions for the two risk domains are sufficiently similar to justify pooling. When extracting four factors, their interpretation is the same for both risk domains as for the mutual analysis. Factor congruency of the corresponding factors in the two domains is .94, .63, .60, and .46 for Threat/Dread, Moral responsibility, Known risk, and Benefits, respectively.
2. https://www.rbb24.de/politik/thema/2020/coronavirus/beitraege/risikoanalyse-robert-koch-institut-rki-bundestag-schutz-szenario.html
3. Survey Germany (Support for measures, trust in health system): https://www.tagesschau.de/inland/deutschlandtrend-extra-blitzumfrage-103.html

4. Survey Citizen Panel (Support for measures, trust in health system and government): https://www.uib.no/
    aktuelt/134902/hva-mener-folk-under-koronakrisen
5. ABC News/Ipsos (Coronavirus Outbreak Triggering Significant Changes to American Society) poll conducted
    April 1-2, 2020, reported April 3, 2020. Accessed April 7 2020 at: https://www.ipsos.com/en-us/news-polls/abc-
    news-coronavirus-poll

Acknowledgement

We thank Frida Ekström, Sven Jeschke, Birgit Mack, Mei Qu, Lynn Rosentrater, Anethe Sandve, and Ingrid
Saelensminde for their support in conducting this study.

Disclosure statement

No potential conflict of interest was reported by the author(s).

ORCID

Ann Bostrom (iD) http://orcid.org/0000-0002-6399-3404
Gisela Böhm (iD) http://orcid.org/0000-0002-5324-6990
Daniel Hanss (iD) http://orcid.org/0000-0001-6692-3316

References

Bassarak, C., H.-R. Pfister, and G. Böhm. 2017. "Dispute and Morality in the Perception of Societal Risks: Extending
    the Psychometric Model." *Journal of Risk Research* 20 (3): 299–325. doi:10.1080/13669877.2015.1043571.
Böhm, G., and H.-R. Pfister. 2017. "The Perceiver's Social Role and a Risk's Causal Structure as Determinants of
    Environmental Risk Evaluation." *Journal of Risk Research* 20 (6): 732–759. doi:10.1080/13669877.2015.1118148.
Bostrom, A., R. E. O'Connor, G. Böhm, D. Hanss, O. Bodi, F. Ekström, P. Halder, et al. 2012. "Causal Thinking and
    Support for Climate Change Policies: International Survey Findings." *Global Environmental Change* 22 (1):
    210–222. doi:10.1016/j.gloenvcha.2011.09.012.
Centers for Disease Control and Prevention (CDC). (2018). Crisis and Emergency Risk Communication (CERC)
    Manual. Center for Preparedness and Response. Messages and Audiences Updated 2018. Accessed 5 April 2020.
    https://emergency.cdc.gov/cerc/manual/index.asp
Edelman, G. 2020. The Analogy Between Covid-19 and Climate Change Is Eerily Precise. Wired, March 25, 2020.
    Accessed 5 April 2020. https://www.wired.com/story/the-analogy-between-covid-19-and-climate-change-is-eerily-
    precise/
Finucane, M. L., A. Alhakami, P. Slovic, and S. M. Johnson. 2000. "The Affect Heuristic in Judgments of Risks and
    Benefits." *Journal of Behavioral Decision Making* 13 (1): 1–17. doi:10.1002/(SICI)1099-0771(200001/03)13:1<1::AID-
    BDM333>3.0.CO;2-S.
Fischhoff, B., N.T. Brewer, N. T., and J. S. Downs, (2011). Communicating Risks and Benefits: An Evidence-Based
    User's Guide. US Dept. of Health and Human Services. Food and Drug Administration, Silver Spring, MD, USA.
    Available at https://www.fda.gov/media/81597/download
Fischhoff, B., and L. Furby. 1983. "Psychological Dimensions of Climatic Change." In *Social Science Research and
    Climate Change*, 177–203. Dordrecht: Springer.
Fischhoff, B., P. Slovic, and S. Lichtenstein. 1982. "Lay Foibles and Expert Fables in Judgments about Risk." *The
    American Statistician* 36 (3): 240–255. doi:10.2307/2683835.
Fischhoff, B., P. Slovic, S. Lichtenstein, S. Read, and B. Combs. 1978. "How Safe is Safe Enough? A Psychometric
    Study of Attitudes towards Technological Risks and Benefits." *Policy Sciences* 9 (2): 127–152. doi:10.1007/
    BF00143739.
Holloway, R., S. A. Rasmussen, S. Zaza, N. J. Cox D. B. Jernigan, and Influenza Pandemic Framework Workgroup.
    2014. "Updated Preparedness and Response Framework for Influenza Pandemics." *Morbidity and Mortality Weekly
    Report: Recommendations and Reports* 63 (6): 1–18.
Homeland Security Council (HSC). (2005). National Strategy for Pandemic Influenza, USA. https://www.cdc.gov/flu/
    pandemic-resources/pdf/pandemic-influenza-strategy-2005.pdf
Howell, J., and J. R. Elliott. 2019. "Damages Done: The Longitudinal Impacts of Natural Hazards on Wealth
    Inequality in the United States." *Social Problems* 66 (3): 448–420. doi:10.1093/socpro/spy016.

Kates, R. W., and J. X. Kasperson. 1983. "Comparative Risk Analysis of Technological Hazards (A Review)." *Proceedings of the National Academy of Sciences* 80 (22): 7027–7038. doi:10.1073/pnas.80.22.7027.

Kunreuther H. & Slovic, P. 2020. What the Coronavirus Curve Teaches Us About Climate Change. Politico: The Big Idea, 03/26/2020. Accessed April 20, 2020 at https://www.politico.com/news/magazine/2020/03/26/what-the-cor-onavirus-curve-teaches-us-about-climate-change-148318

Kunreuther, H. 2016. "Reducing Losses from Catastrophes: Role of Insurance and Other Policy Tools." *Environment: Science and Policy for Sustainable Development* 58 (1): 30–37. doi:10.1080/00139157.2016.1112166.

Leiserowitz, A., E. Maibach, S. Rosenthal, J. Kotcher, P. Bergquist, M. Ballew, M. Goldberg, and A. Gustafson. 2019. *Climate Change in the American Mind*. New Haven, CT: Yale Program on Climate Change Communication, Yale University and George Mason University.

Lunn, P. D., C. A. Belton, C. Lavin, F. P. McGowan, S. Timmons, and D. A. Robertson. 2020. "Using Behavioral Science to Help Fight the Coronavirus." *Journal of Behavioral Public Administration* 3 (1). doi:10.30636/jbpa.31.147.

Mileti, D. S. 1999. *Disasters by Design: A Reassessment of Natural Hazards in the United States*. Washington, DC: Joseph Henry Press.

Oliver-Smith, A., I. Alcántara-Ayala, I. Burton, and A. Lavell. 2017. "The Social Construction of Disaster Risk: Seeking Root Causes." *International Journal of Disaster Risk Reduction* 22: 469–474. doi:10.1016/j.ijdrr.2016.10.006.

Samson, A., ed. 2019. The Behavioral Economics Guide 2019 (with an Introduction by Uri Gneezy). https://www.behavioraleconomics.com

Slovic, P. 1987. "Perception of Risk." *Science* 236 (4799): 280–285. doi:10.1126/science.3563507.

Slovic, P., B. Fischhoff, and S. Lichtenstein. 1984. "Perception and Acceptability of Risk from Energy Systems." *Advances in Environmental Psychology* 3: 155–169.

Tierney, K. 2014. *The Social Roots of Risk: Producing Disasters, Promoting Resilience*. Stanford, CA: Stanford University Press.

Tierney, K. 2019. *Disasters: A Sociological Approach*. Medford, MA: Polity Press (John Wiley & Sons). ISBN-13: 978-0745671024

Van Bavel, J., Baicker, K., Boggio, P., Capraro, V., Cichocka, A., Cikara, M., Crockett, M., Crum, A., Douglas, K., Druckman, J. & Drury, J., 2020. Using social and behavioural science to support COVID-19 pandemic response. Nature Human Behaviour.

World Health Organization (WHO). 2017. Communicating Risk in Public Health Emergencies: A WHO Guideline for Emergency Risk Communication (ERC) policy and practice. https://www.who.int/risk-communication/guidance/download/en/

Zarnett, B. 2020. Covid-19 and Climate Change; Generational Fear Drives Action. Medium: Age of Awareness, March 23 2020. Accessed April 5 2020. https://medium.com/age-of-awareness/covid19-and-climate-change-gener-ational-fear-drives-action-221a5b09bfb7

Predictors of expressing and receiving information on social networking sites during MERS-CoV outbreak in South Korea

Woohyun Yoo and Doo-Hun Choi

ABSTRACT

Social networking sites (SNS) are becoming one of the most significant platforms for social interaction and information exchange in epidemics. Nevertheless, relatively little is known about what facilitates or hinders individuals' engagement in information exchange in the event of an infectious disease outbreak. This study examined the effects of potential predictors that might be associated with the expression and reception of information on SNS during the South Korea Middle East respiratory syndrome (MERS) outbreak. Analysis of an online survey among 1000 adults from the general population of South Korea showed that expressing and receiving MERS-related information were predicted differentially by diverse social-demographic, socio-economic, and psychosocial factors. Among psychosocial characteristics, risk perceptions and self-efficacy interacted with each other to predict the expression and reception of MERS-related information. Theoretical and practical implications of the findings are discussed.

Introduction

In the summer of 2015, South Korea experienced a large outbreak of the Middle East respiratory syndrome coronavirus (MERS-CoV; hereafter MERS). From the outbreak, a total of 186 cases were reported including 38 deaths (KCDCP 2015). One of the causes that worsened the MERS outbreak in the country was the failure of the South Korean government to share important information in a timely manner with the public. This risk communication failure of traditional news media resulted in the increased usage of social networking sites (SNS). SNS may be used as an alternative of traditional media outlets when information from traditional media is perceived to be insufficient. Thus, South Korean citizens utilized SNS to gain a broad access to the important MERS-related information and interacted with others during the outbreak.

Given the dramatic rise in the use of SNS during the South Korea MERS outbreak, it is perhaps unsurprising that the public's engagement in information exchange via SNS might influence their attitudes, beliefs, and behavioral responses regarding MERS. Information seeking, information scanning, and information acquisition have been identified as key influential factors in motivating disease-preventive behaviors (Lee, Zhao, and Pena-y-Lillo 2016; Yoo, Kim, and Lee 2018). With the advances in the new communication technologies, the impact of such information behaviors has become observable on SNS during the South Korea MERS outbreak (Choi et al. 2017; Lee and Choi 2018; Yoo, Choi, and Park 2016).

Despite the influence of online information behaviors on the attitudes and practices regarding infectious diseases, relatively little is known about what facilitates or hinders individuals' engagement in information exchange via SNS in the event of an infectious disease outbreak. Thus, this study aims to examine the effects of potential predictors that might be associated with the expression and reception of MERS-related information on SNS during the South Korea MERS outbreak.

Literature review

The role of SNS in emerging pandemics

SNS offer individuals a tool to acquire and share information and, participate in the social construction of risk-related issues. During the situations of disasters such as the Great East Japan Earthquake and Tsunami in 2011 and Typhoon Haiyan in the Philippines in 2013, SNS contributed a significantly effective venue for exchanging critical information about the disaster (Yi and Kuri, 2016). When an infectious disease spreads within a community or area, SNS have functioned as a public sphere for individuals to exchange a variety of information with their family, friends, and neighbors. Research analyzing the Twitter and Facebook messages during the 2009 H1N1 virus outbreak found active exchanges of information, opinions, and experiences about the pandemic among the users (Chew and Eysenbach 2010; Signorini, Segre, and Polgreen 2011). Notably, the role of the public sphere was prominent when information about the crises was insufficient. During the severe acute respiratory syndrome outbreak in 2003, Chinese individuals heavily used the Internet media platforms as communication tools and alternative resources when critical information was not available from traditional media (Tai and Sun 2007).

In addition, SNS have become an integral part of the risk communication in pandemic crises. They can not only communicate information rapidly to a relatively broad audience, but also enable the real-time dissemination of the latest updates about risk situations (Ding and Zhang 2010). Prior to the occurrence of a crisis, governments and organizations utilize SNS for proactive crisis management that includes the provision of information on preparedness and readiness, warning issuances, provision of news and updates, and solicitation of feedback on public health issues. For example, the Centers for Disease Control and Prevention (CDC) used Facebook and Twitter to communicate over half of the CDC's messages related to the H1N1 outbreak in the United States during 2009 (Ding and Zhang 2010). This approach allows organizations to establish a positive reputation, whereby the public is made aware of their integrity, responsiveness, and preparedness for potential pandemics (Wan and Pfau 2004).

SNS communication: expression and reception of information

SNS are a representative of Web 2.0 applications that allow users to link and communicate with each other, as well as the exchange of information. Based on the ideological and technological foundations of Web 2.0 (Kaplan and Haenlein 2010), SNS have contributed to a shift in the online communication environment. The traditional mass communication comprises one-way, top-down, and sender-centered communications; therefore, audiences consist of passive consumers who receive only the information provided by news organizations, and their content control is very limited (Chaffee and Metzger 2001). SNS users, however, can not only receive information from friends, family, and news organizations, but they can also express their thoughts and ideas throughout their social networks (Weeks and Holbert 2013).

Online expressive behavior is active and interactive, which can encourage people to participate in dialogical and dynamic processes of public involvement (Eveland 2004). The various forms of SNS make the degree of ease of people's expressions of their views, opinions, or emotions more than ever before. The interactive natures of SNS amplify the motivation of expressive behaviors because they readily satisfy the message writer's need to send a message to numerous people simultaneously. These features increase the particularly expressive activities on SNS in public health crises. When an emerging infectious disease occurs, people are likely to share a variety of information with family, friends, colleagues, and even strangers quickly and directly. In this situation, the popular and user-friendly SNS platforms can be attractive to people who wish to engage in expressive behaviors during epidemics. Previous studies found that individuals expressed their perceptions, concerns, and behaviors by posting relevant messages on SNS during infectious disease outbreaks (Signorini, Segre, and Polgreen 2011; Vos and Buckner 2016).

Besides functioning as message expression, SNS also facilitate online message reception. In comparison to expressive behaviors, receptive behaviors are more incidental or passive. According to Weeks and Holbert (2013), the information reception on SNS happens in following four ways: (a) receiving the news organization information that is sent to individual SNS pages, (b) consuming the information posted on the SNS pages of news organizations and public institutes, (c) consuming social network link that is sent from one member's feed to another member's SNS feed, and (d) encountering information that is posted to another user or group page during SNS browsing. People can encounter a variety of information on SNS through such ways. In particular, the amount of information that people are exposed to increases dramatically during infectious disease outbreaks. Chew and Eysenbach (2010) analyzed over two million Twitter posts containing keywords related to 'H1N1' or 'swine flu' during the 2009 H1N1 pandemic and found that H1N1-related tweets increased from 8.8% to 40.5%. In the same period, McNeill, Harris, and Briggs (2016) revealed similar patterns of change regarding the H1N1-related tweets.

Potential predictors of expressing and receiving information

This study uses the comprehensive model of information seeking (CMIS; Johnson 1997) as a theoretical model to explain the potential predictors of expressing and receiving information about an infectious disease (i.e. MERS) on SNS. The CMIS has been originally used to explore cancer-related information seeking particularly for channels such as magazines (Johnson and Meischke 1993) and support groups (Czaja, Manfredi, and Price 2003). Recently, it has been applied to specify a set of antecedent factors in predicting communication behaviors in an online cancer support group (Han et al. 2010; Kim et al. 2011). The CMIS synthesizes three theoretical perspectives that incorporate the uses and gratification theory (UGT) model, the health belief model (HBM), and a model of media exposure and appraisal (MEA; Johnson 1997). Most of the variables included in the CMIS are derived from the more specific HBM and MEA models; however, the dynamics underlying the variables rely on the assumptions of the UGT (Johnson et al. 1995). In other words, the CMIS assumes that the individual's selection of media and information is goral-directed toward solving a variety of questions. Based on the CMIS framework, we focus on two categories of potential predictors of expressing and receiving information: socio-demographic factors and psychosocial factors.

Socio-demographic factors

According to the CMIS, socio-demographic factors lead to differences in accessing, seeking, processing, and using health information in the digital media environment. There is robust evidence that age, gender, education, income, employment, and occupation are associated with the selection of media and information channels for health-related activities. Avery (2010) found that younger adults were more likely to use the Internet as an information source during a health crisis. Socioeconomic status was also primarily influential in the sense that individuals with higher levels of education and income were more likely to seek cancer-related information.

Furthermore, those with higher levels of education had higher likelihood of paying significant attention to health information in the media (Viswanath and Ackerson 2011). Being female was predictive of increased use of eHealth, such as searching for health care providers online, using the Internet to search for health or medical information, and participating in online support groups for people with similar health problems (Kontos et al. 2014).

The link between social determinants and health communication may be persistent in the context of SNS. A growing body of research has documented the social determinants of SNS usage in both the general population (Kontos et al. 2010; Perrin 2015; Pfeil, Arjan, and Zaphiris 2009; Sheldon 2012) and among college students (Hargittai 2007; Hargittai and Hsieh 2010). In particular, age, gender, and income are predictive of SNS communication activities in South Korea. For example, men and younger adults in South Korea were more likely than women and older people, respectively, to participate in self-disclosure on SNS (Kwak, Choi, and Lee 2014). The SNS self-disclosure was more common among Korean college students with lower socioeconomic status (Lee, Lee, and Kwon 2011). In the era of health communication, Korean women and the older generation were each more likely than men and younger generation to share health information on SNS (Kye et al. 2017). Similarly, in the U.S. adult population, people with a regular health care provider, younger people, and females were each more likely to use SNS for health-related activities (Thackeray, Crookston, and West 2013). A more recent study showed that people in younger age groups, women, and those with higher income levels were more likely to use SNS and to search online health information (Feng and Xie 2015). Kontos et al. (2014) also found that younger people and females were more likely to read or share information about medical topics on SNS. These results show the significant role of SNS in mitigating inequalities in public health communication. Given the mixed findings as the relationships between social determinants and communication behaviors on SNS, the following research questions are posed.

Research Question 1. How do socio-demographic and socio-economic factors predict expressing MERS-related information on SNS?

Research Question 2. How do socio-demographic and socio-economic factors predict receiving MERS-related information on SNS?

Psychosocial factors

With the CMIS framework, psychosocial factors, especially perceived risk and self-efficacy, are thought to be important predictors of preventive health behaviors such as information seeking. Risk perceptions can be defined as people's subjective assessments of the possibility that an infectious disease or its negative outcomes may occur (Slovic 1987). They are classified into two distinct dimensions: personal-level risk perception refers to people's estimates of their own vulnerability to potential risks, while societal-level risk perception indicates peoples' risk-based judgment in terms of larger communities or societies in general (Tyler 1980; Tyler and Cook 1984). Self-efficacy refers to an individual's own perceived ability to perform a certain behavior or to produce a certain outcome (Bandura 1986). In the context of health communication, those who feel efficacious are likely to regard potential health risks as surmountable challenges, whereas those who are lacking efficacy typically construe their vulnerability in a fatalistic manner (Maibach and Murphy 1995).

Individuals engage in communication behaviors as they work toward solving problems such as outbreaks of infectious diseases (Kim and Grunig 2011). Specifically, individuals who seek more necessary solutions are likely to receive more useful information regarding certain problems, and deliver obtained information to others, so that their problem is perceived to be a shared one that attracts and mobilizes other people's resources. Considering the predictive roles of risk perceptions and self-efficacy in health information seeking, it is assumed that individuals consider engaging in online communication behaviors when they individually perceive an infectious disease and/or a societal risk issue, and they are confident in their ability to exert per-sonal control. Previous studies found that perceived risks and self-efficacy predicted selective exposure to online health messages (Hastall and Knobloch-Westerwick 2013) and online health information seeking (Cao et al. 2016).

Trust may play a significant role in facilitating the exchange of relevant information on SNS during an epidemic. During an infectious disease outbreak, people's perceptions of the satisfac-toriness of the government and news media to address the public health crisis can determine their willingness to engage in online communication behaviors. The public are inclined to rely on information provided by authoritative organizations and news media such as television, radio, and newspapers. If, however, they doubt the reliability of the government and news organiza-tions, they are more likely to seek alternative information sources that they believe. Supporting this expectation, previous research found that people who perceived government and industry less trustworthy had higher risk perceptions, which predicted information seeking behaviors (Ter Huurne and Gutteling, 2008). Thus, such people may be more likely to congregate online to communicate, share, and discuss information.

During a public health crisis, people experience social stigma and report mental health issues such as anxiety and depression (Ro et al. 2017). In this situation, SNS can be a preferable com-munication platform among people in psychologically distress. Many people use SNS for relation-ship maintenance interactions with social bonds such as friends and family members (Tong and Walther 2011). Regular interactions via SNS tend to strengthen such bonds. That is, SNS play the role of a catalyst to form more robust bonds, thereby reducing stress, depression and other forms of negative psychological distress. Accordingly, it is expected that the emotional distress caused by an infectious disease outbreak is predictive of SNS communication. Overall, it is con-ceivable that various psychosocial characteristics can be the factors that are associated with com-munication behaviors on SNS. Given the dearth of empirical evidence, however, the following research questions are proposed.

Research Question 3. How do psychosocial factors predict expressing MERS-related information on SNS?

Research Question 4. How do psychosocial factors predict receiving MERS-related information on SNS?

Interactions between risk perceptions and self-efficacy

According to Witte's (1992, 1994) extended parallel process model, perceived risk and self-effi-cacy interact with each other to determine individuals' motivation to take preventive actions. If individuals perceive the risk and feel efficacious in their ability to combat it, they engage in risk-ameliorating actions (Witte 1992; Witte et al. 1996). When risk levels are sufficiently aroused, indi-viduals engage in risk-avoidance behaviors if their perceived ability to avert the risk is low (Witte et al. 1996). For example, individuals with high perceived risk and high self-efficacy are likely to make the greatest use of health information, whereas those with low perceived risk and low self-efficacy are likely to use health information the least.

The risk perception attitude (RPA) framework (Rimal and Real 2003) suggests that the impacts of risk perceptions need to be examined in the context of individuals' self-efficacy. Individuals' beliefs in their capabilities to enact a particular behavior motivate people to initiate challenging tasks, set realistic goals, and persevere in the face of barriers across a variety of risk-related behaviors (Bandura 1986). When risk perceptions are high, self-efficacy takes on added import-ance because the heightened levels of personal risk not only act as motivational factors but also tend to provoke anxiety (Witte 1994). When individuals feel anxious about their well-being, their perceived ability to avoid the disease plays a pivotal role in how they decide to behave (Witte 1992). Previous studies showed that high self-efficacy generated risk-reducing behaviors at heightened levels of perceived risk, but low self-efficacy generated counterproductive behaviors

(Rimal 2001; Witte 1994). Another recent study (Turner et al. 2006) found that individuals with higher self-efficacy were more likely to engage in information-seeking behaviors compared to those with lower self-efficacy for each level of perceived risk.

Given the framework discussed above, it is possible to hypothesize the following interaction effects between risk perceptions and self-efficacy on SNS communication behaviors.

Hypothesis 1. The effects of risk perceptions (personal- and societal-level risk perceptions) on expressing MERS-related information will be amplified for those with high self-efficacy for MERS compared with those with low self-efficacy for MERS.

Hypothesis 2. The effects of risk perceptions (personal- and societal-level risk perceptions) on receiving MERS-related information will be amplified for those with high self-efficacy for MERS compared with those with low self-efficacy for MERS.

Method

Procedure and participants

Data were collected from a web survey of South Korean adults from 6 to 13 July 2015. To secure the representativeness of data, we hired a leading research firm, which provided a panel of respondents with nationally representative demographic characteristics, including age, gender, and area of residence. A recruitment e-mail message with the survey's URL was sent to a 10,000-member online panel, which was randomly chosen via a computer algorithm. Of the 1150 completed surveys, those with inadequate or missing answers were removed, and 1000 completed surveys were finally in the analysis. Table 1 shows the socio-demographic and socio-economic characteristics of the final sample.

Measures

To measure the expression of MERS-related information, we asked participants how often they had posted information about MERS on SNS in the past 30 days. The reception of MERS-related information was measured by asking participants to indicate how often they had seen or heard information about MERS on SNS in the past 30 days. Responses were based on a 5-point scale (1 = *never* to 5 = *very often*).

Personal-level and societal-level risk perceptions were measured using four items adapted from previous research (Morton and Duck 2001; Oh, Paek, and Hove 2015) on a 5-point scale (1 = *not at all* to 5 = *very much*). Self-efficacy for MERS was assessed with four items adapted from Han et al. (2014) on a 5-point scale (1 = *strongly disagree* to 5 = *strongly agree*). MERS-related stress was measured using nine items derived from Lee et al. (2010) on a 5-point scale (1 = *not at all* to 5 = *very much*). Respondents were asked to indicate how much they had felt the following statement when they thought MERS in the past 30 days. Trust in government was assessed with five items adapted from Griffin et al. (2008) on a 5-point scale (1 = *strongly disagree* to 5 = *strongly agree*). Trust in news media was measured using three items drawn from Taha, Matheson, and Anisman (2013) on a 5-point scale (1 = *strongly disagree* to 5 = *strongly agree*). Table 2 presents the descriptive statistics for the items and scales of expression, reception, and psychosocial variables used in the current study.

Data analysis

To address the research questions posed above, we performed two separate hierarchical regression analyses. The first hierarchical regression used expressing MERS-related information as the

Table 1. Socio-demographic characteristics of study participants.

Characteristics	Participants ($N = 1000$)
Age (years)	
Mean (SD)	45.24 (13.46)
Gender	
Male	502 (50.2%)
Female	498 (49.8%)
Experience with respiratory diseases	
Yes	86 (8.6%)
No	914 (91.4%)
Perceived health status	
Very poor	9 (0.9%)
Poor	73 (7.3%)
Moderate	341 (34.1%)
Good	499 (49.9%)
Very good	78 (7.8%)
Education	
Did not complete junior/middle high	2 (0.2%)
Did not complete high school	6 (0.6%)
High school diploma	195 (19.5%)
Associate degree	159 (15.9%)
Bachelor's degree	525 (52.5%)
Graduate degree	113 (11.35)
Monthly household income	
Less than $1500	114 (11.4%)
$1501–$2500	153 (15.3%)
$2501–$3500	189 (18.9%)
$3501–$4500	221 (22.1%)
$4500 or more	294 (29.4%)
Don't know	29 (2.9%)
Employment	
Yes	686 (68.6%)
No	290 (29.0%)
N/A	24 (2.4%)

dependent variable. The second hierarchical regression was conducted using receiving MERS-related information as the dependent variable. In each regression model, socio-demographic and socio-economic factors were entered into the first block, followed by psychosocial factors, and finally by two interaction terms: (a) interaction term between personal-level risk perception and self-efficacy and (b) interaction term between societal-level risk perception and self-efficacy. Each of the interaction terms was created by multiplying the centered values of the main effect variables to avoid possible multicollinearity discrepancies between the interaction term and its components (Cohen and Cohen 1983).

Results

Table 3 displays the coefficients from the hierarchical regression models. Research questions 1 and 2 were presented to explore what socio-demographic and socio-economic factors were connected to expressing and receiving MERS-related information on SNS. Older people were more likely to express MERS-related information ($\beta = .10$, $p < .01$). Individuals who suffered from respiratory diseases expressed more information about MERS than those who did not suffer from the diseases ($\beta = .16$, $p < .001$). Those who viewed themselves as healthier were more likely to post information about MERS on SNS ($\beta = .10$, $p < .01$). Employed people expressed more messages about MERS than unemployed people ($\beta = .10$, $p < .01$). Regarding receiving MERS-related information, people who suffered from respiratory diseases received more information about MERS than those who did not suffer from the diseases ($\beta = .11$, $p < .01$). Those who perceived themselves as healthier were more likely to see or hear information about MERS ($\beta = .14$, $p <$

Table 2. Descriptive statistics for key variables.

	M	SD	α
MERS-related information expression (1 item)	2.31	1.15	
How often did you post information about MERS on SNS in the past 30 days?			
MERS-related information reception (1 item)	3.14	1.21	
How often did you see or hear information about MERS on SNS in the past 30 days?			
Personal-level risk perceptions (4 items)	3.27	.77	.82
The problem of MERS is important to me			
I am worried that I would be affected by MERS			
It is likely that I would be affected by MERS			
I have felt risk from MERS			
Societal-level risk perceptions (4 items)	3.59	.76	.87
The problem of MERS is important to Korean			
I am worried that Korean would be affected by MERS			
It is likely that Korean would be affected by MERS			
Korean have felt risk from MERS			
Self-efficacy for MERS (4 items)	3.50	.66	.78
I can avoid MERS infection			
I can figure out how to avoid MERS infection			
I can recover even if I contract MERS			
I am fully informed about MERS			
MERS-related stress (9 items)	3.01	.80	.91
Problems were unsolved and continued to increase when I thought MERS in the past 30 days			
It was hard to relieve the tension when I thought MERS in the past 30 days			
I was angry when I thought MERS in the past 30 days			
I felt that I was being criticized or judged by others when I thought MERS in the past 30 days			
I was mentally exhausted when I thought MERS in the past 30 days			
I was discouraged when I thought MERS in the past 30 days			
I got nervous when I thought MERS in the past 30 days			
I wanted to break something when I thought MERS in the past 30 days I did not feel like thinking anything when I thought MERS in the past 30 days			
Trust in government (5 items)	2.35	.96	.89
I trust government to protect people from MERS			
Government officials cared about minimizing MERS infection			
Government provided sufficient information about MERS			
I believe the government reports on MERS would be true			
I distrust the government responses to the MERS outbreak			
Trust in news media (3 items)	2.94	.87	.90
News media provided accurate information about MERS			
News media provided sufficient information about MERS			
I believe the news media reports on MERS would be true			

Table 3. Hierarchical regression analyses predicting expressing and receiving MERS-related information on SNS ($N = 976$).

Predictors	Expressing MERS-related information		Receiving MERS-related information
Block 1: Socio-demographic and socio-economic factors			
Age	.10**		−.01
Gender[a]		.03	.04
Experience with respiratory diseases[b]	.16***		.11**
Perceived health status	.10**		.14***
Education		−.003	.03
Monthly household income		.04	.07*
Employment[c]	.10**		.02
Incremental R^2(%)	5.3***		4.2***
Block 2: Psychosocial factors			
Personal-level risk perception	.17***		.06
Societal-level risk perception		− .17***	.05
Self-efficacy for MERS	.17***		.13***
MERS-related stress	.23***		.16***
Trust in government	.12**		−.03
Trust in news media		.01	.03
Incremental R^2(%)	11.8***		6.9***
Block 3: Interactions			
Personal-level risk perception × Self-efficacy for MERS	.07*		.04
Societal-level risk perception × Self-efficacy for MERS		.03	.08**
Incremental R^2(%)	.5#		.9**
Total R^2	17.6***		12.0***

Note. Displayed values refer to the standardized regression coefficient.
[a]Gender coded as 0 = male, 1 = female.
[b]Experience with respiratory diseases coded as 0 = no, 1 = yes.
[c]Employment coded as 0 = no, 1 = yes.
#$p < .10$, *$p < .05$, **$p < .01$, ***$p < .001$.

.001). People with higher household income were also more likely to see or hear MERS-related information ($\beta = .07$, $p < .05$).

Research questions 3 and 4 were designed to assess what psychosocial factors were related to expressing and receiving MERS-related information on SNS. People with higher personal-level risk perceptions were more likely to express MERS-related information ($\beta = .17$, $p < .001$), while those with greater societal-level risk perceptions were less likely to express MERS-related information ($\beta = -.17$, $p < .001$). Moreover, individuals with greater self-efficacy for MERS ($\beta = .17$, $p < .001$), MERS-related stress ($\beta = .23$, $p < .001$), and trust in government ($\beta = .12$, $p < .01$) were more likely to post information about MERS. Relevant to receiving MERS-related information, people with higher self-efficacy for MERS were more likely to receive MERS-related information ($\beta = .13$, $p < .001$). Those with higher MERS-related stress were also more likely to see or hear MERS-related information ($\beta = .16$, $p < .001$).

Hypothesis 1 posed the interaction effects between risk perceptions and self-efficacy for MERS on the expression of MERS-related information. As expected, there was a significant interaction effect between personal-level risk perception and self-efficacy on expressing MERS-related information ($\beta = .07$, $p < .05$). Specifically, personal-level risk perception had a significantly stronger relation with information expression for those with high levels of self-efficacy than for those with low levels of self-efficacy (see Figure 1). However, there was no interaction between societal-level risk perception and self-efficacy for MERS. Thus, Hypothesis 1 was partially supported.

Hypothesis 2 proposed the interaction effects between risk perceptions and self-efficacy for MERS on the reception of MERS-related information. On the contrary to the results of testing Hypothesis 1, we found no interaction between personal-level risk perception and self-efficacy, but there was a significant interaction effect between societal-level risk perception and self-efficacy on receiving MERS-related information ($\beta = .08$, $p < .01$). As shown in Figure 2, societal-level risk perception exhibited a significantly stronger association with information reception for those

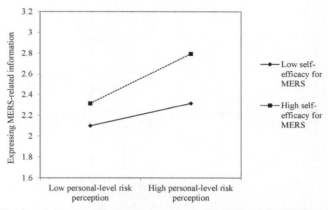

Figure 1. Interaction effect between personal-level risk perception and self-efficacy for MERS on expressing MERS-related information.

with high levels of self-efficacy than for those with low levels of self-efficacy. Thus, Hypothesis 2 received partial support.

Discussion

The purpose of this study was to ascertain potential predictors may be associated with SNS communication in the context of the South Korea MERS outbreak. Specifically, we investigated whether and how socio-demographic, socio-economic, and psychosocial factors predicted two major communication behaviors on SNS: (a) information expression and (b) information reception. In addition, we examined possible interaction patterns between risk perceptions and self-efficacy in predicting expression and reception behaviors. The findings demonstrate the variety of factors that may contribute to SNS communication in the prevention and control of communicable diseases.

First, experience with respiratory diseases was the most predictive social determinant of SNS communication about MERS. People with respiratory illness experience were more likely than those without such experience to express and receive information about MERS on SNS. This result echoes previous research that individuals who have chronic diseases or medical problems are more likely than those who are healthy to engage in online health communication, including online health information seeking (Ayers and Kronenfeld 2007; Rice 2006) and online support group participation (Chou et al. 2009). In general, individuals who suffered from a specific disease have higher uncertainty about similar illnesses than those who did not. According to some theories including uncertainty management theory, problematic integration theory, theory of motivated information management, and the RPA framework, they try to manage and process that uncertainty in some way, and at least in the field of communication, they strive to manage uncertainty through interpersonal communication (Head and Cohen 2015). Information exchange via SNS can be effective in decreasing uncertainty that is far more stressful for people with a similar disease during an infectious disease outbreak.

Second, the digital divide existed in SNS communication during the South Korea MERS outbreak. Employed people were more likely to express MERS-related information than unemployed people. Those with a higher household income were more likely to receive MERS-related information. People with higher levels of socio-economic status tend to use the Internet in more productive and practical ways (DiMaggio et al. 2004), while people with lower levels of socioeconomic status employ the Internet in more general and superficial ways (van Dijk 2005). The digital divide literature encompasses inequalities in the access to and use of information

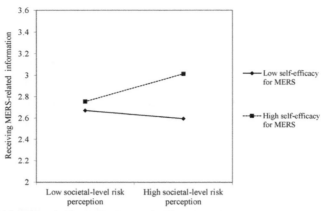

Figure 2. Interaction effect between societal-level risk perception and self-efficacy for MERS on receiving MERS-related information.

communication technologies, which have been called the first-level and the second-level digital divides (Hargittai 2002). During a public health crisis, the digital divide is related to not differences in the access to SNS but differences in the expression and reception of information on SNS.

Third, two communication activities were differentially predicted by psychosocial factors. Expressing MERS-related information included more significant predictors than receiving MERS-related information. In the online communication environment, expressing information is a self-involved and goal-directed behavior that requires conscious and intentional self-regulatory processes. Behavior change theories suggest that knowledge, attitude, risk perception, self-efficacy, and other psychosocial characteristics are crucial for triggering conscious motivation to pursue the goal (Bertrand, Babalola, and Skinner 2012). In this sense, people who post information on SNS have the strong intentions initiated by a variety of psychosocial factors during an infectious disease outbreak. On the other hand, consuming information can be viewed as the basic step to the engagement with an issue (Napoli 2011). During an emerging epidemic, individuals can encounter a great deal of information on SNS in a purely incidental manner (Yoo, Choi, and Park 2016). Accordingly, they may not need the strong intentions to expend effort, mobilize energy, and devote resources for attaining information.

Fourth, we found the distinct roles of personal- and societal-level risk perceptions in predicting the expression of MERS-related information. Personal-level risk perception was positively related to the expression of information, while societal-level risk perception was negatively associated with the expression of information. This finding coincides with some researchers' suggestion that personal-level risk perception may directly result in preventive behaviors, but societal-level risk perception may not have such a direct effect (Sjöberg 2003; Snyder and Rouse 1995). Paek, Oh, and Hove (2016) also found that individuals' intention to talk about a risk was most led by their perception of the risk as serious to themselves rather than to general people. Another possible reason comes from the impersonal-impact hypothesis (Tyler and Cook 1984) that mass media increase societal-level risk perceptions, but they have little impact on personal-level risk perception. Thus, people with high societal-level risk perception might be more likely to rely on mass media than social media as a primary source of information about MERS.

Lastly, the results regarding the interactions between risk perceptions and self-efficacy deserve further attention. Based on individuals' perceptions of risk and personal efficacy, the RPA framework (Rimal and Real 2003) classifies them into four groups: responsive (high risk, high efficacy), avoidance (high risk, low efficacy), proactive (low risk, high efficacy), and indifference (low risk, low efficacy). Applying the RPA four-group clusters to the findings, those with responsive attitude were most likely to express MERS-related information, while those with indifference attitude were least motivated to post information about MERS. Individuals who had responsive attitude were also most likely to receive MERS-related information, while individuals who had avoidance attitude were least likely to see or hear information about MERS. These findings are consistent with previous studies (Rimal and Real 2003; Turner et al. 2006) showing that efficacy moderates the relation between risk perception and information seeking such that when efficacy is high, risk perception is strongly related to information seeking. Conversely, when efficacy is low, risk perception exhibits little impact on information seeking. This implies that the level of efficacy plays an important role in predicting the expression and reception of information on SNS during a pandemic.

On the other hand, in recent years, there have been concerns that the darker side of information flow through SNS can contribute to the proliferation of disinformation or misinformation (Shin et al. 2018). In particular, in public health, misinformation can produce fear and suspicion among people. This may in turn cause negative impact on individual and societal well-being (Chen et al. 2015), such as an increased propensity to engage in harmful behaviors. Indeed, a study on content analysis showed that misinformation on SNS was more popular than relevant public health information about the disease, during the Zika virus pandemic. Misinformation occurred through sharing and receiving information among the users (Sharma et al. 2017). Nevertheless, a recent study showed that expressing and receiving information regarding an infectious disease can play a pivotal role in promoting users' preventive behaviors (Yoo, Choi, and Park 2016). Thus, public health practitioners and officials need to monitor the diffusion of misinformation or disinformation circulating on SNS among the public, especially among the less well-informed individuals. To accomplish this, they should identify rumors and false information on social media and provide verified facts through not only social media but also traditional mass media so that less informed people can easily and timely perceive such information. Also, they need to consider developing educational interventions that help the information poor promote their health information literacy, including the ability to find, evaluate, and interpret health or risk-related information. These will contribute to reducing or preventing the harmful effects of misinformation on people and society.

Overall, these findings help to shed some light on the predictors of information exchange via SNS during public health crises. Nevertheless, the current study has limitations that should be addressed in future research. First, the use of cross-sectional data may not be insufficient to evaluate the predictive values of potential factors for the expression and reception of information on SNS. A longitudinal design would help establish certainty in the causal effects of social determinants, psychosocial characteristics, and their interactions on SNS communication. Second, the present study measured the expression and reception behaviors without considering the conversation topics and the types of participants in risk and crisis communication. In an outbreak of infectious disease, SNS serve as a focal place for expressing and receiving information about a variety of topics among diverse populations. Future studies should improve the SNS communication measurement so as to get an exact understanding of the relationships between predictors and communication activities. Third, this study only focused on predictors from the individual characteristics. Other organizational, situational, and cultural features are likely to have a strong influence on SNS communication. Finally, the expression and reception of MERS-related information were each assessed using a single-item scale. This approach may lead to a problem of a lack of reliability and validity. Future research should replicate the findings with multiple-item scales to measure the expression and reception of risk information on SNS.

Despite these limitations, the present study provides both theoretical and practical implications for risk and crisis communication. This is the first study that has investigated the predictors of expressing and receiving information during an infectious disease outbreak. While factors influencing the use of health-related SNS have been examined from a public health perspective, the similar factors have rarely been explored in the context of public health emergencies. By proving the significant predictors of SNS communication, the current study fills a gap in the literature. In addition, this study extends our understanding of SNS communication by further elaborating two types of communication behaviors and by demonstrating the potential predictors in terms of different communication activities. Passively consuming information is still a major communication behavior on SNS. However, the individuals who formerly only received information provided by traditional news media are now playing the roles of producers and disseminators who create and spread information through SNS platforms (Paek 2016). Reflecting the interactive nature of SNS communication, this study pays some attention to the message expression as well as the message reception on SNS. As for practical implications, this study suggests that risk communicators and public health officials should pay closer attention to disparities in the engagement of SNS communication. SNS have recently been utilized in order to promote infectious disease awareness because they are known to be cost effective and relatively influential (Shariatpanahi et al. 2017). Given the benefits of SNS communication during an emerging epidemic, they need to develop the strategies that encourage people facing a digital divide with SNS (i.e. usage gaps) to participate in communication activities via SNS.

In conclusion, SNS play a critical role in orchestrating and facilitating communication pertaining to a public health crisis, and such communication can have a direct impact on the crisis prevention and management. By identifying individual difference factors that may influence communication activities on SNS, this study helps improve the vitalization of SNS communication in the area of public health and risk communication.

Disclosure statement

No potential conflict of interest was reported by the authors.

Funding

This work was supported by Incheon National University (International Cooperative) Research Grant in 2017.

References

Avery, E. 2010. "Contextual and Audience Moderators of Channel Selection and Message Reception of Public Health Information in Routine and Crisis Situations." Journal of Public Relations Research 22 (4):378–403. doi:10.1080/10627261003801404.

Ayers, S. L., and J. J.Kronenfeld. 2007. "Chronic Illness and Health-Seeking Information on the Internet." Health (London, England: 1997) 11 (3):327–347.

Bandura, A. 1986. Social Foundations of Thought and Action: A Social Cognitive Theory. Englewood Cliffs, NJ: Prentice-Hall.

Bertrand, J. T., S.Babalola, and J.Skinner. 2012. "The Impact of Health Communication." In Handbook of Global Health Communication, edited by R.Obregon and S.Waisbord,97–120. Malden, MA: Wiley.

Cao, W., X.Zhang, K.Xu, and Y.Wang. 2016. "Modeling Online Health Information-Seeking Behavior in China: The Roles of Source Characteristics, Reward Assessment, and Internet Self-Efficacy." Health Communication 31 (9): 1105–1114. doi:10.1080/10410236.2015.1045236.

Chaffee, S. H., and M. J.Metzger. 2001. "The End of Mass Communication?" Mass Communication & Society 4 (4): 365–379. doi:10.1207/S15327825MCS0404_3.

Chen, X., S.-C. J.Sin, Y.-L.Theng, and C. S.Lee. 2015. "Why Students Share Misinformation on Social Media: Motivation, Gender, and Study-Level Differences." The Journal of Academic Librarianship 41 (5):583–592. doi:10.1016/j.acalib.2015.07.003.

Chew, C., and G.Eysenbach. 2010. "Pandemics in the Age of Twitter: Content Analysis of Tweets during the 2009 H1N1 Outbreak." PLoS One 5 (11):e14118.

Choi, D.-H., W.Yoo, G.-Y.Noh, and K.Park. 2017. "The Impact of Social Media on Risk Perceptions during the MERS Outbreak in South Korea." Computers in Human Behavior 72:422–431. doi:10.1016/j.chb.2017.03.004.

Chou, W.-Y. S., Y. M.Hunt, E. B.Beckjord, R. P.Moser, and B. W.Hesse. 2009. "Social Media Use in the United States: Implications for Health Communication." Journal of Medical Internet Research 11 (4):e48.

Cohen, J., and P. Cohen. 1983. *Applied Multiple Regression/Correlation Analysis for the Behavioral Sciences*. 2nd ed. Hillsdale, NJ: Erlbaum.

Czaja, R., C.Manfredi, and J.Price. 2003. "The Determinants and Consequences of Information Seeking among Cancer Patients." Journal of Health Communication 8 (6):529–562. doi:10.1080/716100418.

DiMaggio, P., E.Hargittai, C.Celeste, and S.Shafer. 2004. "Digital Inequality: From Unequal Access to Differentiated Use." In Social Inequality, edited by K.Neckerman,355–400. New York: Russell Sage.

Ding, H., and J.Zhang. 2010. "Social Media and Participatory Risk Communication during the H1N1 Flu Epidemic: A Comparative Study of the United States and China." China Media Research 6 (4):80–91.

Eveland, W. P. Jr. 2004. "The Effect of Political Discussion in Producing Informed Citizens: The Roles of Information, Motivation, and Elaboration." Political Communication 21 (2):177–193.

Feng, Y., and W.Xie. 2015. "Digital Divide 2.0: The Role of Social Networking Sites in Seeking Health Information Online from a Longitudinal Perspective." Journal of Health Communication 20 (1):60–68. doi:10.1080/10810730.2014.906522.

Griffin, R., Z.Yang, E. THuurne, F.Boerner, S.Ortiz, and S.Dunwoody. 2008. "After the Flood: Anger, Attribution, and the Seeking of Information." Science Communication 29 (3):285–315.

Han, G., J.Zhang, K.Chu, and G.Shen. 2014. "Self–Other Differences in H1N1 Flu Risk Perception in a Global Context: A Comparative Study between the United States and China." Health Communication 29 (2):109–123. doi:10.1080/10410236.2012.723267.

Han, J. Y., M.Wise, E.Kim, R.Pingree, R. P.Hawkins, S.Pingree, F.McTavish, and D. H.Gustafson. 2010. "Factors Associated with Use of Interactive Cancer Communication System: An Application of the Comprehensive Model of Information Seeking." Journal of Computer-Mediated Communication 15 (3):367–388.

Hargittai, E. 2002. "Second-Level Digital Divide: Differences in People's Online Skills." First Monday 7 (4). Accessed 9 September 2017. http://firstmonday.org/article/view/942/864

Hargittai, E. 2007. "Whose Space? Differences among Users and Non-Users of Social Network Sites." Journal of Computer-Mediated Communication 13 (1):276–297. doi:10.1111/j.1083-6101.2007.00396.x.

Hargittai, E., and Y. P.Hsieh. 2010. "Predictors and Consequences of Differentiated Practices on Social Network Sites." Information, Communication & Society 13 (4):515–536. doi:10.1080/13691181003639866.

Hastall, M. R., and S.Knobloch-Westerwick. 2013. "Severity, Efficacy, and Evidence Type as Determinants of Health Message Exposure." Health Communication 28 (4):378–388. doi:10.1080/10410236.2012.690175.

Head, K. J., and E. L.Cohen. 2015. "Factors Affecting the Patient." In Health Communication: Theory, Methods, and Application, edited by N. G.Harrington,181–211. New York: Routledge.

Johnson. J. D. 1997. Cancer-Related Information Seeking. Cresskill, NJ: Hampton Press.

Johnson, J. D., W. A.Donohue, C. K.Atkin, and S.Johnson. 1995. "A Comprehensive Model of Information Seeking: Tests Focusing on a Technical Organization." Science Communication 16 (3):274–303. doi:10.1177/1075547095016003003.

Johnson, J. D., and H.Meischke. 1993. "A Comprehensive Model of Cancer-Related Information Seeking Applied to Magazines." Human Communication Research 19 (3):343–367. doi:10.1111/j.1468-2958.1993.tb00305.x.

Kaplan, A. M., and M.Haenlein. 2010. "Users of the World, Unite! The Challenges and Opportunities of Social Media." Business Horizons 53 (1):59–68. doi:10.1016/j.bushor.2009.09.003.

KCDCP (Korea Centers for Disease Control and Prevention). 2015. MERS Statistics. Accessed 2 October 2017. http://www.mers.go.kr/mers/html/jsp/Menu_C/list_C4.jsp?menuIds=&fid=5767&q_type=&q_value=&cid=65812&pageNum=1

Kim, E., J. Y.Han, D.Shah, B.Shaw, F.McTavish, D. H.Gustafson, and D.Fan. 2011. "Predictors of Supportive Message Expression and Reception in an Interactive Cancer Communication System." Journal of Health Communication 16 (10):1106–1121. doi:10.1080/10810730.2011.571337.

Kim, J.-N., and J. E.Grunig. 2011. "Problem Solving and Communicative Action: A Situational Theory of Problem Solving." Journal of Communication 61 (1):120–149. doi:10.1111/j.1460-2466.2010.01529.x.

Kontos, E., K. D.Blake, W.-Y. S.Chou, and A.Prestin. 2014. "Predictors of eHealth Usage: Insights on the Digital Divide from the Health Information National Trends Survey 2012." Journal of Medical Internet Research 16 (7):e172.

Kontos, E., K. M.Emmons, E.Puleo, and K.Viswanath. 2010. "Communication Inequalities and Public Health Implications of Adult Social Networking Site Use in the United States." Journal of Health Communication 15 (suppl3):216–235. doi:10.1080/10810730.2010.522689.

Kwak, K. T., S. K.Choi, and B. G.Lee. 2014. "SNS Flow, SNS Self-Disclosure and Post Hoc Interpersonal Relations Change: Focused on Korean Facebook User." Computers in Human Behavior 31:294–304. doi:10.1016/j.chb.2013.10.046.

Kye, S.-Y., M.Shim, Y.-C.Kim, and K.Park. 2017. "Sharing Health Information Online in South Korea: Motives, Topics, and Antecedents." Health Promotion International. Advance online publication.

Lee, C.-J., X.Zhao, and M.Pena-y-Lillo. 2016. "Theorizing the Pathways from Seeking and Scanning to Mammography Screening." Health Communication 31 (1):117–128.

Lee, E., H. Shin, Y. Yunjun, C. Jeongjin, A. Gwiyeoru, and K. Seokhyun. 2010. Development of the Stress Questionnaire for KNHANES: Report of Scientific Study Service. Osong: Korea Centers for Disease Control and Prevention.

Lee, G., J.Lee, and S.Kwon. 2011. "Use of Social-Networking Sites and Subjective Well-Being: A Study in South Korea." Cyberpsychology, Behavior, and Social Networking 14 (3):151–155. doi:10.1089/cyber.2009.0382.

Lee, J., and Y.Choi. 2018. "Informed Public against False Rumor in the Social Media Era: Focusing on Social Media Dependency." Telematics and Informatics 35 (5):1071–1081. doi:10.1016/j.tele.2017.12.017.

Maibach, E., and D. A.Murphy. 1995. "Self-Efficacy in Health Promotion Research and Practice: Conceptualization and Measurement." Health Education Research 10 (1):37–50. doi:10.1093/her/10.1.37.

McNeill, A., P. R.Harris, and P.Briggs. 2016. "Twitter Influence on UK Vaccination and Antiviral Uptake during the 2009 H1N1 Pandemic." Frontiers in Public Health 4:26.

Morton, T. A., and J. M.Duck. 2001. "Communication and Health Beliefs Mass and Interpersonal Influences on Perceptions of Risk to Self and Others." Communication Research 28 (5):602–626. doi:10.1177/009365001028005002.

Napoli, P. M. 2011. Audience Evolution: New Technologies and the Transformation of Media Audiences. New York: Columbia University Press. [10.1086/ahr/86.5.1102-a]

Oh, S. H., H. J.Paek, and T.Hove. 2015. "Cognitive and Emotional Dimensions of Perceived Risk Characteristics, Genre-Specific Media Effects, and Risk Perceptions: The Case of H1N1 Influenza in South Korea." Asian Journal of Communication 25 (1):14–32. doi:10.1080/01292986.2014.989240.

Paek, H. J. 2016. "Effective Risk Governance Requires Risk Communication Experts." Epidemiology and Health 38: e2016055.

Paek, H. J., S. H.Oh, and T.Hove. 2016. "How Fear-Arousing News Messages Affect Risk Perceptions and Intention to Talk about Risk." Health Communication 31 (9):1051–1062.

Perrin, A. 2015. Social Media Usage: 2005-2015. Accessed 8 October 2017. http://www.pewinternet.org/2015/10/08/social-networking-usage-2005-2015/

Pfeil, U., R.Arjan, and P.Zaphiris. 2009. "Age Differences in Online Social Networking: A Study of User Profiles and the Social Capital Divide among Teenagers and Older Users in MySpace." Computers in Human Behavior 25 (3): 643–654. doi:10.1016/j.chb.2008.08.015.

Rice, R. E. 2006. "Influences, Usage, and Outcomes of Internet Health Information Searching: Multivariate Results from the Pew Surveys." International Journal of Medical Informatics 75 (1):8–28. doi:10.1016/j.ijmedinf.2005.07.032.

Rimal, R. N. 2001. "Perceived Risk and Self-Efficacy as Motivators: Understanding Individuals' Long-Term Use of Health Information." Journal of Communication 51 (4):633–654. doi:10.1111/j.1460-2466.2001.tb02900.x.

Rimal, R. N., and K.Real. 2003. "Perceived Risk and Efficacy Beliefs as Motivators of Change: Use of the Risk Perception Attitude (RPA) Framework to Understand Health Behaviors." Human Communication Research 29 (3): 370–399. doi:10.1111/j.1468-2958.2003.tb00844.x.

Ro, J.-S., J.-S.Lee, S.-C.Kang, and H.-M.Jung. 2017. "Worry Experienced during the 2015 Middle East Respiratory Syndrome (MERS) Pandemic in Korea." PLoS One 12 (3):e0173234.

Sharma, M., K.Yadav, N.Yadav, and K. C.Ferdinand. 2017. "Zika Virus Pandemic-Analysis of Facebook as a Social Media Health Information Platform." American Journal of Infection Control 45 (3):301–302.

Shariatpanahi, S. P., A.Jafari, M.Sadeghipour, N.Azadeh-Fard, K.Majidzadeh-A, L.Farahmand, and A. M.Ansari. 2017. "Assessing the Effectiveness of Disease Awareness Programs: Evidence from Google Trends Data for the World Awareness Dates." Telematics and Informatics 34 (7):904–913. [10.1016/j.tele.2017.03.007] doi:10.1016/j.tele.2017.03.007.

Sheldon, P. 2012. "Profiling the Non-Users: Examination of Life-Position Indicators, Sensation Seeking, Shyness, and Loneliness among Users and Non-Users of Social Network Sites." Computers in Human Behavior 28 (5): 1960–1965. doi:10.1016/j.chb.2012.05.016.

Shin, J., L.Jian, D.Kevin, and F.Bar. 2018. "The Diffusion of Misinformation on Social Media: Temporal Pattern, Message, and Source." Computers in Human Behavior 83:278–287. doi:10.1016/j.chb.2018.02.008.

Signorini, A., A. M.Segre, and P. M.Polgreen. 2011. "The Use of Twitter to Track Levels of Disease Activity and Public Concern in the U. S. during the Influenza a H1N1 Pandemic." PLoS One 6 (5):e19467. doi:10.1371/journal.pone.0019467.

Sjöberg, L. 2003. "The Different Dynamics of Personal and General Risk." Risk Management 5 (3):19–34. doi:10.1057/palgrave.rm.8240154.

Slovic, P. 1987. "Perception of Risk." Science (New York, N.Y.) 236 (4799):280–285.

Snyder, L. B., and R. A.Rouse. 1995. "The Media Can Have More than an Impersonal Impact: The Case of AIDS Risk Perceptions and Behavior." Health Communication 7 (2):125–145. doi:10.1207/s15327027hc0702_3.

Taha, S. A., K.Matheson, and H.Anisman. 2013. "The 2009 H1N1 Influenza Pandemic: The Role of Threat, Coping, and Media Trust on Vaccination Intentions in Canada." Journal of Health Communication 18 (3):278–290. doi:10.1080/10810730.2012.727960.

Tai, Z., and T.Sun. 2007. "Media Dependencies in a Changing Media Environment: The Case of the 2003 SARS Epidemic in China." New Media & Society 9 (6):987–1009. doi:10.1177/1461444807082691.

Ter Huurne, E., and J. M.Gutteling. 2008. "Information Needs and Risk Perception as Predictors of Risk Information Seeking." Journal of Risk Research 11 (7):847–862. doi:10.1080/13669870701875750.

Thackeray, R., B. T.Crookston, and J. H.West. 2013. "Correlates of Health-Related Social Media Use among Adults." Journal of Medical Internet Research 15 (1):e21. doi:10.2196/jmir.2297.

Tong, S., and J. B.Walther. 2011. "Relational Maintenance and CMC." In Computer-Mediated Communication in Personal Relationships, edited by K. B.Wright & L. M.Webb,98–118. New York: Peter Lang.

Turner, M. M., R. N.Rimal, D.Morrison, and H.Kim. 2006. "The Role of Anxiety in Seeking and Retaining Risk Information: Testing the Risk Perception Attitude Framework in Two Studies." Human Communication Research 32 (2):130–156. doi:10.1111/j.1468-2958.2006.00006.x.

Tyler, T. R. 1980. "Impact of Directly and Indirectly Experienced Events: The Origin of Crime-Related Judgments and Behaviors." Journal of Personality and Social Psychology 39 (1):13–28. doi:10.1037/0022-3514.39.1.13.

Tyler, T. R., and F. L.Cook. 1984. "The Mass Media and Judgments of Risk: Distinguishing Impact on Personal and Societal Level Judgments." Journal of Personality & Social Psychology 47 (4):693–708. doi:10.1037/0022-3514.47.4.693.

van Dijk, J. A. G. M. 2005. The Deepening Divide: Inequality in the Information Society. Thousand Oaks, CA: Sage.

Viswanath, K., and S.Ackerson. 2011. "Race, Ethnicity, Language, Social Class, and Health Communication Inequalities: A Nationally-Representative Cross-Sectional Study." PLoS One 6 (1):e14550. doi:10.1371/journal.pone.0014550.

Vos, S. C., and M. M.Buckner. 2016. "Social Media Messages in an Emerging Health Crisis: Tweeting Bird Flu." Journal of Health Communication 21 (3):301–308. doi:10.1080/10810730.2015.1064495.

Wan, H., and M.Pfau. 2004. "The Relative Effectiveness of Inoculation, Bolstering, and Combined Approaches in Crisis Communication." Journal of Public Relations Research 16 (3):301–328. doi:10.1080/1532-754X.2004.11925131.

Weeks, B. E., and R. L.Holbert. 2013. "Predicting Dissemination of News Content in Social Media: A Focus on Reception, Friending, and Partisanship." Journalism & Mass Communication Quarterly 90 (2):212–232. doi:10.1177/1077699013482906.

Witte, K. 1992. "Putting the Fear Back into Fear Appeals: The Extended Parallel Process Model." Communications Monographs 59 (4):329–349. doi:10.1080/03637759209376276.

Witte, K. 1994. "Fear Control and Danger Control: A Test of the Extended Parallel Process Model (EPPM)." Communications." Monographs 61 (2):113–134. doi:10.1080/03637759409376328.

Witte, K., Kenzie, A.Cameron, J. K.Mckeon, Judy, and M.Berkowitz. 1996. "Predicting Risk Behaviors: Development and Validation of a Diagnostic Scale." Journal of Health Communication 1 (4):317–342. doi:10.1080/108107396127988.

Yi, C. J., and M.Kuri. 2016. "The Prospect of Online Communication in the Event of a Disaster." Journal of Risk Research 19 (7):951–963. doi:10.1080/13669877.2015.1115424.

Yoo, S. W., J.Kim, and Y.Lee. 2018. "The Effect of Health Beliefs, Media Perceptions, and Communicative Behaviors on Health Behavioral Intention: An Integrated Health Campaign Model on Social Media." Health Communication 33 (1):32–40. doi:10.1080/10410236.2016.1242033.

Yoo, W., D. H.Choi, and K.Park. 2016. "The Effects of SNS Communication: How Expressing and Receiving Information Predict MERS-Preventive Behavioral Intentions in South Korea." Computers in Human Behavior 62: 34–43. doi:10.1016/j.chb.2016.03.058.

Public health emergency response coordination: putting the plan into practice

Yushim Kim, Minyoung Ku and Seong Soo Oh

ABSTRACT

Insufficient specifications about public health emergency coordination involving government entities have been criticized as a contributing factor in managerial and institutional shortcomings. In response, this study analyzed the coordination plan and actions taken during the 2015 Middle East Respiratory Syndrome Coronavirus (MERS-CoV) outbreak in South Korea. Using network data, we found a low congruence between the planned response coordination networks and those carried out. This result was observed for two reasons. First, unrealized or newly emerging relationships among planned actors contributed to the low congruence. Second, the response plan overlooked the role and relationships of several intermediary actors between the local and national actors in the government system. The broad implication is that public health emergency preparedness and response agencies may be cognizant of the neglected areas in drawing the boundaries between—and the relationships of—core and emergent actors in emergency planning.

Public managers and decision-makers may have done what they should have—or could have—in response to public health emergencies, such as emerging infectious diseases (e.g. SARS, H1N1, Ebola, Zika, and MERS), but the outcomes are often not the ones that they anticipated. An example is found in the difficulty on the part of public health officials of communicating the risks associated with H1N1 to the public (Michelle, Maier, and Jardine 2018; Jehn et al. 2011; Kim et al. 2015). But the challenges are not limited to risk communication. The response to public health emergencies by health authorities may not unfold as planned because of the complexity of the response system itself. The most notable aspect of the response system is not only the fact that different organizations participate in the response to public health emergencies, but also that they share the authority, responsibilities, and resources at all levels of government within the nation's public health system (Davis and Lederberg 2000; Nelson et al. 2007; Hodge, Gostin, and Vernick 2007). Recent studies suggest that, because of insufficient specifications regarding how to coordinate and collaborate with organizations across federal, state, local, and tribal governments, their response has suffered from managerial and institutional frailties when tested, including poor coordination, blurred lines of authority, communication breakdowns, and weak leadership (Hodge, Gostin, and Vernick 2007; Gorman and Stoney 2015).

This article investigates the response to the 2015 Middle East Respiratory Syndrome Coronavirus (MERS-Cov; MERS) in South Korea, which tested the country's public health emergency response system. Before this event, the country had prepared by developing its MERS response plans, which specified detailed response coordination among a small number of crucial stakeholders. The plans were revised and updated multiple times during the response, but the response to MERS revealed critically inadequate emergency response pathologies (MOHW 2016). The case provides a useful context for examining how the government's response plan performs during a public health emergency and to identify insufficient specifications. The research questions of this article are (1) to what extent was the response coordination plan carried out in the actual response? and (2) what contributed to the observed level of congruence in the research context?

Below, we briefly review the challenges of public health emergency preparedness and response and identify an ongoing debate about the roles and limitations of formal policies and response plans in practice. We then overview the MERS response plans in South Korea as our research case. The data and methods section describes how the response coordination network data were collected and constructed from archival materials. We use social network analysis and visualization to map out and analyze the planned and the actual response networks, and the results section presents the level of congruence between the planned and actual response networks, as well as the sources of observation. The article ends with a discussion regarding what insights these findings provide in the effort to improve response planning for public health emergencies.

Response to public health emergencies

Public health emergency preparedness and response has proven to be especially difficult because of 'ambiguous and uncertain preparedness goals, a lack of agreement about what the measures should aim at and how they should be interpreted, and a weak system of accountability for producing results' (Nelson et al. 2007, S9). Most of all, the lack of specifications regarding response coordination across government entities has been an issue in the U.S. (Hodge, Gostin, and Vernick 2007; Gorman and Stoney 2015). The challenge of response coordination among organizations during a public health emergency was also identified as a critical issue in other countries such as the Netherlands (Swaan et al. 2018) and South Korea (Go and Park 2018).

In any disaster response, both organizations and individuals make a series of decisions to achieve the uninterrupted operation of sequential tasks, and the success of a response is largely affected by the achievement of effective coordination and collaboration (Perry and Lindell 2003; Kapucu and Demiroz 2016). Similarly, the response to public health emergencies requires a collective endeavour through inter-organizational networks (Treurniet 2014). However, because public health emergencies are primarily addressed by the nation's public health system (Davis and Lederberg 2000; Hodge, Gostin, and Vernick 2007; Gorman and Stoney 2015; Mars 2013), the role of intergovernmental networks in these emergencies may be more salient than in natural disasters, such as hurricanes and earthquakes. National public health emergencies require considerable effort to collect, assemble, analyze, and make health information available to communities through coordination and collaboration at federal, state, and local levels (CDC 2011; Holloway et al. 2014). Accordingly, the Pandemic and All-Hazard Preparedness Act recognizes that interjurisdictional coordination is pivotal during emergencies, but it does not specify the ways in which federal agencies should work with tribal, local, and state governments (Hodge, Gostin, and Vernick 2007). The same issue is also found in the U.S. government's response guidelines and plans for public health emergencies (e.g. CDC 2011; the Utah Department of Health 2016). How exactly to specify coordination sufficiently for effective emergency response is an ongoing debate in the literature, and response plans are certainly at the centre of this debate.

Response plans in practice

In practice, the stability of response is sought through the development of formal policies and plans (Robinson et al. 2013). These may have a smaller roster of organizations with a higher threshold of participation, because emergency managers can expect benefits in terms of efficiency and robustness from the loss of noncentral entities (Marcum, Bevc, and Butts 2012; Robinson et al. 2013). An unrealistically small set of responsible emergency agencies appears in the plans, but it still provides structure and stability to governmental operations (Schneider 1992). Although formal policies and plans are crucial elements of any emergency response, they are inevitably limited in the response process. Sticking with the plan is recommended if emergency management agencies want their efforts to be perceived as successful by the public (Schneider 1992), whereas flexibility is necessary to make use of decentralized knowledge in highly dynamic environments (Comfort 1994; Takeda and Helms 2005; Hart, Rosenthal, and Kouzmin 1993; Kapucu, Arslan, and Collins 2010). The flexible combination of planning and improvisation is often suggested in the literature (Boin and 'T Hart 2010; Comfort 2007), but the literature does not clarify the specifications with regards to response policies and plans that are necessary to achieve such a goal.

In this situation, the role and limitations of an emergency response plan continue to be debated with nuanced differences regarding their practical utility. For some, emergency response plans are inherently limited, but still useful. In any case, emergency response guidance and plans are developed through societies' and communities' ongoing planning processes for emergency preparedness (Perry and Lindell 2003). Perry and Lindell (2003) called the written documents 'living documents'. While the written plan is a snapshot of the planning process at a specific time, it embodies the principles that have been learned in the planning process. The presence of the written plan is 'an important part of, but not a sufficient condition for, emergency preparedness' (Perry and Lindell 2003, 338). Emergency planning cannot be equated with the presence of a written plan, nor is a written plan evidence of jurisdictional preparedness (Perry and Lindell 2003). However, good planning can help limited plans 'fail gracefully' without surprising their users (Brown and Eriksson 2008). A recent review of 80 empirical studies indicated that an effective plan increases the likelihood of a successful emergency response effort, but implementing a plan still remains challenging, especially for first responders and on-scene staff in response operations (Steigenberger 2016).

Others have challenged the plan's ability to successfully structure emergent and complex operations during disasters and emergencies (Boin and 'T Hart 2010; Brooks, Bodeau, and Fedorowicz 2012; Comfort 2005; Kapucu 2006; Marcum, Bevc, and Butts 2012; Michelle, Maier, and Jardine 2018; Schneider 1992). Clarke (1999) called response plans 'fantasy documents' because they are often 'not functional in the sense of serving as blueprints for coordination and action, but are functional in the sense of asserting to others that the uncontrollable can be controlled' (p. 16). Clarke (1999) stated that it is remarkable to find coherence between organizational coordination and societal simplicity in response plans. In reality, emergency response coordination is messy and dynamic, not straightforward at all, involving decision-making and resource allocation across boundaries. Thus, response coordination requires countless ongoing articulations by organizations and individuals to make the best decisions about the numerous tasks that go beyond the plan (Brooks, Bodeau, and Fedorowicz 2012).

In summary, there are perspectives, anecdotes, and claims about response plans in the literature, but evidence of the performance of response coordination plans in an actual response situation is lacking. It is difficult to know how response plans function in an actual response and where they are limited in terms of guiding that response. Public health emergency response is not exempt from this deficit. This study addresses this shortcoming by examining both planned and actual response coordination networks during the 2015 MERS response in South Korea.

The 2015 MERS response plans in South Korea

In June 2012, the Erasmus University Medical Center in the Netherlands sequenced a previously unknown human coronavirus from a patient in Saudi Arabia (Williams et al. 2015). Three months later, in September 2012, the first case of MERS worldwide was officially reported in Saudi Arabia. MERS is an illness with symptoms that include fever, cough, and shortness of breath, and three or four out of every 10 MERS patients die from the condition.[1] Since that first outbreak, 1,952 MERS cases have been reported in 27 countries, with 693 fatalities.[2] Outside of the Arabian Peninsula, the largest MERS outbreak occurred in South Korea in 2015, where the first MERS case was confirmed in a man who had visited Saudi Arabia on May 20, 2015. Between May 20, 2015 and July 13, 2015, 186 cases were reported in 16 healthcare facilities in South Korea (KCDC 2015b). Until the epidemic ended on December 23, 2015, the country was under considerable stress (MOHW 2016; Choi et al. 2015).

The Ministry of Public Safety and Security is in charge of disaster management in South Korea, but in cases of an infectious disease outbreak, the Ministry of Health and Welfare (MOHW) takes charge (Seo et al. 2015). Disaster and crisis management are based on four government policies and guidelines: The Fundamental Act on National Crisis Management, the Disaster Management Standards Manual, the Crisis Response Manual, and the Situation Action Manual (Seo et al. 2015). The first two high-level policies are primarily for central governments, and include abstract directions, goals, and guidance, while the Situation Action Manual focuses on responses in local settings. The Crisis Response Manual (i.e. MERS Response Manual by KCDC 2014, 2015a) was the appropriate policy guideline with which to examine response coordination across multiple governments and sectors within the country.

In July 2014, the Korea Centers for Disease Control and Prevention (KCDC) prepared its first official MERS response manual, which was revised and updated multiple times (eight revisions) until the end of 2015. The second edition was updated in December 2014, just before the event. Subsequent editions, 3-1 and 3-2, which were updated during the early stages of the event in May-June 2015, focused heavily on controlling the entry of the pathogen through local quarantine stations. Editions 3-3, 3-3-1, and 3-3-2, which were updated at the peak of the epidemic, expand the focus from quarantine to managing patients and close contacts. The last two editions (3-4 and 3-5) were updated in the waning stage of the emergency and shifted the focus back to quarantine, which was similar to editions 3-1 and 3-2.

The MERS response manual structured the response coordination with stakeholders for four key response operations (Table 1). Reporting operations refers to the process of identifying and reporting suspected cases by front-line organizations, such as hospitals and local quarantine stations, up to the KCDC and MOHW. Patient management focuses on requesting and allocating hospital beds for MERS patients, coordinating MERS patients, monitoring their close contacts and suspected cases, as well as sharing and managing their information among the organizations. Laboratory testing handles the collecting, transporting, and testing of samples and specimens, as

Table 1. Key response coordination in the South Korean Government's MERS response manual.

Reporting suspected cases	Patient management	Laboratory testing	Epidemiological investigation
• Report suspected cases	• Transport MERS patients • Request isolated beds • Share MERS patient information • Manage close contacts and suspected cases • Manage MERS hospitals	• Collect samples/specimens • Transport samples/specimens • MERS diagnostic tests • Transport suspected cases • Feedback test results to hospitals • Distribute protective equipment for testing	• Epidemiological investigation • Report investigation results • Acquire flight passengers' information • Monitor suspected cases

Source: KCDC (2014, 2015). MERS Response Manual (editions 1 through 3.5).

well as reporting test results to the appropriate organizations. Epidemiological investigation coordinates the circumstances in which MERS cases occurred, as well as the causes and responses of those circumstances. The manual defines the four key operations and includes additional coordination activities among stakeholders (e.g. distributing a protection guideline from the central government to local governments).

The ways in which the MERS response plan was implemented in the actual response process remains an issue. We answer the research questions stated at the beginning of this article by investigating the congruence between response coordination plans and the realization of health risk management in South Korea. Below, we present the network data extracted from archival materials and methods.

Data and methods

Data sources and collection

To collect network data both in the plan and in action, we relied on the aforementioned editions of the Korean government's MERS response manual, online news articles published by the country's four major newspapers (i.e. the *Kyunghyang Shinmun*, the *Hankyoreh*, *Dong-a Ilbo*, and *Hankook Ilbo*) between 20 May 2015 and 31 December 2015, and a post-event white paper published by the MOHW in December 2016. The manual was used to collect information on *response networks in plans*, 'planned response networks', and the news articles and the white paper on *response networks in practice*, or 'actual response networks'.

Because the government revised the response manual eight times after July 2014 (edition 1) until December 2015 (edition 3–5), and such revisions could alter the information regarding response networks in plans by changing the number of stakeholders and the scope of their roles and interactions, we used all nine versions of the manual to construct 'planned response networks'. The sources of 'actual response network' data were complementary. The news articles reported by journalists during the event contain detailed daily records about the stakeholders associated with it and the various kinds of interactions among them. The Center for Computational Social Science at Hanyang University provided an online data collection tool that allowed us to read, assess, and tag news articles using the term 'MERS'. The white paper, which reports research results by independent researchers at the Korea Institute for Health and Social Affairs after the event, provides rich analytical information about the response process, from pre-event planning to post-event evaluation. The white paper is based not only on government records, but also on surveys of and in-depth interviews with governmental and non-governmental entities who participated in the risk-response planning and process.

There is no well-structured guideline with which to collect inter-organizational network data, especially from archival materials such as government manuals, news articles, and reports. Procedurally, the authors of this article and the graduate research assistants, who are fluent in Korean, went through the data collection process by trial and error. The authors of this article and a graduate research assistant were involved in collecting the manual data between July 2017 and August 2017. The data from news articles were collected through two separate trials (a total of 6,187 news articles from four newspapers were reviewed in both trials). The test trial was run by the authors and a graduate assistant between August 2016 through April 2017. In July 2017, the authors developed a data collection protocol based on the news articles and the white paper (488 pages and an Appendix), which was collected between December 2016 and April 2017. Using the protocol, we re-collected the data from the news articles between August 2017 and September 2017.

Response coordination networks

The network data consist of primary actors and types of relations among them from both the response manual and the actual response process. First, we define the actors as *groups of organizations* that planned to perform or actually participated in the epidemic response. The rationale for this definition rests on the MERS response manual's identification of stakeholders. The manual defines the stakeholders who should be engaged in the MERS response process at the organization level by listing both individual organizations (e.g. the MOHW and the Ministry of Justice) and collectives (e.g. hospitals and municipalities). Such an approach to the response plans is reasonable, particularly in terms of defining the stakeholders in the private and non-profit sectors and at the provincial and local levels, because we cannot foresee in which municipalities an epidemic will occur or which hospitals, cities or towns should be involved in the execution of the plans before the event. As a result, response entities in the manual are mixed units. However, the actual response network data collected from the newspapers and the white paper do not have this problem, and were collected as individual organizations. This creates the 'mixed units' problem for the analysis that we perform.

To resolve this problem, we set a group of organizations as a unit of analysis and identified the groups in two ways: (1) groups that correspond to collectives in the manual (e.g. local police stations), and (2) groups that we assigned to individual organizations in the data sources. In the second grouping method, we categorized organizations according to the following criteria. We first determined whether an individual organization was located inside or outside the country. Second, domestic organizations were separated into governmental or non-governmental entities. Third, governmental entities were further separated according to their jurisdictional levels (e.g. local, provincial, national) as well as the functions they perform (e.g. health care, police, fire). For example, central government departments and agencies that have a leading role in response to the epidemic (e.g. MOHW, KCDC) were grouped together and separated from the other central departments and agencies that support the response (e.g. the Ministry of Justice, the Ministry of Foreign Affairs). Local police stations were separately grouped from provincial police headquarters as well as the national police headquarters. Lastly, non-governmental entities were categorized according to their primary service or function (e.g. hospitals, universities).

The second method was applied for both organizations in the response manual and organizations in the actual response process. By doing so, a total of 34 groups were identified as *actors* (see Table 2). Specifically, 16 groups of organizations appear in both the planned response networks, which are sourced from the nine versions of the MERS response manual, and the actual response networks, which are sourced from the online news articles and the white paper. Table 2 also includes 18 emergent groups of organizations that appeared only in the actual response data. See Appendix[3] for details regarding how actors are defined, and which organizations are included for the actors.

We identified five types of network ties among the actors by following the definitions of necessary key functions in response to the health risks triggered by the epidemic in the MERS response manual, as discussed in the previous section: reporting, patient management, laboratory testing, epidemiological investigation, and the overall response network. Ties in *reporting networks* represent the relationship of reporting suspected cases among the actors. When a suspected MERS case visits a hospital, for example, the hospital must report the case to the local health clinic within the administrative district. *Patient management networks* are collections of ties that show the relationships of requesting and allocating hospital beds for MERS patients, coordinating MERS patients, monitoring their close contacts and suspected cases, and sharing and managing their information among various organizations. For example, a hospital with a suspected MERS case transfers the patient to another hospital designated for MERS patients because it has special equipment, such as isolation beds. *Laboratory testing networks* consist of ties among the actors that show the partnerships between actors in terms of collecting, transporting,

Table 2. Summary of response actors.

Level	Government Entities	Non-Governmental Entities					
		Hospitals	Associations	Universities	Companies	Other	Outside the Country
International							*INT*
Foreign Gov.							*FC(H)*
National	**NSD**, **NHD**, **NPE(TP)**, *NQG(H)*, *NPS*, *NFA*	**H**, **HD**	**A(HA)**, **A(MP)**	*U*	**C(TP)**, **C(MW)**, *C(CC)*, *C(MT)*	*MF*, *V*, *FIP*, *R(F)*	
Provincial	**PG**, **PHR**, *PEO*, *PPA*, *PFD*, *PMH*, *PED*						
Local	**LG**, **LHC**, **LPS**, **LFS**, **LQS**, *LED*						

Label	16 Planned Actors	Label	18 Emergent Actors
NHD	Central Government Health Department and Agencies	*INT*	International Health Organizations
NSD	Other Central Government Departments	*FC(H)*	Foreign Country Heath Departments or Medical Centers
NPE(TP)	Public Enterprises (Transportation)	*NFA*	Korean Embassies and Consulates
PG	Provincial Governments	*NQG(H)*	Quasi-Government Organizations (Health and Welfare)
PHR	Provincial Health and Environment Research Institutes	*NPS*	National Public Safety Agencies
LG	Local Governments	*PEO*	Provincial Emergency Operation Centers
LHC	Local Health Clinics	*PPA*	Provincial Police Agencies
LPS	Local Police Stations	*PFD*	Provincial Fire and Disaster Headquarters
LFS	Local Fire Stations	*PMH*	Provincial Mental Health Centers
LQS	Local Quarantine Stations	*PED*	Provincial Education Offices
H	Hospitals	*LED*	Local Education Office
HD	Designated Hospitals	*U*	Universities
C(TP)	Transportation Companies	*MF*	Clinical Laboratories
C(MW)	Medical Waste Treatment Companies	*V*	Humanitarian Organizations
A(HA)	Academic Associations (Health Academics)	*FIP*	Funeral Industry Professionals
A(MP)	Professional Associations (Medical Professionals)	*R(F)*	Financial Regulators
		C(CC)	Credit Card Companies
		C(MT)	Mobile Telecommunication Companies

Bold fonts are planned actors and *italicized fonts* are emergent actors. For government actors, the first letter of the ID indicates the level of government (N: national level, P: provincial level, and L: local level). Health actors include the letter H or M in the IDs. Some actors' specialty is presented with a parenthesis, such as C(TP) for transportation companies and A(HA) for health academics association.

and testing the samples and specimens, as well as sharing the test results. For example, a designated hospital with a suspected MERS case sends the patient's specimen to KCDC for testing and confirmation, and then KCDC reports the results to the hospital. *Epidemiological investigation networks* capture the cooperative relationships among the actors to investigate the circumstance of the disease occurrence, as well as the response. For example, KCDC dispatches epidemiologists to a hospital for the investigation of a MERS case occurrence or a response to the occurrence. *Overall response networks* are the collections of ties built among the actors with respect to any kind of response interaction that takes place during the MERS outbreak, as defined in the MERS response manual. Each set of the five types of networks are identified for the planned response networks and the actual response networks, respectively.

To gather information about the five types of relations (i.e. ties) among the actors, we first conducted a content analysis by manually parsing sentences in the source texts and reading and interpreting actors (e.g. from a local health clinic to a provincial health and environment research institute), verbs (e.g. transferred), and objects (e.g. a specimen of a MERS patient), as well as adverbs and adjectives (if necessary) that are relevant to each type of relationship. When any working relationship for response was found between organizations, which was later assigned to different actor groups, the actors were considered to be coordinated in our final dataset. The number of actors and ties among actors can be unbalanced, given the organizations that they include. The network data were constructed as directional adjacency matrices that display the binary relationship between the actors, which consist of 0 s and 1 s.

Methods

To analyze the network data, we employed two social network analysis (SNA) techniques: the Quadratic Assignment Procedure (QAP) and network visualization. The utility of SNA in disaster and emergency management research has been well-established (Jones and Faas 2016). The QAP allows researchers to statistically assess the similarity of an actor's behaviour in two networks—the planned response network and the actual response network. Specifically, QAP correlation coefficients concisely measure the direction and strength of congruence between networks among the same set of actors by randomly permuting rows and columns in a network matrix and then calculating the probability that the network observed was produced by chance (Borgatti, Everett, and Johnson 2013). In this article, we report Jaccard's coefficient as a measure of similarity between the planned and the actual networks, given the binary matrices. It should be noted that since the QAP allows for the comparison of network behaviours only among the same sets of actors with regards to both the size and the label of actors, we only used network data from the 16 actors that commonly appeared in both the planned and actual response networks. We also visualized the planned and actual response networks among the 16 actors to examine which actors and relationships were enacted as planned, or planned but not enacted, or newly emerging, which contributed to the level of congruence between the networks planned and enacted.

Results

To provide an overview of the response coordination networks, we first present and contrast *overall response networks* in the manual and in the actual response. Figure 1(a) shows the response coordination network in the MERS manual with the 16 actors, whereas Figure 1(b) shows the actual response network with the 34 actors. Figure 1(b) includes both the planned and the emergent actors that can be distinguished based on the colours of the nodes. Black nodes represent the planned and realized actors, and white nodes represent the emergent actors.

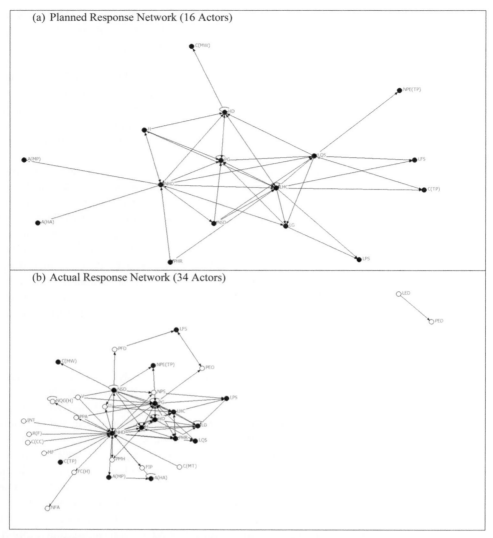

Figure 1. Overall MERS response networks in South Korea. The colours of the symbols represent information on actors' inclusion in the response manual: black = groups of organizations defined in the MERS response manual, and white = groups of organizations emerged during the actual response process. See Table 2 for labels.

Figure 1(b) shows that some planned actors were actively involved in coordinating with emergent actors during the response. Compared to the planned network, for example, the Central Government Health Department and Agencies [NHD] coordinated with a surprisingly high number of actors in the actual response, many of which were emergent actors. Other Central Government Departments [NSD] also coordinated with several emergent actors, such as Universities [U] and Humanitarian Organizations [V]. It also shows that other emergent actors were provincial, such as the Provincial Fire and Disaster Headquarters [PFD] and Provincial Emergency Operation Centers [PEO], which served as intermediaries between local actors and national actors. Local Quarantine Stations [LQS] and Local Health Clinics [LHC] were planned to be the central actors in the manual, but their role and relationships were limited in the actual response. Figure 1(b) seems to derive from the situation that once the first case was confirmed, most attention was focused on addressing and managing confirmed and suspected cases in the country until the epidemic ended.

Congruence of planned and actual response coordination networks

We used QAP to analyze the level of congruence between the planned and actual response coordination networks among the 16 actors for four key response operations. The correlation between the planned and actual response networks was not random, but rather was weak in each operation network. In Table 3, he coordination plans were enacted more successfully in reporting suspected cases (Jaccard coef.: 0.31, $p < 0.001$) and in patient management (Jaccard coef.: 0.33, $p < 0.000$), but to a lesser extent in laboratory testing (Jaccard coef.: 0.27, $p < 0.004$) and epidemiological investigation (Jaccard coef.: 0.18, $p < 0.011$). In short, the coordination plans were realized more successfully in case management operations, but less so in specialized response operations for the epidemic.

We visualized four operation networks separately to examine which actors and relationships were enacted as planned, or planned but not enacted, or newly emerging. For illustration purposes, we present the epidemiological investigation network in Figure 2, which shows the lowest congruence between the plan and the actual response in QAP. The circle nodes are government actors, and the triangle nodes are non-government actors. The black nodes are health actors, and the grey nodes are non-health actors. As expected, the health actors are those organizations in the actor group that specialize in health or medical knowledge and resources (e.g. hospitals, provincial health and environment research institutes, the Korea National Institute of Health).

In Figure 2(a), the manual specified nine actors and the relationships among them for the epidemiological investigation. In Figure 2(b), only four out of the nine (Hospitals [H], NHD, the Provincial Government [PG], and the Local Government [LG])[4] and some relationships were actually realized. Figure 2(c) shows that the manual specified and emphasized the roles and relationships of local actors (e.g. LQS), but that their relationships with other actors were not enacted in this operation. The emphasis on the roles and relationships of the local actors in the plan were consistently evident in the visualization of the planned but not enacted networks in the remaining three operation networks, which was not visually presented in this article. Figure 2(d)

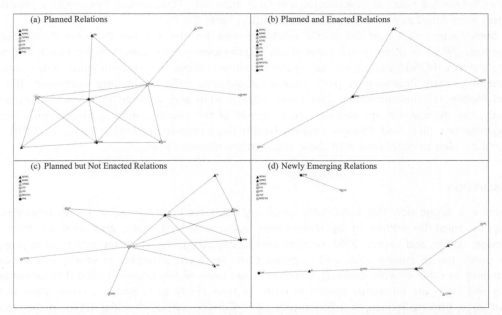

Figure 2. Epidemiological investigation network. The colours of the symbols represent information on actors' affiliation in health sectors: black = a group of organizations in health sectors, and grey = a group of organizations in non-health sectors. The symbol shapes indicate actors' government affiliation: circle = groups of governmental actors, and up triangle = groups of non-governmental actors in the private and non-profit sectors. See Table 2 for labels.

presents newly emerging relations, which the manual did not plan but which appeared in the actual response. For example, it shows that the manual did not specify the role of Provincial Health and Environment Research Institutes [PHR] in the epidemiological investigation and its coordinated effort with LG.

Figure 2 also shows that a relationship between health actors (i.e. from **H** to **NHD**)[5] was enacted in the actual response as planned (Figure 2b), but that several emerging relations in the response were observed between health and non-health actors (e.g. from **P**HR to LG, from PG to Designated Hospitals [**H**D], from NSD to **H**, and from Transportation Companies [C(TP)] to **N**HD) (Figure 2d). Such newly emerging relations between health actors and non-health actors were frequently observed in the laboratory testing network (e.g. from **P**HR to LG, between **P**HR and PG, between LG and **N**HD), as well as in the patient management net-work (e.g. from Local Police Stations [LPS] to L**H**C, from LG to **H**D, from NSD to **N**HD).

Unrealized or newly emerging relations among actors contributed to the low congruence of the planned and actual response networks. The response manual fell short in terms of anticipat-ing and guiding the breadth and complexity of the relationships among the 16 actors in the public health emergency response. In particular, the response manual was designed to empha-size the roles and relationships of first-responding local actors, missing newly emerging relations between health actors and non-health actors, especially in disease-specific operations.

Emergent actors

Table 2 includes the 18 emergent actors that were not identified from the manual but were identified from the actual response data. The MERS response manual identified government actors at the local level relatively well (see bold IDs in government entities), but defined the roles of provincial government actors less clearly (see italicized IDs in government entities). The MERS response manual identified PG as a planned actor, but it did not properly envision the role of other actors at the provincial level that serve as intermediaries (e.g. Provincial Police Agencies [PPA] between a national headquarter and local branches). Thus, several intermediary provincial actors were listed as emergent actors (italicized) in Table 2.

Some actors that perform public safety services for the country (National Public Safety Agencies [NPS]) or other government affairs (Quasi-Governments, especially for health and wel-fare services [NQG(H)]) emerged during the response process. Non-governmental actors such as Funeral Industry Professionals [FIP], Clinical Laboratories [MF], Credit Card Companies [C(CC)], and Mobile Telecommunication Companies [C(MT)] were also involved in the actual response. Lastly, the manual did not include actors outside of the country, such as International Health Organizations [INT] and Foreign Country Health Departments or Medical Centers [FC(H)]. We found no plan to coordinate with these actors in the response manual.

Discussion

There is a suggestion that sufficiently specifying the ways in which public health emergencies respond must be addressed by stakeholders such as federal, state, and local governments (Hodge, Gostin, and Vernick 2007; Gorman and Stoney 2015). This is an important call to prepare for public health emergencies, and response plans are a crucial aspect of emergency response planning. In other disaster contexts, however, it has been widely acknowledged that formal poli-cies and plans are inherently limited in terms of their ability to respond to crises (Boin and 'T Hart 2010; Brooks, Bodeau, and Fedorowicz 2012; Comfort 2005; Schneider 1992). In this article, we used the example of South Korea's MERS response case to build quantitative evidence regarding how a response plan performed in an actual response. Beyond the finding of the low congruence between planned and actual response networks, the analysis also provides three analytical insights into how the response plan was limited in the response, and thus where attention needs to be paid to improve public health emergency preparedness and response.

The response coordination that was planned but not enacted was observed in the coordination surrounding local quarantine stations (e.g. Figure 2c), whereas the role of the national and provincial government actors was significant in the actual response (e.g. Figure 1b). The emphasis on the role of local quarantine stations and local health clinics in the response manual makes sense. This approach implicitly assumes that emerging infectious diseases such as MERS will enter the country from the outside, so controlling the entry of new pathogens is a key response operation. Clearly, if the entry of new pathogens can be successfully controlled, it is highly desirable for the country. In today's globalized and mobile world, however, the risk of a person entering a country with a new pathogen is high. The novelty of new pathogens, their incubation periods, and other unknown parameters can hinder the immediate identification of a disease that enters a country for the first time. Furthermore, the MERS event speaks to the fact that it is crucial to have a plan to control the exit of infected people to other countries, a factor to which we found the response plans to have paid little attention. By failing to monitor and manage MERS patients' travel to other countries, the response to the epidemic became more challenging and caused tensions and confrontations with neighbouring countries, which in turn complicated the response (see Figuie (2014) for the global governance of risk framework).

The response plan can certainly leave out crucial actors or necessary relationships between actors from different sectors. The study identified emergent actors in the response, especially from the plan's perspective, one set of which was intermediary government organizations, whose role is critical in emergencies (Brooks, Bodeau, and Fedorowicz 2012). Several government actors at the provincial level were listed as emergent actors in Table 2, because the manual missed specifying the roles and relationships of those entities. In a similar vein, the manual overlooked the role of important health actors, such as provincial health and environment research institutes (PHR). Additionally, a source of the low congruence in terms of the epidemic-specific operations can be attributed to newly emerging relations between health and non-health actors (Figure 2d). Emerging relations among health actors were also observed in the other response coordination networks, although less frequently than those between health and non-health actors. This finding highlights the uniqueness of public health emergencies that require the involvement of actors from different specialties in the response, and also demonstrates the challenge of coordination between actors at the horizontal as well as at the vertical levels (Davis and Lederberg 2000).

A response plan that focuses on the entry of new infectious diseases may underestimate the coordination burden that may be associated with emergent actors and relationships during the response period. Figure 2(b) shows that the response process can pose high coordination costs for the leading health agency group (e.g. NHD), especially when the response focus shifted to control the spread of the epidemic inside the country. In this research context, emergent actors included international organizations, as well as those that have been considered *expanding* (e.g. social services such as schools) or *extending* (e.g. Red Cross, Salvation Army) organizations in traditional disaster response (Boin and 'T Hart 2010). Funeral industry professionals, financial regulators, credit card companies, and mobile telecom companies can be considered *emerging* organizations, which are difficult to envision until the response is actually performed. It has often been found that the circle of organizations actively involved in emergency response networks is drawn too narrowly and focuses on *established* (e.g. police, fire, ambulance services) and *expanding* organizations, with much patchier participation on the part of *extending* organizations, and insufficient thought devoted to *emerging* organizations during emergencies (Boin and 'T Hart 2010; Briggs and Stern 2007). Although which organizations will emerge will be unclear until sufficient research is conducted, how to work with identified emerging organizations is worth paying attention to in the emergency planning stage, as well as during the response (Table 3).

It is worth noting that the MERS response manual was revised multiple times by KCDC. However, the response coordination structure remained consistent throughout the various

Table 3. Congruence of planned and actual response coordination networks.

Response operations	Jaccard Coefficient	p-value
Reporting suspected cases	0.31	0.001
Patient management	0.33	0.000
Laboratory test	0.27	0.004
Epidemiology investigation	0.18	0.011

editions. A major difference was found from a set of editions 3-3-1 and 3-3-2, which was updated during the peak and which categorized different types of hospitals to test and treat MERS patients and manage MERS patients and their close contacts. In the two versions, local police appeared first to coordinate with local emergency management and the health actors for MERS patients. The health authority (i.e. KCDC) might learn the limitations of their response manual during the event and attempt to incorporate what they have learned as promptly as possible, but the data suggest that the changes were only at the margins, and very conservative. The agency would not have had sufficient time to reflect on and fully revise the manual. While we cannot tell the reasons for the limited changes, this study finds substantial areas for improvement for future public health emergency planning by identifying gaps between the manual and the actual response process from the plan's perspective.

Two limitations are worth noting. We focused on analyzing response coordination in the response manual and in the actual response to the 2015 MERS outbreak in South Korea. As mentioned earlier, the written plans are a snapshot of an ongoing planning process (Perry and Lindell 2003). Our approach narrowly defines the government's public health emergency response planning efforts by focusing on the written plans. Second, the study relies on relational data collected from multiple text sources. We documented the rules, decisions, and processes, but extracting relational data from text materials poses several challenges and issues that need to be addressed and discussed, as it is a labour-intensive, error-prone approach.

In conclusion, this article investigated a critical and ever-present risk to modern societies in the form of emerging infectious diseases, as well as the issue of coordinating actions to deal with such risks with formal response plans. Our study finds that formal policies and response plans can be constrained by the planner's orientation toward first need (e.g. controlling the entry of new pathogens to the country), and that the response plan can overlook coordination with crucial actors at the vertical and the horizontal levels that need to be involved in the actual response, including their responsibility to control the travel of infected people to other countries. When uncertainties surrounding the risk and the response system is high, such as during public health emergencies, learning by trial and error is one way to improve society's response efforts. In any case, from the perspective of public health emergency preparedness and response, the lessons learned from the response to the 2015 MERS outbreak in South Korea are too important to ignore.

Notes

1. https://www.cdc.gov/coronavirus/mers/about/symptoms.html
2. Information retrieved from the WHO website on May 14, 2017: http://www.who.int/emergencies/mers-cov/en/
3. Appendix also shows that 28 entities (individual organizations and collectives) were listed in the response manual, and 1,242 organizations were identified from the actual response network data sources.
4. We used an [ID] for each of the actors using the initials of the actors' names.
5. We used a bold font for H to highlight health actors.

Acknowledgements

We would like to thank Ji Hyun Byeon, Minsang Lee, and Chan Wang for their research assistance. We appreciate comments from Stefan Verweij and Wei Zhong. We are grateful to the Center for Computational Social Science at Hanyang University for their technical support. We are also benefited from a presentation at the Institute of

Governance Design's Social Science Korea colloquium series in Korea University and a workshop at Renmin University of China in 2017 as well as a presentation at the American Society for Public Administration conference in 2018 and the Association of Policy Analysis and Management in 2019. We remain responsible for all errors.

Disclosure statement

No potential conflict of interest was reported by the authors.

Funding

The author(s) disclosed receipt of the following financial support for the research, authorship, and/or publication of this article: This work was supported by the Ministry of Education of the Republic of Korea and the National Research Foundation of Korea (NRF-2016S1A3A2924956). We were also technically and financially supported by the National Research Foundation of Korea (Ministry of Science and ICT) (No.2018R1A5A7059549).

References

Boin, A., and P. 'T Hart. 2010. "Organizing for Effective Emergency Management: Lessons from Research." *Australian Journal of Public Administration* 69(4): 357–371. doi:10.1111/j.1467-8500.2010.00694.x.

Borgatti, S. P., M. G. Everett, and J. C. Johnson. 2013. *Analyzing Social Networks*. Thousand Oaks, CA: Sage.

Briggs, D., and R. Stern. 2007. "Risk Response to Environmental Hazards to Health–towards an Ecological Approach." *Journal of Risk Research* 10(5): 593–622. doi:10.1080/13669870701315799.

Brooks, J. M., D. Bodeau, and J. Fedorowicz. 2012. "Network Management in Emergency Response: Articulation Practices of State-Level Managers–Interweaving up, down, and Sideways." *Administration & Society* 45(8): 911–948. doi:10.1177/0095399712445874.

Brown, C., and K. Eriksson. 2008. "A Plan for (Certain) Failure: Possibilities for and Challenges of More Realistic Emergency Plans." *International Journal of Emergency Management* 5(3–4): 292–310. doi:10.1504/IJEM.2008.025099.

Centers for Disease Control and Prevention (CDC). 2011. *Public Health Emergency Response Guide for State, Local, and Tribal Public Health Directors (Version 2.0)*. Washington, DC: U.S. Department of Health and Human Services. https://emergency.cdc.gov/planning/pdf/cdcresponseguide.pdf.

Choi, J. W., K. H. Kim, Y. M. Cho, and S. H. Kim. 2015. "Current Epidemiological Situation of Middle East Respiratory Syndrome Coronavirus Clusters and Implications for Public Health Response in South Korea." *Journal of the Korean Medical Association* 58(6): 487–497. doi:10.5124/jkma.2015.58.6.487.

Clarke, L. 1999. *Mission Improbable: Using Fantasy Documents to Tame Disaster*. Chicago, IL: The University of Chicago Press.

Comfort, L. K. 1994. "Risk and Resilience: Inter-Organizational Learning following the Northridge Earthquake of 17 January 1994." *Journal of Contingencies and Crisis Management* 2(3): 157–170. doi:10.1111/j.1468-5973.1994.tb00038.x.

Comfort, L. K. 2005. "Risk, Security, and Disaster." *Annual Review of Political Science* 8(1): 335–356. doi:10.1146/annurev.polisci.8.081404.075608.

Comfort, L. K. 2007. "Crisis Management in Hindsight: Cognition, Communication, Coordination, and Control." *Public Administration Review* 67(s1): 189–197. doi:10.1111/j.1540-6210.2007.00827.x.

Davis, J. R., and J. Lederberg. 2000. *Public Health Systems and Emerging Infections: Assessing the Capabilities of the Public and Private Sectors: Workshop Summary*. Washington, DC: National Academy Press.

Figuie, M. 2014. "Towards a Global Governance of Risks: International Health Organizations and the Surveillance of Emerging Infectious Diseases." *Journal of Risk Research* 17(4): 469–482.

Go, D. Y., and J. Park. 2018. "A Comparative Study of Infectious Disease Government in Korea: What we Can Learn from the 2003 SARS and the 2015 MERS Outbreak." *Journal of the Korea Association for Policy Studies* 27(1): 243–280.

Gorman, L., and C. Stoney. 2015. "Missed Opportunities: Public Health Disaster Management in Canada." *Journal of Public Management & Social Policy* 22(2): 6.

Hart, P. 'T., U. Rosenthal, and A. Kouzmin. 1993. "Crisis Decision Making: The Centralization Thesis Revisited." *Administration & Society* 25(1): 12–45. doi:10.1177/009539979302500102.

Hodge, J. G., L. O. Gostin, and J. S. Vernick. 2007. "The Pandemic and All-Hazards Preparedness Act: Improving Public Health Emergence Response." *JAMA* 297(15): 1708–1711. doi:10.1001/jama.297.15.1708.

Holloway, R., S. A. Rasmussen, S. Zaza, N. J. Cox, and D. B. Jernigan. 2014. "Updated Preparedness and Response Framework for Influenza Pandemics." *MMWR* 63(6): 1–18.

Jehn, M., Y. Kim, B. Bradley, and T. Lant. 2011. "Community Knowledge, Risk Perception, Preparedness for the 2009 Influenza a/H1N1 Pandemic." *Journal of Public Health Management Practice* 17(5): 431–438. doi:10.1097/PHH.0b013e3182113921.

Jones, E., and A. J. Faas. 2016. *Social Network Analysis of Disaster Response, Recovery, and Adaptation*. Cambridge, MA: Butterworth-Heinemann.

Kapucu, N. 2006. "Examining the National Response Plan in Response to a Catastrophic Disaster: Hurricane Katrina in 2005." *International Journal of Mass Emergencies and Disasters* 24(2): 271–299.

Kapucu, N., T. Arslan, and M. L. Collins. 2010. "Examining Intergovernmental and Interorganizational Response to Catastrophic Disasters: Toward a Network-Centered Approach." *Administration & Society* 42(2): 222–247. doi:10.1177/0095399710362517.

Kapucu, N., and F. Demiroz. 2016. "Interorganizational networks in disaster management," In *Social Network Analysis of Disaster Response, Recovery, and Adaptation*, edited by E. Jones and A.J. Faas, 25–39. Cambridge, MA: Butterworth-Heinemann.

Kim, Y., W. Zhong, M. Jehn, and L. Walsh. 2015. "Public Risk Perceptions and Preventive Behaviors during the 2019 H1N1 Influenza Pandemic." *Disaster Medicine and Public Health Preparedness* 9(2): 145–154. doi:10.1017/dmp.2014.87.

Korea Centers for Disease Control and Prevention (KCDC). 2014. *MERS Response Manual*. (1st and 2nd ed). Seoul: KCDC.

Korea Centers for Disease Control and Prevention (KCDC). 2015a. *MERS Response Manual*. (3-1, 3-2, 3-3, 3-3-1, 3-3-2, 3-4, and 3-5 ed.). Seoul: KCDC.

Korea Centers for Disease Control and Prevention (KCDC). 2015b. "Middle East Respiratory Syndrome Coronavirus Outbreak in the Republic of Korea, 2015." *Osong Public Health and Research Perspect* 6(4): 269–278.

Marcum, C. S., C. A. Bevc, and C. T. Butts. 2012. "Mechanisms of Control in Emergent Interorganizational Networks." *Policy Studies Journal* 40(3): 516–546. doi:10.1111/j.1541-0072.2012.00463.x.

Mars, D. 2013. "Heterarchy: An Interorganizational Approach to Securing the United States against a Pandemic Threat." *Policy Perspectives* 20: 100–117. doi:10.4079/pp.v20i0.11788.

Michelle, D. S., R. Maier, and C. Jardine. 2018. "Damned If You Do, and Damned If You Don't': Communicating about Uncertainty and Evolving Science during the H1N1 Influenza Pandemic." *Journal of Risk Research*. doi:10.1080/13669877.2018.1459793.

Ministry of Health and Welfare (MOHW). 2016. *2015 MERS White Paper*. Seoul: Korea Institute for Health and Social Affairs.

Nelson, C., N. Lurie, J. Wasserman, and S. Zakowski. 2007. "Conceptualizing and Defining Public Health Emergency Preparedness." *American Journal of Public Health* 97(Supplement_1): S9–S11. doi:10.2105/AJPH.2007.114496.

Perry, R. W., and M. K. Lindell. 2003. "Preparedness for Emergency Response: Guideline for the Emergency Planning Process." *Disasters* 27(4): 336–350. doi:10.1111/j.0361-3666.2003.00237.x.

Robinson, S. E., W. S. Eller, M. Gall, and B. J. Gerber. 2013. "The Core and Periphery of Emergency Management Networks: A Multi-Modal Assessment of Two Evacuation-Hosting Networks from 2000 to 2009." *Public Management Review* 15(3): 344–362. doi:10.1080/14719037.2013.769849.

Schneider, S. K. 1992. "Governmental Response to Disasters: The Conflict between Bureaucratic Procedures and Emergent Norms." *Public Administration Review* 52(2): 135–145. doi:10.2307/976467.

Seo, K. H., J. C. Lee, G. H. Kim, and E. Lee. 2015. "Epidemics Crisis Management Systems in South Korea." *Chung-Ang Public Administration Review* 29(4): 219–242.

Steigenberger, N. 2016. "Organizing for the Big One: A Review of Case Studies and a Research Agenda for Multi-Agency Disaster Response." *Journal of Contingencies and Crisis Management* 24(2): 60–72. doi:10.1111/1468-5973.12106.

Swaan, C. M., A. V. Öry, L. G. C. Schol, A. Jacobi, J. H. Richardus, and A. Timen. 2018. "Ebola Preparedness in The Netherlands: The Need for Coordination between the." *Public Health and the Curative Sector." Journal of Public Health Management and Practice* 24(1): 18–25. doi:10.1097/PHH.0000000000000573.

Takeda, M. B., and M. M. Helms. 2005. "Bureaucracy, Meet Catastrophe: Analysis." *International Journal of Public Sector Management* 19(4): 397–411. doi:10.1108/09513550610669211.

Treurniet, W. 2014. "Shaping Comprehensive Emergency Response Networks," In *Network Topology in Command and Control: Organization, Operation, and Evolution*, edited by H. Monsuur and R.H.P. Janssen, 26–48. Hershey, PA: IGI Global.

Utah Department of Health. 2016. *Infectious Disease Emergency Response Plan*. http://health.utah.gov/epi/IDER_2016.pdf.

Williams, H. A., R. L. Dunville, S. I. Gerber, D. D. Erdman, N. Pesik, D. Kuhar, K. A. Mason, et al. 2015. "CDC's Early Response to a Novel Viral Disease, Middle East Respiratory Syndrome Coronavirus (MERS-Cov), September 2012–May 2014." *Public Health Reports* 130(4): 307–317. doi:10.1177/003335491513000407.

Appendix: Actors (groups of organizations) defined and organizations included.

ID	Actors (34)	Collectives or Organizations in the Response Manual (A total of 28 entities)	Organizations in the Actual Response data (A number of organizations Included: 1,242)
NHD[a]	Central Government Health Department and Agencies	Ministry of Health and Welfare; KCDC; Central MERS Management Headquarters; Korea National Institute of Health (4)	Ministry of Health and Welfare; KCDC; Korea National Institute of Health; Central MERS Management Headquarters; Pan-Government MERS Countermeasures Support Center (5)
NSD[a]	Other Central Government Departments	Ministry of Justice, Korea Customs Service; Ministry of Public Safety and Security; Ministry of Land, Infrastructure and Transport; Ministry of Foreign Affairs; Ministry of Environment (6)	Names are not listed due to space (21)
NPE(TP)	Public Enterprises (Transportation)	Korea Airports Corporation (1)	Korea Airports Corporation; Korea Railroad Corporation (2)
PG	Provincial Governments	Listed as collective (1)	Names are not listed due to space (17)
PHR	Provincial Health and Environment Research Institutes	Listed as collective (1)	Names are not listed due to space (17)
LG	Local Governments	Listed as collective (1)	Names are not listed due to space (227)
LHC	Local Health Clinics	Listed as collective (1)	Names are not listed due to space (255)
LPS	Local Police Stations	Listed as collective (1)	Names are not listed due to space (252)
LFS	Local Fire Stations	Listed as collective (1)	Names are not listed due to space (205)
LQS	Quarantine Stations	Listed as collective (1)	Names are not listed due to space (13)
H[b]	Hospitals	Listed as collective (1)	Names are not listed due to space (61)
HD[b]	Designated Hospitals	Listed as collective such as Designated Hospitals with Isolated Beds; Designated MERS Hospitals; Hospitals that Treated Suspected Cases; MERS Treatment Hospitals (4)	Names are not listed due to space (66)
C(TP)	Transportation Companies	Listed as collective such as Airlines, Ship Companies (2)	Korean Air (1)
C(MW)	Medical Waste Treatment Companies	Listed as collective (1)	Names are not listed due to space (16)
A(HA)	Academic Associations (Health)	Listed as collective (1)	The Korean Society of Infectious Diseases; The Korean Society for Preventive Medicine (2)
A(MP)	Professional Associations (Medical)	Listed as collective (1)	Korean Hospital Association; Korean Medical Association; Korea Association of Regional Public Hospitals (3)
INT	International Health Organizations	Not listed	WHO (1)
FC(H)	Foreign Country Heath Departments or Medical Centers	Not listed	CDC; National Health and Family Planning Commission of the People's Republic of China; Department of Health, The Government of the Hong Kong Special Administrative Region; Erasmus University Medical Center (4)
NFA	Korean Embassies and Consulates	Not listed	Embassy of the Republic of Korea in Beijing; Consulate General of the Republic of Korea in Guangzhou (2)
NQG(H)	Quasi-Government Organizations (Health)	Not listed	Health Insurance Review and Assessment Service; National Health Insurance Service; Social Security Information Service; Korea Human Resource Development Institute for Health and Welfare; Korea Training Institute for Self-Sufficiency (5)

(continued)

NPS	National Public Safety Agencies	Not listed	National Police Agency; National 119 Rescue Services; National Emergency Management Agency (3)
PEO	Provincial Operation Centers	Not listed	120 Dasan Call Center; Seoul Emergency Operation Center (2)
PPA	Provincial Police Agencies	Not listed	Busan Provincial Police Agency; Chungnam Provincial Police Agency (2)
PFD	Provincial Fire and Disaster Headquarters	Not listed	Names are not listed due to space (19)
PMH	Provincial Mental Health Centers	Not listed	Names are not listed due to space (14)
PED	Provincial Education Offices	Not listed	Seoul Metropolitan Office of Education (1)
LED	Local Education Office	Not listed	Seoul Gangnam District Office of Education Support (1)
U	Universities	Not listed	Seoul National University; Kyungpook National University; Korea Armed Forces Nursing Academy; Daegu Health College (4)
MF	Clinical Laboratories	Not listed	Green Cross Laboratories; Samkwang Medical Laboratories; Seoul Clinical Laboratories; Seegene Medical Foundation; EONE Laboratories (5)
V	Humanitarian Organizations	Not listed	Korean Red Cross (1)
FIP	Funeral Industry Professionals	Not listed	Korea Funeral Association; Korea Funeral Culture and Policy Institute (2)
R(F)	Financial Regulator	Not listed	Financial Supervisory Service (1)
C(CC)	Credit Card Companies	Not listed	Organizations are not listed due to space (9)
C(MT)	Mobile Telecommunication Companies	Not listed	KT; LG U-Plus; SK Telecom (3)

[a]We separated health department and health agencies from other central government departments because, unlike other disaster situations, health authorities (i.e. MOWH and KCDC) are in charge of the infectious disease crisis in South Korea (Seo et al., 2015).

[b]The response manual designated special categories of hospitals that are distinguished from hospitals participated in the response process.

Outbreak! Socio-cognitive motivators of risk information sharing during the 2018 South Korean MERS-CoV epidemic

Jisoo Ahn, Lee Ann Kahlor (iD) and Ghee-Young Noh

ABSTRACT

This study examines socio-cognitive motivators of information-sharing behaviors during the 2018 Middle East Respiratory Syndrome Coronavirus (MERS-CoV) outbreak in South Korea. During the outbreak, an online survey was fielded to 988 South Korean adult members of an online research panel. The survey included questions about MERS-CoV-related risk perceptions, and attitudes and beliefs about risk information behaviors during the outbreak. The concepts and relationships sought through those questions were informed by the risk information seeking and processing model and related works. Data analysis suggests that sharing risk information about MERS-CoV was heavily shaped by risk information seeking (such that more seeking led to more sharing) and somewhat shaped by perceived pressure from others to share risk information. Interestingly, perceived level of knowledge and perceived level of risk were not significantly related to sharing. Implications for theory and practice are discussed.

Introduction

In fall of 2018, three years after it first appeared in South Korea, the Middle East Respiratory Syndrome Coronavirus (MERS-CoV) had returned to the country, and was once again spreading mystery and fear throughout the population. The mystery around the disease was (and remains) due to its newness; it was first reported in humans in Saudi Arabia in 2012, and because of that newness, not much is known about the virus compared to other coronaviruses. The fear is related to that 'unknown.' Although MERS-CoV is thought to spread through respiratory secretions (e.g. coughing), how exactly it spreads is still not fully understood. Fear is further exacerbated by the disease's deadly impact: During the 2015 outbreak, the virus caused 186 infections in South Korea, but it resulted in 39 deaths −a 21% fatality rate (Korea Broadcasting Company 2015).

Looking back at the 2015 outbreak and trying to learn from it, scholars have investigated the government's response (Choi et al. 2015) as well as the response of the medical community (Petersen et al. 2015); some attention has also been paid to the spread of information among laypeople during the epidemic (Song et al. 2017). Overall, the still emerging body of work suggests that, throughout the 2015 crisis period, the South Korean government did not adequately track the outbreak across hospital visits, and did not inform the public about their own level of risk regarding the disease. Additional shortcomings, on the part of infected individuals and hospital staff – all of whom who did not take adequate precautions to curb the spread of the virus, further caused the catastrophic results that unfolded over the 217-day 2015 epidemic.

Infection control and health security are, in part, dependent on the effective intertwining of government and citizen information channels, including interpersonal communication on- and off-line. Working in tandem, these channels can increase health knowledge and empower a community with timely information about health promotion and disease prevention practices (Heymann et al. 2015). Quickly and efficiently building public knowledge of a disease or health threat is key when individual health is tied to community health (Covello 2003; Reynolds and Seeger 2005; van Velsen et al. 2014), as is the case with an outbreak such as MERS-CoV. Yet, the 2015 South Korean outbreak is a case study of information dissemination failure: Individuals failed to inform the authorities about possible infections and the government failed to inform the public immediately that people were at risk, all of which led to ineffective early attempts to control the outbreak.

Because of this experience, when a suspected MERS-CoV case was discovered in 2018, the Korean government and the public were highly concerned and ready to react. This study focuses on that concern and how it impacted the public's information sharing during the 2018 outbreak. The 2018 South Korean outbreak began around the first week of September and lasted through mid-October. We collected data during the last week of September that year, mid-epidemic. Thus, our study offers a unique glimpse at risk information sharing behaviors during a health crisis *in situ*. In this way, our study helps heed the call that more attention be paid to individuals' role in the dissemination of disease information during epidemics (Takahashi, Tandoc, and Carmichael 2015). During an outbreak, such individual sharing – which is increasingly happening online - can serve multiple purposes. For example, it can be a way to tell friends and family about the disease and how it spreads, which may help keep them safe (Sharma et al. 2017), and it can be a way to let friends and family know that you are safe in the midst of the chaos (Bhuvana and Aram 2019; Houston et al. 2015). To explore these behaviors more fully, our present study examines Korean's information-sharing behaviors during the 2018 MERS outbreak and the motivators underlying those behaviors. Our work is informed by the risk information seeking and processing model (Griffin, Dunwoody, and Neuwirth 1999) and related works.

Literature review

In the modern information landscape, it can be said that people are often both health information consumers and health information contributors (Li et al. 2018). Indeed, research suggests that people typically seek and share health information synergistically (Lee and Jin 2019; Lin et al. 2016; Myrick 2017), and that these behaviors share similar motivators. Social exchange theory supports this assumption. That is, by exchanging information with others through their own risk seeking and sharing behaviors, individuals are able to seek increased understanding of the risks and benefits of a given situation and then share what they learn, and obtain an increased sense of belonging within their network (Yan et al. 2016).

Indeed, in their study of online information seeking and sharing, Li and colleagues (2018) found that risk and benefit perceptions were significant predictors of individual's intentions to seek and share health information via social media. These findings are consistent with similar research that found support for shared predictors of information seeking and sharing in the contexts of nanotechnology (Kahlor et al. 2016) and climate change (Yang, Kahlor, and Griffin 2014). The latter study specifically suggested the applicability of Griffin, Dunwoody, and Neuwirth (1999) risk information seeking and processing model to information sharing behaviors. That model and related works are detailed below.

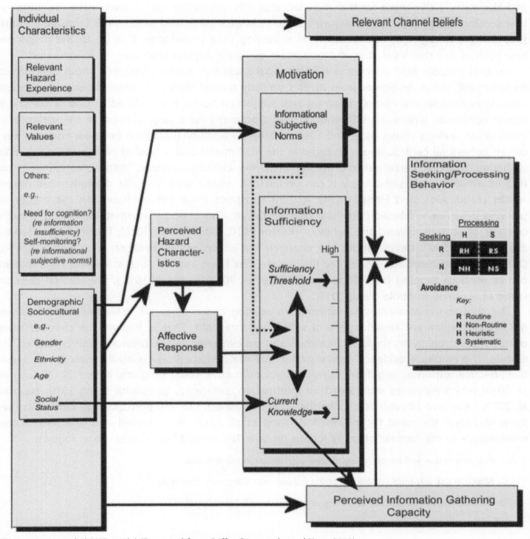

Figure 1. Amended RISP model (Excerpted from Griffin, Dunwoody, and Yang 2013).

Risk information seeking and processing (RISP) model

The risk information seeking and processing model (RISP; Griffin, Dunwoody, and Neuwirth 1999; Griffin, Dunwoody, and Yang 2013) serves as a framework for recognizing the socio-cognitive constructs and complex relationships among those constructs that shape information seeking and processing in risk-related contexts. The model (see Figure 1), which synthesizes its key elements from the heuristic-systematic model (Chaiken and Eagly 1993), the theory of planned behavior (Ajzen 1991; Ajzen and Fishbein 2005), and Slovic's (1987, 2001) work on risk perception and related affect, now has more than 20 years of support behind it (c.f. Griffin et al. 2008; Kahlor et al. 2006; Yang, Aloe, and Feeley 2014; Yang, Chu, and Kahlor 2019). At its core is the sufficiency principle, which is the psychological need for 'sufficient' or adequate knowledge; this need serves as a motivator for the seeking and processing of risk-related information (Yang, Aloe, and Feeley 2014). Information *insufficiency is 'the size of the gap between information held and information needed' (Griffin, Dunwoody, and Neuwirth 1999, 26). Griffin, Dunwoody, and Neuwirth (1999) argue for the importance of this knowledge gap in motivating risk information seeking and processing behaviors; that is, individuals seek and process risk information until they achieve a sufficient confidence level regarding their knowledge. It is up to the individual how high or low that level of confidence needs to be for a given situation.

Another notable RISP concept is informational subjective norms (perceived social pressure to be informed), which originates from Ajzen's similarly named theory of planned behavior concept (also named subjective norms). Informational subjective norms has surfaced as one of the more robust constructs within the RISP model, and it accounts for a large portion of the variance in information seeking (Yang, Aloe, and Feeley 2014). An additional planned behavior concept, perceived behavioral control, also is featured in the RISP model and is labeled perceived information gathering capacity. Perceived information gathering capacity captures both accessibility (I can find information) and self-efficacy (I can understand what I find), and has demonstrated mixed results (Yang, Aloe, and Feeley 2014). A third construct, more loosely based on the theory of planned behavior, is labeled perceived channel beliefs. This concept is something akin to Ajzen's concept of attitude toward the behavior (Kahlor 2010; Kahlor et al. 2016), but it is intended to capture individual's beliefs about the channels via which risk information is available (Griffin, Dunwoody, and Neuwirth 1999). The RISP model has been applied successfully across a myriad of risk contexts ranging from flooding (Griffin et al. 2008) to the 2016 U.S. Presidential Election (Yang et al. 2019) to Ebola (Yang 2019).

The common relationships for information seeking and sharing are risk perception, affective risk responses, current knowledge, and sufficiency threshold. That is, beyond the characteristics of information behavior, those relationships can be explained in the previous RISP or related literature. The empirical evidence demonstrates that risk perception is positively related with negative affective responses (e.g. fear, anger, worry; Griffin et al. 2008; Yang and Kahlor 2013; Yang et al. 2019) which enhances more need for information (sufficiency threshold) (Yang 2019; Yang et al. 2019; Yang and Zhuang 2019). For the cognitive aspect, the low perception of current knowledge increases the need for information (Yang et al. 2019). We adopted and examined those relationships in the context of an infectious disease. The related hypotheses are as follows:

H1: Risk perception will be positively related with affective risk response.

H2: Affective risk response will be positively related with sufficiency threshold.

H3: Current knowledge will be negatively related with sufficiency threshold.

RISP and information sharing

As mentioned earlier, a number of information-sharing studies assert that seeking and sharing behaviors share motivational antecedents (Kahlor et al. 2016; Lee and Jin 2019; Lin et al. 2016; Myrick 2017; Yang, Kahlor, and Griffin 2014). Among the most notable motivators of information sharing to emerge from that body of work were: information seeking (Lin et al. 2016; Yang, Kahlor, and Griffin 2014); informational subjective norms (Kahlor et al. 2016; Yang, Kahlor, and Griffin 2014), attitude toward sharing (akin to RISP's relevant channel beliefs; Kahlor et al. 2016; Lin et al. 2016), negative affect (Yang, Kahlor, and Griffin 2014), and prior knowledge and insufficiency (Yang, Kahlor, and Griffin 2014).

Despite of the interdependency between information seeking and sharing (Wood et al. 2012), the mechanism inducing information sharing is different (Ajzen 1991). In other words, although information insufficiency is known as the primary motivator of information seeking, different motivational factors are anticipated for sharing risk information. Therefore, the consideration of 'sharing' and the specific risk situation is needed to understand individuals' risk information sharing behavior.

Affective risk response

Within the original conceptualization of the RISP model, affective response to risk is depicted as directly impacting information insufficiency, which then positively impacts information seeking (Griffin, Dunwoody, and Neuwirth 1999). However, more recent studies also have shown support for a direct relationship from affective risk response to information seeking (Noh, Lee, and Choi 2016; Pokrywczynski, Griffin, and Calhoun 2019). This direct link was found in information sharing studies as well (e.g. Kim and Lai 2020; Yang, Kahlor, and Griffin 2014); furthermore, affect has a more pronounced role in sharing behavior than in does in seeking behavior. Specifically, in situations where individuals forward and share information (regardless of whether the information is correct)[1], individuals tend to spread information when they feel more uncertain (Valente, Poppe, and Merritt 1996), stressed (Ryfe 2005), or anxious (DiFonzo et al. 2012). Therefore, we hypothesize that:

> H4: Affective risk response will be positively related with information sharing, such that stronger affect will lead to more sharing.

Sufficiency threshold

Shared responsibility is an important consideration in communal risk information sharing contexts (Liao, Yuan, and McComas 2018). This is especially the case when the collaboration of the community is needed to prevent a disease or deal with a disaster. In such cases, individuals may want others to be knowledgeable of the disease or the situation, and he/she also may want to participate in the creation of a collective, relevant information pool from which the community can draw knowledge as needed (Yang and Zhuang 2019). This altruistic behavior (Andreoni 1990; He and Wei 2009) occurs voluntarily without the expectation of receiving a tangible (personal) payback. For example, members of organizations tend to share information within an organization when they perceive that the information has some benefit to the collective whole (Yuan et al. 2005). Similar information sharing phenomena have been observed within nations when dealing with national disasters; in the case of a 2009 typhoon in Taiwan, information sharing via social networks facilitated the coordination of volunteers and the flow of relief supplies, as well as the sharing of disaster relief information as it became available (Huang, Chan, and Hyder 2010).

However, in a comparison of information sharing related to climate change in the U.S. and China (Yang, Kahlor, and Griffin 2014), researchers found that the sufficiency threshold was significantly and negatively associated with information sharing, at least in the US sample, which suggests that a higher sufficiency threshold led to less sharing. The relationship was not significant in the Chinese sample (Yang, Kahlor, and Griffin 2014). The negative relationship in the U.S. sample may indicate that people who feel uninformed are not likely to share what they know (or don't know). However, our understanding of this relationship is still limited; thus, we approached it as a research question in this study.

> RQ1: How does the sufficiency threshold relate to information sharing?

Information sharing-related subjective norms

One of the most powerful variables in the RISP model is informational subjective norms (Griffin, Dunwoody, and Neuwirth 1999; Kahlor 2007), which has emerged as a strong positive predictor of both information seeking intentions and information sharing (Yuan et al. 2005; Wittenbaum, Hollingshead, and Botero 2004). However, findings have not been consistent. Specifically, in Yang and Zhuang (2019), which employed a U.S. sample, a non-significant relationship surfaced between informational subjective norms and the sharing of information about Hurricane Harvey; however, a significant positive relationship was found within the subsample representing

Houston, TX, which was where the hurricane occurred. Similarly, when an incident is prevalent and visible within a community, for example, haze and air pollution in Singapore, subjective norms related to information sharing were positively related with the sharing intention (Kim and Lai 2020). In addition, sharing norms (perceptions that others expect one to share the information) were found to positively impact perceived information need (Yang and Zhuang 2019). Considering the 'spreading' characteristic of the infectious disease, MERS-CoV, and the potential range of the risk (all of South Korean society), information sharing-related subjective norms can influence both sufficiency threshold and information sharing positively.

H5: Information sharing-related subjective norms will be positively related with sufficiency threshold.

H6: Information sharing-related subjective norms will be positively related with information sharing.

Perceived information-sharing capacity
Also consistent with the theory of planned behavior (Ajzen 1991) is the concept of perceived behavioral control, or perceived information gathering capacity in the RISP model, which captures the perception of one's ability to perform certain (information) behaviors. In sharing studies, this construct has been used inconsistently. For example, perceived information gathering capacity had a positive relationship with information sharing in one study which focused on Hurricane Harvey (Yang and Zhuang 2019). In another study, this construct was specifically tailored to sharing (perceived information sharing capacity), and applied to information sharing behavior (Kim and Lai 2020). Consistent with the latter, we tailored our constructs specifically to information sharing behavior in our model. We propose a research question focused on how perceived information-sharing capacity is related to information sharing due to limited prior research on this relationship and the inconsistent relationship between perceived information gathering capacity and information seeking; on the latter relationship, both positive (ter Huurne, Griffin, and Gutteling 2009; Yang et al. 2019) and negative relationships (Kahlor 2010; Yang and Kahlor 2013) have surfaced.

RQ2: How does perceived information-sharing capacity relate to information sharing?

Attitude toward information sharing
Within the original iteration of the RISP model was a construct intended to account for the influence of individual's perceptions related to information channels – or the channels via which they seek and process risk information (Griffin, Dunwoody, and Neuwirth 1999). Over time, some researchers have moved away from the focus on channels to approach this construct following a conceptualization more closely aligned with the theory of planned behavior concept of attitude toward the behavior (Ajzen 1991; Kahlor 2010). Working alongside subjective norms and perceived behavioral control, this attitudinal construct focuses on one's attitudes towards the act of seeking information. This construct has also been tested within sharing contexts, and is intended to capture intrinsic motivation, which is beyond the management of affective responses, the fulfillment of cognitive needs, or the consciousness of others' expectation (Veinot 2009). In information sharing contexts, the behavior can be motivated by relying on the pleasure and the satisfaction from one's actions, (Yan et al. 2016). The empirical research also supports that favorable sharing attitudes increase information sharing intention (Kim and Lai 2020; Kuttschreuter and Hilverda 2019).

H7: Attitude toward information sharing will be positively related with information sharing.

Information seeking
Although the focus of this study is information sharing, as opposed to information seeking, we assert that information seeking still plays a role in shaping sharing behaviors. For example, one purpose of information sharing is to confirm the quality or credibility of one's information by

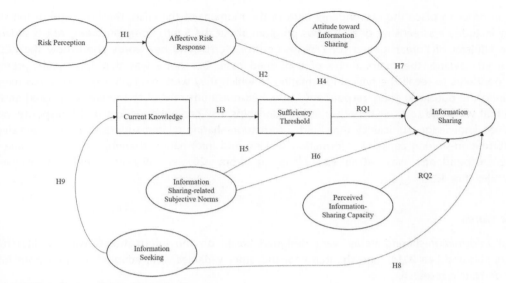

Figure 2. Hypotheses and research questions.

sharing it with others to gauge their reaction to it (Veinot 2009). And during interactions with others, while giving and receiving valuable information as social support, the process benefits the individual, as well as others. Although information seeking and sharing are distinct behaviors, information seeking is suggested as a determinant of information sharing, helping to build the content (and confidence in the content) that is shared and a few studies have shown that information seeking contributes to information sharing (Hilverda and Kuttschreuter 2018; Kuttschreuter and Hilverda 2019; Yang, Kahlor, and Griffin 2014). Therefore, we added the construct of information seeking to capture the synergistic role that seeking plays alongside sharing behaviors, and we proposed a positive relationship between information seeking and information sharing. In addition, we proposed a positive relationship between information seeking and perceived knowledge such that more seeking information about a risk leads to feeling more knowledgeable about that risk.

H8: Information seeking will be positively related with information sharing.

H9: Information seeking will be positively related with perceived current knowledge.

To summarize, in this study, we are interested in the socio-cognitive motivators of risk information sharing during the 2018 South Korean outbreak of MERS-CoV. Our hypotheses were primarily informed by the RISP model, which, although developed with seeking and processing in mind, has been applied (at least in part) to two risk-information sharing contexts as well (Kahlor et al. 2016; Yang, Kahlor, and Griffin 2014). Our 9 hypotheses and 2 research questions are depicted in Figure 2.

Method

In September 2018, in the midst of the South Korean outbreak of MERS-CoV, we contracted with a research company to field an online panel survey. The company emailed to 13,762 South Korean adults and 2,235 registrars participated in the survey. The complete responses were 1,318. After removing the insincere responses (e.g. clicking the same answer for all questions), the final data from 988 responses were used in the analysis. Participants received compensation in the form of credit from the company after completing our 15-20-minute survey.

In order to place the respondents back in the moment of the crisis, the first page of the survey included a screenshot of a TV news program about the South Korea outbreak, which showed the Minister of Korean Center for Disease Control (KCDC) and her words about how the KCDC worked towards the quarantining of confirmed case. Our hope was that this would prompt respondents to recall the typical information to which they were regularly exposed across media during the outbreak. Then, respondents answered questions related to the variables listed above so that we could test our hypothesized relationships (risk perception, affective risk response, perceived knowledge, sufficiency threshold, information sharing-related subjective norms, perceived information-sharing capacity, information seeking and information sharing). The average age of the respondents was 40.46 years (ranging from 20 to 59 years), and 48.7% were females (n = 481).

Measures

Our information-sharing items were designed based on the information-forwarding literature (e.g. Kim and Lee 2014), and the items for the other variables were adapted from previous RISP or derivative research.

Information sharing
Sharing MERS-CoV information was assessed with four 5-point scale items (1: not at all, 5: very much) that were adapted from Kim and Lee (2014) information forwarding study. The items were worded as follows: 'I talked about my opinions regarding MERS with my friends and coworkers,' 'If it was possible, I took the time to explain this problem to others,' 'I looked for chances to share my knowledge and thoughts about this problem,' and 'I volunteered to inform others about the problem' (M = 2.90, SD = .95, α = .90).

Risk perception
Similar to prior research (Yang, Kahlor, and Griffin 2014), we measured risk likelihood, in this case the likelihood of MERS-CoV infecting the respondents, and risk seriousness using the following four items with a 5-point scale (1: not at all, 5: very much): 'Did you perceive MERS as a serious risk to yourself?' 'Did you feel that you would have chances of contracting MERS?' 'Did you think that MERS would pose a severe threat to you?' and 'Did you think that you would become infected with MERS?' (M = 3.29, SD = .83, α = .86).

Affective risk response
We focused on respondents' negative feelings toward MERS using five items adapted from the previous information-seeking and emotion research (Yang and Kahlor 2013; Yang et al. 2019): 'When I received information from the government during the early stages of the MERS outbreak, I was worried/anxious/scared/fearful/frightened of contracting the disease' (M = 3.24, SD = .89, α = .93). The items were presented as 5-point Likert scales (1: not at all, 5: very much).

Current knowledge
The perception of respondents' knowledge during the outbreak regarding MERS was measured by one item (Yang, Kahlor, and Griffin 2014): 'Keeping in mind the period during which you received the information about MERS (during the early stages of infection control), please estimate your knowledge regarding MERS on a scale from 0 (knowing nothing) to 100 (knowing everything you could possibly know about the topic)' (M = 62.02, SD = 19.13).

Sufficiency threshold

Sufficiency threshold was assessed based on the extent of information required to have sufficient knowledge regarding the disease; a scale from 0 to 100 was used for this assessment. As with prior research (Kahlor 2007; Yang, Kahlor, and Griffin 2014), the impact of perceived knowledge on the sufficiency threshold was controlled in the analysis to assess information insufficiency ($M = 71.25$, $SD = 15.79$).

Attitude toward information sharing

Respondents' evaluations of the information-sharing behavior regarding MERS were assessed, using three 7-point bipolar scale items selected from Yang and Kahlor (2013): 'Please indicate whether you felt that sharing information about MERS was harmful/beneficial, bad/good, worthless/valuable' ($M = 5.24$, $SD = 1.14$, $\alpha = .91$).

Information sharing-related subjective norms

These sharing norms, which contain injunctive norms (i.e. others' expectations regarding one's information sharing) and descriptive norms (i.e. others' information-sharing behavior), were assessed using five items adapted from Kahlor and Rosenthal (2009): 'Most of the people who are important to me thought that I should share information about MERS,' 'I was expected to share information about MERS,' 'People whose opinions I value would approve of my sharing information about MERS,' 'I thought that people whose opinions I value had also shared information about MERS,' and 'The people I spend most of my time with were likely to share information related to MERS' ($M = 3.20$, $SD = .72$, $\alpha = .89$) (1: strongly disagree, 5: strongly agree).

Perceived information-sharing capacity

The confidence derived from one's ability to share MERS information is defined as perceived information-sharing capacity. Three items adapted from Kahlor and Rosenthal (2009) were used: 'It was easy to deliver accurate information about MERS to others,' 'When I wanted to, I was easily able to share information about MERS with others,' and 'I could easily share MERS information with others' ($M = 3.35$, $SD = .66$, $\alpha = .80$) (1: strongly disagree, 5: strongly agree).

Analysis

Data were analyzed by performing structural equation modeling with AMOS 22 software. This analysis provides the results of the measurement model—convergent and discriminant validity (Kline 2016) and model fit indices—and hypotheses testing.

Results

Measurement model

The factor loading scores and average variance extracted (AVE) were calculated to assess construct validity. All factor loading scores and AVE were greater than .7 and .6, respectively (Table 1); they were well over the cutoff point of .5 (Hair et al. 2006). The results indicate that the items of each construct obtained convergent validity.

Discriminant validity is used to determine the presence or lack of correlation between two different constructs; for this purpose, AVE and the squared correlations between two constructs (i.e. shared variance) are compared. As shown in Table 2, most of AVE values were greater than the shared variance pairs; this implies that discriminant validity was achieved.

Table 1. Summary of the confirmatory factor analysis.

Construct and item	Factor loading	SE	C.R.	AVE
Risk perception			.87	.62
RP1	.74	.40		
RP2	.85	.30		
RP3	.72	.45		
RP4	.80	.36		
Affective risk response			.93	.74
ARR1	.70	.41		
ARR2	.81	.32		
ARR3	.90	.20		
ARR4	.93	.15		
ARR5	.91	.18		
Attitude toward information sharing			.86	.67
ATIS1	.85	.40		
ATIS2	.89	.34		
ATIS3	.88	.37		
Information sharing-related subjective norms			.91	.67
ISSN1	.74	.33		
ISSN2	.79	.30		
ISSN3	.81	.25		
ISSN4	.79	.31		
ISSN5	.78	.29		
Perceived information-sharing capacity			.87	.68
PISC1	.74	.29		
PISC2	.80	.24		
PISC3	.73	.26		
Information seeking				
ISK1	.79	.41	.89	.68
ISK2	.87	.29		
ISK3	.84	.34		
ISK4	.85	.31		
Information sharing			.90	.69
ISR1	.73	.49		
ISR2	.89	.27		
ISR3	.89	.26		
ISR4	.87	.28		

Several model fit indices of the measurement model, including χ^2/df ratio, standardized root-mean-square residual (SRMR), comparative fit index (CFI), Tucker-Lewis index (TLI), and root mean square error of approximation (RMSEA), were checked using confirmatory factor analysis. Instead of χ^2, which is sensitive to sample size (Bollen 1989), the χ^2/df ratio was reported. Determined by the conventions (Kline 2016; Hooper, Coughlan, and Mullen 2008; Hu and Bentler 1999), the indices showed that the proposed model fits well with the data (Table 3).

Hypothesis testing

Figure 3 shows that, as we had predicted, most of the paths and directions were significant. The detailed results are reported in Table 4. The relationship between risk perception and affective risk response was positive ($\beta = .85$, $p < .001$; H1 supported). Sufficiency threshold was not significantly related to affective risk response ($\beta = -.01$, $p = .84$; H2 not supported) but was positively related to current knowledge ($\beta = .31$, $p < .001$; H3 supported) and information sharing-related subjective norms ($\beta = .12$, $p = .001$; H5 supported). Information sharing was positively related to information sharing-related subjective norms ($\beta = .13$, $p < .001$; H6 supported) and information seeking ($\beta = .84$, $p < .001$; H8 supported). However, sharing was negatively related to attitude toward information sharing ($\beta = -.05$, $p = .01$; H7 disconfirmed) and sufficiency threshold ($\beta = -.03$, $p < .05$; RQ1). The relationship between sharing and affective risk response was not significant ($\beta = .04$, $p = .05$; H4 not supported) whereas the relationship between sharing

Table 2. Summary of discriminant validity.

Variable	1	2	3	4	5	6	7	8	9
1. RP	.79								
2. ARR	.82	.86							
3. ATIS	.27	.20	.82						
4. ISR	.69	.67	.19	.83					
5. PISC	.40	.27	.33	.50	.83				
6. ISSN	.58	.54	.30	.76	.62	.82			
7. ISK	.72	.68	.21	.96	.47	.73	.82		
8. CK	.27	.23	.23	.38	.42	.35	.39	–	
9. ST	.15	.12	.31	.15	.22	.22	.18	.35	–

Note: Discriminant validity of knowledge was not inserted in the table because the variable was measured by using one item.

Table 3. Summary of fit indices.

Models	χ^2 /df (< 5)	SRMR (< .08)	CFI (> .95)	TLI (> .95)	RMSEA (< .08)
Baseline CFA model	3.75	.04	.95	.95	.05, [90% CI: .05, .06]
Revised CFA model	3.46	.04	.96	.95	.05, [90% CI: .047, .053]
Final structural model	4.07	.05	.95	.94	.06 [90% CI: .053, .059]

Note: CFA model was revised by adding error covariance between two affective risk response measures.

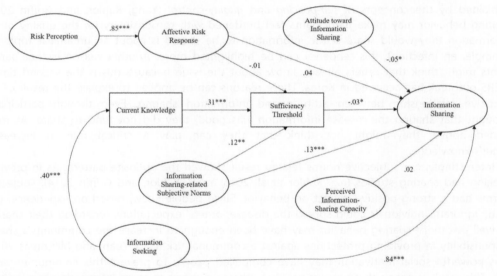

Figure 3. The results of hypotheses testing.

Table 4. The results of structural equation model analysis.

			Estimate	S.E.	C.R.(t)	P
Risk perception	→	Affect	0.85	0.04	20.11	<.001
Information seeking	→	Current Knowledge	0.40	0.73	12.49	<.001
Affect	→	Sufficiency threshold	−0.01	0.90	−0.20	.84
Current knowledge			0.31	0.03	9.71	<.001
Subjective norms			0.12	0.95	3.23	.001
Subjective norms	→	Information sharing	0.13	0.04	4.26	<.001
Attitude			−0.05	0.01	−2.64	.01
Affect			0.04	0.03	1.94	.05
Sufficiency threshold			−0.03	0.001	−2.25	.03
Capacity			0.02	0.03	1.02	.31
Information seeking			0.84	0.04	19.48	<.001

and perceived information-sharing capacity was not significant ($\beta = .02$, $p = .31$; RQ2). Lastly, information seeking was positively related to current knowledge ($\beta = .40$, $p < .001$; H9 supported).

Discussion

This study investigated the socio-cognitive motivators of risk information sharing during the 2018 South Korean outbreak of MERS-CoV. The framework for this investigation was Griffin, Dunwoody, and Neuwirth (1999) well-established risk information seeking and processing model. However, based on recent research, which has emphasized the synergistic qualities of informa-tion seeking and information sharing behaviors (Lee and Jin 2019; Lin et al. 2016; Myrick 2017), we also integrated information seeking into our sharing framework as both a positive correlate of perceived knowledge and information sharing. We also added to our RISP-informed frame-work, a positive relationship between affective risk response and information sharing.

One interesting result is about the negative relationship between sufficiency threshold and information sharing. Even though participants felt that they should have a higher level of know-ledge, they were not likely to share their knowledge to others. There are two possible explana-tions. First, people who need more information may be more careful to deliver their knowledge. Explained by the concepts of *self-policing* and *quality-control* (Yang, Kahlor, and Griffin 2014), sharing behavior may make participants feel burdened with responsibility for the quality of the information they would share. If the information to be shared is about an unfamiliar topic (for example, an infection), this tendency can be highlighted more. Another reason is that partici-pants might think that others already know about the issue because this is the second time a MERS outbreak has occurred in Korea. These reasons can be applied to explain the result of the negative relationship between attitude and information sharing. Even though participants thought that sharing the disease information was good, they did not tend to share. As men-tioned above, they might not think that they can play a critical role in increasing other's knowledge.

Interestingly, our subjective norms related result showed the opposite pattern. As in previous seeking and sharing studies (e.g. Kahlor et al. 2016; Yang, Kahlor, and Griffin 2014), subjective norms had a strong positive impact on behavior. Since people knew, based on experience, that some ignorant individuals could spread the disease, others' expectations regarding their sharing, as well as others' sharing behavior may have been enough to increase the community's shared responsibility in providing protections against a communal risk (Liao, Yuan, and McComas 2018). This powerful social motivation may have compelled people to prevent this community-based risk. This result suggests that perceptions that others want one to share information can increase one's need for information (maybe to share more confident information) and prompt information sharing.

Similar with information-seeking research, we found that perceived hazard characteristics (i.e. risk perception) induces feelings of worry and fear regarding MERS. We also sought a direct rela-tionship between those feelings and sufficiency threshold and information sharing and found no significant relationships. A previous study showed that negative affect was positively related to information sharing in the U.S., whereas it was not significantly related to information sharing in China, at least on the topic of climate change (Yang, Kahlor, and Griffin 2014). Rather than cul-tural characteristics, we suspect our results may be due to the difference in the characteristic of the topic. Different from climate change, infectious disease is a more sensitive and immediate topic with more direct implications – thus people may be more careful to deliver the related information. Another possible reason for the relationship between affective risk response and sharing is that since Koreans already experienced the disease, they might not be as fearful of the disease as the first time they encountered it; this may be reflected in the relatively low mean for affective risk response (3.25 out of 7). In such a circumstance, they may not have been highly motivated to share MERS information, or may have needed more information about it.

The positive relationship between perceived knowledge and sufficiency threshold was expected and consistent with previous research (e.g. Yang, Kahlor, and Li 2014). People already had a fair amount of prior knowledge (given there had been an outbreak only a few years earlier) and they wanted to learn more information to prevent illness. Future research can focus on how this relationship might be impacted when respondents are faced with a health risk and have little experience with it, as this might alter the relationship and its role in information sharing. The relationship between past seeking and perceived knowledge also was expected and consistent with prior work (Kahlor and Rosenthal 2009).

Our insignificant result regarding capacity was unexpected. Comparing the two types of behavior, seeking health information versus sharing health information, seeking requires cognitive ability to find and understand health information, whereas sharing is less dependent on cognitive ability. That is, someone else can find and write the information, and the sharer need only to show that information to others. The sharing behavior is more dependent on whether the individual wants to share information about the infectious disease or not, which can come from the desire to protect others, to protect oneself (by informing others), or the desire to simply keep the information until they feel confident they have enough to share, etc.

The significant positive relationship between seeking and sharing is consistent with Yang, Kahlor, and Griffin (2014). Participants who tended to seek more MERS information were more likely to share information; this finding can be explained from an information exchange perspective (Yan et al. 2016) and is consistent with prior work on online health communities (Maloney-Krichmar and Preece 2005). In online health communities, 'information, emotional support, and encouragement can dominate the exchanges between community members' (Maloney-Krichmar and Preece 2005, 26), which suggests that there may be a reciprocal relationship between seeking and sharing such that people seek so that they can actively share, and they share to seek still (and obtain) more information. Interestingly, the impact of seeking was stronger than other predictors in this study.

Practical implications

Our results contribute to the growing body of work dedicated to managing information about infectious diseases, particularly in the era of social media (Charles-Smith et al. 2015). One particularly practical insight from this study is our finding related to informational subjective norms, which is consistent with the robust support found for this social psychological factor in prior RISP research. Similar with models of risk information seeking, we found that in the case of risk information sharing, people are particularly motivated by expectations from others that they share risk information. To build on this finding, infectious disease information providers can emphasize in their messaging strategies that there is an expectation within families and social groups that individuals will do their part to keep the group healthy and that sharing helpful information about health risks is an expected way to do that. In addition, considering the importance of seeking information, the importance of the information exchange process could also be highlighted in this strategy, given that these informational subjective norms also motivate information seeking as well.

Limitations and future research

Looking at some of our study's limitations can help to explain the findings and develop related research. As an early information-sharing study, we applied information seeking models and the relevant variables to explain sharing behavior. In the process, we found unexpected patterns in the information-processing mechanism. We presumed that the results may have been caused by the recurrence of the disease, but more potential reasons should be considered. Another limitation may be our reliance on self-report items, particularly when it comes to self-reported perceptions of one's own knowledge. Self-report measurements tend to suffer from a number of biases, including social desirability bias; that is, respondents might be sensitive to portraying themselves as being naïve or uninformed (Cook and Selltiz 1964). There are also limits to how well individuals can consciously know or access their preferences or attitudes (Kahlor et al. 2020), thus attitudes or estimates of ones' own knowledge may be inaccessible or skewed.

In addition, we suggest that the type of information shared should be examined. For example, it would be interesting to contrast what information individuals tend to share when they go through cognitive processing, as opposed to affective processing. One possible assumption is that, if individuals perceive that their information is not sufficiently comprehensive enough to share, they may share only confirmed information; however, if they are not aware of their knowledge level and are being aroused by the immediacy of the situation, they will have a higher likelihood of disseminating ambiguous information. Thus, in order to deliver the right information to the right people, the relationship between types of information and sharing should be further elucidated.

Conclusion

Making risk information available to the public during a disease outbreak is a key part of controlling the spread of disease. Also important in the dissemination of risk information is the potential role that the public can play in helping to share accurate information throughout their social networks. This study focused on socio-cognitive motivators of risk information sharing during an outbreak, and suggests factors that might impact our ability to harness those networks to more effectively spread risk mitigation messages. The core findings indicate that individuals were more likely to share MERS-CoV information when they frequently sought related information and when they recognized others' expectation for them to share. However, attitude or sufficiency threshold had a weak and negative relationship with information sharing. The unexplainable relationships need to be examined in other infectious disease contexts.

Note

1. Unfortunately, the rapid spreading of information during fearful situations, such as disasters, can contribute to the spread of inaccurate and false information (Kongthon et al. 2012).

Disclosure statement

No potential conflict of interest was reported by the author(s).
Funding
This work was supported by the Ministry of Education of the Republic of Korea and the National Research Foundation of Korea (NRF-2018S1A3A2074932).

ORCID

Lee Ann Kahlor ⓘ http://orcid.org/0000-0003-3372-9589

References

Ajzen, I. 1991. "The Theory of Planned Behavior." *Organizational Behavior and Human Decision Processes* 50 (2): 179–211. doi:10.1016/0749-5978(91)90020-T.

Ajzen, I., and M. Fishbein. 2005. "The Influence of Attitudes on Behavior." In *The Handbook of Attitudes*, edited by Blair T. Johnson and Mark P. Zanna, 173–221. Mahwah, NJ: Erlbaum.

Andreoni, J. 1990. "Impure Altruism and Donations to Public Goods: A Theory of Warm-Glow Giving." *The Economic Journal* 100 (401): 464–477. https://www.jstor.org/stable/2234133. doi:10.2307/2234133.

Bhuvana, N., and I. A. Aram. 2019. "Facebook and Whatsapp as Disaster Management Tools during the Chennai (India) Floods of 2015." *International Journal of Disaster Risk Reduction* 39: 101135–101135. doi:10.1016/j.ijdrr.2019.101135.

Bollen, K. A. 1989. *Structural Equations with Latent Variables*. New York, NY: John Wiley.

Chaiken, S., and A. Eagly. 1993. *The Psychology of Attitudes*. Fort Worth, TX: Harcourt Brace Jovanovich.

Charles-Smith, L. E., T. L. Reynolds, M. A. Cameron, M. Conway, E. H. Lau, J. M. Olsen, J. A. Pavlin, et al. 2015. "Using Social Media for Actionable Disease Surveillance and Outbreak Management: A Systematic Literature Review." *PloS One* 10 (10): e0139701. doi:10.1371/journal.pone.0139701.

Choi, J. W., K. H. Kim, J. M. Moon, and M. S. Kim. 2015. "Public Health Crisis Response and Establishment of a Crisis Communication System in South Korea: Lessons Learned from the MERS Outbreak." *Journal of the Korean Medical Association* 58 (7): 624–634. doi:10.5124/jkma.2015.58.7.624.

Cook, S. W., and C. Selltiz. 1964. "A MULTIPLE-INDICATOR APPROACH TO ATTITUDE MEASUREMENT ." *Psychol Bull* 62 (1): 36–55. doi:10.1037/h0040289.

Covello, V. T. 2003. "Best Practices in Public Health Risk and Crisis Communication." *Journal of Health Communication* 8 (sup1): 5–8. doi:10.1080/713851971.

DiFonzo, N., N. M. Robinson, J. M. Suls, and C. Rini. 2012. "Rumors about Cancer: Content, Sources, Coping, Transmission, and Belief." *Journal of Health Communication* 17 (9): 1099–1115. doi:10.1080/10810730.2012.665417.

Griffin, R., S. Dunwoody, and K. Neuwirth. 1999. "Proposed Model of the Relationship of Risk Information Seeking and Processing to the Development of Preventive Behaviors." *Environmental Research* 80 (2): S230–S245. doi:10.1006/enrs.1998.3940.

Griffin, R. J., S. Dunwoody, and Z. J. Yang. 2013. "Linking Risk Messages to Information Seeking and Processing." *Annals of the International Communication Association* 36 (1): 323–362. doi:10.1080/23808985.2013.11679138.

Griffin, R. J., Z. J. Yang, E. ter Huurne, F. Boerner, S. Ortiz, and S. Dunwoody. 2008. "After the Flood: Anger, Attribution, and the Seeking of Information." *Science Communication* 29: 285–315. doi:10.1177/1075547007312309.

Hair, J., B. Black, B. Babin, R. Anderson, and R. Tatham. 2006. *Multivariate Data Analysis*. 6th ed. Upper Saddle River, NJ: Prentice Hall.

He, W., and K. Wei. 2009. "What Drives Continued Knowledge Sharing? an Investigation of Knowledge-Contribution and -Seeking Beliefs." *Decision Support Systems* 46 (4): 826–838. doi:10.1016/j.dss.2008.11.007.

Heymann, D. L., L. Chen, K. Takemi, D. P. Fidler, J. W. Tappero, M. J. Thomas, T. A. Kenyon, et al. 2015. "Global Health Security: The Wider Lessons from the West African Ebola Virus Disease Epidemic." *Lancet (*London, England) 385 (9980): 1884–1901. doi:10.1016/S0140-6736(15)60858-3.

Hilverda, F., and M. Kuttschreuter. 2018. "Online Information Sharing about Risks: The Case of Organic Food." *Risk Analysis : An Official Publication of the Society for Risk Analysis* 38 (9): 1904–1920. doi:10.1111/risa.12980.

Hooper, D., J. Coughlan, and M. Mullen. 2008. "Structural Equation Modelling: Guidelines for Determining Model Fit." *Electronic Journal of Business Research Methods* 6 (1): 53–60. http://arrow.dit.ie/cgi/viewcontent.cgi?article=1001&context=buschmanart.

Houston, J. Brian, Joshua Hawthorne, Mildred F. Perreault, Eun Hae Park, Marlo Goldstein Hode, Michael R. Halliwell, Sarah E. Turner McGowen, et al. 2015. "Social Media and Disasters: A Functional Framework for Social Media Use in Disaster Planning, Response, and Research." *Disasters* 39 (1): 1–22., . doi:10.1111/disa.12092.

Hu, L., and P. M. Bentler. 1999. "Cutoff Criteria for Fit Indexes in Covariance Structure Analysis: Conventional Criteria versus New Alternatives." *Structural Equation Modeling: A Multidisciplinary Journal* 6 (1): 1–55. doi:10.1080/10705519909540118.

Huang, C. M., E. Chan, and A. A. Hyder. 2010. "Web 2.0 and Internet Social Networking: A New Tool for Disaster management?-lessons from Taiwan." *BMC Medical Informatics and Decision Making* 10: 57doi:10.1186/1472-6947-10-57.

Kahlor, L. 2007. "An Augmented Risk Information Seeking Model: The Case of Global Warming." *Media Psychology* 10 (3): 414–435. doi:10.1080/15213260701532971.

Kahlor, L. A. 2010. "Prism: A Planned Risk Information Seeking model." *Health Commun* 25 (4): 345–356. doi:10.1080/10410231003775172.

Kahlor, L. A., A. Dudo, M. C. Liang, A. J. Lazard, and N. AbiGhannam. 2016. "Ethics Information Seeking and Sharing among Scientists: The Case of Nanotechnology." *Science Communication* 38 (1): 74–98. doi:10.1177/1075547015617942.

Kahlor, L., S. Dunwoody, R. Griffin, and K. Neuwirth. 2006. "Seeking and Processing Information about Impersonal Risk." *Science Communication* 28 (2): 163–194. doi:10.1177/1075547006293916.

Kahlor, L., and S. Rosenthal. 2009. "If we Seek, Do we Learn? Predicting Knowledge of Global Warming." *Science Communication* 30 (3): 380–414. https://doi.org/ doi:10.1177/1075547015617942.

Kahlor, L. A., J. Yang, X. Li, W. Wang, H. C. Olson, and L. Atkinson. 2020. "Environmental Risk (and Benefit) Information Seeking Intentions: The Case of Carbon Capture and Storage in Southeast Texas." *Environmental Communication* 14 (4): 555–572. doi:10.1080/17524032.2019.1699136.

Kim, H. K., and C. H. Lai. 2020. "Seeking and Sharing Information about Transboundary Air Pollution in Singapore: Effects of Own and Others' Information Insufficiency." *Environmental Communication* 14 (1): 68–81. doi:10.1080/17524032.2019.1597751.

Kim, J. N., and S. Lee. 2014. "Communication and Cybercoping: Coping with Chronic Illness through Communicative Action in Online Support Networks." *Journal of Health Communication* 19 (7): 775–794. doi:10.1080/10810730.2013.864724.

Kline, R. B. 2016. *Principles and Practice of Structural Equation Modeling*. 4th ed. New York, NY: Guilford.

Kongthon, A., C. Haruechaiyasak, J. Pailai, and S. Kongyoung. 2012. "The Role of Twitter during a Natural Disaster: Case Study of 2011 Thai Flood." In Technology Management for Emerging Technologies (PICMET), 2012 Proceedings of PICMET'12, 2227–2232. IEEE.

Korea Broadcasting Company. 2015. *The current situation of Mers infection*. https://dj.kbs.co.kr/resources/2015-06-08/

Kuttschreuter, M., F. Hilverda. 2019. "Listen, Did You Hear … ? A Structural Equation Model Explaining Online Information Sharing on the Risks of Nanotechnology in Food." *Food Quality and Preference* 76: 118–132. doi:10.1016/j.foodqual.2019.03.011.

Lee, Y. I., and Y. Jin. 2019. "Crisis Information Seeking and Sharing (CISS): Scale Development for Measuring Publics' Communicative Behavior in Social-Mediated Public Health Crises." *Journal of International Crisis and Risk Communication Research* 2 (1): 13–38. doi:10.30658/jicrcr.2.1.2.

Liao, W., Y. C. Yuan, and K. A. McComas. 2018. "Communal Risk Information Sharing: Motivations behind Voluntary Information Sharing for Reducing Interdependent Risks in a Community." *Communication Research* 45 (6): 909–933. doi:10.1177/0093650215626981.

Li, Y., X. Wang, X. Lin, and M. Hajli. 2018. "Seeking and Sharing Health Information on Social Media: A Net Valence Model and Cross-Cultural Comparison." *Technological Forecasting and Social Change* 126: 28–40. doi:10.1016/j.techfore.2016.07.021.

Lin, W. Y., X. Zhang, H. Song, and K. Omori. 2016. "Health Information Seeking in the Web 2.0 Age: Trust in Social Media, Uncertainty Reduction, and Self-Disclosure." *Computers in Human Behavior* 56: 289–294. doi:10.1016/j.chb.2015.11.055.

Maloney-Krichmar, D., and J. Preece. 2005. "A Multilevel Analysis of Sociability, Usability, and Community Dynamics in an Online Health Community." *ACM Transactions on Computer-Human Interaction (TOCHI)* 12 (2): 201–232. doi:10.1145/1067860.1067864.

Myrick, J. G. 2017. "The Role of Emotions and Social Cognitive Variables in Online Health Information Seeking Processes and Effects." *Computers in Human Behavior* 68: 422–433. doi:10.1016/j.chb.2016.11.071.

Noh, G. Y., S. Y. Lee, and J. Choi. 2016. "Exploring Factors Influencing Smokers' Information Seeking for Smoking Cessation." *Journal of Health Communication* 21 (8): 845–854. doi:10.1080/10810730.2016.1177140.

Petersen, E., D. S. Hui, S. Perlman, and A. Zumla. 2015. "Middle East Respiratory Syndrome - advancing the public health and research agenda on MERS - lessons from the South Korea outbreak ." *International Journal of Infectious Diseases : IJID : official Publication of the International Society for Infectious Diseases* 36: 54–55. doi:10.1016/j.ijid.2015.06.004.

Pokrywczynski, J., R. J. Griffin, and G. J. Calhoun. 2019. "Information Seeking among Women Aged 18 to 25 about the Risk of Sexual Aggression." *Journalism & Mass Communication Quarterly* 96 (1): 239–263. doi:10.1177/1077699018801315.

Reynolds, B., and M. Seeger. 2005. "Crisis and Emergency Risk Communication as an Integrative Model." *Journal of Health Communication* 10 (1): 43–55. doi:10.1080/10810730590904571.

Ryfe, D. 2005. "Does Deliberative Democracy Work?" *Annual Review of Political Science* 8 (1): 49–71. doi:10.1146/annurev.polisci.8.032904.154633.

Sharma, M., K. Yadav, N. Yadav, and K. C. Ferdinand. 2017. "Zika Virus pandemic-analysis of Facebook as a social media health information platform." *American Journal of Infection Control* 45 (3): 301–302. doi:10.1016/j.ajic.2016.08.022.

Slovic, P. 1987. "Perception of Risk." *Science (New York, N.Y.)* 236 (4799): 280–285. doi:10.1126/science.3563507.

Slovic, P. 2001. *The Perception of Risk*. London, England: Earthscan Publications Ltd.

Song, J., T. M. Song, D. C. Seo, D. L. Jin, and J. S. Kim. 2017. "Social Big Data Analysis of Information Spread and Perceived Infection Risk during the 2015 Middle East Respiratory Syndrome Outbreak in South Korea." *Cyberpsychology, Behavior, and Social Networking* 20 (1): 22–29. doi:10.1089/cyber.2016.0126.

Takahashi, B., E. C. Tandoc, Jr., and C. Carmichael. 2015. "Communicating on Twitter during a Disaster: An Analysis of Tweets during Typhoon Haiyan in the Philippines." *Computers in Human Behavior* 50: 392–398. doi:10.1016/j.chb.2015.04.020.

ter Huurne, E. F. J., R. J. Griffin, and J. M. Gutteling. 2009. "Risk Information Seeking among U.S. and Dutch Residents." *Science Communication* 31 (2): 215–237. doi:10.1177/1075547009332653.

Valente, T. W., P. R. Poppe, and A. P. Merritt. 1996. "Mass-Media-Generated Interpersonal Communication as Sources of Information about Family Planning." *Journal of Health Communication* 1 (3): 247–265. doi:10.1080/108107396128040.

van Velsen, L., D. J. Beaujean, J. E. van Gemert-Pijnen, J. E. van Steenbergen, and A. Timen. 2014. "Public Knowledge and Preventive Behavior during a Large-Scale Salmonella Outbreak: results from an Online Survey in The Netherlands." *BMC Public Health* 14: 100doi:10.1186/1471-2458-14-100.

Veinot, T. C. 2009. "Interactive Acquisition and Sharing: Understanding the Dynamics of HIV/AIDS Information Networks." *Journal of the American Society for Information Science and Technology* 60 (11): 2313–2332. doi:10.1002/asi.21151.

Wittenbaum, G. M., A. B. Hollingshead, and I. Botero. 2004. "From Cooperative to Motivated Information Sharing in Groups: Going beyond the Hidden Profile Paradigm." *Communication Monographs* 71 (3): 286–310. doi:10.1080/0363452042000299894.

Wood, M. M., D. S. Mileti, M. Kano, M. M. Kelley, R. Regan, and L. B. Bourque. 2012. "Communicating Actionable Risk for Terrorism and Other hazards." *Risk Analysis : An Official Publication of the Society for Risk Analysis* 32 (4): 601–615. doi:10.1111/j.1539-6924.2011.01645.x.

Yan, Z., T. Wang, Y. Chen, and H. Zhang. 2016. "Knowledge Sharing in Online Health Communities: A Social Exchange Theory Perspective." *Information & Management* 53 (5): 643–653. doi:10.1016/j.im.2016.02.001.

Yang, J. Z. 2019. "Whose Risk? Why Did the US Public Ignore Information about the Ebola Outbreak?" *Risk Analysis : An Official Publication of the Society for Risk Analysis* 39 (8): 1708–1722. doi:10.1111/risa.13282.

Yang, Z. J., A. M. Aloe, and T. H. Feeley. 2014. "Risk Information Seeking and Processing Model: A Meta-Analysis." *Journal of Communication* 64 (1): 20–41. doi:10.1111/jcom.12071.

Yang, J. Z., H. Chu, and L. Kahlor. 2019. "Fearful Conservatives, Angry Liberals: Information Processing Related to the 2016 Presidential Election and Climate Change." *Journalism & Mass Communication Quarterly* 96 (3): 742–766. doi:10.1177/1077699018811089.

Yang, Z. J., and L. Kahlor. 2013. "What, Me Worry? the Role of Affect in Information Seeking and Avoidance." *Science Communication* 35 (2): 189–212. doi:10.1177/1075547012441873.

Yang, Z. J., L. A. Kahlor, and D. J. Griffin. 2014. "I Share, Therefore I Am: A US – China Comparison of College Students' Motivations to Share Information about Climate Change." *Human Communication Research* 40 (1): 112–135. doi:10.1111/hcre.12018.

Yang, Z. J., L. Kahlor, and H. Li. 2014. "A United States-China Comparison of Risk Information–Seeking Intentions." *Communication Research* 41 (7): 935–960. doi:10.1177/0093650213479795.

Yang, J. Z., and J. Zhuang. 2019. "Information Seeking and Information Sharing Related to Hurricane Harvey." *Journalism & Mass Communication Quarterly* 1–26. doi:10.1177/1077699019887675.

Yuan, Y.,. J. Fulk, M. Shumate, P. R. Monge, J. A. Bryant, and M. Matsaganis. 2005. "Individual Participation in Organizational Information Commons: The Impact of Team Level Social Influence and Technology-Specific Competence." *Human Communication Research* 31 (2): 212–240. doi:10.1093/hcr/.31.2.212.

Risk communication in a double public health crisis: the case of Ebola and cholera in Ghana

Esi E. Thompson

ABSTRACT

During 2014–2016 Ebola epidemic, many West African countries experienced perennial outbreaks of various infectious diseases. Given the geographic dynamics of disease outbreaks in the region, it seems obvious that research on risk communication needs to contemplate how these countries manage risk communication about simultaneously occurring infectious diseases. Yet, this is missing in risk communication scholarship. I draw on insights from the social amplification of risk framework to assess how three amplification stations responded to risk signals about proximate Ebola and cholera outbreaks in 2014 in Ghana. Based on in-depth interviews and focus group discussions with risk communicators, media workers, and community members, I argue that the differing individual and social experiences of Ebola and cholera in Ghana were shaped by historical, religious, socio-cultural, and institutional processing of risk signals, which guided judgements about risks. This study contributes to the literature on the social amplification of risk framework and risk and crisis communication by showing how the context of an impending crisis can lead to a health crisis for a preventable and treatable disease through the amplification and attenuation of risks signals. The study recommends the inclusion of lay people perspectives in the development of risk and crisis communication campaigns.

Infectious disease outbreaks can be counted on to occur with some regularity in Sub-Saharan Africa, given weak health systems and structures (Fenollar and Mediannikov 2018). Given the geographical dynamics of disease outbreaks, it seems obvious that research on risk communication would contemplate how these countries might manage communication about simultaneous disease outbreaks. But scholars have paid less attention to risk communication about simultaneous health risk events.

Simultaneous health risk events, or what others call overlapping outbreaks, are situations in which more than one disease outbreak occurs in a context, such as the Dengue and Covid 19 epidemics in Columbia (Cardona-Ospina et al. 2020), and Ebola, measles, and Covid 19 outbreaks in the DR Congo (Nachega et al. 2020). Such situations put a strain on health resources and services, and may result in lack of funds and resources, or a focus on one health risk to the detriment of the other (Cardona-Ospina et al. 2020; Milko and Ghosal 2020).

Ghana is one of such countries that had to manage communication about two outbreaks. During the height of 2014–2016 proximate Ebola outbreak in some West African countries,

Ghana experienced its worst cholera outbreak with 28, 975 cases and 243 deaths (Ghana Health Services, 2015).

The purpose of this study is to extend scholarship about simultaneous health risk events by exploring the responses of three amplification stations to the cholera and proximate Ebola outbreaks in Ghana. Guided by the social amplification of risk framework (SARF) and adopting in-depth interviews and focus group discussions with risk communicators, media workers, and community members, this exploratory study argues that each amplification station's response reflects multidimensional socio-contextual influences on the construction of each risk.

The study makes three contributions to scholarship. First the study suggests that the more diverse the roles played at each station (sources, transmitters or receivers), the more likely amplification will occur. Secondly, I show the limited influence of the media's amplification and argue that the media's ability to amplify risk signals for audiences is effective when there is existing heightened concern among audiences. Furthermore, the differing individual and social responses to the two risk events were shaped by socio-cultural, institutional, and individual processes and structures. I also show how the context of an impending crisis can lead to a health crisis for a preventable and treatable disease through the amplification or attenuation of each risk. By focusing on simultaneous risk events in a developing context, the study better reflects the challenges of risk communication in real life.

Ebola and cholera in Ghana

In June 2014, when the Ebola outbreak was confirmed in Guinea, Liberia, and Sierra Leone (WHO 2015), an outbreak of cholera was confirmed in the capital of Ghana, Accra. In August 2014, the WHO declared the Ebola outbreak as a public health emergency of international concern (PHEIC; WHO 2014) and the Ghana Health Service (GHS) declared the cholera outbreak in the Greater Accra region as an epidemic (Mordy 2014). One thousand seven hundred cases of Ebola had been recorded in the affected countries, while 3000 cases of cholera had been recorded in the Greater Accra region alone (Mordy 2014). Of course, the two diseases are incomparable: ingesting contaminated food and water causes cholera, while Ebola is caused by contact with infected fluids and spreads through care-giving practices and social contact. But the fact that a country had to deal with both at the same time, makes them worthy of study.

Ghana constitutes a good context because of its proximity to the 2014–2016 Ebola outbreak sites and its role as the hub for the international Ebola relief effort (Thompson 2019). Ghana also has a public health insurance scheme (NHIS) that fully covers the treatment costs of cholera for Ghanaians in public health facilities.

Literature review

Social amplification of risk framework

The social amplification of risk framework (SARF) is an integrative framework that addresses the social experience of risk in addition to its psychological factors. The framework argues that "events pertaining to hazards interact with psychological, social, institutional, and cultural processes in ways that can heighten or attenuate individual and social perceptions of risk and shape risk behavior" (Renn et al. 1992, 139). It also seeks to understand why certain events are amplified and receive high attention even though they might not be very risky, while others which are more serious receive less focus and are minimized (Kasperson et al. 2003).

SARF has as a start point a real or hypothesized risk which becomes a signal i.e., messages, pictures etc. about an event that influence people's perceptions about the manageability or seriousness of a risk event (Kasperson et al. 2003). This risk signal is then transferred through amplification stations including the media, politicians/government, individuals, social groups, and even international agencies and bodies, who communicate the risk to either heighten or constraint it. Amplification or attenuation of signals could occur in the transfer of the information or in response to the signals (interpretations and perception of the signals) which could lead to further outcomes or fallouts from the main risk events called secondary or even tertiary impacts, and further amplification (Kasperson, 2012; Machlis and Rosa 1990). These secondary and tertiary impacts could be economic (loss of trade or income), symbolic (stigma), or policy (passing of new policies and laws) etc.

Renn et al. (1992) argues that because messages are transmitted and received in a social context, assessing the amplification process should not be restricted to studying only the messages or signals. He suggests that social groups and agencies are critical in moving risk signals into prominence, but all three amplification groups (individual action, social groups, and the media) are essential for the amplification process. Therefore, the current study focuses on the responses of news workers as media, social mobilization and risk communication subcommittee members as an expert social group, and individual community members as amplification stations.

Media as an amplification station

Studies of SARF have often focused on the media as an amplification station. Such studies suggest that the media heighten risk through the volume of information published, frames used, and dramatization of facts, among others (Rossmann, Meyer, and Schulz 2018; Wirz et al. 2018; see Binder et al. 2015 for a review of Media in SARF). Rossmann, Meyer, and Schulz (2018) analyzed the content of press releases and news media to show that the media amplified the A/H1N1 risk by emphasizing conflict, presenting information in emotion-based and dramatized ways, and adopting risk-amplifying frames. Strekalova (2017) analyzed content from the Centers for Disease Control and Prevention (CDC) Facebook channel and found that commenters of social media posts can serve as amplification stations on particular topics.

Early risk communicators viewed media as mainly transmitters, but recent scholars have shown that communicating a risk is "a collection of endeavors by news organizations and individuals" (Raupp 2014, 568). Media sociologists, who study how news organizations and news workers produce the news, suggest that media content is a complex process of social construction (Shoemaker and Reese 2013). If news content is a social creation and news workers are actively involved in constructing risks, then understanding how news workers prioritize, construct, and transmit risk signals is critical to understanding the media as an amplification station.

I use insights from sociology of media to unearth specific practices and functionalities of the media that lead to constructing certain events as risk requiring prioritization. Specifically, I use individual *routine* practices from the hierarchy of influences model (Shoemaker and Reese 2013) to guide the discussion. Here, the focus is on how media organizational processes for news delivery, audience knowledge and preferences, and the sources of information influence the news product. The current study therefore asks:

RQ1: What was news workers role in amplification or attenuation of the two risk events

Risk communicators and lay people as amplification stations

Even though the original conceptualization of SARF considered individuals as amplification stations, earlier studies focused on experts (individuals with authoritative knowledge in a particular field) as the repositories of "accurate" risk assessments which lay people amplify or attenuate (Duckett and Busby 2013). This was drawn from risk perception research, that suggested that experts' judge risk differently from lay people because expert risk assessment was more veridical, objective, and based on mortality and probability, while lay risk assessment were subjective, hypothetical, and emotional based (see Rowe and Wright 2001; Wright, Bolger, and Rowe 2002). Earlier studies thus rarely focused on the individual as an amplification station, but rather as secondary sources and as affected by amplification signals (e.g., Wiedemann et al., 2003). But this position has been criticized for privileging expert risk judgment over lay risk judgement and ignoring that all risk judgements are socially constructed.

Recent studies have addressed individual and social factors in signal amplification. Binder et al. (2011) assessed how interpersonal discussions serve as amplification stations for risk signals. Moussaïd, Brighton, and Gaissmaier (2015) experimentally investigated how risk perceptions change in transmission from one person to the other. They found that individuals' preconceptions influenced information that is received and passed on. Boyd and Jardine's (2011) study of public perspectives about BSE in Canada showed that public risk perspectives reflected actual health and economic consequences.

Expert and lay risk perceptions may thus more adequately be viewed as "competing discourses each having concrete effects" (Duckett and Busby 2013, 142). If that is the case, then exploring these competing discourses would enhance our understanding of risk judgments at each station. Experts in this case could include medical doctors, risk communicators, healthcare providers, epidemiologists etc. I focus on members of the social mobilization and risk communication subcommittee (risk communicators), as the government's risk communication apparatus. The current study explores how risk communicators and community members assessed and responded to the cholera and Ebola outbreaks. The next two research questions ask:

RQ2. How did risk communicators assess and communicate the risk of Ebola and cholera?

RQ3. How did community members perceive and respond to the risk signals they received about Ebola and cholera?

Method

This qualitative study is situated in social constructivism and uses an interpretivist approach in data analysis. Specifically, in-depth interviews were used to get at individual experiences, knowledge, meanings, explanations, and perspectives (Lindlof and Taylor 2011), while focus group discussions were used to exploit group dynamics and to draw out both convergent and divergent viewpoints (Lindlof and Taylor 2011). The study forms part of a larger study on health risk and crisis communication in West Africa. The data presented here pertains to Ebola and cholera communication in Ghana. The author's institutional review board approved the study.

The author is a Ghanaian educated health risk and crisis communication researcher and has worked as a communication consultant with various national, international, and local partners in the field including the media. This helped the author to gain access and to build trust with the respondents.

Population and recruitment

For in-depth interviews, media workers in legacy media (radio, television and newspaper; Thompson 2019) in the Greater Accra region, who published stories about both outbreaks were recruited. Members of the Ebola main committee and the social mobilization and risk communication subcommittee (set up to manage risk communication about the proximate Ebola outbreak)[1] were also recruited.

I sent recruitment emails and letters to all registered media in the Greater Accra region that had published stories about both outbreaks. Emails and letters were also sent to individual journalists based on their by-lines. I followed these with calls and emails and in-person visits to confirm participation and schedule interviews. Journalists who agreed to be interviewed recommended and invited other journalists who had done stories on Ebola and cholera to participate. For risk communicators, I reached out to contacts in the Ministry of Health (MoH) who introduced me to some members of the subcommittee and then through snowballing I recruited other members of the subcommittee. In both cases I used purposive and snowball sampling approaches.

I recruited community members in the Shai Osodoku district of the Greater Accra region for the focus group discussions. The district was purposively selected from the 16 municipalities, metropolises, and districts in the region because the region is endemic to cholera, and the district has fruit bats which at the time was the focus of possible animal-to-man transmission of the Ebola virus. Both Ebola and cholera were issues of concern to residents in the district.

In-depth interviews

Interviews were conducted in person between August 1 and September 22, 2015. Each interview lasted between 60 minutes and 90 minutes and was held at respondent's chosen venue. Respondents provided written consent to participate in the study and for the interviews to be audio recorded. After interviews were held, respondents provided recommendations of others who fit the study purpose. In all, I held 14 interviews made up of eight risk communicators and six media workers.

Interview protocols

The interview protocols consisted of four main questions each with probes and prompts. The risk communicator interview guide addressed how decisions about the risk of each disease were made; how communication about the two outbreaks was designed, developed, and disseminated; approaches for campaign implementation; and existing knowledge and perceptions about both diseases. The media worker interview guide addressed news workers knowledge about the risks of Ebola and cholera; how decisions about the news values of the two risk events were made; coverage of Ebola and cholera; and perceptions about audience response to coverage. Both protocols were pretested with representatives from the MoH and two journalists respectively not involved with the study. Modifications were done based on the pretest prior to data gathering. All interviews were held in the English language and were audio recorded.

Focus group discussions (FGD)

A community volunteer helped to purposively recruit participants through announcements at the Dodowa market and contacting church leaders to announce the discussion in their meetings. Twenty-one community members participated in three focus group discussions. Participants had to be 18 years and above, lived in the district during the simultaneous outbreaks, and received communication about both Ebola and cholera. Each group was made up of between six and ten participants. The adult male group (36 years and above) had six members, the adult female group (36 years and above) had seven members and the youth group (males and females between 18 and 25 years) had eight members. Cultural and gender norms, and age deference in Ghana required grouping individuals of similar gender and age together to facilitate discussion and to ensure that respondents could freely share their views (Amoakohene 2005). Discussions were held in a central location in the Dodowa township on a market day.

The women's group was made up of two traders, an orphanage manager, a retiree, a teacher, a business owner, and a women's group leader. The men's group had a businessman, a catechist, a phone operator, security guards, and a carpenter. The youth group was made up of college students, recent college graduates, high school graduates, hairdresser, interns, and government employees.

Focus group protocol

Participants first provided verbal or written consent to participate and for audio recording. Five main questions made up the focus group guide: how participants describe a health risk; knowledge about Ebola and cholera; how they received information about the Ebola and cholera outbreaks; behaviors and practices changed or modified; and perceptions about how communication about the two health conditions was done. I conducted the discussions in both English and the Twi language (default lingua franca) to ensure that participants were able to express themselves without restraint.

In both methods, I adopted the researcher-as-instrument approach, the idea that researcher's characteristics and attributes can potentially influence data gathering and interpretation (Pezalla, Pettigrew, and Miller-Day 2012), and actively participated in the process while encouraging interactions and conversations. I constantly reflected on who I am and how my characteristics influence the participants, the conversation, the data gathered, and my interpretation of the data. An assistant also took notes. After the discussion, respondents were provided refreshments and their compensation.

Although the sample size of 35 may be regarded as small, it is consistent with studies elsewhere (e.g., Sacilotto and Loosemore 2018; Tanner, Friedman, and Zheng 2015). Considering homogeneity of the interview sample and guided by Morse' (2000) criteria for qualitative samples, the scope of this explorative study was specific to the groups studied and was clear and relevant to the respondents. With the limited number of risk communication subcommittee members and the limited number of journalists who covered both outbreaks, saturation was deemed to have been achieved when no new information was received and recommendations were of people who had already been interviewed. The findings are not intended to be representative of the views of the media or Ghanaians or even of all community members in the Shai Osudoku district. Rather, they give an indication of how individuals make and transfer risk meaning in their context.

Coding and analysis

Data from both interviews and focus group discussions were transcribed verbatim. Focus group transcripts were then back translated to check the authenticity of the transcripts. I used Braun and Clark's (2006) deductive thematic analysis to analyze and report themes. First, initial or open codes (actual words and phrases used by respondents), were generated. These codes were then related to the theoretical framework, as "analytic induction tools" (Miller and Sinclair 2012, p. 488) to develop themes. The themes were further reviewed with the data and then abstracted and named through selective coding.

Results

The results are organized according to research questions. I present how each amplification station received, processed, and transmitted the risk signals and how this led to amplification or attenuation of each risk. I use quotations as illustrative examples of what respondents said and numbers or designations to protect the identity of respondents.

RQ1: What was news workers role in amplification or attenuation of the two risk events?

Media workers received initial Ebola signals through stories about a strange disease outbreak in the three affected countries in March 2014. They sought clarification from the Ghana MoH and the WHO-Ghana. Concern and suspicion for lack of information from the health ministry became new risk signals that led media workers to speculate and publish stories about the outbreak using information from international and social media sources. At this stage, not much filtering was done as news workers could not verify the information. A television and radio journalist explained, "It was lack of information. The ministry and researchers were not open from the beginning. But they later started talking to the media because we [media] were misinforming."

The media used pictures of hemorrhaging patients, increasing case counts, and suspected cases to raise concern among Ghanaians about the "strange disease." Such presentations increased the concern among the public and put pressure on the public health system to provide information on preparedness and suspected cases. Some media workers transmitted Ebola risk signals by developing in-house programs or segments of programs that focused on Ebola and its prevention as one television journalist explained, "We developed our own ads and LPMs. We also made sure that every news program had something on Ebola." For other media workers, sanitizers and handwashing stations set up in-house by their management became signals that led to stories on the preparedness of different organizations including churches and mosques.

The approach to cholera was a little different. Media workers received an initial alert about the impending rainy season and published this initial signal as a routine practice. As a radio and newspaper journalist explained, "When the alert came, we wrote about it, but that is all that we got."

Reports about increasing cases of cholera in a suburb of the Greater Accra region became new risk signals for the media. The main sources of information were health workers and directors of overwhelmed health facilities and family members of patients. Media workers reached out to the health ministry but did not get much information about how the cholera outbreak was being addressed. This information (or rather lack of information) attained signal value for sections of the media who decided to focus on the outbreak.

> We set up camp at La and Arts Center, where there were a lot of cases and broadcast from there. It was like they [Health Ministry] didn't even know about the outbreak. They did nothing. We had to talk about it [cholera]. The health centers were overflowing. (Radio and Television journalist 3)

At the media station, signals about both Ebola and cholera were deemed important enough for further transfer and amplification. In both cases, news workers explained their focus as two pronged: 1) provide information to the public to guide good decision making and prevent infections, and 2) keep an eye on government surveillance, preparedness and case management.

Media workers did this through publishing stories about suspected cases, state of medical facilities to handle patients, water and sanitation, hosting interviews with experts and members of the risk communication subcommittee and the main Ebola response committee, and following up on government stated efforts or inactions (e.g., building holding centers, providing training for doctors etc.). A radio and television journalist expressed their frustration with the lack of focus on the cholera epidemic thus, "The government did nothing about cholera. They did nothing. No resources were focused on cholera. We had to bash them before they took any action. We had to educate the public." The media used vox-pop, and phone-in sessions to provide audiences the opportunity to share their concerns about both Ebola and cholera.

RQ2. How did risk communicators assess and communicate the risk of Ebola and cholera?

The MoH first received information about a strange disease in Guinea, Sierra Leone, and Liberia in March 2014. The Ministry checked the authenticity of these signals with the WHO country office as well as the West African Health Organization (WAHO). When indications showed that these sources were also figuring out things, the Ministry published alerts cautioning citizens about an unknown disease in those countries.

> We decided to do our checks and learn properly before we come out with our communication messages. It was as if nothing was happening in those countries. We thought we were going to get information from

those countries. We did not get the right information because this was a new disease even though it had happened before. (RC 7)

The lack of information from the WHO, WAHO and increasing news stories with gruesome pictures from the affected countries raised concern within the health system in Ghana. In processing and transferring risk signals, respondents expressed their own fears and concerns instigated by the increasing case counts and visuals of hemorrhaging patients, and messages about the lack of treatment.

As the government's risk communication apparatus, the social mobilization and risk communication subcommittee developed a communication strategy to guide its efforts. The campaign focused on transmitting information through recognized groups and associations, mass media and communication materials to amplify the risks of Ebola and to facilitate adoption of protective measures.

So, we started using the radio stations and later went in to do TV and radio ads, docudrama, jingles, to just dramatize some of the things. We had animations being used on mass media and also on social media. (RC 5)

They also targeted recognized groups to build trust and use them as ambassadors and advocates to reach different communities and counter misinformation and rumors that were rife during the period.

From the beginning there wasn't trust so messages were bouncing back. We went to organized groups by way of public education and by way of advocacy. We went to key places like GNAT, Trades Union Congress and engaged their top hierarchy, letting them know the facts about Ebola and the role they can play in the fight against Ebola. One of the first groups we trained were the media because they were misinforming the public. (RC 4)

Initial messages that projected Ebola infection as a death sentence had to be modified to communicate the need for early identification and treatment of symptoms as ways of addressing the infection.

Those messages brought some panic reaction... that if you get it, death, or if you see someone oozing blood, it means the person has Ebola. We were using the wrong messages from the beginning and we had to change the message to: if you report early, it can be managed. (RC 1)

The case for cholera was different. The Ghana Health Service (GHS) publishes an annual alert that details the signs and symptoms of cholera, how to prevent infection, and treatment options available, prior to the start of the rainy season and also undertakes sensitization activities in some communities. A cholera alert was sent out in April 2014. Media reports provided the first risk signals of cholera in a suburb of the Greater Accra region in July 2014. The reports included pictures of overwhelmed health facilities, car parks turned into holding stations, and soundbites of frustrated medical workers and patients' family members.

We did not handle it [cholera] well at all. It was bad. Very embarrassing. The hospitals were choked with cholera patients. God gave us cholera to spare us Ebola because we can manage cholera somehow. To the extent that you know the treatment is free but they [patients] had to buy infusion. It went to all the regions. (RC 6)

However, because the country was still in preparatory mode for Ebola, it seems these risk signals were filtered out as one respondent alluded to, "It was a tricky situation. Sometimes, we would be queried 'why is it that cholera is killing people in Ghana and you are talking about Ebola which hasn't even come yet?' Cholera went viral. It was so bad." (RC, 2).

There were no financial resources to address the cholera outbreak until the GHS declared the cholera outbreak in the Greater Accra region as an epidemic (Mordy 2014). Subsequently, the Minister of Health (Mr. Kweku Agyeman Mensah) indicated that money would be taken from Ebola to fight cholera (Gadugah 2014). Communication about cholera was later added to the Ebola communication but respondents indicated that Ebola was the main issue of focus.

Risk communicators described the differing responses to the two diseases in terms of strangeness and novelty.

> Ebola is strange, not known in Ghana and we were scared, so comparing the two you could see that there was a difference. Cholera was here overwhelming us, but cholera was not a strange disease, it is not a strange disease. It has been known to us and we have been handling it. (RC 3)

In addition, risk communicators explained the government's response to Ebola and cholera in terms of international/national dichotomy. Because Ebola had received international focus, it was viewed as risky and deserving of attention compared to cholera which was mainly a national issue.

> As for Ebola, it was more like an international thing and all countries were being watched as to what to do to prevent it from coming to your country. There were standard prescriptions for every country and that is exactly what we were doing. Cholera was more or less a national issue; not as international as Ebola. (RC 2)

RQ3. How did community members perceive and respond to the risk signals they received about Ebola and cholera?

For community members, Ebola risk signals were received initially through social media and mass media as a male participant shared, "At first, I heard on the radio that Ebola has come, then TV, how it affects people and then on Whatsapp." Other signal sources included suspected case reports from interpersonal networks. The increasing case counts in the affected countries reported on these channels along with pictures of patients, health workers in PPEs, burial teams, and interviews with health experts on radio and television also served as risk signals. But as the signals were contradictory, respondents indicated ascertaining the truth from friends, neighbors, and other health experts in processing the signals. A participant in the youth FGD shared, "We have a relative in Liberia, and they called to tell us that it is not a spiritual issue, but a new disease. So, we also started telling our friends and neighbors."

These signals, which increased with media publications, talks in churches and social groups and through interpersonal networks, coupled with visuals through social and mass media and posters and flyers, attained enough signal value to warrant amplification among community members. There was also increased reporting of suspected cases on radio phone-in programs. In addition, respondents indicated making personal, behavioral, and social changes due to the risks of Ebola, some of which had negative social repercussions.

> In the past, when we have communion [a Christian religious ritual], we use glasses but because of Ebola, we started using disposable cups so that when you take and drink it you drop it in a bowl. We also stopped shaking hands with the priest after communion and with each other. (Male 3, FGD)

> That thing … not shaking hands … really became a bother for us, because you see someone you can greet but it became scary. So, for some people after shaking hands, the person takes something out of their bag and use it to sanitize their hands (Female 1, FGD)

For others, processing and transferring Ebola risk signals involved relating the risk of Ebola to HIV/AIDS, gonorrhea, and syphilis when such diseases were first encountered in their communities. Others used cultural, religious, and their lived realities to make sense of the risk signals.

> When HIV/AIDS came at first, we thought that it is when people who travel to places such as Abidjan and return without keeping the vows they made to the god of the river they crossed. For me what I heard is that in places where there was conflict, and people died and were not buried properly but just thrown away, it is through that process that the Ebola virus came out and is infecting people. (Female 3 FDG)

> Well it is in the bible that it will get to a time that due to disobedience, a certain disease will come that people will never find a cure for it. (Male 6, FDG)

Around July, there was no bird disease outbreak but 17 of my chickens died. I woke up one morning and they were dead so I started wondering if Ebola is there or not. (male 3 FDG)

Respondents did not recall receiving information about the impending cholera season prior to the outbreak. Some respondents mentioned seeing or hearing news stories about a cholera outbreak in a suburb of Accra, but when they talked about cholera, it was in passing and almost in a dismissive manner explaining that it is a well-known disease. "For cholera, we know cholera. If you are dirty you will get it, but as for the Ebola, it is not like that," a participant in the youth FGD explained.

Participants did not recall discussing cholera in their networks besides admonishing children to eat only hot food. All respondents had good knowledge about cholera, its causes, symptoms, and treatment. Respondents attributed this depth of knowledge to earlier public health campaigns.

When cholera first came, we were young, … Then they did the campaign in every place, on TV, on the radio, at the schools, even at this market, they came to tell us. That is how I know so much about cholera. (Female 5 FGD)

Cholera is from food and water. If you keep your surroundings clean, drink clean water and eat hot food you will not get it. For cholera, if someone gets it, you can hold them, give them ORS [oral rehydration salt] and take them to the clinic, but for Ebola they say you should not even touch them. (female 4, FGD)

Participants expressed limited knowledge about Ebola and compared risk communication about Ebola to communication about other diseases such as HIV/AIDS and cholera. Also expressed was the need for risk and crisis communication about Ebola to adopt more interpersonal communication approaches, which were found to be effective in previous health communication campaigns.

So, for us we want them to do the teachings [about Ebola] well so that we would know. And then they should move like when they moved during the HIV campaign, house to house, village to village, cottage to cottage, hamlet to hamlet, church to church, group to group. Even our market, they should come and do it here and they should specially select people and give them education and those people should take the education into the community. (female 1 FGD)

Discussion

I investigated how risk and crisis communication was produced and received during the simultaneous proximate Ebola and cholera outbreaks in Ghana. Below, I discuss the three main themes and five sub-themes drawn from the findings as they relate to and extend the SARF.

Constructing a health risk

Respondents described Ebola as a risk in terms of its novelty to the subregion, lack of cure at the time, fatality rate at the time, and its strangeness. In contrast, cholera was not viewed as a risk, but rather in terms of a condition that is known. The findings from this study are consistent with studies that suggest that characteristics of risks such as familiarity, catastrophic potential, controllability, dread, and uncertainty shape how risks are evaluated (Covello and Sandman 2001; Kreps 2009). This may be related to the novelty of Ebola to the sub-region, its virulence and fatality, and specialized care requirement. These attributes created a sense of dread and panic about Ebola, but cholera was viewed as a well-known, endemic, "man-caused," preventable, and treatable condition. As the psychometric paradigm suggests, risks that are novel, unfamiliar, and dreaded ignite higher risk perception than risk that are well known and familiar (Slovic, 1987). This may also suggest that risk perception is determined less by mortality and morbidity (though important) and more by how the disease is constructed as a threat (McInnes

2016) supporting Covello and Sandman's assertion that "the risks that kill people and the risks that alarm them are often completely different," (2001, 1).

Furthermore, community members' use of previous communication campaigns to justify their knowledge levels and as benchmarks for assessing the effectiveness of other campaigns suggests that community members discourses warrant examination as they provide insights into how risk are constructed, and which communication approaches and channels work for specific community members. Indeed the perspectives of the target audience needs to be incorporated into risk and crisis communication dialog (Árvai 2014; Hambach et al. 2011).

Processing and signal transmission

When people receive risk signals, they engage in a process of sensemaking to decode the signals in the context of their lived experiences and then either filter the information, recode the signals for further transfer, or ignore them.

Processing risk signals through religion, culture, and lived realities

Both risk communicators and community members, used religion and their socio-cultural context to make sense of the Ebola risk signals. While risk communicators viewed cholera as given by God in place of an Ebola outbreak, community members saw Ebola as a predicted biblical outbreak due to transgression. Community members related the risk of Ebola to previously experienced health risk events such as HIV/AIDS, gonorrhea, and syphilis. Others viewed Ebola as a result of a transgression of cultural norms. In the absence of medical explanations as is common with new and emerging diseases, socio-cultural and religious explanations operate to fill the gap and provide a sense of control over causes and to suggest solutions. It also shows that buried experiences of other risk events can resurface to serve as decoding content for making sense of a current risk. Thus, both risk communicators and community members' processing of risks illustrate that "local values, social identities, and experiences of 'place attachment' shape the local constructions of risk," (Wardman and Löfstedt, 2018).

Community members and risk communicators' use of "we know cholera" suggests their agency in addressing cholera. This sense of agency and knowledge served to attenuate the risk signals from cholera. If as Renn (1991) suggests, changes in amplification station reflect information received and processed, then it stands to reason that individuals who had received messages about cholera were confident in their ability to address it and therefore attenuated its risks while heightening concern about Ebola. All these factors suggest that a risk is only a risk if it is constructed and processed as such in a specific context and time.

Risk communicators processed Ebola and cholera risks in terms of international/national dynamics. International/global requirements, funding, and monitoring were provided for Ebola, but similar resources were unavailable for cholera. Cholera was viewed as a local outbreak of a familiar, treatable, and vaccine preventable disease. International agencies such as the WHO thus became Ebola risk amplifiers for risk communicators through instituting standard preparedness requirements for Ebola.

Transmitting signals- inaction or coordinated action

With no specific interventions from the health system for the cholera outbreak, the impression was that the cholera outbreak was unimportant. Thus, community members and risk communicators filtered out cholera risk signals in favor of Ebola risk signals. Although information about cholera was later included in Ebola communication, cholera still did not seem to be amplified among risk communicators and community members.

Risk communicators used the stereo effect by disseminating Ebola information through various channels in a complimentary manner including interpersonal and small group meetings, mass media programs and ads, communication materials, a call-center and training sessions. This strategy amplified the risks of Ebola while diminishing the risks of cholera. Thus, stereo effect may work to both amplify and attenuate risk signals when there are overlapping health risks.

Transmitting risk- routines facilitate amplification

Through the use of consistent and increased reporting, the media amplified the risks of both Ebola and cholera. A purposive sampling of Ghanaian legacy media (radio, television, and newspapers) showed that coverage about both Ebola and cholera were voluminous, consistent, and sustained from April/May 2014 until January 2015 when coverage about both issues tapered down. The consistency in coverage shows the media's effort to make both issues salient for their audiences. This means that beyond volume, consistency in reporting plays a role in how news workers amplify risk signals.

From the routines perspective (Shoemaker and Reese 2013), news values played a role in news workers' decisions to cover the two risk events. Both Ebola and cholera were valued for their human interest, mortality, unexpectedness, and proximity to the target audience. In addition, Ebola was novel and strange with many uncertainties while cholera received focus partly because of failings of government to address the needs of constituents. Both risk events therefore qualified for sustained focus based on the routinization of news worthiness, which addresses what media think audiences want from the media. The focus on Ebola and cholera signified that either news workers were responding to the perceived interest and agenda of their audiences or setting the agenda for audiences.

Another routinization that ensured that both Ebola and cholera were amplified was sourcing patterns (Shoemaker and Reese 2013). Thompson (2019) has documented how Ghanaian news workers generally rely on official sources for information but adopt different strategies including culling stories from international media and using the flushing out strategy during information scarcity. The media filtered very little at the initial stages of the outbreak and transmitted different kinds of risk signals. The media generally, and local language media in particular, may have heightened fear and panic through their translation and transmission efforts during this period (Thompson 2019). Drawing from this, it seems that in a time of high uncertainty during a risk event, the media may reduce the filtering process instituted by their organizational routines to allow various risk signals to be further transferred in an effort to provide information or to force authority to provide the needed information. This form of routinization ensured that news workers had a constant flow of information to enable them to perform their normative duties of informing audiences and holding authority accountable.

Amplification or attenuation-

Knowledge or attribution of responsibility

The different responses to the media's amplification suggest the media's limited ability to amplify risks among the public. A reason for the attenuation of cholera may relate to the risk appraisal hypothesis, which suggests that adopting a preventive behavior leads to reduced risk perception (Brewer et al. 2004; Renner et al., 2008). In that sense, community members and risk communicators' high knowledge about cholera and its management may have lowered their risk perception leading to attenuation of cholera risk signals.

Attribution of responsibility (Kim and Anne Willis, 2007) or who is blamed for causing the outbreak and solving it, may also explain the differing responses to the two risk events. While respondents attributed the cause of Ebola to various factors including the unknown, nature, religion, and conflicts, cholera was viewed as caused by individual unhygienic behaviors. Individuals were blamed for the cholera outbreak without considering the structural and systemic failings (the lack of structures and resources for managing garbage, inadequate places of convenience, and poor drainage systems) that create a conducive context for the cholera bacteria to spread. These inadequacies necessitate annual sensitization activities including public education, durbars, and community mobilization on the need to follow personal hygienic practices, eating hot food, clearing surroundings and desilting clogged drains, home treatment remedies for diarrheal related illness, and reporting any incidences of suspected cholera or diarrheal cases (e.g., Agbey 2016). While not minimizing individual responsibility in the spread of any disease, it is well known that many of the cholera affected communities in Ghana lack adequate toilet and waste disposal facilities (Bagah, Osumanu, and Owusu-Sekyere 2015), coupled with poor drainage systems that lead to annual flooding and resultant disease outbreaks (Songsore 2017). By assigning the individual as the cause of cholera, (Fife-Schaw and Rowe 1996) individuals are indirectly assigned responsibility for solving cholera outbreaks, absolving government, and lessening the social attention to the epidemic.

Amplification and attenuation- Diverse roles lead to amplification

Although the traditional SAR framework has been criticized for static categories of sources, transmitters, and receivers, the current study shows an iterative process for these roles. For Ebola, risk communicators acted in the traditional position of sources when they developed and implemented the communication campaign, but they were receivers when individual citizens and the media informed them about suspected cases requiring attention. News workers played their traditional transmission role of channels by transmitting information from risk communicators to the public and by informing risk communicators about suspected cases from the public. But the media were also sources when they developed their own inhouse campaigns to inform the public about protective and preventive measures. As receivers, news workers were the target of trainings and workshops to prepare them to handle information about the outbreak well. Individuals in the general public were the receivers of communication about Ebola from risk communicators and the media, but were sources of information on suspected cases and transmitters of information within their interpersonal and social networks.

For cholera, the media were both sources and transmitters of information about the outbreak but not receivers. Risk communicators were receivers of information when the media targeted them to address the cholera outbreak and became sources of information when they included cholera information in their communication. For the general public, some were sources of information then they reached out to the media about the cholera outbreak and then receivers of information from the media and later the health system. The situation presented here seems to suggest that the more dynamic the roles played at each station, the higher the likelihood of amplification.

Conclusion and limitations

This study has limitations that need to be acknowledged. First, this is an exploratory qualitative study with non-probabilistic samples. Caution must be exhibited in generalizing beyond the respondents of the study. Second, the study relied on respondents' ability to recall information and behaviors during the outbreaks because fieldwork was conducted after both outbreaks had curbed. Also, the district of focus was purposively selected to avoid over sensitization of one disease condition. A study in a high cholera incidence area using a communication studies lens may produce interesting results.

The SARF seems to reflect a multi-layered, multi-dimensional endeavor that influences and is influenced by various factors. Amplification was achieved through various mechanisms including how a health risk is constructed, international pressure, disease characteristics, and routines that guide media workers. In decoding risk signals, religious, cultural, historical, and even suppressed risk events may find articulation in the processing and sensemaking of new risk signals. Stereo effect may work to simultaneously amplify and attenuate competing risk signals. The study showed that the more diverse the roles assumed at each station, the more likely the risk signals will be amplified. I argue that the context of an impending crisis can lead to a crisis for a preventable and treatable disease based on how the risk is amplified or attenuated and the characteristics associated with the risk.

It is therefore recommended that risk communication about new diseases be made a part of and not replace existing health communication policy and interventions in order to avoid the possibility of existing risks receiving less attention. Secondly risk and crisis communication needs to be designed as a process guided by feedback from laypeople and their conceptions of risk as well as their preferred channels of communication. Interpersonal channels and sources as well as radio need to be respected and used in developing contexts. Finally, in contexts where infectious diseases are common, the end of an outbreak should be an opportunity to provide accurate information about risks, because such information will become respondents baseline information for judging and making decisions about other outbreaks.

Note

1. The committee was set up to address the Ebola outbreak, but was later requested to include cholera in its communication. The members include representatives from the Ghana Health Services, the National Health Promotion Unit, National Disaster Management Organization, Ministry of Information, MoH, Veterinary Services, and international partners such as UNICEF Ghana, Red Cross, and the WHO.

Acknowledgements

I would like to thank God for the grace to complete this paper. I would also like to thank Radhika Parameswaran, Annie Lang, and James Kelly (Indianan University) for providing feedback on initial drafts. I am also indebted to two reviewers who provided insightful feedback to improve the paper. Some of the data in the manuscript is based on research previously used as part of the authors doctoral dissertation. (Thompson, E. E. (2017). *Communicating in a public health crisis: The case of Ebola in West* Africa (Doctoral dissertation). ProQuest Dissertations & Theses Global. (Order No. 10279436).

Disclosure statement

I have no conflict of interest to disclose.

Funding

There is no funding to report for this submission.

ORCID

Esi E. Thompson (iD) http://orcid.org/0000-0002-0772-0997

References

Agbey, G. M. 2016. "NADMO intensifies education on cholera, yellow fever in Agona East." The Daily Graphic, September 16. www.graphic.com.gh

Amoakohene, M. I. 2005. "Focus Group Research: Towards an Applicable Model for Africa." In *Topical Issues in Communications and Media Research*, edited by Kwansah-Aidoo. NY: Nova Science Publishers.

Árvai, J. 2014. "The End of Risk Communication as We Know It." *Journal of Risk Research* 17 (10): 1245–1249. doi:10.1080/13669877.2014.919519.

Bagah, D. A., I. K. Osumanu, and E. Owusu-Sekyere. 2015. "Persistent "Cholerization" of Metropolitan Accra, Ghana: Digging into the Facts." *American Journal of Epidemiology and Infectious Disease* 3 (3): 61–69.

Brewer, N. T., N. D. Weinstein, C. L. Cuite, and J. E. Herrington. 2004. "Risk Perceptions and Their Relation to Risk Behavior." *Annals of Behavioral Medicine* 27 (2): 125–130. doi:10.1207/s15324796abm2702_7.

Binder, A. R., M. A. Cacciatore, D. A. Scheufele, and D. Brossard. 2015. "The Role of News Media in the Social Amplification of Risk." In *The SAGE Handbook of Risk Communication*, edited by H. Cho and T. Reimer (vol. 69). Thousand Oaks, CA: Sage.

Binder, A. R., D. A. Scheufele, D. Brossard, and A. C. Gunther. 2011. "Interpersonal Amplification of Risk? Citizen Discussions and Their Impact on Perceptions of Risks and Benefits of a Biological Research Facility." *Risk Analysis: An Official Publication of the Society for Risk Analysis* 31 (2): 324–334. doi:10.1111/j.1539-6924.2010.01516.x.

Boyd, A., and C. Jardine. 2011. "Did Public Risk Perspectives of Mad Cow Disease Reflect Media Representations and Actual Outcomes?" *Journal of Risk Research* 14 (5): 615–630. doi.org/ doi:10.1080/13669877.2010.547258.

Braun, Virginia, and, Victoria Clarke. 2006. "Using Thematic Analysis in Psychology." *Qualitative Research in Psychology* 3 (2): 77–101. doi:10.1191/1478088706qp063oa.

Cardona-Ospina, J. A., K. Arteaga-Livias, W. E. Villamil-Gómez, et al. 2020. "Dengue and COVID-19, Overlapping Epidemics? an Analysis from Colombia." *Journal of Medical Virology*: 1–6. doi:10.1002/jmv.26194.

Covello, V. T., and P. M. Sandman. 2001. "Risk Communication: Evolution and Revolution." In *Solutions to an Environment in Peril*, edited by A. Wolbarst, 164–178. Baltimore, MD: Johns Hopkins University Press.

Duckett, D., and J. Busby. 2013. "Risk Amplification as Social Attribution." *Risk Management* 15 (2): 132–153. doi:10.1057/rm.2013.2.

Gadugah, N. 2014. "Gov't Squeezes Cash from Ebola Find to Fight Cholera." *Myjoy Online*, August 18. www.myjoyonline.com.

Ghana Health Services. 2015. "2014 Annual report"

Fenollar, F., and O. Mediannikov. 2018. "Emerging Infectious Diseases in Africa in the 21st Century." *New Microbes and New Infections* 26: S10–S18. doi:10.1016/j.nmni.2018.09.004.

Fife-Schaw, C., and G. Rowe. 1996. "Public Perceptions of Everyday Food Hazards: A Psychometric Study." *Risk Analysis* 16 (4): 487–500.

Hambach, R., P. Mairiaux, G. François, L. Braeckman, A. Balsat, G. Van Hal, C. Vandoorne, P. Van Royen, and M. van Sprundel. 2011. "Workers' Perception of Chemical Risks: A Focus Group Study." *Risk Analysis: An Official Publication of the Society for Risk Analysis* 31 (2): 335–342. doi:10.1111/j.1539-6924.2010.01489.x.

Kasperson, Roger E. 2012. "The Social Amplification of Risk and Low-Level Radiation." *Bulletin of the Atomic Scientists* 68 (3): 59–66. doi:10.1177/0096340212444871.

Kasperson, J., R. Kasperson, N. Pidgeon, and P. Slovic. 2003. "The Social Amplification of Risk: Assessing Fifteen Years of Research and Theory." In *The Social Amplification of Risk*, edited by N. Pidgeon, R. Kasperson, and P. Slovic, 13–46. Cambridge: Cambridge University Press.

Kim, Sei-Hill, and, L Anne Willis. 2007. "Talking about Obesity: News Framing of Who is Responsible for Causing and Fixing the Problem." *Journal of Health Communication* 12 (4): 359–376. doi:10.1080/10810730701326051.

Kreps, G. 2009. "Health Communication Theories." In *Encyclopedia of Communication Theory*, edited by S. Littlejohn and K. Foss, 464–469. California, CA: Sage Publications.

Lindlof, T., and B. C. Taylor. 2011. *Qualitative Communication Research Methods*. 3rd ed. USA: Sage.

Machlis, G. E., and E. A. Rosa. 1990. "Desired Risk: Broadening the Social Amplification of Risk Framework." *Risk Analysis* 10 (1): 161–168. doi:10.1111/j.1539-6924.1990.tb01030.x.

McInnes, C. 2016. "Crisis! What Crisis? Global Health and the 2014–15 West African Ebola Outbreak." *Third World Quarterly* 3 (37): 380–400. doi:10.1080/01436597.2015.1113868.

Milko, V., and A. Ghosal. 2020. "Dengue Prevention Efforts Stifled by Coronavirus Pandemic." *Associated Press*, July 12. www.apnews.com.

Miller, B., and J. Sinclair. 2012. "Risk Perceptions in a Resource Community and Communication Implications: Emotion, Stigma, and Identity." *Risk Analysis* 32 (3): 483–495. doi:10.1111/j.1539-6924.2011.01685.x.

Mordy, J. T. 2014. "Cholera Outbreak in Accra Declared an Epidemic as More Die." Myjoy Online, August 13. www.myjoyonline.com

Morse, J. M. 2000. "Determining Sample Size." *Qualitative Health Research* 10 (1): 3–5. doi:10.1177/104973200129118183.

Moussaïd, M., H. Brighton, and W. Gaissmaier. 2015. "The Amplification of Risk in Experimental Diffusion Chains." *Proceedings of the National Academy of Sciences of the United States of America* 112 (18): 5631–5636. doi:10.1073/pnas.1421883112.

Nachega, J. B., P. Mbala-Kingebeni, J. Otshudiema, A. Zumla, and J. J. M. Tam-Fum. 2020. "The Colliding Epidemics of COVID-19, Ebola, and Measles in the Democratic Republic of the Congo." *The Lancet. Global Health* 8 (8): e991–e992. doi:10.1016/S2214-109X(20)30281-3.

Pezalla, A. E., J. Pettigrew, and M. Miller-Day. 2012. "Researching the Researcher-as-Instrument: An Exercise in Interviewer Self-Reflexivity." *Qualitative Research: QR* 12 (2): 165–185. doi:10.1177/1468794111422107.

Raupp, J. 2014. "Social Agents and News Media as Risk Amplifiers: A Case Study on the Public Debate about the E. coli Outbreak in Germany 2011." *Health, Risk & Society* 16 (6): 565–579.

Renn, O., W. J. Burns, J. X. Kasperson, R. E. Kasperson, and P. Slovic. 1992. "The Social Amplification of Risk: Theoretical Foundations and Empirical Applications." *Journal of Social Issues* 48 (4): 137–160. doi:10.1111/j.1540-4560.1992.tb01949.x.

Renn, O. 1991. "Risk Communication and the Social Amplification of Risk." In *Communicating Risk to the Public*, edited by R.E. Kasperson and P.J.M. Stallen, 287–324. Dordrecht: Kluwer Academic publishers.

Renner, Britta, Benjamin Schüz, and Falko F Sniehotta. 2008. "Preventive Health Behavior and Adaptive Accuracy of Risk Perceptions." *Risk Analysis* 28 (3): 741–748. doi:10.1111/j.1539-6924.2008.01047.x.

Rossmann, C., L. Meyer, and P. J. Schulz. 2018. "The Mediated Amplification of a Crisis: Communicating the a/H1N1 Pandemic in Press Releases and Press Coverage in Europe." *Risk Analysis: An Official Publication of the Society for Risk Analysis* 38 (2): 357–375. doi:10.1111/risa.12841.

Sacilotto, J., and M. Loosemore. 2018. "Chinese Investment in the Australian Construction Industry: The Social Amplification of Risk." *Construction Management and Economics* 36 (9): 507–520. doi:10.1080/01446193.2018.1457222.

Shoemaker, P. J., and S. D. Reese. 2013. *Mediating the Message in the 21st Century: A Media Sociology Perspective.* 3rd ed. New York, N.Y: Routledge.

Slovic, P. 1987. "Perception of Risk." *Science* 236 (4799): 280–285. doi:10.1126/science.3563507.

Songsore, J. 2017. "The Complex Interplay between Everyday Risks and Disaster Risks: The Case of the 2014 Cholera Pandemic and 2015 Flood Disaster in Accra, Ghana." *International Journal of Disaster Risk Reduction* 26: 43–50. doi:10.1016/j.ijdrr.2017.09.043.

Strekalova, Y. A. 2017. "Health Risk Information Engagement and Amplification on Social Media: News about an Emerging Pandemic on Facebook." *Health Education & Behavior: The Official Publication of the Society for Public Health Education* 44 (2): 332–339. doi:10.1177/1090198116660310.

Tanner, A. H., D. B. Friedman, and Y. Zheng. 2015. "Influences on the Construction of Health News: The Reporting Practices of Local Television News Health Journalists." *Journal of Broadcasting & Electronic Media* 59: 359–376.

Thompson, E. E. 2019. "Communicating a Health Risk/Crisis: Exploring the Experiences of Journalists Covering a Proximate Epidemic." *Science Communication* 41 (6): 707–731. doi:10.1075/547019878875.

Wardman, Jamie K, and Ragnar Löfstedt. 2018. "Anticipating or Accommodating to Public Concern? Risk Amplification and the Politics of Precaution Reexamined." *Risk Analysis* 38 (9): 1802–1819. doi:10.1111/risa.12997.

Wirz, C. D., M. A. Xenos, D. Brossard, D. Scheufele, J. H. Chung, and L. Massarani. 2018. "Rethinking Social Amplification of Risk: Social Media and Zika in Three Languages." *Risk Analysis* 38 (12): 2599–2624. doi:10.1111/risa.13228.

World Health Organization (WHO). 2015. "One Year into the Ebola Epidemic: A Deadly, Tenacious and Unforgiving Virus." https://www.who.int/csr/disease/ebola/one-year-report/ebola-report-1-year.pdf?ua=1

World Health Organization (WHO). 2014. "Statement on the 1st Meeting of the IHR Emergency Committee on the 2014 Ebola Outbreak in West Africa," August 8. https://www.who.int/mediacentre/news/statements/2014/ebola-20140808/en/

Wiedemann, P. M., Clauberg, M., & Schutz, H.2003. "Understanding amplification of complex risk issues: The risk story model applied to the EMF case. In The Social Amplification of Risk" edited by N. Pidgeon, R. Kasperson, and P. Slovic, 286. Cambridge Cambridge University Press

Wright, G., F. Bolger, and G. Rowe. 2002. "An Empirical Test of the Relative Validity of Expert and Lay Judgments of Risk." *Risk Analysis: An Official Publication of the Society for Risk Analysis* 22 (6): 1107–1122. doi:10.1111/1539-6924.00276.

Rowe, G., and G. Wright. 2001. "Differences in Expert and Lay Judgments of Risk: Myth or Reality?" *Risk Analysis: An Official Publication of the Society for Risk Analysis* 21 (2): 341–356. doi:10.1111/0272-4332.212116.

From information to intervention: connecting risk communication to individual health behavior and community-level health interventions during the 2016 Zika outbreak

Rachael Piltch-Loeb and David Abramson

ABSTRACT

Emerging disease threats are on the rise. Risk communication in an emerging threat is used by public health officials to reach the population in a timely and effective manner. However, limited research has drawn on data gathered during an emerging threat to understand how risk communication shapes intervention perceptions. This analysis examines the relationship between risk communication, especially where information comes from, and receptivity to individual-level and community-level health interventions in an emerging threat using evidence from the 2016 rise of Zika. Data comes from a repeat cross-sectional survey conducted three times in 2016, representative of the United States population. Drawing on leading theories of risk communication, a structural model (SEM) is used to measure the relationships of interest. Two distinct SEMs are used to compare and contrast the relationship between source of information and individual health behavior change and community-level health interventions while also exploring the role of knowledge, perceived risk, and demographics. Results of both direct and indirect SEM pathways show different sources of information may be more effective in promoting particular interventions. Promoting community-level interventions can be accomplished through dissemination of information in print news to increase knowledge and ultimately receptivity. However, there is a far more complex relationship between risk communication and personal intervention receptivity. With a more nuanced understanding of the way information from a particular source effects intervention receptivity, communicators can reach the public more effectively to limit the consequences of an emerging public health threat.

Introduction

Emerging disease threats pose a risk to naïve populations, creating unique challenges due to a lack of scientific knowledge on the threat itself and the most effective measures to control the consequences of the disease (Gubler 1998; GAO 2017; Fauci and Morens 2016). The COVID-19 pandemic in 2020 has only served to highlight this. During an emerging disease event, public health officials take measures to mitigate the potential impact of the threat. The success of intervention implementation is dependent on the willingness of the population at large or subsets of the population to take action themselves or accept governmental action to limit the impact of the emerging threat (Sadique et al. 2007; Bults et al. 2010; Rudisill 2013). Risk communication is one of the primary mechanisms by which the public health community informs the public of these recommended actions or governmental policies. However, there is little evidence in the context of recent emerging disease threats on how risk communication actually influences intervention uptake.

Interventions in emerging threats

Generally, there are two types of interventions that can be implemented to control an emerging threat- individual level interventions and community level or policy oriented interventions. Past examples of individual level interventions in an emerging threat that have been employed have included quarantine, which was recommended for people returning from West Africa during the Ebola outbreak in 2014, and throughout many states to control COVID-19 or the use of precautionary protective behaviors, such as wearing masks to prevent the spread of COVID-19 or the use of condoms and reduction in risky sex to prevent transmission of HIV/AIDS. In contrast, community level interventions are those that do not require individual health behavior change for implementation. These types of interventions broadly refer to policies, directives, or actions taken by governmental actors to limit disease spread. Historic examples have included workplace vaccination requirements to control smallpox, screening for symptoms at airports to limit the spread of COVID-19 or SARS, or limiting mass gathering such as with the closure restaurants and sports venues to prevent COVID-19 transmission or closure of schools which were used to prevent transmission of H1N1. These interventions can also be community-level interventions to control particular vectors such as aerial spraying to control mosquito vectors such as in multiple West Nile Virus outbreak. Consistent with other public health efforts, the control of emerging threats typically involve both behavioral interventions and community level interventions (Bell et al. 2006; Aledort et al. 2007).

Individual interventions

In the past there has been a wide range of compliance with public health promotion campaigns related to emerging disease threats, suggesting the need for further research into the factors that promote or inhibit individual intervention uptake. The consequences of noncompliance with recommended disease control measures include increased disease spread, higher morbidity, and higher mortality. There are many examples of this, but one of the more recent examples prior to the COVID-19 pandemic, is the 2017 flu season. An estimated 80,000 people died from this flu, 172 of them being children. CDC reports this is in part attributable in part to historically low flu vaccine uptake among children under 5 (Garten et al. 2018; Sun 2018). In this case, limited compliance led to increased flu morbidity and mortality.

Despite the recognition that protective actions by the public are necessary to control a threat, there is a practical challenge to understanding who is most likely to take these actions when a threat is happening. The majority of public health efforts are on controlling the disease rather than on predicting who is likely to engage in individual control measures. Because compliance with public health measures can be the difference between a small and large disease burden, there have been efforts to study predictors of intervention compliance. To study compliance with individual public health measures, researchers commonly look to other threats that perhaps required similar actions by the public and measure willingness to engage in behavior change. Typically, this is done because of 1) the challenge of measuring health behavior change in real time in an emerging threat (per the flu example) and 2) the utility for not only the current event (or future events) to understanding public willingness to engage in behaviors in designing interventions and communication campaigns (Blendon et al. 2008; Savoia, Testa, and Viswanath 2012; Diepeveen et al. 2013).

Looking across recent emerging disease threats including SARS, H1N1, West Nile Virus, and Ebola, the primary focus of research has been on demographic differences that relate to possible preventive behavior, and in a limited fashion drawing on traditional models of behavior change, how risk perception and knowledge can contribute to intervention receptivity (Brug et al. 2004; Smith 2006; Cheng and Ng 2006; de Zwart et al. 2009; Sastry and Lovari 2017; Gidado et al. 2015). Examining willingness to engage in personal behavior change, women and those with high levels of self-efficacy have been found to be more willing to make health behavior changes both in an emerging threat (and generally) while older adults appear to be less willing to do so (Brewer et al. 2007; Cheng and Ng 2006; Quinn et al. 2013). Beyond demographics, authors have found during the H1N1 pandemic, mixed support for H1N1 population interventions by perceived risk, and understanding of disease characteristics (Quinn et al. 2013; Hilyard et al. 2014; Quinn et al. 2009). Across events, the limited evidence suggests gender, age, self-efficacy, perceptions of risk, and knowledge of threat are predictors of individual behavior change in an emerging threat.

Community interventions

Community-level interventions operate differently than individual interventions. They do not require action by the public but instead require inaction. This is because the success of community based interventions is dependent on the public not opposing their implementation. For example, during the Ebola outbreak, the governors of the tristate area collectively suggested a quarantine policy at the airports in the region (Greer and Singer 2017). The decision was met with mixed public reactions. Some suggested the policy violated the individual rights of the individuals returning who were not symptomatic with Ebola disease while others were concerned about disease spread (Gesser-Edelsburg and Shir-Raz 2015). This public backlash was widely covered in the media and prompted a shift in policy (Greer and Singer 2017). While there were no direct connections to the spread of Ebola domestically, the point is, public response can dictate success of community level interventions. Similarly, public opposition to aerial spraying to control the West Nile Virus outbreak in the Dallas, TX area in 2012 lead to spraying only occurring in one particular county and a higher burden of West Nile Virus in the area than in outbreaks over the prior two decades (Roehrig 2013; Piltch-Loeb et al. 2014). And most recently, policies that have been implemented across states to close businesses to prevent COVID-19 transmission, have been met by protests and defiance, limiting their potential success.

There is noted variation in public support of community interventions and little research as to why in emerging threats. The research that does exist on community interventions in emerging threats has also examined hypothetical support for community interventions. These efforts are consistent with decades of research that have examined policy preferences among the population to determine how the public may react to a variety of national or local decisions before they are undertaken to prevent backlash and promote optimal implementation. This literature historically exploring policy preferences among the population has shown two relevant things: there are strong gendered differences in policy preferences, and available information that is accurate and helpful can shift collective policy preferences (a form of community intervention) in meaningful ways (Page and Shapiro 2010; Shapiro and Mahajan 1986). In recent emerging disease threats these efforts to understand public perception of community-level disease control measures have included the following. During the H1N1 pandemic of 2009, a survey by Blendon and colleagues asked hypothetical disease control questions, and found most adults support government implemented policies such as quarantine, but results varied based on financial status (Blendon et al. 2008). Similarly, Paek and colleagues found in a statewide survey of Michigan residents, residents showed strong support for many proposed government actions in a pandemic, except for offering non-fully approved drugs as long as their economic livelihood was not threatened (Paek et al. 2008). Taken together, gender, understanding of threat, and income appear to be key factors related to perceptions of community-interventions.

Promoting interventions through risk communication

All types of interventions must be communicated effectively to the public or subsets of the public for adoption. Risk communication is the means by which public officials share with the public information about the threat and potential interventions. Risk communication in emerging disease threats is somewhat distinct from other types of risk communication, such as risk communication on chronic health issues or natural hazards.

Compared to chronic health issues, the scientific uncertainty during emerging diseases, attributable to the lack of medical and public health information available as the threat emerges, complicates messaging (Vaughan and Tinker 2009; Reynolds and Crouse Quinn 2008). Most health promotion efforts for a chronic disease are based on having the 'right' factual information to tell a patient. While interventions that fall within this domain are incredibly varied such as individual health behavior changes to diet and exercise or breast self-examination, and communal health changes such as bans on smoking in work places or public spaces, there are some common strategies to increase preventive behavior (Bandura 2004; Perry et al. 1992; Maibach, Flora, and Nass 1991; Sparling et al. 2000). Mechanisms for altering health behaviors that authors have explored include transmitting information on how habits affect health, arousing fear of disease, increasing perceptions of one's personal vulnerability or risk, or raising people's beliefs in their efficacy to alter their habits (Meyerowitz and Chaiken 1987). These tools are most effectively implemented when mediated by social pathways of influence (Bandura 2004). Years if not decades of research are drawn upon to share information with a patient, often in one-to-one counseling from a physician or health educator. Unless there is novel content, the information itself remains fairly consistent, and it often becomes the individual context of an information seeker that is influencing who is getting that information, such as if a new patient is diagnosed with diabetes and then looks for diabetes information resources.

Once information on a suggested intervention reaches a target population, predictors of public support for these interventions included self-efficacy, perceived risk, perceived benefit, and knowledge of health impacts (Rothman and Salovey 1997; Johnson, Scott-Sheldon, and Carey 2010). Though this evidence is helpful to understanding information influence on intervention receptivity in emerging threats, it may be insufficient given particular characteristics related to emerging threats.

In natural hazards, often there is a short time frame between when a threat emerges and the need to communicate emergency information the public, though the threat itself is more familiar and determined in its potential impacts (i.e. a hurricane is comprised of wind and rain). For example, once the National Oceanic and Atmospheric Association (NOAA) identifies an emerging storm and can predict its potential path with some, but not perfect certainty, local governments and emergency managers must communicate evacuation and sheltering plans to given communities (Demuth et al. 2012). The time frame to do this is possibly a week, but typically days (Lindell, Lu, and Prater 2005). More extreme community mobilization efforts can be used to get the word out. Beyond traditional mass media and social media, there are an increasing the number of information channels that may include door to door communication, telephone trees, or emergency alarm systems (Gladwin et al. 2007). This level of communication is both not sustainable in an emerging disease threat, and may be too localized to be effective on a population level.

Emerging disease threats sit at the intersection of these two domains: they are health issues, but they often require population level compliance to mitigate consequences; they occur over a period of time that is longer than a natural hazard, but without adequate time for the research on transmission and consequences that chronic disease threats often have. Emerging disease communication typically must convey the best public health information available at the time, amid a dynamic situation (Kapucu, Arslan, and Demiroz 2010; Pechta, Brandenburg, and Seeger 2010; Steelman et al. 2014). This is especially a concern when the information being communicated is time-sensitive, such as the need to take preventive measures before an outbreak becomes localized. Multiple factors complicate the risk communication process in an emerging threat. Among them is the scientific uncertainty surrounding the threat which means communication must by dynamic in order to be successful (Young, Rao, and Rosamilia 2016). Because of these considerations of time and disease uncertainty, to reach the public in a timely and effective manner to promote public health interventions, risk communication becomes increasingly important but also increasingly complex (Houston et al. 2015; Pechta, Brandenburg, and Seeger 2010; Steelman et al. 2014).

Further complicating communication in recent emerging threats is a shifting information landscape including the breadth of information sources currently available to the public and the speed with which the public can access information (Fox 2015). In some research on prior threats, results have shown particular sources of information including forms of mass media and one's social network, can promote knowledge of disease and perceived risk for disease (Lampi 2011; Fang et al. 2012). Prior work, including on emerging threats, has also demonstrated that familiar information sources, which tend to be more trusted, are more likely to increase perceived risk, and in turn may increase behavioral intentions (Fang et al. 2012; Taha, Matheson, and Anisman 2013; Sheeran, Harris, and Epton 2014). Therefore, source of information is a key piece of the information landscape to explore when considering the effect of risk communication, and one that is focused on here.

Theoretical foundations

Bish and Michie (2010) describe in their review of behavioral intentions in emerging threats that most of the studies in this space have been a-theoretical, and when the studies have involved theoretical constructs they have drawn only in part on theory, either from the health belief model, theory of planned behavior, or precaution adoption model (Bish and Michie 2010). As previously described, because emerging threats sit at the intersection of the health and hazards literature, both fields offer a theoretical foundation to understand how risk communication from a given source may reach the population and influence intervention receptivity. Theoretical models of health and hazards behavior including the health belief model and the protective action decision model (PADM) have shown risk communication typically can operate to promote intervention engagement by increasing understanding of a threat and perceived risk for that threat (Lindell and Perry 2012). As described by Lindell and Perry (2012), the nature of the 'warning network' or set of sources that a receiver gets information from has a significant impact on protective action decision making because multiple sources can deliver conflicting or different messages. The transmission of a message can lead to further information seeking in a feedback loop that continues until there is information sufficiency to proceed to a protective action.

Beyond characteristics of the information transmission pathway, past research that has applied PADM has shown the factors in the model are important in shaping perceptions and action but there is extensive variation in people's protective actions (Lindell and Perry 2012). Work has demonstrated that risk perception is an important determinant of protective action behavior but that other perceptions like perceived efficacy are also important (Maloney, Lapinski, and Witte 2011). However, there is limited evidence on what these other perceptions are and if they specifically relate to understanding of the threat. Risk communication research has found that feeling both personally and societally threatened by an event can influence behavior (Sears and Funk 1991).

Case study: risk communication to promote Zika interventions

The Zika virus which emerged in the Americas in 2016 provides a relatively recent case study to examine the role of risk communication in willingness to support individual and community interventions. Zika has multiple viral vectors- it is both mosquito borne and sexually transmitted. Zika can also be transmitted from mother to fetus and cause significant birth defects, especially microcephaly. Individual control measures included abstaining from sexual activity or use condoms consistently if having traveled to a Zika endemic area, particularly if there was a pregnant partner, reducing travel to Zika endemic areas, or considering delaying pregnancy altogether (Goldfarb, Jaffe, and Lyerly 2017). Community level interventions included aerial or local ground spraying for mosquitoes in areas where transmission was possible based on climate or recognized cases (Cáceres 2016).

The evolving nature of the science around Zika and need for both personal interventions and community-level interventions created the opportunity to explore how information reached the public and related to intervention receptivity and to examine if there are unique ways in which information shapes intervention receptivity for individual level versus community level interventions. Existing work in the context of the Zika virus has explored the sources of information accessed, that information related to Zika knowledge and perceived risk, and that intervention receptivity varied. This analysis uses structural equation modeling to compare and contrast the relationship between source of information, knowledge, risk perception, and intervention receptivity, while also exploring demographics that have been found to relate to willingness to support individual or community level interventions. Two separate models are fit- one that explores community level Zika interventions the other which explores individual level Zika interventions to understand if the similarities and differences in intervention promotion. Because prior research has demonstrated that different demographic groups, levels of knowledge, and perceived risk relate to distinct interventions, the authors deliberately use two models to further identify these unique pathways (Piltch-Loeb, Abramson, and Merdjanoff 2017). The specific research questions are:

1.   How does risk communication operate both directly and indirectly to influence individual level intervention receptivity?
2.   How does risk communication operate both directly and indirectly to influence community level intervention receptivity?
3.   Which theoretical characteristics including knowledge and perceived risk, as well as demographics age, income, gender, and efficacy directly and indirectly influence individual and community intervention receptivity?

The results will improve the public health community's understanding of the relationship between sources of information and intervention receptivity, the relationship between knowledge and risk, and ultimately the drivers of interventions more broadly.

Methods

Data collection

Data comes from a representative sample of U.S. households collected using a fully-replicated, single-stage, random-digit-dialing (RDD) sample households supplemented by a list of randomly generated cell phone numbers. Data were collected at three time points: Spring (April/May), Summer (July/August), and Fall (October/November) of 2016. The first structured telephone survey was of 1,233 US residents, subsequent surveys sampled 1,231 residents and 1,234 residents respectively. The AAPOR response rate was approximately 4% at each wave. The data were weighted to represent the U.S. adult population using inverse probability sample weights. Further information on sampling and weighting procedures has previously been described by the author (reference removed for identification). The study was found to be exempt by the author's institution's Institutional Review Board.

Measures

Latent variables

Receptivity to community-level interventions (Outcome 1) is a latent factor comprised of the responses to support for community-wide outdoor spraying of insecticides; indoor spraying of insecticide by local officials; and provision of larvicide tablets to residents to be deployed on personal property. Receptivity to individual interventions (Outcome 2) is a latent factor built comprised of the responses to willingness to delay pregnancy for six months or more due to Zika concerns; willingness to take a Zika vaccine should one become available; willingness to change travel plans due to Zika concerns; and willingness to use condoms with a sexual partner. In addition to intervention receptivity, there are two proximal outcomes examined in this model related to answering research question (RQ) 3: knowledge of Zika and perceived risk of Zika. Actual knowledge of Zika is a latent factor related to respondents correctly responding to one of three survey items that the Zika virus could be sexually transmitted, could be carried asymptomatically, or could cause birth defects. Perceived risk of Zika is comprised of responses to perceptions of personal Zika risk and community Zika risk based on self-report of respondents. All items that were used to comprise these latent measures were dichotomous. Model fit statistics for all latent variables were examined in a CFA that showed good model fit before fitting the structural model components.

Observed variables

Sources of information: Sources of influence for the Zika virus were determined based on the following survey question. 'People may have heard or read about the Zika virus from a number of sources. I am going to name a source of information and would like to know whether you got any information about Zika from this source in the past two weeks. Have you gotten information about the Zika virus from ... '? The response options analyzed here are getting information from print news and from family or friends. These two sources of information are specifically being examined because they have been found to be the most utilized, and distinct sources of information drawn on by the public for Zika information in prior work by the authors (citation removed for anonymity). Print news in particular was found to be the most common source of Zika information, likely to increase knowledge of Zika; and therefore could be related to both types of intervention receptivity; while information from family and friends has been related to increasing perceived risk (citation removed for anonymity). Further, in unsaturated models, other sources included TV news and social media, had no relationship with the proximal or distal outcomes of interest, suggesting their inclusion would not add to the goodness of fit and may lead to oversaturation by adding theoretically unfounded pathways to outcomes of interest. A metric of breadth of information sources was also tested but ultimately not included as it decreased model fit indices. Specific demographic variables were included in this model based on the prior literature. These included a proxy measure of self-efficacy (dichotomized as yes/no based on the response to the survey item 'I have control over whether or not I get the Zika virus'), and demographic variables of female gender, age measured continuously, and income measured continuously. Point in time of data collection was also examined in the model to see if there was decay in intervention receptivity.

Analytic plan

Associations and pathways of factors leading to intervention receptivity were tested by combining the measurement (latent variables) and structural components (multiple path analysis) of the model into a simultaneous SEM. Consistent with the literature, to assess goodness of model fit, the following criteria were examined (Hooper, Coughlan, and Mullen 2008): Comparative Fit Index (CFI); Root mean square error of approximation (RMSEA); Standardized root mean square residual (SRMR); Chi-squared metrics are also typically used to assess goodness-of-fit, though with large sample sizes and weighted data, the results of these tests are typically discounted, so they were therefore not included as a criterion for judging model fit in this study. SEMs were tested both with and without indirect pathways to identify if model fit improved with the inclusion of mediating effects. In all cases, mediation not only fit with the hypotheses of the author but also improved model fit. Final models that included mediating effects are reported below. SEM was conducted using standard procedures in Mplus Version 8 (Muthén and Muthén 2015).

Results

Structural equation model of personal intervention receptivity

The significant pathways to personal intervention receptivity are noted in Table 1, along with all standardized total, total indirect, and specific indirect and direct effects. Results from the structural equation model showed excellent fit (CFI = 0.98, RMSEA = 0.01, and SRMR = 0.02). These indices validate the statistical fit of the model to infer that the theorized model matches the empirical data well.

There was a small, positive effect of information from print news on personal intervention receptivity (TE 0.098, SE 0.029), of which, 30% of the effect was a significant indirect effect through knowledge of Zika (IDE 0.031, SE 0.012) and 20% of the effect was an indirect effect through information from family and friends (IDE 0.019, SE 0.005). The direct effect of information from family and friends on personal intervention receptivity was 0.118 (TE 0.118, SE 0.028), which was primarily attributable to a direct effect. Overall, knowledge of Zika had an effect of 0.180 on intervention receptivity (TE 0.180, SE 0.051), of which a small but significant portion operated through increasing perceived risk to influence personal intervention receptivity. Perceived risk had a direct effect, increasing personal intervention receptivity by 0.109 (TE 0.109, SE 0.028). Examining the impact of the demographic characteristics of interest: age (TE −0.097, SE 0.026) and income (TE −0.178, SE 0.035) each had a small, significant negative impact on personal intervention receptivity, while female gender had a small, positive impact (TE 0.104, SE 0.028). Time of data collection significantly decreased personal intervention receptivity (TE −0.098, SE 0.028), suggesting that as time passed, the public became less receptive to personal interventions.

Structural equation model of community level intervention receptivity

The significant pathways to community-level intervention receptivity are shown in Table 2, along with all standardized total, total indirect, and specific indirect and direct effects. Results from the structural equation model showed strong indicators of model fit (CFI = 0.94, RMSEA = 0.02, and SRMR = 0.02). These indices validate the statistical fit of the model to infer that the model matches the empirical data well.

Table 1. Standardized total, total indirect, specific indirect, and direct effects.

Factor affecting support of personal intervention	Effect	Specific indirect	Estimate	S.E.
Information from News	Total		0.098**	0.029
	Total Indirect		0.054**	0.013
	Indirect	Knowledge	0.031**	0.012
		Risk	−0.001	0.003
		Family/Friends	0.019**	0.005
	Direct		0.044	0.031
Information from family and friends	Total		0.118***	0.028
	Total Indirect		0.003	0.009
	Indirect	Knowledge	−0.008	0.007
		Risk	0.012*	0.006
	Direct		0.115***	0.029
Age (cont.)	Total		−0.097***	0.026
	Total indirect		−0.059**	0.020
	Indirect	Knowledge	0.019*	0.009
		Risk	0.000	0.004
		Income	−0.093***	0.018
		Family/Friends	−0.002	0.003
		Print news	0.004	0.003
	Direct		−0.037*	0.032
Female	Total		0.104***	0.028
	Total indirect		0.040***	0.011
	Indirect	Knowledge	0.017*	0.008
		Risk	−0.004	0.003
		Income	0.019***	0.005
		Family/Friends	0.007*	0.003
		Print news	0.000	0.001
	Direct		0.064	0.028
Time of data	Total		− 0.098**	0.028
	Total indirect		−0.019*	0.008
	Indirect	Knowledge	−0.001	0.006
		Risk	−0.002	0.004
		Family/Friends	−0.007*	0.003
		Print news	−0.004	0.003
	Direct		−0.079**	0.028
Income (cont)	Total		−0.178***	0.035
	Total indirect		0.013	0.011
	Indirect	Knowledge	0.018*	0.009
		Risk	−0.003	0.004
		Family/Friends	−0.010**	0.004
		Print news	0.003	0.002
	Direct		−0.191***	0.036
Health efficacy	Total		0.006	0.028
	Total indirect		−0.005	0.012
	Indirect	Knowledge	0.014	0.007
		Risk	−0.021**	0.008
		Family/Friends	− 0.002	0.002
		Print news	0.001	0.001
	Direct		0.011	0.029
Knowledge	Total		0.180***	0.051
	Total Indirect		0.017*	0.008
		Risk	0.017*	0.008
	Direct		0.163**	0.130
Risk	Total	0.109**		0.038
	Direct	0.109**		0.038

*p < 0.01.
**p < 0.01.
***p < 0.001.

Information from print news had a small, significant effect on support of community-level interventions (total effect estimate of 0.127, SE 0.035), close to half of which was attributed to an indirect effect through knowledge of Zika (IDE 0.056, SE 0.001) and directly (DE 0.062, SE 0.006).

Table 2. Standardized total, total indirect, specific indirect, and direct effects.

Factor affecting support of environmental intervention	Effect	Specific indirect	Estimate	S.E.
Information from news	Total		0.127***	0.035
	Total Indirect		0.065***	0.018
	Indirect	Knowledge	0.056**	0.001
		Risk	0.000	0.002
		Family/Friends	0.009**	0.006
	Direct		0.062	0.038
Information from family and friends	Total		0.045	0.034
	Total Indirect		−0.009	0.012
	Indirect	Knowledge	−0.015	0.011
		Risk	0.007	0.006
	Direct		0.054	0.035
Age (cont.)	Total		0.048	0.032
	Total Indirect		0.039	0.026
	Indirect	Knowledge	0.034*	0.014
		Risk	0.000	0.002
		Income	−0.023	0.021
		Family/Friends	−0.001	0.001
		Print news	0.005	0.004
	Direct		0.009	0.041
Female	Total		−0.009	0.038
	Total Indirect		0.032*	0.014
	Indirect	Knowledge	0.031*	0.012
		Risk	−0.002	0.003
		Income	0.005	0.005
		Family/Friends	0.003	0.003
		Print news	0.000	0.001
	Direct		−0.042	0.039
Time of data	Total		−0.071*	0.036
	Total Indirect		−0.016	0.011
	Indirect	Knowledge	−0.001	0.010
		Risk	−0.001	0.002
		Family/Friends	−0.003	0.002
		Print news	−0.006	0.004
	Direct		−0.056	0.037
Income (cont)	Total		−0.010	0.043
	Total Indirect		0.037*	0.015
	Indirect	Knowledge	0.032*	0.014
		Risk	−0.003	0.002
		Family/Friends	−0.005	0.003
		Print news	0.004	0.003
	Direct		−0.047	0.043
Health efficacy	Total		0.048	0.036
	Total Indirect		0.015	0.016
	Indirect	Knowledge	0.024*	0.011
		Risk	−0.012	0.010
		Family/Friends	−0.001	0.001
		Print news	0.002	0.002
	Direct		0.033	0.036
Knowledge	Total		0.296***	0.065
	Total Indirect		0.010*	0.008
	Indirect	Risk	0.010	0.008
	Direct		0.286***	0.066
Risk	Total		0.064	0.050
	Direct		0.064	0.050

*$p < 0.01$.
**$p < 0.01$.
***$p < 0.001$.

Information from family and friends did not have a significant effect on the outcome. Overall, knowledge of Zika had the greatest total effect on community-level intervention receptivity (TE 0.296, SE 0.065), largely attributable to a direct effect, with a small indirect effect through perceived risk (IDE 0.010, SE 0.008). Perceived risk alone did not have a significant direct or indirect

effect. Turning to other model constructs that were explored: age, income, gender, and self-efficacy did not have significant total effects on community-level intervention receptivity, but each
had a, slight significant indirect effect through knowledge. Time of data collection significantly
decreased intervention receptivity (TE −0.071, SE 0.036).

Discussion

This analysis is the first of its kind. It identifies not only that source of Zika information relates to
receptivity to Zika interventions (both personal and community-level), but also identifies how
that relationship operates, while exploring the role of knowledge, perceived risk and demographic characteristics. This analysis highlights different sources of information may be more
effective in promoting particular interventions. This discussion returns to the research questions
proposed by the authors in the introduction.

*How does risk communication operate both directly and indirectly to influence individual level
intervention receptivity?*

Information from family and friends has an effect on personal intervention receptivity. The direct pathway from information from family and friends to personal intervention receptivity suggests people may have specifically discussed likelihood to engage in particular behavioral public
health actions with their networks. Information from print news flows to information from family
and friends and knowledge, and in turn has an effect on personal level intervention receptivity.
We hypothesize that as the population sought information from the news, they may have then
discussed it with family and friends, prompting an increase in personal intervention receptivity.
This re-packaging or exchange of information in turn influenced personal intervention receptivity
both directly and by heightening perceived risk.

*How does risk communication operate both directly and indirectly to influence community level
intervention receptivity?*

These findings show that the effect and flow of information varies depending on where it
comes from. The pathway from information from print news to community-level interventions
highlights these interventions may be promoted in the mass media and directly shape knowledge and then receptivity. Information from print news may have also provided sufficient depth
in content to prompt support for community interventions. The lack of relationship between
information from family and friends on community level intervention receptivity is also meaningful. Social networks may not discuss interventions that do not directly require a behavior change.
This may mean the voice of the media is more important when it comes to community level
interventions, and that these interventions do not rise to the same level of personal concern or
discourse because they do not involve a personal calculation related to behavior.

*Which theoretical characteristics including knowledge and perceived risk, as well as demographics
age, income, gender, and efficacy directly and indirectly influence individual and community intervention receptivity?*

The paths to intervention receptivity for individual level and community-level interventions
are distinct. Knowledge of a threat and perceived risk of that threat are two constructs consistently identified in the theoretical literature to influence action. In the model of personal intervention receptivity, knowledge of Zika, and perceived risk of Zika both had strong direct effects on
intervention receptivity for personal interventions, while in the model of community-level intervention receptivity, there was no effect (indirectly or directly) of perceived risk of Zika, and an
even stronger effect of knowledge of Zika on intervention receptivity. These findings demonstrate that increasing knowledge matters for community interventions while increasing both
knowledge and perceived risk matters can increase receptivity to personal interventions. If the
population understands the threat, they are more receptive to community-level interventions,
where as personal action requires both an understanding of threat and a sense of risk.

Various demographic characteristics have previously been found to influence the intervention receptivity and thus tested here. In the model of personal intervention receptivity, income, age, and gender each had an effect- with those with higher income and age less likely to be receptive and females increasingly receptive. The results related to age and gender are expected-adults who are beyond their child bearing years and males had less of a reason to engage in protective behavior related to Zika. These results show that when personal action is expected, individual characteristics become increasingly important to examine. Engaging particular demographics to promote individual interventions may be necessary.

In contrast, there were no direct pathways from demographics or self-efficacy to community-level intervention receptivity. Instead, age, gender, income, and self-efficacy each operated indirectly through knowledge, though the effect was not significant on receptivity. In the context of community-level interventions, individual sociodemographic characteristics have a negligible effect on receptivity. Promoting knowledge is therefore increasingly important and related to intervention support.

Finally, point in time of data collection was included in the model. For both personal intervention receptivity and community-level intervention receptivity, there was a negative direct effect of time of data collection. The population may have experienced fatigue with Zika as time passed and therefore become less receptive to all interventions related to the threat. As time went on, scientific certainty increased in terms of Zika's transmission pathways and effects. The threat also did not materialize as expected across the continental United States during mosquito season. These two factors likely decreased the dread factor associated with the disease and may have contributed to 'Zika fatigue' and decreasing intervention support.

Limitations

First, this study relied upon an existing survey of primarily binary observed variables to operationalize latent constructs which means some constructs may be under specified. This can increase the standard errors in factor loadings and in the path analysis, and suggests future work should work to refine and expand the findings using more robust constructs. Despite this concern, factor loadings operated significantly and as expected. Some factor loadings were less robust than others. Measures also would have been improved had they quantified information use, efficacy, perceived risk, and level of intervention receptivity. Second, other communication scholars have explored the role of message content and channel of information dissemination in the context of risk communication. This study did not measure these concepts, but future analyses should consider the impact of these constructs.

Implications

To control an emerging threat, the public must be effectively engaged through various information sources, yet there is currently a limited understanding of this process and the result it has in promoting a given activity. There are two key implications from this study. This study presents the first attempt to measure the direct effect of two sources of information on intervention receptivity. Prior work has focused on knowledge and perceived risk but not connected a source of information to either construct. These results directly show that a portion of the effect of both knowledge and risk is attributable to where the public gets information. With a more nuanced, and operationalized understanding of the way information from a particular source effects intervention receptivity, public health communicators can refine their approaches to shape behavior.

The second implication is in the distinction between personal intervention receptivity and community-level intervention receptivity. There is a far more complex relationship between risk communication and personal intervention receptivity which is shaped by information from print news as well as family and friends, impacted by demographics, and especially driven by perceived risk. In contrast, promoting community-level intervention receptivity can be accomplished effectively through dissemination of information in print news to increase knowledge and ultimately receptivity. The results show the pathways to personal intervention receptivity are clearly distinct from community level intervention receptivity, and highlight the need for distinct risk communication mechanisms to promote one or the other. Given the current COVID-19 pandemic, the direct implications here are to focus the promotion of community-level control measures in the print, mass media rather than through social media channels. This suggests both the theory and practice of public health must take more nuanced approaches depending on the type of intervention that is most important to promote in an emerging disease threat.

Disclosure statement

No potential conflict of interest was reported by the authors.

Funding

This research was with funding support awarded to New York University's College of Global Public Health from the National Science Foundation grant number 1638545.

References

Aledort, Julia E., Nicole Lurie, Jeffrey Wasserman, and Samuel A. Bozzette. 2007. "Non-Pharmaceutical Public Health Interventions for Pandemic Influenza: An Evaluation of the Evidence Base." *BMC Public Health* 7 (1): 208. doi:10.1186/1471-2458-7-208.

Bandura, Albert. 2004. "Health Promotion by Social Cognitive means." *Health Education & Behavior* 31 (2): 143–164. doi:10.1177/1090198104263660.

Bell, David, Angus Nicoll, Keiji Fukuda, Peter Horby, Arnold Monto, Frederick Hayden, Clare Wylks, Lance Sanders, and J. Tam Van. 2006. "Non-Pharmaceutical Interventions for Pandemic Influenza, International Measures." *Emerging Infectious Diseases* 12 (1): 81–87. doi:10.3201/eid1201.051370.

Bish, A., and S. Michie. 2010. "Demographic and Attitudinal Determinants of Protective Behaviours during a Pandemic: A Review." *British Journal of Health Psychology*. 15.4 (2010): 797–824.

Blendon, Robert J., Lisa M. Koonin, John M. Benson, Martin S. Cetron, William E. Pollard, Elizabeth W. Mitchell, Kathleen J. Weldon, and Melissa J. Herrmann. 2008. "Public Response to Community Mitigation Measures for Pandemic Influenza." *Emerging Infectious Diseases* 14 (5): 778–786. doi:10.3201/eid1405.071437.

Brewer, Noel T., Gretchen B. Chapman, Frederick X. Gibbons, Meg Gerrard, Kevin D. McCaul, and Neil D. Weinstein. 2007. "Meta-Analysis of the Relationship between Risk Perception and Health Behavior: The Example of Vaccination." *Health Psychology* 26 (2): 136–145. doi:10.1037/0278-6133.26.2.136.

Brug, Johannes, Anke Oenema, Jan Hendrik Richardus, Aria R. Aro, Onno De Zwart, and George D. Bishop. 2004. "SARS Risk Perception, Knowledge, Precautions, and Information Sources, The Netherlands." *Emerging Infectious Diseases* 10 (8): 1486–1489. http://ezproxy.library.nyu.edu:2048/login?url=http. ://search.ebscohost.com/login. aspx?direct = true&db = a9h&AN = 14054182&site = eds-live. doi:10.3201/eid1008.040283.

Bults, Marloes, Desiree Beaujean, Onno de Zwart, Gerjo Kok, Pepijin van Empelen, Jim E. van Steenbergen, Jan Hendrik Richardus, and Helene A. C. M. Voeten. 2010. "Mexican Flu: Risk Perceptions of the General Public, Precautionary Measures and Trust in Information Provided by the Government." *Dutch Journal of Medicine* 154: A1686

Cáceres, Marco. 2016. "Controversial Pesticide Naled Sprayed over Miami to Combat Zika." *The Vaccine Reaction*. August 22.

Cheng, Cecilia, and Aik-Kwang Ng. 2006. "Psychosocial Factors Predicting SARS-Preventive Behaviors in Four Major SARS-Affected Regions." *Journal of Applied Social Psychology* 36 (1): 222–247. doi:10.1111/j.0021-9029.2006.00059.x.

de Zwart, Onno, Irene K. Veldhuijzen, Gillian Elam, Arja R. Aro, Thomas Abraham, George D. Bishop, Helene A. C. M. Voeten, Jan Hendrik Richardus, and Johannes Brug. 2009. "Perceived Threat, Risk Perception, and Efficacy Beliefs

Related to SARS and Other (Emerging) Infectious Diseases: Results of an International Survey." *International Journal of Behavioral Medicine* 16 (1): 30–40. doi:10.1007/s12529-008-9008-2.

Demuth, Julie L., Rebecca E. Morss, Betty Hearn Morrow, and Jeffrey K. Lazo. 2012. "Creation and Communication of Hurricane Risk Information." *Bulletin of the American Meteorological Society* 93 (8): 1133–1145. doi:10.1175/BAMS-D-11-00150.1.

Diepeveen, Stephanie, Tom Ling, Marc Suhrcke, Martin Roland, and Theresa M. Marteau. 2013. "Public Acceptability of Government Intervention to Change Health-Related Behaviours: A Systematic Review and Narrative Synthesis." *BMC Public Health* 13 (1): 756. doi:10.1186/1471-2458-13-756.

Fang, David, Chen-Ling Fang, Bi-Kun Tsai, Li-Chi Lan, and Wen-Shan Hsu. 2012. "Relationships among Trust in Messages, Risk Perception, and Risk Reduction Preferences Based upon Avian Influenza in Taiwan." *International Journal of Environmental Research and Public Health* 9 (8): 2742–2757. doi:10.3390/ijerph9082742.

Fauci, Anthony S., and David M. Morens. 2016. "Zika Virus in the Americas-Yet Another Arbovirus Threat." *The New England Journal of Medicine* 374 (7): 601–604. doi:10.1056/NEJMp1600297.

Fox, S. 2015. *The Social Life of Health Information, 2011.* Washington, DC: Pew Internet & American Life Project.

GAO. 2017. *Actions Needed to Address the Challenges of Responding to Zika Virus Disease Outbreaks.* Washington, DC: Government Accountability Office (GAO).

Garten, Rebecca, Lenee Blanton, Anwar Isa Abd Elal, Noreen Alabi, John Barnes, Matthew Biggerstaff, Lynnette Brammer, et al. 2018. "Update: Influenza Activity in the United States during the 2017-18 Season and Composition of the 2018-19 Influenza Vaccine." *MMWR. Morbidity and Mortality Weekly Report* 67 (22): 634–642. doi:10.15585/mmwr.mm6722a4.

Gesser-Edelsburg, Anat, and Yaffa Shir-Raz. 2015. "Science vs. Fear: The Ebola Quarantine Debate as a Case Study That Reveals How the Public Perceives Risk." *Journal of Risk Research* 20 (5): 1–633. doi:10.1080/13669877.2015.1100659.

Gidado, Saheed, Abisola, M. Oladimeji, Alero Ann Roberts, Patrick Nguku, Iruoma, Genevieve Nwangwu, Ndadilnasiya Endie Waziri, Faisal, et al. 2015. "Public Knowledge, Perception and Source of Information on Ebola Virus Disease–Lagos, Nigeria; September, 2014." *PLoS Currents*: 7.

Gladwin, Hugh, Jeffrey K. Lazo, Betty Hearn Morrow, Walter Gillis Peacock, and Hugh E. Willoughby. 2007. "Social Science Research Needs for the Hurricane Forecast and Warning System." *Natural Hazards Review* 8 (3): 87–95. doi:10.1061/(ASCE)1527-6988(2007)8:3(87).

Goldfarb, I. T., E. Jaffe, and A. D. Lyerly. 2017. "Responsible Care in the Face of Shifting Recommendations and Imperfect Diagnostics for Zika Virus." *JAMA* 318 (21): 2075. https://doi.org/. doi:10.1001/jama.2017.15680..

Greer, Scott L., and Phillip M. Singer. 2017. "The United States Confronts Ebola: suasion, Executive Action and Fragmentation." *Health Economics, Policy, and Law* 12 (1): 81–104. doi:10.1017/S1744133116000244.

Gubler, Duane J. 1998. "Resurgent Vector-Borne Diseases as a Global Health Problem." *Emerging Infectious Diseases* 4 (3): 442–450. doi:10.3201/eid0403.980326.

Hilyard, Karen M., Sandra Crouse Quinn, Kevin H. Kim, Don Musa, and Vicki S. Freimuth. 2014. "Determinants of Parental Acceptance of the H1N1 Vaccine." *Health Education & Behavior* 41 (3): 307–314. doi:10.1177/1090198113515244.

Hooper, Daire, Joseph Coughlan, and Michael Mullen. 2008. "Structural Equation Modelling: Guidelines for Determining Model Fit." *Electronic Journal on Business Research Methods* 2: 53–60.

Houston, J. Brian, Joshua Hawthorne, Mildred F. Perreault, Eun Hae Park, Marlo Goldstein Hode, Michael R. Halliwell, Sarah E. Turner McGowen, et al. 2015. "Social Media and Disasters: A Functional Framework for Social Media Use in Disaster Planning, Response, and Research." *Disasters* 39 (1): 1–22. doi:10.1111/disa.12092.

Johnson, Blair T., Lori A. J. Scott-Sheldon, and Michael P. Carey. 2010. "Meta-Synthesis of Health Behavior Change Meta-Analyses." *American Journal of Public Health* 100 (11): 2193–2198. . http://www.ncbi.nlm.nih.gov/pmc/articles/PMC2951968/. doi:10.2105/AJPH.2008.155200.

Kapucu, Naim, Tolga Arslan, and Fatih Demiroz. 2010. "Collaborative Emergency Management and National Emergency Management Network." *Disaster Prevention and Management: An International Journal* 19 (4): 452–468. doi:10.1108/09653561011070376.

Lampi, Elina. 2011. "What Do Friends and the Media Tell Us? How Different Information Channels Affect Women's Risk Perceptions of Age-Related Female Infertility." *Journal of Risk Research* 14 (3): 365–380. doi:10.1080/13669877.2010.541560.

Lindell, Michael K., Jing-Chein Lu, and Carla S. Prater. 2005. "Household Decision Making and Evacuation in Response to Hurricane Lili." *Natural Hazards Review* 6 (4): 171–179. doi:10.1061/(ASCE)1527-6988(2005)6:4(171).

Lindell, Michael K., and Ronald W. Perry. 2012. "The Protective Action Decision Model: theoretical Modifications and Additional Evidence." *Risk Analysis* 32 (4): 616–632. doi:10.1111/j.1539-6924.2011.01647.x.

Maibach, Edward, June A. Flora, and Clifford Nass. 1991. "Changes in Self-Efficacy and Health Behavior in Response to a Minimal Contact Community Health Campaign." *Health Communication* 3 (1): 1–15. doi:10.1207/s15327027hc0301_1.

Maloney, Erin K., Maria K. Lapinski, and Kim Witte. 2011. "Fear Appeals and Persuasion: A Review and Update of the Extended Parallel Process Model." *Social and Personality Psychology Compass* 5 (4): 206–219. doi:10.1111/j.1751-9004.2011.00341.x.

Meyerowitz, Beth E., and Shelly Chaiken. 1987. "The Effect of Message Framing on Breast Self-Examination Attitudes, Intentions, and Behavior." *Journal of Personality and Social Psychology* 52 (3): 500–510. doi:10.1037/0022-3514.52.3.500.

Muthén, L. K., and B. Muthén. 2015. "Mplus." In *The Comprehensive Modelling Program for Applied Researchers: User's Guide*, vol. 5. Los Angeles, CA.

Paek, H. J., K. Hilyard, V. S. Freimuth, J. K. Barge, and M. Mindlin. 2008. "Public Support for Government Actions during a Flu Pandemic: Lessons Learned from a Statewide Survey." *Health Promotion Practice* 9 (4_suppl): 60S–72S. doi:10.1177/1524839908322114.

Page, Benjamin I., and Robert Y. Shapiro. 2010. *The Rational Public: Fifty Years of Trends in Americans' Policy Preferences*. Chicago, IL: University of Chicago Press.

Pechta, Laura E., Dale C. Brandenburg, and Matthew W. Seeger. 2010. "Understanding the Dynamics of Emergency Communication: Propositions for a Four-Channel Model." *Journal of Homeland Security and Emergency Management* 7 (1). doi:10.2202/1547-7355.1671.

Perry, C. L., S. H. Kelder, D. M. Murray, and K. I. Klepp. 1992. "Communitywide Smoking Prevention: long-Term Outcomes of the Minnesota Heart Health Program and the Class of 1989 Study." *American Journal of Public Health* 82 (9): 1210–1216. doi:10.2105/ajph.82.9.1210.

Piltch-Loeb, Rachael, David M. Abramson, and Alexis A. Merdjanoff. 2017. "Risk Salience of a Novel Virus: US Population Risk Perception, Knowledge, and Receptivity to Public Health Interventions regarding the Zika Virus Prior to Local Transmission." *PLoS One* 12 (12): e0188666. doi:10.1371/journal.pone.0188666.

Piltch-Loeb, Rachael N., Christopher D. Nelson, John D. Kraemer, Elena Savoia, and Michael A. Stoto. 2014. "A Peer Assessment Approach for Learning from Public Health Emergencies." *Public Health Reports* 129 (6_suppl4): 28–34. doi:10.1177/00333549141296S405.

Quinn, Sandra Crouse, Supriya Kumar, Vicki S. Freimuth, Kelly Kidwell, and Donald Musa. 2009. "Public Willingness to Take a Vaccine or Drug under Emergency Use Authorization during the 2009 H1N1 Pandemic." *Biosecurity and Bioterrorism: Biodefense Strategy, Practice and Science* (7): 275–290. doi:10.1089/bsp.2009.0041.

Quinn, Sandra Crouse, John Parmer, Vicki S. Freimuth, Karen M. Hilyard, Donald Musa, and Kevin H. Kim. 2013. "Exploring Communication, Trust in Government, and Vaccination Intention Later in the 2009 H1N1 Pandemic: results of a National survey." *Biosecurity and Bioterrorism* 11 (2): 96–106. doi:10.1089/bsp.2012.0048.

Reynolds, B., and S. Crouse Quinn. 2008. "Effective Communication during an Influenza Pandemic: The Value of Using a Crisis and Emergency Risk Communication Framework." *Health Promotion Practice* 9 (4_suppl): 13S–17S. doi:10.1177/1524839908325267.

Roehrig, John T. 2013. "West Nile Virus in the United States - A historical perspective." *Viruses* 5 (12): 3088–3108. doi:10.3390/v5123088.

Rothman, Alexander J., and Peter Salovey. 1997. "Shaping Perceptions to Motivate Healthy Behavior: The Role of Message Framing." *Psychological Bulletin* 121 (1): 3–19. doi:10.1037/0033-2909.121.1.3.

Rudisill, Caroline. 2013. "How Do we Handle New Health Risks? Risk Perception, Optimism, and Behaviors regarding the H1N1 Virus." *Journal of Risk Research* 16 (8): 959–980. doi:10.1080/13669877.2012.761271.

Sadique, M. Z., W. J. Edmunds, R. D. Smith, W. J. Meerding, O. de Zwart, J. Brug, and P. Beutels. 2007. "Precautionary Behavior in Response to Perceived Threat of Pandemic Influenza." *Emerging Infectious Diseases* 13 (9): 1307–1313. doi:10.3201/eid1309.070372.

Sastry, S., and A. Lovari. 2017. "Communicating the Ontological Narrative of Ebola: An Emerging Disease in the Time of "Epidemic 2.0"." *Health Communication* 32 (3): 329–338. doi:10.1080/10410236.2016.1138380.

Savoia, Elena, Marcia A. Testa, and Kasisomayajula Viswanath. 2012. "Predictors of Knowledge of H1N1 Infection and Transmission in the US Population." *BMC Public Health* 12 (1): 328doi:10.1186/1471-2458-12-328.

Sears, David O., and Carolyn L. Funk. 1991. "The Role of Self-Interest in Social and Political Attitudes." In *Advances in Experimental Social Psychology*, edited by Mark Zanna, 1–91. San Diego, CA: Elsevier.

Shapiro, Robert Y., and Harpreet Mahajan. 1986. "Gender Differences in Policy Preferences: A Summary of Trends from the 1960s to the 1980s." *Public Opinion Quarterly* 50 (1): 42–61. doi:10.1086/268958.

Sheeran, Paschal, Peter R. Harris, and Tracy Epton. 2014. "Does Heightening Risk Appraisals Change people's intentions and behavior? A meta-analysis of experimental studies." *Psychological Bullettin* 140 (2): 511–543. doi:10.1037/a0033065.

Smith, R. D. 2006. "Responding to Global Infectious Disease Pandemics: lessons from SARS on the Role of Risk Perception, Communication and Management." *Social Science & Medicine* 63 (12): 3113–3123. doi:10.1016/j.socscimed.2006.08.004.

Sparling, P. B., N. Owen, E. V. Lambert, and W. L. Haskell. 2000. "Promoting Physical Activity: The New Imperative for Public Health." *Health Education Research* 15 (3): 367–376. doi:10.1093/her/15.3.367.

Steelman, Toddi A., Branda Nowell, Deena Bayoumi, and Sarah McCaffrey. 2014. "Understanding Information Exchange during Disaster Response: Methodological Insights from Infocentric Analysis." *Administration & Society* 46 (6): 707–743. doi:10.1177/0095399712469198.

Sun, L. 2018. "Flu Broke Records for Deaths, Illnesses in 2017-2018, New CDC Numbers Show." *The Washington Post*, September 27.

Taha, Sheena Aislinn, Kimberly Matheson, and Hymie Anisman. 2013. "The 2009 H1N1 Influenza Pandemic: The Role of Threat, Coping, and Media Trust on Vaccination Intentions in Canada." *Journal of Health Communication* 18 (3): 278–290. doi:10.1080/10810730.2012.727960.

Vaughan, E., and T. Tinker. 2009. "Effective Health Risk Communication about Pandemic Influenza for Vulnerable Populations." *American Journal of Public Health* 99 (S2): S324–S332. https://doi.org/. http://dx.doi.org/10.2105/AJPH.2008.154609. doi:10.2105/ajph.2008.154609..

Young, Cory, Aditi Rao, and Alexis Rosamilia. 2016. "Crisis and Risk Communications: Best Practices Revisited in an Age of Social Media." In *Communicating Climate-Change and Natural Hazard Risk and Cultivating Resilience*, edited by Jeanette L. Drake, John C. Eichelberger, Karen M. Taylor, T. Scott Rupp, and Yekaterina Y. Kontar, 27–36. New York, NY: Springer.

Risk perceptions of COVID-19 around the world

Sarah Dryhurst ⓘⒹ, Claudia R. Schneider ⓘⒹ, John Kerr ⓘⒹ, Alexandra L. J. Freeman ⓘⒹ, Gabriel Recchia ⓘⒹ, Anne Marthe van der Bles ⓘⒹ, David Spiegelhalter and Sander van der Linden ⓘⒹ

ABSTRACT
The World Health Organization has declared the rapid spread of COVID-19 around the world a global public health emergency. It is well-known that the spread of the disease is influenced by people's willingness to adopt preventative public health behaviors, which are often associated with public risk perception. In this study, we present the first assessment of public risk perception of COVID-19 around the world using national samples (total $N = 6{,}991$) in ten countries across Europe, America, and Asia. We find that although levels of concern are relatively high, they are highest in the UK compared to all other sampled countries. Pooled across countries, personal experience with the virus, individualistic and prosocial values, hearing about the virus from friends and family, trust in government, science, and medical professionals, personal knowledge of government strategy, and personal and collective efficacy were all significant predictors of risk perception. Although there was substantial variability across cultures, individualistic worldviews, personal experience, prosocial values, and social amplification through friends and family in particular were found to be significant determinants in more than half of the countries examined. Risk perception correlated significantly with reported adoption of preventative health behaviors in all ten countries. Implications for effective risk communication are discussed.

Introduction

"We're deeply concerned both by the alarming levels of spread and severity, and by the alarming levels of inaction." We have rung the alarm bell loud and clear. – Tedros Adhanom Ghebreyesus, Director-General, World Health Organization (Ghebreyesus 2020).

The new coronavirus (SARS-CoV-2) is a highly infectious disease that caused an epidemic of acute respiratory syndrome (COVID-19). Between January and April 2020, the epidemic turned into a global pandemic from its centre of origin in Wuhan, China to now having reached most countries around the world. As of April 14th, 2020, over 126,000 people have died from COVID-19 globally. Men are at higher risk of dying than women (Caramelo, Ferreira, and Oliveios 2020; Jin et al. 2020) and there are signs that in some countries, ethnic minorities may also be at higher risk (Garg, Kim, and Whitaker 2020; Rimmer, 2020). On January 30th, 2020, the World Health Organization declared the outbreak a "public health emergency of international concern". In this paper, we ask two critical questions; a) how concerned are people around the world? and b) what psychological factors determine their level of concern?

As the number of deaths from the disease rises around the world, it is becoming increasingly important to understand public risk perception (Van Bavel et al. 2020). Current governmental responses range from social distancing and hygiene advice (e.g. Sweden) to complete lockdowns of the general population (e.g. Italy). These measures aim to prevent national health services from becoming overwhelmed by a sudden onslaught of cases. Yet, we know from past pandemics that the success of policies to slow down the rapid transmission of a highly infectious disease rely, in part, on the public having accurate perceptions of personal and societal risk factors. In fact, collectively, people's behavior can fundamentally influence and alter the spread of a pandemic (Epstein et al. 2008; Funk et al. 2009; Reluga 2010; Van Bavel et al. 2020). Threat appraisal and risk perception are core features of protection-motivation theory (Floyd, Prentice-Dunn, and Rogers 2000; Rogers 1975) and as such, are known to be important determinants of the public's willingness to cooperate and adopt health-protective behaviors during pandemics, including frequent hand washing, physical distancing, avoiding public places, and wearing face masks (Bish and Michie 2010; Leppin and Aro 2009; Poletti, Ajelli, and Merler 2011; Rubin et al. 2009; Rudisill 2013; van der Weerd et al. 2011). In other words, accurate public risk perceptions are critical to effectively managing public health risks.

Yet, although official health organizations have now established the pandemic to be an objective threat to public health, ringing the alarm bell "loud and clear", as Slovic (1992) once stated, "risk does not exist independent of our minds and culture" (p. 690). Indeed, a large body of research over the last decades has shown that risk perception is a subjective psychological construct that is influenced by cognitive, emotional, social, cultural, and individual variation both between individuals and between different countries (Douglas and Wildavsky 1983; Loewenstein et al. 2001; Leiserowitz 2006; Joffe 2003; Kasperson et al. 1988; Sjöberg 2002; Wildavsky and Dake 1990; Slovic 2010; Slovic, Fischhoff, and Lichtenstein 1982; van der Linden 2015, 2017; Wåhlberg 2001).

Contagion: Risk perception during pandemics

Compared to other risk domains, such as environmental risks, far less is known about how the public perceives risks associated with emerging infectious diseases (de Zwart et al. 2009). Most of the evidence on risk perception has come from studies during previous pandemics, most notably the H1N1 swine flu pandemic in 2009 (e.g. Fischhoff et al., 2018; Rudisill 2013; Prati, Pietrantoni, and Zani 2011), the Ebola outbreak (e.g. Prati and Pietrantoni 2016; Yang and Chu 2018) and the SARS and Avian influenza (bird flu) epidemics (Leppin and Aro 2009). Although this research has been important and informative, reviews have pointed out that a common characteristic of rapid-response studies is that many of them are exploratory and descriptive in nature and therefore a) do not rely on established theory-based models of risk perception, b) almost exclusively rely on single-item measures of risk perception selectively tapping into either cognitive or emotional dimensions, and c) fail to include important international comparisons (de Zwart et al. 2009; Leppin and Aro 2009).

Accordingly, here we adopt a theory-based approach to the study of risk perception. In an attempt to integrate over 50 years of risk perception research, van der Linden's (2015, 2017) risk perception model recommends the inclusion of clusters of variables that correspond to the cognitive tradition (e.g. people's knowledge and understanding about risks), the emotional and experiential tradition (e.g. personal experience), the social-cultural paradigm (e.g. the social amplification of risk, cultural theory, trust, and values), and relevant individual differences (e.g. gender, education, ideology). This "holistic" approach to modelling the determinants of risk perception prevents overreliance on a single paradigm, helps mitigate concerns about the questionable reliability of single-item constructs, and has also been adopted in recent studies of disease outbreaks (e.g. see Prati and Pietrantoni 2016). As such, we measure risk perception with an index covering the cognitive (likelihood), emotional (worry), and temporal-spatial dimensions of risk (see also Leiserowitz 2006; Xie et al. 2019). In short, in the current paper we are the first—to the best of our knowledge—to report an international analysis of COVID-19 holistic risk perception amongst $N = 6,991$ individuals surveyed across 10 different countries between mid-March and mid-April 2020.

Methods

Participants and procedure

We surveyed people in 10 different countries around the world (United Kingdom, United States, Australia, Germany, Spain, Italy, Sweden, Mexico, Japan, and South Korea). These countries were chosen for their cultural and geographic diversity and to represent countries at different stages of the pandemic, with different government policies. Data collection took place between mid-March and mid-April 2020 (Table S21). Participants were recruited through several different platforms/agencies: Prolific (US and UK; prolific.co), Dynata (AU; Dynata.com) and Respondi.com (all other countries). Prolific provided nationally representative quota samples of the US and UK stratified by age, gender, and ethnicity. We employed interlocking age and gender quotas in all other countries to ensure broadly representative samples, with a target of 700 participants per country (exact sample sizes and demographic characteristics for all samples are listed in Table S1 of the supplementary materials). The survey was conducted in a web browser via Qualtrics and took about 20 minutes to complete. Participants were paid £0.80-£2.05 ($1.00-$2.57), varying between countries. Participants completed the surveys in their native local language. Translators were fluent in both English as well as each local language to help ensure appropriate adaptation of the survey items in each country.

Measures. Following Leiserowitz (2006), van der Linden (2015), and Xie et al. (2019), our dependent measure "COVID-19 Risk Perception" was measured as an index, covering affective, cognitive, and temporal-spatial dimensions to provide a holistic measure of risk perception. The index included items capturing participants' perceived seriousness of the COVID-19 pandemic, perceived likelihood of contracting the virus themselves over the next 6 months, perceived likelihood of their family and friends catching the virus, and their present level of worry about the virus (pooled alpha across countries, $\alpha = .72$; alphas per country, αs .60-.82). All risk perception items are detailed in Table 1. For a full list of all items, correlations, and alphas across countries please see Tables S2–S14, supplementary material.

Psychological predictors. Our psychological predictor variables were broadly mapped based on the model by van der Linden (2015), and included measures of cognition, affect/personal experience, and social/cultural norms (Table 1). Specifically, we included items on knowledge, both personal knowledge and social knowledge, direct personal experience with the virus[1] (ranging from 9% to 28% of the sample depending on the country), a measure of social amplification of risk (via friends and family), as well as prosocial values and individualistic worldviews (via the individualism-communitarianism dimension of the cultural cognition scale (Kahan 2012)). We further extended the model of van der Linden (2015) by including measures of trust (trust in government, trust in science, trust in medical professionals), and efficacy (personal and collective), as recommended by van der Linden (2015) and Xie et al. (2019), especially since these were

Table 1. Dependent and independent variables (example items).

Type	Variable name	Example item	Scale
DV	Risk perception	How worried are you personally about the following issues at present? - Coronavirus/COVID-19	7 point Likert scale, 1 = not at all worried, 7 = very worried
		How likely do you think it is that you will be directly and personally affected by the following in the next 6 months? - Catching the coronavirus/COVID-19	7 point Likert scale, 1= not at all likely, 7 = very likely
		How likely do you think it is that your friends and family in the country you are currently living in will be directly affected by the following in the next 6 months? - Catching the coronavirus/COVID-19	7 point Likert scale, 1= not at all likely, 7 = very likely
		How much do you agree or disagree with the following statements? - The coronavirus/COVID-19 will NOT affect very many people in the country I'm currently living in	Reverse coded, 5 point Likert scale, 1 = strongly disagree, 5 = strongly agree
		How much do you agree or disagree with the following statements? - I will probably get sick with the coronavirus/COVID-19	5 point Likert scale, 1 = strongly disagree, 5 = strongly agree
		How much do you agree or disagree with the following statements? - Getting sick with the coronavirus/COVID-19 can be serious	5 point Likert scale, 1 = strongly disagree, 5 = strongly agree
Predictors	Personal knowledge	How much do you feel you understand the government's strategy to deal with the coronavirus/COVID-19 pandemic?	7 point Likert scale, 1 = not at all, 7 = very much
	Social knowledge	To what extent do you think scientists have a good understanding of the coronavirus/COVID-19?	7 point Likert scale, 1 = very limited understanding, 7 = very good understanding
	Direct experience	Have you ever had, or thought you might have, the coronavirus/COVID-19?	binary yes-no coding
	Social amplification	Have you come across information about coronavirus/COVID-19 from: - Friends and family	binary yes-no coding
	Prosociality	To what extent do you think it's important to do things for the benefit of others and society even if they have some costs to you personally?	7 point Likert scale, 1 = not at all, 7 = very much so
	Individualism worldview	The government interferes far too much in our everyday lives.	6 point Likert scale, 1 = strongly disagree, 6 = strongly agree
	Trust in government	How much do you trust the country's politicians to deal effectively with the pandemic?	7 point Likert scale, 1 = not at all, 7 = very much
	Trust in science	How much do you trust each of the following? – Scientists	5 point Likert scale, 1 = cannot be trusted at all, 5 = can be trusted a lot
	Trust in medical professionals	How much do you trust each of the following? - Medical doctors and nurses	5 point Likert scale, 1 = cannot be trusted at all, 5 = can be trusted a lot
	Personal efficacy	To what extent do you feel that the personal actions you are taking to try to limit the spread of coronavirus make a difference?	7 point Likert scale, 1 = not at all, 7 = very much
	Collective efficacy	To what extent do you feel the actions that your country is taking to limit the spread of coronavirus make a difference?	7 point Likert scale, 1 = not at all, 7 = very much
	Political ideology	Where do you feel your political views lie on a spectrum of left wing (or liberal) to right wing (or conservative)?	7 point Likert scale, 1 = very left wing/ liberal, 7 = very right wing/ conservative

deemed important in the context of risk perception of COVID-19 and previous pandemics (de Zwart et al. 2009; Prati and Pietrantoni 2016). Lastly, basic demographic variables known to influence risk perception were also incorporated into the model. These included gender (binary: male, female), age, political ideology (liberal-conservative), and education (ranging from "no formal education above 16" to "PhD"). A full list of items with details on item inter-correlations, reliabilities, and variable distributions across countries are available in the supplementary materials.

Results

We start by plotting mean risk perception scores around the world (Figure 1). Risk perception across the ten sampled countries varied between 4.78 and 5.45 on a 7-point scale, and were thus fairly high across all countries in Europe, Asia, and North America. A one-way analysis of variance on the risk perception index across countries showed a significant difference in risk levels ($F(9, 6904) = 33.12$, $p < 0.001$, $\eta^2 = 0.041$). Tukey HSD pairwise-comparisons revealed several significant differences between countries (please see Supplementary Table S15). Notably, risk perception was highest in the UK ($M = 5.45$, $SD = 0.98$), followed by Spain ($M = 5.19$, $SD = 0.87$, $p < 0.001$). Both countries were significantly higher in risk perception compared to all other countries.

Next, we ran a pooled linear regression model[2] across all countries to provide a 'big picture' overview of the predictors that play a role in COVID-19 risk perception (Table 2). To provide detail on the determinants of risk perception in each country we also ran separate models per country[3]. We investigated the determinants of risk perception in the pooled model first. Within the full predictor model pooled across all countries, our indicators of experience with the virus, social amplification through information received from family and friends, prosociality, individualistic worldviews, personal as well as collective efficacy, all trust variables, as well as personal knowledge, were all significantly associated with risk perception, in addition to a gender effect, such that males perceive less risk compared to females (please refer to Table 2 for regression outputs and statistics).

Specifically, people who have had direct personal experience with the virus perceive more risk compared to those who have not had direct experience ($\beta = 0.39$, [95%CI; 0.34, 0.45]) and people who have received information on the virus from family and friends perceive more risk compared to those who have not ($\beta = 0.24$, [95%CI; 0.18, 0.30]). The more people think that it is important to do things for the benefit of others and society even if they have some costs to them personally, the more risk they perceive ($\beta = 0.12$, [95%CI; 0.10, 0.15]). Conversely, the more individualistic worldviews people hold the less risk they perceive ($\beta = -0.18$, [95%CI; -0.20, -0.15]). Efficacy results show a positive correlation of personal efficacy with risk perception ($\beta = 0.10$, [95%CI; 0.07, 0.13]) but a negative correlation for collective efficacy ($\beta = -0.15$, [95%CI; -0.19, -0.12]). Trust in science ($\beta = 0.08$, [95%CI; 0.05, 0.11]), medical practitioners ($\beta = 0.09$, [95%CI; 0.06, 0.12]) and personal knowledge ($\beta = 0.09$, [95%CI; 0.06, 0.12]) were all positively correlated with risk perception, while trust in government was negatively correlated such that on average, people have lower risk perceptions when they have higher trust in government ($\beta = -0.06$, [95%CI; -0.09, -0.03]). The only significant demographic was gender such that males generally displayed lower risk perceptions than females ($\beta = -0.15$, [95%CI; -0.19, -0.10]). The patterns that emerged in the overall pooled model are also reflected in the per country models. The signs of the reported effects are consistent between the pooled model and all country models in which those predictors play a role, i.e. the way in which the predictors are correlated with risk perception is stable across countries. In addition, although each country shows a unique set of significant predictors, many predictors emerge to have an effect in several countries (for a detailed overview please see Table S18 in the supplementary materials).

Although results from multiple regression models are informative on their own, scholars now frequently recommend to supplement regression analyses with additional indicators of variable

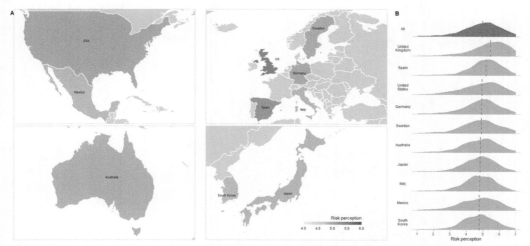

Figure 1. Map of COVID − 19 risk perception around the world (A) with density plots (B). *Note*: The risk perception colour gradient is truncated to better visualize variation on the higher end of the scale (full range 1–7).

importance (Darlington 1968; Tonidandel and LeBreton 2011). Accordingly, to assess the relative contribution of our predictor variables for the pooled and per country models in more detail, we followed Pratt's (1987)[4] variance partitioning method. Figure 2 details the contribution of each variable to the R^2 of our models.

Several of our predictors emerged as important in our pooled and per country models (see Figure 2 for full details). In particular, the extent to which people hold individualistic views explained the most variance in our pooled model (4.78%, 95% CI [3.77, 6.01]) and in five out of the ten countries surveyed (UK, Germany, Sweden, Spain and Japan; full results of all analyses are reported in supplementary Table S17). It also explained a substantial proportion of variance in four of the remaining ten countries. The notable exception was South Korea, where this construct did not appear to be an important predictor (0.18%, [-0.04, 1.65]). Prosociality was the second most important predictor in the pooled model, explaining 3.19% [2.32, 4.18] of the total variance. At the country level, prosociality explained the most variance in the models for Italy, Australia, and Mexico, and was also a comparatively important predictor in our other countries. Again South Korea was an exception; prosociality was of comparatively little importance as a predictor (0.54%, [0.04, 2.42]).

Direct experience with the virus was the third most important predictor in the pooled model (2.34%, [1.73, 3.03]) and emerged as the most important predictor in the US (5.65% [3.02, 8.99]) and comparatively important in most countries surveyed, including South Korea (2.39% [0.78, 4.90]), although it appeared a less important predictor in Australia (0.81% [0.11, 2.28]) and Sweden (0.75%, [-0.02, 2.5]), perhaps due, in part, to the relatively low number of confirmed cases in these countries at the time of the survey. Various trust variables were also important in the pooled model (trust in medical practitioners: 1.73%, [1.02, 2.51]; trust in science: 1.62%, [0.86, 2.51]) and some were also important in South Korea (trust in government: 2.87% [0.77, 5.9]; trust in medical professionals: 2.47% [0.45, 5.59]). However, out of the other countries, trust was only of some importance in the US (trust in medical practitioners: 2.28%, [0.03, 5.28]).

Personal efficacy explained 1.62% of the variance in the pooled model [0.98, 2.42] but appeared to only have substantial importance in Germany (4.13% [1.07, 8.7] and Sweden (7.3% [3.6, 12.14]), and to a lesser extent Spain (1.72%, [0.1, 4.41]) and the US (1.67% [0.26, 4.4]). Collective efficacy was far less important in the pooled model (0.41% [0.02, 1.00]) and indeed only emerged as a comparatively important predictor in Japan (1.98% [0.19, 5.19]), Mexico (2.87% [0.53, 7.42]) and the US (4.33% [1.38, 8.69].

Table 2. Regression outputs and statistics.

Predictors	All std. Beta (standardized CI)	Australia std. Beta (standardized CI)	Germany std. Beta (standardized CI)	Spain std. Beta (standardized CI)	Italy std. Beta (standardized CI)	Japan std. Beta (standardized CI)	South Korea std. Beta (standardized CI)	Mexico std. Beta (standardized CI)	Sweden std. Beta (standardized CI)	United Kingdom std. Beta (standardized CI)	United States std. Beta (standardized CI)
Gender [Male]	-0.15 *** (-0.19 – -0.10)	-0.08 (-0.23 – 0.07)	-0.16 * (-0.29 – -0.02)	-0.28 *** (-0.41 – -0.14)	-0.09 (-0.25 – 0.07)	-0.11 (-0.26 – 0.04)	-0.16 * (-0.30 – -0.02)	-0.18 * (-0.34 – -0.03)	-0.11 (-0.25 – 0.04)	-0.18 * (-0.32 – -0.04)	-0.05 (-0.19 – 0.08)
Age	-0.01 (-0.04 – 0.01)	0.00 (-0.08 – 0.08)	-0.08 * (-0.16 – -0.01)	0.06 (-0.12 – 0.01)	-0.12 ** (-0.20 – -0.04)	-0.12 ** (-0.20 – -0.05)	0.02 (-0.05 – 0.09)	-0.01 (-0.09 – 0.06)	0.06 (-0.01 – 0.13)	-0.02 (-0.09 – 0.06)	0.03 (-0.04 – 0.09)
Education	-0.01 (-0.04 – 0.01)	-0.03 (-0.11 – 0.05)	-0.02 (-0.09 – 0.05)	0.04 (-0.03 – 0.11)	0.06 (-0.02 – 0.14)	-0.05 (-0.13 – 0.02)	-0.03 (-0.10 – 0.05)	0.01 (-0.06 – 0.09)	-0.06 (-0.13 – 0.01)	-0.05 (-0.12 – 0.02)	0.00 (-0.07 – 0.07)
Political ideology (liberal-conservative)	0.01 (-0.01 – 0.03)	-0.05 (-0.13 – 0.02)	0.02 (-0.05 – 0.09)	0.01 (-0.06 – 0.08)	0.07 (-0.01 – 0.15)	0.01 (-0.07 – 0.09)	0.11 ** (0.03 – 0.19)	0.07 (-0.01 – 0.14)	0.02 (-0.05 – 0.09)	-0.05 (-0.12 – 0.03)	-0.08 (-0.16 – -0.01)
Personal knowledge	0.09 *** (0.06 – 0.12)	0.16 ** (0.06 – 0.26)	0.07 (-0.02 – 0.16)	0.21 *** (0.12 – 0.30)	0.04 (-0.07 – 0.15)	0.10 * (0.02 – 0.19)	0.14 ** (0.03 – 0.25)	0.03 (-0.07 – 0.14)	0.06 (-0.04 – 0.16)	0.06 (-0.03 – 0.14)	0.07 (-0.01 – 0.15)
Social knowledge	-0.01 (-0.03 – 0.02)	-0.05 (-0.14 – 0.03)	-0.08 (-0.16 – 0.00)	0.02 (-0.05 – 0.09)	-0.04 (-0.12 – 0.04)	0.02 (-0.07 – 0.11)	0.05 (-0.03 – 0.13)	0.06 (-0.02 – 0.14)	-0.03 (-0.12 – 0.05)	-0.05 (-0.12 – 0.03)	-0.05 (-0.12 – 0.02)
Direct experience	0.39 *** (0.34 – 0.45)	0.32 * (0.06 – 0.58)	0.38 *** (0.21 – 0.55)	0.48 *** (0.33 – 0.63)	0.45 *** (0.27 – 0.63)	0.36 *** (0.19 – 0.53)	0.40 *** (0.22 – 0.59)	0.37 *** (0.15 – 0.58)	0.23 ** (0.07 – 0.40)	0.37 *** (0.19 – 0.55)	0.61 *** (0.42 – 0.80)
Social amplification [Yes]	0.24 ** (0.18 – 0.30)	0.35 *** (0.17 – 0.53)	0.26 * (0.04 – 0.49)	0.39 *** (0.15 – 0.63)	0.00 (-0.17 – 0.18)	0.23 * (0.05 – 0.41)	0.16 (-0.05 – 0.36)	0.17 (-0.10 – 0.44)	0.30 ** (0.12 – 0.48)	0.26 * (0.00 – 0.17)	0.08 (-0.14 – 0.30)
Prosociality [Yes]	0.12 *** (0.10 – 0.15)	0.15 *** (0.06 – 0.23)	0.11 ** (0.04 – 0.19)	0.12 ** (0.04 – 0.20)	0.23 *** (0.14 – 0.32)	0.12 ** (0.03 – 0.20)	0.06 (-0.01 – 0.14)	0.17 *** (0.09 – 0.25)	0.10 ** (0.03 – 0.18)	0.17 *** (0.10 – 0.25)	0.10 ** (0.02 – 0.18)
Individualism worldview	-0.18 *** (-0.20 – -0.15)	-0.14 *** (-0.22 – -0.06)	-0.29 *** (-0.37 – -0.21)	-0.19 *** (-0.27 – -0.11)	-0.17 *** (-0.27 – -0.07)	-0.15 *** (-0.23 – -0.07)	-0.04 (-0.11 – 0.04)	-0.11 ** (-0.19 – -0.03)	-0.23 *** (-0.31 – -0.16)	-0.21 *** (-0.29 – -0.13)	-0.15 *** (-0.23 – -0.07)
Trust in government	-0.06 *** (-0.09 – -0.03)	0.00 (-0.11 – 0.10)	-0.03 (-0.13 – 0.07)	-0.21 *** (-0.31 – -0.12)	0.01 (-0.09 – 0.12)	-0.07 (-0.18 – 0.04)	-0.21 *** (-0.30 – -0.12)	-0.01 (-0.12 – 0.10)	-0.07 (-0.18 – 0.04)	-0.04 (-0.14 – 0.06)	0.00 (-0.09 – 0.09)
Trust in science	0.08 *** (0.05 – 0.11)	0.08 (-0.01 – 0.17)	0.03 (-0.06 – 0.12)	0.09 (-0.00 – 0.18)	0.01 (-0.10 – 0.11)	0.05 (-0.04 – 0.15)	0.06 (-0.04 – 0.15)	0.07 (-0.02 – 0.17)	0.04 (-0.05 – 0.13)	0.08 (-0.00 – 0.17)	0.09 (-0.01 – 0.18)
Trust in medical professionals	0.09 *** (0.06 – 0.12)	-0.01 (-0.10 – 0.08)	0.05 (-0.03 – 0.14)	0.04 (-0.04 – 0.13)	0.08 (-0.02 – 0.18)	0.09 (-0.00 – 0.18)	0.12 ** (0.03 – 0.21)	0.07 (-0.02 – 0.16)	0.05 (-0.04 – 0.14)	0.08 (-0.00 – 0.17)	0.10 * (0.01 – 0.19)
Personal efficacy	0.10 *** (0.07 – 0.13)	0.08 (-0.02 – 0.17)	0.16 *** (0.07 – 0.25)	0.10 * (0.01 – 0.18)	0.03 (-0.08 – 0.14)	-0.02 (-0.11 – 0.07)	0.09 (-0.01 – 0.19)	0.07 (-0.01 – 0.16)	0.24 *** (0.15 – 0.32)	0.04 (-0.04 – 0.11)	0.12 ** (0.04 – 0.19)
Collective efficacy	-0.15 *** (-0.19 – -0.12)	-0.07 (-0.19 – 0.05)	-0.04 (-0.15 – 0.06)	-0.13 * (-0.23 – -0.02)	-0.03 (-0.16 – 0.09)	-0.15 ** (-0.26 – -0.04)	-0.1 (-0.22 – 0.01)	-0.20 ** (-0.32 – -0.08)	-0.08 (-0.20 – 0.04)	-0.11 * (-0.21 – -0.01)	-0.20 *** (-0.30 – -0.10)
Observations (N)	6482	646	656	669	531	617	690	621	656	699	697
R² / R² adjusted	0.181 / 0.179	0.166 / 0.146	0.233 / 0.215	0.262 / 0.245	0.199 / 0.176	0.154 / 0.132	0.157 / 0.139	0.166 / 0.145	0.240 / 0.222	0.198 / 0.181	0.263 / 0.247

Note: * $p < 0.05$ ** $p < 0.01$ *** $p < 0.001$

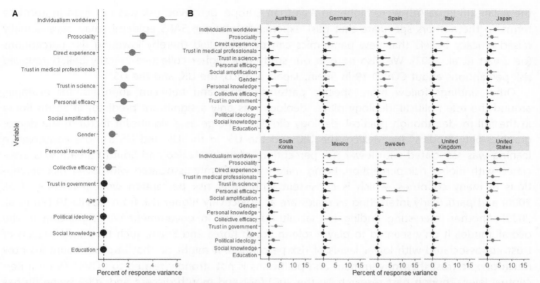

Figure 2. Relative importance of individual predictors for the pooled and per country models with 1,000 bootstrapped 95% confidence intervals. Red dots denote confidence intervals that do not include zero. *Note*: The figure visualizes the percent that each variable contributes out of the total variance explained in each model (R^2).

Social amplification explained 1.21% [0.75, 1.80] of the variance in the pooled model and showed some predictive importance in six of our ten countries (Australia, Germany, Spain, Sweden, Japan, UK). While, in the pooled model, gender (0.7% [0.39, 1.11]) and personal knowledge (0.6% [0.24, 1.07]) displayed some predictive importance, they were only relevant as predictors in a few countries (gender: Germany, Spain and the UK; personal knowledge: Australia and Spain).

Discussion

In this paper, we set out to map and model risk perception of COVID-19 in ten countries around the world. Across all of our national surveys, we find that risk perception of COVID-19 is uniformly high. Several psychological factors emerged as significant predictors across countries. Consistent with the literature in the domain of environmental risk (e.g. see Leiserowitz 2006; van der Linden 2015; Xie et al. 2019), experiential and socio-cultural factors explained most of the variance in our risk perception models across all countries in comparison to cognition (knowledge) and socio-demographic characteristics. Several specific predictors proved important, including the role of prosocial versus individualistic values and to a lesser extent our measure of social amplification (hearing about the virus from friends and family). Most notably, experience with the virus stands out across all countries, such that people who have had personal and direct experience perceive significantly higher risk.

These findings are generally consistent with the literature on "risk as analysis vs risk as feelings", where having had visceral contact with the virus strongly engages the affective experiential system which is known to be more dominant in the processing of risk under these conditions (Loewenstein et al. 2001; Leiserowitz, 2006; Slovic et al. 2004; van der Linden 2014, 2015; Weber 2006). Although not directly evaluated here, it could also be the case that experience with the virus helps to construe the situation as more concrete and closer to the self and thus heightens risk perceptions through construal level (Trope and Liberman 2010).

Interestingly, although comparative risk perception research on pandemics remains scant (de Zwart et al. 2009; Leppin and Aro 2009), existing research finds that whilst risk perceptions of the Asian influenza (AI) were higher in Asia than Europe, perceived risk was not high in absolute terms so the authors speculate that past experience with the SARS epidemic may have actually raised efficacy beliefs that new pandemics can be controlled thereby lowering risk perceptions (de Zwart et al. 2007). We also note in our study that higher collective efficacy beliefs reduced risk perceptions about COVID-19 in Spain, Japan, Mexico, the UK, and the US.

Other findings follow more specific patterns within and between countries, for example, around the role political ideology plays. Ideology was only a significant predictor in South Korea in the full model, though political ideology did also emerge as a significant factor in the demographics-only models[5] for Mexico, the UK, and the US. In the UK and US a more conservative leaning was associated with lower risk perception, while in Mexico and South Korea it was associated with higher risk perception. Being male was uniformly associated with lower risk perceptions in many countries, which is consistent with other risk perception work (Finucane et al. 2000) and particularly interesting as males are at objectively higher risk from COVID-19 (Jin et al. 2020). Another interesting finding is that although trust in government was significant in the overall model, it only seemed to play a role in South Korea and Spain, such that higher levels of trust are associated with lower levels of risk perception. It might be that in other countries how much people trust their government and politicians is not strongly related to COVID-19 on a perceptual level. Though past research on the 2001 foot and mouth disease and 2009 swine flu has shown that perceptions of government handling were related to trust judgments (Poortinga et al. 2004; van der Weerd et al. 2011) and failed risk management has generally contributed to declining trust in regulators (Löfstedt 2005; Slovic 1993). Importantly, recent research finds that being transparent about scientific uncertainty does not necessarily undermine public trust in facts or the communicator (van Der Bles et al. 2020). Nonetheless, it may be that compared to trust in government and scientific understanding, other factors play a more salient role.

Lastly, consistent with the literature on the important role of risk perception in motivating health protection behaviors (Floyd, Prentice-Dunn, and Rogers 2000), especially during pandemics (Bish and Michie 2010; Rudisill 2013; van der Weerd et al. 2011; Wise et al. 2020), we find that risk perception correlated positively and significantly with an index of preventative health behaviors (Tables S19-S20) such as washing hands, wearing a face mask, and physical distancing (r_{pooled} = 0.28, and $r = 0.24$ to $r = 0.39$ per country, $p < 0.001$). At the same time, it is important to note that both downplayed and exaggerated perceptions of risk can potentially undermine the adoption of protective health behaviors (Leppin and Aro 2009). Causality can also run both ways so that higher risk perceptions lead to more protective behaviors but that taking effective action can, in turn, also reduce risk perceptions (Brewer et al. 2004). We therefore stress the importance of evaluating accuracy in public risk perceptions.

Of course, this research is not without limitations. It is important to note that although our samples were balanced on national quotas, they were not probability samples and therefore are not truly representative of the population in each country. In addition, some constructs, such as the individualism-collectivism dimension of the cultural cognition scale (Kahan 2012) proved less reliable in the Asian cultural context, consistent with other recent research (Xue et al. 2016) and the explained variance of the regressions (up to 26%) suggests that a significant portion of variation in risk perceptions of COVID-19 remains yet to be explained. Although we covered several major dimensions of risk perception research, our measures were imperfect, for example, we did not assess objective knowledge of COVID-19 nor include multi-item measures of social norms and values or affective evaluations about COVID-19. Thus, future research is well-advised to consider expanding upon our research.

Conclusion

Policy-makers often conceptualize risk as the probability of catching a disease multiplied by the magnitude of the consequences. Yet, our findings—which present the first comparative evidence of how people perceive the risk of COVID-19 around the world—clearly illustrate that risk perceptions of COVID-19 consistently correlate strongly with a number of experiential and socio-cultural factors across countries. At the same time, we also note the need to attend to cross-cultural variation in risk perception. In fact, our holistic approach to understanding the nature of risk perception is consistent with research that has identified important "sociocultural vectors" for effective risk communication (Wardman 2014), which involves much more than just "getting the numbers right" (Fischhoff 1995). The idea that risk is socially negotiated based on people's experiences, values, and trust in institutions (Rickard 2019) is reinforced here. More specifically, across multiple countries and analyses, we show that people's perception of the risk is higher in those with direct personal experience of the virus, and in those who hold more prosocial world-views. The act of making sacrifices for the greater benefit of society is relevant to risk communication as it reveals the social nature of risk. As Fischhoff (1995) notes, "effective risk communication can fulfil part of the social contract between those who create risks and those who bear them" (p. 144). In fact, appealing to altruistic and prosocial motives can be an important aspect of solving social dilemmas during pandemics (Van Bavel et al. 2020). Relatedly, those who receive information about the virus from friends and family, those who think that their government's action is not being effective, and those who say that they believe it's important for governments to intervene and take collective action all perceive a higher risk. Health risk communication messages therefore tend to be most effective when they include information about the effectiveness of measures designed to protect people from the disease at both a personal and societal level (Leppin and Aro 2009; Bish and Michie 2010; Witte, Meyer, and Martell 2001). Thus, although the current evidence is only observational and could benefit from experimental testing, what does seem clear is that a better understanding of not only the knowledge that people have, but also the experiential, social, and cultural factors that drive COVID-19 risk perceptions around the world (and their role in motivating preventative health behaviors) could help policy-makers design evidenced-based risk communication strategies, and that insights from different countries around the world could be of relevance and use in designing those.

Notes

1. Participants who reported they had tested positive for the virus, or suspected that they were infected were coded as having direct experience with the COVID-19 virus. Suspected infections were included here as many countries do not undertake tests for low risk cases.
2. We checked for multi-collinearity between variables, as well as for homogeneity of variance, normal distribution of residuals, and the presence of influential outliers for all our models. Please see Figure S1 and the section "Model Diagnostics" in the supplement for more details. We tested the robustness of our pooled and individual country regressions by running all models using robust standard errors. Results were consistent with the OLS regressions reported here.
3. We also tested the appropriateness of a multi-level model (MLM) by including country as a random intercept (as the pooled model can mask significant between-country heterogeneity). However, the resulting ICC was near zero (0.04) indicating that most variability lied within groups (Gelman and Hill 2007). Furthermore, multi-level models can be unreliable when n is large for individuals in comparison to the second-level predictor (country). Specifically, Bryan and Jenkins (2016) recommend at least $n = 25$ for linear models. We therefore proceed with separate OLS regressions and discuss between-country differences qualitatively with caution.
4. The relative importance of an independent variable is defined as the product of its bivariate correlation with the dependent variable and its standardised coefficient in the multiple regression, with the sum of each variable's contribution equalling the R^2 of the overall model (see Pratt 1987; van der Linden 2015).
5. Please refer to Table S16 in the supplement for details on the demographic models.

Acknowledgments

This study was funded by the Winton Centre for Risk and Evidence Communication which is supported by the David and Claudia Harding Foundation. We would like to thank María del Carmen Climént Palmer, Ullrika Sahlin, Ban Mutsuhisa, Jin Park, and Giulia Luoni for translations and the University of Tokyo for their collaboration. We also thank Eric Kennedy at the University of York, Canada for sharing their questionnaire from which some of our risk perception measures were taken as well as all the participants and those who helped to administer the study.

Disclosure statement

No potential conflict of interest was reported by the author(s).

ORCID

Sarah Dryhurst ⓘ http://orcid.org/0000-0002-7772-8492
Claudia R. Schneider ⓘ http://orcid.org/0000-0002-6612-5186
John Kerr ⓘ http://orcid.org/0000-0002-6606-5507
Alexandra L. J. Freeman ⓘ http://orcid.org/0000-0002-4115-161X
Gabriel Recchia ⓘ http://orcid.org/0000-0002-0210-8635
Anne Marthe van der Bles ⓘ http://orcid.org/0000-0002-7953-9425
Sander van der Linden ⓘ http://orcid.org/0000-0002-0269-1744

Data availability statement

All data are publicly available on the Open Science Framework (OSF) website: https://osf.io/jnu74

References

Bish, A., and S. Michie. 2010. "Demographic and Attitudinal Determinants of Protective Behaviours during a Pandemic: A Review." *British Journal of Health Psychology* 15 (4): 797–824. doi:10.1348/135910710X485826.
Brewer, N. T., N. D. Weinstein, C. L. Cuite, and J. E. Herrington. 2004. "Risk Perceptions and Their Relation to Risk Behavior." *Annals of Behavioral Medicine* 27 (2): 125–130. doi:10.1207/s15324796abm2702_7.
Bryan, M. L., and S. P. Jenkins. 2016. "Multilevel Modelling of Country Effects: A Cautionary Tale." *European Sociological Review* 32 (1): 3–22. doi:10.1093/esr/jcv059.
Caramelo, F., N. Ferreira, and B. Oliveios. 2020. "Estimation of Risk Factors for COVID-19 Mortality – Preliminary Results." *MedRxiv*
Darlington, R. B. 1968. "Multiple Regression in Psychological Research and Practice." *Psychological Bulletin* 69 (3): 161–182. doi:10.1037/h0025471.
de Zwart, Onno, Irene K. Veldhuijzen, Gillian Elam, Arja R. Aro, Thomas Abraham, George D. Bishop, Jan Hendrik Richardus, and Johannes Brug. 2007. "Avian Influenza Risk Perception, Europe and Asia." *Emerging Infectious Diseases* 13 (2): 290–293. doi:10.3201/eid1302.060303.
de Zwart, Onno, Irene K. Veldhuijzen, Gillian Elam, Arja R. Aro, Thomas Abraham, George D. Bishop, Hélène A. C. M. Voeten, Jan Hendrik Richardus, and Johannes Brug. 2009. "Perceived Threat, Risk Perception, and Efficacy Beliefs Related to SARS and Other (Emerging) Infectious Diseases: Results of an International Survey." *International Journal of Behavioral Medicine* 16 (1): 30–40. doi:10.1007/s12529-008-9008-2.
Douglas, M., and A. Wildavsky. 1983. *Risk and Culture: An Essay on the Selection of Technological and Environmental Dangers*. California, United States: University of California Press.
Epstein, J. M., J. Parker, D. Cummings, and R. A. Hammond. 2008. "Coupled Contagion Dynamics of Fear and Disease: Mathematical and Computational Explorations." *PLoS One.* 3 (12): e3955. doi:10.1371/journal.pone.0003955.
European Centre for Disease Control COVID-19 Situation Update. (n.d.). Retrieved April 15, 2020, from https://www.ecdc.europa.eu/en/geographical-distribution-2019-ncov-cases
Finucane, M. L., P. Slovic, C. K. Mertz, J. Flynn, and T. A. Satterfield. 2000. "Gender, Race, and Perceived Risk: The 'White Male' Effect." *Health, Risk & Society* 2 (2): 159–172. doi:10.1080/713670162.
Fischhoff, Baruch, Gabrielle.Wong-Parodi, Dana Rose.Garfin, E. Alison.Holman, and Roxane Cohen.Silver. 2018. "Public Understanding of Ebola Risks: Mastering an Unfamiliar Threat." *Risk Analysis* 38 (1): 71–83. doi:10.1111/risa.12794.
Fischhoff, B. 1995. "Risk Perception and Communication Unplugged: twenty Years of Process." *Risk Analysis* 15 (2): 137–145. doi:10.1111/j.1539-6924.1995.tb00308.x.
Floyd, D. L., S. Prentice-Dunn, and R. W. Rogers. 2000. "A Meta-Analysis of Research on Protection Motivation Theory." *Journal of Applied Social Psychology* 30 (2): 407–429. doi:10.1111/j.1559-1816.2000.tb02323.x.

Funk, S., E. Gilad, C. Watkins, and V. A. A. Jansen. 2009. "The Spread of Awareness and Its Impact on Epidemic Outbreaks." *Proceedings of the National Academy of Sciences of Sciences* 106 (16): 6872–6877. doi:10.1073/pnas.0810762106.

Garg, S., L. Kim, and M. Whitaker. 2020. Hospitalization Rates and Characteristics of Patients Hospitalized with Laboratory-Confirmed Coronavirus Disease 2019 — COVID-NET, 14 States, March 1–30, 2020. *MMWR Morb Mortal Wkly Rep*, 8 April. 10.15585/mmwr.mm6915e3

Gelman, A., and J. Hill. 2007. *Data Analysis Using Regression and Multi Level Hierarchical Models* (Vol. 1). New York City, NY: Cambridge University Press.

Ghebreyesus, T. A. (2020). WHO Director-General's opening remarks at the media briefing on COVID-19 - 11 March 2020, New York, USA.

Jin, J.-M., P. Bai, W. He, F. Wu, X.-F. Liu, D.-M. Han, … J.-K. Yang. 2020. "Gender Differences in Patients with COVID-19: Focus on Severity and Mortality." *MedRxiv*. 10.1101/2020.02.23.20026864.

Joffe, H. 2003. "Risk: From Perception to Social Representation." *British Journal of Social Psychology* 42 (1): 55–73. doi:10.1348/014466603763276126.

Kahan, D. M. 2012. "Cultural Cognition as a Conception of the Cultural Theory of Risk." In. *Handbook of Risk Theory: Epistemology, Decision Theory, Ethics, and Social Implications of Risk*, 725–759. 10.1007/978-94-007-1433-5_28.

Kasperson, Roger E., Ortwin Renn, Paul Slovic, Halina S. Brown, Jacque Emel, Robert Goble, Jeanne X. Kasperson, and Samuel Ratick. 1988. "The Social Amplification of Risk: A Conceptual Framework." *Risk Analysis* 8 (2): 177–187. doi:10.1111/j.1539-6924.1988.tb01168.x.

Leiserowitz, A. 2006. "Climate Change Risk Perception and Policy Preferences: The Role of Affect, Imagery, and Values." *Climatic Change* 77 (1-2): 45–72. doi:10.1007/s10584-006-9059-9.

Leppin, A., and A. R. Aro. 2009. "Risk Perceptions Related to SARS and Avian Influenza: Theoretical Foundations of Current Empirical Research." *International Journal of Behavioral Medicine* 16 (1): 7–29. doi:10.1007/s12529-008-9002-8.

Loewenstein, G., E. Weber, C. Hsee, and N. Welch. 2001. "Risk as Feelings." *Psychological Bulletin* 127 (2): 267–286. doi:10.1037/0033-2909.127.2.267.

Löfstedt, R. E. 2005. *Risk Management in Post-Trust Societies*. London: Palgrave Macmillan UK. 10.1057/9780230503946.

Poletti, P.,. M. Ajelli, and S. Merler. 2011. "The Effect of Risk Perception on the 2009 H1N1 Pandemic Influenza Dynamics." *PLoS One*. 6 (2): e16460. doi:10.1371/journal.pone.0016460.

Poortinga, W., K. Bickerstaff, I. Langford, J. Niewöhner, and N. Pidgeon. 2004. "The British 2001 Foot and Mouth Crisis: A Comparative Study of Public Risk Perceptions, Trust and Beliefs about Government Policy in Two Communities." *Journal of Risk Research* 7 (1): 73–90. doi:10.1080/1366987042000151205.

Prati, G., and L. Pietrantoni. 2016. "Knowledge, Risk Perceptions, and Xenophobic Attitudes: Evidence from Italy during the Ebola Outbreak." *Risk Analysis* 36 (10): 2000–2010. doi:10.1111/risa.12537.

Prati, G., L. Pietrantoni, and B. Zani. 2011. "A Social-Cognitive Model of Pandemic Influenza H1N1 Risk Perception and Recommended Behaviors in Italy." *Risk Analysis* 31 (4): 645–656. doi:10.1111/j.1539-6924.2010.01529.x.

Pratt, J. W. 1987. "Dividing the Indivisible: Using Simple Symmetry to Partition Variance Explained." *Proceedings of the Second International Tampere Conference in Statistics* 245–260. Tampere, Finland: University of Tampere.

Reluga, T. C. 2010. "Game Theory of Social Distancing in Response to an Epidemic." *PLoS Computational Biology* 6 (5): e1000793–9. doi:10.1371/journal.pcbi.1000793.

Rickard, L. N. 2019. "Pragmatic and (or) Constitutive? on the Foundations of Contemporary Risk Communication Research." *Risk Analysis (Analysis)* doi:10.1111/risa.13415.

Rimmer A. Covid-19: Disproportionate impact on ethnic minority healthcare workers will be explored by government. BMJ 2020;369:m1562. 10.1136/bmj.m156232303494

Rogers, R. D. 1975. "A Protection Motivation Theory of Fear Appeals and Attitude Change." *The Journal of Psychology* 91 (1): 93–114. doi:10.1080/00223980.1975.9915803.

Rubin, G. J., R. Amlôt, L. Page, and S. Wessely. 2009. "Public Perceptions, Anxiety, and Behaviour Change in Relation to the Swine Flu Outbreak: Cross Sectional Telephone Survey." *Bmj (Bmj* 339 (3): b2651–b2651. doi:10.1136/bmj.b2651.

Rudisill, C. 2013. "How Do we Handle New Health Risks? Risk Perception, Optimism, and Behaviors regarding the H1N1 Virus." *Journal of Risk Research* 16 (8): 959–980. doi:10.1080/13669877.2012.761271.

Sjöberg, L. 2002. "Are Received Risk Perception Models Alive and Well?." *Risk Analysis* 22 (4): 665–669. doi:10.1111/0272-4332.00058.

Slovic, P. 1992. "Perception of Risk: Reflections on the Psychometric Paradigm." In *Theories of Risk*, edited by D. Goldingand and S. Krimsky. New York: Praeger.

Slovic, P. 1993. "Perceived Risk, Trust, and Democracy." *Risk Analysis* 13 (6): 675–682. doi:10.1111/j.1539-6924.1993.tb01329.x.

Slovic, P. 2010. *The Feeling of Risk: New Perspectives on Risk Perception*. New York: Routledge.

Slovic, Paul, M. L. Finucane, E. Peters, and D. G. MacGregor. 2004. "Risk as Analysis and Risk as Feelings: Some Thoughts about Affect, Reason, Risk, and Rationality." *Risk Analysis* 24 (2): 311–322. doi:10.1111/j.0272-4332.2004.00433.x.

Slovic, Paul, B. Fischhoff, and S. Lichtenstein. 1982. "Why Study Risk Perception?". *Risk Analysis* 2 (2): 83–93. doi:10.1111/j.1539-6924.1982.tb01369.x.

Tonidandel, S., and J. M. LeBreton. 2011. "Relative Importance Analysis: A Useful Supplement to Regression Analysis." *Journal of Business and Psychology* 26 (1): 1–9. doi:10.1007/s10869-010-9204-3.

Trope, Y., and N. Liberman. 2010. "Construal Theory." *Psychological Review* 117 (2): 440–463. https://doi.org/10.1037/a0018963.Construal-Level. doi:10.1037/a0018963.

Van Bavel, J. J., P. Boggio, V. Capraro, A. Cichocka, M. Cikara, M. Crockett, … N. Ellemers. 2020. "Using Social and Behavioural Science to Support COVID-19 Pandemic Response." *Nature Human Behaviour*

Van Der Bles, A. M., S. van der Linden, A. L. Freeman, and D. J. Spiegelhalter. 2020. "The Effects of Communicating Uncertainty on Public Trust in Facts and Numbers." *Proceedings of the National Academy of Sciences* 117 (14): 7672–7683. doi:10.1073/pnas.1913678117.

van der Linden, S. 2014. "On the Relationship between Personal Experience, Affect and Risk Perception: The Case of Climate Change." *European Journal of Social Psychology* 44 (5): 430–440. doi:10.1002/ejsp.2008.

van der Linden, S. 2015. "The Social-Psychological Determinants of Climate Change Risk Perceptions: Towards a Comprehensive Model." *Journal of Environmental Psychology* 41: 112–124. doi:10.1016/j.jenvp.2014.11.012.

van der Linden, S. 2017. "Determinants and Measurement of Climate Change Risk Perception, Worry, and Concern." In *Oxford Research Encyclopedia of Climate Science*, edited by M. Nisbet, 1-49. Oxford, UK: Oxford University Press. 10.1093/acrefore/9780190228620.013.318.

van der Weerd, W.,. D. R. Timmermans, D. J. Beaujean, J. Oudhoff, and J. E. van Steenbergen. 2011. "Monitoring the Level of Government Trust, Risk Perception and Intention of the General Public to Adopt Protective Measures during the Influenza A (H1N1) Pandemic in The Netherlands." *BMC Public Health* 11 (1): 575. doi:10.1186/1471-2458-11-575.

Wåhlberg, A. E. 2001. "The Theoretical Features of Some Current Approaches to Risk Perception." *Journal of Risk Research* 4 (3): 237–250. 10.1080/13669870152023791.

Wardman, J. K. 2014. "Sociocultural Vectors of Effective Risk Communication." *Journal of Risk Research* 17 (10): 1251–1257. doi:10.1080/13669877.2014.942498.

Weber, E. U. 2006. "Experience-Based and Description-Based Perceptions of Long-Term Risk: Why Global Warming Does Not Scare us (yet)." *Climatic Change* 77 (1/2): 103–120. doi:10.1007/s10584-006-9060-3.

Wildavsky, A., and K. Dake. 1990. "Theories of Risk Perception: Who Fears What and Why?." *Daedalus* 119 (4): 41–60.

Wise, T., T. D. Zbozinek, G. Michelini, and C. C. Hagan. 2020. "Changes in Risk Perception and Protective Behavior During the First Week of the COVID-19 Pandemic in the United States."

Witte, K., G. Meyer, and D. Martell. 2001. *Effective Health Risk Messages: A Step-by-Step Guide*. Thousand Oaks, CA: Sage.

Xie, B., M. B. Brewer, B. K. Hayes, R. I. McDonald, and B. R. Newell. 2019. "Predicting Climate Change Risk Perception and Willingness to Act." *Journal of Environmental Psychology* 65: 101331. doi:10.1016/j.jenvp.2019.101331.

Xue, W., D. W. Hine, A. D. G. Marks, W. J. Phillips, and S. Zhao. 2016. "Cultural Worldviews and Climate Change: A View from China." *Asian Journal of Social Psychology* 19 (2): 134–144. doi:10.1111/ajsp.12116.

Yang, J. Z., and H. Chu. 2018. "Who is Afraid of the Ebola Outbreak? the Influence of Discrete Emotions on Risk Perception." *Journal of Risk Research* 21 (7): 834–853. doi:10.1080/13669877.2016.1247378.

Mismanagement of Covid-19: lessons learned from Italy

Maria Laura Ruiu

ABSTRACT

Maria Laura Ruiu is lecturer at Northumbria University (Newcastle upon Tyne). She has recently completed her second PhD in Social Sciences (Northumbria University). She also acted as post-doctoral researcher at the Desertification Research Centre (University of Sassari, Italy) investigating the adaptive capacity of some communities to climate change impact. This paper analyses the first phases of the Covid-19 (Coronavirus) outbreak management in Italy by exploring the combination of political, scientific, media and public responses. A lack of coordination between political and scientific levels, and between institutional claim-makers and the media, suggests a mismanagement of the crisis during the first phases of the outbreak. The outbreak management suffered from the five communication weaknesses identified by Reynolds, related to i) mixed messages from multiple messengers; ii) delay in releasing information; iii) paternalistic attitudes; iv) lack of immediate reaction to rumours; and v) political confusion. This supports that the communication of uncertainty around an unknown threat should be accompanied by both political and scientific cohesion. However, both political and scientific dysfunctions caused the failure of several government efforts to contain the outbreak. This paper contributes towards informing policymakers on some lessons learned from the management of the Covid-19 in one of the most affected countries in the world. The Italian case study offers the opportunity for other countries to improve the management of the outbreak by limiting the spread of both chaos and panic.

Introduction

This paper reflects on crisis management practices by exploring the combined effort of political, media and scientific responses to the Covid-19 outbreak in Italy. On 31 December 2019, the Chinese authorities reported a cluster of pneumonia cases of unknown aetiology in Wuhan (Hubei Province, China) (Corman et al. 2020) and on 7 January 2020 a novel Covid-19 was identified (WHO 2020a). In one month, the outbreak was declared a Global Public Health Emergency by the World Health Organisation (WHO) and classified as a pandemic on the 11th of March (WHO 2020c). Since the Covid-19 was a novel pathogen, high degrees of uncertainty characterised scientific results, particularly during the earliest phases. For example, on the 23rd of January, scientists classified the infection as "more than just a cold" given its association with both severe acute respiratory syndrome (SARS) and Middle East respiratory syndrome (MERS) (Paules, Marston, and Fauci 2020). However, the trajectories of the outbreak were classified as impossible to predict, but effective countermeasures and prompt actions were encouraged to contain the spread of the infection (Li et al. 2020). The WHO (2020b) announced the global imperative for the scientific community to broadly share scientific advances and create collaborations to effectively and rapidly inform decisionmakers (Public Health Emergency of International Concern [PHEIC] 2020). This paper investigates the Italian case study, which soon became one of the most affected country in the world. Given that both containment measures and transparency of information are essential to control the spread of the virus, this paper investigates the effects of some emergency response strategies adopted in Italy. This is important in a risk-management perspective due to a potential spread of panic and stigmatisation of people affected (or suspected to be) by the disease (Weiss and Ramakrishna 2006). The Italian case study offers the opportunity to other countries to identify some missteps in managing the same and future crises.

The first section reviews the literature related to crisis management. The second section reports the methods adopted to identify the main events and the actors involved in the communication process. The third section and its related sub-sections describe the responses of the Italian government, the scientific community, the media and other political actors. Finally, these results will help identify the elements that undermined the success of the government response during the preliminary phases of the outbreak.

Literature review

The literature recognises a fundamental value played by the interrelationships between the media, authorities and public perception in crisis/disaster management (Schultz, Utz, and Goritz 2011). Communication strategies are an essential component of disaster planning, response, and recovery (Houston et al. 2015). Four main forces might affect the communication of a crisis related to its perception, process and metabolization of information, tendency to put greater attention on losses than gains, and trust-building processes (Covello et al. 2001; Glik 2007). These processes are interconnected and can determine the success of a crisis response operation. In fact, the literature highlights that crisis-communication (Seeger, Sellnow, and Ulmer 1998, 2001) must be "timely, accurate, direct, and [...] give people hope" (Glik 2007). Therefore, a crisis/disaster communication deals with an emergency (Seeger, Sellnow, and Ulmer 1998) and involves huge and scared audiences (Sandam 2003). Specifically, a disaster can be defined as a time-delimited collective experience that is potentially traumatic (McFarlane and Norris 2006). This means that when an unexpected health crisis occurs, governments, scientists and the media deal with uncertainty (Lofstedt 2006), public fear, and rely upon reciprocal support/coordination (Reynolds and Seeger 2005). Previous case studies, such as e.g. anthrax risk in 2001 (Robinson and Newstetter 2003), spread of West Nile Virus (see e.g. Covello et al. 2001), SARS outbreak in 2003 (Brug et al. 2004; Washer 2004) and H1N1 in 2009 (Durodié 2011; Klemm, Das, and Hartmann 2016) gave the opportunity to define effective crisis communication standards (Glik 2007). For example, the severe acute respiratory syndrome (SARS) in 2003 affected 26 countries and resulted in more than 8000 cases and 774 deaths with a fatality rate of 9.6% (WHO 2003). Soon after the SARS crisis, between 2003 and 2015, the H5N1 virus affected 826 individuals and caused 440 fatalities (WHO 2015). In 2009, the H1N1 influenza mainly affected young people with high mortality rates and, for the first time, a global effort was initiated by implementing the plans designed after the SARS outbreak and H5N1 flu (Keil, Schönhöfer, and Spelsberg 2011). However, compared to these previous outbreaks, the Covid-19 is extremely contagious. On January 2020, 22580 cases were recorded globally, and on March 11 the number of affected raised to 126214 (Worldometers 2020).

The literature highlights that the spread of panic is one of the most frequent causes of failure of crisis communication, and can result from high degrees of uncertainty surrounding an unknown threat (Frewer et al. 2003), incapacity of leaders to channel people fears into specific actions, speculation and multiple contrasting messages sent to the public (Covello et al. 2001; Robinson and Newstetter 2001), lack of transparency and lack of trust and credible claim-makers (Fessenden-Raden, Fitchen, and Heath 1987; Peters, Covello, and McCallum 1997; Renn and Levine 1991; Reynolds 2005). Given these premises, the first research question (RQ) relates to the role of both government and scientists in managing the communication of the emergent Covid-19 crisis, and it is split in two sub-questions:

RQ1a: How did Italian governmental agencies manage the communication of an emergent and unknown health crisis?

RQ1b: Did Italian scientists represent a unique voice in reporting scientific advances related to the Covid-19?

During health/disaster crises the use of both mainstream media and the Internet increases exponentially (Glass 2002). Eriksson (2018) identifies some lessons that show the importance of combining the use of both traditional media and social media in time of crisis. Even though several studies highlight that traditional media are considered more credible sources of information (see, e.g. Eriksson 2018; Schultz, Utz, and Goritz 2011), social media and blogs often provide "information-sharing behaviors" (Ng, Yang, and Vishwanath 2018) and real-time updates (Husain et al. 2014; Liu 2010), which in turn can influence the content of mainstream media (Houston et al. 2015). Accordingly, social media have been increasingly integrated in crisis management planning to anticipate public reaction (Fraustino, Liu, and Jin 2012; Freberg, Palenchar, and Veil 2013; Keim and Noji 2011; Taylor and Kent 2007). Therefore, a second research question relates to the use of the media by institutional voices to inform the public.

Q2: How did institutional actors (e.g. government representatives, political voices and scientists) use the media to manage the crisis?

The literature identifies four main frames used by the media during crises to help the public interpret the situation (Cho and Gower, 2006; Liu 2010; Neuman, Just, and Crigler, 1992). These frames include the attribution of responsibility, representation of conflicts, economic impact and human interest. Therefore, these elements are investigated by the following research questions:

Q3a: Who are the actors held responsible for managing the crisis?

Q3b: What are the aspects that cause conflicts?

Q3c: What are the consequences on the economic asset?

Q4d: What are the consequences on humans?

Answering these questions will help explore the effectiveness of an emergency response strategy resulting from the interrelationships between political institutions, scientists and the media during the emergence of the Covid-19 crisis in Italy. The analysis will be guided by the five elements identified by Reynolds (2005) as potential threats to the success of an emergency response operation. These are: i) Mixed messages from multiple messengers; ii) delay in releasing information; iii) paternalistic attitudes; iv) lack of immediate reaction to rumours; and v) political confusion. In fact, during health crises, timely and precise communication facilitates public understanding of the events and provides recommendations/instructions about protective measures, symptoms, and practical information (Reynolds and Seeger 2005). By contrast, a lack of coordination between the guidelines provided by governmental agencies and information reported by other mediators (e.g. media) can undermine the success of the crisis management (Sellnow et al. 2019).

Methods

To explore the combined efforts of politics, science and the media in informing people and containing the spread of the Covid-19, one of the most read Italian newspaper, *La Repubblica* (Statista 2019), guided the identification of the main events that characterised the management of the first phases of the outbreak. *La Repubblica* dedicated an online page to update news about the Covid-19 hour by hour (Stabile and Matteucci 2020). The time frame included in the analysis is between February 22, 2020 and March 11, 2020. On the 21st of February, around 20 cases were identified in Italy and the day after the Government isolated the most affected areas. On the 10th of March, the entire country was locked down and, the day after, the WHO declared the global pandemic status. The sources referenced by *La Repubblica* were verified and the national law-decrees were analysed to identify government's efforts to contain the spread of the virus.

Results

The Italian Government declared the "state of emergency" soon after the identification of the first two cases of Covid-19 in Rome on January 31. On February 22, the government enforced restrictions to contain the outbreak, which included quarantine for over 50000 people in 11 towns of northern Italy (Gazzetta Ufficiale 2020a). In three weeks (21 February-11 March), the virus affected 12462 people and caused 827 fatalities (Worldometers 2020). The restrictions imposed by the government involved fines on anyone entering or leaving outbreak areas, suspension of public events, ban of people gatherings, closure of schools and Universities, suspension of public transport and closure of "not essential" shops. In the same days, new cases of people who visited Italy were found in other countries. Several countries either envisaged (or forced) 14 days self-isolation for people returning from northern Italy. Other countries suspended flights to the affected areas.

To answer the RQs the following sub-sections identify the main steps in the crisis management in terms of governmental and political efforts (Q1a), scientific contribution (Q1b), media communication (Q2), and attribution of responsibility (Q3a), raise of conflicts (Q3b), economic (Q3c) and human consequences (Q3d).

Governmental agencies efforts and political debate

On February 22, the Italian government approved a first law-decree that imposed draconian measures, such as the lock down of 11 towns in the North of Italy. Between the 23rd and the 24th of February, several governmental representatives sent reassuring messages about the government readiness to deal with the crisis. The Minister of Health stated that the virus could only be contracted by a direct contact with an affected person. Both the Minister of Economy and the Minister of Infrastructure and Transport announced efforts to contain the economic damage. The Department of Civil Protection confirmed that the victims of the virus presented a compromised health status. The Minister of foreign affairs, Luigi Di Maio, engaged into a dialogue with neighbouring countries. However, starting from the 25th of February a misalignment between regional decisions and government guidelines generated confusion in the management. From this point, a fracture between official communications, fake news and local reactions can be identified. Internal and external pressures increased in the following days and required several official statements by ministers. For example, on February 27, Di Maio invited foreign countries to trust the data published by the Civil Protection Department. In fact, only 0.01% of the territory was locked down and there was no reason to suspend flight connections with other regions. In this confusion, the Lombardy governor appeared on a Facebook live wearing a protective mask. Scientists condemned this action as setting a wrong example because the protective mask was not necessary. Moreover, the mask used by the governor was non-conformed to the EU standards. On February 28, a second decree was approved to provide economic support to people and businesses in the affected areas. While the virus spread to several regions, some schools reopened, and some public events were organised by bars and shops to attract customers.

On March 2, a third decree classified three areas as "red" (locked down), "yellow" (medium-high risk), and a low risk zone. A fourth decree approved on the 8th of March locked down the Lombardy region and additional 14 provinces of the North of Italy (Gazzetta Ufficiale 2020b). Finally, another decree entered in force on the 10th of March (Gazzetta Ufficiale 2020c) and imposed the lockdown of the entire country.

Scientific responses

A constellation of scientific voices provided contrasting information throughout the process. An Italian physician and Professor of Virology at the San Raffaele Hospital in Milan, Roberto Burioni, immediately warned that the outbreak was a serious threat. On both his Twitter account (more than 172k followers) and national TV, the expert often gave indications on the restrictive measures needed to contain the outbreak. Both the Spallanzani hospital and the Superior Institute of Infective diseases stated that the mortality was connected to underlying serious illness and age of people affected. The Civil Protection ensured that around 50% of the cases did not need hospitalisation. Moreover, other experts, such as e.g. the director of the microbiology department of the Sacco Hospital in Milan, stated that the virus was slightly more serious than a flu in terms of affected people and fatalities (https://www.la7.it/laria-che-tira/video/coronavirus-myrta-merlino-alla-virologa-maria-rita-gismondo-pensa-ancora-che-sia-poco-piu-di-04-03-2020-311139). Professor Burioni counter-stated that the virus could not be classified as a flu and needed aggressive containment measures. These contrasting voices inflamed the debate around what to do on both social media and national TV. In addition to these internal forces, external pressures were represented by the WHO and the European Centre for Disease Prevention and Control (ECDPC), which increased the level of alert in the country and started an investigation around the procedures followed by a hospital in Codogno to deal with the first cases of Covid-19. Therefore, Italian scientists and doctors had to deal with several issues related to i) curing patients; ii) informing policymakers; iii) informing people; iv) advancing research; v) dealing with a lack of equipment, personnel and structures; and iv) contrasting rumours. Several times, a misalignment between political and scientific statements was reported by La Repubblica. For example, when the governor of Lombardy appeared on Facebook wearing a protective mask, the scientific community had to release a statement for two reasons. First, scientists repeatedly recommend to use protective masks in case of symptoms or high-risk exposure. Second, that mask was not approved by the European regulation. This point is also connected to a lack of protective equipment and illegal selling of overpriced and unchecked products. In fact, the increasing panic triggered assaults to supermarkets and pharmacies, which in turn caused a lack of necessary products for those in need. Another example is represented by the choice of closing all schools across the country. The scientific committee instituted by the government dissociated themselves from this decision. However, after the publication of a new decree on March 8, scientists univocally asked people to stay at home because of a lack of resources to deal with the increasing number of affected people. In fact, in three days (March 6-8) the number of patients in need of intensive care increased from 462 to 650. Doctors and nurses released statements and posted on social media that the health system was due to collapse (see e.g. https://www.facebook.com/photo.php?fbid=10221963451383805&set=a.10200987625721273&type=3).

Media reaction

La Repubblica reports that the discussion on coronavirus massively populated both traditional and social media. The day after the identification of the first case in Codogno, the hashtag #coronavirusitalia became the second trending hashtag with 31thousands of tweets. On March 4, Mediamonitor.it reported that the main national radio and tv used the word "coronavirus" once every two minutes since the 20th of February. Governmental agencies and government representatives used social media such as Facebook and Twitter to point people to official sources of information and inform them about government decisions. However, despite these efforts to control the flow of information, fake news and rumours spread on the Web. During the first days of the outbreak a fake logo of the newspaper VeneziaToday was used to report a Covid-19 case in Venice. Moreover, given the scarce availability of protective equipment and sanitising products the Internet and social media became the ideal platform to sell overpriced products.

Social media also became platforms for political conflicts. In fact, throughout the crisis the leader of the Lega Nord party (currently the first party in Italy), Matteo Salvini, accused the Government to do too little too late. On February 24, he posted on Facebook that the restrictions were implemented when the problem was already out of control; on the 26th, he disapproved the investigations into Codogno hospital relative to the management of the first case of Covid-19; on the same day, he advanced the hypothesis of new elections; on the 28th, he condemned the government for limiting the implementation of economic concessions to the red areas. In a similar attempt to destabilise the government, the leader of the Viva Italia party (part of the Government coalition) and former Prime Minister, Matteo Renzi, attacked the government for its incapacity to communicate with regions. Every time both Salvini and Renzi posted accuses against the Government, other political actors replied to these provocations by further inflaming the debate. For example, the Minister of Transport accused Salvini to use the coronavirus as a propaganda tool. Moreover, Salvini, interviewed by *El Pais*, condemned the governmental management. In turn, these debates were echoed by both social and national mainstream media, e.g. by giving space to the disagreement between the national and regional governments on the course of action to be implemented. On a national radio, Renzi held the government responsible for the economic failure of the country and stated that the situation was worse than the post 11/09 (Ansa 2020).

Social media and online magazines also reported disagreements between scientists and decisionmakers. The virologist Burioni attacked the political choice to open museums in Florence on his online magazine *Medical Facts*. Moreover, a conflict on Facebook involved a Professor of Microbiology and Virology at the San Raffaele Hospital, who posted that the virus was slightly more severe than a flu, and the Councillor for Welfare, who expressed his indignation for such underestimation of the problem.

Finally, throughout the crisis, the prime minister, Giuseppe Conte, invited journalists to avoid inflaming controversies on the measures implemented by the Government (Corriere della Sera 2020). He also invited the country to be united in tackling the problem, implicitly encouraging the media to support decision making without spreading alarmism. Several times, representatives of the government asked to stop sterile political debates on the media and to put aside political rivalry. However, a member of the Rai Supervisory Commission (national tv) and member of Viva Italia party, stated that the prime minister could not pretend a de-escalation of tones since he was the first to spread alarmism on media platforms.

Attribution of responsibility, raise of conflicts, economic and human consequences

The results connected to the RQs3 related to i) attribution of responsibility, ii) raise of conflicts, iii) prediction of economic and human consequences, should be explored in the light of both internal and external pressures.

Attribution of responsibility

The events described in the previous sections show a general internal political chaos. Even though the government followed the procedures recommended by the WHO to manage outbreaks, several issues emerged in the communication between i) the central government and regional authorities, between ii) the government and scientists, and between iii) the government and the public. The previous sections highlighted an initial misalignment between government decisions and regional implementation of restrictions. On February 26, the Governor of Marche authorised the closure of schools without government approvals. A mayor in Calabria (South of Italy) closed the town boarders to people arriving from the North of Italy. The governor of Sicily asked people from northern Italy not to visit the region. This suggests that even though the government asked for internal cohesion, some political actors undermined its credibility. Furthermore, other regional governors and political representatives inflamed controversies in several occasions. For example, the leader of the Fratelli di Italia party (right-wing party) accused the Prime minister to be a "criminal" for the management of the crisis (https://www.ilfattoquotidiano.it/2020/03/05/coronavirus-meloni-su-la7-giuseppe-conte-e-un-criminale-ha-responsabilita-gravissime-myrta-merlino-la-riprende-e-lei-rettifica/5726787/). The day after, the prime minister replied to this accusation during a press conference (https://www.ilfattoquotidiano.it/2020/03/05/coronavirus-conte-a-meloni-io-criminale-parole-gravi-dannose-per-il-paese-e-uno-schiaffo-a-tutti-i-cittadini-a-cui-abbiamo-chiesto-sacrifici/5726935/). Therefore, the government was held responsible for tackling the emergency, but constantly criticised for the decisions taken throughout the process.

Moreover, some choices taken by local and regional governments to support local businesses (such as e.g. promotion of aperitives and cultural/entertainment events) were strongly criticised by scientists on social media. Some government representatives, e.g. Nicola Zingaretti (governor of the Lazio region and leader of the main governmental political party), demonstrated not to be completely aware of the severity of the situation. In fact, even though Zingaretti supported the government throughout the process, he also promoted initiatives such as #Milanodoesn'tstop and #Italylloveyou, which invited people to socialise and consume aperitives in Milan. Soon after these events, and given the acceleration of the outbreak, Zingaretti supported the implementation of restrictive measures, and, around ten days later, he resulted positive to the virus.

Finally, the government was not capable to communicate a sense of responsibility to citizens. This confusion at multiple levels generated two opposite public reactions. On the one hand, an underestimation of the problem caused that some businesses did not respect the restrictions, thus contributing to the spread of the virus. Several people were investigated for leaving the red area; illegal parties were organised in several cities; a private nursery school in Sicily continued ordinary activities after the government order to close schools; patients with fever visited ERs forcing the hospitals to shut down in several areas. The situation was aggravated by several prison riots across the country due to a ban on family meetings, which culminated with the death of 6 people (Radighieri 2020).

On the other hand, some panic reactions increased the exposure of the South of the country to the virus. The content of the government plan to lockdown the Lombardy region leaked on the 7th of March. The CNN published the content of the decree draft (https://edition.cnn.com/asia/live-news/coronavirus-outbreak-03-08-20-intl-hnk/h_f28ad3a7c6c653b1fe04a628870946d1), as well as the Italian media. This leak jeopardised the government attempts to deal with the crisis - thousands of people assaulted train stations to flee to the south and forced other regions to implement more restrictions. The new decree in force from March 8 (Gazzetta Ufficiale 2020b), locked down the Lombardy region plus additional 14 provinces in the North of Italy. In this chaotic flow of information, some regional and local government representatives supported the restrictions while some others continued to complain about the too severe measures.

Despite these conflicts, the lockdown of Lombardy (economic core of the country) coincided with the raise of a collective voice. Policymakers, politicians, scientists, celebrities and social media users collectively started to ask people to respect the rules despite huge sacrifices. However, to contain the internal conflicts and preserve the image of the country, on March 10 the government was forced to lock down the entire country (Gazzetta Ufficiale 2020c)

In terms of attribution of responsibility by external actors, the Italian mismanagement soon became responsible for the spread of the virus. A member of the WHO, Walter Ricciardi, claimed that Italy should have stopped flights that could arrive from China through multiple connections (Berberi 2020; La Stampa 2020). Moreover, the fact that the WHO started an investigation into the management of the first cases of Covid-19, increased the external perception of a chaotic management. An article published by the *New York Times* identified the Italian "furbizia" (capacity to break the rules in a clever way) as the cause of the Italian failure in managing the crisis (Horowitz and Bubola 2020). This is also connected to a second point related to the raise of conflicts.

Raise of conflicts

Not only the management of the crisis was conditioned by political rivalry, but also by debates related to football and investigations into illegal acts and fake news. Football teams and supporters questioned the necessity to suspend football matches by accusing some teams (e.g. Juventus) to pollute the Serie A results. The internal conflictual situation and the impossibility of controlling the flow of information created an image of fragmentation outside. This progressively contributed towards limiting movements of people inside and outside the country and imposing quarantine for Italian citizens in foreign countries. This hostility was further inflamed by discriminatory statements released by some institutional voices. The governor of Lombardy advocated a stricter control of immigration flows in the future; some areas denied access to Chinese tourists; the president of Veneto, Luca Zaia, asked to stop people arriving from the countries that did not accept Italian people; Zaia also held China responsible for the global disaster because, he stated, "we have all seen the Chinese eat live mice" (https://video.repubblica.it/dossier/coronavirus-wuhan-2020/luca-zaia-president-of-veneto-region-we-have-all-seen-the-chinese-eat-live-mice/354888/355455).

Another critical aspect related to the Health care system. In 8 days, the intensive care unit in Lombardy increased its capacity from 50 to 244 beds. Additional 150 spaces were also created in the Lazio region. on March 8, the Lombardy region was forced to move some patients to other regions. Hospitals suffered from a lack of personnel and protective equipment. Doctors and healthcare personnel started to release statements, video and interviews about the unbearable conditions in the hospitals in Lombardy. The Chinese Government and several Chinese enterprises donated equipment to help manage the crisis (The Straits Times 2020). By contrast, some countries such as France and Germany suspended the export of protective masks (Guarascio and Blenkinsop 2020). Therefore, even though Italy immediately became a case study to produce knowledge about the virus and how to manage it, the government had to repeatedly request support from the EU to the point that the director of the EU crisis management commission, urged EU countries to cooperate and to "put solidarity above national interests" (Associate Press 2020).

Therefore, these internal and external controversies caused consequences in both economic and human terms.

Economic and human consequences

In economic terms, on February 24, Milan bourse closed 5.4% down. On the 28th, the spread between Italy's 10-year BTP bond and the German Bund raised to 180 basis points. The

President of the Italian Federation of Public Exercises estimated a loss of 2billions of euros in the first 4 months of the year. *La Repubblica* reported that the tourist sector (that represents the 13% of the Italian GDP) lost 200millions in March. The agricultural consortium Coldiretti announced a decrease of 27% in demand of "made in Italy" agri-food products. On the March 9, the bourse of Milan plunged 10.8%. The bond spread to 216 basis points.

In terms of human consequences, the stigmatisation was increasingly inflamed inside and outside the country. Some Italian regions discriminated people arriving from the affected areas. In the same way, foreign countries restricted or stopped connections with the country. In some countries, cruise ships were no allowed to dock due to the presence of Italian passengers. Moreover, foreign media contributed to stigmatisation. For example, a private French tv canal (Canal +) mocked the Italian situation and the CNN identified Italy as responsible for the global crisis (https://www.ilfattoquotidiano.it/2020/03/05/coronavirus-la-cnn-pubblica-una-mappa-in-cui-italia-e-il-principale-focolaio-del-mondo-di-maio-visione-distorta-della-realta/5726671/).

Discussion and conclusions

Following Reynolds (2005), the Covid-19 crisis communication in Italy failed in several directions. A first weakness can be identified in the communication of mixed messages from multiple sources. To answer QR1a related to the management of the crisis, formally the government implemented all the measures recommended by the WHO and those that helped slow the crisis in China (e.g. lockdown of areas and quarantine obligations, see She et al. 2020). However, these efforts were undermined by a lack of coordination between scientific and governmental messengers. In turn, the media reported multiple and competing versions of the events causing a public polarisation between "believers" and "sceptics". The literature review highlighted that the Covid-19 presents similarities with previous health crisis, however, this outbreak caused a shock in the global system and needed a quick reaction by governments at all scales (from local to global levels). Therefore, a first lesson learned relates to the failure of a "step by step strategy" adopted by the Italian government, which led to a spread of the virus in the entire territory. However, the Italian government was eventually forced to adopt draconian measures to contain the outbreak. In fact, the conflicting information reported by multiple messengers, plus the spread of fake news, caused a lack of respect of rules. People struggled to change their habits. Some bars and shops did not respect the restrictions and people underestimated the importance of reducing their social contacts. This public reaction resulted from an institutional miscommunication, which in turn undermined the credibility of the recommendations provided by the government (Holmes et al. 2009). Neither the government nor the scientific community provided coherent explanations. Therefore, to answer RQ2a, scientists provided mixed messages that contributed to chaos (Zoeteman et al. 2010) and triggered opposite public responses. The second lesson learned from the Italian case supports the necessity to replace these competing messages with a consistent narrative to successfully resolve the crisis (Sellnow et al. 2019).

The delay in releasing information is identified by Reynolds (2005) as a second weakness, as well as the need for outlining specific patterns of action and providing accurate information (Glik 2007). The delay in implementing the decree that locked down the Lombardy region, and a leak of its content, caused chaos and panic. This chaos pushed people to flee outside the region. This is directly connected to RQ2b related to the flow of information between institutions and the media. The Italian case shows that the management of the crisis was conditioned by a need to respond to some public reactions that were generated by a chaotic media communication. The mainstream media reported a polarisation in both political and scientific terms by giving space to both contrasting voices and social media disputes between politicians and government representatives. Moreover, social media offered a fertile ground for political disputes that fostered distrust in government and scientists. Therefore, social media increased exposure to multiple and competing messages and made it difficult the creation of a dominant narrative (Sellnow et al. 2019). However, as highlighted by Keil, Schönhöfer, and Spelsberg (2011) in analysing the H1N1 crisis management, the media alone cannot be considered responsible for spreading panic. In fact, both traditional and social media combine information provided by several sources (including scientists, government and global agencies). In the case of Covid-19, even though the media contributed towards increasing confusion by e.g. emphasising potential catastrophic consequences or, by contrasts, underestimating the problem, they mirrored internal conflicts and external pressures. Therefore, a third lesson learned is that, while an "interpretative pluralism" is vital to understand a crisis, collective efforts to reconcile these differences should also involve the media. In fact, the media actively contribute towards the definition of crisis narratives (Sellnow et al. 2019). By contrast, in the Italian case, the lack of collaboration between governmental agencies, politicians, health organisations/operators and the media undermined the public trust (Covello 2003; Holmes et al. 2009).

Moreover, paternalistic attitudes, represented by a simple request of not panicking (Reynold 2005), promoted opposite reactions. Repeatedly, local authorities questioned central government decisions without providing alternatives. Reynolds suggest that a reasonable amount of fear is inevitable. However, the fourth lesson learned is that this should be channelled in a specific course of actions. In fact, as Leslie (2006) suggests, in uncertain conditions, people might react instinctively, and, in the Italian case, this caused assaults to supermarkets, shortage of masks and overprice of sanitising products.

Following Reynolds, not responding to rumours in real time might reinforce the impression that multiple interpretations exist. Moreover, if fake news or conflicts persist on social media, the mainstream media will be likely to report these rumours unless they are quickly demonstrated to be false. The spread of fake news and the disputes triggered by some political actors caused this confusion, which in turn was often reported by national television and newspapers. This is also connected to RQ3a related to the attribution of responsibility, which was both internally and externally attributed to the national government. At the same time, all decisions were strongly criticised by specific agents. Therefore, the fifth lesson is that internal conflicts (such as those created by Salvini and Renzi, plus the decision of some regional governors not to follow the national guidelines), severely undermine the management of the crisis, increase confusion, and create an image of chaos outside. Several times, the government was forced to adjust in relation to these controversies. For example, the decision of locking down Lombardy resulted from the imprudence of people who did not respect the government recommendations to keep social distance and respect the rules. This is also connected to the sub-question related to the controversial aspects that caused conflicts. The leak of information about the imminent closure of Lombardy caused that people fled to the south and islands. In addition to this, the lack of respect of the roles (e.g. self-quarantine) forced the lock down of the entire country.

Finally, a sixth lesson relates to the misalignment between the central government and regional authorities, which promoted people distrust. The importance of public communication has become clear in the management of health crises (Koplan 2003; Prue et al. 2003). For example, the West Nile virus risk communication management by New York City showed that the misalignment between some city's decisions (spraying pesticides) and different advises given by health and environmental experts promoted mistrust (Covello et al. 2001).

The mismanagement of the preliminary phases of the Covid-19 crisis produced consequences in both economic (RQ3c) and human terms (RQ3c). The National Association of Italian Industries (Confindustria) predicted a loss around 7.4 billion in the trimester March-May only in the tourism sector (https://www.repubblica.it/cronaca/2020/03/01/news/coronavirus_in_italia_aggiornamento_ora_per_ora-249954540/). The chief economist at the German bank stated that the measures adopted by Italy and potentially by other European countries in the future would produce global impact (Baynes 2020). On the one hand, the global economic consequences will be negative but still uncertain, on the other hand, the human consequences in terms of stigmatisation of people are concrete. The attribution of responsibility to Italy for spreading the virus by other countries, such as in the case of the French canal and CNN, triggered stigmatisation processes that might last even after the crisis. In a similar way, stigmatisation of people also happened during SARS (Person et al. 2004). The literature highlights that fear associated with health problems, such as e.g. in mental illness (Schulze and Angermeyer 2003), HIV/AIDS (Chesney and Smith 1999; Herek 2002) and other chronic conditions, causes stigmatisation. This in turn undermines public efforts to tackle the problem. In fact, to prevent stigmatisation, people at risk of either being affected by or transmitting the condition, might avoid voluntary testing (Person et al. 2004).

In conclusion, the Italian crisis has been conditioned by a mismanagement of communication (Rodríguez et al. 2007) at different. This case study suggests that governments need to direct the communication process in a more univocal direction. All five weaknesses identified by Reynolds characterised the management of the preliminary phases of the crisis in Italy. This case suggests that the inherent uncertainty of health crisis should be supported by political and scientific cohesion (Sellnow et al. 2019). However, in the first phases of the outbreak, the country's political dysfunction, plus a "scientific war" (Ferraresi 2020), caused the failure of several government efforts to tackle the problem. Matteo Salvini's call for elections in a moment of national crisis, in addition to other attempts of some members of the government to destabilise the political asset, shows that several Italian political actors are ready to sacrifice international credibility and internal safety to prioritise individual political gains.

References

Ansa 2020. "Coronavirus: Renzi, peggio di 11 settembre." Ansa, March 2. http://www.ansa.it/sito/notizie/politica/2020/03/02/coronavirusrenzipeggio-di-11-settembre_9b93453b-54a8-4312-ab5c-77695f63393b.html

Associate Press 2020. "EU Seeks United Front to Tackle Medical Shortages from Virus." New York Times, March 6. https://www.nytimes.com/aponline/2020/03/06/world/europe/ap-eu-virus-outbreak-europe.html

Baynes, C. 2020. "Coronavirus 'pushing Europe into recession', say economists." The Independent, March 10. https://www.independent.co.uk/news/business/news/coronavirus-latest-eurozone-recession-morgan-stanley-berenberg-forecasts-a9388566.html

Berberi, L. 2020. "Coronavirus, l'Italia ferma i voli con la Cina, gli ultimi aerei sono arrivati a Roma e Milano." Il Corriere della Sera. January 30. https://www.corriere.it/cronache/20_gennaio_30/coronavirus-l-italia-ferma-voli-la-cina-ma-5-aerei-stanno-arrivando-roma-milano-4c159766-43a8-11ea-bdc8-faf1f56f19b7.shtml

Brug, J., A. R. Aro, A. Oenema, O. de Zwart, J. H. Richardus, and G. D. Bishop. 2004. "SARS Risk Perception, Knowledge, Precautions, and Information Sources, The Netherlands." Emerging Infectious Diseases 10 (8): 1486–1489. doi:10.3201/eid1008.040283.

Chesney, M. A., and A. W. Smith. 1999. "Critical Delays in HIV Testing and Care: The Potential Role of Stigma." American Behavioral Scientist 42 (7): 1162–1174. doi:10.1177/00027649921954822.

Cho, Seung Ho, and Karla K.Gower. 2006. "Framing Effect on the Public's Response to Crisis: Human Interest Frame and Crisis Type Influencing Responsibility and Blame." Public Relations Review 32 (4): 420–422. doi:10.1016/j.pubrev.2006.09.011.

Corman, V. M., O. Landt, M. Kaiser, R. Molenkamp, A. Meijer, D. K. W. Chu, T. Bleicker, et al. 2020. "Detection of 2019 Novel Coronavirus (2019-nCoV) by Real-Time RT-PCR." Eurosurveillance 25 (3). Advance online publication. https://www.eurosurveillance.org/content/10.2807/1560-7917.ES.2020.25.3.2000045. doi:10.2807/1560-7917.ES.2020.25.3.2000045.

Covello, V. T. 2003. "Best Practices in Public Health Risk and Crisis Communication." Journal of Health Communication 8 (sup1): 5–8. doi:10.1080/713851971.

Covello, V. T., R. G. Peters, J. G. Wojtecki, and R. C. Hyde. 2001. "Risk Communication, the West Nile Virus Epidemic: responding to the Communication Challenges Posed by the Intentional and Unintentional Release of a Pathogen in an Urban Setting." Journal of Urban Health: Bulletin of the New York Academy of Medicine 78 (2): 382–391. doi:10.1093/jurban/2.382.

Durodié, B. 2011. "H1N1 – the Social Costs of Élite Confusion." Journal of Risk Research 14 (5): 511–518. doi:10.1080/13669877.2011.576767.

Eriksson, M. 2018. "Lessons for Crisis Communication on Social Media: A Systematic Review of What Research Tells the Practice." International Journal of Strategic Communication 12 (5): 526–551. doi:10.1080/1553118X.2018.1510405.

Ferraresi, M. 2020. "Italy's Politicians Are Making the Coronavirus Crisis Worse." *Foreign Policy*, March 9. https://foreignpolicy.com/2020/03/09/italy-covid19-coronavirus-conte-salvini-epidemic-politicians-are-making-crisis-worse/

Fessenden-Raden, J., J. M. Fitchen, and J. S. Heath. 1987. "Providing Risk Information in Communities: factors Influencing What is Heard and Accepted." *Technical and Ethical Aspects of Risk Communication* 12: 94–101.

Fraustino, J. D., B. F. Liu, and Y. Jin. 2012. *Social Media Use during Disasters: A Review of the Knowledge Base and Gaps*. Maryland: U.S. Department of Homeland Security. National Consortium for the Study of Terrorism.

Freberg, K., M. J. Palenchar, and S. R. Veil. 2013. "Managing and Sharing H1N1 Crisis Information Using Social Media Bookmarking Services." *Public Relations Review* 39 (3): 178–184. doi:10.1016/j.pubrev.2013.02.007.

Frewer, L., S. Hunt, M. Brennan, S. Kuznesof, M. Ness, and C. Ritson. 2003. "The Views of Scientific Experts on How the Public Conceptualize Uncertainty." *Journal of Risk Research* 6 (1): 75–85. doi:10.1080/1366987032000047815.

Gazzetta Ufficiale 2020b. "Decreto Del Presidente del Consiglio dei Ministri, 8 marzo 2020." Accessed March 9, 2020. https://www.gazzettaufficiale.it/eli/id/2020/03/08/20A01522/sg.

Gazzetta Ufficiale 2020c. "Decreto Del Presidente del Consiglio dei Ministri, 9 marzo 2020." Accessed March 9, 2020.https://www.gazzettaufficiale.it/eli/gu/2020/03/09/62/sg/pdf

Glass, A. J. 2002. "The War on Terrorism Goes Online: Media and Government Response to First Post Internet Crisis." The Joan Shorenstein Center on the Press, Politics and Public Policy. https://shorensteincenter.org/wp-content/uploads/2012/03/2002_03_glass.pdf

Glik, D. C. 2007. "Risk Communication for Public Health Emergencies." *Annual Review of Public Health* 28 (1): 33–54. doi:10.1146/annurev.publhealth.28.021406.144123.

Guarascio, F., and P. Blenkinsop. 2020. "EU fails to Persuade France, Germany to Lift Coronavirus Health Gear Controls." *Reuters*, March 6. https://www.reuters.com/article/us-health-coronavirus-eu/eu-fails-to-persuade-france-germany-to-lift-coronavirus-health-gear-controls-idUSKBN20T166

Herek, G. M. 2002. "Thinking about AIDS and Stigma: A Psychologist's Perspective." *The Journal of Law, Medicine & Ethics* 30 (4): 594–607. doi:10.1111/j.1748-720X.2002.tb00428.x.

Holmes, B. J., N. Henrich, S. Hancock, and V. Lestou. 2009. "Communicating with the Public during Health Crises: experts' Experiences and Opinions." *Journal of Risk Research* 12 (6): 793–807. doi:10.1080/13669870802648486.

Horowitz, J., and M. Bubola. 2020. "On Day 1 of Broad Lockdown, a Debate Arises: Can Italians Follow the Rules?" *New York Times*, March 9, 2020. https://www.nytimes.com/2020/03/08/world/europe/italy-coronavirus-quarantine.html

Houston, J. Brian, Joshua Hawthorne, Mildred F. Perreault, Eun Hae Park, Marlo Goldstein Hode, Michael R. Halliwell, Sarah E. Turner McGowen, et al. 2015. "Social Media and Disasters: A Functional Framework for Social Media Use in Disaster Planning, Response, and Research." *Disasters* 39 (1): 1–22. doi:10.1111/disa.12092.

Husain, K., A. N. Abdullah, M. Ishak, M. F. Kamarudin, A. Robani, M. Mohin, and S. N. S. Hassan. 2014. "A Preliminary Study on Effects of Social Media in Crisis Communication from Public Relations Practitioners' Views." *Procedia – Social and Behavioral Sciences* 155: 223–227. doi:10.1016/j.sbspro.2014.10.283.

Keil, Ulrich, Peter Schönhöfer, and Angela Spelsberg. 2011. "The Invention of the Swine-Flu Pandemic." *European Journal of Epidemiology* 26 (3): 187–190. (https://link.springer.com/article/10.1007%2Fs10654-011-9573-6. doi:10.1007/s10654-011-9573-6.

Keim, M. E., and E. Noji. 2011. "Emergent Use of Social Media: A New Age of Opportunity for Disaster Resilience." *American Journal of Disaster Medicine* 6 (1): 47–54. doi:10.1017/S1049023X11003190.

Klemm, C., E. Das, and T. Hartmann. 2016. "Swine Flu and Hype: A Systematic Review of Media Dramatization of the H1N1 Influenza Pandemic." *Journal of Risk Research* 19 (1): 1–20. doi:10.1080/13669877.2014.923029.

Koplan, J. P. 2003. "Communication during Public Health Emergencies." *Journal of Health Communication* 8 (sup1): 144–145. doi:10.1080/713851967.

La Stampa 2020. "Ricciardi (Oms): 'L'Italia ha sbagliato, chiudere i voli dalla Cina non serve quando ci sono quelli indiretti'." *La Stampa*, February 22. https://www.lastampa.it/cronaca/2020/02/22/news/ricciardi-oms-l-italia-ha-sbagliato-chiudere-i-voli-dalla-cina-non-serve-quando-ci-sono-quelli-indiretti-1.38503026

Leslie, M. 2006. "Fear and Coughing in Toronto: SARS and the Uses of Risk." *Canadian Journal of Communication* 31 (2): 367–389. doi:10.22230/cjc.2006v31n2a1544.

Li, Qun, Xuhua Guan, Peng Wu, Xiaoye Wang, Lei Zhou, Yeqing Tong, Ruiqi Ren, et al. 2020. "Early Transmission Dynamics in Wuhan, China, of Novel Coronavirus–Infected Pneumonia." *The.* New England Journal of Medicine 382 (13): 1199–1207.,. doi:10.1056/NEJMoa2001316.

Liu, B. F. 2010. "Distinguishing How Elite Newspapers and A-List Blogs Cover Crises: Insights for Managing Crises Online." *Public Relations Review* 36 (1): 28–34. doi:10.1016/j.pubrev.2009.10.006.

Lofstedt, R. E. 2006. "How Can We Make Food Risk Communication Better: Where Are We and Where Are We Going?" *Journal of Risk Research* 9 (8): 869–890. doi:10.1080/13669870601065585.

McFarlane, A. C., and F. H. Norris. 2006. "Definitions and Concepts in Disaster Research." *In Methods for Disaster Mental Health Research*, edited by F. H. Norris, S. Galea, M. J. Friedman, and P.J. Watson, 3–19. New York, NY: Guilford Publications Inc.

Neuman, W. R., M. R. Just, and A.N. Crigler. 1992. *Common Knowledge*. Chicago: The University of Chicaho Press.

Ng, Y. J., Z. J. Yang, and A. Vishwanath. 2018. "To Fear or Not to Fear? Applying the Social Amplification of Risk Framework on Two Environmental Health Risks in Singapore." *Journal of Risk Research* 21 (12): 1487–1415. doi: 10.1080/13669877.2017.1313762.

Paules, C. I., H. D. Marston, and A. S. Fauci. 2020. "Coronavirus Infections—More than Just the Common Cold." *Jama* 323 (8): 707. doi:10.1001/jama.2020.0757.

Person, Bobbie, Francisco Sy, Kelly Holton, Barbara Govert, Arthur Liang, Brenda Garza, Deborah Gould, Meredith Hickson, Marian McDonald, Cecilia Meijer, Julia Smith, and the NCID. 2004. "NCID/SARS Emergency Outreach Team. Fear and Stigma: The Epidemic within the SARS Outbreak." *Emerging Infectious Diseases* 10 (2): 358–363. doi:10.3201/eid1002.030750.

Peters, R. G., V. T. Covello, and D. B. McCallum. 1997. "The Determinants of Trust and Credibility in Environmental Risk Communication: An Empirical Study." *Risk Analysis* 17 (1): 43–54. doi:10.1111/j.1539-6924.1997.tb00842.x.

PHEIC. 2020. "Global Research and Innovation Forum: Towards a Research Roadmap." Geneva, Accessed February 11-12. https://www.who.int/blueprint/priority-diseases/key-action/Global_Research_Forum_FINAL_VERSION_for_web_14_feb_2020.pdf?ua=1

Prue, C., C. Lackey, L. Swenarski, and J. Gantt. 2003. "Communication Monitoring: Shaping CDC's Emergency Risk Communication Efforts." *Journal of Health Communication* 8 (sup1): 35–49. doi:10.1080/713851975.

Radighieri, M. 2020. "Coronavirus, violenta rivolta nel carcere di Modena: morti sei detenuti". La Repubblica, March 8. https://bologna.repubblica.it/cronaca/2020/03/08/news/coronavirus_violenta_rivolta_nel_carcere_di_modena-250646974/

Renn, O., and D. Levine. 1991. "Credibility and Trust in Risk Communication." In *Communicating Risks to the Public*, edited by R. Kasperson, and P. Stallen, 175–217. Dordrecht, The Netherlands: Kluwer Academic Publishers.

Reynolds, B. 2005. "Crisis and Emergency Risk Communication." *Applied Biosafety* 10 (1): 47–56. doi:10.1177/153567600501000106.

Reynolds, B., and M. W. Seeger. 2005. "Crisis and Emergency Risk Communication as an Integrative Model." *Journal of Health Communication* 10 (1): 43–55. doi:10.1080/10810730590904571.

Robinson, S. J., and C. W. Newstetter. 2003. "Uncertain Science and Certain Deadlines: CDC Responses to the Media during the Anthrax Attacks of 2001." *Journal of Health Communication* 8 (sup1): 17–34. doi:10.1080/713851980.

Rodríguez, H., W. Díaz, J. M. Santos, and B. E. Aguirre. 2007. "Communicating Risk and Uncertainty: science, Technology, and Disasters at the Crossroads." In *Handbook of Disaster Research*, edited by H. Rodríguez, E.L. Quarantelli, and R.R. Dynes, 476–488. New York, NY: Springer.

Sandam, P. M. 2003. "Four Kinds of Risk Communication." Accessed March 3 2020. https://www.psandman.com/col/4kind-1.htm

Schultz, F., S. Utz, and A. Goritz. 2011. "Is the Medium the Message? Perceptions of and Reactions to Crisis Communication via Twitter, Blogs, and Traditional Media." *Public Relations Review* 37 (1): 20–27. doi:10.1016/j.pubrev.2010.12.001.

Schulze, B., and M. C. Angermeyer. 2003. "Subjective Experiences of Stigma. A Focus Group Study of Schizophrenic Patients, Their Relatives and Mental Health Professionals." *Social Science & Medicine* 56 (2): 299–312. doi:10.1016/S0277-9536(02)00028-X.

Seeger, M. W., T. L. Sellnow, and R. R. Ulmer. 1998. "Communication, Organization and Crisis." *Annals of the International Communication Association* 21 (1): 231–275. In edited by M.E. Roloff, Thousand Oaks, CA: Sage. doi: 10.1080/23808985.1998.11678952.

Seeger, M. W., T. L. Sellnow, and R. R. Ulmer. 2001. "Public Relations and Crisis Communication: Organizing and Chaos." In *Public Relations Handbook*, edited by R.L. Heath, 155–166. Thousand Oaks, CA: Sage.

Sellnow, T. L., D. D. Sellnow, E. M. Helsel, J. M. Martin, and J. S. Parker. 2019. "Risk and Crisis Communication Narratives in Response to Rapidly Emerging Diseases." *Journal of Risk Research* 22 (7): 897–908. doi:10.1080/13669877.2017.1422787.

She, J., J. Jiang, L. Ye, L. Lijuan, B. Chunxue, and Y. Song. 2020. "Novel Coronavirus of Pneumonia in Wuhan, China: emerging Attack and Management Strategies." *Clinical and Translational Medicine* 9 (1). Advance online publication. https://clintransmed.springeropen.com/articles/10.1186/s40169-020-00271-z. doi:10.1186/s40169-020-00271-z.

Stabile, E., and P. Matteucci. 2020. "Coronavirus in Italia: aggiornamento ora per ora." La Repubblica. MATTEUCCI https://www.repubblica.it/cronaca/2020/02/22/news/coronavirus_in_italia_aggiornamento_ora_per_ora-249241616/.

Statista 2019. "Most Used Online News Sources on a Weekly Basis in Italy in 2019." Accessed March 5, 2020. https://www.statista.com/statistics/730125/top-online-news-sources-in-italy/

Taylor, M., and M. L. Kent. 2007. "Taxonomy of Mediated Crisis Responses." *Public Relations Review* 33 (2): 140–146. doi:10.1016/j.pubrev.2006.11.017.

The Straits Times. 2020. "China offers Italy medical aid as province donates masks to help overseas Chinese." *The Straits Times*, March 11. https://edition.cnn.com/asia/live-news/coronavirus-outbreak-03-08-20-intl-hnk/h_f28ad3a7c6c653b1fe04a628870946d1

Ufficiale, Gazzetta. 2020a. "Disposizioni attuative del decreto-legge 23 febbraio 2020, n. 6." Decreto Del Presidente del Consiglio dei Ministri, 23 febbraio 2020. Accessed February 25, 2020. https://www.lastampa.it/cronaca/2020/02/22/news/ricciardi-oms-l-italia-ha-sbagliato-chiudere-i-voli-dalla-cina-non-serve-quando-ci-sono-quelli-indiretti-1.38503026

Washer, P. 2004. "Representation of SARS in the British Newspapers." *Social Science & Medicine* 59 (12): 2561–2571. doi:10.1016/j.socscimed.2004.03.038.

Weiss, Mitchell G., and J.Ramakrishna. 2006. "Stigma Interventions and Research for International Health." *The Lancet* 367 (9509): 536–538. doi:10.1016/S0140-6736(06)68189-0.

WHO 2003. "SARS (Severe Acute Respiratory Syndrome)." Accessed March 2, 2020. https://www.who.int/ith/diseases/sars/en/

WHO 2020a. "Live from Geneva" – January 7." Accessed January 7, 2020. https://www.pscp.tv/WHO/1OdJrqEvgaeGX

WHO 2020b. "World Health Organization Holds News Conference on Coronavirus Outbreak – February 10." Accessed February 25, 2020. https://www.youtube.com/watch?v=a0Nu5MURFe4&feature=youtu.be&t=2166

WHO 2020c. "WHO Director-General's opening remarks at the media briefing on COVID-19 - 11 March 2020." Accessed March 11, 2020. https://www.who.int/dg/speeches/detail/who-director-general-s-opening-remarks-at-the-media-briefing-on-covid-19—11-march-2020

WHO. 2015. "Cumulative Number of Confirmed Human Cases for Avian Influenza A(H5N1) reported to WHO, 2003–2015." Accessed March 5, 2020. https://www.who.int/influenza/human_animal_interface/EN_GIP_201503031cumulativeNumberH5N1cases.pdf

Worldometers 2020. "Coronavirus Cases – March 11." Accessed March 11, 2020. https://www.worldometers.info/coronavirus/coronavirus-cases/#cases-growth-factor

Zoeteman, B., W. C. Kersten, W. F. Vos, L. de Voort, and B. J. Ale. 2010. "Communication Management During Risk Events and Crises in a Globalized World: Predictability of Domestic Media Attention for Calamities." *Journal of Risk Research* 13 (3): 279–302. doi:10.1080/13669870902955427.

The paradox of trust: perceived risk and public compliance during the COVID-19 pandemic in Singapore

Catherine Mei Ling Wong and Olivia Jensen

ABSTRACT

Public trust in the authorities has been recognised in risk research as a crucial component of effective and efficient risk management. But in a pandemic, where the primary responsibility of risk management is not centralised within institutional actors but defused across society, trust can become a double-edged sword. Under these conditions, public trust based on a perception of government competence, care and openness may in fact lead people to underestimate risks and thus reduce their belief in the need to take individual action to control the risks. In this paper, we examine the interaction between trust in government, risk perceptions and public compliance in Singapore in the period between January and April 2020. Using social media tracking and online focus group discussions, we present a preliminary assessment of public responses to government risk communication and risk management measures. We highlight the unique deployment of risk communication in Singapore based on the narrative of 'defensive pessimism' to heighten rather than lower levels perceived risk. But the persistence of low public risk perceptions and concomitant low levels of compliance with government risk management measures bring to light the paradox of trust. This calls for further reflection on another dimension of trust which focuses on the role of the public; and further investigation into other social and cultural factors that may have stronger influence over individual belief in the need to take personal actions to control the risks.

1. Introduction

Over the last two decades, risk researchers noted that public trust in policy-makers and corporate leaders were declining in western societies and began to interrogate 'trust' as a concept more deeply (Lofstedt 2005). Trust has since been recognised in risk research as a crucial component of effective and efficient risk management. If the public trusts the authorities to fulfil their duty of care, the persuasiveness of risk information will be higher, the public will be more accepting of risks and uncertainties, and discursive conflicts will be significantly reduced (Freudenburg 2003; Renn 2008; Poortinga and Pidgeon 2003; Wardman and Mythen 2016).

But in the case of a pandemic, where the primary responsibility of risk management is not centralised within institutional actors (e.g. the corporation, the regulator, local government, etc.)

but defused across society, trust can become a double-edged sword. Under these conditions, public trust based on a perception of government competence, fairness, care and openness (Poortinga and Pidgeon 2003) may in fact lead people to underestimate risks and thus reduce their compliance with government risk management measures. This in turn may undermine efforts to control the risks and drive the need for stricter institutional enforcement and more stringent government measures.

In this paper, we examine the interaction between trust in government, risk perceptions and public compliance in Singapore in the period between January 2020 when the first COVID-19 case was reported in the country and April 2020. Singapore is distinguished by a high level of public trust in government compared to other high-income countries: 24% of people in Singapore report having a 'great deal of confidence' in their government, compared to 5.8% in South Korea, 5.5% in Germany or 3.7% in the US (World Values Survey Wave 2014). In the context of the severe challenges posed by COVID-19, this is a very favourable position, and the government appears to have sought to build on this trust by initially adopting a more advisory stance on 'social distancing' to slow the spread of the virus. Government communications consistently emphasised the seriousness of the risk rather than seeking to downplay it, with the expectation that the public would make appropriate changes in their behaviour. However, public compliance with institutional guidance has been variable and the government has had to incrementally tighten controls on activity and movement.

Singapore's experience suggests a tension for governments seeking simultaneously to demonstrate competence and trustworthy management, and to communicate to the public a level of risk that would induce behavioural compliance with risk management measures at the same time.

2. Singapore's risk communication approach

2.1. Pre-crisis communication: 'defensive pessimism'

Singapore's approach to risk communication during COVID-19 draws heavily on the country's experience during the SARS outbreak of 2003. In that earlier crisis, the government's attitude was one of 'defensive pessimism', as the then Director General of the WHO described it (Lanard 2004). Government communications maintained throughout the crisis period that risks were serious and should not be under-estimated, were likely to persist and that it was the responsibility of government to consider and prepare for negative scenarios in the context of high levels of uncertainty.

During SARS, Health Minister, Lim Hng Kiang, presented the risks related to the epidemic thus: 'We're facing an unprecedented situation, this is a 9/11 for health.... We're not going to go back to the pre-SARS situation for some time. We're in for the long haul' (Quoted in Lanard 2004). This message of the persistent nature of the risk and a refusal to adopt an optimistic spin in communicating risk assessments has been echoed in COVID-19. In an interview with CNN in late March 2020, Prime Minister Lee Hsien Loong explained his reluctance to describe Singapore's approach as a success: 'I hesitate to talk about success because we are right in the midst of a battle, which is intensifying. We have tried very hard, right from the beginning, to take this very seriously ... I am under no illusions that we have won. We are just going in, and there is a long battle ahead' (Prime Minister's Office 2020).

There are numerous other examples that demonstrate a consistent pattern of 'defensive pessimism' in the Singapore government's risk communication approach. The interesting point here is the rather counter-intuitive deployment of risk communication, in the case of Singapore, not for the purpose of making people feel safer, but rather to prepare them mentally for future risks. In other words, risk communication was applied with the inverse objective of heightening risk perceptions and raising public concern in order to prepare the public for future government interventions. This expectation is consistent with the findings of studies on the adoption of risk management behaviours by individuals in Singapore and Hong Kong during the SARS crisis, which found that individuals who were more anxious about SARS risk were more likely to adopt risk management behaviours (Leung et al. 2003).

2.2. Early crisis communication

At least two key pillars of communications can be observed in the initial period of the outbreak in Singapore: (1) conventional media; and (2) digital and social media. The first pillar relied on the conventional medium of weekly press conferences by key government officials where the same narrative of 'defensive pessimism' was deployed. But in addition to that, two things stand out: first, great care was given to the multi-lingual and multi-cultural context of Singapore. For example, when the Prime Minister addressed the nation on April 3rd to announce the partial lockdown, he spoke in English, Bahasa Melayu and Mandarin.[2] When infection clusters began to emerge in some of the foreign worker dormitories housing workers mostly from South Asia, Minister for Communications and Information S. Iswaran conducted a dialogue with workers at one of the dormitories in English and Tamil (Lim 2020), the latter being one of the languages widely spoken in that community. Direct address by the country's leaders speaking in the language of the targeted audience without the use of translators is crucial in building trust and triggering the affective beliefs about institutional behaviour and competence (Metlay 1999) in a multi-cultural society such as Singapore.

Second, officials openly addressed the scientific uncertainties around the virus, such as the mode of transmission, effectiveness of wearing masks, the search for a vaccine, etc. Even when the numbers of new infections seemed to be under control in early March, the government warned that the uncertainties around the virus particularly the mode, and extent of transmission globally and locally meant that Singapore was still in the midst of the crisis and that numbers were expected to rise again (see the timeline of virus prevalence provided in supplementary material, Annexe B). This is very much in keeping with the recommended *resilience-based* communication strategy for risk problems characterised by uncertainty and complexity (Renn, Klinke, and Asselt 2011, Rosa, Renn, and McCright 2014) and the transparent reporting of uncertainty information (Petersen et al. 2013).

The second pillar of communication drew heavily on digital and social media. One of the key instruments the government deployed very early in the crisis was WhatsApp. With some 4 million users out of Singapore's population of 5.7 million (Basu 2020), the government recognised very early that WhatsApp would be the main conduit of reliable information as well as fake news and false information. As the first COVID-19 cases started to appear in the country in late January 2020, the government established a meticulous contact tracing procedure which included detailed case information for every confirmed patient, including the location of their residence and workplace. A detailed summary of contact tracing was then communicated widely to the public through WhatsApp (as well as twitter, Facebook, Telegram and designated websites) which sent two to three daily updates via the Gov.sg account along with other key public messages. These included counter-fake news and scam alerts; links to websites for credible information about the latest medical information, government advisories, financial aid packages, and support programmes; and messages to inspire community spirit and familial responsibility.

2.3. During crisis communication

As the virus began to unfold in Singapore, other apps and websites were rapidly deployed within a matter of weeks to facilitate more rapid and accurate contact tracing, as well as to manage other risk factors emanating from mobility, crowding in public spaces, loss of business and

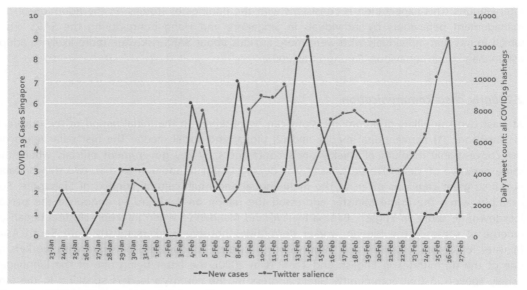

Figure 1. COVID-19 Case information & Twitter salience.

loss of employment. While these online and digital tools are crucial, their efficacy relied heavily on people to be honest in their reporting and to make responsible decisions based on the information provided by these online and digital platforms. The implicit assumption in the deployment of these tools was that with adequate information, people would make the 'right' decision to behave in ways that would reduce collective risk. And while we do not yet know the level of public uptake of these apps and websites, anecdotal evidence of the mixed response to the government's communication strategies discussed in the next section highlights the perennial problem of interpretive and moral ambiguity in risk communication (Renn, Klinke, and Asselt 2011).

3. Public perceptions of government risk management & communication

In seeking to understand how the public perceived the messaging from the government, we conducted two preliminary investigations using: (1) social media tracking; and (2) online Focus Group Discussions (FGDs). This section presents the approach and initial findings.

3.1. Social media tracking using the risk pulse monitor

As noted above, regular, detailed information on individual confirmed COVID-19 cases has been a key part of the Singapore government's communication approach since the beginning of the outbreak. This high level of transparency is meant to support individuals to make risk-informed decisions but it could also induce panic or lead to the stigmatisation of enterprises or localities associated with infections. As a first step in examining the reactions of the public to detailed information on virus prevalence, we tracked social media activity in Singapore relating to COVID-19. From a dataset of 3.47 million global Tweets using hashtags related to the coronavirus in the period 29 January to 28 February 2020, we identified Tweets from 1.89 million Singapore-linked accounts.[3] Preliminary analysis was conducted for a final dataset of 200,002 Tweets meeting these criteria.

Figure 1 plots announcements of new COVID-19 cases against the level of Twitter activity during this period. The data suggest that there may be a link between new case announcements and Twitter activity, with greater numbers of new cases echoed in higher levels of Twitter

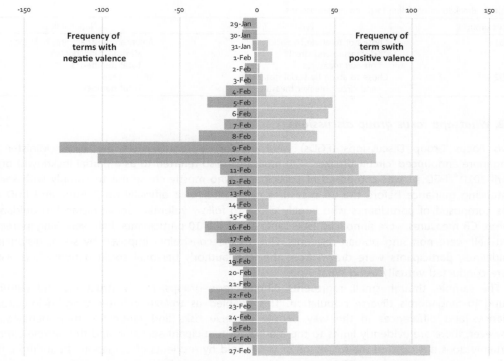

Figure 2. Emotional Valence of COVID-19-related Tweets from Singapore-linked Twitter accounts.

activity in the following days. Twitter users appear to be sensitive to the release of information and to share this with their networks. However, the relationship seems to weaken in the latter part of the period. This may be due to the rapid globalisation of the spread of the virus at that time, which might increase the salience of international prevalence information compared to local information. We have continued to collect Twitter data as the crisis has evolved, which will allow for further analysis in the future.

We also conducted a preliminary analysis of Tweet content, counting occurrences of keywords evoking negative and positive emotional valence. An initial coding of the content of a set of 100 Tweets with COVID-related hashtags using the 'near this place' location filter was conducted by the authors to identify sub-topics and modes of expression in Tweets in Singapore. The manual coding revealed that emotions were more likely to be expressed in relation to the behaviour of other people or organisations. This formed the basis for the selection of keywords and their classification as negative or positive. Most keywords are in English, reflecting the dominant language of communication among Singapore Twitter users, but several common colloquial terms and abbreviations derived from the Hokkien dialect were also included. The full set of keywords used in this round of analysis is provided in Annexe 1 (supplementary material).

The analysis by keyword count suggests that a majority of Tweets relating to COVID-19 are purely informational. Of those Tweets containing markers of emotional valence, we found that a majority (62%) were of positive valence, as shown in Figure 2. These findings are very preliminary but give a first indication that the detailed communications issued by government in the first month of the COVID-19 crisis did not induce predominantly negative emotional reactions. However, further work will be needed to refine the set of key words, to extend the period of analysis, and ideally to cover additional social media platforms in order to investigate these issues more thoroughly.

Table 1. Breakdown of online focus group discussions.

Focus group #	Type	Nationalities
FGD1	Chose not to abide by social distancing and circuit breaker measures	American, Austrian, British, French, Mexican, Singaporean **Total number: 8**
FGD2	Chose to abide by social distancing and circuit breaker measures	Singaporean **Total number: 2**

3.2. Whatsapp focus group discussions

Two Focus Group Discussions (FGDs) were conducted shortly after the Prime Minister of Singapore announced 'circuit breaker' (CB) measures (also referred to as a partial lockdown) on 3 April 2020.[4] FGD #1 was composed of participants who mostly chose not to comply with social distancing guidance before the CB measures came into force officially on 7 April; and FGD #2 was composed of participants who largely chose to follow voluntary social distancing guidance before CB measures were annouced (see Table 1). Of the 10 participants, half were Singaporeans and half were non-Singaporean residents. Due to the constraints imposed by social distancing guidelines, participants were drawn from the lead author's personal social network and FGDs were conducted virtually using WhatsApp.

The sample, though small, represents different age groups, family structures and cultures found in Singapore's diverse population. This enabled us to extract interesting socio-cultural nuances and differences in the way people perceive risks and rationalise their behaviours. However, there are evidently limits to the method of participant selection and the sample almost certainly does not capture the full range of views held by residents of Singapore. In addition, the online administration of the FGDs meant that many of the physical nuances of expression are not captured in the discussion and were limited to available gifs and emojis. Nevertheless, the FGDs did produced some interesting contextual insight to what people thought about the government's communication approach and why they chose to follow or not follow the government's advisories. Hence, this particular assemblage of participants and range of perspectives raises interesting leads for future, more extensive research into the relationships between trust, perceived risk and behavioural compliance.

Finding 1: Trust in the government

Most participants expressed a high level of trust in the government, though there were key variations between the two groups. The more diverse FGD1 had a very positive perception of the government's risk management and communication efforts, and expressed a very high level of confidence in the Singapore government. They mostly considered their risk of exposure to be very low because they felt that the government has been transparent; they considered the authorities to be highly competent and effective; and they had strong confidence in the health-care system. Further, many of them compared the number of infections and fatalities with the US, UK and other European countries as a point of reference for how well the Singapore government and healthcare system was managing the risks. FGD2 participants, however, were more sceptical and found the government's approach to be confusing at times. They expressed higher levels of anxiety and, on occasion, denialism (see Table 2).

This difference in perception was also reflected in the vastly different *stated* behavioural responses of participants. The Singaporeans across both FGDs stated that they had reduced their social activities, stayed home more and worked from home more even before the partial lockdown was announced. Participants from FGD1, however, expressed less inclination to comply even after the partial lockdown was announced.

That said, it is important to note that this difference is not simply a function of 'foreigner' versus 'local' perceptions. All participants in FGD2 were young parents with extended families in Singapore while FGD1 participants were mostly expats living in Singapore with no, to limited, family members. The Singaporeans in FGD1 also had extended family and elderly parents in

Table 2. Public perception of government's risk management and communication.

FGD1 indicative quotes	FGD2 indicative quotes
P1: 'We have true leadership here [...] Do you believe the numbers coming out of Russia or China are accurate? Hell no. I believe the numbers in Singapore and would bet on it'.	P10: 'Haha I feel its like ... whatever the govt say lor ... first surgical mask better, then no need mask, now give cloth mask [...] Then social distancing ... like [P9] said, [lockdown] was overdue ... so bo bian⁵ lockdown ... In the end I'm very confused now haha'
P5: 'The government does more tests (compared to low testing in Japan or US or Indonesia), checks on SHN [Stay-Home-Notice], does contact tracing, and good healthcare ... '	P10: 'I'm starting to think the virus is bogus! Lol the stupid test kit bogus [...] Erm sorry to say ... they [the government] like gasak gasak⁶ ... guess only leh'.
P2: 'Leadership learn from SARS -> Leadership does better now and people listen and do their thing -> lower risk'	P9: 'Partial lockdown is way overdue imo [in my opinion]'.

Singapore and express greater inclination to comply with social distancing. A more important observation to be made here, therefore, is that the presence of family and vulnerable members of the household is likely to have an effect on individuals' parameters of concern and, thus, evaluation of risks and compulsion to comply with circuit breaker measures.

Indeed, since the circuit breaker measures came into effect, it became clear that incomplete compliance was a widespread phenomenon. Government officials noted with frustration that many people continued to congregate in high risk locations such as food markets, contravening distancing requirements. Authorities issued 10,000 advisories, 3100 warnings and 40 fines to members of the public for social distancing violations in just three days after the CB was announced (Heng and Rajendran 2020; Toh 2020). This prompted the government to impose tighter restrictions such as closing outdoor exercise spaces and sports stadiums and, prohibiting parents from sending their children to be looked after by their grandparents (Lai and Sin 2020).

Finding 2: Acceptable social distancing is mediated by trust

This problem of apparent non-compliance of the public could at least be partly explained by the second finding: that participants had very different understandings of 'acceptable social distancing'. In the minds of both groups of participants, they considered themselves to have already taken acceptable social distancing measures, commensurate with their evaluation of the risks. As Table 3 shows, participants from FGD1 felt that by confining their social activities to a limited group of *trusted* friends, they were already engaging in social distancing, and were reducing their risk of exposure to the virus. When asked to consider the risk that their small group of trusted friends may be infected by COVID-19, FGD1 participants considered that possibility to be an uncontrollable unknown, a risk they were willing to take:

P3: How can you be sure you won't get hit by a car when you go outside?

P6: Or strike by lightning?

FGD2 participants, despite their lower levels of trust, also continued to go out every day and patronised cafes and restaurants, but were more strict in limiting their socialising to family members and began restricting social life earlier than FGD1. They attributed their inability to maintain social distancing in public spaces to the lack of space in Singapore rather than a function of their individual choices. This indicates that there are important nuances in public interpreations of government risk management measures and their perception of compliance.

4. Discussion

4.1. The paradox of trust

Under normal circumstances, a high level of public trust in the authorities and a low level of perceived risk is, generally, a desirable condition. However, in a pandemic like COVID-19, this is highly problematic for public compliance. Our FGD and social media data suggest that while

Table 3. Interpretations of social distancing.

FGD1 indicative quotes	FGD2 indicative quotes
P7: 'I'm not meeting other people so I think besides this group it's sort of isolation?'	P10: 'I have been out ah … every day. But to less crowded n open places … Don't cook at home mah so gotta go out eat … haven't been socialising much though haha'
P5: 'I've reduced my activities. When I go out, I take safety precautions & do social distancing'.	P9: 'I think Singapore social distancing tough la no space'.
P1: 'If we all agree to sacrifice other interaction for [name of small group activity] (which is what I am doing), then you folks are my only known risk'.	

there was a high level of public trust in the government, concomitant low levels of perceived risk resulted in low compliance with the government's risk management measures. This challenges the assumption in risk research that transparent communication, particularly of uncertainties enables the public to make informed decisions (see e.g. Frewer et al. 2002; Petersen et al. 2013). In this case, it seems factors other than risk and uncertainty information informs individual choices to comply or otherwise.

4.2. Uncertainty communication and trust

The efficacy of uncertainty communication in building trust remains hotly debated. While some contend that uncertainty communication is, more often than not, desirable and effective (Funtowicz and Ravetz 1993; Petersen et al. 2013; van der Sluijs 2012), others find that it causes greater confusion, reduces trust in the authorities and faith in their competence (Johnson and Slovic 1995; Lofstedt and Bouder 2017; Lofstedt et al., 2017). We find in the case of Singapore, that uncertainty communication was conducted in a highly selective manner, and in a way that conveyed strong institutional consensus, competency and effectiveness. Hence, we did not see the kind of negative effects of uncertainty communication that Johnson and Slovic (1995), Johnson and Slovic (1998) found in their studies. Where there was confusion expressed by FGD2 participants, that was more in response to the adaptive risk management approach used by the government than with its uncertainty communication per se.

4.3. Trust in the public

The FGD and social media data also brings to light the challenges when trust is placed on the public to make appropriate evaluations of the risks and take appropriate actions. In the first two months of the outbreak, the emphasis was on government authorities trusting members of the public to take responsibility for their own actions. This was well illustrated in the response of government ministers to questions about the enforcement of rules to limit the size of social gatherings to no more than 10, prior to the circuit breaker measures. Health Minister, Gan Kim Yong, in response to a question from a member of the public who asked whether he could invite nine friends to his home if his brother, who lived in the same house, stayed inside his room for the duration of the gathering, replied, 'It's not a question of whether you can or cannot. The key question is whether you need to or not. Even if you need to have interactions with close friends, do you need so many at the same time? If you can avoid it, avoid it during this period of time' (TODAY 2020). But as public non-compliance remained high, stricter measures were subsequently imposed in early April.

This highlights the importance of public belief in the need to take individual actions to control the risks, and, by extension, to build trust within the community during a pandemic, whereby the onus of risk management is not concentrated in the institutions of government, but diffused across society.

5. Conclusion

Trust is an essential component of what holds society together, especially in a time of crisis. There is an implicit assumption in the risk scholarship that trust is a boon for risk communication and risk management. Emphasis has, thus, been placed on the systems and processes in which governments, regulators and corporations earn the trust of the public. The COVID-19 pandemic reveals another dimension of trust – one in which high levels of public trust results in lower levels of compliance and a belief that individual action is not required to manage the risks effectively.

The very preliminary assessment of public perceptions in Singapore shows that high levels of trust in the government and authorities present other challenges of public complacency and the relegation of responsibility to control the risks to the authorities. In this case, the high level of public trust in the government has resulted in the underestimation of risk by the public and non-compliant behaviour.

Certainly, we do not suggest that efforts be directed at lowering trust in order to increase perceived risk and compliant behaviour in a pandemic or any other risk situation for that matter. But this observation calls for further reflection on trust from a different vantage point – one that focuses on the role of the public in building trust and its relationship with risk perception and risk management. It also calls for more investigation into other strategies for risk communication that can simultaneously build trust while maintaining a high level of perceived risk and compulsion for individual action to control the risks. In relation to this, deeper reflection is need as to the contexts in which such forms of communication are needed, such as a pandemic. The different interpretations of risk management measures such as 'social distancing' and the variations in participants' willingness to comply also reveals the myriad other factors that inform peoples' choices and decisions that warrant further investigation.

The Chinese have a saying, '天下无难事, 只怕有心人' [tiān xià wú nán shì, zhǐ pà yǒu xīn rén], which means nothing is unachievable under the heavens, but the heart stands in the way. Perhaps it is not *hard* information but *heart* information that ultimately determines the success and effectiveness of risk communication and risk management measures in a pandemic or any other risk event.

Notes

1. Trust in other individuals, meanwhile, is on par with other countries: 37.3% of people in Singapore say that 'most people can be trusted', compared to 44.6% in Germany, 34.8% in the US, or 26.5% in South Korea.
2. See full speech here: https://www.youtube.com/watch?v=j3nrBanbbaw
3. Risk Pulse Monitor project (IPUR Grant #LRFI_FY2018_RES_01_KAN). Analysis of Tweets matching the following criteria: hashtags: #coronavirus, #COVID19, #COVID2019, #19NCoV, #wuhanvirus, #wuhancoronavirus; Twitter accounts which follow at least 1 of 59 Singapore government or Singapore media Twitter accounts.
4. 'Circuit breaker' measures apply to the period 7 April–4 May. They include the closure of physical workplaces and school premises and require residents to 'minimize movements and interactions in public and private places and stay home unless necessary for essential purposes'. The announcement of these measures stipulated that 'entities that are able to comply immediately are strongly encouraged to do so', https://www.moh.gov.sg/news-highlights/details/circuit-breaker-to-minimise-further-spread-of-covid-19
5. 'Bo bian' is a Hokkien dialect expression for not having a choice.
6. 'Gasak gasak' is a Malay expression for someone doing a job hurriedly.

Disclosure statement

No potential conflict of interest was reported by the authors.

Disclaimer

The views, thoughts and opinions expressed in this paper belong solely to the authors, and do not necessarily represent the views of the author's employer.

References

Basu, Medha. 2020. "How Singapore Sends Daily Whatsapp Updates on Coronavirus." Govinsider.asia, 3 March. Accessed 10 April 2020. https://govinsider.asia/innovation/singapore-coronavirus-whatsapp-covid19-open-government-products-govtech/

Freudenburg, William. 2003. "Institutional Failure and the Organizational Amplification of Risks: The Need for a Closer Look." In *The Social Amplification of Risk*, edited by Nick Pidgeon, Roger E. Kasperson, and Paul Slovic, 102–120. Cambridge: Cambridge University Press.

Frewer, Lynn J., Susan Miles, Mary Brennan, Sharon Kuznesof, Mltchell Ness, and Christopher Ritson. 2002. "Public Preferences for Informed Choice under Conditions of Risk Uncertainty." *Public Understanding of Science* 11 (4): 363–372. doi:10.1088/0963-6625/11/4/304.

Funtowicz, Silvio O., and Jerome R. Ravetz. 1993. "Science for the Post-Normal Age." *Futures* 25 (7): 739–755. doi:10.1016/0016-3287(93)90022-L.

Heng, Melissa, and Shivraj Rajendran. 2020. "Roads Empty but Some Still Break the New Rules." *The Straits Times*, April 9.

Johnson, Branden B., and Paul Slovic. 1995. "Presenting Uncertainty in Health Risk Assessment: Initial Studies of Its Effects on Risk Perception and Trust." *Risk Analysis* 15 (4): 485–494. doi:10.1111/j.1539-6924.1995.tb00341. x.

Johnson, Branden B., and Paul Slovic, 1998. "Lay Views on Uncertainty in Environmental Health Risk Assessment." *Journal of Risk Research* 1 (4): 261–279. doi:10.1080/136698798377042.

Lai, Linette, and Yuen Sin. 2020. "More Stringent Measures Imposed as New Virus Cases Reach High of 287." *The Straits Times*, April 10.

Lanard. 2004. "WHO Expert Consultation on Outbreak Communications – Singapore's SARS Outbreak Communications." Keynote presentation, World Health Organization conference "Outbreak Communications," Singapore, September 21, 2004. Accessed 12 April 2020. https://www.psandman.com/articles/sarscomm.htm

Leung, G. M., T. H. Lam, L. M. Ho, S. Y. Ho, B. H. Y. Chan, I. O. L. Wong, and A. J. Hedley. 2003. "The Impact of Community Psychological Responses on Outbreak Control for Severe Acute Respiratory Syndrome in Hong Kong." *Journal of Epidemiology & Community Health* 57 (11): 857–863. doi:10.1136/jech.57.11.857.

Lim, Min Zhang. 2020. "Singapore to Take Care of Foreign Workers." *The Straits Times*, April 5.

Lofstedt, Ragnar, Maeve.Mcloughlin, and Magda.Osman. 2017. "Uncertainty Analysis: results from an Empirical Pilot Study. A Research Note." *Journal of Risk Research* : 1–11. doi:10.1080/13669877.2017.1313768.

Lofstedt, Ragnar. 2005. *Risk Management in Post-Trust Societies*. New York: Palgrave Macmillan.

Lofstedt, Ragnar, and Frederic Bouder. 2017. "Evidence-Based Uncertainty Analysis: What Should We Now Do in Europe? A View Point." *Journal of Risk Research*, 4(2017): 1–20. doi:10.1080/13669877.2017.1316763.

Lofstedt, Ragnar, Maeve McLoughlin, and Magda Osman. 2017. "Uncertainty Analysis: Results from an Empirical Pilot Study. A Research Note." *Journal of Risk Research*, 5(2017): 1–11. doi:10.1080/13669877.2017.1313768.

Metlay, Daniel. 1999. "Institutional Trust and Confidence: A Journey into a Conceptual Quagmire." In *Social Trust and the Management of Risk*, edited by G. T. Cvetkovich and R. E. Lofstedt, 100–116. London: Earthscan.

Petersen, A. C., Peter H. M. Janssen, J. P. Van Der Sluijs, J. S. Risbey, Jerome R. Ravetz, J. Arjan Wardekker, and H. Martinson Hughes. 2013. *Guidance for Uncertainty Assessment and Communication*. 2nd ed. The Hague: BPL Netherlands Environmental Assessment Agency.

Poortinga, Wouter, and Nick F. Pidgeon. 2003. "Exploring the Dimensionality of Trust in Risk Regulation." *Risk Analysis* 23 (5): 961–972. doi:10.1111/1539-6924.00373.

Prime Minister's Office. 2020. "PM Lee Hsien Loong's Interview with CNN." Accessed 10 April 2020. https://www.pmo.gov.sg/Newsroom/PM-interview-with-CNN

Renn, Ortwin. 2008. *Risk Governance: Coping with Uncertainty in a Complex World*. New York: Earthscan Publishing.

Renn, Ortwin, Andreas Klinke, and Marjolein Asselt. 2011. "Coping with Complexity, Uncertainty and Ambiguity in Risk Governance: A Synthesis." *Ambio* 40 (2): 231–246. doi:10.1007/s13280-010-0134-0.

Rosa, Eugene A, Ortwin Renn, and Aaron M. McCright. 2014. *The Risk Society Revisited: Social Theory and Governance*. Philadelphia: Temple University Press.

TODAY. 2020. "Covid-19: Many Abiding by Safe Distancing Rules but Some Still 'Missing the Point', Says Lawrence Wong." Accessed 10 April 2020. https://www.todayonline.com/singapore/covid-19-many-abiding-safe-distancing-rules-some-still-missing-point-says-lawrence-wong

Toh, T. W. 2020. "PM makes special appeal to older Singaporeans to stay home." *The Straits Times*, 11 April.

van der Sluijs, Jeroen P. 2012. "Uncertainty and Dissent in Climate Risk Assessment: A Post-Normal Perspective." *Nature and Culture* 7 (2): 174–195. doi:10.3167/nc.2012.070204.

Wardman, Jamie K., and Gabe Mythen. 2016. "Risk Communication: Against the Gods or against All Odds? Problems and Prospects of Accounting for Black Swans." *Journal of Risk Research* 19 (10): 1220–1230. doi:10.1080/13669877.2016.1262002.

World Values Survey Wave. 2014. http://www.worldvaluessurvey.org/WVSOnline.jsp

Managing the Covid-19 pandemic through individual responsibility: the consequences of a world risk society and enhanced ethopolitics

Katarina Giritli Nygren and Anna Olofsson

ABSTRACT
At the end of March 2020, international media present Swedish management of the ongoing Covid-19 pandemic as soft and irresponsible. Thus, Sweden, which is usually regarded as exceptionally risk averse and cautious, has chosen an unexpected risk management approach. The aim of this article is to reflect on how the Swedish government has managed the Covid-19 pandemic until early April 2020 from two theoretical perspectives, the risk society thesis and governmentality theory. We make a brief review of how previous pandemics have been managed compared to Covid-19 and try to understand the consequences of the Swedish handling of present pandemic with a particular focus on the governance of the pandemic and the exercise of power rather than definite risk management strategies during the pandemic.

The world seems shocked by Sweden's relaxed approach to the Covid-19 pandemic. A headline in the Daily Mail on 31 March 2020 read 'Is softly, softly Sweden heading for catastrophe?' (Connolly 2020), and on 4 April, an article in The Economist stated:

> While Sweden's fellow Scandinavians and nearly all other Europeans are spending most of their time holed up at home under orders from their governments, Swedes last weekend still enjoyed the springtime sun sitting in cafés and munching pickled herrings in restaurants. Swedish borders are open, as are cinemas, gyms, pubs and schools for those under 16. Restrictions are minimal: the government recommends frequent handwashing for all, working from home for those who can, and self-isolation for those who feel ill or are older than 70...Only on March 29th did Sweden ban gatherings of more than 50...During other pandemics, such as the outbreak of cholera at the end of the 19th century or the aids pandemic in the 1980s, Sweden imposed more stringent restrictions than its neighbours. So far the public is supportive of [Prime minister] Mr Lofven's contrarian strategy—but once the death toll rises this may quickly change.

In this short article, we reflect on how the Swedish government has managed the Covid-19 pandemic until early April 2020 from two theoretical perspectives: a realist risk theory based on Ulrich Beck's risk society thesis (1992) and a critical risk theory grounded in the work of Michel Foucault ([1976] 2003). At the end of the article, we also reflect on the risks related to Covid-19 from an intersectional perspective. Thus, we focused on the governance of the pandemic and the exercise of power rather than definite risk management strategies during the pandemic.

Compared to the governments of many European countries and other countries around the world, the Swedish government has managed the Covid-19 pandemic in a slightly different manner. By the end of March 2020, we had witnessed lockdowns in cities, regions, and whole countries worldwide. In Sweden, schools were open, and gatherings of up to 49 people were still allowed. Compared to our neighbouring countries, Finland, Norway, and Denmark, Sweden had less regulation of and restrictions on people's daily lives. To mention a few examples, the capital region has been contained in Finland, and schools have been closed since 16 March in Denmark and Norway. Furthermore, the Norwegian government also decided to restrict its citizens from visiting their holiday cottages, and municipalities closed all large ski resorts. In Sweden, the government decided on the 18th of March that all education at upper secondary levels and higher, including university education, should be conducted via distance learning. The following day, unnecessary travel to Sweden was forbade, and unnecessary travel from Sweden to other countries was discouraged by the Ministry of Foreign Affairs. On the 28th of March, any gathering of more than 49 people was prohibited. Still, restaurants, shops, gyms, etc. were open. Thus, the Swedish strategy to manage Covid-19 has been largely based on the responsibility of the citizens who receive daily information and instructions for individually targeted self-protection techniques by the Public Health Agency of Sweden's website and press conferences held by state epidemiologist Anders Tegnell, Prime Minister Stefan Löfven, and other representatives of the government. They continue to underline the importance of all citizens playing their part to stop the virus from spreading and avoiding the enhancement of law enforcement's restrictions on citizens' rights as long as possible.

Swedish management of previous pandemics

In a recent article, Mulinari and Vilhelmsson (2020) showed how Sweden, and particularly the Public Health Agency of Sweden, managed the 2009 H1N1 (swine flu) pandemic. Sweden differed from other countries in the management of that pandemic as well. However, Sweden was, as it usually is, on the other end of the spectrum of precautionary action in 2009 and decided to vaccinate the whole population remarkably early in the process. As a result, Sweden reached the highest level of vaccination coverage among all countries at 60 percent. Both then and in the current situation, the Swedish government and expert authorities focused on recourses and communication to protect risk groups and fundamental societal structures. Mulinari and Vilhelmsson (2020) showed that these measures were achieved in 2009 by encouraging people's solidarity with vulnerable people, and they argue that high levels of trust in institutions and the health care system support the process. Furthermore, mass media worked together with expert authorities and the government to create a strong alliance in 2009 that promoted mass vaccination for the common good, even though it meant downplaying that the vaccination only benefitted a minority of the population and might even harm some individuals. Mulinari and Vilhelmsson (2020, 337) concluded that this action was a quite remarkable exertion of power that saved some lives while devastating others, since the vaccine used (Pandemrix) had an unknown adverse effect of narcolepsy, which is a chronic disorder of excessive daytime sleepiness, among hundreds of Swedish children and adolescents.

The current situation differs from the situation in 2009. In the current situation, there is no available vaccine, and Sweden has not applied its usual precautionary approach to risk and crisis. Possibly because of the latter, we have not observed a strong alliance among mass media, the government, and expert authorities as we did in 2009. In contrast, Peter Wolodarski, editor in chief of Sweden's largest morning newspaper, Dagens Nyheter, has heavily criticized the government's decisions and recommendations from the Public Health Agency (Wolodarski 2020). In addition, the Public Health Agency appears to have a stronger position than before, and the government has openly shown that it makes decisions based on expert authorities' assessments.

What is similar to previous crises is the way the government has relied on citizens' trust in the state and how it has appealed to people's accountability and solidarity. Sociological risk theory may help us understand this situation.

The consequences of a world risk society

In risk society, risk is the driving force of social change; it is political in terms of liability (see also Douglas 1990) and provides power to those with the ability to avert and manage risks. The key pillars on which the risk society thesis rests are (Beck 1992) (1) the development of new, man-made, mega risks that threaten the existence of humanity on a global scale; (2) globalization with a world risk society; (3) expert dependence: the insensibility and complexity of risk that leave both politicians and the individual dependent on scientific knowledge; (4) individualization: old social structures such as social class are replaced, or at least hidden by, a new political self-fulfilling subject; and (5) risk positions: although social class and other social structures diminish, inequality remains but in the shape of risk positions.

At first glance, the Swedish situation, in which the responsibility for managing the Covid-19 pandemic is characterized by expert judgments and individual responsibility, seems to reflect what Ulrich Beck (1992) already described at the end of the 1980s as a risk society: a more modern globalized society derived by the management of risk and uncertainty. Furthermore, the interconnectedness of the Covid-19 pandemic with the global economy makes this pandemic a late modern complex mega risk, where our dependence on experts is evident. What could then be questioned is whether the inequalities that we can observe are individualized risk positions or if social inequalities are still classed, gendered, racialized, and aged. Building on Beck's early claim that risk (or bads) is an object of distribution comparable to the distribution of wealth, creating risk and class positions, respectively, Dean Curran's (2016) theorisation of structural inequalities in terms of social class within the risk society manages to combine the strength of Beck's theory with social class theory. He flips the discussion about resources, discusses the risk and inequality nexus, in which risk intensifies class differences, and argues that there is a systemic process structuring contemporary power relations resulting from the distribution of these bads.

The consequences of enhanced ethopolitics

Following the writings of Foucault ([1976] 2003) and his followers, it is possible that Sweden's management of Covid-19 falls under the description of the governing of conduct and individual responsibilisation, a political rationality that has a long history in the Swedish welfare state (Olsson 1997; Berg 1914). Reviewing the Swedish strategy, the public communication goals and recommendations of the health agency have emphasized adherence to and trust in infection control techniques informed by scientific and biomedical experts. The tacit implication is that specialized scientific and medical knowledge is somehow more or the most appropriate to guide pandemic planning and responses. Such an assumption about the legitimacy of scientific knowledge guiding public health and medical interventions is not unique to this pandemic. The Public Health Agency of Sweden provides recommendations for diverse health-related habits in relation to different risk groups not only on how to behave in relation to infectious diseases topics but also on more general health topics. Thus, risk discourses also enable individual identities to be linked to the biopolitical apparatus in disciplining, normalising, and protecting citizens. Nicholas Rose expanded on Foucault's writing, arguing that biopolitics are merging with what he called ethopolitics, a politics of life itself and how it should be lived (Rose 1999, X). Ethopolitics refers to the ethos of human existence—the sentiments, moral nature, or guiding beliefs of persons, groups, or institutions—which provides the medium within which self-government of the autonomous individual can be connected with the imperatives of good government. The moral component means that individuals are expected to self-regulate in accordance with the norms of a moral, or rather ethical, righteous life (Rose 2001), where responsibility for the avoidance of risk is bestowed upon individuals, who are supposed to regulate themselves in line with the directions of health authorities.

Intersectional vulnerability in the face of the governing of conduct

At the time this paper was written, we did not yet know the consequences of a soft lockdown in Sweden during the Covid-19 pandemic in terms of the number of patients infected and the mortality rate. What we have witnessed is that this pandemic, as with all risks, strikes differently, and already existing inequalities soar (Curran 2016). During the first phase of the pandemic, before the number of people infected started to rise more quickly, we witnessed the governing of conduct by the government. With recommendations rather than prohibitions, the individual becomes the unit of decision making towards whom claims of liability are directed if he or she does not manage to act ethically according to social expectations (Douglas 1990). This kind of governing of conduct, which has been characteristic of the Swedish risk management strategy during the pandemic thus far, targets the self-regulating individual in terms of not only trust but also solidarity. This type of governing was explicitly made by the prime minister in his speech to the nation on the 22nd of March (speeches that are extremely rare in Sweden) in which he particularly emphasized individual responsibility not only for the sake of personal safety but for the sake of others. Throughout the speech, this call for conduct was present, and he ended his speech by stating (Regeringen.se 2020), 'I am sure that everyone in Sweden will take on their responsibility. Do your utmost to ensure the health of others. To help each other and therefore be able to look back on this crisis and be proud of your particular role, your efforts. For your fellow human beings, for our society and for Sweden. Thanks.'

The focus on the individual in the self-management of epidemiological risk is also a key tenet of Sweden's health promotion strategy, and it relies on an assumption that appropriate information is being provided and individuals are able to make scientifically informed, risk-minimizing or risk-managing, correct choices. This management of responsible selves does, however, rest on a particular conception of the self, an assumption that people have the same potential to protect themselves, and that to be responsible in relation to Covid-19 does not expose you to other risks, which is similar to the risk society thesis (Beck 1992). However, decades of social science risk and crisis research have shown that the ability to manage risks and crises by conduct is largely related to social inequality. Previous risk and crisis communication studies have also emphasised the importance of considering people's differences, not least with regard to functional ability and language skills, which is something that is not often sufficiently considered (e.g. Kvarnlöf and Montelius 2020). Returning to our previous theoretical discussion, one can ask if this is a matter of the distribution of bads *per se* (Beck 1992), if the vulnerabilities are based on the uneven distribution of wealth (Curran 2016), or if the governing of conduct based on scientific and epidemic knowledge hides and black boxes underlying inequalities (Rose 2001).

Both risk rationalisation and governance mask and sometimes strengthen the structures of power underpinning the uneven distribution of both good and bad emerging from the production process. To better understand what is happening during a pandemic like Covid-19, we also need to analyse how risk is entangled with spatial gendered, racialised, and classed experiences of these and other hierarchal ordered categories (Giritli Nygren, Olofsson, and Öhman 2020) because the recommended infection control practices can also be understood as points of reference for individuals in which they have to negotiate different risks. We have, for example, already witnessed how people in already quite privileged positions are the ones who have the ability to work from home, which means that they also have more potential to act according to health recommendations, while others run the risk of being dismissed from their work or of their businesses going bankrupt.

Then, there are those in positions identified as socially important functions that cannot choose to avoid risks, particularly in the care sector, where the risk of infection is the largest and shortages of protective equipment exist. Last, not everyone has the resources that are required to participate in pandemic self-governance (knowledge of how and when to shop, having people who can help you, the hospital closest to you having enough respirators, etc.). This feature has already been evident in the Swedish mortality statistics because of the Covid-19 pandemic.

In early April 2020, the Swedish government proposed temporary changes in the constitution to be able to implement fast and extensive changes in citizens' and companies' rights to meet the challenges of the pandemic. There were protests from opposition parties, and the government reframed the proposition to include immediate approval by the parliament after making these kind of decisions. Thus, we are witnessing how Sweden prepares to leave the risk society and soft risk governance of conduct for a more radical securitization path while still protecting democracy thus far. The social contracts that regulate the relationship between the state and citizens is still built on trust in Sweden more than in many other countries. Although there are some voices calling for the necessity of being able to open up for state of emergency situations, there are others that while having seen what can be changed under this situation, do not want to threaten democracy. The question is what the long-term consequences will be if Sweden changes to more restrictive securitization with extensive lockdowns and penalties and a form of governance that increases the power of the government. With Covid-19, we face an ambivalent situation when the constant presence of risk and uncertainty increases our daily dependence on expertise, which in turn heightens the demand for alternative explanations, even to the extent of questioning expert and democratic systems (Giritli Nygren, Olofsson, and Öhman 2020).

Disclosure statement

No potential conflict of interest was reported by the authors.

References

Beck, Ulrich. 1992. *Risk Society: Towards a New Modernity*. London: Sage Publications.
Berg, Fridtjuv. 1914. "Uppfostran till Självstyre." *Social Tidskrift* 6: 241–259.
Connolly, Paul. 2020. "Is Softly, Softly Sweden Heading for Catastrophe?" *The Daily Mail*, March 31. https://www.dailymail.co.uk/debate/article-8173691/Is-softly-softly-Sweden-heading-catastrophe.html.
Curran, Dean. 2016. *Risk Power and Inequality in the 21st Century*. London: Palgrave Maximilian.
Douglas, Mary. 1990. "Risk as a Forensic Resource." *Daidalos* 119 (4): 1–16.
Foucault, Michel. (1976) 2003. *Lecture 11, 17 March 1976, in Society Must Be Defended: Lectures at the College de France*, 239–264. New York: Picador Press.
Giritli Nygren, Katarina, Anna Olofsson, and Susanna Öhman. 2020. *A Framework for Intersectional Risk Theory in an Ambivalent World*. London: Palgrave Maximilian.
Kvarnlöf, Linda, and Elin Montelius. 2020. "Militariseringen av Covid-19." *Dagens Arena* https://www.dagensarena.se/essa/militariseringen-av-coronapandemin/.
Mulinari, Shai, and Andreas Vilhelmsson. 2020. "Revisiting the Pharmaceuticalisation of Pandemic Influenza Using Lukes' Framework of Power." *Sociology of Health & Illness* 42 (2): 327–341. doi:10.1111/1467-9566.13006.
Olsson, Ulf. 1997. *Folkhälsa som pedagogiskt projekt*. Uppsala: Acta Universitatis, Uppsala Studies in Education 72.
Regeringen.se. 2020. "22 March Statsministerns tal till nationen [The Primeminister's speech to the nation]." https://www.regeringen.se/tal/2020/03/statsministerns-tal-till-nationen-den-22-mars-2020/.
Rose, Nicholas. 1999. *Powers of Freedom. Refraiming Political Thought*. Cambridge: CUP.
Rose, Nicholas. 2001. "The Politics of Life Itself." *Theory, Culture & Society* 18 (6): 1–30. doi:10.1177/02632760122052020.
Wolodarski, Peter. 2020. "Ursäkta måste vi vara plågsamt långsamma [Excuse me do we have to be painfully slow]." *Editorial in Dagens Nyheter*, March 8. https://www.dn.se/ledare/peter-wolodarski-ursakta-maste-vi-vara-plagsamt-langsamma/.

Be alarmed. Some reflections about the COVID-19 risk communication in Germany

Peter M. Wiedemann and Wolfgang Dorl

ABSTRACT

This article addresses six typical communication traps regarding COVID-19 which can also be observed with respect to other risk topics. First, we argue that risk communication can slide into what is known as 'risk kitsch'. This refers to the misconception that avoiding risk automatically results in safety. However, the avoidance of one risk always leads to other risks. Life without risk is not possible. We go on to scrutinize the unquestioning belief in numbers. It would seem that describing risks in terms of numbers promises to overcome chaos, provide order, and create a sense of agency over the threatening health risks. However, is this really so? Don't numbers also lie, lead astray, or misrepresent? The third issue we examine is the impact of pictures and individual cases on risk perception. What key picture – or rather what particular graphic – shapes the risk perception of COVID-19? What message does it convey? Does it bias and mislead us? The fourth issue involves the use of COVID-19 modeling studies which aim to provide answers to a number of essential questions: How bad can it get? What does it depend on? What can be done? Yet it is clear that not all assumptions underlying modeling computations are valid. Information content is not necessarily the same as reality content. The fifth section examines the question of how politics can navigate through the crisis. Is it navigating with a faulty compass? How defective is the compass? We then consider the question of morality, which is a crucial issue during a pandemic with its life- and-death stakes. Are moral evaluations always helpful? Or does a rigorously moral discourse hinder the necessary consideration of alternative options in dealing with the pandemic? Finally, we will draw some conclusions. What could better risk communication on COVID-19 look like? What can be improved, and how?

In the following we focus on the practice of risk communication concerning the coronavirus epidemic in Germany. What and how does the scientific community communicate about the COVID-19 risks to the general public, media, and politics? This communication should be evaluated. Does it meet recognized standards for effective risk communication (Albrecht and Steckelberg 2014; Lühnen et al. 2017)? Or does it contain gaps, biases, and distortions?

This article addresses six typical communication traps regarding COVID-19 which can also be observed with respect to other risk topics. First, we argue that risk communication can slide into what is known as 'risk kitsch'. This refers to the misconception that avoiding risk automatically results in safety. However, the avoidance of one risk always leads to other risks. Life without risk is not possible. We go on to scrutinize the unquestioning belief in numbers. It would seem that describing risks in terms of numbers promises to overcome chaos, provide order, and create a sense of agency over the threatening health risks. However, is this really so? Don't numbers also lie, lead astray, or misrepresent? The third issue we examine is the impact of pictures and individual cases on risk perception. What key picture – or rather what particular graphic – shapes the risk perception of COVID-19? What message does it convey? Does it bias and mislead us? The fourth issue involves the use of COVID-19 modeling studies which aim to provide answers to a number of essential questions: How bad can it get? What does it depend on? What can be done? Yet it is clear that not all assumptions underlying modeling computations are valid. Information content is not necessarily the same as reality content. The fifth section examines the question of how politics can navigate through the crisis. Is it navigating with a faulty compass? How defective is the compass? We then consider the question of morality, which is a crucial issue during a pandemic with its life- and-death stakes. Are moral evaluations always helpful? Or does a rigorously moral discourse hinder the necessary consideration of alternative options in dealing with the pandemic? Finally, we will draw some conclusions. What could better risk communication on COVID-19 look like? What can be improved, and how?

Risk kitsch

According to Kulka, the German word Kitsch is something that triggers an unreflective emotional response that ignores the hardness of reality (Kulka 1996, cited by Ortlieb and Carbon 2019). Kitsch is also evident in science (Kaeser 2013), for instance as pop science that turns science into a spectacle. Kitsch can be found in thinking about risks as well, either exaggerating them or putting them in the realm of evil or promises salvation and redemption. For example, it is kitsch to assume that whoever minimizes or even eliminates risk is on the safe side. Keeney (1995) pointed out this misperception in an essay published in the journal 'Risk Analysis' in 1995: *Whenever one risk is eliminated, another takes effect.*

A fitting example is the death of the writer Ödön von Horváth. He was killed by a falling branch during a thunderstorm in Paris in 1938. He had previously declined the offer to be chauffeured because he was afraid of motoring. Hence, it always depends on the net risk: Which measure involves the higher risk? Of course, it is not always possible to know this precisely in advance. Nevertheless, the risk of risk avoidance should always be kept in mind.

Risk kitsch is also a part of covid-19 reporting. The lockdown from March to May 2020 prevented people from being infected with the virus. Nevertheless, imposed social distancing also causes stress. Not surprisingly, it may even result in mental disorders. But the real problem does not become apparent until after the contact ban has been lifted. Fatal consequences of social distancing such as depression, insomnia, and anxiety may persist. The lockdown also amplifies somatic susceptibility to disease and the death risk (Hakulinen et al. 2018; Leigh-Hunt et al. 2017; Holt-Lunstad, Smith, and Layton 2010). There are already indications of hidden deaths due to the lockdown. In England and Wales, mortality increased for about 6,000 cases in the 14th calendar week compared with previous years. In about 42% of these cases, the death was not related to COVID-19 (Office for National Statistics 2020).

These additional deaths make it evident that the alternatives are not 'saving lives' versus 'selfish adherence to parties, major events and carefree social contact' or even 'saving lives' versus 'saving the economy'. Instead, it is a matter of risk-risk evaluation in equal dimensions: What counts are declines in quality of life and the risk of illness and death. This is why any moral argument that the lockdown of public life must be maintained without any ifs and buts until a vaccine is found is a risky strategy that also causes suffering and costs human lives.

The literature on the consequences of economic recessions makes it clear that no good can be expected from an economic lockdown (Karanikolos et al. 2016). When economic output declines, diseases become more frequent, and the risk of death increases, (Catalano et al. 2011). For example, to enable a transparent and evidence-based pandemic policy, the Network for Evidence-Based Medicine in Germany calls for rigorous evaluation of the effectiveness and collateral damage of the measures currently being implemented to protect the population and COVID-19 risk groups (EbM Netzwerk – Deutsches Netzwerk Evidenzbasierte Medizin e. V 2020). The Academy of Sciences Leopoldina has also made corresponding recommendations (Leopoldina 2020).

Keeney (1995) draws attention to another point that is rarely considered when weighing up the risks of measures to combat the corona pandemic. It concerns the noble goal of 'saving lives'. Unfortunately, we all die. Only the time of death and its cause are at stake, not death itself. If infant mortality is reduced, then the number of deaths from heart disease may increase, and if heart fatalities decrease, deaths from Alzheimer's disease may increase. Life remains risky and finite.

It is crucial to prevent infections and to cure diseases and thus prolong life. However, in addition to the number of deaths, age statistics must always be taken into account, and it would be more reasonable to report the average years of life lost rather than counting lost lives. To make this a bit clearer: In Italy, the average life expectancy in 2018 was about 83 years (www.worldlifeexpectancy.com/italy-life-expectancy). For comparison: The average age of COVID-19 deceased in Italy at the end of March 2020 was over 80 years, and only 1% of the deceased had no previous illnesses (Instituto Superiore di Sanità 2020). In Germany, the numbers are similar. The median age of people who died with SARS-CoV-2 was 82. In other words, for many patients, death was close even without COVID-19. A look at the mortality tables of Germans shows that 80-year-olds have, on average, 8 (men) and 9.5 (women) years to live (Statista, 2019). However, if we take the premorbidity of the COVID-19 fatalities into account, the average life expectancy of those over 80 might be lower than 8-9.5 years.

The mess of risk numbers

Quantification is one of the foundations of all exact science, including medicine and risk research. The question is, are we getting the right risk figures in the current corona pandemic? Are these figures also understandable to laypersons? It is noteworthy that most people prefer numerical risk figures over qualitative risk figures (e.g. 1 in 100 persons is at risk rather than 'the risk is high'). However, when it comes to characterizing the magnitude of risk itself, most people prefer qualitative claims (Wallsten et al. 1986).

The Robert Koch Institute (RKI), Germany's central institution in the field of disease surveillance and prevention, is not much different. It evaluates the health risk situation for the population qualitatively. Until 3 March 2020, the RKI assessed the risk situation as moderate, but shifted on March 17 when it declared: 'The RKI currently assesses the risk to the health of the population in Germany as high overall' (RKI Daily Management Report on Coronavirus Disease). As of 26 March 2020, it changed to: 'The risk to the health of the population in Germany is currently estimated to be high overall and very high for risk groups' (www.rki.de/DE/Content/InfAZ/N/Neuartiges_Coronavirus/Risikobewertung.html). What led to this reassessment is not discussed in detail. The precise meaning of 'health risk is high' also remains unclear. Interpretation of such qualitative expressions vary considerably (Wiedemann, Boerner, and Repacholi 2014). A numerical risk description would probably be more appropriate.

Not surprisingly, even quantitative formats have their pitfalls. Public understanding of numbers is limited. Most people do not understand numerical data very well and fail even at simple numerical tasks. For example, a German survey indicates that about 30% of the participants gave a wrong answer to the question as to which of the numbers indicates the greater risk of illness: 1 in 100 people die every day, 1 in 1000 people die every day, or 1 in 10 die every day (Galesic,

Olsson, and Rieskamp 2012). This reduced numeracy opens the door to misunderstandings. It makes a difference whether a risk is described as '100 people die of cancer every day' or '36,500 people die of cancer every year'. The larger the number, the higher the risk perception, since the reference terms – here day vs. year – is mostly ignored (Bonner and Newell 2008).

The reporting on COVID-19 risks is susceptible to this bias. In Germany, crude data – the number of known infected cases and COVID-19 deaths – are highlighted. Such crude data are also provided for the entire world population. For example, on 17 March 2020, the Worldometer indicated 2,197,174 COVID-19 cases and 147,512 deaths (www.worldometers.info/coronavirus/?). Most important, these figures refer to cumulative numbers, which are summed up over time. The actual number of cases is always much lower. But large numbers, void of any interpretative aid, amplify the perception of risk and cause fear. This is because only few people know that, on average, 150,000 people die every day worldwide and 54 million every year. People must be provided with a context that supports understanding. In this regard, comparisons play a crucial. They are essential for ascertaining whether the reported deaths due to COVID-19 are significant. There is a range of options to provide such information. One would be a reference to excess mortality: Have more people died than usual? Is the COVID-19 mortality noticeable?

Let us look at the data to make this more clear. In the last week of March 2020, there was a slight excess mortality in Switzerland for the over-65 age group. However, for people aged 0 to 65, there were no deviations in the expected frequency of deaths (FSO 2020). In Italy, excess mortality occurred from the 11th calendar week 2020, in Spain from the 12th calendar week. Excess mortality was also observed in France and England from the 13th calendar week. Worth mentioning, excess mortality disappeared at the 18th calendar week (www.EuroMOMO.eu, 8 September 2020).

Since excess mortality has also been repeatedly observed in connection with waves of influenza, one way to put COVID-19 deaths into perspective is to compare the numbers with flu deaths in recent years. During winter 2017/18 about 25,000 flu deaths were estimated for Germany alone. If one assumes a case fatality rate of 0.5% of those infected during this flu epidemic (as the RKI does), then approximately 5 million people in Germany were likely to become infected by the flu. It follows that within the 15-week core period of the 2017/18 flu wave, flu cases would have had to have doubled every 4.4 days in order to reach the predicted 5 million cases. This growth rate is comparable to the first weeks of the current corona virus pandemic in Germany (EbM Netzwerk – Deutsches Netzwerk Evidenzbasierte Medizin e. V 2020; RKI 2019). The accusation that this comparison is misleading and plays down the seriousness of the situation is false. We are not saying that SARS-CoV-2 is less dangerous than the known influenza viruses. Nor do we claim that the 2017/18 influenza wave in Germany had more severe consequences than the COVID-19 epidemic will ever have. However, the comparison does reveal something about the state of affairs up to April 2020 by showing that the more recent situation is not worse. Whether and how the development of COVID-19 fatalities will continue, we do not know. However, exploiting this ignorance to fuel fears is an unwarranted attempt to influence the general public (Bolsen and Druckman 2015). One question suggests itself: Why are such comparisons rarely used? This may be due to the fear of encouraging skeptics who assume that the new coronavirus is only half as bad.

Finally, it is important to avoid traps caused by framing (Levin, Schneider, and Gaeth 1998). Risk perceptions and decisions under uncertainty are particularly susceptible to framing traps. It makes a difference whether a statement specifies that 2% of infected people have died (to give a fictitious percentage) or 98% of infected people have survived. The risk perception will be higher for the loss variant than for the rescue variant (Rothman and Salovey 1997).

The perils of narratives and pictures

Stories of individual fates have an immense influence on the perception of risk. A quotation attributed to Josef Stalin sums it up, regardless of the authorship: The death of one man is a tragedy, the death of millions is a statistic. It is the individual fate that causes people to care. An individual case triggers far more emotions than a series of numbers (Slovic and Slovic 2015). The closer the individual case is to us, the stronger the emotions triggered. Closeness can be defined in terms of time and space, but also similarity (Trope and Liberman 2010). COVID-19 in China felt far away; only when we learned that people in Lombardy were affected did it become clear that the risk was on its way to us. However, in science, the weight of the evidence for individual cases is low. Anecdotal evidence does not allow any valid and reliable conclusions – especially in pandemics. Hence media reporting, which often refers to narratives such as dramatic single cases, can be problematic. This is how fuel is feared and panic is promoted (Garfin, Silver, and Holman 2020).

Images play a decisive role in media coverage. They stimulate risk perception because they facilitate imagination and identification (Shen, Sheer, and Li 2015). They help us put ourselves in the place of those affected and enable us to experience their worries and concerns. One example is the photograph depicting the transport of coffins containing COVID-19 victims in Bergamo. This image has shaped our collective memory of Europe's corona crisis. Even abstract images can be powerful, as they are used as argumentative instruments (Pörksen 1997).

The power of images is illustrated in COVID-19 communication by the graphic depicting the exponential growth of newly infected cases. This graphic reinforces the impression of an uncontrollable disaster by showing rising growth figures in terms of an explosion. The graphic triggers the imagination that the number of humans expected to become ill could reaches tens of millions if COVID-19 is allowed to spread unhindered among the population. The message is that it will not take long before COVID-19 infects the majority of the population. This image is also associated with the horror of the imminent overloading of hospitals.

Such visual depictions are so powerful because of their selectivity. Only the worst-case information is highlighted. A balanced view would underline the fact that not every infected person falls ill, and not every infected person has to be hospitalized and will die. Furthermore, the number of convalescences has to be taken into account, as is recently practiced by the RKI in its overview information on COVID-19 cases. This additional information would lead to a figure that no longer appears quite so threatening. The emotional impact of the visual argument of the unlimited growth in SARS CoV-2 infections would disappear.

Another way to amplify risk perception by a graphic display is to overstate the size of effect shown in the display by spreading the scale (Tufte 2001). The effect size simply looks bigger than the data indicate. A closer look at media reporting reveals many examples of that bias (Lauer 2020).

Overconfidence in computational modeling

People place trust outside themselves when their own knowledge is not sufficient to make informed decisions. Someone who trusts is a believer. Moreover, those who believe can eliminate uncertainty and contingency and make decisions. However, trust is a risky advance performance (Luhmann 2014). Trust can be disappointed, especially when it comes to the prognosis of the course of pandemics. One example is the swine flu in 2009, whose spread was massively overestimated. Psychological research points to a particular cause: experts have more confidence in their models than these models usually deserve. The keyword here is 'overconfidence', i.e. excessive confidence of the modelers in their ability to make correct judgments (Hoffrage 2004).

To give an example, probably no computation has had more influence on political decisions in the UK and the USA during the corona pandemic than the mathematical model developed by Neil Ferguson and colleagues of the Imperial College London (Ferguson et al. 2020). Their modeling was the argument for lockdown in the UK. Based on several plausible assumptions, the team of scientists calculated that only a radical strategy of contact restriction could restrain the spread of the virus and thus save human lives.

Strict measures, they said, would slow down the pandemic and thus prevent the health care system from being overloaded. Ferguson predicted approximately 500,000 deaths in the UK by August 2020 if measures such as contact restrictions, school closures, and quarantine for infected people were not applied. He claimed that such measures would keep the numbers down to only 20,000 deaths. However, this does not mean that 480,000 lives could be saved. In an interview with the *Telegraph* (Knapton 2020), on 25 March 2020, Ferguson himself called his estimates into question by admitting that up to 2/3 of the assumed 500,000 deaths would have occurred in the near future anyway.

Nevertheless, the real dilemma is that the strict measures to restrain SARS-CoV-2 virus infections cannot be maintained for months or years without immense damage to society. And yet, a rash relaxation of the strict measures could lead to a second wave of COVID-19 cases, which in turn could result in a considerable number of deaths. To make matters worse, the immunity of convalescents from COVID-19 might be limited. Reliable data are still lacking, but it may only last about 6 to 18 months. The convalescents could – after this period – fall ill again if they come into contact with the virus (Hartmann 2020).

In this context, one particular assessment of the RKI is also interesting: 'A challenge for communication arises in particular from the problem: the more successful we are [...], the longer we have to wait before a substantial part of the population has acquired immune protection against SARS-CoV-2 due to a past infection' (RKI 2020a).

In line with Albert (1963), it can be argued that model computations of the course of COVID-19 diseases have high information value. It is precisely this characteristic that makes them so popular in politics. However, and this is the decisive point, such models do not provide any information about their validity. Whether or not their conclusions actually come true is not their business. Computational models explore only the logical consequences of their assumptions and not the real-world connections and developments the computations aim to describe. Reality can be more surprising and completely different.

To prevent surprises, the model designers think in scenarios, i.e. they present several possible developments. One could think of it as a kind of immunization strategy to prevent criticism of the modeling. Nonetheless, this line of thinking limits the information content of the models. The more open the model is, the lower the orientation value. Potential users are forced to choose their particular scenario out of the various ones presented in the model. In most cases, users pick the scenario that matches their own beliefs and convictions. In this way, models become all-purpose weapons that support the users' already existing preferences and intentions.

Another phenomenon to consider is called defensive pessimism (Norem 2007). It works on the premise that the best way to be prepared is to expect the worse. This strategy can also be used as a preventive strategy to avert possible criticism later, especially in the event of accusations of acting carelessly and putting human lives at risk. Anyone who takes defensive precautions will escape this criticism (Artinger, Artinger, and Gigerenzer 2019). However, this practice is not always beneficial, especially if we consider the potential damage of excessive precautionary actions (Graham 2004). Models should also take the consequences of the lockdown on mortality, disease, and economic welfare into account. It should be noted that first scenarios regarding the economic costs of the corona shutdown for Germany are now available (Dorn et al. 2020).

Poor navigation

To be able to steer through a pandemic, one should be well informed about the following issues: (1) How many people are infected? (2) How many people are newly infected per time unit (day or week)? (3) How many of those infected do not develop symptoms, and how many fall seriously ill? (4) How many have to be treated in intensive care units, and how many have to be ventilated? (5) How many of the infected are dying?

To the first question: How many are infected? We have no answer because only the reported infections are counted. Those who are infected with the virus but have no or only mild symptoms will not go to a doctor and are thus not registered in the statistics. Moreover, the tests used can only identify acute SARS-COV-2 infections. They cannot detect whether someone may have had the virus earlier and recovered. Unfortunately, we will not have the full picture until a reliable antibody test has been developed.

The reported number of acutely infected people thus depends on two factors: first, how many tests are conducted, and second, who is tested. Statistics based on reported cases do not provide reliable information about the population's actual number of infections. As a result, all other key figures which are based on the number of reported infections are also unreliable. Hence the so-called doubling time, or how many days it will take for the number of infected persons to double, a value that policymakers relied on at the beginning of the pandemic in Germany (Homburg 2020), is mostly a blind indicator. If more tests for suspected COVID-19 cases are conducted, the number of infected persons identified will increase. This bias will occur even if the actual number of infected persons in the population remains unchanged. Far-reaching decisions on to manage the pandemic – whether to tighten or loosen contact restrictions – thus lack a solid foundation.

The reported number of positive tested persons does not say anything about how severely these persons are affected by the virus. Regrettably, the RKI does not provide any information in its statistics on the variation of COVID-19 disease's severity in addition to information on fatalities. For risk communication, differentiated statistics on the number of hospitalized cases, for example, would be desirable. Such information would help to get a more accurate picture of the threat COVID-19 poses to our society.

Recently, the RKI has started providing information on the number of hospital admissions and the occupation of intensive care units with COVID-19 patients by referring to the newly established DIVI Intensive Care Register of the German Interdisciplinary Association for Intensive and Emergency Medicine (DIVI). This register lists 2,405 COVID-19 patients in intensive care treatment on 12 April, based on reports from 752 hospitals. This is slightly less than one-third of the 1,942 hospitals in Germany. A total of 2,978 treatments were completed. On the same day, 8,235 beds were available in intensive care units (DIVI 2020). Therefore, there was no cause for concern at this particular point in time.

Some reservations concerning the information about the COVID-19 death toll are justified. The mere indication of the crude numbers – i.e. the reported number of deaths – has little meaning. In order to determine how severe COVID-19 lethality is, the number of deaths must be related to the number of people infected. However, if the number of unreported infections is very large, the COVID-19 lethality will be probably overestimated. The reverse error is also possible. It is just as likely that there are infected deceased persons who have not been recorded. We assume that this error occurs less frequently, especially if we include the following consideration: People who died due to the virus infection must be distinguished from those who died with the virus. This distinction is by no means trivial. At present, the RKI includes in its statistics all deaths of persons who tested positive for the virus regardless of whether the virus was the cause of death. This procedure leads to an overestimation of the number of COVID-19 deaths.

Finally, tests on a sufficiently large random sample of the population are absolutely essential. Only they can provide certainty about the severity and course of COVID-19 diseases, e.g. to indicate how large the percentage of infected persons in the population is. On 10 April 2020, the RKI announced to conduct such a prevalence study, although demands from the scientific community had been voiced for some time (cf. for example, EbM Netzwerk – Deutsches Netzwerk Evidenzbasierte Medizin e. V 2020). The Free State of Bavaria has already launched a similar project, and in North Rhine-Westphalia virologists from the University of Bonn (Streeck et al. 2020) studied the community of Gangelt (1,000 persons in 400 households). A report is now available

(Streeck et al. 2020). Austria also already presents figures. In the test period from 1–6 April 2020, about 28,500 persons in Austria were infected, three times the number reported as testing positive in the official case statistics (SORA 2020).

Morality on slippery ground

The risk communication on COVID-19 is essentially based on scientific, i.e. virological and epidemiological arguments. In the media and in political debates, however, talking about COVID-19 risks is morally charged. The good people are afraid of COVID-19, the bad deny the threat. The moral turn in the public discourse helps to reduce complexity. Psychological research proves that COVID-19 communication becomes so better understandable, will be better processed and remembered, and will be seen as more credible (Schwarz et al. 2007). But moral arguments also have their disadvantages. Research on populism (Reinemann et al. 2016) can help us better understand these disadvantages. Populist communication is propaganda with emotional arguments, black-and-white thinking, a focus on existential crisis and threat, and clear distinctions between good and evil (Bloch and Negrine 2017; Meyer 2006). Luhmann's famous remark that it is the task of ethics to warn against morality (Luhmann 2008) indicates what it is all about: Morality prevents tradeoffs and the weighing of alternatives.

The dilemma is that in the corona crisis, losses have to be weighed against losses. Decisions makers can only aim at limiting losses. There is no way out of the corona crisis without sacrifice. At the moment, this inconvenient truth is being ignored. Worse, every critique of the lockdown, even those that have empirical arguments on their side, is being fended off. This corral mentality itself violates fairness. A study by Mahoney (1977) already refers to this in another context. He demonstrated that the assessment of a scientific study is much more rigorous if one does not like its results. One is more generous with studies whose findings agree with one's own convictions.

An example of this bias was the media criticism of the study by the virologist Streeck (Streeck et al. 2020) in Gangelt – a community profoundly affected by COVID-19. The main focus of objection was the reported death rate, which did not match the prevailing view of the risks of SARS-CoV-2. The media favored the figures on the COVID-19 case fatality rate in Germany from Johns Hopkins University (3.1% as of 17 April) and the Robert Koch Institute (1% as of 4 April, RKI 2020b). They are rather unquestioningly accepted as a 'gold standard'. However, the available statistical evidence of both data sets is weak, and the uncertainties are considerable. More openness regarding these issues should have been exercised.

In fact, some prevalence studies from the US are in line with the Streeck study (Bendavid et al. 2020; USC., 2020). The fatality rate of infected persons in Santa Clara County amounts to 0.12–0.2% (Bendavid et al. 2020), which corresponds to approximately the same order of magnitude as indicated by the Streeck group for Gangelt.

Conclusion

Risk communication should provide information and enable informed decisions. This is why it is crucial to determine whether it stirs up fears or counteracts them with reliable information. No doubt, fears can activate protective actions, but whenever people are unable to act, fear leads to panic. By using evidence-based risk information, diffuse fears should be transformed into circumscribed and directed fears. The aim should be to enable a tailored evaluation of the Covid-19 risks for the various risk groups in the population.

A good practice of risk communication in the COVID-19 pandemic also requires a risk intelligence that takes into both the risks of the pandemic and the risk of the related containment measures into account. Risk communication should be balanced, scrutinizing the risks of the risk measures, and not lead to uncritical acceptance of civil liberties restrictions without proof of their necessity. Of course, in an emergency situation, politics cannot wait for 5-year research projects that might support the success of its measures implemented to fight the COVID-19 pandemic. However, without any evaluation whatsoever politics will act blindly. An on-sight steering through the pandemic is only possible if the view is cleared.

Whether this practice of good risk communication is actually pursued depends on how the addressees of the communication are viewed. Are they seen as fearful wards who need to be directed and managed? Or are they assumed to be reasonable, mature individuals who can make informed decisions even under difficult circumstances if they receive the right information? Doubt is justified. Politics tends toward paternalism in times of crisis.

What could be done better?

1. There is a need for a national health portal that brings together the relevant evidence-based information on COVD-19.
2. In addition to specialist information on risk and risk reduction measures, appropriate information should also be made available to the general public.
3. The following indicators of COVID-19 risks should be communicated: (1) the number of infected persons minus the number of convalescents, (2) the number of deaths and their age distribution, (3) the number of hospitalized cases, and (4) the cases in intensive care units. Information on immunization of the population would also be desirable.
4. Interpretation aids for these basic indicators should be provided in the form of comparisons.
5. Ad hoc summaries and insights of relevant new findings such as those provided by the Centre for Evidence-Based Medicine (CEBM) in the United Kingdom should be made more easily accessible to the public.
6. Missing data and uncertainties regarding COVID-19 should be pointed out repeatedly and prominently in the statistics. For laypersons, a kind of traffic light system could be used to indicate the strength of the available evidence.
7. The measures to combat the COVID-19 pandemic should be assessed in terms of their benefits as well as their collateral damage. This information should also be communicated to the public.

Instead of trying to limit diffuse fears, most of the COVID-19 risk communication reinforces the panic mode. A worst-case-oriented and defensive policy that does not want to be accused later of playing down the hazards of the coronavirus encounters a public that is already enraged. It would be better if risk communication aimed to empower people to make evidence-based judgements on COVID-19 risks.

Disclosure statement

No potential conflict of interest was reported by the authors.

References

Albert, H. 1963. "Modell-Platonismus – Der neoklassische Stil des ökonomischen Denkens in kritischer Beleuchtung." In: *Logik der Sozialwissenschaften, hrsg*, edited by von E. Topitsch, 406–434. Berlin: Kiepenhauer und Witsch.
Albrecht, M., and A. Steckelberg. 2014. "Manual für die Erstellung von evidenzbasierten Informationen für Arbeitnehmerinnen und Arbeitnehmer." Accessed April 17, 2020. www.baua.de/DE/Angebote/Publikationen/Berichte/Gd78.pdf?__blob=publicationFile&v=8
Artinger, F. M., S. Artinger, and G. Gigerenzer. 2019. "Frequency and Causes of Defensive Decisions in Public Administration." *Business Research* 12 (1): 9–25. doi:10.1007/s40685-018-0074-2.
Bendavid, E., B. Mulaney, N. Sood, S. Shah,E. Ling, R. Bromley-Dulfano, C. Lai, Z. Weissberg, R. Saavedra-Walker, J. Tedrow, D. Tversky, A. Bogan, Th. Kupiec, D. Eichner, R. Gupta, J. Ioannidis, AND J. Bhattacharya. 2020. COVID-19 Antibody Seroprevalence in Santa Clara County, California. medRxiv 2020.04.14.20062463. doi: https://doi.org/10.1101/2020.04.14.20062463
Bloch, E., and R. Negrine. 2017. "The Populist Communication Style: Toward a Critical Framework." *International Journal of Communication* 11: 178–197.

Bolsen, T., and J. N. Druckman. 2015. "Counteracting the Politicization of Science." *Journal of Communication* 65 (5): 745–769. doi:10.1111/jcom.12171.

Bonner, C., and B. R. Newell. 2008. "How to Make a Risk Seem Riskier: The Ratio Bias versus Construal Level Theory." *Judgment and Decision Making* 3 (5): 411–416.

Catalano, R., S. Goldman-Mellor, K. Saxton, C. Margerison-Zilko, M. Subbaraman, K. LeWinn, and E. Anderson. 2011. "The Health Effects of Economic Decline." *Annual Review of Public Health* 32: 431–450. doi:10.1146/annurev-publhealth-031210-101146.

DIVI. 2020. "Tagesreport-Archiv." Accessed April, 17, 2020. https://www.divi.de/divi-intensivregister-tagesreport-archiv

Dorn, F., C. Fuest, M. GöTtert, C. Krolage, S. Lautenbacher, S. Link, A. Peichl, et al. 2020. "Die volkswirtschaftlichen Kosten des Corona-Shutdown für Deutschland: Eine Szenarienrechnung." ifo-Schnelldienst 4/2020.

EbM Netzwerk – Deutsches Netzwerk Evidenzbasierte Medizin e. V. 2020. "COVID-19: Wo ist die Evidenz? Stellungnahme des EbM-Netzwerks vom 20.03.2020 (Aktualisierung 21.03.2020)." Accessed April 17, 2020. www.ebm-netzwerk.de

Ferguson, N., D. Laydon, G. Nedjati Gilani, N. Imai, K. Ainslie, M. Baguelin, S. Bhatia, et al. 2020. "Report 9: Impact of Non-Pharmaceutical Interventions (NPIs) to Reduce COVID19 Mortality and Healthcare Demand." Accessed April 17, 2020. https://spiral.imperial.ac.uk/handle/10044/1/77482

FSO. 2020. "Weekly Number of Death in 2020." Accessed April 17, 2020. https://www.bfs.admin.ch/bfs/en/home/statistics/health/state-health/mortality-causes-death.html

Galesic, M., H. Olsson, and J. Rieskamp. 2012. "Social Sampling Explains Apparent Biases in Judgments of Social Environments." *Psychological Science* 23 (12): 1515–1523. doi:10.1177/0956797612445313.

Garfin, D. R., R. C. Silver, and E. A. Holman. 2020. "The Novel Coronavirus (COVID-2019) Outbreak: Amplification of Public Health Consequences by Media Exposure." *Health Psychology* 39 (5): 355–357. doi:10.1037/hea0000875.

Graham, J. 2004. "The Perils of the Precautionary Principle: Lessons from the American and European Experience." Accessed April 17, 2020. https://www.heritage.org/government-regulation/report/the-perils-the-precautionary-principle-lessons-the-american-and

Hakulinen, C., L. Pulkki-Råback, M. Virtanen, M. Jokela, M. Kivimäki, and M. Elovainio. 2018. "Social Isolation and Loneliness as Risk Factors for Myocardial Infarction, Stroke and Mortality: UK Biobank Cohort Study of 479 054 Men and Women." *British Medical Journal*. Accessed April 17, 2020. https://heart.bmj.com/content/104/18/1536

Hartmann, G. 2020. "Heinsberg Protokoll Pressekonferenz." Accessed April 17, 2020. www.facebook.com/hbergprotokoll. http://diskussionspapiere.wiwi.uni-hannover.de/pdf_bib/dp-670.pdf

Hoffrage, U. 2004. "Overconfidence." In *Cognitive Illusions*, edited by R. Pohl, 235–254. New York: Psychology Press.

Holt-Lunstad, J., T. B. Smith, and J. B. Layton. 2010. "Social Relationships and Mortality Risk: A Meta-Analytic Review." *PLoS Medicine* 7 (7): e1000316. doi:10.1371/journal.pmed.1000316.

Homburg, Stefan, 2020. "Effectiveness of Corona Lockdowns: Evidence for a Number of Countries," Hannover Economic Papers (HEP) dp-671, Leibniz Universität Hannover, Wirtschaftswissenschaftliche Fakultät.

Instituto Superiore di Sanità. 2020. "Sorveglianza Integrata COVID-19 in Italia [09.03.2020]." Accessed April 17, 2020. www.iss.it/documents/20126/0/Infografica_09marzo.pdf/1f62ad0a-e156-cf27-309d-26adcb1b52b4?t=1583782049035

Kaeser, E. 2013. "Science Kitsch and Pop Science: A Reconnaissance." *Public Understanding of Science* 22 (5): 559–569. doi:10.1177/0963662513489390.

Karanikolos, M., P. Heino, M. McKee, D. Stuckler, and H. Legido-Quigley. 2016. "Effects of the Global Financial Crisis on Health in High-Income OECD Countries: A Narrative Review." *International Journal of Health Services* 46 (2): 208–240. doi:10.1177/0020731416637160.

Keeney, R. L. 1995. "Understanding Life-Threatening Risks." *Risk Analysis* 15 (6): 627–637. web.iitd.ac.in/~arunku/files/CEL899_Y14/Understanding%20life%20threatening%20risks_Keeney.pdf

Knapton, S. 2020. "Two Thirds of Coronavirus Victims May Have Died This Year Anyway, Government Adviser Says." *Telegraph*, 25.3.2020. Accessed April 17, 2020. https://www.telegraph.co.uk/news/2020/03/25/two-thirds-patients-die-coronavirus-would-have-died-year-anyway/.

Kulka, T. 1996. *Kitsch and Art*. University Park, PA: Pennsylvania State University Press.

Lauer, J. 2020. "You're Telling the Truth, but Your Visualization Isn't." Accessed September 9, 2020. https://towardsdatascience.com/youre-telling-the-truth-but-your-visualization-isn-t-eef69298f1af

Leigh-Hunt, N., D. Bagguley, K. Bash, V. Turner, S. Turnbull, N. Valtorta, and W. Caan. 2017. "An Overview of Systematic Reviews on the Public Health Consequences of Social Isolation and Loneliness." *Public Health* 152 (11): 157–171. doi:10.1016/j.puhe.2017.07.035.

Leopoldina. 2020. "Ad-hoc-Stellungnahmen zur Coronavirus-Pandemie." Accessed April 17, 2020. www.leopoldina.org/uploads/tx_leopublication/2020_Leopoldina-Stellungnahmen_zur_Coronavirus-Pandemie.pdf.

Levin, I. P., S. L. Schneider, and G. J. Gaeth. 1998. "All Frames Are Not Created Equal: A Typology and Critical Analysis of Framing Effects." *Organizational Behavior and Human Decision Processes* 76 (2): 149–188. doi:10.1006/obhd.1998.2804.

Luhmann, N. 2008. *Die Moral der Gesellschaft. Hrsg. von D. Horster*. Frankfurt/M: Suhrkamp.

Luhmann, N. 2014. *Vertrauen. Ein Mechanismus zur Reduktion sozialer Komplexität. 5. Aufl.* Konstanz: UVK Verlagsgesellschaft.

Lühnen, J., M. Albrecht, I. Mühlhauser, and A. Stueckelberg. 2017. "Leitlinie evidenzbasierte Gesundheitsinformation." Version 1.0. Erstellungsdatum: 20.02.2017. Accessed April 17, 2020. www.ebm-netzwerk.de/de/medien/pdf/leitlinie-evidenzbasierte-gesundheitsinformation-fin.pdf

Mahoney, M. J. 1977. "Publication Prejudices: An Experimental Study of Confirmatory Bias in the Peer Review System." *Cognitive Therapy and Research* 1 (2): 161–175. doi:10.1007/BF01173636.

Meyer, T. 2006. "Populismus und Medien." In *Populismus. Gefahr für die Demokratie oder nützliches korrektiv?*, edited by F. Decker, 86–91. Wiesbaden: Verlag für Sozialwissenschaften.

Norem, J. K. 2007. "Defensive Pessimism, Anxiety, and the Complexity of Evaluating Self-Regulation." *Social and Personality Psychology Compass* 2 (1): 121–134.

Office for National Statistics. 2020. "Deaths Registered Weekly in England and Wales, Provisional." Accessed April 17, 2020. www.ons.gov.uk/peoplepopulationandcommunity/birthsdeathsandmarriages/deaths/datasets/weeklyprovisionalfiguresondeathsregisteredinenglandandwales

Ortlieb, S. A., and C. C. Carbon. 2019. "A Functional Model of Kitsch and Art: Linking Aesthetic Appreciation to the Dynamics of Social Motivation." *Frontiers in Psychology* 9. doi:10.3389/fpsyg.2018.02437.

Pörksen, U. 1997. *Weltmarkt der Bilder.* Stuttgart: Klett Cotta.

Reinemann, C., T. Aalberg, F. Esser, J. Strömbäck, and C. H. de Vreese. 2016. "Populist Political Communication. Toward a Model of Its Causes, Forms, and Effect." In *Populist Political Communication in Europe*, edited by T. Aalberg, F. Esser, C. Reinemann, J. Strömbäck, and C. H. de Vreese, 12–25. New York: Routledge.

RKI. 2019. "Bericht zur Epidemiologie der Influenza in Deutschland Saison 2018/19." Accessed April 17, 2020. https://influenza.rki.de/Saisonberichte/2018.pdf

RKI. 2020a. "Modellierung von Beispielszenarien der SARS-CoV-2-Epidemie 2020 in Deutschland (20.3.2020)." Accessed April 17, 2020. www.rki.de/DE/Content/InfAZ/N/Neuartiges_Coronavirus/Modellierung_Deutschland.html

RKI. 2020b. "Vorläufige Bewertung der Krankheitsschwere von COVID-19 in Deutschland basierend auf übermittelten Fällen gemäß IfSG." *Epidemiologisches Bulletin* 17: 3–9. https://www.rki.de/DE/Content/Infekt/EpidBull/Archiv/2020/Ausgaben/17_20.pdf?__blob=publicationFile

Rothman, A. J., and P. Salovey. 1997. "Shaping Perceptions to Motivate Healthy Behavior: The Role of Message Framing." *Psychological Bulletin* 121 (1): 3–19. https://pdfs.semanticscholar.org/eac3/e2171d06097b21f2d6e628ab09fd5f273922.pdf doi:10.1037/0033-2909.121.1.3.

Schwarz, N., L. J. Sanna, I. Skurnik, and C. Yoon. 2007. "Metacognitive Experiences and the Intricacies of Setting People Straight: Implications for Debiasing and Public Information Campaigns." *Advances in Experimental Social Psychology* 39: 127–161. https://dornsife.usc.edu/assets/sites/780/docs/07_aep_schwarz_et_al_setting-people-straight.pdf

Shen, F., V. C. Sheer, and R. Li. 2015. "Impact of Narratives on Persuasion in Health Communication: A Meta-Analysis." *Journal of Advertising* 44 (2): 105–113. doi:10.1080/00913367.2015.1018467.

Slovic S., and P. Slovic, eds. 2015. *Numbers and Nerves.* Corvallis: Oregon Stat University Press.

SORA. 2020. "SORA-Ergebnisse der repräsentativen Stichprobe COVID-19." Accessed April 17, 2020. https://www.sora.at/nc/news-presse/news/news-einzelansicht/news/covid-19-praevalenz-1006.html

Statista. 2019. https://de.statista.com/statistik/daten/studie/1783/umfrage/durchschnittliche-weitere-lebenserwartung-nach-altersgruppen/

Streeck, H., G. Hartmann, M. Exner, and M. Schmid. 2020. "Vorläufiges Ergebnis und Schlussfolgerungen der COVID-19 Case-Cluster-Study (Gemeinde Gangelt)." Accessed April 17, 2020. www.land.nrw/sites/default/files/asset/document/zwischenergebnis_covid19_case_study_gangelt_0.pdf

Trope, Y., and N. Liberman. 2010. "Construal-Level Theory of Psychological Distance." *Psychological Review* 117 (2): 440–463. doi:10.1037/a0018963.

Tufte, E. R. 2001. *The Visual Display of Quantitative Information.* Cheshire: Graphics press.

USC. 2020. Early antibody testing suggests COVID-19 infections in L.A. County greatly exceed documented cases. Accessed April 17, 2020 https://news.usc.edu/168987/antibody-testing-results-covid-19-infections-los-angeles-county/

Wallsten, T., D. Budescu, A. Rapoport, R. Zwick, and B. Forsyth. 1986. "Measuring the Vague Meanings of Probability Terms." *Journal of Experimental Psychology: General* 115 (4): 348–365. doi:10.1037/0096-3445.115.4.348.

Wiedemann, P. M., F. Boerner, and M. Repacholi. 2014. "Do People Understand IARC's 2B Categorization of RF Fields from Cell Phones?" *Bioelectromagnetics* 35 (5): 373–378. doi:10.1002/bem.21851.

Did the world overlook the media's early warning of COVID-19?

King-wa Fu 🆔 and Yuner Zhu 🆔

ABSTRACT

This perspective is written to give a rapid response to discuss the role of media in risk communication in the first three months of the COVID-19 pandemic. We analyze two sets of media data, China's social media and global news event, and draw a few initial observations in relation to the impacts of China's information control policy, global risk governance, and the role of WHO.

COVID-19 is striking the world on an unprecedented scale. Cities are locked down, schools and businesses are closed, airlines are cancelled, tens of thousand people were killed globally, and many people and their family members, especially the underprivileged class, are suffering. It remains uncertain how long the global pandemic will last and not to mention an end.

The first batch of coronavirus cases was reported in Wuhan, China in late 2019. China's local health authority first claimed the virus had "no apparent pattern of human-to-human transmission" on December 31, 2019 (Wuhan Municipal Health Commission 2019). Then, the spokesperson of China's Ministry of Foreign Affair said China had notified the World Health Organization (WHO) and the United States multiple times in early January (Ministry of Foreign Affairs and the People's Republic of China 2020). However, nothing official was done to inform or warn the public at that moment. On January 14, WHO tweeted a post citing the investigation of Chinese authorities that there was "no clear evidence of human-to-human transmission of the disease," (World Health Organization 2020) and the tweet is still accessible on the current WHO's Twitter timeline. In less than a week on 20 January, the Chinese government officially announced the coronavirus epidemic to the world (Phillips, Mallapaty, and Cyranoski 2020) and a group of leading Chinese virologists confirmed the virus can be passed between people (National Health Commission 2020). Even though confirmed cases of coronavirus had skyrocketed between late January and early March in many parts of the world, WHO finally acted on March 12 to make an announcement to declare the novel coronavirus a pandemic, indicating a global spread of virus and major public health threat.

Despite uncertainty, early warning in a crisis is known as a significant move to engage the public (Zhu et al. 2020). The world has learned the lessons in previous pandemics that transparency and proactive communication are keys to inform the public for crisis preparation. For example, WHO once discontinued its routine press conference during the 2009 H1N1 pandemic and the move is considered as a "misstep." (Fineberg 2014, 1340) Mass media has been playing a critical role in sending risk signals to the world, even though the crisis is yet to be formally recognized, helping the public make informed responses to take necessary precautionary measures. Despite inevitably resulting in some overreaction and spread of misinformation, in one WHO's published handbook, the organization recommends "panic avoidance should never be used as a rationale for false reassurance or for lack of transparency on the part of authorities." (World Health Organization 2005, 11) Transparency is considered as a best practice of risk communication to inform and build trust with the public. No legitimate reason should stop the free press to report about crises, especially in its early stage.

Unfortunately, making early warning in a non-transparent social system poses particular challenges. Ophthalmologist Dr. Li Wenliang, a Chinese "whistleblower" who sent a warning message to his friend circle of medical doctors in late December 2019, was accused of disturbance of public order (Green 2020). In an authoritarian state like China, public conversation on many critical issues is restricted, media outlets are state-controlled, and dissidents and independent journalists are routinely silenced. Chinese citizens often resort to social media to receive and share news (including using proxy servers to access news outside China) but the authorities have a sophisticated censorship system to filter information (Fu, Chan, and Chau 2013), including messages related to the crisis (Zeng, Chan, and Fu 2017).

For instance, a Chinese social media message, which read (in English translation), "Wuhan pneumonia cannot be judged to be SARS. Wuhan has the only virus laboratory in the country and is also a world-class virology laboratory. There are ways to deal with the virus. If Wuhan can't figure it out, no one can handle it" was published in the afternoon of December 31, 2019. The post was swiftly censored within an hour, according to our monitoring system, Weiboscope.

Censorship social media in China

We analyze a unique dataset of Chinese social media and aim to evaluate how online information about the COVID-19 outbreak was restricted in China. Weibo is China's answer to Twitter and is the largest microblog service provider, with 497 million active monthly users in 2019 (Weibo Corporation 2019). We have been collecting Weibo data since 2011 via our research project Weiboscope (Fu, Chan, and Chau 2013). Weiboscope samples a list of high-profile users and a group of randomly selected users, whose posts are programmatically retrieved every 15-20 minutes by a cluster of computer servers. When the system detects a once-published post is missing in an attempt to retrieve a user's timeline, the post is then confirmed to be censored by the platform, i.e. return of error message of "permission denied" indicating fully censored message. Through such a process, social media posts made by 66,126 high-profile users and 52,268 randomly selected accounts are longitudinally traced and their post-publication censored messages are recorded. Since the high-profile users generate the vast majority of social media contents (Fu and Chau 2013) and the randomly sampled accounts represent the voice of general users, a combination of these two constitutes a fairly representative sample of the whole user population of Weibo. A censored message is defined as either a "permission denied" post or a retweet of a "permission denied" post. Ethical aspect of this project was approved by the Human Research Ethics Committee at the University of Hong Kong (EA260113).

Between December 1, 2019 and February 27, 2020, Weiboscope collected 11,362,502 posts, among which 1,230,353 (https://doi.org/10.6084/m9.figshare.12199038) contain at least an outbreak-related keyword[1] and 2,104 (1.7 per 1,000) have been censored. The daily censorship ratio (Figure 1) indicates a few early spikes, referring to some non-local coronavirus cases in Thailand, Japan, and South Korea, before the Chinese government's full disclosure on January 20. The spikes after January 20 correspond to the censorship of public reactions to Wuhan's lockdown (Jan 24), an alleged coverup by the Chinese Center for Disease Control and Prevention (Jan 30), whistleblower Dr. Li Wenliang's death (Feb 6), logistic problem of medical resources (Feb 10), and a patient's suicide (Feb 26).

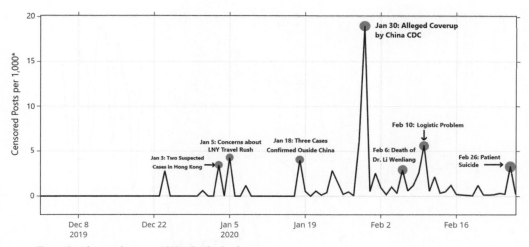

* The number of censored posts per 1,000 outbreak-related posts.

Figure 1. Daily censorship ratio (per 1,000 posts related to coronavirus outbreak).

Covering coronavirus in the global news

The above data analysis indicates online discussion on China social media was restricted. But how did the news media respond at the global level? To what extent was the world informed by the news media about the coronavirus even though the information about the first outbreak in China was limited? We then draw on another large dataset Global Database of Events, Language, and Tone (GDELT, Leetaru and Schrodt 2013), which records the world events reported by all national and international news on Google News. We aim to examine to what extent the mass media reported the coronavirus at the global level.

We downloaded the GDELT data between December 1, 2019 and March 31, 2020. We took advantage of each event item's first news report whose hyperlink contains the article title. For example, The Guardian's story titled "China's Sars-like illness worries health experts" on January 9, 2020 is structured like: https://www.theguardian.com/world/2020/jan/09/chinas-sars-like-illness-worries-health-experts. We identified all such news items whose title carries at least one of the following patterns in case-insensitive manner: "-coronavirus-", "-pneumonia-", or "-sars-". We excluded the events dated before December 1, 2019 and obtained 759,191 event entries from the database which linked to 163,714 unique news articles, i.e. multiple distinct events can link to the same article.

Figure 2 presents the daily trend of the events related to "coronavirus," "pneumonia," or, "SARS" as reported by the global news. As seen in the chart, there was almost a flat line before January 20, 2020 but indeed a few hundred events on average took place per day. Altogether, there were 3,155 events that happened before January 20, 2020, among which 1,616 (51.5%) happened in China, 317 (10.1%) in the United States, 182 (5.8%) in Thailand, 166 (5.3%) in Hong Kong, 142 (4.5%) in Japan, and 717 (29%) in other locations. This suggests that, even though the Chinese government did not make any official announcement about the coronavirus and only released very limited information to the public before January 20, a certain number of stories about coronavirus in China and the cases exported to other places were reported in the news media. Having said that, media attention is deemed relatively low.

Global media coverage on coronavirus began to rise after January 20, when Chinese government officially confirmed the local outbreak to the world. The number of news covered events, which were mainly related to the epidemic in China, increased drastically, and peaked at January 31, 2020, but the trend did not sustain in February. Starting from early February, the events count exhibited a declining trend until February 23. After that, the situations in Italy, Iran, South

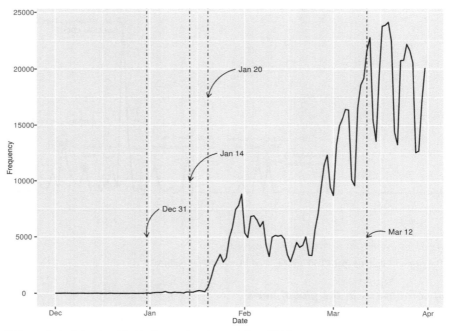

Figure 2. Daily numbers of events related to Coronavirus, Pneumonia, or SARS.

Korea, and many other places were getting worse and the event count skyrocketed between the last week of February and the first week of March. After the number of events almost reached the new height in early March, WHO declared the pandemic on March 12, 2020.

At the time of writing, the coronavirus pandemic is developing and the situation is changing every day. So this short perspective does not intend to give a comprehensive media analysis or a full account for the ultimate role of the mass media in crisis communication. Future in depth research into this subject is definitely warranted. We instead aim to offer a few observations on the basis of the above preliminary data analysis. First, Chinese authorities censored online discussion on the coronavirus and restricted the public access to early warning on social media. This is in contrast to the lesson learned in previous pandemics that transparency and proactive communication are essential to early detection and containment of pandemics (Fineberg 2014). The information control policy in China not only limited Chinese people to make necessary and timely responses to the outbreak, but it may have also delayed the global media attention to the upcoming crisis, according to the chart which shows very few news reports covered the coronavirus-related events before China broke the silence on January 20. In a global society, China's local information control policy is no longer locally impactful but has significant global implication; Second, the world seems to have missed or overlooked the early but weak warning signal before January 20, when the outbreak was developing in China and a growing number of cases were being exported to other places. Later in early February, in view of a reduction of news reports of events, the world also did not pay sufficient attention to the developing pandemic that was globally widespread. These time intervals are both critical periods for governments to develop risk preparedness and management strategies; Third, at least from a risk communication perspective, in considering the global attention was rising in the first two months of Year 2020, the WHO appeared to be too passive to give an official warning to the global society in response to the apparent escalation of reported coronavirus events around the world. Based on the data in the chart, the world had been well notified about the global epidemic from the mass media and social media before the WHO's declaration on March 12, which seems to be lagging behind the global epidemic as well as many people's expectations.

Note

1. Weibo posts pertinent to COVID-19 were identified according to a set of predefined keywords: '疫情' epidemic situation, '口罩' mask, '病毒' virus, '肺炎' pneumonia, '冠状' coronavirus,'感染' infected, '确诊' confirmed case, '隔离' quarantine, '防疫' combat the outbreak, '传染' infection, '新冠' novel coronavirus, '钟南山' Zhong Nanshan, '封城' lockdown, '非典' SARS, 'N95' N95, '李文亮' Li Wenliang, '蝙蝠'bat, '防护服'hazmat suit, '卫健委' 'health commission, '世卫' WHO (abbr), '重症' severe, '疾控中心' CDC, '李兰娟' Li Lanjuan, '流行病' epidemiology, '华南海鲜市场' Huanan Seafood Market, '人传人' human-to-human transmission, '管轶' Guan Yi, '世界卫生组织' WHO, '消毒液' bleach, '洗手液' hand sanitizer, '危重' critically ill, '张文宏' Zhang Wenhong, 'CDC' CDC, '高福' Gao Fu, '穿山甲' pangolin, '粪口传播' fecal–oral transmission, 'WHO' WHO, '飞沫传播' droplets transmission, '疑似病例' suspected case, '潜伏期' incubation period. The keyword list was checked and confirmed by both bilingual authors to be sufficiently inclusive and specific.

Disclosure statement

No potential conflict of interest was reported by the authors.

ORCID

King-wa Fu ⓘ http://orcid.org/0000-0001-8157-5276
Yuner Zhu ⓘ http://orcid.org/0000-0003-2772-2188

References

Fineberg, Harvey V. 2014. "Pandemic Preparedness and Response — Lessons from the H1N1 Influenza of 2009." *New England Journal of Medicine* 370 (14): 1335–1342. doi:10.1056/NEJMra1208802.

Fu, King-wa, Chung-hong Chan, and Michael Chau. 2013. "Assessing Censorship on Microblogs in China: Discriminatory Keyword Analysis and the Real-Name Registration Policy." *IEEE Internet Computing* 17 (3): 42–50. doi:10.1109/MIC.2013.28.

Fu, King-wa, and Michael Chau. 2013. "Reality Check for the Chinese Microblog Space: A Random Sampling Approach." *PloS One* 8 (3): e58356–e58356. doi:10.1371/journal.pone.0058356.

Green, Andrew. 2020. "Li Wenliang." *The Lancet* 395 (10225): 682. doi:10.1016/S0140-6736(20)30382-2.

Leetaru, Kalev, and Philip A. Schrodt. 2013. "GDELT: global data on events, location, and tone, 1979–2012." In *ISA annual convention*. http://data.gdeltproject.org/documentation/ISA.2013.GDELT.pdf

Ministry of Foreign Affairs, the People's Republic of China. 2020. "Foreign Ministry Spokesperson Hua Chunying's Daily Briefing Online on February 3, 2020." 2020. https://www.fmprc.gov.cn/mfa_eng/xwfw_665399/s2510_665401/2511_665403/t1739548.shtml.

National Health Commission. 2020. "Press Conference of the National Health Commission High-Level Expert Group Regarding the Pneumonia Caused by the Novel Coronavirus Infection." http://www.nhc.gov.cn/xcs/s7847/202001/8d735f0bb50b45af928d9944d16950c8.shtml.

Phillips, Nicky, Smriti Mallapaty, and David Cyranoski. 2020. "How Quickly Does the Wuhan Virus Spread?" *Nature, January* 10.1038/d41586-020-00146-w.

Weibo Corporation. 2019. "Weibo Reports Third Quarter 2019 Unaudited Financial Results." https://weibocorporation.gcs-web.com/news-releases/news-release-details/weibo-reports-third-quarter-2019-unaudited-financial-results.

World Health Organization. 2005. "Effective Media Communication during Public Health Emergencies." WHO. http://www.who.int/csr/resources/publications/WHO_CDS_2005_31/en/.

World Health Organization 2020. "Preliminary Investigations Conducted by the Chinese Authorities Have Found No Clear Evidence of Human-to-Human Transmission of the Novel #coronavirus (2019-NCoV) Identified in #Wuhan, #China." https://twitter.com/WHO/status/1217043229427761152.

Wuhan Municipal Health Commission. 2019. "Wuhan Municipal Health Commission's Situation Report of the Epidemic of Pneumonia in Our City (in Chinese)." http://wjw.wuhan.gov.cn/front/web/showDetail/2019123108989.

Zeng, Jing, Chung-hong Chan, and King-wa Fu. 2017. "How Social Media Construct 'Truth' around Crisis Events: Weibo's Rumor Management Strategies after the 2015 Tianjin Blasts." *Policy & Internet* 9 (3): 297–320. doi:10.1002/poi3.155.

Zhu, Yuner, King-Wa Fu, Karen A. Grépin, Hai Liang, and Isaac Chun-Hai Fung. 2020. "Limited Early Warnings and Public Attention to COVID-19 in China, January-February, 2020: A Longitudinal Cohort of Randomly Sampled Weibo Users." *Disaster Medicine and Public Health Preparedness* : 1–9. https://doi.org/10.1017/dmp.2020.68.

Fact-checking as risk communication: the multi-layered risk of misinformation in times of COVID-19

Nicole M. Krause (iD), Isabelle Freiling (iD), Becca Beets (iD) and Dominique Brossard (iD)

ABSTRACT

The emergence of the 2019 novel coronavirus has led to more than a pandemic—indeed, COVID-19 is spawning myriad other concerns as it rapidly marches around the globe. One of these concerns is a surge of misinformation, which we argue should be viewed as a risk in its own right, and to which insights from decades of risk communication research must be applied. Further, when the subject of misinformation is itself a risk, as in the case of COVID-19, we argue for the utility of viewing the problem as a multi-layered risk communication problem. In such circumstances, misinformation functions as a meta-risk that inter-acts with and complicates publics' perceptions of the original risk. Therefore, as the COVID-19 "misinfodemic" intensifies, risk communication research should inform the efforts of key risk communicators. To this end, we discuss the implications of risk research for efforts to fact-check COVID-19 misinformation and offer practical recommendations.

The information environment on COVID-19 is constantly evolving, with inconsistent and unclear messages regarding risk levels and appropriate protective behaviors coming from the media, employers, public health officials, and all levels of government, as well as friends and family. The World Health Organization (WHO) has characterized the COVID-19 information landscape as an "over-abundance of information," ultimately declaring the existence of a "massive infodemic" (World Health Organization 2020b). Unfortunately, woven into this rapidly-expanding tapestry of messages is a plethora of misinformation (Frenkel, Alba, and Zhong 2020).

The "misinfodemic" surrounding COVID-19 is the focus of our discussion, and one key purpose of this paper is to illustrate the importance and utility of viewing misinformation as a risk in its own right, to which decades of insight from risk communication research must be applied. Further, we argue that the COVID-19 misinformation risk interacts with the risks of the pandemic itself, creating a *multi-layered risk*. Ultimately, we show that multi-layered risks involving misinformation pose unique communication challenges that fact-checking (the current mitigation strategy of choice) will fail to sufficiently address. We conclude with recommendations to researchers and risk communicators.

A tale of two risks: the COVID-19 misinfodemic

At the outset, it is worth emphasizing that the risk of misinformation should not be taken lightly. In the case of the COVID-19 misinfodemic—where the subject of misinformation is a health risk—misinformation can literally be a matter of life and death. Consider, for example, that an Arizona resident died after consuming chloroquine (that was intended for use in aquariums) after hearing on the news that the substance might be a good treatment for COVID-19 (Waldrop, Alsup, and McLaughlin 2020). Furthermore, misinformation about COVID-19 can encourage people to shirk experts' recommendations for protective behaviors such as social distancing, thus accelerating the spread of the virus. Concerned about this possibility, a large collection of journalism professors and journalists recently raised the alarm about COVID-19 misinformation on Fox News, arguing that its misreporting "endangers" both their own viewers and others (Gitlin 2020).

Clearly, experts are concerned about COVID-19 misinformation and see Fox News as one source of the risk. However, recent poll data indicate that the supposedly at-risk public does not view the misinfodemic the same way as the experts: 84% of Fox News viewers said they believed the network covered the coronavirus outbreak somewhat to very well (Pew Research Center 2020). We are not suggesting with these data that Fox News viewers see no risk of COVID-19 misinformation whatsoever, but only that they do not see Fox News as the problem. Meanwhile, many Americans are aware of misinformation about COVID-19, and many more have exhibited concern about misinformation more broadly. In a nationally-representative survey conducted in mid-March 2020, 47% of Americans said they had come across some to a lot of news on COVID-19 that seemed completely made up (Pew Research Center 2020). Further, regarding misinformation in general, recent research shows that "more Americans view made-up news as a very big problem for the country than identify terrorism, illegal immigration, racism and sexism that way" (Pew Research Center 2019a).

The latter data reveal that, for many Americans, misinformation is indeed perceived as a risk, or "the possibility that an undesirable state of reality … [may] occur as the result of natural events or human activities" (Renn 1992, 56). However, the discrepancy between experts' and some lay publics' concerns about Fox News as a source of misinformation is one of many examples that, in addition to the variation in risk perceptions that seasoned risk researchers expect about COVID-19, *we should expect similarly varied perspectives on the definitions and attributes of misinformation risks*. Before arguing this point, we will clarify some key concepts.

First, there are different ways to define "misinformation" (Southwell, Thorson, and Sheble 2018, Scheufele and Krause 2019). Our operating definition of misinformation does not differentiate between (a) incorrect information that a communicator believes is true and (b) information that a communicator *knows* is false but purveys as true (sometimes referred to as "disinformation"). Instead, we define misinformation broadly as any messages that conflict with the best-available evidence about COVID-19, and that would likely *not* be corrected if they were challenged. To identify misinformation about COVID-19, it is noteworthy that we must consider the "best available evidence," because notions of "scientific consensus" or "established scientific facts" are tenuous in this context. For example, there is not yet agreement on the biology of the novel SARS-CoV-2 virus and the COVID-19 disease it produces—there is uncertainty about the processes of disease transmission and treatment strategies (Service 2020).

Beyond our definition of "misinformation," our understanding of "fact-checking" also requires clarification. For our purposes, "fact-checking" refers to efforts to "investigate claims that are *already* in the news" (Graves 2016, 7-8) or on social media. Examples of fact-checking include work by Snopes.com, CheckYourFact.com, and FactCheck.org, as well as the efforts of fact-checking departments within established journalistic outlets, and those working in partnership with social media platforms (Graves 2016). Our definition of fact-checking also includes myth-busting efforts by institutions and scientific agencies. For example, the WHO has set up a website dedicated to COVID-19 "myth busting" (World Health Organization 2020a), and the Centers for Disease Control and Prevention (CDC) now publishes a webpage titled "Stop the Spread of Rumors," which encourages people to "know the facts about COVID-19" (Centers for Disease Control and Prevention 2020). As COVID-19 spreads, fact-checking efforts are multiplying, with the number of English-language fact-checks about COVID-19 increasing by more than 900% from January to March 2020 (Brennan et al. 2020).

Misinformation and fact-checking, through the lens of risk

At first glance, fighting falsehoods with facts may seem like a straightforward strategy to miti-gate misinformation. Unfortunately, while fact-checking can sometimes correct individuals' mis-perceptions, there is ample evidence from political communication and social psychology showing that fact-checking can be of limited utility—or worse, it can backfire—in contexts where audiences are motivated to defend their pre-existing beliefs (Scheufele and Krause 2019). Complementing this work, we argue that risk communication research offers another useful framework for understanding why fact-checking can sometimes be problematic.

Specifically, we argue for the necessity and utility of viewing fact-checking as a form of risk communication in which the "risk" is misinformation. Through this lens, we draw on well-estab-lished risk research to assess the complexity of the COVID-19 misinfodemic, and we argue that: (a) misinformation risks are difficult to define, particularly when they are *multi-layered* and when subgroups of the population define misinformation risks differently; (b) attempts to fact-check misinformation will be complicated by varying levels of trust in the communicators behind such efforts; and (c) risks are, by definition, related to "uncertainties," which means that articulating "the facts" about COVID-19 may be insufficient (or, in some cases, impossible).

Defining the misinfodemic risk: a multi-layered problem

Risk research has long asserted that risks are difficult to define, and that different publics—oper-ating with different ideologies, value systems, and cultural backgrounds—tend to define them very differently (Hansson 2010, Renn 1992, Rayner 1992). To illustrate this point, consider public opinion in the United States pertaining broadly to the issue of misinformation. Two thirds of Americans (67%) "are worried about what is real and fake on the internet" (Newman et al. 2019, 10). This suggests, as discussed earlier, that Americans broadly view misinformation as a "risk." Taking a closer look, however, it is clear that definitions and perceptions of the misinformation risk are not the same for everyone.

For example, there are strong, partisan-based cleavages in the United States. Whereas nearly two-thirds of Republicans and Republican-leaning independents (62%) view "made-up news [a]s a very big problem in the country today," only two in five Democrats and Democratic-leaning independents (40%) say the same (Pew Research Center 2019a). Further, "Republicans [are] about three times as likely as Democrats to blame journalists" for the problem (Pew Research Center 2019a). Clearly, partisans in the United States have divergent perspectives on key constitutive elements of the misinformation threat, including its magnitude and its source.

When it comes to perceived risks of COVID-19, these divergent understandings of the misin-formation risk seem to be interacting with COVID-19 risk perceptions in ways that will surely complicate risk communications about the pandemic. First, a nationally-representative survey in the United States conducted in mid-March shows aggregate-level agreement about the risks posed by the pandemic: Two-thirds of Americans (66%) considered COVID-19 a major threat to the health of the population; about nine in ten saw it as a major threat to the US economy (88%); and half of Americans (49%) saw it as a major threat to their personal financial situation (Pew Research Center 2020). Further, nearly two thirds (63%) also said that the CDC has properly

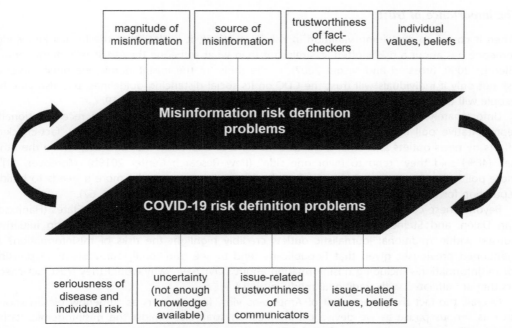

Figure 1. A multi-layered problem of risk definition in the context of the COVID-19 pandemic. (Note: This graphic does not aim to be all-encompassing.).

communicated the risks of COVID-19 (Pew Research Center 2020). Despite these indicators of broad agreement, partisan-based cleavages begin to emerge when publics are asked about who seems to be exaggerating—i.e., misreporting—the risks of COVID-19: Three quarters of Republicans and Republican-leaning independents (77%) say the media have exaggerated the risks of the coronavirus outbreak at least slightly, whereas only half (49%) of Democrats and Democratic-leaning independents say so (Pew Research Center 2020).

Clearly, when COVID-19 risks and misinformation risks are considered in combination, complexities arise as individuals' COVID-19 risks perceptions influence their misinformation risk perceptions. With two different sets of risk perceptions layered on top of each other, individuals who trust that the CDC will not exaggerate COVID-19 risks can still simultaneously trust media sources or other actors who are accused of misrepresenting the CDC's position and recommendations on the pandemic. Thus, efforts to combat misinformation about COVID-19 will confront a multi-layered problem of risk definition, as illustrated in Figure 1.

Recognizing the multi-layered nature of the misinfodemic risk is helpful for understanding why ongoing efforts to fact-check misinformation about COVID-19 are unlikely to succeed in their current form. Indeed, the psychometric paradigm of risk research has demonstrated that what people think should be done about a given risk can depend largely on how they define the characteristics of the hazard (e.g., its magnitude and source) (Slovic 1992).

For example, in the case of misinformation about COVID-19, the above data suggest that Republicans who see journalists as the origin of misinformation will likely expect two things: (a) That fact-checking organizations will scrutinize false COVID-19 claims made by traditional news media, and (b) That risk communicators will tell them how traditional media will be held accountable for COVID-19 misinformation. Comparatively, Democrats will be less likely to have these expectations. If parts of the public feel that fact-checkers are disregarding or simply misunderstand the nature of the misinformation risk, then fact-checkers' credibility will be harmed among those parts of the public in times of crisis (Covello et al. 2001). This brings us to the issue of trust.

The importance of trust

When it comes to explaining variation in risk perceptions, it is clear that the factual knowledge someone has about a risk is often less relevant than what someone they trust tells them about it (Siegrist 2000, Brossard and Nisbet 2007). In the midst of the misinfodemic, we must therefore ask not only if individuals will trust the CDC on its social distancing guidelines, but also whether people will trust the fact-checkers seeking to dispel rumors about COVID-19.

Unfortunately, fact-checkers are not uniformly trusted by Americans. In a recent nationally-representative poll in the United States, only half of the respondents said that "fact-checking efforts by news outlets and other organizations tend to deal fairly with all sides," while the other half (48%) said they "tend to favor one side" (Pew Research Center 2019b). Moreover, "[t]he more political or controversial issues a fact-checking service covers, the more it needs to build a reputation for usefulness and trustworthiness" (Brandtzaeg and Følstad 2017, 67).

Beyond these concerning figures, a low level of trust in the press in United States (Hanitzsch, Van Dalen, and Steindl 2018) also raises an important question: can fact-checking initiatives housed within traditional journalistic outlets credibly highlight the risks of misinformation? As mentioned previously, given that Republicans tend to see traditional journalists as responsible for misinformation—including misinformation about COVID-19—why would they trust fact-checkers that are affiliated with traditional media outlets?

Overall, the fact that almost half of Americans view fact-checkers as somehow biased should give us serious pause as we devise communication strategies amidst the misinfodemic. Rather than hastily ramping up existing fact-checking efforts, we would be better served to investigate how we can shore up fact-checkers' credibility or how existing fact-checking operations can partner with highly-trusted organizations to deliver messages more effectively. Further, as risk researchers, we should recognize that if we want to effectively address future crises that misinformation is sure to complicate, then we need to better understand how fact-checkers (and "corrective" communications more generally) are perceived by various publics.

The problem of uncertainty

Another unique challenge that fact-checkers will face during this misinfodemic is uncertainty. Fact-checking in the context of risks—which are, by definition, uncertainties—is not easy. New information is continually emerging, and old information is often discovered to be inaccurate. For example, given the novelty of the SARS-CoV-2 virus, there is ongoing uncertainty about its origins and the nature of the disease it produces (Kuznia and Griffin 2020).

Another example of the uncertainties connected to COVID-19 are the predictive models of infection and death rates. Models are just models, but they are often presented as "the truth" in media representations (Tufekci 2020), even though it is often unclear to the public which assumptions and data the models are based on. For instance, as individuals' compliance with protective behaviors evolves over time, the models evolve as well. Beyond this, uncertainty can also stem from misinformation spread by non-experts. For example, a COVID-19 article published on *Medium* garnered millions of views before it was taken down because the author's "number-crunching [was] riddled with inconsistencies and entry-level errors" (Requarth 2020).

The limits of knowledge

A problematic assumption often put forward is that people who believe misinformation have a "knowledge" problem—i.e., they lack sufficient exposure to the facts, or they mistake falsehoods for facts. Often, this is where fact-checking enters the picture. However, the notion of a single, mass public struggling to understand "the facts" is known as the "knowledge deficit model," and it has been mostly debunked as an effective model for bringing individuals' views in line with expert consensus (Scheufele 2013). In part, this is because of the roles that psychological biases and information processing tendencies play in shaping how people respond to uncertainty and risk (see, e.g., Kahneman and Tversky 1979, Trumbo 2002).

When processing scientific (mis)information, individuals often rely on "heuristics" that can make complex information easier or more efficient to digest (Scheufele and Krause 2019). In the context of risk communication, individuals sometimes form attitudes about complex risk-related information by relying on their existing value systems (Ho, Scheufele, and Corley 2011, Kim et al. 2014). When new information contradicts individuals' pre-existing values or beliefs—such as when they are told a risk-related belief they hold is false, via a fact-checking effort—they are likely to engage in "motivated reasoning" to defend their prior beliefs (Kunda 1990). Further, even if the corrective message succeeds in correcting misperceptions, there is no guarantee that updated beliefs will lead to a change in behavior.

Finally, risk and benefit perceptions are heavily influenced by message content that has little to do with facts. Instead, emotions tend to matter more, with some risk scholars offering evidence that hazards characterized by more "outrage factors" (e.g., the uncontrollability of the risk or its involuntariness) tend to elicit emotive reactions that can heighten risk perceptions (Sandman 1987). Put simply, "the greater the outrage, the higher the risk perception" (Ju et al. 2015, 880). Thus, as has happened with misinformation about vaccines, emotionally-flat "fact-checks" about COVID-19 will struggle to win hearts and minds as they compete against misinformation that is replete with emotionally-stirring human interest stories (Kata 2012, Offit and Coffin 2003).

Recommendations

Throughout this paper, we have argued for the utility and importance of viewing fact-checking efforts as forms of risk communication, in that they implicitly attempt to define the risk of misinformation and to establish the fact-checkers as trustworthy risk mitigators. Further, we demonstrated then when fact-checkers are communicating about a risk—such as COVID-19—they are engaged in a multi-layered risk communication effort, in which two sets of risk perceptions are at play.

Risk communication researchers have long demonstrated that different publics view risks differently, and that varied risk perceptions can have consequences for how people respond to communications, including how they take action to mitigate risks. Misinformation is no exception, and we must account for this fact during the COVID-19 misinfodemic, as well during future moments of crisis in which risks are likely to be multi-layered. Thus, we have argued that it is important and useful to think about misinformation from a risk communication perspective.

In making this argument, we have listed several challenges facing risk communicators in the COVID-19 misinfodemic. Addressing each challenge, we offer the following recommendations:

Problems of trust

Fact-checkers should build trust instead of just saying or implying they are trustworthy. This could be done by working with actors that are trusted among most of the public, such as the CDC or WHO, in the case of COVID-19 (Kaiser Family Foundation 2020).

The limits of knowledge

Fact-checkers should not assume that objectivity will win against emotive and value-laden misinformation. They should make careful use of emotions, possibly by trying to connect corrective information to *values* many people hold, to concerns that audiences have, and to what they deem important.

Fact-checking a state of uncertainty

When fact-checking *likely-false* information, make it very clear that definite answer may not be known, if that's the case. Highlighting uncertainties does not impact trust levels (Van Der Bles et al. 2020).

Disclosure statement

No potential conflict of interest was reported by the author(s).

ORCID

Nicole M. Krause (iD) http://orcid.org/0000-0003-0550-9546
Isabelle Freiling (iD) http://orcid.org/0000-0002-6046-4005
Becca Beets (iD) http://orcid.org/0000-0002-3323-1281
Dominique Brossard (iD) http://orcid.org/0000-0002-9188-8388

References

Brandtzaeg, P. B., and A. Følstad. 2017. "Trust and Distrust in Online Fact-Checkig Services." *Communications of the ACM* 60 (9): 65–71. doi:10.1145/3122803.

Brennan, J. S., F. Simon, P. N. Howard, and R. K. Nielsen. 2020. "Types, sources, and claims of COVID-19 misinformation." *Reuters Institute*, April 7. Accessed April 10. https://reutersinstitute.politics.ox.ac.uk/types-sources-and-claims-covid-19-misinformation.

Brossard, D., and M. C. Nisbet. 2007. "Deference to Scientific Authority among a Low Information Public: Understanding U.S. opinion on Agricultural Biotechnology." *International Journal of Public Opinion Research* 19 (1): 24–52. doi:10.1093/ijpor/edl003.

Centers for Disease Control and Prevention. 2020. "Stop the spread of rumors 2020", April 3. Accessed 10 April 2020. https://www.cdc.gov/coronavirus/2019-ncov/daily-life-coping/share-facts.html.

Covello, V. T., R. G. Peters, J. G. Wojtecki, and R. C. Hyde. 2001. "Risk Communication, the West Nile Virus Epidemic, and Bioterrorism: responding to the Communication Challenges Posed by the Intentional or Unintentional Release of a Pathogen in an Urban Setting." *Journal of Urban Health: Bulletin of the New York Academy of Medicine* 78 (2): 382–391. doi:10.1093/jurban/78.2.382.

Frenkel, S., D. Alba, and R. Zhong. 2020. "Surge of virus misinformation stumps Facebook and Twitter." *New York Times*, March 3, 2020. Accessed 10 April 2020. https://www.nytimes.com/2020/03/08/technology/coronavirus-misinformation-social-media.html.

Gitlin, T. 2020. "Open letter to the murdochs." *Medium.com*, April 3, 2020. Accessed 10 April 2020. https://medium.com/@journalismprofs/open-letter-to-the-murdochs-9334e775a992.

Graves, Lucas. 2016. *Deciding What's True: The Rise of Political Fact-Checking in American Journalism*. New York: Columbia University Press.

Hanitzsch, Thomas, Arjen Van Dalen, and Nina Steindl. 2018. "Caught in the Nexus: A Comparative and Longitudinal Analysis of Public Trust in the Press." *The International Journal of Press/Politics* 23 (1): 3–23. doi:10.1177/1940161217740695.

Hansson, Sven Ove. 2010. "Risk: objective or Subjective, Facts or Values." *Journal of Risk Research* 13 (2): 231–238. doi:10.1080/13669870903126226.

Ho, S. S., D. A. Scheufele, and E. A. Corley. 2011. "Value Predispositions, Mass Media, and Attitudes toward Nanotechnology: The Interplay of Public and Experts." *Science Communication* 33 (2): 167–200. doi:10.1177/1075547010380386.

Ju, Y., J. Lim, M. Shim, and M. You. 2015. "Outrage Factors in Government Press Releases of Food Risk and Their Influence on News Media Coverage." *Journal of Health Communication* 20 (8): 879–887. doi:10.1080/10810730.2015.1018602.

Kahneman, D., and A. Tversky. 1979. "Prospect Theory: An Analysis of Decision under Risk." *Econometrica* 47 (2): 263–291. doi:10.2307/1914185.

Kaiser Family Foundation. 2020. KFF coronavirus poll – March 2020.

Kata, A. 2012. "Anti-Vaccine Activists, Web 2.0, and the Postmodern Paradigm–an Overview of Tactics and Tropes Used Online by the anti-Vaccination Movement." *Vaccine* 30 (25): 3778–3789. doi:10.1016/j.vaccine.2011.11.112.

Kim, J., S. K. Yeo, D. Brossard, D. A. Scheufele, and M. A. Xenos. 2014. "Disentangling the Influence of Value Predispositions and Risk/Benefit Perceptions on Support for Nanotechnology among the American Public." *Risk Analysis* 34 (5): 965–980. doi:10.1111/risa.12141.

Kunda, Z. 1990. "The Case for Motivated Reasoning." *Psychological Bulletin* 108 (3): 480–498. doi:10.1037/0033-2909. 108.3.480.

Kuznia, R., and D. Griffin. 2020. "How did coronavirus break out? Theories abound as researchers race to solve genetic detective story." *CNN.com*, April 6, 2020. Accessed 10 April 2020. https://www.cnn.com/2020/04/06/us/coronavirus-scientists-debate-origin-theories-invs/index.html.

Newman, N.,. R. Fletcher, A. Kalogeropoulos, and R. K. Nielsen. 2019. Reuters Institute digital news report 2019. Reuters Institute.

Offit, Paul A., and Susan E. Coffin. 2003. "Communicating Science to the Public: MMR Vaccine and Autism." *Vaccine* 22 (1): 1–6. doi:10.1016/S0264-410X(03)00532-2.

Pew Research Center. 2019a. "Many Americans say made-up news is a problem that needs to be fixed," June 5. Accessed 12 December 2019. https://www.journalism.org/2019/06/05/many-americans-say-made-up-news-is-a-critical-problem-that-needs-to-be-fixed/.

Pew Research Center. 2019b. "Republicans far more likely than Democrats to say fact-checkers tend to favor one side," June 27. Accessed 12 December 2019. https://www.pewresearch.org/fact-tank/2019/06/27/republicans-far-more-likely-than-democrats-to-say-fact-checkers-tend-to-favor-one-side/.

Pew Research Center. 2020. "Explore the data." Accessed 10 April 2020. https://www.pewresearch.org/pathways-2020/covidcover2/main_source_of_election_news/us_adults/.

Rayner, S. 1992. "Cultural Theory and Risk Analysis." In *Social Theories of Risk*, edited by S. Krimsky and D. Golding, 83–115. Westport, CT: Praeger.

Renn, O. 1992. "Concepts of Risk: A Classification." In *Social Theories of Risk*, edited by S. Krimsky and D. Golding, 53–79. Westport, CT: Praeger.

Requarth, T. 2020. "Please, let's stop the epidemic of armchair epidemiology," *Slate*, March 26, 2020. Accessed 20 April 2020. https://slate.com/technology/2020/03/armchair-epidemiology-coronavirus.html.

Sandman, P. M. 1987. "Risk Communication: Facing Public Outrage." *Epa J* 13 : 21–22.

Scheufele, D. A. 2013. "Communicating Science in Social Settings." *Proceedings of the National Academy of Sciences* 110 (Supplement_3): 14040–14047. doi:10.1073/pnas.1213275110.

Scheufele, D. A., and N. M. Krause. 2019. "Science Audiences, Misinformation, and Fake News." *Proceedings of the National Academy of Sciences* 116 (16): 7662–7669. doi:10.1073/pnas.1805871115.

Service, R. F. 2020. "NAS Letter Suggests 'Normal Breathing' Can Expel Coronavirus." *Science* 368 (6487): 119–119. doi:10.1126/science.368.6487.119.

Siegrist, M. 2000. "The Influence of Trust and Perceptions of Risks and Benefits on the Acceptance of Gene Technology." *Risk Analysis* 20 (2): 195–203. doi:10.1111/0272-4332.202020.

Slovic, P. 1992. "Perception of Risk: Reflections on the Psychometric Paradigm." In *Social Theories of Risk*, edited by S. Krimsky and D. Golding, 117–152. Westport, CT: Praeger.

Southwell, B. G., E. Thorson, and L. Sheble, eds. 2018. *Misinformation and Mass Audiences*. Austin, TX: University of Texas Press.

Trumbo, C. W. 2002. "Information Processing and Risk Perception: An Adaptation of the Heuristics Systematic Model." *Journal of Communication* 52 (2): 367–382. doi:10.1111/j.1460-2466.2002.tb02550.x.

Tufekci, Z. 2020. "Don't Believe the COVID-19 Models." *The Atlantic*, April 2, 2020. Accessed 20 April 2020. https://www.theatlantic.com/technology/archive/2020/04/coronavirus-models-arent-supposed-be-right/609271/?fbclid=IwAR3Sz117_0qniVmCbkWV1JxP1OtiNWm2XCfhRrf2aisM5W6RfMBBt3X1_Q8.

Van Der Bles, A. M., S. van der Linden, A. L. Freeman, and D. J. Spiegelhalter. 2020. "The Effects of Communicating Uncertainty on Public Trust in Facts and Numbers." *Proceedings of the National Academy of Sciences* 117 (14): 7672–7683. doi:10.1073/pnas.1913678117.

Waldrop, T., D. Alsup, and E. McLaughlin. 2020. "Fearing coronavirus, Arizona man dies after taking a form of chloroquine used to treat aquariums." *CNN.com*, March 25, 2020. Accessed 10 April 2020. https://www.cnn.com/2020/03/23/health/arizona-coronavirus-chloroquine-death/index.html.

World Health Organization. 2020a. "Coronavirus disease (COVID-19) advice for the public: Myth busters." Accessed 10 April 2020. https://www.who.int/emergencies/diseases/novel-coronavirus-2019/advice-for-public/myth-busters.

World Health Organization. 2020b. "Novel Coronavirus (2019-nCoV). situation report - 13." Accessed 10 April 2020. https://www.who.int/docs/default-source/coronaviruse/situation-reports/20200202-sitrep-13-ncov-v3.pdf.

Pandemic democracy: elections and COVID-19

Todd Landman and Luca Di Gennaro Splendore

ABSTRACT
This article provides an initial assessment of the many risks posed by the COVID-19 pandemic on the conduct of genuine and transparent elections in the world. It begins with explaining why elections are a vital part of democracy, and then using the notion of the electoral cycle, constructs a risk matrix that assesses the relative impact and likelihood of risks to the cycle, as well as proposes a number of potential mitigations to these risks. The variety and number of elections, dimensions of the electoral cycle that can be disrupted, and the need for solutions raises significant questions about the future of democracy itself.

Introduction

On 7 April 2020, the state of Wisconsin held its primary election in the run up to the November Presidential Elections in the United States. The primary was held at a time when the global pandemic COVID-19 was on its upward trajectory in the US, where cases of infection and death were increasing at a dramatic rate, most notably in New York City, the hardest hit region in the country. The conduct of the primary was hotly contested across the political spectrum, as significant concerns were raised about the health risks to voters, the conduct of the election using traditional ballot paper methods of voting, and the possibility of biased results that would compromise the ability for the state to guarantee a genuine and transparent election.

In contrast to Wisconsin, 14 other states postponed their primaries: Alaska, Connecticut, Delaware, Georgia, Hawaii, Indiana, Kentucky, Louisiana, Maryland, New York, Ohio, Pennsylvania, Rhode Island, and Wyoming, as well as Puerto Rico. Outside the United States, The Republic of Korea voted on April 15 and set out various measures so that voters were able to participate in the election without safety concerns, where a turnout of more than 66% was the highest in the last three decades. In Mali, first round elections were held on 29 March, the day its first coronavirus death was announced with very low turnout and its second-round was held on 19 April. France cancelled its second round of local elections due to be held on 29 March, and turnout in the first round on March 22 was much lower than in the previous election.

These different approaches to managing elections during a pandemic raise a number of questions about the risks to democracy in the presence of an external threat of the kind the world has experienced with the spread of COVID-19, and join a wide range of questions concerning risk, democracy, and public participation (see, e.g. Webler and Tuler 2018). In this article, we argue that the COVID-19 pandemic poses significant risks to the ability for countries to

Table 1. Elections during COVID-19, March–May 2020.

Country	Type of election	Date of election
Israel	Parliamentary elections	2 March 2020
Taiwan	Kuomintang Chairperson election	7 March 2020
France	Local elections	15 March 2020[a]
Germany	Local elections (Bavaria)	15 March 2020
Moldova	Local elections (Hâncesti)	15 March 2020
Dominican Republic	Municipal elections	15 March 2020
United States	Primaries (Arizona, Florida, Illinois)	17 March 2020
Vanuatu	General elections	19 March 2020
Zimbabwe	Municipal elections	14-22 March 2020
Poland	By-election	22 March 2020
Guinea	Constitutional referendum	22 March 2020
Canada	Shoal Lake 39 council elections	26 March 2020
Mali	General elections	29 March 2020
Australia	Local elections (Queenstown)	29 March 2020
Switzerland	Local elections (Luzern)	29 March 2020
United States	Presidential primary (Wisconsin)	7 April 2020[a]
South Korea	Legislative elections	15 April 2020
Russian Federation	Referendum	22 April 2020[b]
Chile	Referendum	26 April 2020[b]
Kazakhstan	Kazakh House of Representatives	30 April 2020
Bolivia	Chamber of Deputies, Senate, Referendum	3 May 2020[b]

Source: Election Guide, available at http://www.electionguide.org/digest/post/17597/
[a]Partially postponed (14 states in the US and Puerto Rico postponed primary elections)
[b]Postponed

guarantee genuine and transparent elections, and that without well-considered and appropriate measures, the conduct of elections may have significant impact on both public health protection and electoral integrity. We illustrate how the pandemic may affect critical elements that constitute the electoral cycle and consider different measures to mitigate the electoral risks from the pandemic, including cancellation, postponement, postal voting, and electronic voting.

Elections and democracy

Elections are a mainstay feature and 'basic predicate' of democracy (Ginsburg and Huq 2018), which provide the primary mechanism through which political leaders are chosen and held to account and through which individuals participate in the governance of their country (see Dahl 1971; Lijphart 1999; Lindberg 2006, Landman 2013; Webler and Tuler 2018; Pzreworski 2019). The ability for countries to conduct elections is further bolstered by a robust regime of human rights protection; rights such as freedom of movement, freedom of assembly, freedom of association, and freedom of speech (Dahl 1971; Landman 2013).[1] Elections aggregate citizen interests and mediate their relationship to government across several different dimensions: (1) the electoral unit (local, regional, and national), (2) the branch of government (executive and legislature, which can be bicameral or unicameral), and (3) the timing and type of elections (mid-term, primary, and general). The rise in the number of democracies, despite a recent backslide (see Chu et al. 2020), over the 'third' and 'fourth' waves of democracy since the 1970s (Huntington 1991; Doorenspleet 2005; Landman 2013) means that any given year has seen a very large number of elections across all continents of the world, and as the pandemic runs its course, political leaders will need to focus on measures that mitigate the worst and most probable risks facing these processes.

According to the latest figures for 2020, 28 countries have had national elections in which more than 88 million people have voted, while at the height of the pandemic between March and May 2020 there have been 22 elections scheduled (see Table 1). Between April and October 2020, the world is scheduled to have more than 30 national elections, and many more elections at the local and state level,[2] while the United States Presidential Elections are scheduled to be held on 3 November 2020, when in addition to the executive, all seats in the House of Representatives and two-thirds of seats in the Senate will be contested. While some elections are scheduled to take place as the pandemic reaches its peak in many countries, the measures to manage the worst risks during the subsidence of the virus will continue to have widespread impact on subsequent elections around the world.

COVID-19, government response, and the electoral cycle

The January outbreak and subsequent global spread of the coronavirus pandemic has claimed a significant number of lives across the world with varying degrees of severity and prevalence. Data collected by the Centre for Systems Science and Engineering at Johns Hopkins University, for example, have tracked the time-series and cross-national spread of reported cases, deaths, and recoveries.[3] Government responses to the pandemic tracked, for example, by the Blavatnik School of Government at Oxford University, include lockdowns restricting freedom of movement, a variety of social distancing measures to reduce community transmission, and severe restrictions on economic freedom, business operations, and other organizational activity;[4] the combination of which may have significant implications for the conduct of genuine elections for the foresee-able future. Stay at home measures have reduced productivity, led to stock market convulsions, consumer stockpiling, rising levels of unemployment,[5] disproportionate impact on vulnerable populations and minority communities,[6] and some instances of civil unrest (e.g. in Michigan, Virginia, Colorado, parts of South Africa, and in certain suburbs of Paris).[7]

Mainstream media reporting, social media commentary, and 'fake news' have fuelled a large number of conspiracy theories about the origin of the virus, debates about 'flattening the curve'[8] through tough measures, and pleas from national health services for personal protective equip-ment (PPE),[9] rapid development of a vaccine,[10] and the deployment of emergency testing sites to manage the worst periods of the pandemic.[11] Travel restrictions imposed during the crisis have affected 100 countries and any relaxation in any of these measures has varied according to the vagaries of the pandemic and the national political contexts in which it spreads. The inter-sections between scientific debate and guidance, public awareness and acceptance of the pan-demic, and the trade-off between concerns over public health and economic sustainability have affected government consideration for so-called 'exit-strategies' from life under lockdown.[12]

The spread of the virus and various government responses may have a significant impact on what is known as the *electoral cycle*, or the set of steps and processes involved in the conduct of elections. The electoral cycle involves a number of elements relating to: (1) the pre-electoral period (training, information, and voter registration), (2) the electoral period (nominations, cam-paigns, voting, and results), and (3) the post-electoral period (review, reform, and strategies).[13] Under more normal circumstances, these elements should be in place to provide the appropriate processes, provide opportunities for voters to inform themselves, and to conduct elections in ways that allow for the maximisation of democratic participation and for the arrival at trusted and legitimate results.

There are several ways in which the pandemic and government response can affect any one of these processes. First, the virus itself could discourage voters from casting their votes and affect overall levels of turnout. Voter turnout is seen by many as a crucial factor underpinning the legitimacy of an election, providing electoral mandates to leaders, and as a barometer for the health of democracy in general. Mature democracies have been experiencing a secular decline in voter turnout over the last several decades, a trend which may well worsen as a result of the pandemic in these democracies, as well as affecting newer democracies around the world.

Second, the consequences of formal postponement varies by regime type. For example, in full or 'flawed' democracies (The Economist Intelligence Unit 2019),[14] postponement can lead to intensifying polemics, e.g. in US, France, Italy, and Poland. In the US, the outbreak has plunged

Table 2. Electoral cycle risk matrix.

Electoral cycle	Risk	Impact	Likelihood	Possible mitigations
Pre-electoral period				
Planning	Limited potential for physical meetings	Low	High	On-line meetings for planning
Training	Limited potential for physical training	Low	High	On-line training
Information	Limited leafletting	Low	High	On-line messaging, social media, news media (restricted)
Registration	Limited access to registration offices	Medium	High	One-line and postal registration
Electoral period				
Nomination	Disruption to primaries	High	High	Postal voting On-line voting Hybrid models of voting
Campaign	Limited physical campaigning and party conventions	High	High	On-line campaigning Paid media advertisements One-line conventions
Voting	Limited potential for physical voting	High	High	Postal voting On-line voting Hybrid models of voting
Results	Disrupted vote counts and processing	High	High	Electronic voting integrity Postal vote verification Physical/virtual vote tallies
Post-electoral period				
Review	Limited potential for physical meetings	Low	High	On-line review meetings and stakeholder interviews On-line documentation archives
Strategy	Limited potential for physical meetings	Low	High	On-line meetings and stakeholder strategy sessions On-line documentation archives
Reform	Limited potential for physical meetings	Low	High	On-line reform meetings and stakeholder consultations One-line legislative drafting and passage; virtual parliaments

Source: compiled by the authors, using the electoral cycle model: https://aceproject.org/electoral-advice/electoral-assistance/electoral-cycle

the 2020 political campaign calendar into uncertainty. The discussion on alternative voting methods has become a partisan political dispute. In hybrid systems with some presence of electoral processes (Levitsky and Way 2010), postponement can lead to increased political uncertainty and an undermining of the rule of law. In Bolivia the pandemic emergency overlaps with the political crisis triggered after the controversial elections held in October 2019 (Human Rights Watch 2020). On 21 March the planned elections for 3 May were postponed. The electoral administration body sent parliament a proposal for the new elections to take place between 7 June and 6 September, which will decide on the new date when confinement measures are lifted. In elected authoritarian regimes (Schedler 2006; Levitsky and Way 2010), postponement can create a power vacuum, abuse of power, and the abuse of state of emergency measures, which further consolidate authoritarian rule, undermine the rule of law, and further threaten the protection of human rights (e.g. as has occurred in Hungary, where a slate of authoritarian measures have been passed under the premiership of Victor Orbán).[15]

Third, many different elements in the electoral cycle may be affected. Voting operations on Election Day and campaigns in the run up to an election can be disrupted. Already, in the United States, the Biden campaign is appealing to voters remotely, while the national party conventions will be unlikely to take place in their normal format.[16] Training and voter registration can be affected, as has been in the case in the Wisconsin primary. There is also speculation that the November Presidential Elections could be postponed, as the Republicans under the leadership of President Donald Trump weigh up the costs and benefits of staging the election on time.[17]

Mitigating the risk of electoral disruption

Talking a formal risk-based approach to the disruption of the electoral cycle demonstrates that there are significant risks with a high likelihood of causing disruption. Table 2 is a risk matrix that sets out the different elements of the electoral cycle and the possible mitigations that could be implemented to reduce these risks. The table shows that the electoral period has risks with the highest impact and highest likelihood for candidate nomination processes, campaigning, voting, and tallying results. For the pre-electoral and post-electoral periods, there is less impact of the risks, but high likelihood. The final column of mitigations shows that there are a number of on-line and pragmatic ways to address these risks. For the pre-electoral period, it is possible to have on-line planning, training, information, and registration processes developed. For the electoral period, there are on-line, postal, and hybrid solutions available, while for the post-electoral period, there are on-line solutions and 'virtual parliament' solutions available for reviews, stakeholder engagement, and the promulgation of electoral reform legislation. Remote working and on-line solutions that have been implemented quickly during the pandemic by business organisations, universities, and other organisations can be adapted for the electoral cycle.

These and other challenges require a set of solutions that will need to be in place relatively quickly as the uncertainty of the virus continues. There are on-line and mail solutions for training, registration, and voting itself, each of which has a number of problems that need to be overcome, and that will be subject to the influence of political self-interest from political parties and candidates. Any on-line solution faces problems relating to information security, the threat of cyber attacks, and hacking more generally, as well as questions over the integrity of the results, as was seen during the Iowa caucuses before COVID-19. Postal voting, while used for absentee ballots, has become highly contentious in the US owing to the belief that such a system may be biased to particular party affiliations. Online and mail voting can generate mistrust in elections and the rejection of an unfavourable outcome (in these systems, the full secrecy of the vote is not guaranteed).

Procedures for "early voting" in South Korea, as well as many precautionary measures, provided conditions in which the turnout reached 66% in 2020 (58% in 2016). The turnout of early voting in 2020 hit 26% (12% in 2016). A special "code of conduct of voters" was implemented due to COVID-19 (i.e. Spinelli 2020). The system itself may have generated new voters by providing different ways of voting, while also creating some form of voting substitution effects. Every context is unique, the South Korean case certainly cannot be generalised all over the world. Nevertheless it appears that a mixed voting possibility led to higher turnout.

These legal and procedural provisions to facilitate inclusion and participation of voters were already part of the South Korean electoral framework. Nevertheless in Poland, the lack of multiple modes of voting created many political disputes. Under virulent political polemics on April 6, the Parliament voted to conduct the next presidential elections completely through postal voting or to delay the date of the election, if necessary.[18] Both decisions by parliament required approval from the Senate.

Quite apart from the technical details relating to the conduct of genuine and transparent elections, there are additional concerns over public health and public security that require more holistic solutions and inter-agency cooperation at levels that have not been present in pre-COVID-19 elections. The recent popular (and in some cases armed) protests against stay at home restrictions in Michigan and other states illustrate this intersection of concerns that may well affect forthcoming elections.

Conclusion

This brief overview of the many challenges for the conduct of elections during the time of the pandemic shows that there remain many unknowns as the pandemic progresses and as governments respond. There are clearly no single or simple solutions to the election quandaries we set

out here; however, given the number of elections, some of which are very significant for global politics, due to take place under the shadow of COVID-19, make it imperative that solutions need to be
found, tested, and legitimacy secured if democratic institutions and accountability are not to be dam-
aged. All electoral authorities need to focus on an election risk management plan in case of an outbreak. In the medium term perspective, every country needs a backup plan to hold the election. A
solid electoral framework needs to contemplate pandemic solutions. It is crucial to avoid delaying the
election and to incentivize participation under an outbreak.

For the electoral period, Table 2 suggests a mixed system of voting as a potential solution.
Such a mixed system of voting may include, for example, (1) postal voting for out-of-country
people and those who are over 65, (2) online voting for people with certificate electronic signa-
ture, and (3) standard voting in polling stations under strict safety measures for the rest of people (i.e. polling stations disinfection, social distancing, compulsory masks for voters and
temperature checking upon arrival). The trade-off whether to hold or postpone scheduled elections is complex, resulting in controversies in either case. Introducing reforms to the electoral
law shortly ahead of the election is not compatible with the principles of stability of electoral
legislation and legal certainty (OSCE 2020). Postponement or electoral law reforms need a high
level of consensus among political parties, civil society and all stakeholders.

Given the centrality of elections to democracy and the large number of elections scheduled
around the world during the pandemic, it is vital that solutions for the conduct of genuine and
transparent are found quickly. Failure to find suitable and effective solutions can undermine the
health of democracy and compromise the fundamental human rights to vote and participate in
the governance of a country.

Notes

1. In addition to these civil and political rights, enshrined most notably in the 1948 Universal Declaration of
   Human Rights and the 1966 International Covenant on Civil and Political Rights, human rights to education
   and health as set out in the 1966 International Convention on Economic, Social, and Cultural Rights are also
   important for maximising participation in elections, since provisions for and fulfilment of state obligations on
   these rights provides the necessary capacity and capability for individuals to take part in elections
   meaningfully. Limits to the fulfilment of these rights can lead to the de facto disenfranchisement of many
   eligible voters. For more on the human rights implications of COVID-19, see https://www.un.org/sites/un2.un.
   org/files/un_policy_brief_on_human_rights_and_covid_23_april_2020.pdf.
2. See: https://aceproject.org/today/upcoming-elections/.
3. See the Center for Systems Science and Engineering here: https://systems.jhu.edu/.
4. The Blavatnik School of Government tracking of government response to COVID-19 is available here: https://
   www.bsg.ox.ac.uk/research/research-projects/coronavirus-government-response-tracker.   The   school's
   'Stringency Index' (OxCGRT) collects publicly available information on 17 indicators of government responses,
   including containment and closure policies, economic policies, and health system policies.
5. For an analysis of the socio-economic impact of COVID-19 on the UK, see the analysis of scenarios available
   from PwC: https://www.pwc.co.uk/services/economics-policy/insights/uk-economic-update-covid-19.html.
6. See, for example: https://www.un.org/sites/un2.un.org/files/un_policy_brief_on_human_rights_and_covid_23_
   april_2020.pdf.
7. See, for example, Mudde, C. (2020) 'The "Anti-Lockdown' Protests are About More Than Just Quarantines,' *The
   Guardian*, 21 April 2020, London: The Guardian. Available at: https://www.theguardian.com/us-news/
   commentisfree/2020/apr/21/anti-lockdown-protests-trump-right-wing.
8. Spektor, B. (2020) 'Coronavirus: What is 'flattening the curve,' and will it work?' Livescience, 16 March 2020;
   Available at: https://www.livescience.com/coronavirus-flatten-the-curve.html.
9. See, for example, The Royal College of Nurses (RCN) statement on personal protection equipment (PPE),
   available at: https://www.rcn.org.uk/covid-19/rcn-position/ppe-position-statement.
10. See, for example, Gartner, A. and Roberts, L. (2020) 'How close are we to a coronavirus vaccine? Latest news
    on UK trials,' *The Telegraph*, 1 May 2020, London: The Telegraph; Available at: https://www.telegraph.co.uk/
    global-health/science-and-disease/coronavirus-vaccine-latest-news-trial-covid-19/.
11. The availability and accessibility of testing sites for COVID have been hotly debated in the press and vary
    significantly by country. See, for example, the guidance issued by the Centers for Disease Control and
    Prevention (CDC); Available at: https://www.cdc.gov/coronavirus/2019-ncov/symptoms-testing/testing.html.

12. All governments across different jurisdictions face a number of challenges in devising exit strategies. See for example, Highfield, R. (2020) 'Coronavirus: Exit Strategies,' The Science Museum Group; Available at: https://www.sciencemuseumgroup.org.uk/coronavirus-exit-strategies/.
13. Election Guide, available at http://www.electionguide.org/digest/post/17597/.
14. Full democracies have a long history of legitimate elections, peaceful transfers of power between political leaders, and a strong regime of human rights protection in place that allow for the maximisation of citizen participation in the political system. Flawed democracies have many elements missing, where elections take place, but there are significant shortcomings with respect to media laws, freedom of expression, and the arbitrary use of coercion and repression to affect electoral outcomes. See, for example, Zakaria (2007), Landman (2013, 2018).
15. See, for example, Euronews (2020) 'Hungary's Viktor Orbán handed sweeping new powers with COVID-19 law;' Available at: https://www.euronews.com/2020/03/30/blank-cheque-hungary-expected-to-pass-controversial-covid-19-law.
16. See, for example, Lange, J. (2020) 'Democrats delay presidential convention until August, citing coronavirus,' Reuters, London: Tomson Reuters; Available at: https://uk.reuters.com/article/uk-usa-election-biden-convention/democrats-delay-presidential-convention-until-august-citing-coronavirus-idUKKBN21K36C.
17. See, for example, Zurcher, A. (2020) 'Coronavirus: Could Donald Trump delay the presidential election?' BBC, London: BBC; Available at: https://www.bbc.co.uk/news/world-us-canada-52326166.
18. See, for example, Dalhusen, J. (2020) 'EU must call out the follies of Poland's Covid-19 election,' The Financial Times, London: The Financial Times; Available at: https://www.ft.com/content/b1a6457c-7a5c-11ea-bd25-7fd923850377.

Disclosure statement

No potential conflict of interest was reported by the author(s).

References

Chu, Y., K.-P. Huang, M. Lagos, and R. Mattes. 2020. "A Lost Decade for Third-Wave Democracies?" *Journal of Democracy* 31 (2): 166–181. doi:10.1353/jod.2020.0029.
Dahl, R. 1971. *Polyarchy: Participation and Opposition*. New Haven: Yale University Press.
Doorenspleet, R. 2005. *Democratic Transitions: Exploring the Structural Sources of the Fourth Wave*, Boulder, CO: Lynne Rienner.
Ginsburg, T., and A. Z. Huq. 2018. *How to Save Constitutional Democracy*. Chicago: University of Chicago Press.
Human Rights Watch. 2020. *Bolivia: COVID-19 Decree Threatens Free Expression*. New York: Human Rights Watch. https://www.hrw.org/news/2020/04/07/bolivia-covid-19-decree-threatens-free-expression.
Huntington, S. 1991. *The Third Wave: Democratization in the Late Twentieth Century*. Oklahoma: University of Oklahoma Press.
Landman, T. 2013. *Human Rights and Democracy: The Precarious Triumph of Ideals*. London: Bloomsbury Press.
Landman, T. 2018. "Democracy and Human Rights: Concepts, Measures and Relationships." *Politics and Governance* 6 (1): 48–59. doi:10.17645/pag.v6i1.1186.
Levitsky, S., and L. Way. 2010. *Competitive Authoritarianism: Hybrid Regimes after the Cold War*. Cambridge: Cambridge University Press.
Lijphart, A. 1999. *Patterns of Democracy*. New Haven: Yale University Press.
Lindberg, S. 2006. *Democracy and Elections in Africa*. Baltimore: Johns Hopkins University Press.
Organisation for Security and Cooperation in Europe (OSCE). 2020. "Opinion on the Draft Act on Special Rules for Conducting the General Election of the President of the Republic of Poland Ordered in 2020" (Senate Paper No. 99). https://www.osce.org/odihr/elections/poland/450856
Pzreworski, A. 2019. *Crises of Democracy*. Cambridge: Cambridge University Press.
Schedler, A. 2006. *Electoral Authoritarianism: The Dynamics of Unfree Competition*. Boulder: Lynne Rienner.
Spinelli, A. 2020. "Managing Elections under the COVID-19 Pandemic: The Republic of Korea's Crucial Test". International IDEA Technical Paper 2/2020. https://www.idea.int/publications/catalogue/managing-elections-under-covid-19-pandemic-republic-korea-crucial-test
The Economist Intelligence Unit. 2019. *Democracy Index 2019*. London: The Economist Intelligence Unit.
Webler, T., and S. Tuler. 2018. "Four Decades of Public Participation in Risk Decision Making." *Risk Analysis* 39(6). doi:10.1111/risa.13250.
Zakaria, F. 2007. *The Future of Freedom: Illiberal Democracy at Home and Abroad* (Revised Edition). New York: Norton and Company.

Survival at the expense of the weakest? Managing modern slavery risks in supply chains during COVID-19

Alexander Trautrims (iD), Martin C. Schleper, M. Selim Cakir and Stefan Gold

ABSTRACT

This paper reflects on the implications of the Coronavirus (COVID-19) pandemic on modern slavery risks in supply chains. We first reason that the global supply and demand shock resulting from COVID-19 exacerbates workers' vulnerability to modern slavery. Then, we discuss challenges firms face to detect, prevent, and mitigate increasing modern slavery risks in supply chains during COVID-19. We conclude our paper by arguing that proactive, value-oriented, and long-term supply chain management approaches increase firms' resilience to cope with highly volatile and extreme events, such as COVID 19.

Introduction

An estimated 40 million people worldwide live in modern slavery[1]; many of them work for products and services produced in global supply chains. Despite policy and law advancement over the past years, the G20 countries alone continue importing products at-risk of being made by slave labour worth 354 billion US dollars annually (Global Slavery Index (GSI) 2018).

The COVID-19 pandemic is increasing the vulnerability of workers to find themselves in exploitative conditions and in modern slavery as the most extreme form of exploitation. Within a highly dynamic environment with daily updates from different analyses, the latest economic forecasts draw a bleak picture. At the time of writing in early May 2020, the International Monetary Fund (2020) already assumes the pandemic to induce the worst economic recession since the Great Depression, resulting in world economy losses of 9 trillion dollars and additional unemployment of 305 million people globally. With labour in the informal economy hit even worse – around 1.6 billion workers are expected to lose their livelihoods (International Labour Organization 2020) – the most vulnerable workers are becoming susceptible to severe forms of exploitation including modern slavery.

Detecting, preventing, and mitigating modern slavery in supply chains has been a challenge even for more proactive businesses and it is recognised that modern slavery may be present in every supply chain. In response, most businesses have taken a risk-based approach, identifying where they are more exposed to modern slavery in their supply chains and where they have opportunities to reduce and mitigate this risk (Gold, Trautrims, and Trodd 2015). This article discusses the potential implications of the sudden shock of COVID-19 to supply chains, which has caused extreme shifts in demand patterns, disrupted supply flows, and diminished the effective-ness of risk management and mitigation mechanisms while increasing workers' vulnerability to exploitation. Taking foremost a firm-level view, we also recognise the systemic forces that are impacting modern slavery exposure. We conclude by arguing that this pandemic could prove proactive, value-oriented, and long-term supply chain management to be a superior risk man-agement approach than traditional approaches.

Impact of COVID-19 on operations and supply chain management

It has been widely acknowledged that the economic repercussions of the pandemic are twofold: the COVID-19 outbreak and subsequent mitigation policies, such as social distancing, have sev-ered the flow of goods and people, resulting in a global supply and demand shock. Besides changing consumer behaviour, disrupted global supply chains have had the biggest impact on operations and the global economy in general. Whereas some firms were not able to meet surg-ing demands for certain products from their existing supply base, other product lines suddenly carried significant obsolete stock, reverting power imbalances in some supply chains and ampli-fying the possibilities for abuse of these imbalances in others.

Sudden demand surges

Due to abrupt changes in consumer behaviour, and an obvious surge in demand for other prod-ucts (e.g. from the pharmaceutical and medical industry), some supply chains faced insufficient supply availability. For example, the urgent need for personal protective equipment (PPE) meant a prioritisation of availability over the risk of due diligence for modern slavery that is well-docu-mented in the manufacturing of medical gloves (Feinmann 2020) alongside the drop of essential procurement practices such as quality checks with the consequence of buying faulty and some-times dangerous kits and face masks (BBC. 2020).

Other products experienced not necessarily an overall rise in demand, but a shift in demand patterns, including tendencies such as hoarding (e.g. toilet paper). For instance, when restau-rants, cafes, and bars were closed, unsurprisingly cooking and baking at home increased and products such as flour – despite enough supply overall – were not available in supermarkets as consumer products have packaging and labelling requirements different from business custom-ers. Diverting supply routes meant the need for rapid onboarding of suppliers that were never used before as most businesses and public institutions, such as the National Health Service in the UK, had opted for efficiencies through lean supply chain practices such as single sourcing as well as cutting buffer inventory and slack capacity (Hendricks, Singhal, and Zhang 2009; Mackay, Munoz, and Pepper 2019; Bryce et al. 2020). The need for an urgent extension of their supplier base left buyers without the opportunity for comprehensive modern slavery risk assessments.

Obsolete stock

Whilst demand surged for some products, it collapsed for others and businesses were left with unsellable stock and idle capacity in their supply chains. Particularly in the garment industry with its global supply chains that predominately produce in countries with already high risks of labour exploitation, orders were cancelled and payments withheld, sometimes for products that were already on their way (The Guardian 2020). Power imbalances in global supply chains entail that suppliers have difficulties to resist such unfair practices, for remaining in the business (Schleper, Blome, and Wuttke 2017). They are expected to shoulder major parts of business risk; and they are often left alone by business partners in wealthy economies as well as the political system when trying to buffer detrimental consequences for workers as the weakest stakeholders. This may imply that garment workers as well as (midlevel) managers are left without income, which jeopardises their livelihood and thus make workers and their families even more vulnerable for exploitative employment practices, in the same or other sectors.

Workforce

Although COVID-19 has been and will be causing serious job losses in global economies overall, the pandemic has also been leading to labour shortages in some sectors. Border closures have considerably affected the availability of migrant workers. One of the most affected sectors, especially in developed countries, is agriculture which heavily relies on seasonal migrant workers, raising fears of a looming food systems crisis if farmers cannot recruit workers. Despite much political noise around filling vacancies with workers who lost their jobs in other sectors, only 150 workers started harvesting jobs in UK agriculture as part of a scheme for which initially 50,000 UK workers had signed up (Financial Times 2020). Germany even allowed agriculture companies to fly in harvest workers from Eastern European countries despite its borders being officially closed (Time 2020). One major reason for this is that agricultural work indeed requires a combination of endurance and skill-set that is not abundant and cannot be easily acquired, although agricultural labour has often been labelled as "unskilled".

Other industries may find that workers who have been furloughed or left without income altogether during lockdowns are not available afterwards as they have found work in other sectors, increasing the pressure to bring in new contractors and hire new workers without thorough checks as pressure mounts to get businesses operating again and clear a backlog of work.

Disruption to usual modern slavery mitigation mechanisms

Apart from a rise in worker vulnerability and supply chains slavery risks, the COVID-19 outbreak also disrupts the usual mechanisms taken to prevent and tackle modern slavery in supply chains. Given that many firms struggle to survive and to secure their financial bottom line, this 'emergency mode' might have shifted priorities away from social and environmental considerations, at least temporarily.

Moreover, due to travel restrictions, physical audits of suppliers and their workforces are impossible and in many businesses staff across the organisations have been moved to other functions focussed on business continuity, such as filling shelves in stores and onboarding supplier, thus reducing organisational capacity to detect and remediate instances of labour exploitation. This means that some supply chains have become less transparent altogether, and that tracing risky supplier behaviour, such as unauthorised subcontracting of orders, has become more difficult due to resource constraints and policy-induced mobility restrictions.

Besides businesses, governments have also sporadically relaxed some modern slavery prevention measures. In the UK, for example, labour providers can temporarily provide workforce into sectors with high modern slavery risks without requiring the usual gangmasters licence to make workers more readily accessible (GLAA (Gangmaster and Labour Abuse Authority) 2020). In the US, an import ban on a large Malaysian manufacturer of medical gloves accused of using forced labour has been lifted to access additional supply (US Customs and Border Protection 2020).

With physical distancing and other lockdown measures in place, it became much more difficult for victims of modern slavery to access support and disclose their situation. They have fewer opportunities to visit faith and community organisations, attend in-person site instructions, speak to fellow workers, or call helplines that are essential infrastructure of modern slavery detection for many businesses.

Leading the way forward: benefits of proactive, value-oriented, and long-term supply chain management

Despite this gloomy diagnosis of the effects of the COVID-19 pandemic on working conditions and workers' rights in upstream supply chains, this crisis has certainly also disrupted "common wisdom" of doing business and human interaction in general, and may thus represent a window of opportunity to rethink current supply chain designs and trade relationships.

Increased mindfulness among consumers and customers might provide a silver lining that could uplift the weakest in the global workforce. Still, it remains to be seen if purchasing and consumption patterns will permanently change; exceeding selfishness and status-orientation towards more ethical purchasing and consumption. From a managerial perspective, this can be the time where sustainable supply chain management approaches demonstrate their benefits. Firms that have taken a proactive, value-oriented, and long-term supply chain management approach prior to COVID-19 may prove their superiority compared to arm-length, transactional, and oftentimes myopically economically incentivised approaches. Collaboration with external stakeholders is crucial for sustainable supply chain management, and beneficial in the response to volatile and extreme events, such as COVID-19. Finding and working with new suppliers at short notice can be more safely achieved if these are already supplying other businesses (e.g. competitors or supply chain actors in your own network) with similar sustainability standards (but also in regards to classical procurement KPIs, such as quality or lead time). Supply chain management approaches, in which buying firms participate in sustainability initiatives and industry consortia (e.g. Responsible Business Alliance, Roundtable for Sustainable Palm Oil) allow firms to indirectly manage lower tier suppliers through the implementation of industry-wide standards and guidelines or even to directly exchange auditing and assessment information (e.g. 'Together for Sustainability' in the chemical industry) (Meinlschmidt, Schleper, and Foerstl 2018). Furthermore, more intensive information exchange and collaboration with unions, NGOs, and other expert stakeholders increase supply chain transparency and allow for a proactive detection of early warning signals on deteriorating conditions even when physical audits are disrupted (Gold, Trautrims, and Trodd 2015).

In risk management in general, but especially in times of emergencies and crises, decision-makers benefit from trust, effective communication and information exchange, and close relationships (Balog-Way and McComas 2020). Highly volatile and extreme events in the past, such as the financial crisis, have put organisational resilience through its paces and the current COVID-19 pandemic will not be different (Bryce et al. 2020). Studies conducted after the 2008 financial crisis have shown that strategically formulated social and environmental practices that base on long-term relationships and commitments – rather than mere tick-box compliance exercises – can significantly increase organisational resilience and thus better prepare for these exceptional states (DesJardine, Bansal, and Yang 2019; Sajko, Boone, and Buyl 2020) that shock events such as the COVID-19 pandemic create. So far supply chain resilience has been taken largely a supply continuity view, but COVID-19 may show us that supply chain resilience goes hand in hand with environmental and social sustainability (Fahimnia and Jabbarzadeh 2016; Rajesh 2018). Recent supply chain risk management studies clearly emphasise relational approaches and proactiveness to gain transparency during turbulent times (e.g. Sodhi and Tang 2019), which is also essential for sustainability-related risks and for improving sustainability across supply chains overall (Foerstl et al. 2015).

Taking a more macroeconomic perspective on supply chain management and COVID-19, it may be noted that on the one hand, the COVID-19 pandemic may accelerate protectionist developments that have been on the political agenda already before, for example in the US, Russia, or the UK, which has led to ongoing frictions in global trade in recent years. Whether this reversion of globalisation helps improving the situation of workers hinges not the least on related legal framework conditions set by political systems. On the other hand, the COVID-19 pandemic and its effects on societies and supply chains will likely reinforce already existing tendencies of reshoring production to industrialised countries, due to the experience of supply disruptions; the political aim of controlling production that is considered systemically important; and ethical concerns regarding new supply chains quickly set up during and after the COVID-19 crisis. This means that production and consumption is brought closer together, holding the potential of increasing transparency of value creation as well as closer scrutiny of labour supply chains and their intermediaries such as temporary employment agencies.

COVID-19 highlights the wicked problems that sustainable supply chain management faces and the assumed prioritisation of economic sustainability when confronted with disruptive shocks that threaten firm survival. Tightly coupled supply chains prioritising short-term efficiency goals are proven to be particularly weak for handling shock events, such as COVID-19 and cause firms to take untested measures with greater social risks, including modern slavery. Thus, despite the abovementioned concerns about the increase in modern slavery risks in supply chains as a consequence of COVID-19, future research will need to show if this pandemic and its expected economic repercussions will change the prioritisation of the different triple-bottom-line dimensions (i.e. economic, social, environmental). More precisely, an interesting avenue for future research will be whether the pandemic and the economic crisis will lead to a focus on financial survival and thereby a neglect of social and environmental concerns or, contrarily, we will see a shift in supply chain networks towards value-based supply chain management away from the short-term, arms-length cost focus.

Like disruptive crises in the past, the COVID-19 pandemic creates uncertainty and has the potential to challenge existent political and economic institutions as well as overall societal structures. Yet, besides this bleak outlook, this crisis also provides an opportunity to reflect on our attitudes towards supply chain management, external stakeholders and especially the weakest in the global society and production process. The time to prove that proactive, value-oriented, and long-term supply chain management is a superior risk management approach than traditional approaches is now.

Note

1. In absence of a globally agreed definition, we use modern slavery as an umbrella term encompassing slavery, servitude, forced or compulsory labour and human trafficking. Victims of modern slavery are unable to leave their situation of exploitation, controlled by threats, punishment, violence, coercion, and deception (see Nicholson, Dang, and Trodd 2018 for a comprehensive debate on modern slavery definitions).

Disclosure statement

No potential conflict of interest was reported by the author(s).

ORCID

Alexander Trautrims (iD) http://orcid.org/0000-0001-8428-3682

References

Balog-Way, D. H. P., and K. A. McComas. 2020. "COVID-19: Reflections on Trust, Tradeoffs, and Preparedness." *Journal of Risk Research*. doi: 10.1080/13669877.2020.1758192.

BBC. 2020. "Coronavirus: Countries Reject Chinese-Made Equipment." Accessed 30 March 2020. https://www.bbc.com/news/world-europe-52092395

Bryce, C., P. Ring, S. Ashby, and J. K. Wardman. 2020. "Resilience in the Face of Uncertainty: early Lessons from the COVID-19 Pandemic." *Journal of Risk Research*. doi: 10.1080/13669877.2020.1756379.

DesJardine, M., P. Bansal, and Y. Yang. 2019. "Bouncing Back: Building Resilience through Social and Environmental Practices in the Context of the 2008 Global Financial Crisis." *Journal of Management* 45 (4): 1434–1460. doi:10. 1177/0149206317708854.

Fahimnia, B., and A. Jabbarzadeh. 2016. "Marrying Supply Chain Sustainability and Resilience: A Match Made in Heaven." *Transportation Research Part E: Logistics and Transportation Review* 91(C): 306–324. doi:10.1016/j.tre. 2016.02.007.

Feinmann, F. 2020. "The Scandal of Modern Slavery in the Trade of Masks and Gloves." *BMJ (Clinical Research ed.)* 369: m1676. doi:10.1136/bmj.m1676.

Financial Times. 2020. "Time Runs Short for UK to Recruit Tens of Thousands of Fruit Pickers." Accessed 29 April 2020. https://www.ft.com/content/e3713342-c883-483a-956f-41cd6ec5367e

Foerstl, K., A. Azadegan, T. Leppelt, and E. Hartmann. 2015. "Drivers of Supplier Sustainability: moving beyond Compliance to Commitment." *Journal of Supply Chain Management* 51 (1): 67–92. doi:10.1111/jscm.12067.

GLAA (Gangmaster and Labour Abuse Authority). 2020. "Temporary Licences to Be Issued during Coronavirus Outbreak." Accessed 31 March 2020. https://www.gla.gov.uk/whats-new/latest-press-releases/31032020-temporary-licences-to-be-issued-during-coronavirus-outbreak/.

Global Slavery Index (GSI). 2018. www.globalslaveryindex.org

Gold, S., A. Trautrims, and Z. Trodd. 2015. "Modern Slavery Challenges to Supply Chain Management." *Supply Chain Management: An International Journal* 20 (5): 485–494. doi:10.1108/SCM-02-2015-0046.

Hendricks, K. B., V. R. Singhal, and R. Zhang. 2009. "The Effect of Operational Slack, Diversification, and Vertical Relatedness on the Stock Market Reaction to Supply Chain Disruptions." *Journal of Operations Management* 27 (3): 233–246. doi:10.1016/j.jom.2008.09.001.

International Labour Organization. 2020. "ILO Monitor: COVID-19 and the World of Work. Second edition." Accessed 30 April 2020. https://www.ilo.org/wcmsp5/groups/public/—dgreports/—dcomm/documents/briefingnote/wcms_740877.pdf

International Monetary Fund. 2020. "The IMF's Response to COVID-19." Accessed 30 April 2020. https://www.imf.org/en/About/FAQ/imf-response-to-COVID-19

Mackay, J., A. Munoz, and M. Pepper. 2019. "Conceptualising Redundancy and Flexibility towards Supply Chain Robustness and Resilience." *Journal of Risk Research*: 1–21. doi: 10.1080/13669877.2019.1694964

Meinlschmidt, J., M. C. Schleper, and K. Foerstl. 2018. "Tackling the Sustainability Iceberg: A Transaction Cost Economics Approach to Lower Tier Sustainability Management." *International Journal of Operations & Production Management* 38 (10): 1888–1914. doi: 10.1108/IJOPM-03-2017-0141.

Nicholson, A., M. Dang, and Z. Trodd. 2018. "A Full Freedom: Contemporary Survivors' Definitions of Slavery." *Human Rights Law Review* 18 (4): 689–704. doi:10.1093/hrlr/ngy032.

Rajesh, R. 2018. "Pseudo Resilient Supply Chains: Concept, Traits, and Practices." *Journal of Risk Research* 21 (10): 1264–1286. doi:10.1080/13669877.2017.1304977.

Sajko, M., C. Boone, and T. Buyl. 2020. "CEO Greed, Corporate Social Responsibility, and Organizational Resilience to Systemic Shocks." *Journal of Management*. doi: 10.1177/0149206320902528

Schleper, M. C., C. Blome, and D. D. Wuttke. 2017. "The Dark Side of Buyer Power: Supplier Exploitation and the Role of Ethical Climates." *Journal of Business Ethics* 140 (1): 97–114. doi:10.1007/s10551-015-2681-6.

Sodhi, M. S., and C. S. Tang. 2019. "Research Opportunities in Supply Chain Transparency." *Production and Operations Management* 28 (12): 2946–2959. doi:10.1111/poms.13115.

The Guardian. 2020. "Primark and Matalan among Retailers Allegedly Cancelling £2.4bn Orders in 'Catastrophic' Move for Bangladesh." Accessed 02 April 2020. https://www.theguardian.com/global-development/2020/apr/02/fashion-brands-cancellations-of-24bn-orders-catastrophic-for-bangladesh.

Time. 2020. "Germany Flies in Seasonal Farm Workers to Help Agriculture Sector Hit by Coronavirus Travel Bans." Accessed 09 April 2020. https://time.com/5818428/germany-farm-workers-coronavirus/

US Customs and Border Protection. 2020. "CBP Revokes Withhold Release Order on Disposable Rubber Gloves." Accessed 2 May 2020. https://www.cbp.gov/newsroom/national-media-release/cbp-revokes-withhold-release-order-disposable-rubber-gloves

COVID-19 risk governance: drivers, responses and lessons to be learned

Aengus Collins, Marie-Valentine Florin (iD) and Ortwin Renn

ABSTRACT
The COVID-19 outbreak was neither unpredictable nor unforeseen, yet it blind-sided policymakers when it emerged, leading to unprecedented global restrictions on human activity and almost certainly triggering the first global economic contraction since WWII. This paper considers the key factors in the eruption of the crisis, as well as the lessons that should be learned from it. The paper begins with an outline of COVID-19's spread, highlighting six key drivers that have determined its severity: the exponential pace of transmission, global interconnectedness, health-sector capacity, wider state capacity, the economic impact of suppression measures, and fragilities caused by the 2008 financial crisis. The paper then proceeds by considering the steps that have been taken in response to five key challenges, corresponding to elements of the IRGC risk governance framework: technical assessment, risk perception, evaluation, management and communication. While acknowledging that only tentative conclusions can be drawn at this early stage, the paper ends with a series of ten recommendations designed to increase preparedness for future crises.

The COVID-19 outbreak was neither unpredictable nor unforeseen (Sansonetti 2020).[1] Many organisations warned about the vulnerability of our increasingly tightly interconnected world to the spread of infectious diseases (Cabinet Office 2017; Global Preparedness Monitoring Board 2019). Reservoirs of coronaviruses in animal populations have long been identified as a problem (W. Li et al. 2005). So too have the 'wet markets' which appear once again to have been responsible for zoonotic transmission in the case of COVID-19 (Webster 2004). The nexus of animals, humans and pathogens has been recognised as a 'time bomb' waiting to go off (Cheng et al. 2007). Despite this, a sense of complacency about pandemic risks has prevailed among policymakers, perhaps because of the comparatively low death tolls and the limited geographic spread of recent outbreaks (SARS and MERS).

As the COVID-19 crisis erupted, policymakers were blind-sided by the disease's combination of SARS-like severe lower-respiratory impacts with the transmissibility of common-cold coronaviruses (Kormann 2020). The result has been a dramatic spread across the world, aided by failures or delays at key junctures. The first four cases were officially reported in Wuhan on 29 December 2019 (Q. Li et al. 2020). By mid-April 2020 there were more than 2 million confirmed cases and almost 150,000 deaths globally, despite the introduction of unprecedented restrictions on human travel and interaction (Hale and Webster 2020). Modelling published by Imperial College London in March 2020 suggested that in the absence of policy measures, COVID-19 would have spread to infect 7 billion and kill 40 million people globally (Walker et al. 2020). Such figures may appear to be on the high side given that stringent restrictions have led to a fall in new infections in countries including Italy, Spain, Germany and France are in decline. However, developments in several other countries, in particular the US, remain unclear, and in all countries sustainable success depends on the continuing effectiveness of confinement measures. On top of its direct health impacts, COVID-19 has caused immediate and severe economic damage; it is set to trigger the first contraction of global GDP since World War II (Economist Intelligence Unit 2020). The longer-term economic impacts are unclear, but a recent study of 12 major historical pandemics argues that the adverse economic consequences of pandemics last for about 40 years and greatly exceed those of wars (Jorda, Singh, and Taylor 2020). Again, given the severe measures that are now in place, the economic repercussions may not be as severe as in previous pandemics.

Drivers of the crisis

A number of factors have played a particularly important role in the rapid escalation of the crisis since the start of the year:

i.   The **pace** of the disease's spread has been a critical consideration. As the Imperial College model mentioned above highlights, in the absence of mitigation measures, exponential propagation can swiftly engulf almost the entire population of the world. This requires policymakers to act—and to collaborate internationally—extremely swiftly. Those countries with preparedness plans in place have enjoyed a significant advantage, including countries with recent experience from SARS and other outbreaks.

ii. The basic reproduction number (R0) of a virus is partly a reflection of its inherent properties of transmissibility, but it also reflects the degree of contact between people (Jackson 2019). A second factor in the spread of COVID-19 has therefore been the deepening of global **interconnectedness** in recent decades (not least because of the integration of China into the world economy). The biggest outbreak hotspots have been close to major airport hubs, and air travel is the paradigmatic example of increasing global network densities: between 2000 and 2018 the number of air passengers each year increased from 1.7 billion to 4.2 billion (World Bank 2020).

iii. A third factor in shaping the scale of the current crisis has been **health-sector capacity**. Like flood defences threatened by a tsunami, the exponential growth in confirmed cases of COVID-19 has threatened to overwhelm limited supplies of critical healthcare resources, including hospital beds, personal protective equipment (PPE), testing materials, medication, ventilators and specialist personnel. Constraints in the health sector have been exacerbated by efforts to boost short-term operational and financial efficiency, to the detriment of investments that would have bolstered the long-term resilience of the sector.

iv. A fourth factor to consider is the role of **state capacity** more generally in responses to the spread of the virus. A proper assessment will not be possible for many months until relative performances can be judged, but particular concerns have already been raised about state capacity in weaker, poorer countries in sub-Saharan Africa if caseloads begin to mount in that region (Nordling 2020). It should also be noted, however, that the erosion of state capacity (albeit from a much higher base) has also been cited to explain the vast variability in mortality in advanced Western countries (Smith 2020).

v.   A further driver has been the immediacy with which risk has **cascaded** from the health system to the economy. This is for obvious reasons. Suppression of the outbreak has focussed on measures (distancing, quarantine, isolation, etc) that lead inexorably to an immediate slowdown in economic activity. In the US, for example, the weekly number of new unemployment claims was around ten times higher than had ever previously been recorded (US Department of Labor 2020).

vi.   Finally, the COVID-19 crisis has emerged at a time when the political, economic and societal **fragilities** produced by the 2008 financial crisis are still being felt in many countries and regions. It is notable that in some countries patterns of societal polarisation and fragmentation appear to be shaping attitudes and responses to COVID-19 (Coppins 2020). In some countries, the financial crisis has also contributed directly to healthcare and other capacity constraints, as a result of the austerity measures taken over the past decade (Portes 2020).

Responses to the crisis

In this section, we focus on five key elements in the developing response to the COVID-19 outbreak: scientific assessment, risk perception, evaluation, management and communication. These are drawn from the IRGC risk governance framework (Florin and Bürkler 2017).

Technical assessment

The technical assessment of COVID-19 hazards, exposures and vulnerabilities does not start from scratch, but builds on a large body of evidence and analysis relating to previous coronaviruses (Paules, Marston, and Fauci 2020). The full genetic sequence of the virus was available globally within just ten days of the first WHO alert (National Center for Biotechnology Information 2020). The pace of scientific research into the virus since then has continued at breakneck speed and medical preprint servers have been flooded with research. Important early policy-relevant discoveries include the significant level of asymptomatic transmission of SARS-CoV-2, information that has shaped epidemiological models and management strategies (Ma et al. 2020). There have been blind spots, however. Early evidence from Taiwan about human-to-human transmission was reportedly disregarded by the WHO because of political considerations (*Financial Times* 2020).

Despite the pace of research, significant scientific uncertainties remain about COVID-19. It is still unclear how many people are infected or have recovered. It is even unclear how many people have died of the disease—testing and reporting standards differ and evolve, and there may be deliberate mis-reporting. Other uncertainties include whether infection confers immunity (Branswell 2020), and how the virus might be affected as weather patterns change over the course of the year. As with previous infectious disease outbreaks, a comprehensive scientific assessment will only be possible retrospectively. This creates obstacles to designing and implementing optimal risk management strategies. So too does the even greater difficulty of assessing accurately any second- and third-order effects of the outbreak on the economy, society, domestic politics, international relations and so on (Baldwin and di Mauro 2020).

Risk perceptions

Assessing risk perceptions complements the scientific assessment by taking account of individual and societal opinions, concerns and preferences. Risk perceptions play an important role in shaping individual protective behaviours, which is of particular importance in a case like COVID-19, where protective behaviours are at the heart of most response strategies (van der Pligt 1996). Moreover, a number of factors may skew perceptions of COVID-19, including cognitive biases (Fisher 2020)[2], anxiety (American Psychological Association 2020; Rubin et al. 2009), the unintuitive nature of exponential growth (Wagenaar and Sagaria 1975), experience of previous outbreaks, and indications that individuals pay more attention to media timelines of pandemics than to the underlying epidemiological timelines (Reintjes et al. 2016). Conflicting values among both policymakers and the public are another important factor in risk perceptions—for example over the balancing of health and economic impacts, or the level of isolation that it is appropriate for the state to enforce. It is still very early to draw firm empirical conclusions about perceptions of this particular disease and responses to it. Research is under way, however, and preliminary results point to marked variation between countries on dimensions such as trust in governments' ability to protect citizens, and the specific behavioural changes that individuals have made (International Survey on Coronavirus 2020).

Evaluation

A key task facing decision-makers is the evaluation of risks to determine whether they are (i) acceptable without any mitigation measures, (ii) intolerable no matter what precautions are taken, or (iii) tolerable if risk reduction measures are taken (Florin and Bürkler 2017, 20). This judgement should be grounded in the results of the scientific assessment and the perception assessment (as well as wider considerations such as societal values, resource constraints and trade-offs). In the case of COVID-19 there have been instances—including in the US—where this process has broken down and policy-makers' evaluation of the risk has been at odds with the scientific consensus. However, the vast majority of countries have imposed stringent risk reduction measures, while tolerating significant residual risk rather than curtail civil liberties too completely or for too long. According to the available data, China appears to have evaluated the risk of the disease spreading as being closer to intolerable, taking comprehensive and intrusive steps to suppress the Wuhan outbreak and prevent it from spreading to the rest of the country. At the other end of the spectrum, a small number of countries appear at times to have been willing to accept a much greater degree of COVID-19 risk, foregoing widely implemented suppression measures in order to allow the infection to spread, seemingly in the hope that herd immunity could be achieved. In the case of the UK, this evaluation appears to have rested on an underestimation of the number of deaths that such a strategy would entail (Horton 2020). When the potential for 250,000 deaths was highlighted in another Imperial College modelling paper (Ferguson et al. 2020) the government swiftly changed course. Another crucial issue is the trust of governments in voluntary or enforced measures for self-protection. Sweden has been pioneering an approach of relying on voluntary compliance while most other countries promulgated legally enforced measures to assure compliance.

Risk management

Risk management begins with taking decisions about the measures needed to deal with risks evaluated as tolerable. It involves designing, selecting and implementing strategies to reduce the adverse consequences associated with the risk (Florin and Bürkler 2017, 23). The decisions taken after appropriate evaluation are instrumental in determining how much harm a risk will ultimately cause. In the context of the current outbreak, the pace of the infection's spread has been a key constraint in the decision-making process, forcing policymakers to decide on unprecedented mass restrictions at great speed, under ongoing uncertainty and in the knowledge that the cost of failure (or even delayed success) could be very high numbers of deaths. Despite the complexity and uncertainty of the epidemiology, strong scientific consensus has resulted in a high degree of agreement among policymakers on the kind of measures needed to suppress it (Hale and Webster 2020). This emerging policy consensus was strengthened as increasing data became available from the earliest-affected countries, notably China and Italy (Phull 2020). Timing has therefore emerged as a key differentiator between responses in different countries. Thus far, two delays in particular have played an important role in determining the trajectory and scale of the global outbreak: an initial three-week delay in China after the first cases were seen, and a later delay in suppressing the virus in the United States (Shear et al. 2020). A further source of variation in the way countries have managed COVID-19 has been the healthcare capacity constraints mentioned earlier. For example, a lack of key materials in some Western countries has hampered their adoption of large-scale testing strategies that appear to have been successful when deployed elsewhere, notably in South Korea. Furthermore, there is an ongoing debate about the extent to which civil rights can be compromised in order to reduce the health risks. While South Korea reported to have success with a tracing app that would warn people if a positive tested person would come near to them, most European countries felt that such an app would not be compatible with the existing civil rights legislation unless it could be entirely anonymized. Hence, policymakers are forced to decide on further measures to manage risk-risk trade-offs— the additional risks created or exacerbated by the measures taken to manage COVID-19. In particular, huge financial commitments have been made to mitigate the potential economic harm caused by the steps taken to suppress the outbreak (IMF 2020). It is too early to judge either the cost or the effectiveness of the management strategies that policymakers are pursuing. It is also too early to judge what unintended consequences these strategies might lead to. In light of the scientific evidence about COVID-19, policymakers have had little choice but to intervene rapidly and forcefully in multiple interconnected complex systems (healthcare, economy, society, global transport, etc). It should not come as a surprise if these interventions trigger further spill-overs, including potential nonlinear effects.[3]

Communication

By risk communication we mean the process of sharing risk-related information within and between different groups, such as scientists, policymakers and the public, both nationally and internationally. It is crucial for effective risk governance (Florin and Bürkler 2017, 27), particularly in the context of a crisis as far-reaching as COVID-19 (Boin and Lodge 2020). The transparent communication of reliable scientific data among scientists is central to reducing uncertainty and facilitating robust risk assessments. The effective communication between scientists and policymakers is key to the formulation (and modification where necessary) of evidence-based management strategies. And clear channels for communication between policymakers and the public are needed in order to ensure the legitimacy and durability of management strategies as disruptive and sustained as those that are currently being implemented. A large body of research has established clear guiding principles for communicating about *risk* (Renn 2010). However, COVID-19 has presented policymakers in particular with numerous communication challenges related to *crisis* communication: how to communicate the severity of the risk (particularly given the combination of exponential dynamics and asymptomatic transmission); how to instil urgency without creating panic or despair; how to acknowledge uncertainty across multiple dimensions of the risk governance process;[4] and how to maintain confidence if changes in management strategies are required.

Compounding all of these challenges is the need to communicate consistent messages to very different audiences. Very broadly speaking, people's responses to crisis can be grouped into three categories: freeze, flight and fight (Bracha 2004, 679). Each of these patterns require different forms of communication. The freeze cluster requires clear incentives to make people more alert to the risks they are facing. The flight cluster needs to be informed that even within isolation there are risks that will need to be addressed—for example, health risks such as dehydration or social risks such as isolation. Finally, the fight cluster requires good advice on how to channel their need for action into behavioural responses that reduce the risk to themselves and others (such as helping the elderly to get food), while avoiding the scapegoating of individuals who are alleged to be causing or amplifying the risk (Renn 2015). Methods of communicating effectively with one of these groups may not work (or may be actively counter-productive) for the other two. Therefore, it is crucial to design consistent but also audience-specific risk and crisis communication programmes.

Where there have been failures of risk-related communication in relation to COVID-19 they have been costly. The two important risk management delays noted above, in China and the US, both involved failures of communication. In the Chinese case, early risk-related information was actively supressed, notably in the case of Dr Li Wenliang who had warned colleagues about COVID-19 (Green 2020). In the US case, damaging delays flowed from key policymakers' disregard for scientific advice until it was too late to contain the outbreak. Another area of missing or confused guidance has been in relation to the benefits or otherwise of members of the public wearing masks when they are outdoors (Tufekci 2020).

Lessons to be learned from the crisis

It is far too early to be definitive about the lessons that should be learned from the COVID-19 outbreak. However, tentative conclusions can be drawn as fresh evidence about this crisis accumulates. Previous crises suggest that COVID-19 may open a 'window of opportunity' during which otherwise infeasible changes might be tabled, agreed and implemented. Notwithstanding the fact that the crisis response is ongoing, now is also the time to assess what the priorities should be.

1. **Deal with similar risks at source.** It remains the case that bats and other animals are a reservoir of potential infectious diseases. To prevent further outbreaks, opportunities for zoonotic transmission will need to be reduced. Among other things, this would seem to require steps to shut down transmission via the 'wet markets' that have been responsible for both the SARS and COVID-19 outbreaks.
2. **Act on warnings**. A global infectious disease outbreak was predicted but not adequately prepared for. One obvious lesson is to review national and international risk assessments (or conduct new ones) and put better protections in place for high-impact risks that have been warned about. In the wake of COVID-19 there will be a temptation to focus disproportionate resources on strengthening pandemic preparedness. While remedying key deficiencies in this area will be important, the next shocks are likely to come from other directions. What other risk warnings have not received the attention they deserve?
3. **Pay attention to risk-risk trade-offs.** Whatever steps are taken to reduce the risks of COVID-19 are likely to have unexpected consequences. With high-stakes decisions currently being taken at speed and under conditions of uncertainty, there is a danger of these consequences being overlooked. As far as possible, build these second-round effects into assessments, evaluations and management strategy decisions.
4. **Consider the role of technology.** How can powerful computing technologies be safely used to predict, identify and help respond to infectious disease outbreaks and other emergencies? This is the first 'smartphone pandemic'. How can phones be used for contact tracing, while protecting privacy (Troncoso et al. 2020)? Similarly, what more can be safely done to leverage machine learning and other technologies as tools for pandemic assessment, preparedness and response (Hao 2020)?
5. **Invest in resilience.** Great gains in organisational efficiency over recent decades have resulted in a lack of resilience in some critical systems, such as healthcare. Investing in resilience needs to focus on three elements: redundancy, diversity and adaptive management (Linkov et al. 2014). We have seen the spread of COVID-19 exacerbated by supply-chain blockages (for example, for protective clothing and face masks, 80% of which is manufactured in China). Similarly, relying on only one line of products or services can lead to

collapse if no alternatives are readily available. And being trapped in rigid managerial structures, institutional silos and administrative rules can make the situation much worse than if a flexible and system-oriented approach is in place.

6. **Focus on key nodes in the system.** As noted above, the rapid growth of air travel is a key enabler of the global transmission of infectious diseases (Epstein et al. 2007). Future preparedness efforts should reflect this. Sharply restricting air travel as early as possible is an important way of slowing or halting the spread of an outbreak. To facilitate this kind of rapid disruption, a global emergency fund could be established to provide immediate compensation to affected parties, such as airlines and airport operators.

7. **Strengthen the science-policy nexus.** In many cases during this outbreak, the transmission of information and advice from the scientific assessment to policymakers' decisions about risk evaluation, management and communication has worked well. However, in the context of an exponentially spreading disease, when policymakers have ignored scientific advice, or delayed acting upon it, the human costs have been high. Every country should review the effectiveness of its current model of science-policy integration in light of COVID-19 experiences, and international bottlenecks should also be assessed.

8. **Build state capacity.** Two global systemic risks have crystallised since 2007—dealing with such risks perhaps needs to be considered an ongoing part of normal government rather than a periodic emergency response function. The aftermath of the upheaval caused by COVID-19 may offer an important opportunity for institutional and regulatory change to strengthen future responses.(Balleisen et al. 2017) Where public money is being used to bolster the economy, it should have conditions attached that seek to reduce the likelihood of future crises emerging. These conditions might involve the kind of resilience-boosting measures mentioned above (recommendation 3) or steps to tackle climate change or enhance sustainable practices (Hsu, Chia, and Vasoo 2020).

9. **Communicate better.** The pace of the COVID-19 crisis has required management strategies to be chosen and implemented without the time for careful engagement with the public. The communication part of the response to COVID-19 has been slow and/or flawed in a number of countries. One solution for this would be to establish national and international risk information and communication units tasked responding as soon as a potential crisis arises.[5] To address the point raised earlier about communicating to groups with very different risk responses (freeze, flight, fight), centralised crisis communications should be complemented by decentralised hotlines and similar services, with staff trained to recognise the different groups and communicate accordingly.

10. **Reflect on current societal disruptions.** The COVID-19 crisis is forcing a large number of people and organisations to experiment with new patterns of living and working, involving among other things: less consumption, less traffic, more time spent with family, less time spent with colleagues and employers, greater reliance on virtual communication (Wise et al. 2020). If the crisis persists, preferences may begin to shift, leading to some of these changes becoming entrenched. Now is the time to consider which changes might be desirable over the long-term (for example, because they accelerate changes that climate change is likely to require in any case), and which changes should be resisted (for example, because they involve a deleterious reduction in social interaction and individual well-being.

Notes

1. This paper draws on a recent document from the EPFL International Risk Governance Center. See Collins (2020)
2. Perception research has been able to prove many biases that can lead either to overestimation or underestimation of risks. For example, risks are overestimated when the potential consequences are illustrated in a particularly drastic way (such as television images of overcrowded hospitals or morgues). Another pattern revealed by research is that threats that can be statistically characterized by a bell-curve distribution of health

effects per triggering event tend to polarize reactions. On the one hand, there are those who self-locate on the left of the curve ("There's no way it will get me!"). On the other, there are those who self-locate on the right ("I'm so unlucky, someone is certain to infect me!"). Communicating simultaneously to these two groups is extremely difficult. See Science Advice for Policy by European Academies (2019).

3. Hungary's indefinite suspension of elections is an example of a nonlinear social/political effect of COVID-19. The collapse of oil prices (now cheaper than supermarket water) and the near-total grounding of many airlines are examples of non-linear business and economic impacts, which in turn may cause further spillover effects.

4. Uncertainties must be communicated because silence about them can undermine credibility. However, incautious communication of uncertainties can lead to fear and exaggerated negative risk perceptions. For this reason, the imperatives are to (i) communicate uncertainties as precisely as possible, and (ii) make clear what steps are being taken to reduce the degree of uncertainty. See Han (2013).

5. For principles of clear risk communication, see Environmental Protection Agency (1988).

Acknowledgements

The authors would like to thank the following individuals for their insightful comments on an earlier version of this article: Gérard Escher (EPFL), James Larus (EPFL), Granger Morgan (Carnegie Mellon University and IRGC Foundation), Arthur Petersen (University College London), Stephan Schreckenberg (Swiss Re).

Disclosure statement

No potential conflict of interest was reported by the author(s).

ORCID

Marie-Valentine Florin 🆔 http://orcid.org/0000-0003-2263-3928

References

American Psychological Association. 2020. "Speaking of Psychology: Coronavirus Anxiety." American Psychological Association. 2020. https://www.apa.org/research/action/speaking-of-psychology/coronavirus-anxiety.

Baldwin, Richard, and B. Weder di Mauro. 2020. *Economics in the Time of COVID-19*. London: CEPR Press VoxEU. org.

Balleisen, Edward J., Lori S. Bennear, Kimberly D. Krawiec, and Jonathan Baert Wiener, eds. 2017. *Policy Shock: Recalibrating Risk and Regulation after Oil Spills, Nuclear Accidents and Financial Crises*. New York, NY: Cambridge University Press.

Boin, Arjen, and Martin Lodge. 2020. "Making Sense of an Existential Crisis: The Ultimate Leadership Challenge." TransCrisis. March 20, 2020. https://www.transcrisis.eu/making-sense-of-an-existential-crisis-the-ultimate-leadership-challenge/.

Bracha, H. Stefan. 2004. "Freeze, Flight, Fight, Fright, Faint: Adaptationist Perspectives on the Acute Stress Response Spectrum." *CNS spectrums* 9 (9): 679–685. doi:10.1017/s1092852900001954.

Branswell, Helen. 2020. "What We've Learned about the Coronavirus — and What We Need to Know." STAT. March 26, 2020. https://www.statnews.com/2020/03/26/what-weve-learned-about-the-coronavirus-and-what-we-still-need-to-know/.

Cabinet Office. 2017. National Risk Register of Civil Emergencies. Cabinet Office London. https://www.gov.uk/government/publications/national-risk-register-of-civil-emergencies-2017-edition.

Cheng, Vincent C. C., Susanna K. P. Lau, Patrick C. Y. Woo, and Kwok Yung Yuen. 2007. "Severe Acute Respiratory Syndrome Coronavirus as an Agent of Emerging and Reemerging Infection." *Clinical microbiology reviews* 20 (4): 660–694. doi:10.1128/CMR.00023-07.

Collins, Aengus. 2020. "COVID-19: A Risk Governance Perspective." 10.5075/EPFL-IRGC-276934.

Coppins, McKay. 2020. "The Social-Distancing Culture War Has Begun." The Atlantic. March 30, 2020. https://www.theatlantic.com/politics/archive/2020/03/social-distancing-culture/609019/.

Economist Intelligence Unit. 2020. "COVID-19 to Send Almost All G20 Countries into a Recession." Economist Intelligence Unit. March 26, 2020. https://www.eiu.com/n/covid-19-to-send-almost-all-g20-countries-into-a-recession/.

Environmental Protection Agency 1988. "Seven Cardinal Rules of Risk Communication." https://archive.epa.gov/care/web/pdf/7_cardinal_rules.pdf.

Epstein, Joshua M., D. Michael Goedecke, Feng Yu, Robert J. Morris, Diane K. Wagener, and Georgiy V. Bobashev. 2007. "Controlling Pandemic Flu: The Value of International Air Travel Restrictions." *PLoS One* 2 (5): e401. Edited by Maurizio Del Poeta. doi:10.1371/journal.pone.0000401.

Ferguson, N., D. Laydon, G. Nedjati Gilani, N. Imai, K. Ainslie, M. Baguelin, S. Bhatia, et al. 2020. "Report 9: Impact of Non-Pharmaceutical Interventions (NPIs) to Reduce COVID19 Mortality and Healthcare Demand." Report. 10.25561/77482.

Financial Times 2020. "Taiwan Says WHO Failed to Act on Coronavirus Transmission Warning," March 20, 2020. https://www.ft.com/content/2a70a02a-644a-11ea-a6cd-df28cc3c6a68.

Fisher, Max. 2020. "Coronavirus 'Hits All the Hot Buttons' for How We Misjudge Risk." *The New York Times*, February 13, 2020, sec. World. https://www.nytimes.com/2020/02/13/world/asia/coronavirus-risk-interpreter.html.

Florin, Marie-Valentine, and Marcel Thomas Bürkler. 2017. "Introduction to the IRGC Risk Governance Framework." REP_WORK. International Risk Governance Center 10.5075/epfl-irgc-233739.

Global Preparedness Monitoring Board 2019. *A World at Risk: Annual Report on Global Preparedness for Health Emergencies.* Geneva: World Health Organization.

Green, Andrew. 2020. "Li Wenliang." *The Lancet* 395 (10225): 682. doi:10.1016/S0140-6736(20)30382-2.

Hale, Thomas, and Samuel Webster. 2020. "Oxford COVID-19 Government Response Tracker." 2020. https://www.bsg.ox.ac.uk/research/research-projects/oxford-covid-19-government-response-tracker.

Han, Paul K. J. 2013. "Conceptual, Methodological, and Ethical Problems in Communicating Uncertainty in Clinical Evidence." *Medical care research and review : MCRR* 70 (1 Suppl): 14S–36S. doi:10.1177/1077558712459361.

Hao, Karen. 2020. "This Is How the CDC Is Trying to Forecast Coronavirus's Spread." MIT Technology Review. March 13, 2020. https://www.technologyreview.com/s/615360/cdc-cmu-forecasts-coronavirus-spread/.

Horton, Richard. 2020. "Offline: COVID-19—a Reckoning." *The Lancet* 395 (10228): 935. doi:10.1016/S0140-6736(20)30669-3.

Hsu, Ly, Py Chia, and S. Vasoo. 2020. "A Midpoint Perspective on the COVID-19 Pandemic." *Singapore Medical Journal.* doi:10.11622/smedj.2020036.

IMF2020. 2020. "Policy Responses to COVID19." IMF. 2020. https://www.imf.org/en/Topics/imf-and-covid19/Policy-Responses-to-COVID-19.

International Survey on Coronavirus. 2020. "International Survey on Coronavirus." 2020. https://covid19-survey.org/index.html.

Jackson, MatthewO. 2019. *The Human Network: How We're Connected and Why It Matters.* London: Atlantic Books.

Jorda, Oscar, Sanjay R. Singh, and Alan M. Taylor. 2020. "Longer-Run Economic Consequences of Pandemics." 2020-09. Federal Reserve Bank of San Francisco. https://www.frbsf.org/economic-research/publications/working-papers/2020/09/.

Kormann, Carolyn. 2020. "From Bats to Human Lungs, the Evolution of a Coronavirus." The New Yorker. March 27, 2020. https://www.newyorker.com/science/elements/from-bats-to-human-lungs-the-evolution-of-a-coronavirus.

Li, Qun, Xuhua Guan, Peng Wu, Xiaoye Wang, Lei Zhou, Yeqing Tong, Ruiqi Ren, et al. 2020. "Early Transmission Dynamics in Wuhan, China, of Novel Coronavirus–Infected Pneumonia." *New England Journal of Medicine* 382 (13): 1199–1207. January. doi:10.1056/NEJMoa2001316.

Linkov, Igor, Todd Bridges, Felix Creutzig, Jennifer Decker, Cate Fox-Lent, Wolfgang Kröger, James H. Lambert, et al. 2014. "Changing the Resilience Paradigm." *Nature Climate Change* 4 (6): 407–409. doi:10.1038/nclimate2227.

Li, Wendong, Zhengli Shi, Meng Yu, Wuze Ren, Craig Smith, Jonathan H. Epstein, Hanzhong Wang, et al. 2005. "Bats Are Natural Reservoirs of SARS-Like Coronaviruses." *Science (New York, N.Y.)* 310 (5748): 676–679. doi:10.1126/science.1118391.

Ma, Shujuan, Jiayue Zhang, Minyan Zeng, Qingping Yun, Wei Guo, Yixiang Zheng, Shi Zhao, Maggie H. Wang, and Zuyao Yang. 2020. "Epidemiological Parameters of Coronavirus Disease 2019: A Pooled Analysis of Publicly Reported Individual Data of 1155 Cases from Seven Countries." Preprint. Infectious Diseases (except HIV/AIDS). 10.1101/2020.03.21.20040329.

National Center for Biotechnology Information 2020. "Severe Acute Respiratory Syndrome Coronavirus 2 Data Hub." NCBI Virus. 2020. https://www.ncbi.nlm.nih.gov/labs/virus/vssi/#/virus?SeqType_s=Nucleotide&VirusLineage_ss=Wuhan%20seafood%20market%20pneumonia%20virus,%20taxid:2697049.

Nordling, Linda. 2020. "A Ticking Time Bomb': Scientists Worry about Coronavirus Spread in Africa." Science | AAAS March 15, 2020. https://www.sciencemag.org/news/2020/03/ticking-time-bomb-scientists-worry-about-corona-virus-spread-africa. [Mismatch

Paules, Catharine I., Hilary D. Marston, and Anthony S. Fauci. 2020. "Coronavirus Infections—More Than Just the Common Cold." *JAMA* 323 (8): 707. . [Mismatch] doi:10.1001/jama.2020.0757.

Phull, Amit. 2020. "What We Must Learn From Wuhan." Op-Med. March 20, 2020. https://opmed.doximity.com/articles/what-we-must-learn-from-wuhan?_csrf_attempted=yes.

Pligt, Joop van der. 1996. "Risk Perception and Self-Protective Behavior." *European Psychologist* 1 (1): 34–43. 10.1027/1016-9040.1.1.34.

Portes, Jonathan. 2020. "And so the Appalling Human Consequences of the Austerity Experiment Become Clear." Prospect. March 25, 2020. https://www.prospectmagazine.co.uk/economics-and-finance/and-so-the-appalling-human-consequences-of-the-austerity-experiment-become-clear-george-osborne-economy-coronavirus-covid-19-recession.

Reintjes, Ralf, Enny Das, Celine Klemm, Jan Hendrik Richardus, Verena Keßler, and Amena Ahmad. 2016. "Pandemic Public Health Paradox': Time Series Analysis of the 2009/10 Influenza A/H1N1 Epidemiology, Media Attention, Risk Perception and Public Reactions in 5 European Countries." *PloS One* 11 (3): e0151258. doi:10.1371/journal.pone.0151258.

Renn, Ortwin. 2010. "Risk Communication: Insights and Requirements for Designing Successful Communication Programs on Health and Environmental Hazards." In *Handbook of Risk and Crisis Communication*, edited by Robert Heath and Dan O' Hair, 92–110. London: Routledge.

Renn, Ortwin. 2015. "Are We Afraid of the Wrong Things? Statistics, Psychology and the Risk Paradox." In *The Measurement of Risk*, edited by Union Investment, 24–35. Frankfurt am Main: Union Investment International.

Rubin, G. James, Richard Amlôt, Lisa Page, and Simon Wessely. 2009. "Public Perceptions, Anxiety, and Behaviour Change in Relation to the Swine Flu Outbreak: Cross Sectional Telephone Survey." *BMJ (Clinical research ed.)* 339: b2651. doi:10.1136/bmj.b2651.

Sansonetti, Philippe. 2020. "Web conférence : Covid-19 ou la chronique d'une émergence annoncée." Inserm - La science pour la santé. 2020. https://www.inserm.fr/actualites-et-evenements/actualites/web-conference-covid-19-ou-chronique-emergence-annoncee.

Science Advice for Policy by European Academies. 2019. *Making Sense of Science for Policy under Conditions of Complexity and Uncertainty*. Germany: Science Advice for Policy by European Academies. 10.26356/masos.

Shear, MichaelD, Abby Goodnough, Sheila Kaplan, Sheri Fink, Katie Thomas, and Noah Weiland. 2020. "The Lost Month: How a Failure to Test Blinded the U.S. to Covid-19." *The New York Times*, March 28, 2020, sec. U.S. https://www.nytimes.com/2020/03/28/us/testing-coronavirus-pandemic.html.

Smith, Noah. 2020. "Coronavirus Makes America Seem Like a Civilization in Decline." Bloomberg.Com. March 29, 2020. https://www.bloomberg.com/opinion/articles/2020-03-29/coronavirus-makes-america-seem-like-a-civilization-in-decline.

Troncoso, Carmel, Mathias Payer, Jean-Pierre Hubaux, Marcel Salathé, James Larus, Edouard Bugnion, Wouter Lueks, et al. 2020. "Decentralized Privacy-Preserving Proximity Tracing: Overview of Data Protection and Security." https://github.com/DP-3T.

Tufekci, Zeynep. 2020. "Why Telling People They Don't Need Masks Backfired." *The New York Times*, March 17, 2020, sec. Opinion. https://www.nytimes.com/2020/03/17/opinion/coronavirus-face-masks.html.

US Department of Labor 2020. "Unemployment Insurance Weekly Claims (Week Ending March 28)." US Department of Labor. https://www.dol.gov/sites/dolgov/files/OPA/newsreleases/ui-claims/20200551.pdf.

Wagenaar, William A., and Sabato D. Sagaria. 1975. "Misperception of Exponential Growth." *Perception & Psychophysics* 18 (6): 416–422. doi:10.3758/BF03204114.

Walker, P., C. Whittaker, O. Watson, M. Baguelin, K. Ainslie, S. Bhatia, S. Bhatt, et al. 2020. "Report 12: The Global Impact of COVID-19 and Strategies for Mitigation and Suppression." Report 19. 10.25561/77735.

Webster, Robert G. 2004. "Wet Markets—a Continuing Source of Severe Acute Respiratory Syndrome and Influenza?" *The Lancet* 363 (9404): 234–236. https://doi.org/. [Mismatch] doi:10.1016/S0140-6736(03)15329-9..

Wise, Toby, Tomislav Damir Zbozinek, Giorgia Michelini, Cindy C. Hagan, and Dean Mobbs. 2020. "Changes in Risk Perception and Protective Behavior during the First Week of the COVID-19 Pandemic in the United States." Preprint. PsyArXiv. 10.31234/osf.io/dz428.

World Bank. 2020. "Air Transport, Passengers Carried." World Bank. 2020. https://data.worldbank.org/indicator/IS.AIR.PSGR.

'A monstrous threat': how a state of exception turns into a 'new normal'

Jens O. Zinn

ABSTRACT

This article explores the factors that helped COVID-19 to become a 'monstrous threat' to humanity, which legitimises significant restrictions to people's freedom and is justified by the ethics to keep everyone safe. It analyses how rigid means increase old inequalities and produce secondary risks and significant side-effects and demonstrates how, with social and economic costs soaring, governments seek ways back – not to the old normal – but new social practices and attitudes towards infectious diseases, thereby transforming the state of exception into a 'new normal'.

In 1986, shortly after the Chernobyl nuclear power disaster, Ulrich Beck (1986) published his book 'Risikogesellschaft' (translation: Risk Society, Beck 1992), describing a new social condition, in which the state of exception becomes the new normal. He later developed his approach into his theses on the World Risk Society (Beck 1999, 2009) – a society challenged by managing the new catastrophic global risks accompanying the technological and social advancements of the modernisation process. From the early days of technological disasters, through to the financial crisis, international terrorism and climate change, cosmopolitan spaces open up for international collaboration, necessary to successfully manage such global challenges. However, it is an empirical question whether governments collaborate and confront the challenge or allow it to grow into a 'monstrous threat' that necessitates extreme measures, and requires an answer to the question in which world we want to live.

SARS-CoV-2 and the related illness COVID-19 is an example of such a threat, which grew from a local infection to a monstrous global risk utilising intensified mobility of human bodies to travel quickly locally, regionally and worldwide through major events and to faraway places.

This article explores (I) the factors that helped COVID-19 to become a 'monstrous threat' to humanity, which legitimises significant restrictions to people's freedom and is justified by the ethics to keep everyone safe, (II) On this basis, it suggests that even though epidemiological knowledge is crucial for informing political action, the evidence provides a general direction rather than precision. At the same time, while playing a metaphorical role for the dominant ethics to protect everyone from the virus, the article argues that (III) epidemiological recommendations support rigid means, which increase old inequalities and produce secondary risks and significant side-effects. (IV) It demonstrates further, how, with social and economic costs soaring, governments seek ways back – not to the old normal – but new social practices and attitudes towards infectious diseases, thereby transforming the state of exception into a 'new normal'.

How COVID-19 became a 'monstrous threat'

This section argues that, (i) the reality of the spread of the virus combines with, (ii) media coverage illustrating the impact of the virus, (iii) psychological tendencies in human responses to uncertain, unknown and involuntary risks, and (iv) epidemiology developing authoritative knowledge and tools how to manage infectious diseases. These different forces combined constitute a 'monstrous threat' (Latour 2005, Mol 2003) that pressures governments to respond and defines their success and failure.

The reality of the virus

As other corona viruses before, SARS-CoV-2 emerged from the ways how we live and work and used the opportunity to jump the boundary between animals and humans (NIH 2020). COVID-19 developed first unobserved, was quickly transferred and carried by human bodies to distant places and, when finally discovered, it had already developed into a major social threat not mainly due to its ability to kill but by challenging our way of living and the social institutions, which have been developed to protect and manage human health and well-being.

COVID-19 got a head start with China first silencing her concerned doctors. When recognising the ability of the coronavirus to spread quickly and to cause a severe illness, Chinese authorities responded with the relentless power of totalitarian regime, by isolating Wuhan, a major travel hub of more than 11 million population from China and the world. They also applied rigid mobility restrictions and enforced behavioural changes. Similarly, the World Health Organisation (WHO), as well as other national governments, when being informed about the discovery of a new coronavirus were initially slow to respond, allowing the virus to spread further and developing into a major force.

The media

During March 2020, with infection rates and deaths soaring, and the media reporting about an overloaded health care system, first in Italy and soon after in Spain, the originally Chinese virus had become a powerful global agent. The daily press briefings of the director general of the WHO, Tedros Adhanom Ghebreyesus and experts from national institutes responsible for disease control and prevention were given prime time in television news to promote the most recent data and advice on how to protect against the virus. Similarly online platforms such as the 'worldometer' provided regular updates on coronavirus infection rates and fatalities worldwide.[1]

The media complemented data with pictures of desperate nurses and doctors being overwhelmed by the number of patients, the lack of protective gear, the traumatised relatives just heaving lost a loved one, the piling of coffins, the death of famous people, and the sense that everyone could become infected and die. Thus, COVID-19 had most characteristics necessary for becoming a major news event (Kitzinger 1999), and the media played its part to spread the news, inform the public and provide pictures and reports sharing what it means and feels like to be in the centre of a crisis. Sometimes, martial language that compared hospitals with 'war zones' and political measures with a 'war against the virus' heightened the feeling of urgency and disaster. At the same time, they played a vital role in promoting the message of the medical experts, which are commonly amongst the most trustworthy professional groups (IPSOS MORI 2020; Funk et al. 2019), emphasising the lack of cure, the deadly danger we are facing, and the need to act fiercely to stop the virus spreading.

Thereby, the media reporting from people experiencing the virus as well as the experts' judgements, amplified risk consciousness in the public sphere (Pidgeon, Kasperson, and Slovic 2003). This consciousness was the backdrop providing politicians with legitimacy for extraordinary measures and restrictions, thus distracting debate from political negligence (e.g. savings in the health care system, slow response to the virus), secondary risks and deeper socio-structural issues (Ribeiro et al. 2018; Wallis and Nerlich 2005).

Psychological mechanisms

The social acceptance of highly restricted measures was also supported by psychological mechanisms of risk perception. When risks are experienced as catastrophic, people tend not to accept any likelihood of a potentially catastrophic event occurring (e.g. death of a loved one, high number of fatalities). The degree of unfamiliarity with a risk as well as the involuntary exposure increases the perceived risk (Slovic 2000; Starr 1969) and fosters the acceptance of even highly restricting measures of social distancing. Many might feel even more vulnerable as intuitive responses to crisis, such as sticking together with the loved one at times of crisis, became itself a source of high risk, thereby eroding feelings of ontological security (Giddens 1991).

Socio-historical dynamics

The experts' authority in the debate builds on the institutionalisation and spread of epidemiological knowledge that had become increasingly influential within the medical profession (Skolbekken 1995) and the public sphere since World War Two (Zinn 2020). The proliferation of risk language, the reporting of medical research in the news and the authority of medical research in the definition and management of health risk are connected (Zinn and McDonald 2018). For a long time, experts have warned that it is not a question of if but when a next deadly pandemic would strike (DW 2019). While in many cases it is possible to geographically contain a virus (e.g. Ebola and MARS), the H1N1 swine flu in 2009 mobilised fantasies of the next Spanish flu threatening humanity (Shaban 2020). Such concerns of how to prepare for the next pandemic have been nourished by a growing body of expert knowledge.

The political power of coronavirus

These different factors combined provided the virus with political power that pressured governments such as in the UK and recently Sweden with an initially relatively relaxed approach to controlling the spread to engage in more rigid approaches (Boseley 2020; Nikel 2020). Equally, at the outset hesitant leaders, who tried to oppose the evidence such as Donald Trump in the US joined the global fight. In contrast, Brazil Jair Bolsonaro's resistance to acknowledge the threat triggered growing resistance and opposition, destablising his leadership (Londoño, Andreoni, and Casado 2020).

Governments of different countries restricted people's freedoms to different degrees by shutting down businesses, imposing lockdowns and further social distancing measures, often enforced by punishing noncompliance. Despite varying in their degree of restrictions, these measures where regularly introduced as "without alternative", prompting the impression that the more restrictive the means the better. Measures were legitimised by a continuous stream of numbers – such as on daily new numbers of infected or death persons – that was employed to illustrate the severity of the thread and how well countries managed the spread of the virus.

The numbers

However, numbers as such are not sufficient to determine a risk, they require interpretation and valuation (Renn 2008). With an estimated 1% to 3% fatalities, COVID-19 is clearly not as fatal as Ebola Virus Disease (EVD: 25%-90%), Middle East Respiratory Syndrome (MERS: 34%) or Severe Acute Respiratory Syndrome (SARS: 9.6%)[2]. The major concerns were the impact of the virus when spreading to a large part of the population (Guarner 2020) and health care systems becoming overburdened and unable to meet the demand (OECD 2020). It were therefore less the concrete numbers but their general tendency and the illustrated possibility of negative outcomes that shaped the political responses, based on the sense that everyone should be saved if possible, since in face of death, no argument is acceptable to justify preventable fatalities.

Therefore, the lack of comparability of the presented data of infected people for different countries were not problematic. They reflected the different national capacity for testing, their specific testing regimes or attempts to downplay the risk. Some countries tested less than others and therefore received lower official infections. Even confirmed fatalities, which can be expressed in concrete figures, do not easily compare. The UK, for example, only included in its COVID-19 figures hospital deaths where there has been a positive COVID-19 test - but not people who died in care homes (Doyle 2020). However, there are suggestions that about half of the people who died in Italy, Spain, France, Ireland and Belgium from COVID-19 lived in care homes (Booth 2020b).

Further difficulties to interpret the numbers arose from the fact that the reasons why patients die are not clearly distinguished (Vincent and Taccone 2020). Already severely ill patients might die with COVID-19 whereas previously healthy patients may die from COVID-19. Good estimates about the overall fatalities of the crisis can only be made retrospectively by measuring the excess mortality of a year compared with average mortality. But it is difficult to interpret the data when the large proportion that dies (Zhang, et al. 2020; WHO 2020a) is not the group which is mainly infected. Even though there are high infections in all age groups from 15 to 80+ years old, fatalities cumulate mainly in the oldest age groups as the example of Italy shows, where almost 80% of deaths occurred amongst the age group of 70 years and above and almost 55% of the death were in their 80s or beyond.[3]. This observation is shared by countries such as Australia, where the median age of deaths was 80 years (range 55 to 94 years, AusGov (Australian Government and Department of Health) 2020) and Germany, where the median age of deaths was 82 years (range 28 to 105 years, RKI 2020: 4). The likelihood to die increases when suffering any of the common civilisation diseases such as cardiovascular diseases, diabetes, chronic respiratory disease, hypertension and cancer, which are all typical for old age (Zhang, et al. 2020).

While the numbers do not question the basic message of the experts, the possibility of severe impact and the uncertainty of knowledge, the uncertainty around their overall validity mainly allocates them an illustrative purpose. Statements such as COVID-19 "can kill healthy adults in addition to elderly people with existing health problems" (Gates 2020) might be misleading since even though possible the likelihood for such an incident happening is very low, but it is underpinned by our shared ethical commitment. Consequently, reporting focussed on measuring the spread of the virus and the increase of overall fatalities and the very real consequences this had on struggling health systems. The worst scenario hospital doctors spoke about when describing the crisis was the possibility or necessity to allocate limited medical resources via a triage system, thus creating the ethically unacceptable situation of balancing the value of one's life against another.

This ethical commitment, however, remains on an abstract epidemiological level and neglects the normalised socio-structural patterns of health inequalities and secondary risks caused by the measures of managing COVID-19.

Social inequalities and secondary risks

The experiences of the COVID-19 pandemic have shown that social inequalities surface in different ways and therefore require different approaches to identify and tackle them. Inequalities can directly relate to the resources available to manage (i) the pandemic, (ii) the structure and organisation of care and health care necessary to look after vulnerable populations, and (iii) the impact of the means to manage the virus such as social distancing measures, on everyday life, which may intensify the experience of disadvantage. These inequalities are visible on a global level as well as nationally and within the social structure of society.

COVID-19 has challenged the national resources available to accommodate the large number of patients in need of intensive care. When Italy and Spain struggled under the demand it became clear that they both had relatively low numbers of intensive care beds available (Spain: 9.7 per 100,000 population; Italy 8.6) in contrast to other countries (Germany: 33.9; Austria: 28.9 and the US: 25.8). The picture was similar for acute care hospital beds that are important to manage a higher load at times of crisis with the exception of the US, which is amongst the lowest (2.4 beds per 1000 population, OECD 2020a: 11-2) and Japan (7.8) and Korea (7.1) leading the table. These and other data highlight differences both in investments in the health sector, inequalities in national wealth but there are also significant differences in who has access to health care with the US being known for being more exclusive. With COVID-19 spreading to countries with large parts of their population living in poverty and health care systems already struggling, there are growing concerns to what extent they will manage the pandemic (WHO. 2020b).

Inequalities are also observable in the affectedness of the virus drawing attention to differences in the health status of different populations within a society. The higher COVID-19 fatality rates of African Americans in the US (Evelyn 2020) are a telling example suspected to reflect deep social inequalities of the US characterised by differences in health status, access to health support and average life expectancy (Wilkinson and Pickett 2009). Similarly, the overproportionate number of none-white Covid-19 patients in intensive care in the UK asks for explanations (Booth 2020a).

The means to manage COVID-19 can also bring to light unsolved social issues in the care system of a society. For example, aging societies such as Germany require and attract a large number of foreign care workers from Eastern Europe, which profit from the comparatively high income. Since foreign care workers are essential for the underfunded and understaffed elderly care system in Germany, they are exempt from the travel ban for foreigners but must prove their work contract at the border. However, since adhering to legal home care arrangements is expensive, many people in need of care revert to work arrangements in the grey or black market (Horn et al. 2019). These estimated 150,000 to 300,000 carers (Löffelholz 2017) cannot continue their work during the travel ban, losing income and leaving vulnerable people and their relatives without support, and adding additional problems to the coronavirus crisis. In this way, the means managing the COVID-19 worsens unsolved social issues and further exposes vulnerable people.

The lockdowns many governments have imposed cause additional stress for the mental well-being of both single people living in as well as people living together under cramped conditions. For already disadvantaged people being required to stay at home for an unknown time span may have negative effects on a number of levels. This situation has been linked to a worldwide surge in domestic violence (Townsend 2020; Taub 2020). Children's opportunities to continue their education also vary during lockdown. Some might get support from their middle-class parents while others lack the supportive environment needed to successfully learn from home (e.g. educated or available parents, hardware/internet access). The longer the lockdown, the more negative these effects are.

Economic costs equally have been high as social lockdown directly influences one's opportunity for gainful employment. Particularly employees in unprotected and casual work who are not system relevant and who may not be able to work from home are affected by a sudden loss of income, jeopardizing them and their families. The expected economic downturn and recession following from the closure of businesses as part of the coronavirus lockdown will have negative effects for large social groups. There are already soaring numbers of people looking for work in many countries (UN News 2020), while there are warnings that half a billion people worldwide could be pushed into poverty by the corona virus (Oxfam 2020) likely to have long term effects on their overall well-being.

Considering and balancing such risks when responding to a pandemic can improve outcomes, but general socio-structural risks, which might 'silently kill' are more difficult to judge and to balance against immediate threats of an illness. Therefore, significant interventions into the social

and economic life have not only immediate but also long-term negative effects for a large proportion of the members of a society important to take into account.

Conclusions and consequences

From an epidemiological perspective, COVID-19 is a test case for even more serious infectious diseases spreading globally. It has exposed weaknesses in national health systems and of governments' responses as well as national and international inequalities. It also evidenced the influence
of global live styles with high mobility patterns and global dependencies. The response is framed
by the sense that no one should be exposed to the risk of dying by a virus if preventable, supported by subjective risk perceptions and institutional zero-risk priorities. However, such ethical
standards tend to neglect the reality of competing risks and favour more immediate over socio-
structural and individualised risks such as ill health and reduced life-expectancies, which tend to
kill more 'silently'. Indeed, the case of COVID-19 has proved the importance of governments
responding swiftly in face of a pandemic to prevent viruses becoming a monstrous agent.
Nevertheless, the undifferentiated top down approach proves a lack of confidence in the public to
respond reasonably in the face of crisis. Prioritising the epidemiological measures to control the
spread of a deadly virus such as comprehensive lockdown of social life affects social groups
unequally and produces secondary risks. It is rather questionable whether compelling people to
stay at home over a lengthy time improves population health. School closures will affect the children of the already disadvantaged people most, thereby further dividing social groups. The application of broader ethical standards to evaluate and take into account the social and economic
implications are the basis for developing more flexible tools, which combine effective disease control with the application of self-responsible hygiene and social distancing measures to keep social
and economic costs low. Because of these costs, in many countries where the infection rates slow
down, the social pressure increases to scale down the COVID-19 restrictions (EU 2020).

Managing an infectious disease and at the same time keeping the economic and social
impact comparatively low might include (voluntary) tracing apps to more efficiently control the
spread of a virus right from the beginning (Ferretti et al. 2020). Where possible, organisations
might increasingly replace face-to-face meetings by online meetings and virtual mobility. In
many countries, COVID-19 has pushed the use of online tools to manage everyday tasks (e.g.
teaching, meeting, planning, home office). These examples have demonstrated how such tools
could be used more efficiently not only at times of crisis. Indeed, changing mobility patterns
with a greater emphasis of virtual mobility could also contribute to reduce other problems such
as climate change by reducing carbon emissions.

However, it is less the technical support but the attitudinal change, which will be required.
Even though the pressure is growing to scale down restrictions to public life, it is not yet clear
when and whether COVID-19 will fully disappear (Devlin 2020). The way back to normal life might
be longer than originally expected and demand significant changes of ethical standards and
behavioural patterns regarding both hygiene and individual management of illness more generally.
Responsibility and greater awareness of distant but potentially vulnerable others are crucial.

The desire to come back to normal live sooner rather than later might encourage and promote a fundamental shift in the way how we live together and care for each other, which goes
far beyond the current COVID-19 crisis. It is a necessity to prepare efficiently for future pandemics to avoid new viruses developing into a 'monstrous threat'. Such a general change could also
contribute to better managing well-known risks, such as during the annual flu seasons. While
preparation for annual flu seasons is well institutionalised in many countries with comprehensive
provision of vaccination keeping fatalities marginal, the flu regularly claims high numbers of lives
(e.g. in Germany the 2017/18 flu season caused approx. 25,000 deaths, RKI 2019). A stronger
awareness and virus sensitised attitudes might contribute to keep these known threats at bay as

much as preparing for the unknown pandemics of the future. It would constitute a new social condition characterised by a heightened responsibility not only for individual health but the health of others as well.

Notes

1. https://www.worldometers.info/
2. https://www.worldometers.info/coronavirus/coronavirus-death-rate/
3. With one of the highest death rates in Europe, the age distribution of Covid-19 fatalities in Italy reads as follows: 0-29 years: 10 (0.2%), 30-39 years: 39 (0.4%), 40-49 years: 170 (0.9), 50-59 years: 712 (2.5%), 60-69: 2142 (9.3%), 70-79: 5874 (23.8%), 80-89: 7534 (30.5%), 90+ years: 2161 (25%), all as of April 13 (ISdS 2020).

Disclosure statement

No potential conflict of interest was reported by the author(s).

References

AusGov (Australian Government, Department of Health). 2020. "Coronavirus (COVID-19) at a glance." Infographic. Accessed 10/04/2020 at: https://www.health.gov.au/resources/publications/coronavirus-covid-19-at-a-glance.

Beck, U. 1986. *Risikogesellschaft. Auf Den Weg in Eine Andere Moderne*. Frankfurt/Main: Suhrkamp.

Beck, U. 1992. *Risk Society. Towards a New Modernity*. London, UK, Thousand Oaks, CA: Sage

Beck, U. 1999. *World Risk Society*. Cambridge, UK, Malden, MA: Polity.

Beck, U. 2009. *World at Risk*. Cambridge, UK, Malden, MA: Polity.

Booth, R. 2020a. "BAME groups hit harder by Covid-19 than white people, UK study suggests". *The Guardian online*. 7 April 2020. Accessed 14/04/2020 at https://www.theguardian.com/world/2020/apr/07/bame-groups-hit-harder-covid-19-than-white-people-uk.

Booth, R. 2020b. "Half of coronavirus deaths happen in care homes, data from EU suggests." *The Guardian online*, 13 April 2020. Accessed 14/04/2020 at https://www.theguardian.com/world/2020/apr/13/half-of-coronavirus-deaths-happen-in-care-homes-data-from-eu-suggests.

Boseley, S. 2020. "Coronavirus: health experts fear epidemic will 'let rip' through UK." *The Guardian online*, 15 March 2020. Accessed 14/04/2020 at https://www.theguardian.com/world/2020/mar/15/coronavirus-health-experts-fear-epidemic-will-let-rip-through-uk.

Devlin, H. 2020. "Coronavirus distancing may need to continue until 2022, say experts." *The Guardian online*. Accessed 14/04/2020 at https://www.theguardian.com/world/2020/apr/14/coronavirus-distancing-continue-until-2022-lockdown-pandemic?.

Doyle, E. 2020. "Why is coronavirus killing so many more people in the UK than in Ireland." *The Guardian online*. Accessed 14/04/2020 at https://www.theguardian.com/commentisfree/2020/apr/14/coronavirus-uk-ireland-delay?.

DW 2019. 'Next flu pandemic 'a metter of when, not if' says WHO." *DW*, 11 March 2019. Accessed 14/04/2020 at https://www.dw.com/en/next-flu-pandemic-a-matter-of-when-not-if-says-who/a-47853367.

EU 2020. "COVID-19: EU Commission Suggests Gradual Return to Normalcy." *Schengen visa info* 12 Apr 2020. Accessed 15/04/2020 at https://www.schengenvisainfo.com/news/covid-19-eu-commission-suggests-gradual-return-to-normalcy/.

Evelyn, K. 2020. "'It's a racial justice issue': Black Americans are dying in greater numbers from Covid-19." *The Guardian online*. Accessed 14/04/2020 at https://www.theguardian.com/world/2020/apr/08/its-a-racial-justice-issue-black-americans-are-dying-in-greater-numbers-from-covid-19.

Ferretti, L., C. Wymant, M. Kendall, L. Zhao, A. Nutray, L. Abeler-Dörner, M. Parker, D. Bonsall, and C. Fraser. 2020. "Quantifying SARS-CoV-2 Transmission Suggests Epidemic Control with Digital Contact Tracing." *Science* 31 March 2020. doi:10.1126/science.abb6936.

Funk, C., M. Hefferon, B. Kennedy, and C. Johnson. 2019. "Trust and Mistrust in Americans' Views of Scientific Experts", August 2, *PEW Research Centre, Science and Society*, accessed 10/04/2020 at: https://www.pewresearch.org/science/2019/08/02/trust-and-mistrust-in-americans-views-of-scientific-experts/.

Gates, B. 2020. "Responding to Covid-19 – a Once-in-a-Century Pandemic?" *The New England Journal of Medicine* 378: 2057–2060.

Giddens, A. 1991. *Modernity and Self-Identity. Self and Society in the Late Modern Age*. Cambridge: Polity.

Guarner, J. 2020. "Three Emerging Coronaviruses in Two Decades. The Story of SARS, MERS, and Now COVID-19." *American Journal of Clinical Pathology* 153 (4): 420–421. doi:10.1093/ajcp/aqaa029.

Horn, V., C. Schweppe, A. Böcker, and M. Bruquetas-Callejo. 2019. "Live-in Migrant Care Worker Arrangements in Germany and The Netherlands: motivations and Justifications in Family Decision-Making." *International Journal of Ageing and Later Life* 13 (2): 83–113. doi:10.3384/ijal.1652-8670.18410.

IPSOS MORI. 2020. *"Trust in Professions: Long-term trends"*. Accessed 10/04/2020 at: https://www.ipsos.com/ipsos-mori/en-uk/trust-professions-long-term-trends?view=wide.

ISdS (Instituto Superiore di Sanita). 2020. "Sorveglianza Integrata COVID-19 in Italia". Accessed 14/04/2020 at https://www.epicentro.iss.it/coronavirus/bollettino/Infografica_13aprile%20ITA.pdf.

Kitzinger, J. 1999. "Researching Risk and the Media." *Health, Risk & Society* 1 (1): 55–69. doi:10.1080/13698579908407007.

Latour, B. 2005. *Reassembling the Social: An Introduction to Actor-Network-Theory*. Oxford New York: Oxford University Press.

Löffelholz, J. 2017. "Schwarzarbeit ab 800 Euro". *Süddeutsche Zeitung*, 23 Jan 2017. Accessed 14/04/2020 at https://www.sueddeutsche.de/wirtschaft/illegal-schwarzarbeit-ab-800-euro-1.3345286.

Londoño, E., M. Andreoni, and L. Casado. 2020. "Bolsonaro, Isolated and Defiant, Dismisses Coronavirus Threat to Brazil." *The New York Times*. Accessed 14/04/2020 at https://www.nytimes.com/2020/04/01/world/americas/brazil-bolsonaro-coronavirus.html.

Mol, A. 2003. *The Body Multiple*. Durham, N.C.: Duke University Press.

NIH (National Institute of Allergy and Infectious Diseases). 2020. *COVID-19, MERS & SARS*. Accessed 12/04/2020 at https://www.niaid.nih.gov/diseases-conditions/covid-19.

Nikel, D. 2020. "Sweden: 22 Scientists Say Coronavirus Strategy Has Failed As Deaths Top 1,000." *Forbes*. Accessed 14/04/2020 at https://www.forbes.com/sites/davidnikel/2020/04/14/sweden-22-scientists-say-coronavirus-strategy-has-failed-as-deaths-top-1000/#7dfa8f047b6c.

OECD. 2020. *"Beyond Containment: health systems responses to COVID-19 in the OECD"*. Updated 31 March 2020. Accessed 10/04/2020 at: https://read.oecd-ilibrary.org/view/?ref=119_119689-ud5comtf84&Title=Beyond%20Containment:Health%20systems%20responses%20to%20COVID-19%20in%20the%20OECD.

OECD. 2020. *"Hospital beds"*. (indicator). doi:10.1787/0191328e-en.(Accessed on 07 April 2020)

Oxfam. 2020. *"Half a billion people could be pushed into poverty by coronavirus, warns Oxfam"*. Accessed 15/04/2020 at https://www.oxfam.org/en/press-releases/half-billion-people-could-be-pushed-poverty-coronavirus-warns-oxfam.

PEW. 2020. https://www.pewresearch.org/science/2019/08/02/trust-and-mistrust-in-americans-views-of-scientific-experts/.

Pidgeon, N., R. E. Kasperson, and P. Slovic. 2003. *The Social Amplification of Risk*. Cambridge: CUP.

Renn, O. 2008. *Risk Governance. Coping with Uncertainty in a Complex World*. London, Sterling, VA: Earthscan.

Ribeiro, B., S. Hartley, B. Nerlich, and R. Jaspal. 2018. "Media Coverage of the Zika Crisis in Brazil: "the Construction of a 'War' Frame That Masked Social and Gender Inequalities." *Social Science & Medicine* 200: 137–144. doi:10.1016/j.socscimed.2018.01.023.

RKI. 2019. Pommes für die Grippeschutzimpfung? Neuer Influenza-Saisonbericht erschienen. *"Pressemitteilung des Robert Koch Instituts"*. Accessed 15 Apr 2020 at https://www.rki.de/DE/Content/Service/Presse/Pressemitteilungen/2019/10_2019.html.

RKI. 2020. "Coronavirus Disease 2019 (COVID-19)". *Daily Situation Report of the Robert Koch Institute*. 04/04/2020 – Updated Status for Germany. Accessed 10/04/2020 at: https://www.rki.de/DE/Content/InfAZ/N/Neuartiges_Coronavirus/Situationsberichte/2020-04-04-en.pdf?__blob=publicationFile.

Shaban, A. R. A. 2020. "Throwback: Bush, Obama pandemic warning, Gadaffi's vaccine caution." *africanews.com*. Accessed 14/04/2020 at https://www.africanews.com/2020/04/11/throwback-bush-obama-pandemic-warning-gadaffi-s-vaccine-caution/.

Skolbekken, J.-A. 1995. "The Risk Epidemic in Medical Journals." *Social Science & Medicine* 40 (3): 291–305. doi:10.1016/0277-9536(94)00262-R.

Slovic, P. 2000. *The Perception of Risk*. Earthscan, London.

Starr, C. 1969. "Social Benefits versus Technological Risk." *Science* 165 (3899): 1232–1238. doi:10.1126/science.165.3899.1232.

Taub, A. 2020. "A New Covid-19 Crisis: Domestic Abuse Rises Worldwide." *The New York Times*. Accessed 14/04/2020 at https://www.nytimes.com/2020/04/06/world/coronavirus-domestic-violence.html.

Townsend, M. 2020. "Revealed: surge in domestic violence during Covid-19 crisis. *"The Guardian online*. Accessed 14/04/2020 at https://www.theguardian.com/society/2020/apr/12/domestic-violence-surges-seven-hundred-per-cent-uk-coronavirus.

UN News. 2020. "COVID-19. impact could cause equivalent of 195 million job losses, says ILO chief." 8 April 2020. Accessed 14/04/2020 at https://news.un.org/en/story/2020/04/1061322.

Vincent, J.-L., and F. S. Taccone. 2020. "Understanding pathways to death in patients with COVID-19". *The Lancet*. Online First: doi:10.1016/S2213-2600(20)30165-X.

Wallis, P., and B. Nerlich. 2005. "Disease Metaphors in New Epidemics: The UK Media Framing of the 2003 SARS Epidemic." *Social Science & Medicine* 60 (11): 2629–2639. doi:10.1016/j.socscimed.2004.11.031.

WHO. 2020a. *Report of the WHO-China Joint Mission on Coronavirus Disease 2019 (COVID-19)*. Accessed 14/04/2020 at https://www.who.int/docs/default-source/coronaviruse/who-china-joint-mission-on-covid-19-final-report.pdf.

WHO. 2020b. *"WHO concerned as COVID-19 cases accelerate in Africa"*. WHO regional office for Africa, Brazzaville, 2 April 2020. Accessed 04/04/2020 at https://www.afro.who.int/news/who-concerned-covid-19-cases-accelerate-africa.

Wilkinson, R., and K. Pickett. 2009. *The Spirit Level*. London: Allen Lane.

Zhang, Y, et al. 2020. "The Epidemiological Characteristics of an Outbreak of 2019 Novel Coronavirus Diseases (COVID-19) – China, 2020." *CCdC Weekly* 2 (8): 113–122.

Zinn, J. O. 2020. *The UK ,at Risk'. A Corpus Approach to Historical Social Change 1785-2009*. Cham Switzerland: Palgrave Macmillan.

Zinn, J. O., and D. McDonald. 2018. *Risk in the New York Times (1987-2014). a Corpus-Based Exploration of Sociological Theories*. Cham Switzerland: Palgrave Macmillan.

Recalibrating pandemic risk leadership: thirteen crisis ready strategies for COVID-19

Jamie K. Wardman

ABSTRACT
Good leadership is widely regarded as a crucial component of risk and crisis management and remains an enduring theme of more than 40 years of inquiry into emergencies, disasters, and controversies. Today, the question of good leadership has come under the spotlight again as a key factor shaping how successfully nations have dealt with the COVID-19 global health crisis. Amidst plummeting levels of public trust, the worst recession of the G7, and the highest death toll in Europe, the UK's pandemic leadership response has faced especially stern accusations of incompetence and culpability for what has been described as the most catastrophic science policy failure for a generation. Addressing these issues, this paper argues for the adoption of a more pluralised UK leadership approach for handling COVID-19. Particularly, it is contended that as COVID-19 is a multifaceted problem that presents many varied and distributed challenges, UK leadership should employ a differentiated range of strategic mechanisms and processes to help improve substantive understandings and decision-making, support collective resilience, and build adaptive capacities as the crisis continues. The paper accordingly identifies and elaborates thirteen strategies, drawing on lessons and insights from the risk and crisis management field, that are proposed to serve as a useful heuristic to help guide UK pandemic leadership in this endeavour. To illustrate the value and application of each strategy, examples are provided of noteworthy leadership responses to COVID-19 observed internationally thus far, as well as leadership problems that have hampered the UK's pandemic response. In conclusion, it is suggested that in as far as the conduct expected of leaders during a pandemic, or any other crisis, should maintain and be reflective of democratic values and standards of legitimacy, these strategies may also provide broadly applicable normative criteria against which leadership performance in handling COVID-19 may be judged as crisis ready.

1. Introduction

First, they went fast, speed meant so much. Secondly, to get that speed, they mobilised the whole population, the population, the people, became their surveillance system to help find this disease, prevent the disease, but when it did occur, rapidly get isolated so that they didn't spread it to others. And that was because the population knew what the problem was, and they were a big part of the solution. That is the big, big lesson: you cannot do this by government, you cannot do it by the health authorities alone, you need it all working in synch, that's the critical piece.

Dr. Bruce Aylwood, Assistant-Director General, World Health Organisation, Amanpour, 9 March, 2020

In times of emergency leadership matters. When a crisis occurs, citizens look to elected leaders with the expectation that they will help avert danger or chart a path to safety (Boin et al. 2016). If leaders are clear sighted, proactive, inclusive, and respond decisively, it is thought that harm and damages can be minimised, and trust can be gained (Fischhoff 2005; Löfstedt 2005; Löfstedt et al. 2011; Nyenswah, Engineer, and Peters 2016). When leaders do not take the job of addressing threats seriously and fail in these duties, they can quickly lose public support and vulnerabilities can be exacerbated with devastating consequences (Boin et al. 2016; Fischhoff 1995; Johansson and Bäck 2017).

Yet, despite being served by more than 40 years of research insights and 'best practice' guidance, the risk and crisis management field continues to document regular accounts of frustrated leadership efforts and the re-treading of past strategic failings whenever a new risk problem is encountered (Fischhoff 1995; Leiss 1996; Löfstedt 2005; Wardman and Löfstedt 2018). If leaders perform responsibly, and risk and crisis management is practiced effectively, this tends to be considered more the exception than the rule (Kasperson 2014; Wardman 2014). It should perhaps be of no small surprise then, that with the advent of the COVID-19 global health crisis, while some leaders can be credited for the measures they have taken to avert the virus and its impacts, other leaders can be seen to have proceeded with questionable strategies that have limited the possibilities for productively tackling the threats posed by the pandemic.

Against this backdrop, the UK government's mishandling of COVID-19 arguably stands out as a particularly poor pandemic leadership response, with official statistics indicating that the nation has variously suffered the highest recorded total deaths and excess deaths per 100,000 in Europe, and amongst the worst worldwide, along with the hardest economic impact of the G7 having plunged into the worst recession since records began (Islam 2020; Scally, Jacobson, and Abbasi 2020). This is despite official assessments having previously pinpointed a pandemic threat as 'number one' on the national risk register for more than a decade (Cabinet Office 2017; Freedman 2020a), not to mention the UK being considered the second most well-prepared nation after the US for such an eventuality by the Global Health Security Index (Collins, Florin, and Renn 2020). Leadership absences, incapacities, a lack of direction, and serial incompetence 'at the head' of pandemic response efforts have especially come under fire for contributing to what some health experts have described as 'the greatest science policy failure for a generation' (Horton 2020). This damning criticism of an unfolding yet avoidable catastrophe stands very starkly in contrast to the portrayal of the 'great success' regularly hailed by the British Prime Minister, Boris Johnson, in his repeated acclamations of the UK government supposedly 'following the science' and introducing 'world beating' initiatives to 'defeat coronavirus', for which he feels the nation should be 'very proud' (Dalglish 2020). Meanwhile, comparable nations, along with those ostensibly thought to be far less well-resourced and prepared for a pandemic, continue to fare much better than the UK across a host of health, social, and economic indicators (Abbey et al. 2020; Islam 2020; Scally, Jacobson, and Abbasi 2020).

In view of the current resurgence and record daily totals of coronavirus infections across the country, more than half of the population entering a wave of further lockdowns and restrictions, and the winter NHS crisis looming with many months – if not years – of the pandemic still left to run, questions therefore abound concerning what lessons might be learned from current strategic failings thus far, and what more can be done to help make the UK leadership response to COVID-19 more 'crisis ready' as the pandemic continues? Addressing these issues, this paper argues that if UK leaders wish to proceed less haphazardly in their handling of COVID-19 in future, a deeper engagement with the strategic insights and lessons of the past 40 years of risk and crisis management research and best practice is urgently warranted. Particularly, I contend that as COVID-19 is a multifaceted problem that presents many varied and distributed challenges, this requires a pluralised leadership approach that strategically draws from a wider range of differentiated mechanisms and processes to help increase the substantive decision-making capabilities of UK leaders, as well as to support the collective resilience and adaptive capacities of the nation in its efforts to stem the transmission and impacts of the virus.

The paper proceeds by first outlining a conceptual framework supporting the idea and role of pluralised leadership in risk and crisis management. Next, I specify thirteen inter-related strategies, drawn from across the risk and crisis management literature, that are proposed to serve as a useful heuristic for anchoring focal leadership priorities and practices for addressing the coronavirus outbreak. To help illustrate the value of each strategy, accompanying examples are provided from internationally noteworthy leadership responses observed thus far, along with instances in which UK leadership has gone awry that underscore the problems and difficulties that can arise when failing to take these wider considerations into account. In closing, it is suggested that in as far as the conduct expected of pandemic risk leadership should maintain and reflect democratic values and standards of legitimacy, these strategies may also provide broadly applicable normative criteria against which leader risk and crisis management performance in handling COVID-19 might be judged as 'crisis ready'.

2. Conceptualising risk and crisis leadership: towards a pluralised approach

Ideas and understandings of 'effective leadership' have been a conceptually contested and continually evolving topic of research. Interpretations of key leadership features and dynamics located within this body of work can be broadly delineated according to the respective emphasis placed on such aspects as: transactional rewards and punishments (Fairhurst and Connaughton 2014a); personal qualities and value commitments (Fairhurst and Connaughton 2014b; Jaques 2012); social identity processes and the management of interpersonal relations (Haslam, Reicher, and Platow 2010; van Dick et al. 2018); and communicative mechanisms, processes and procedures (Hyvärinen and Vos 2015; Johansson and Bäck 2017). Nowadays, however, it is common to 'state-of-the-art' thinking for leadership to be considered as part of a reciprocal group or social process for expressing and supporting a particular collective identity and attaining mutually desired goals (Haslam, Reicher, and Platow 2010). In this view, leadership is understood to operate through such mechanisms as communication, influence and persuasion, not by force or coercion wielded through centralised power by a stand-alone figure 'at the top' (Haslam, Reicher, and Platow 2010; Müller and Van Esch, 2020).

This perspective suggests that leadership practices and processes are as such best understood as being variously 'meaning centred', 'symbolic', 'ideational' and 'networked' activities, that are constituted through dialogue, contestation, negotiation, and language games, which serve to shape, direct, and facilitate collective acts of organising towards a goal (Boin and Hart 2003; Fairhurst and Connaughton 2014b; Johansson and Bäck 2017). While different forms of hard and soft power might variously make up part of the execution of authority in particular leadership domains, a group 'bond' also has to be identified and maintained, both within inner-group circles and wider groups of followers, for leadership to operate and be considered legitimate (Fairhurst and Connaughton 2014a; Jaques 2012; Muller and van Esch 2020). This also means that the perceived legitimacy of inputs and outputs associated with leadership decisions, communications, and policy impacts is dependent upon, and must be understood within, the context in which leadership is practiced (Boholm, Corvellec, and Karlsson 2012; Wardman 2014).

In terms perhaps more familiar to risk and crisis management scholars, this pluralised view essentially parallels developments in understanding within the field that have rejected mechanistic hierarchical formulations of 'leader-follower' relations evoked by widely known and criticised – albeit still widely practiced – 'decide-announce-defend' (DAD) and 'public deficit' models

(Rickard 2019; Wardman 2008). In such models, the associations between leadership and risk and crisis management would typically be construed in reductionist individualistic terms (Jetten et al. 2020), being confined to simple acts of 'announcing' an official view or mandate regarding whether a particular hazard is of concern and what to do about it, that has already been decided upon, is then passed down to others, and defended if it is questioned. Follower compliance with the leader's wishes or instructions would comprise the expected goal (Jetten et al. 2020). This would accordingly depend on perceptions of the leader's personal attributes being found to be admirable, compelling and persuasive by followers, but leaving little scope for reciprocal dialogue or negotiation (Jaques 2012). Were deviation from a leader's wishes to arise this would perhaps only occur if the personal qualities of the leader were found to be uninspiring, or there was considered to be some deficit in understanding on the part of message receivers (Wardman 2008).

Contemporary 'state-of-the-art' views of risk and crisis management have equally moved on from the idea of simply ensuring follower compliance through centralised unidirectional communication, and now emphasise the importance of inclusive partnership for generating substantive improvements in understanding and the quality of knowledge that is held and informs decision making (Jetten et al. 2020; Johansson and Bäck 2017; Webler and Tuler 2018). For emergency preparedness and response actions to work well, people in authority are required to play a responsible leadership role in enacting and integrating inclusive and transformational communicative processes and mechanisms to help bridge critical gaps in risk knowledge and understanding (Hyvärinen and Vos 2015; Reynolds and Seeger 2005). Well designed and coherent messaging that is prominently and publicly conveyed would be considered only one of many important tasks (Fischhoff 2005; Rickard 2019). Leaders also need to be involved in crafting a sense of shared identity and image of togetherness (Jetten et al. 2020), such as by making salient how a particular hazard or event poses a risk to all, and how in turn everyone may need to unite in action in the collective interest to mitigate a shared threat (Breakwell 2001; Drury et al. 2019). To ensure collective engagement and support are integrated with domain expertise and opinion obtained from different sources, responsive mechanisms and inclusive processes would need to be 'designed into' risk and crisis management (Collins, Florin, and Renn 2020). The shared distribution and co-ordination of tasks across different locations and varying levels of responsibility, employed in a reflective and open way, would as such also be beneficial to helping build integrative collective understanding, mutual support, and collaboration.

Taken together, these broader substantive ideas of leadership and risk and crisis management underscore how pluralised components and processes play a generative role in ensuring responses are well informed and clear sighted, allowing for comprehensive views of the information and mutual support needed to direct and shape actions that best safeguard against a looming threat or imminent new danger (Fischhoff 1995; Rickard et al. 2013; Webler and Tuler 2018). In this pluralised view, leadership would accordingly be legitimately positioned to address critical gaps in knowledge and focus attention on 'what matters most' allowing for 'honest disagreements' and robust discussion to inform decisions and action (Fischhoff 1995; Wardman 2008). This would help to ensure public needs and priorities are identified, preparations are made to address them, plans are executed, and that operations quickly change track as the situation changes, or when it becomes clear that outcomes are playing out in unexpected or undesirable ways (Wardman and Mythen 2016).

3. Thirteen crisis ready strategies for confronting COVID-19

Addressing a new deadly infectious disease outbreak is never easy, viruses such as COVID-19 quickly spread and are difficult to control. However, it has also been remarked, to quote one global health expert, that deciding what to do in response to an outbreak not 'rocket science'

(Sridhar 2020). This is meant in the sense that possible response options are not only broadly well-established through decades of research and applied practice in the field, but also essentially limited to four choices. These include: to 'suppress' the virus, through control measures such as 'test, trace and isolate' systems that break the chains of transmission and aim to halt virus spread completely; to 'delay', or dampen, the spread of virus through measures such as 'social distancing' and 'shielding' the most vulnerable such that health systems can cope while not aiming to eliminate the virus completely; to 'mitigate' the spread and impacts of the virus typically when it escapes control, or looks set to do so, through the use of stringent measures including lockdowns and circuit breaker restrictions that help buy more time for further planning and control preparations to be made; or to simply 'do nothing', letting the disease run its natural course, albeit this would not normally be the preferred choice for a deadly outbreak given an option to do otherwise. Added to this, the 'ramping up' of a comprehensive testing and surveillance system would generally be considered essential for helping to monitor the emergence and spread of an outbreak along with the effects of any measures taken in response to reduce the incidence of the disease, hence the WHO's repeated call to 'test, test, test' (Scally, Jacobson, and Abbasi 2020).

However, while this range of possible responses is easy to distinguish, this is not to say that the timing and structure of their use in the event of an outbreak is necessarily clear or intuitive from the outset, to which it may also be added each choice has a downside and their implementation is not problem free (Fischhoff 2020b). The appropriateness and applicability of each approach can vary depending on the characteristics of the virus, which may not always be clear, along with the structural conditions into which an outbreak emerges. Suffice to say, with the spread of infectious disease being dependent on human interaction, emergency response plans must draw from across a range of behavioural, biomedical, epidemiological, and logistical considerations when devising specific measures to prevent or bring outbreaks under control (Ruggeri et al. 2020; Smith and Gibson 2020). For instance, simple behavioural changes, such as increased handwashing and reducing interpersonal contact through social distancing, are considered vital to helping stave off the spread of the virus (Michie et al. 2020). Likewise, the wearing of face masks and coverings has been widely embraced by some nations in order to help further reduce the spread of infection. At the same time, the levels of individual and social protection offered by such measures can vary according to such aspects as public awareness of the need for behavioural change, the settings in which changes are implemented, and that appropriate procedures are followed (Greenhalgh 2020). The use and effectiveness of each response will therefore depend on there being adequate levels of political will, preparedness planning and resources, along with the collective mobilisation of a health infrastructure that can put plans into action once a threat is identified (Reynolds 2006).

Difficulties in 'ramping up' the supply of face masks and other Personal Protective Equipment (PPE) in light of disrupted supply lines and depleted reserves are illustrative of the kind of problems that can be encountered through a lack of foresight and forward planning, or simply being slow to respond (Bryce et al. 2020). The use of any selected response measures may additionally face social, cultural and political barriers. This is especially true if the interventions prescribed are bluntly introduced or construed as draconian, as might be the case with the imposition of an invasive surveillance system or the use of restrictive quarantines and curfews (Drury et al. 2019). Collective engagement, resolve, and support would therefore ordinarily be considered necessary to implementing emergency response measures effectively once the level of response required is assessed and appropriate response measures are devised and initiated (Jetten et al. 2020). Some nations might prefer to employ 'hard measures' that are made enforceable and punishable by law, while other nations may baulk at the use of strict mandates and so adopt less stringent approaches that rely on communication and dialogue, with still others employing a combination of both. Responsive leadership is therefore thought to be important to determining the appropriate level of response, the selection of appropriate emergency measures, ensuring that decisive

Table 1. Thirteen pandemic risk leadership strategies and guidelines.

Strategy	Guidelines
1. Plan and prepare	Anticipate major events, assess risk, specify areas of concern, identify warning signs and trigger points to mobilise action. Integrate risk communication into planning, make it part of training and preparedness exercises and embed it as part of harm mitigation strategies.
2. Narrate a clear-sighted strategy	Narrate the strategy for how the threat is to be addressed and the role people can play. Set the tone from the top, lead by example. Don't give mixed messages.
3. Meaning making	Describe the risk, explain and contextualise its significance at opportune moments of public connection.
4. Direction giving	Give clear, coherent, concise and comprehensible decision-relevant information and instructions. Emphasise efficacy.
5. Differentiating people's needs	Obtain, understand and address the varying information and support needs, preferences and concerns of different individuals, groups and cultures.
6. Credibility and trustworthiness	Show competence and commitment. Align with credible sources and use experts well. Communicate in ways that build trust. Do not over-protect or over promise, do not stretch the truth. Be accountable.
7. Transparency	Make information ascertainable, comprehensible, verifiable in a timely way.
8. Openness	Be candid, honest, and factual. Accept uncertainty. Enable critical input, allow hard truths to be aired. Admit mistakes, apologise when get it wrong. Be receptive to and listen to external concerns.
9. Partnership and co-ordination	Establish networks integrating internal and external members and agencies at all levels. Identify the needs of stakeholders, partner up and provide support where it is needed. Work together with communities, co-ordinate and pool respective strengths and resources.
10. Empathy	Show situational awareness. Acknowledge and respect others and show that feel as they do. Do not be aloof and dismissive.
11 Solidarity	Express solidarity. Emphasise and enact a sense of 'we-ness', identify that everyone is 'in it together' including leaders 'at the top'. Share the burden of risk and responsibility for dealing with it.
12. Be responsive and adaptive	Act quickly and decisively. Continuously evaluate and update plans and impacts and react promptly to change. Conduct dynamic risk assessments to identify wider interdependencies, needs and practical constraints. Involve stakeholders at all stages.
13. Media engagement across traditional and digital platforms	Initiate lines of communication. Meet the needs of the media. Monitor sentiment, interact with and proactively engage across traditional and digital platforms and technologies.

actions are taken, accompanying instruction is provided, and advice is followed, with power, influence and legitimacy all playing a role in bringing any selected interventions into effect (Jetten et al. 2020).

Following a pluralised concept of leadership and its role in risk and crisis management, what specific strategies and mechanisms might then be considered important for aiding such processes? Drawing on current lessons and insights from the risk and crisis management field, in the following sections I outline thirteen inter-related leadership strategies for tackling COVID-19 (see Table 1). These strategies are elaborated with a view to underscoring the value of adopting a differentiated range of cross-cutting processes and mechanisms by which to support pluralised pandemic leadership response capacities and collective resilience. In particular, the aim is to illustrate the benefits of moving away from narrow centralised 'top-down' approaches that currently predominate. As articulated here, these strategies can as such be taken to complement existing frameworks that place communication at the centre of the developmental stages (Fischhoff 1995), progressive phases (Reynolds and Seeger 2005), specific procedures and mechanisms (Drury et al. 2019; Jetten et al. 2020; Michie et al. 2020), and wider societal contexts (Rickard et al. 2013) of risk and crisis management. To help demonstrate the applicability of each strategy, noteworthy international examples are also provided that are illustrative of well-conceived and executed pandemic risk leadership responses to COVID-19, along with cases of ill-founded or badly executed practices, exemplified by the UK government's poor handling of the outbreak in England especially.

3.1. Planning and preparedness

Planning broadly refers to the process of assessing the risks faced across different areas and domains of activity and identifying the corresponding actions and resources needed. This would ideally be accompanied by preparations to prevent or reduce the likely harm suffered should an adverse event happen (Seeger 2006). Planning therefore typically takes place as part of horizon scanning and modelling processes before an event has happened, but plans also need to be updated and can evolve as a threat emerges and unfolds in unpredictable ways and new knowledge and data about the threat grows (Wardman and Mythen 2016). One beneficial outcome of planning and preparing ahead of an event is that broad protocols can be established concerning how to proceed and what procedures need to be initiated, such as opening lines of communication and identifying where responsibilities reside for taking specific actions following a surprising or unexpected event (Holmes et al. 2009; Reynolds 2002). Having a plan, updating assessments, rehearsing response measures, and keeping emergency stocks and resources well supplied can also mean that leaders remain mindful of known dangers (Seeger 2006). Best practice advice also suggests that planning processes should necessarily be inclusive and allow for advice and information exchange between multiple community sources to help ensure that respective components of the plan are representative, well integrated, and operate efficiently to help realise a common purpose when initiated (Drury et al. 2019).

3.1.1. Examples

The UK has historically been credited for its horizon scanning capabilities and having identified the risk of pandemic as the 'no.1 threat' on the national risk register for more than a decade. Previous UK governments also conducted comprehensive crisis and emergency simulations, such as 'Winter Willow' and 'Exercise Cygnus' to stress test emergency response capacities and capabilities in order to identify weaknesses in the event of an infectious respiratory disease outbreak (Bryce et al. 2020). These initiatives led to key warnings and spotlighted practical recommendations advising what preparations subsequently needed to be made, including ensuring pandemic supplies were well stocked to help mitigate the possible impacts of an outbreak.

Despite these best efforts and claims to be an 'international exemplar in terms of preparedness', as made by the Deputy Chief Medical Officer, Dr Jenny Harries, the UK turned out not to be as well prepared as presumed (Sky News 2020a). For reasons that are not wholly clear, the UK government first suppressed, then subsequently failed to sufficiently act on the warnings and advice of the pre-planning assessments and exercises that it undertook (Bryce et al. 2020). One specific problem concerned that pandemic stockpiles of personal protective equipment (PPE) and other safety equipment had been allowed to run low and out of date. It also transpired that a decade of austerity and public sector reforms had eroded public health infrastructure capacity and civil emergency response capabilities (Scally, Jacobson, and Abbasi 2020). For instance, health and social care services were left chronically understaffed and poorly equipped, with little autonomy or established lines of communication, and in the months prior to the outbreak, Public Health

England disbanded its own network of regional labs that were ostensibly intended to support the NHS during a nationwide infectious disease outbreak.

However, perhaps the gravest error in UK government planning and foresight occurred when, far from putting a *'protective ring'* around people in care homes as claimed by the Health Secretary Matt Hancock, COVID-19 was allowed to spread through care homes resulting the deaths of more than 20,000 elderly residents. Instead, care home managers were instructed to take elderly patients discharged from hospitals who were possibly infected with coronavirus while care homes were at the same time struggling with supplies of PPE. A key part of the problem seems to have been an apparent lack of public health and emergency planning expert involvement in forming COVID-19 response plans that would otherwise have likely made a strong case for addressing these sorts of counterveiling risks. Worryingly, the Prime Minister, Boris Johnson, was himself also absent from essential planning for COVID-19, having missed the first five 'Cobra' national crisis committee meetings convened in late January and throughout February, leading to accusations that he was 'missing in action' along with the charge that the UK had been allowed to 'sleepwalk into disaster' (Calvert, Arbuthnott, and Leake 2020). In response to questions about the robustness of the UK's pandemic response, Lord Sedwill, who recently stepped down as the most senior civil servant in government, commented that, 'Although we had exercised and prepared for pandemic threats, we didn't have in place the exact measures, and we hadn't rehearsed the exact measures, for the challenge COVID-19 presented. I think there is a genuine question about whether we could have been better prepared in the first place and that is obviously a very legitimate challenge' (BBC 2020a).

3.2. Narrating a clear-sighted strategy

Related to emergency response planning is the communicative task which could perhaps be best termed as 'narrating a strategy' (Campbell 2020). This essentially involves not only having a plan but also publicising 'what the plan is' (Sellnow et al. 2019). Being proactive about letting people know what lies ahead is important to keep them informed, but also so as not to leave information vacuums that can otherwise invite unhelpful speculation and second guessing as to 'what comes next', alongside doubts about whether public leaders really know what they are doing (Leiss 1996). Narrating a strategy may therefore include conveying a clear-sighted and coherent aim that guides what the key objectives are for tackling the crisis and why (Sellnow et al. 2019). Further information can also be conveyed on how they are to be achieved, and what role different parties may respectively play in achieving 'the plan' (Drury et al. 2019). This may also include providing information about what criteria will be used for different emergency response measures, such as bringing lockdowns into effect, as opposed to simply giving instructions with vital information 'dripped down' to implement specific parts of the plan on a 'need to know' basis (Bakker et al. 2019).

3.2.1. Examples
The New Zealand Prime Minister, Jacinda Ardern, has been credited for expertly narrating a firm national COVID-19 strategy in the early stages of the pandemic in order to take advantage of a 'window of opportunity' to stop the spread of virus before it took hold. This was exemplified through such statements as *'We go hard, we go early'* and that New Zealand *'would not accept any deaths'* (McGuire et al. 2020; Wilson 2020). Public addresses notably outlined the overall strategy accompanied by explanations of how essential services would stay open, along with how measures such as contact tracing and testing would work once the country entered lockdown. A simple easy to follow 'Four Stages of Alert' system was also employed to indicate how the spread and control of the virus was strategically linked to corresponding public health

measures that would be taken, such as the criteria denoting when a lockdown would be intro-duced and eased (Wilson 2020).

Insofar as a UK government strategy for COVID-19 can be discerned, its communication has tended to be vague, seeming to reflect indecisiveness and lack a firm direction. Policies have often flip-flopped back and forth on a weekly basis with Ministers performing major policy U-turns across a range of matters. This indecisiveness and lack of clear-sightedness is perhaps best exemplified by the UK Prime Minister Boris Johnson having initially expressed the wish for the UK to try to 'strike a balance' between meeting the competing priorities of public health, civil liberties, and the economy. In one widely criticised TV interview, the Prime Minister stated: 'one of the theories is that perhaps you could take it on the chin, take it all in one go and allow the disease, as it were, to move through the population, without taking as many draconian measures' (ITV 2020). While not intended to sound callous, this nonetheless demonstrated that neither a direct aim nor clear path for tackling COVID-19 had been determined.

The design and implementation of the UK 'alert system' has been similarly criticised for containing vague and incoherent criteria concerning COVID-19 risk levels and the basis for initiating and easing national lockdown measures respectively. What could initially have been a useful public information tool quickly fell into disuse then became a public irrelevance for months on end. Subsequently, the alert system was revised and, after several abortive attempts, reintroduced as a simpler 'three-tier' system for initiating local regional lockdowns. However, this new 'flagship policy' for dealing with COVID-19 in England immediately fell into disarray after being contested by local city mayors and MPs on both sides of the political spectrum on the basis that the benefits of a national lockdown were not demonstrably the case for local lockdowns when the virus is in wide in circulation. In particular, it was not made clear how local lockdowns would bring rates of infection ('R') down around the country down, indeed this had long proved elusive in areas with tight restrictions. It also meant that those areas denoted as 'tier-three' could remain so indefinitely. The insufficiency of the new three-tier system had in fact been previously pointed out at a public briefing by the Chief Medical Officer, Professor Chris Whitty, who stated that it was not likely to control the spread of virus without additional measures. This view was then confirmed to regional leaders by the Deputy Chief Medical Officer, Jonathan Tam in later communications.

Meanwhile, the Mayor of Greater Manchester, Andy Burnham, outlined the objection that the government was willing to sacrifice jobs, livelihoods, health and well-being in the North West of England to save them elsewhere without giving any assurance that this would in fact be an effective health intervention. Demands for higher financial compensation to be awarded to local people and businesses suffering as a consequence were only partially met amidst much acrimony towards government leaders that the new system was divisive and represented the 'worst of all worlds', both in terms of the heavy death toll exacted alongside draconian measures that have significantly impacted on the economy and civil liberties. In short, the local lockdowns and restrictive measures imposed by the three-tier system met with fierce objections for seeming at once arbitrary, capricious, and insufficient. As the UK government looks set to press ahead with enforced tier-three restrictions, local leaders have united in protest across the North of England. In the event, questions still remain concerning what the broader strategy is for tackling COVID-19, what the long-term objectives are, and how this new 'flagship' scheme fits in as part of an overall plan.

3.3. Meaning making

The concept of 'meaning making' refers to how a leader represents and 'makes sense' of risk related events in public communications (Boin and Hart 2003). This involves making risk information salient, comprehensible, and relevant, which is to say 'meaningful', for those affected, and is thought to benefit from seizing an 'opportune moment' for public connection (Boin and Hart 2003). Meaning making is particularly important because public appraisals of uncertain and unfamiliar threats can often serve to 'psychologically distance' people from 'far flung' harm, especially when they have little experiential knowledge of threats such as disease outbreaks to draw upon and so may not see the personal relevance (Joffe and Haarhoff 2002). Leaders can therefore play a constructive role not only in sounding the alarm, but also describing a new threat and contextualising its implications for individuals and wider society (Burgess 2019; Seeger 2006).

This is not to say that the meanings publicly ascribed to risks by leaders will necessarily be replicated or easily controlled because impressions are formed and mediated by multidirectional interactions and exchanges between many interlocutors who may have varying opinions (Ruben and Gigliotti 2016; Sellnow et al. 2019; Wardman and Löfstedt 2018). Making new risks seem more familiar can also be a tricky process as making comparisons with other risks can backfire particularly if they are seen to try to trivialise threats encountered (Wardman and Löfstedt 2009; Bostrom 2008). Nevertheless, leaders can still play an important role in the sensemaking processes by which social representations of risk are formed and communicated. Protocols for communicating risk and uncertainty can also be pre-tested and established to help make communications clearer and easier to understand (Drury et al. 2019; Fischhoff 2005; Fischhoff 2020a; Reynolds and Seeger 2005). For example, as an aid to clarification, Spiegelhalter (2020) has recently outlined how the representation of 'normal risk' can help people to make a comparative estimate of their statistical chances of dying from COVID-19 at a given age in a given year, as contrasted with all other risk in their life as a means to help put this new risk into perspective. Leaders also typically benefit from being supported by extensive government apparatus and resources, including expert advisors that confer leaders with an 'authoritative' point of view (Reynolds and Seeger 2005). Leaders can also help to establish new social norms as to what is appropriate by being a role model and demonstrating such behaviour to the wider public (Van Bavel et al. 2020).

3.3.1. Examples

The New Zealand Prime Minister Jacinda Ardern, has proven notably adept at giving meaning to and contextualising the significance of the risks posed by COVID-19. Amongst many public addresses that resonated well with New Zealand citizens, the New Zealand Prime Minister made a timely reference to adverse events happening elsewhere in the world to help justify avoiding complacency to the threat of coronavirus at home: *'We only have 102 cases, but so did Italy once. We could see the greatest loss of life in history. We are not going to make the same mistake as others'* (Jetten et al. 2020; Wilson 2020).

The UK government's warnings and instructions about COVID-19 have, by contrast, been markedly ambiguous and confusing, with leaders often fudging or contradicting key messages on such issues as the level of risk posed by the coronavirus outbreak, the gravity of the crisis, and the corresponding requirements for action. Despite initially making the sober announcement that *'families are going to lose loved ones before their time'*, the UK Prime Minster, Boris Johnson, subsequently seemed to attempt to downplay concerns by claiming that he had in any case not stopped shaking hands with COVID-19 patients on hospital wards, thereby undermining a key health message to maintain social distancing and hand hygiene (Freedman 2020b). These comments did not go unremarked when the Prime Minster subsequently contracted and unfortunately became very ill with COVID-19. The Prime Minister also attended an England rugby match at the beginning of the crisis, which was subsequently taken as a sign by organisers of the Cheltenham Festival to justify their controversial decision to go ahead with the annual race meeting. The event registered over 60,000 racegoers in attendance each day and was later subject to calls for an inquiry into what has been described as a 'super-spreader' event after health trust figures showed the coronavirus death toll to be double that of neighbouring health trusts (Tucker and Goldberg 2020).

3.4. Direction giving

Leaders can play a pivotal role in ensuring that people's information needs are met by advising not only on the likelihood, impact, and gravity of potential threats, but also providing direction and instructions concerning what specific actions they need to take in response when safeguarding against harm. Simply stated, direction giving refers to telling people 'what to do' and 'why' during a crisis, typically by providing factual, authoritative, reliable and actionable advice along with the basis for following behavioural instructions that people might need to act on during crisis events and emergencies (Boin and Hart 2003; van Bavel et al. 2020; Michie et al. 2020). However, this need not mean trying to coerce people into specific action. Leader communications can adopt 'non-persuasive' language focusing on providing 'decision-relevant' information and messaging that is clear, concise, and comprehensible (Fischhoff 2013; Michie et al. 2020; Wardman and Löfstedt 2009). This type of messaging would ordinarily be focused at the individual, or 'Me' level, with an emphasis on trying to facilitate self-efficacy, coping, and survival by helping people identify who is at risk, how they might themselves minimise such risk in advance, and what specific things to do to minimise risk or following exposure (Finucane et al. 2020). In the case of coronavirus, this might include providing behavioural guidance such as to engage in self-isolation and social distancing, the appropriate use of facemasks, to engage in hand hygiene practices, when and how to follow lockdown rules, as well as with regards what to include in emergency kits and whether there is a need or not to gather certain personal provisions when preparing for different eventualities of an outbreak (Michie et al. 2020).

3.4.1. Examples

One of the few examples of action undertaken by the UK government that was broadly well received was the early 'behaviourally focused' messaging that repeatedly directed people to 'wash hands', and to 'Stay at Home, Protect the NHS, Save Lives'. These communications were credited initially for achieving 'cut-through' with UK citizens by being simple, unambiguous, clear, easy to follow, thereby contributing to high levels of compliance with safety advice in the early stages of the outbreak. For instance, advice to 'stay at home' is much easier to understand and follow than 'self-isolate'.

Conversely, subsequent revision of this behavioural messaging to 'Stay Alert, Control the Virus, Save Lives' when the lockdown was eased was widely derided for sliding into meaningless 'sloganeering' rather than offering a semblance of clear instruction or direction (BBC 2020b). A jumbled public address on the easing of the lockdown by the British Prime Minster was widely parodied as people were left unsure as to whether they should 'Go to work. Don't go to work. Go outside. Don't go outside' (Mee 2020; Torjesen 2020). When asked for clarification about what government guidance to 'stay alert' actually meant, the Prime Minister rebuffed questions with the response that the public could be trusted 'to continue to apply good solid British common sense'. Confused and unhelpful messaging lacking in clear detail has regrettably continued unabated in government communications throughout the crisis.

3.5. Differentiating and supporting people's needs

Risk and crisis management does not take place within an undifferentiated social space (Wardman 2008; Wardman 2014). Populations are characteristically made up of people with varied understandings, cultural values, and beliefs, as well as language and physical differences that may warrant specific consideration (Reynolds 2007; Crouse Quinn 2008). Failing to take the necessary efforts to recognise, acknowledge, and accommodate people's differences, and the barriers they face, means that essential information may not reach those in need, that vulnerabilities are increased, and that health disparities and social divisions are further deepened for those who are already disadvantaged (Blumenshine et al. 2008). The inherent variety within populations therefore necessitates that different 'user groups' are not only targeted but that their views are sought, rather than stereotyped, in order to understand how their requirements might differ from normative policy models and how best to meet them (Goulden et al. 2018). However, a further complicating issue often missed is that many communities with health disparities have not historically been well served by public institutions, and that this has contributed to their predicament. For instance, minority groups have often suffered systemic discrimination and marginalisation that has left them disenfranchised, feeling neglected, and deeply distrustful of authorities (Crouse Quinn 2008). Health advocates have accordingly argued that social justice and inequality should be a core focus of risk and crisis management efforts so as to ensure health disparities are addressed, and moreover that emergency response efforts do not result in further discrimination and exclusion through narrow design and delivery (Crouse Quinn 2008; Reynolds 2007). To avoid this, extra attention may need to be applied to community outreach efforts in order to open communication channels and overcome unrecognised historic barriers that have built up with official authorities over time that can frustrate efforts to 'level up' health outcomes (Reynolds 2007; Crouse Quinn 2008).

3.5.1. Examples

The more 'progressive' political leaders of some nations have recognised that COVID-19 impacts upon different people in different ways, and have accordingly sought to adopt measures and communications that are broadly attentive to addressing all those affected both by the pandemic and particular response measures. Speaking to one segment of the population that is typically neglected during crises, the Prime Minister of Norway, Erna Solberg, notably told children *'it is ok feel scared'* and to miss hugging friends. Similarly, the New Zealand Prime Minister Jacinda Ardern was credited for holding informal video conferences on Facebook, including specifically for children, to provide them with information and reassurance, such advising that the Easter Bunny was considered a keyworker (McGuire et al. 2020).

UK leaders have at various times notably struggled to recognise and address population differences. In one ongoing scandal, the government has become embroiled in controversy regarding the disproportionate number of deaths from COVID-19 affecting Black, Asian and Minority Ethnic (BAME) groups, including those who provide frontline services for the NHS. While an investigation was being conducted into the issue objections arose because its remit did not include addressing the question of why COVID-19 had such a disproportionate effect on BAME communities, or indeed to provide recommendations on the way forward. Subsequently, a leak of the report to journalists brought to light that recommendations were being withheld from the publication of the main report findings identifying the need for people from BAME communities to be given targeted health advice, particularly with respect to key workers in the advent of a second wave of the COVID-19 pandemic (Scally, Jacobson, and Abbasi 2020). News channels reported that the release of the report findings was also pushed back due to worries surrounding global tensions following the killing of George Floyd and subsequent Black Lives Matter protests. UK government officials denied this to be the case, stating that there were issues surrounding poor data collection, and in particular data on ethnicity, which was not being systematically documented when someone died of COVID-19 outside a hospital in the community. Critics responded that the lack of communication, action, and policy implementation in relation to the findings nonetheless reflected a patent neglect by government leaders to fulfil their obligation to ensure the protection of all workers and members of the public regardless of race or ethnicity. At the time of writing many months into the crisis, the mandatory recording of ethnicity data on death certificates for COVID-19 victims still has not been implemented.

In another case, the UK government failed in its guidance and communications to vulnerable people considered at 'high risk'. In particular, a central database was found to have missed off large numbers of the elderly along with many severely disabled people due to using highly selective criteria. Those omitted from the national register included people with terminal illnesses, such as severe motor neurone disease, along with more than 100,000 children with serious medical conditions (BBC 2020c). Subsequently, they were told that this was because their illness was not serious enough for them to qualify for help, and so they should rely instead on friends or local councils. At the same time, many vulnerable individuals who had received letters instructing them that they should be shielded and to stay indoors because they were at 'high risk' were nonetheless left without accompanying support to access food without leaving their homes. Meanwhile, family doctors (GPs) in turn have raised concerns about not being able to help high risk patients due to receiving very little information other than that trailed in newspapers ahead of government policy briefings. The Department of Health and Social Care later admitted 'operational delays' to their notification system.

3.6. Credibility

Credibility has long been recognised as a crucial component of risk and crisis management. The attribution of credibility generally stems from a leader being thought of as competent, fair, and able to deliver promised outcomes efficiently and effectively (Löfstedt 2005). Ideas of credibility in these regards are thus broadly encompassing, but in practical terms primarily include a leader being able to demonstrate that they are able to handle scientific details astutely, spend economic resources without waste, and make decisions with equitable outcomes following impartial procedures and due process (Löfstedt 2005; Renn and Levine 1991). The use of structural processes that ensure leaders are held accountable for their actions can also help to confer a sense of legitimacy on their right to be in a position of authority. A leader may also obtain some credibility through aligning with credible scientific authorities and using expertise wisely (Löfstedt 2005; Wardman and Löfstedt 2009).

3.6.1. Examples

The German Chancellor Angela Merkel has been praised throughout the pandemic for giving calm, competent, and authoritative explanations, making good use of a background in science to show a command of the facts. This notably included what was widely regarded as a highly clear and coherent description of the virus rate of reproduction number 'R', and why reducing it was a key aim for slowing the spread of COVID-19 in Germany. Initially, public addresses and press briefings about the crisis in the UK were also well regarded with the Prime Minister, or a Cabinet Minister, usually being flanked by a health expert on either side. Placing experts 'front and centre stage' alongside Ministers meant that they could offer support when fielding technical questions from journalists, as well as provide further detailed scientific explanations of the risk and the need for specific measures. These experts were in turn also credited for conducting themselves in calm and authoritative manner. All in all, this was seen to be a positive leadership move that offered public reassurance at the beginning of the crisis that the government was in fact 'following the science' as was repeatedly being claimed.

However, the careful staging of UK science and politics as working 'hand in glove' began to ring hollow. The repeated statements to be 'following the science' or 'being led by the science' gradually began to wear thin and came to be seen as meaningless sloganeering, particularly as government scientists and scientific evidence became increasingly at variance with the Ministerial accounts of the virus and what to do about it. After initial reassurances, it was becoming increasingly apparent that being led by science meant leaders could dodge questions and avoid accountability for decisions while the newly 'politicised' scientists could then later be blamed for any policy errors and mistakes being made (Morgan 2020). Growing discord between science and politics eventually culminated in the Chief Medical Officer Chris Whitty stating at an awkward press briefing that expert advisors had an even stronger wish than the Prime Minister not to be 'drawn into the politics'.

In a later controversy, it emerged that the government had departed from the science altogether when it decided to go against the government's Scientific Advisory Group for Emergency (SAGE) recommendations on 21st September to immediately activate a raft of measures to avert a 'catastrophic' second wave. These measures included a short 'circuit breaker' national lockdown to slow the spread of the virus and give time for the struggling 'test, trace and isolate' system to get on track. Commenting on the insufficiency of the new 'three-tier' system of local restrictive measures elected by the Prime Minister and other Cabinet members instead, the Chief Medical Officer Chris Whitty stated plainly that he was not confident that the baseline measures of the three tiers would go far enough to stem the virus spread, and so further measure would inevitably be needed. Defending the decision to ignore the warnings from SAGE, the UK Communities Secretary, Robert Jenrick justified inaction on the basis that the government not only needed to 'take a balanced judgement' on such matters as health, education and employment, but also that 'scientific opinion' was divided on how far measures should go in any case. With this, the gradual phasing out of the 'following the science' slogan has seemingly come to a head, with Ministers now happy to readily admit going against the scientific advice offered by the government's own experts.

3.7. Transparency

The concept of transparency typically denotes the practice of making information accessible and available to public scrutiny broadly regarding data, rules, operations, procedures, inputs, and outputs (Hood 2007). Following the adage that 'sunlight is the best disinfectant' transparency is hoped to help dissuade corruption, strengthen democracy, and promote efficiency and effectiveness in government, thereby leading to greater public trust (Löfstedt and Bouder 2014). While this is appealing in principle, the public exposure of information is not straightforward and requires detailed consideration of a range of factors relating to such issues as what information is required, to whom it should be provided, in what form, when, and for what purposes (Löfstedt and Wardman 2016). This then typically requires balancing competing priorities such as timeliness against accuracy or accessibility (Garbett et al. 2011; Hood 2007). For example, technical information may need certain expertise to make use and sense of information, or else it may need to be translated or curated in such a way as to make it broadly accessible and meaningful (Garbett et al. 2014). Providing information immediately in 'real time' may require compromises on the completeness and the certainty with which information is assumed to correspond to actual events (Garbett et al. 2014). Sometimes a delay built into the public release of information can therefore be helpful, such that more reliable information can be provided retrospectively, or alternatively that information might be released immediately following an understanding that later updates may be required (Lancaster, Rhodes, and Rosengarten 2020). Answers to the question of what form transparency takes are as such dependent on the purposes for which the public provision of information is needed (Heald 2006), which can benefit from being established through engagement and dialogue with potential users of such information about what their needs and preferences might be (Foster et al. 2012).

3.7.1. Examples

The Singapore government has placed 'radical transparency' at the forefront of its handling of COVID-19, providing public outbreak data concerning disease clusters and the demographics of those who test positive for the virus, including where they travelled and sought medical help, and when they were discharged. Outlining the basis of this approach, Deputy Prime Minister Heng Swee Keat explained: *'First and foremost, we need to provide information as clearly as possible. Because when people trust the information that we put out is accurate, then there's no need for that panic. So transparency is important in this regard, and building a high level of trust with our people'* (Tham 2020).

UK government leaders have faced a number of criticisms over a lack of transparency ranging across a host of issues, including questions about the data and advise upon which decisions have been made, as well as the suppression of key reports on preparedness planning, and the redaction of key sections of a report investigating the impact of COVID-19 on BAME workers. At one point, the advisory board for the UK's coronavirus tracking app publicly expressed concerns that the project would be compromised by a lack of transparency in the rush to deploy the technology. In Leicester, local authority officials and the City Mayor complained of Ministers taking too long to communicate with them about a lockdown extension despite repeated requests for information and consultation, only being given notice about the plans at 1am on the day the lockdown was instigated. The government decision had followed the early discovery of a spike in cases of infection by Public Health England, but Ministers did not share any detailed evidence with local officials about who had been infected (in terms of age and ethnicity) and where they occurred (such as the postcode area). This meant that local health services lacked vital granular information to understand and act on the outbreak and to provide targeted messages to communities specifically affected.

Another transparency policy problem concerned the composition of expert advisory groups and the opaque basis upon which government acts on scientific and other advice provided. Particular controversy surrounded the public clamour for the government to release SAGE meeting minutes and membership details – something the Chairs of SAGE had themselves requested early on in the crisis – when it transpired that Dominic Cummings, the Prime Minister's Special Advisor, and another Number 10 aid, were attending some of the meetings. When this 'unprecedented' breach of protocol came to light, it led to the strong admonishment by a former Chief Scientific Advisor, Sir David King, that having a powerful policy advisor present at expert meetings would inevitably compromise the impartiality and freedom with which scientific opinion could be expressed (Carrell et al. 2020). Subsequently, a breakaway 'Independent SAGE' group of scientists was formed by Sir David King comprising members with wider ranging expertise, and notably including some current SAGE advisors, in order to provide trusted timely information and independent advice that was more publicly accessible.

3.8. Openness

While closely associated with transparency, the concept of openness can be distinguished as the manner in which risk and crisis management is conducted honestly, candidly, and receptively (Seeger 2006). Openness can accordingly be regarded as a process of active listening and communication that can help to bring new problems or potential difficulties to light, but for this to happen leaders may need to instil a cultural environment that is conducive to lifting barriers to free expression and critique from others (Turner and Pidgeon 1997). In practical terms, this means incorporating feedback mechanisms into systems and networks that allow hard truths and alternative views to be aired without prejudicing those who do so. Informational structures that encourage the reporting of problems can then allow for leaders to handle them responsively and constructively, whereas those that dissuade honesty or fail to provide opportunities for upwards communication can lead to important warning information being obscured, and a greater likelihood that 'whistle-blowers' feel they have no choice but to 'go public' with their concerns (Noort, Reader, and Gillespie 2019). During a crisis, being open also means not trying to 'protect' citizens from change by over-promising or stretching the truth, as when making unsubstantiated claims that normality will soon resume when this is an unlikely or uncertain scenario (Fischhoff 1995; Seeger 2006). Rather, leaders also need to acknowledge the uncertainties faced and accept the difficulties that lie ahead (Seeger 2006). They should also readily admit to errors and issue public apologies for mistakes, as opposed to trying to cover them up, pretend everything is okay, or deflect blame elsewhere when things go awry (Heath 2006). It also means not seeing crises as 'opportunities' to try and capitalise on for personal favour, such as using the timing of adverse incidents to 'bury bad news', or to push through personal projects while due process and accountability procedures are diluted or have been disrupted (Freudenburg 2003).

3.8.1. Examples

France has had its fair share of difficulties in handling the pandemic, but the French President, Emmanuel Macron, was commended for making a televised public address to more than 35 million in which he apologised that the country had *not being prepared enough* for the coronavirus crisis and *mistakes had been made* (Allen 2020). In his announcement, the President expressed that lessons were being learned, and continued efforts were required, but also that more sacrifices were yet to come. This candid admission and assessment were broadly welcomed and as a result public trust in government leadership was able to bounce back from an earlier decline.

The UK government has been accused of being patronising and defensive, often objecting to reasonable inquiries, or avoiding questions altogether about such matters as the nation's levels of preparedness and crisis response strategies. Notably, on the rare occasion when either the Prime Minister or a Cabinet member has issued an apology, this has stood as an 'exception to the rule' of never admitting error or taking responsibility for mistakes, and has only seemed to fitting in an attempt to diffuse a public row (Dinnen 2020). Instead, government leaders have preferred to go on the attack against critics, rebuffing detractors and variously accusing them of *'sniping from the side-lines'*, being *'obstructive'*, adopting *'the wrong tone'*, attempting to *'distract the public'*, and making *'endless attacks on public confidence'*. This tendency to retaliate and shift blame to has not gone unnoticed or unanswered. The Prime Minister, Boris Johnson, was roundly criticised and accused of cowardice for appearing to blame care home workers for the deaths of elderly people in their care after he claimed the government had discovered they did not *'follow procedures as they could have'*, comments which subsequently drew the fire of the care industry who pointedly responded that they had in fact followed the rules and guidance issued to them by the government to admit residents without testing amidst national PPE shortages (Chakelian 2020). Similarly, the Health Secretary appeared to be suggesting at another point that NHS staff and other health workers were wasting scarce supplies of PPE, and that this was in part responsible for shortages (Scally, Jacobson, and Abbasi 2020). Again this was much to the consternation of health workers when in fact the government was having difficulties in procuring enough PPE for the crisis having let supplies dwindle and then failed to ramp up supplies once the COVID-19 crisis emerged (Bryce et al. 2020). In another incident, requests from local authorities and MPs in seaside towns for government assistance to deal with immense crowds of day trippers and holiday makers flocking to the beach over the summer were met with the Prime Minister admonishing them to *'show some guts and determination to champion their communities as venues for people to return and support'* (Woodcock 2020). Subsequently, a major incident was declared on the south coast as roads became blocked and local services were overwhelmed, but rather than apologising for not listening to local leader concerns beforehand, the Prime Minister condemned beach goers for *'taking too many liberties'* (Allegretti 2020).

Meanwhile, over the course of the crisis there has been a regular stream of announcements made by Ministers concerning the introduction of new 'world beating' initiatives, 'game changing' developments, and 'moon-shot' solutions. While floating the idea of rapid and widespread tests dubbed 'Operation Moonshot', the Prime Minister has also been happy to publicly convey his hope that such initiatives will help get *lives back to normal by Christmas*' (Merrick 2020). At the same time however, repeated claims of the government's 'success' in fighting off COVID-19 became increasingly at odds with its own figures regarding the health and economic damages suffered. Slides relating to international league table comparisons were quickly dropped from presentations once the UK was shown to be topping the tables in terms of the worst number of COVID-19 cases and deaths. Announcements concerning world beating new initiatives have subsequently come to be regarded by critics as a 'diversionary tactic' to grab newspaper headlines and deflect from current criticism, rather than serious attempts fix major problems with the UK's pandemic response. The resulting scandals over broken promises and vast sums of money wasted either on defective equipment or on secretive outsourced projects procured uncompetitively through contracts with political party donors has become the focus of several media exposes (Monbiot 2020). All of which contributes to the distinct public impression that the political careers of certain Cabinet Members have 'continued to win the battle with their conscience', as one political sketch writer aptly surmised (Crace 2020).

3.9. Partnership

As the risks, damages and emergency response activities associated with infectious disease outbreaks tend to be distributed across multiple locations, agencies, and networks, pandemic leadership involves the national orchestration of partnering arrangements requiring lateral understanding, co-ordination, and power sharing to help mobilise joined-up responses and direct and resources where they are needed (Boin and Hart 2003; Ruben and Gigliotti 2016). At this community – or 'We' – level, risk and crisis management efforts thus recognise that disasters and catastrophes, along with individual resilience to such events, are shaped by social processes, and so using decentralised mechanisms can be helpful in identifying and addressing local community vulnerabilities as well as building social capital to help facilitate collective responses (Finucane et al. 2020). Decentralisation does not mean abdicating responsibility, but rather requires communication and co-ordination with local representatives working together with key stakeholder groups and local community leaders, to listen to concerns, learn from experiences and take different viewpoints into consideration (Krieger 2016). This helps to enable mutual understanding, connectedness and shared sense-making as a crisis situation unfolds and takes a new track. Partnering arrangements also benefit from engaging with communities early on during the planning stage to offer support and guidance where it might be needed, such as with the development of community disaster response plans and guidance, thereby helping to strengthen connections and integrate central authorities with community networks both in preparedness and to help deliver those plans when and if required (Finucane et al. 2020).

3.9.1. Examples

Following the advice of the WHO to make test trace and isolate the backbone of COVID-19 response strategies, the German government along with the Koch Institute, the national body in charge of infectious diseases, quickly moved to make widespread testing a priority. Germany has a highly decentralised health system meaning that responsibility is devolved below central government first to state government, then below that to districts, which run hospitals and health services relatively autonomously. However, with support and advice from central government, these partners managed to implement a co-ordinated, flexible and prepared response that set up comprehensive test and trace systems quickly and aggressively, using 170 labs across the country, to help stall the outbreak and prevent health systems from becoming overwhelmed.

The UK response to COVID-19 can be characterised as having been largely fragmented and disjointed across regions, businesses, and public sectors at all levels. Having initially worked closely together, the so-called 'four nation' strategy for dealing with coronavirus was subsequently under-mined by Number 10 marginalising the devolved administrations of Wales, Scotland and Northern Ireland from policy deliberations and decisions. The First Minister of Scotland, Nicola Sturgeon, raised specific complaints about only finding out when key policy changes had been introduced when the announcement was made in the Sunday newspapers, revealing significant fractures to the four nations approach. As a spokesperson for Nicola Sturgeon put it, if the preference is to 'go in lockstep', whereby all the four nations move together in a co-ordinated fashion, then for this to be meaningful each nation has to be ready, which could only occur if each nation is party to policy discussions at Number 10. Subsequently, whilst the government pressed ahead with its easing of the lockdown, the latest *'stay alert'* messaging was only applied to England as other regions chose instead to retain the message to *'stay at home'* (BBC 2020d).

Perhaps the foremost illustration of the tendency of UK leadership towards 'turning inwards' is the management of its centralised 'test, trace and isolate' system. Far from being 'world beating', this system, variably described as 'shambolic' and 'disastrous' by critics, has suffered a series of blun-ders and bordered on near collapse while continually failing to trace the 80% of contacts needed to make a meaningful difference to stemming the spread of the virus (Monbiot 2020). Initially, unlike Germany, the UK government ignored the advice of the WHO to 'test test test' leading to weeks of inaction, then after the belated decision to 'ramp up' testing capacity, there was a further three-week delay while the government undertook to develop its own 'in house' test when other testing options were already available. The government also ignored or rebuffed the offers of 50 testing labs across the country that could otherwise have helped to process up 100,000 tests per day, and instead of making use of local and regional health services and other existing infrastructure to con-duct testing and contact tracing, chose to centralise then outsource this responsibility to private contractors to develop an entirely new system with no prior expertise or experience of testing and contact tracing requirements (Scally, Jacobson, and Abbasi 2020).

When testing and tracing stopped at the end of March, it was claimed in what were considered patronising remarks made by the Deputy Chief Medical Officer, Dr Jennie Harries, that this was because WHO advice on testing *'was not an appropriate mechanism as we go forward'* essentially due to the UK being professed to have a 'developed' health system (Sky News 2020a). It has also been proposed that the lack of focus on testing perhaps represented a mischaracterisation of COVID-19 as behaving as a 'flu-like' virus (Freedman 2020c). Six weeks later it was conceded at a House of Commons Select Committee inquiry that testing had in fact been a preferable strategy for the UK all along, but that it was halted due to a lack of testing and tracing capacity. In another blun-der for test trace and isolate system run by Baroness Dido Harding in conjunction with companies including Serco, a rudimentary IT error associated with using outdated and insufficient software was held to be responsible for nearly 16,000 positive cases of COVID-19 being excluded from the weekly totals, which also alarmingly resulted in serous delays to tracing over 50,000 contacts. Critical observers noted that while it might be understandable to make such errors in the heat of the first outbreak, it was certainly not acceptable to make such a basic blunder many months down the line after £12bn had been spent on developing a supposedly world beating system (Monbiot 2020). With cases of COVID-19 rising, the testing system has come under increasing strain and is still struggling to meet demand, now tracing less than 60% of contacts (Booth and Parveen 2020). Meanwhile, where local authorities have taken the reigns, despite belated additional funds of only £300 million and having no central government data access, local test trace and isolate has func-tioned much more effectively, successfully reaching 97% of contacts (Booth and Parveen 2020).

3.10. Empathy

Empathy is understood to encompass the inter-personal processes of shared situational awareness, understanding, and feeling that someone might have with others and can be important during a crisis to engender trust in leaders (Reynolds and Quinn 2008). Which is to say, empathising with another person comprises cognitive and affective components that requires a 'projection of the self into the other' in a broadly congruent way that can make them seem trustworthy (Van Bavel et al. 2020). In a communicative sense, the public expression of empathy is also a socially grounded act of emotional sharing that functionally adds, connects and endorses a particular meaning ascribed to people's understandings and experiences of events (Wardman 2006). Empathy can therefore be vital to successful communication, as when politicians often talk of 'reading the room' or the need to judge the 'public mood' when deciding how to pitch a public address. Being unduly casual or dismissive of others during emergencies can lead to public leaders being judged as callous if their actions are considered to breach the social contract of care towards citizens. It can also evoke an image of cold rationale bureaucracy, which may in turn give rise to a strong public backlash forcing retractions and apologies from chastened leaders (Boin and Hart 2003). Sometimes such attentiveness may be disingenuous if it is 'faked' simply to garner favour or trust. Nonetheless, public leaders should recognise social distress and behave respectfully. They can empathise through showing that they care and feel as others do by publicly articulating the 'shared pain' of victims whom have been affected by adverse events (Van Bavel et al. 2020).

3.10.1. Examples

The New Zealand Prime Minister Jacinda Ardern was commended for recognising the difficulties imposed on citizens by government crisis and crisis response measures. In her address to the nation the Prime Minister acknowledged *'We may not have experienced anything like this in our lifetimes'* but appealed to New Zealander's sense of being *'creative, practical, country minded'* saying *'Thank you for all that you're about to do. Please, be strong, be kind and unite against COVID-19'* in her appeal for New Zealanders to support one another through the hard times ahead (Jetten et al. 2020).

UK government leaders have been accused of being nonchalant and even callous at times in response to COVID-19. The apparent aim of adopting a 'herd immunity' strategy not only sounded callous but would have reportedly led to several 100,000 s of deaths according to modelling estimates reported the team at Imperial College London who were instrumental in reversing the government's course. Commentators observed that while herd immunity may not have been the intended emergency response strategy per se, muddled briefings nevertheless gave the distinct impression that it was the plan (Freedman 2020c). Government communications have also faced a backlash for insensitive messages. One such Tweet by The Treasury to *'raise a glass'* while hailing the re-opening of pubs was hastily deleted after it was accused of being irresponsible in adopting a celebratory tone following thousands of deaths from coronavirus. Similarly, a campaign supporting a job retraining scheme was withdrawn after circulating posters promoting the notion that ballerinas and those in other arts based careers should change their life ambitions to retrain in 'cyber'. Government ministers were also accused of turning a blind eye to the needs of the most vulnerable children, including 2.2 million qualifying for free school meals due to low income, who would not otherwise be provided with enough food during the school summer holidays. Some additional provision was made only after a high-profile child food poverty campaign by the England footballer Marcus Rashford, but not extended for half term apparently due to such reasons as not wishing to increase children's dependency on the state or that food was being sold to buy hard drugs (Weale and Adams 2020). The government is now mired in public controversy for being 'tone-deaf' to the issue of starving children.

3.11. Solidarity

The concept of solidarity refers to the social cohesion and mutual support that is shown for one another. It is important during crises because collective threats often demand collective responses. In the case of COVID-19, for instance, the actions of individuals can increase the risks faced by others. Research indicates that a sense of 'common fate' can act as a natural spur to shared social identities that foster a sense of solidarity (Drury et al. 2019). Public leaders can work with these identities by such means as emphasising the 'we' in tackling problems together to emerging group norms that valuing inclusivity help support (Drury, Reicher, and Stott 2020; Reicher and Stott 2020). This may in turn prompt people into acting with compassion and to provide help and support to others where it is needed (Van Bavel et al. 2020). However, punitive measures that position people problematically as potential rule breakers can have the opposite effect by essentially setting authorities against citizens rather than with them (Reicher and Stott 2020).

3.11.1. Examples

The leadership of the First Minister for Scotland, Nicola Sturgeon, has been praised for being able to secure public trust and adherence to coronavirus response measures largely through fostering a spirit of solidarity. In particular, the Minister stressed the importance of community and acting together while offering support instead of harsh punishment in relation to compliance with lockdown measures (Reicher 2020). Elsewhere in the UK, the Queen gave a well-received public address also emphasising the need for solidarity, stating that, *Together we are tackling this disease, and I want to reassure you that if we remain united and resolute, then we will overcome it'* (Jetten et al. 2020). In this collective spirit, citizens up and down the country engaged in acts of mutual support including for ten weeks during the lockdown many thousands of people taking to their front doorsteps every Thursday evening to 'clap for careers' and show appreciation for the NHS, care staff, and other keyworkers. However, the clap for carers gesture of solidarity was brought to a halt by the person who introduced the initiative after it became 'politicised' by UK Ministers who, having appeared in 'photo ops' showing support on their door steps, were criticised for what was regarded as an empty gesture when hospitals were not being provided with the material equipment and support they needed to perform their jobs safely.

The most unreserved criticismm was levelled at the UK government for its poor handling of the *'Cummingsgate'* scandal. In this incident, the Chief Special Advisor, Dominic Cummings, was reported to have flouted the lockdown rules several times without facing reprimand, which as a result is credited with severely undermining public solidarity and compliance with response measures and restrictions (Sky News 2020b). The scandal focused on a 260-mile trip to stay in at family owned residence in Durham during the height of the March lockdown when his wife was suffering symptoms of coronavirus despite this being banned in government guidance. A second trip while in Durham involved driving to Barnard Castle, a picturesque tourist spot, on his wife's birthday, also with his child, apparently to check his eyesight was functioning well enough to drive all the way back to London. In his subsequent Downing Street 'rose garden' press statement made in response to calls for him to be sacked, Dominic Cummings insisted his actions were allowed under the rules, and moreover he was only doing what any responsible parent would do. This version of events was then later endorsed by the Prime Minister, along with other Cabinet members, all agreeing that he did 'what any responsible parent would have done'. One Cabinet member, Michael Gove MP, even went as far as to make the farcical claim on a national radio talk show interview that he had himself also previously driven his car to test his eyesight. This unfortunate incident, bizarre justification, and series of endorsements are thought to have established in the public mind the view that it is *'one rule for them, and another rule for everyone else'*. Consequently, *Cummingsgate* led to a dramatic plunge in trust levels and possibly more than any other event destroyed the moral authority of government to request citizens to follow the rules or criticise them if they failed to do so. Following incidences of poor compliance with social distancing and isolation requirements, the government has since resorted to heavier policing measures. This has included the use of marshals and punitive fines of up to £10,000 to try to ensure compliance with lockdown rules, a move that if anything is likely to undermine any slim sense of solidarity that might have remained amongst the general population that was needed for compliance with measures such as downloading the coronavirus contact tracing app and self-isolating (Reicher and Stott 2020).

3.12. Responsiveness and adaptiveness

While experience of past events can help inform and guide responses to current crises, new events do not always follow the same patterns, so it is often the case that creative and inventive ideas and solutions are required so as to address problems as they unfold (Hardy and McGuire 2020). This means being responsive to the dynamics of emergencies, and being able to adapt to changing circumstances. In practical terms, this requires making 'research' and 'outreach' core functions of risk and crisis management so as to gain wide-reaching and timely information and feedback about current problems and the impacts of interventions. Following an 'adaptive systems' view, risk and crisis management must therefore take a broad view which accounts for individual understandings and behaviour, as well as the wider socioecological conditions and community contexts that shape local realities, practical constraints, and the interdependencies between them, such that material possibilities for action are factored into plans and support for collective resilience and (Finucane et al. (2020). The adaptiveness of leadership can, however, be undermined by what might be termed the 'myth of perfection', which can sometimes stand as a barrier to decisive action, as summed up by Dr Mike Ryan (2020) of the WHO:

> Be fast. Have no regrets. You must be the first mover. The virus will always get you if you don't move quickly. And you need to be prepared. One of the great things in emergency response – and anyone who is involved in emergency response will know this – if you need to be right before you move, you will never win. Perfection is the enemy of the good when it comes to emergency management. Speed trumps perfection and the problem in society at the moment is everyone is afraid of making a mistake, everyone is afraid of the consequence of error. But the greatest error is not to move. The greatest error is to be paralyzed by the fear of failure. And I think that is the single biggest lesson I have learned in Ebola responses in the past.

A second barrier that might be termed the 'myth of maladaptive behaviour', regards misplaced assumptions that portray citizens as 'prone to panic', 'helplessness', 'civil disorder', or 'fatigue' during crises (Drury et al. 2019; Reicher and Stott 2020). These myths are commonly found in the media portrayals and political discourse that individualises and pathologizes behaviour, typically harbouring a dismissive view of citizens capabilities and capacities during crises. Resisting these myths may then at first seem counter-intuitive. However, the prevalence of maladaptive and undesirable group behaviour is overexaggerated. If and when problems do 'occur', it often has a reasonable alternative basis for explanation when considered in the context of practical constraints that people face (Fischhoff 2005; Reicher and Stott 2020). This is not to say that poor conduct or errors within groups never occur, but such acts are given more coverage than they necessarily warrant. Underneath the headlines, people are commonly found to act intelligibly and adaptively when faced with crises, even in the most extreme circumstances, with research findings showing responses such as 'panic' and 'rioting' tend to be more the exception than the rule (Sheppard et al. 2006). Isolated instances of maladaptive responses tend to be just that and can be typically avoided provided that people are issued with the information, physical, social and financial support they need, rather than dismissed as lazy or irrational (Michie et al. 2020; Sheppard et al. 2006; Reicher and Stott 2020).

3.12.1. Examples

The Greek government acted decisively on first news of the pandemic. The testing and isolating of citizens began before the first national cases were confirmed, and an early lockdown was initiated despite economic difficulties. Officials prioritised science over politics and placed its focus on 'state-sensitivity, co-ordination, resolve and swiftness'. Greek government officials also enacted rapid comprehensive digital reforms to change the way citizens interact with public services and government to help reduce risks to vulnerable populations. This notably included allowing the elderly to obtain digital prescriptions so they could stay at home while social distancing.

Emergency management of COVID-19 in the UK has regularly been accused of being sluggish in response to events and then acting without prior warning or clear communication, leading to a sense that measures have been rushed, panicked or contrived on little evidence supporting their use. For example, amidst ample prior warnings, the UK government emergency response was initially dithering and notably failed to act decisively either on the advice of the WHO or lessons emerging from Italy and Spain. Subsequently, the UK was slow to enter state of emergency and initiated only a partial lockdown while borders remained open. For example, on key misstep was to allow 20,000 fans to travel to Liverpool football club from Madrid, likely helping to seed the virus in the UK when Spain was thought to be the epicentre of the virus (Scally, Jacobson, and Abbasi 2020).

There was also evidence of the UK government falling prey to a disaster myth resulting in the delay of firm measures justified on the grounds that people would soon tire of them leading to further problems down the line. In particular, in early statements made by Chief Medical Officer for England, Chris Whitty, argued that 'If you move too early [with containment measures], people get fatigued. This is a long haul.' Later it was acknowledged this was a mistake that needlessly cost thousands of lives, first given that entering lockdown just one week earlier would have saved 20,000 lives, and second that the general population had responded incredibly positively to complying with lockdown measures despite considerable personal hardships in keeping with the British mantra to 'keep clam and carry on' (Sky News 2020c). At the time of writing, it is still not clear where the idea of 'behavioural' or 'lockdown' fatigue first arose though it was clearly factored into early modelling of the pandemic which helped to shape the choice of policy responses. Dr David Halpern, the director of the 'Nudge Unit' which provides advice to the UK government on behavioural policy, used the term in interviews before lockdown measures were announced, but said that the idea had not originated with them (Malnick 2020). Members of the advisory panel on behavioural science (SPI-B) have since also publicly stated that they had in fact argued against such a notion, being that it was not actually a scientific concept or a representation of behaviour borne out by the research evidence they had before them.

3.13. Media engagement

The media are understood to represent the primary means by which both institutions reach out to publicly communicate and wider society hears about crises (Heath 2006). This has led to the view that the media should be treated as a partner in risk and crisis management (Seeger 2006). This means that institutions must be accessible and be proactive in trying to meet the media's informational needs, and that these relations should be built up in advance of a crisis event and maintained when one occurs (Reynolds 2010). Failing in these tasks means that media outlets will likely seek information elsewhere. The fast-paced developments and advances of the 'Information Age' also present a challenging techno-cultural reality for risk and crisis management that extends beyond dealing with traditional media (Gaspar et al. 2016; Panagiotopoulos et al. 2016). Essentially, online channels and social media means that citizens no longer necessarily rely on centralised communications handed from the top down, and it is possible that myth, rumour and disinformation are more easily circulated (Krause et al. 2020). Online communication does however also provide additional channels and formats for government to communicate 'unfiltered' messages to the masses (Wardman 2017). This has in turn yielded 'best practices' with regards to instructive lessons having emerged. Particularly, social media should not simply be seen as an instrument for broadcasting information. While it is unrivalled for providing timely announcements and alerts, social media are perhaps best understood as contributing to an ongoing interactive dialogue that has to be cultivated, curated, and maintained (Austin and Jin 2017; Eriksson 2018). For public leaders and practitioners, this has meant having to understanding and gain mastery of social media tools, techniques, and online cultures, so as to be able to 'go where the audience is', 'grab attention' and engage with others, amidst competing information providers (Brossard and Scheufele 2013; Wardman 2017). In the process, as with the traditional media, authorities have learned the value of growing a community of followers in advance of crises. In the event, they should not forget or neglect the importance of traditional media, which is still regarded by many as a more credible source of information, and also provide much of the content that is subsequently shared and discussed online (Eriksson 2018).

3.13.1. Examples

The communications team at Doncaster Council in the UK gained national praise for its engaging use of social media to advise citizens about COVID-19. One official Twitter post concerning the issue of following expert advice about social distancing notably went viral after recounting analogous lessons from an infamous 1970s exploding whale incident in Oregon. The post ended on the observation that *'When you ignore expert advice and act like an idiot, you cover everyone else with decaying whale blubber #StayHome'*. The Tweet was praised for achieving wide reach in the local community and nationally through its use of humour whilst also providing a constructive lesson from history on the value of following scientific advice.

The UK government has been widely criticised for failing to meet the needs of the media as part of an apparent strategy to centralise control over media messaging and output. From the beginning of the crisis, the government has maintained a long boycott of several news and media outlets and morning talk show television programmes, as well as restricting some journalists from access to press briefings. Ministers have been especially sensitive to media criticism, muting and cutting off follow-up questions from journalists at press conferences. They have also been accused of gagging civil servants and blocking them from responding to questions from journalists that they did not want to be asked or answered by others present. For example, England's Chief Nurse, Ruth May, was apparently dropped from government coronavirus press briefings after refusing to give support for the actions of the Prime Minister's chief advisor Dominic Cummings (Lintern 2020). In press briefings it has been common practice only to allow one question from a journalist without allowing a follow-up question, meaning that the first question often has not been answered or answers could not be subjected to cross-checking. The government also took the unusual step at one point of making a pointed rebuttal of an article featured in The Times newspaper and accusing journalists of 'serious errors' and 'making up falsehoods'. The UK government's digital media communications strategy has also come under fire for being sluggish, such as being initially slow to run adverts on social media, and for being poorly co-ordinated with telecoms companies such that there were problems and delays sending text message alerts. The most notable piece of UK government social media was a 'rogue' tweet from the official Twitter account of the UK Civil Service, which apparently being critical of government Press Briefings, went viral after stating: 'Arrogant and offensive. Can you imagine having to work for these truth twisters'. The Tweet was quite understandably widely shared and liked before it was quickly taken down.

4. Recalibrating pandemic risk leadership: Conclusions and recommendations

While no nation could expect to be fully prepared for COVID-19, the onset of the pandemic has nonetheless evidently revealed misplaced confidence and a number of false assumptions undergirding government assurances about the capacity of the UK to withstand and respond effectively in the event of a health crisis of such magnitude. As frailties in the UK's health and social care infrastructure were laid bare, COVID-19 also exposed an array of leadership deficiencies as the British Prime Minister and Cabinet members showed what might be described, at best, as a predilection for inadequate preparation and a poor basic grasp of emergency response 'fundamentals' such as responsiveness, openness and partnership required to navigate the pandemic in difficult circumstances. The UK emergency response was thus marred initially by being slow to act, then subsequently by a series of reactive initiatives and practices that largely ran counter to what would otherwise be prescribed by health professionals, emergency planners and other risk and crisis experts and lessons learned from past infectious disease outbreaks in recent history.

Inasmuch as the current direction of the UK's pandemic risk leadership response to COVID-19 concerns questions not only of health and the economy, but also of 'how we want to live' and 'by what means' we can hold decisions democratically accountable during a crisis (Burgess et al. 2018; Fiorino 1990), judgements of 'bad' pandemic leadership performance can equally be said to reflect judgements of 'bad' pandemic politics on the part of leaders (Mythen et al. 2018). The characteristically narrow and centralised response adopted, has, at its worst, been considered absent or dithering at key junctures, incoherent and confused throughout, as well as being equally indifferent and combative, and repeating the same errors time and again. Meanwhile, vast sums of money have been wasted on ineffectual programmes and initiatives outsourced under opaque arrangements. Most criticism, let alone constructive advice, has been ignored or discarded, even though the poor performance displayed is plain to see.

In view of the scale and scope of the national health, economic, social, and political damages suffered so far, let alone those that are still to come, and that much of which could have been avoidable, the series of failings and deficiencies exhibited undoubtedly looks set to become a 'textbook example' of how *not* to lead through a health crisis of such magnitude. In view of these observations, this paper closes by arguing that the UK government would do better in future by recalibrating the current leadership response strategy. The concepts, strategic considerations, and exemplars outlined by this paper elaborate the benefits of adopting a more pluralised model of leadership and risk and crisis management – as shown both internationally and sometimes at home – one that is necessarily broadly attuned to the rich amalgam of transactions, individual qualities, social identity dynamics, and communicative mechanisms and exchanges that both comprise and are required of 'good' leadership in a crisis (Fairhurst and Connaughton 2014a; Hyvärinen and Vos 2015; van Dick et al. 2018). In closing, these lessons strongly point to the need for government to move away from an over-reliance on narrow centralisation and diktat and adopt a more differentiated suit of strategies in order to make fuller use of the many substantive and inter-personal levers which could be collectively employed to tackle COVID-19 more productively and adaptively as the crisis continues. Doing so would go some way towards ensuring that the UK leadership decisions shaping the pandemic response are founded on robust knowledge, socially representative, collectively promoted, democratically supported, and crisis ready.

Disclosure statement

No potential conflict of interest was reported by the author(s).

ORCID

Jamie K. Wardman http://orcid.org/0000-0002-3609-7591

References

Abbey, E. J., B. A. Khalifa, M. O. Oduwole, S. K. Ayeh, R. D. Nudotor, E. L. Salia, O. Lasisi, et al. 2020. "The Global Health Security Index is Not Predictive of Coronavirus Pandemic Responses among Organization for Economic Cooperation and Development Countries." *PloS One* 15 (10): e0239398. doi:10.1371/journal.pone.0239398.

Allegretti, A. 2020. "Coronavirus 'Still out there': PM Condemns People 'Taking too Many Liberties' after Crowded Beach Scenes. *Sky News*, June 26. https://news.sky.com/story/coronavirus-still-out-there-pm-condemns-people-taking-too-many-liberties-after-crowded-beach-scenes-12015376

Allen, P. 2020. "French President Macron Extends Lockdown for a MONTH until May 11 but Promises 'Joyous Days are Ahead' - as he Apologises for 'Not being Prepared Enough' for Coronavirus Battle." *Daily Mail*, April 13, 09: 03. https://www.dailymail.co.uk/news/article-8213535/President-Macron-warn-France-brace-extended-lockdown-May.html

Amanpour. 2020. "WHO: Coronavirus not Unstoppable." *CNN* March 9. https://edition.cnn.com/videos/world/2020/03/10/coronavirus-china-italy-world-health-organisation.cnn

Austin, L. L. and Jin, Y. eds. 2017. *Social Media and Crisis Communication*. New York: Taylor & Francis.

Bakker, M. H., J. H. Kerstholt, M. van Bommel, and E. Giebels. 2019. "Decision-Making during a Crisis: The Interplay of Narratives and Statistical Information before and after Crisis Communication." *Journal of Risk Research* 22 (11): 1409–1424. doi:10.1080/13669877.2018.1473464.

BBC. 2020a. "'We didn't have Exact Measures' in Place for Covid Says Ex-Civil Service Head." *BBC News*, October 21. https://www.bbc.co.uk/news/uk-politics-54617148

BBC. 2020b. "Coronavirus: Minister Defends 'Stay Alert' Advice Amid Backlash." *BBC News*. https://www.bbc.co.uk/news/uk-52605819

BBC. 2020c. "Coronavirus: 'High risk' list misses off thousands of people". *BBC News*, April 7. https://www.bbc.co.uk/news/uk-england-52123446

BBC. 2020d. "Coronavirus in Scotland: Stay at Home Message Remains as Exercise Rules Ease." *BBC News*, May 10. https://www.bbc.co.uk/news/uk-scotland-52605959

Blumenshine, P., A. Reingold, S. Egerter, R. Mockenhaupt, P. Braveman, and J. Marks. 2008. "Pandemic Influenza Planning in the United States from a Health Disparities perspective." *Emerging Infectious Diseases* 14 (5): 709–715. doi:10.3201/eid1405.071301.

Boholm, Å., H. Corvellec, and M. Karlsson. 2012. "The Practice of Risk Governance: Lessons from the Field." *Journal of Risk Research* 15 (1): 1–20. doi:10.1080/13669877.2011.587886.

Boin, A., and P. T. Hart. 2003. "Public Leadership in Times of Crisis: mission Impossible?" *Public Administration Review* 63 (5): 544–553. doi:10.1111/1540-6210.00318.

Boin, A., E. Stern, P. Hart, and B. Sundelius. 2016. *The Politics of Crisis Management: Public Leadership under Pressure*. Cambridge: Cambridge University Press.

Booth, R., and N. Parveen. 2020. "Plans to Hand Contact Tracing to England's Local Authorities 'Too Late'." *The Guardian*, October 11. https://www.theguardian.com/world/2020/oct/11/plans-to-hand-contact-tracing-to-england-local-authorities-come-too-late-covid

Bostrom, A. 2008. "Lead is like Mercury: Risk Comparisons, Analogies and Mental Models." *Journal of Risk Research* 11 (1): 99–117. doi:10.1080/13669870701602956.

Brossard, D., and D. A. Scheufele. 2013. " Social science. Science, new media, and the public." *Science (New York, N.Y.)* 339 (6115): 40–41. doi:10.1126/science.1232329.

Breakwell, G. M. 2001. "Mental Models and Social Representations of Hazards: The Significance of Identity Processes." *Journal of Risk Research* 4 (4): 341–351. doi:10.1080/13669870110062730.

Bryce, C., P. Ring, S. Ashby, and J. K. Wardman. 2020. "Resilience in the Face of Uncertainty: Early Lessons from the COVID-19 Pandemic." *Journal of Risk Research* : 1–8.

Burgess, A. 2019. "Environmental Risk Narratives in Historical Perspective: From Early Warnings to 'Risk Society' Blame." *Journal of Risk Research* 22 (9): 1128–1142. doi:10.1080/13669877.2018.1517383.

Burgess, A., J. Wardman, and G. Mythen. 2018. "Considering Risk: Placing the Work of Ulrich Beck in Context." *Journal of Risk Research* 21 (1): 1–5. doi:10.1080/13669877.2017.1383075.

Cabinet Office. 2017. "National Risk Register of Civil Emergencies." *Cabinet Office London*. https://www.gov.uk/government/publications/national-risk-register-of-civil-emergencies-2017-edition

Calvert, J., G. Arbuthnott, and J. Leake. 2020. "Coronavirus: 38 Days when Britain Sleepwalked into Disaster." *The Sunday Times*, April 19. https://www.thetimes.co.uk/article/coronavirus-38-days-when-britain-sleepwalked-into-disaster-hq3b9tlgh

Campbell, A. 2020. "Jacinda Ardern's Covid 19 Coronavirus Response puts UK to Shame." *New Zealand Herald*, June 9, 03:07. https://www.nzherald.co.nz/nz/alastair-campbell-jacinda-arderns-covid-19-coronavirus-response-puts-uk-to-shame/UPFTYETDUFQ7T5S6COY5K22NFE/

Carrell, S., D. Pegg, F. Lawrence, P. Lewis, R. Evans, D. Conn, H. Davies, and K. Proctor. 2020. "Revealed: Dominic Cummings on Secret Scientific Advisory Group for COVID-19." The Guardian, April 24. https://www.theguardian.com/world/2020/apr/24/revealed-dominic-cummings-on-secret-scientific-advisory-group-for-covid-19

Chakelian, A. 2020. A Close Reading: When Boris Johnson Blames Care Homes over COVID-19 He's Really Blaming Himself." *New Statesman,* July 7. https://www.newstatesman.com/2020/07/boris-johnson-blames-care-homes-cor-onavirus-covid-19

Collins, A., M. Florin, and O. Renn. 2020. "COVID-19 Risk Governance: Drivers, Responses and Lessons to Be Learned." *Journal of Risk Research* : 1–10. doi:10.1080/13669877.2020.1760332.

Crace, J. 2020. "Matt Hancock's Career Continues to Win the Battle with his Conscience. *Guardian,* Tuesday, May 5, 17.04. https://www.theguardian.com/politics/2020/may/05/matt-hancocks-career-continues-to-win-the-battle-with-his-conscience?

Crouse Quinn, S. 2008. "Crisis and Emergency Risk Communication in a Pandemic: A Model for Building Capacity and Resilience of Minority Communities." *Health Promotion Practice* 9 (4 Suppl): 18S–25S. doi:10.1177/1524839908324022.

Dalglish, S. L. 2020. "COVID-19 Gives the Lie to Global Health Expertise." *The Lancet* 395 (10231): 1189. doi:10.1016/S0140-6736(20)30739-X.

Dinnen, C. 2020. "Boris Johnson Apologises Saying He 'Misspoke' when Asked to clarify North East England Covid rules." *ITV News,* September 29. https://www.itv.com/news/2020-09-29/boris-johnson-apologises-saying-he-mis-spoke-when-asked-to-clarify-north-east-england-covid-rules

Drury, J., H. Carter, C. Cocking, E. Ntontis, S. Tekin Guven, and R. Amlôt. 2019. "Facilitating Collective Resilience in the Public in Emergencies: Twelve Recommendations Based on the Social Identity Approach." *Frontiers in Public Health* 7: 181. doi:10.3389/fpubh.2019.00181.

Drury, J., S. Reicher, and C. Stott. 2020. " COVID-19 in Context: Why do People Die in Emergencies? It's Probably not because of Collective Psychology." *The British Journal of Social Psychology* 59 (3): 686–693. doi:10.1111/bjso.12393.

Eriksson, M. 2018. "Lessons for Crisis Communication on Social Media: A Systematic Review of What Research Tells the Practice." *International Journal of Strategic Communication* 12 (5): 526–551. doi:10.1080/1553118X.2018.1510405.

Fairhurst, G. T., and S. L. Connaughton. 2014a. "Leadership: A Communicative Perspective." *Leadership* 10 (1): 7–35. doi:10.1177/1742715013509396.

Fairhurst, G. T., and S. L. Connaughton. 2014b. "Leadership Communication." *The SAGE Handbook of Organizational Communication: Advances in Theory, Research, and Method* : 401–423. New York: SAGE.

Finucane, Melissa L., Michael J. Blum, Rajeev Ramchand, Andrew M. Parker, Shanthi Nataraj, Noreen Clancy, Gary Cecchine, et al. 2020. "Advancing Community Resilience Research and Practice: moving from "Me" to "We" to "3D." *Journal of Risk Research* 23 (1): 1–10. doi:10.1080/13669877.2018.1517377.

Fiorino, D. J. 1990. "Citizen Participation and Environmental Risk: A Survey of Institutional Mechanisms." *Science, Technology, & Human Values* 15 (2): 226–243. doi:10.1177/016224399001500204.

Fischhoff, B. 1995. "Risk Perception and Communication Unplugged: twenty Years of Process." *Risk Analysis: An Official Publication of the Society for Risk Analysis* 15 (2): 137–145. doi:10.1111/j.1539-6924.1995.tb00308.x.

Fischhoff, B. 2005. "Scientifically Sound Pandemic Risk Communication." *US House Science Committee Briefing: Gaps in the National Flu Preparedness Plan, Social Science Planning and Response* 14.

Fischhoff, B. 2013. "Non-Persuasive Communication about Matters of Greatest Urgency." *Risk Analysis and Human Behavior* : 223.

Fischhoff, B. 2020a. "The Importance of Testing Messages." *World Health Organization. Bulletin of the World Health Organization* 98 (8): 516–517.

Fischhoff, B. 2020b. "Making Decisions in a COVID-19 World." *JAMA* 324 (2): 139. doi:10.1001/jama.2020.10178.

Foster, D., S. Lawson, J. Wardman, M. Blythe, and C. Linehan. 2012. "Watts in It for Me?" Design Implications for Implementing Effective Energy Interventions in Organisations. In Proceedings of the SIGCHI Conference on Human Factors in Computing Systems, May, 2357–2366.

Freedman, L. 2020a. "Strategy for a Pandemic: The UK and COVID-19." *Survival* 62 (3): 25–76. doi:10.1080/00396338.2020.1763610.

Freedman, L. 2020b. "Scientific Advice at a Time of Emergency. SAGE and Covid-19." *The Political Quarterly* 91 (3): 514–522. doi:10.1111/1467-923X.12885.

Freedman, L. 2020c. "The Real Reason the UK Government Pursued "Herd Immunity"—and Why It Was Abandoned." *New Statesman.*

Freudenburg, W. R. 2003. "Institutional Failure and the Organizational Amplification of Risks: The Need for a Closer Look." *The Social Amplification of Risk* 102: 120.

Garbett, A., J. K. Wardman, B. Kirman, C. Linehan, and S. Lawson. 2014. "Anti-Social Media: communicating Risk through Open Data, Crime Maps and Locative Media." *HCI* 회 순대회 : 145–152.

Garbett, A., C. Linehan, B. Kirman, J. Wardman, and S. Lawson. 2011. "Using Social Media to Drive Public Engagement with Open Data." *Digital Engagement* 11: 15–17.

Gaspar, R., C. Pedro, P. Panagiotopoulos, and B. Seibt. 2016. "Beyond Positive or Negative: Qualitative Sentiment Analysis of Social Media Reactions to Unexpected Stressful Events." *Computers in Human Behavior* 56: 179–191. doi:10.1016/j.chb.2015.11.040.

Goulden, M., A. Spence, J. Wardman, and C. Leygue. 2018. "Differentiating 'the User'in DSR: Developing Demand Side Response in Advanced Economies." *Energy Policy* 122: 176–185. doi:10.1016/j.enpol.2018.07.013.

Greenhalgh, T. 2020. "Laying Straw Men to Rest: author's Reply to "urgency and Uncertainty: covid-19, Face Masks, and Evidence Informed Policy." *BMJ* 369.

Haslam, S. A., S. D. Reicher, and M. J. Platow. 2010. *The New Psychology of Leadership: Identity, Influence and Power.* London: Psychology Press.

Hardy, C., and S. Maguire. 2020. "Organizations, Risk Translation, and the Ecology of Risks: The Discursive Construction of a Novel Risk." *Academy of Management Journal* 63 (3): 685–716. doi:10.5465/amj.2017.0987.

Heald, D. A. 2006. "Varieties of Transparency." In *Transparency: The Key to Better Governance?: Proceedings of the British Academy*, vol. 135, 25–43. Oxford: Oxford University Press.

Heath, R. L. 2006. "Best Practices in Crisis Communication: Evolution of Practice through Research." *Journal of Applied Communication Research* 34 (3): 245–248. doi:10.1080/00909880600771577.

Holmes, B., N. Henrich, S. Hancock, and V. Lestou. 2009. "Communicating with the Public during Health Crises: experts' Experiences and Opinions." *Journal of Risk Research* 12 (6): 793–807. doi:10.1080/13669870802648486.

Hood, C. 2007. "What Happens When Transparency Meets Blame-Avoidance?" *Public Management Review* 9 (2): 191–210. doi:10.1080/14719030701340275.

Horton, R. 2020. *The COVID-19 Catastrophe: What's Gone Wrong and How to Stop It Happening Again.* London: John Wiley & Sons.

Hyvärinen, J., and M. Vos. 2015. "Developing a Conceptual Framework for Investigating Communication Supporting Community Resilience." *Societies* 5 (3): 583–597. doi:10.3390/soc5030583.

Islam, F. 2020. "Coronavirus: UK Hardest Hit by Virus among Leading G7 Nations. *BBC*, June 29. https://www.bbc.co.uk/news/business-53222182

ITV. 2020. "This Morning – Interview with Boris Johnson." *ITV*, March 5, 10:00.

Jaques, T. 2012. "Crisis Leadership: A View from the Executive Suite." *Journal of Public Affairs* 12 (4): 366–372. doi:10.1002/pa.1422.

Jetten, J., S. D. Reicher, S. A. Haslam, and T. Cruwys, eds. 2020. *Together apart: The Psychology of COVID-19.* New York: SAGE.

Joffe, H., and G. Haarhoff. 2002. "Representations of Far-Flung Illnesses: The Case of Ebola in Britain." *Social Science & Medicine (1982)* 54 (6): 955–969. doi:10.1016/S0277-9536(01)00068-5.

Johansson, C., and E. Bäck. 2017. "Strategic Leadership Communication for Crisis Network Coordination." *International Journal of Strategic Communication* 11 (4): 324–343. doi:10.1080/1553118X.2017.1341889.

Kasperson, R. 2014. "Four Questions for Risk Communication." *Journal of Risk Research* 17 (10): 1233–1239. doi:10.1080/13669877.2014.900207.

Krause, N. M., I. Freiling, B. Beets, and D. Brossard. 2020. "Fact-Checking as Risk Communication: The Multi-Layered Risk of Misinformation in Times of COVID-19." *Journal of Risk Research* : 1–8.

Krieger, K. 2016. "Resilience and Risk Studies." In *Routledge Handbook of Risk Studies*, edited by Adam Burgess, Alberto Alemanno, and Jens Zinn, 335–343. London: Routledge.

Lancaster, K., T. Rhodes, and M. Rosengarten. 2020. "Making Evidence and Policy in Public Health Emergencies: Lessons from COVID-19 for Adaptive Evidence-Making and Intervention." *Evidence & Policy: A Journal of Research, Debate and Practice* 16 (3): 477–490. doi:10.1332/174426420X15913559981103.

Leiss, W. 1996. "Three Phases in the Evolution of Risk Communication Practice." *The Annals of the American Academy of Political and Social Science* 545 (1): 85–94. doi:10.1177/0002716296545001009.

Lintern, S. 2020. "Chief nurse dropped from Downing Street coronavirus briefing 'after refusing to back Dominic Cummings'". *The Independent*, June 12. https://www.independent.co.uk/news/uk/politics/coronavirus-chief-nurse-dominic-cummings-ruth-may-daily-briefing-downing-street-a9562741.html

Löfstedt, R. 2005. *Risk Management in Post-Trust Societies.* New York: Palgrave Macmillan.

Löfstedt, R., F. Bouder, J. Wardman, and S. Chakraborty. 2011. "The Changing Nature of Communication and Regulation of Risk in Europe." *Journal of Risk Research* 14 (4): 409–429. doi:10.1080/13669877.2011.557479.

Löfstedt, R., and F. Bouder. 2014. "New Transparency Policies: Risk Communication's Doom?" *Earthscan Risk in Society*.

Löfstedt, R., and J. Wardman. 2016. "State of the Art Transparency: lessons from Europe and North America." *Journal of Risk Research* 19 (9): 1079–1081. doi:10.1080/13669877.2016.1249713.

Malnick, E. 2020. "Government scientists talked up herd immunity despite warnings about early reinfection". *The Telegraph*, May 17. https://www.telegraph.co.uk/news/2020/05/17/government-scientists-talked-herd-immunity-despite-warnings/

McGuire, D., J. E. Cunningham, K. Reynolds, and G. Matthews-Smith. 2020. "Beating the Virus: An Examination of the Crisis Communication Approach Taken by New Zealand Prime Minister Jacinda Ardern during the Covid-19 Pandemic." *Human Resource Development International* 23 (4): 361–379. doi:10.1080/13678868.2020.1779543.

Mee, E. 2020. "Coronavirus: Matt Lucas' Video Mocking Boris Johnson's Speech to the Nation Goes Viral. *Sky News*, May 11. https://news.sky.com/story/coronavirus-matt-lucas-video-mocking-boris-johnsons-speech-to-the-nation-goes-viral-11986438

Merrick, R. 2020. "Boris Johnson Hopes for Return to Normal by Christmas - Despite Whitty Warning of 'Difficult' Period Until Spring." *The Independent,* September 9. https://www.independent.co.uk/news/uk/politics/boris-johnson-coronavirus-christmas-xmas-uk-lockdown-covid-cases-b421098.html

Michie, S., R. West, M. B. Rogers, C. Bonell, G. J. Rubin, and R. Amlôt. 2020. "Reducing SARS-CoV-2 Transmission in the UK: A Behavioural Science Approach to Identifying Options for Increasing Adherence to Social Distancing and Shielding Vulnerable People." *British Journal of Health Psychology.*

Monbiot, G. 2020. "The Government's Secretive Covid Contracts are Heaping Misery on Britain." *The Guardian.* October 21. https://www.theguardian.com/commentisfree/2020/oct/21/government-covid-contracts-britain-nhs-corporate-executives-test-and-trace

Müller, Henriette, and, Femke A. W. J Van Esch. 2020. "The Contested Nature of Political Leadership in the European Union: conceptual and Methodological Cross-Fertilisation." *West European Politics* 43 (5): 1051–1071. doi:10.1080/01402382.2019.1678951.

Mythen, G., A. Burgess, and J. K. Wardman. 2018. "The Prophecy of Ulrich Beck: Signposts for the Social Sciences." *Journal of Risk Research* 21 (1): 96–100. doi:10.1080/13669877.2017.1362029.

Noort, M. C., T. W. Reader, and A. Gillespie. 2019. "Speaking up to Prevent Harm: A Systematic Review of the Safety Voice Literature." *Safety Science* 117: 375–387. doi:10.1016/j.ssci.2019.04.039.

Nyenswah, T., C. Y. Engineer, and D. H. Peters. 2016. "Leadership in Times of Crisis: The Example of Ebola Virus Disease in Liberia." *Health Systems and Reform* 2 (3): 194–207. doi:10.1080/23288604.2016.1222793.

Panagiotopoulos, P.,. J. Barnett, A. Z. Bigdeli, and S. Sams. 2016. "Social Media in Emergency Management: Twitter as a Tool for Communicating Risks to the Public." *Technological Forecasting and Social Change* 111: 86–96. doi: 10.1016/j.techfore.2016.06.010.

Reicher, S. 2020. "Johnson should Learn from Sturgeon and Treat the Public as a Partner, not a Problem." *The Guardian,* September 25. https://www.theguardian.com/commentisfree/2020/sep/25/johnson-sturgeon-public-compliance

Reicher, S., and C. Stott. 2020. "On Order and Disorder during the COVID-19 pandemic." *The British Journal of Social Psychology* 59 (3): 694–702. doi:10.1111/bjso.12398.

Renn, O., and D. Levine. 1991. "Credibility and Trust in Risk Communication." In *Communicating Risks to the Public,* 175–217. Dordrecht: Springer.

Reynolds, B.2007. *Crisis and emergency risk communication: Pandemic influenza.* Atlanta, GA: Centers for Disease Control and Prevention.

Reynolds, B. 2002. *Crisis and Emergency Risk Communication.* Atlanta, GA: Centers for Disease Control and Prevention.

Reynolds, B. 2006. "Response to Best Practices." *Journal of Applied Communication Research* 34 (3): 249–252. doi:10. 1080/00909880600771593.

Reynolds, B. 2010. "Principles to Enable Leaders to Navigate the Harsh Realities of Crisis and Risk Communication." *Journal of Business Continuity & Emergency Planning* 4 (3): 262–273.

Reynolds, B., and M. Seeger. 2005. "Crisis and Emergency Risk Communication as an Integrative Model." *Journal of Health Communication* 10 (1): 43–55. doi:10.1080/10810730590904571.

Reynolds, B., and S. C. Quinn. 2008. "Effective Communication during an Influenza Pandemic: The Value of Using a Crisis and Emergency Risk Communication Framework." *Health Promotion Practice* 9 (4 Suppl): 13S–17S. doi:10. 1177/1524839908325267.

Rickard, L. N., K. A. Mccomas, C. E. Clarke, R. C. Stedman, and D. J. Decker. 2013. "Exploring Risk Attenuation and Crisis Communication after a Plague Death in Grand Canyon." *Journal of Risk Research* 16 (2): 145–167. doi:10. 1080/13669877.2012.725673.

Rickard, L. N. 2019. "Pragmatic and (or) constitutive? On the foundations of contemporary risk communication research." *Risk analysis.* doi:10.1111/risa.13415

Ruben, B. D., and R. A. Gigliotti. 2016. "Leadership as Social Influence: An Expanded View of Leadership Communication Theory and Practice." *Journal of Leadership & Organizational Studies* 23 (4): 467–479. doi:10. 1177/1548051816641876.

Ruggeri, K., S. Linden, C. Wang, F. Papa, J. Riesch, and J. Green. 2020. *Standards for Evidence in Policy Decision-Making.* doi:10.31234/osf.io/fjwvk

Ryan, M.2020. 'Be fast, have no regrets' – Dr Michael Ryan on what's been learned from Ebola. Independent.ie 17 March. Accessed at-https://www.independent.ie/videos/be-fast-have-no-regrets-dr-michael-ryan-on-whats-been-learned-from-ebola-39051117.html

Scally, G., B. Jacobson, and K. Abbasi. 2020. "The UK's Public Health Response to Covid-19." *BMJ (Clinical Research ed.)* 369: m1932–m1932.

Seeger, M. W. 2006. "Best Practices in Crisis Communication: An Expert Panel Process." *Journal of Applied Communication Research* 34 (3): 232–244. doi:10.1080/00909880600769944.

Sellnow, T. L., D. D. Sellnow, E. M. Helsel, J. M. Martin, and J. S. Parker. 2019. "Risk and Crisis Communication Narratives in Response to Rapidly Emerging Diseases." *Journal of Risk Research* 22 (7): 897–908. doi:10.1080/ 13669877.2017.1422787.

Sheppard, B., G. J. Rubin, J. K. Wardman, and S. Wessely. 2006. "Terrorism and Dispelling the Myth of a Panic Prone Public." *Journal of Public Health Policy* 27 (3): 219–245. doi:10.1057/palgrave.jphp.3200083.

Sky News. 2020a. "Coronavirus: Jenny Harries Criticised for 'Patronising' Remark about 'Exemplar Preparedness'." *Sky News*, Monday, April 20, 05.58, UK. https://news.sky.com/story/coronavirus-jenny-harries-criticised-for-patronising-remark-about-exemplar-preparedness-11975652

Sky News. 2020b. Coronavirus: Cummings Row 'Undermines Trust in Government and More People will Die' – Scientist." *Sky News*, May 25. https://news.sky.com/story/scientific-experts-advising-government-criticise-boris-johnson-after-he-backed-dominic-cummings-11994132

Sky News. 2020c. "Coronavirus: 'I Speak Scientific Truth to Power' says Chief Scientific Adviser for England." *Sky News*, March 13. https://news.sky.com/video/coronavirus-i-speak-scientific-truth-to-power-says-chief-scientific-adviser-for-england-11956851

Smith, LauraG. E, and Stephen Gibson. 2020. "Social Psychological Theory and Research on the Novel Coronavirus Disease (COVID-19) Pandemic: Introduction to the Rapid Response Special Section." *British Journal of Social Psychology* 59 (3): 571–583. doi:10.1111/bjso.12402.

Spiegelhalter, D. 2020. "Use of "Normal" Risk to Improve Understanding of Dangers of Covid-19." *BMJ* 370: m3259.

Sridhar, D.2020. This is what you should be demanding from your government to contain the virus. Guardian 4 May. Accessed at: https://www.theguardian.com/commentisfree/2020/may/04/eight-lessons-controlling-corona-virus-east-asian-nations-pandemic-public-health

Tham, Y. C. 2020. "Transparency Key to Allaying People's Fears During Covid-19 Outbreak, Says DPM Heng." *Straits Times*, March 11, 19:16. https://www.straitstimes.com/politics/transparency-key-to-allaying-peoples-fears-during-covid-19-outbreak

Torjesen, I. 2020. "Covid-19: England Plan to Ease Lockdown is "Confusing" and "Risky," Say Doctors." *BMJ (Clinical Research ed.)"* 369: m1877.

Tucker, M., and A. Goldberg. 2020. "Coronavirus: Sports Events in March 'caused Increased Suffering and Death'. *BBC*, May 26. https://www.bbc.co.uk/news/uk-52797002

Turner, B. A., and N. F. Pidgeon. 1997. *Man-Made Disasters*. Oxford: Butterworth-Heinemann.

Van Bavel, J. J., K. Baicker, P. S. Boggio, V. Capraro, A. Cichocka, M. Cikara, M. J. Crockett, et al. 2020. "Using Social and Behavioural Science to Support COVID-19 Pandemic Response." *Nature Human Behaviour* 4: 460–471.

van Dick, Rolf, Jérémy E. Lemoine, Niklas K. Steffens, Rudolf Kerschreiter, Serap Arslan Akfirat, Lorenzo Avanzi, Kitty Dumont, et al. 2018. "Identity Leadership Going Global: Validation of the Identity Leadership Inventory across 20 Countries." *Journal of Occupational and Organizational Psychology* 91 (4): 697–728. doi:10.1111/joop.12223.

Wardman, J. K. 2006. "Toward a Critical Discourse on Affect and Risk Perception." *Journal of Risk Research* 9 (2): 109–124. doi:10.1080/13669870500454773.

Wardman, J. K. 2008. "The Constitution of Risk Communication in Advanced Liberal Societies." *Risk Analysis: An Official Publication of the Society for Risk Analysis* 28 (6): 1619–1637. doi:10.1111/j.1539-6924.2008.01108.x.

Wardman, J. K. 2014. "Sociocultural Vectors of Effective Risk Communication." *Journal of Risk Research* 17 (10): 1251–1257. doi:10.1080/13669877.2014.942498.

Wardman, J. K. 2017. "Nothing to Fear but Fear Itself? Liquid Provocations for New Media and Fear of Crime." In *The Routledge International Handbook on Fear of Crime*, edited by M. Lee and G. Mythen, 121–134. London: Routledge.

Wardman, J. K., and R. Löfstedt. 2018. "Anticipating or Accommodating to Public Concern? Risk Amplification and the Politics of Precaution Reexamined." *Risk Analysis: An Official Publication of the Society for Risk Analysis* 38 (9): 1802–1819. doi:10.1111/risa.12997.

Wardman, J. K., and R. Lofstedt. 2009. *European Food Safety Authority-Risk Communication Annual Review*. Parma: European Safety Authority.

Wardman, J. K., and G. Mythen. 2016. "Risk Communication: Against the Gods or against All Odds? Problems and Prospects of Accounting for Black Swans." *Journal of Risk Research* 19 (10): 1220–1230. doi:10.1080/13669877.2016.1262002.

Weale, S., and R. Adams. "Marcus Rashford in 'Despair' as MPs Reject Free School Meal Plan." *The Guardian*, October 21. https://www.theguardian.com/education/2020/oct/21/marcus-rashford-in-despair-as-mps-reject-free-school-meal-plan

Webler, T., and S. Tuler. 2018. "Four Decades of Public Participation in Risk Decision Making." *Risk Analysis*. doi:10.1111/risa.13250.

Wilson, S. 2020. "Pandemic Leadership: Lessons from New Zealand's Approach to COVID-19." *Leadership* 16 (3): 279–293. doi:10.1177/1742715020929151.

Woodcock, A. 2020. "Boris Johnson Rejects Demand for Urgent Inquiry into Government's Handling of Coronavirus Pandemic." *Independent*, June 23. https://www.independent.co.uk/news/uk/politics/boris-johnson-coronavirus-uk-government-independent-inquiry-a9581586.html

Index

Note: Figures are indicated by *italics*. Tables are indicated by **bold**. Endnotes are indicated by the page number followed by 'n' and the endnote number e.g., 20n1 refers to endnote 1 on page 20.

Risk Communication Advisory Committee 11
risk communicators 8, 138; Ebola and cholera 136–8, 140–1
risk comparisons 71, 73, 77, 82, 103, 117, 163, 169, 206, 207, 276; influenza 43–5
risk governance 2–3, 203, 243, 245
risk information seeking and processing model (RISP) 115–16, 118–19, 124, 125; affective risk response 117; attitude toward information sharing 118; informational subjective norms 117–18; and information sharing 116; perceived information-sharing capacity 118; sufficiency threshold 117
risk kitsch 204–9
risk management 189–90
risk perception 3, 19–20
risk science 19, 20
risk society 201–3, 251
Robert Koch Institute (RKI) 206, 210
role crafting 58–60, 64
root mean square error of approximation (RMSEA) 122, 153
Rottenstreich, Y. 25
Russia 57
Ryan, Mike 280

Salmon, C. T. 10
Sandman, P. M. 140
Santa Clara 44, 45
SARS-CoV-2 virus 209
Saudi Arabia 99
Schein, Edgar Henry 57
Schönhöfer, Peter 184
Scientific Advisory Group for Emergency (SAGE) 273
scientific consensus 17–18
sensitivity 36, 37, **37**, 42–3
serological antibody tests, Covid-19 35–7, 39, 44–5
serological surveys **40**
severe acute respiratory syndrome (SARS) 7, 48, 49, 51, 96, 147, 148, 170, 175, 176, 190, 207, 208, 217, 218, 241, 251, 253
Singapore: during crisis communication 191–2; early crisis communication 191; paradox of trust 195–6; pre-crisis communication 190–1; social media tracking 192–4; trust in the public 196; uncertainty communication and trust 196; Whatsapp focus group discussions 194–5
single information processing system 60–1
Slovic, Paul 7, 115, 163, 196
Snopes.com 221
social amplification of risk framework (SARF) 131–3, 139, 142, 164
social distancing 17, 190, 195; *Cura Italia* 56; and quarantine 56
social inequalities 254–6
socialization 57, 64; approaches, strategies and tools **65**; collective *vs.* individual 57–8; fixed *vs.*

variable 58; formal *vs.* informal 58; investiture *vs.* divestiture 58; newcomers of 57–8; sequential *vs.* random 58; serial *vs.* disjunctive 58
social media tracking 192–4
social mobilization 132, 137
social network analysis (SNA) 97, 103
social networking sites (SNS) 80; communication 81–2, 89, 91–2; emerging pandemics 81; misinformation 91; potential predictors 82; psychosocial factors 83–4; public health crisis 91, 92; risk perceptions and self-efficacy 84–5; socio-demographic factors 82–3; South Korea MERS 80–1
social sustainability 238
society for risk analysis (SRA) 21
socio-cognitive motivators: information-seeking research 124; literature review 114; perceived knowledge and sufficiency threshold 125; risk information sharing 124, 126; RISP model (*see* risk information seeking and processing (RISP) model); sufficiency threshold and information sharing 124
sociology 132
solidarity 278–80
South Korea 97, 167, 190
Spain 40, 57, 167, 169, 170, 242, 252, 281
specificity **37**
Spelsberg, Angela 184
Spiegelhalter, D. 269
spring-breakers 10
standardized root mean square residual (SRMR) 122, 153
Stango, V. 24
state capacity 242
statistics stalkers 10
'Stay Home—Stay Safe' 77
"Stop the Spread of Rumors" 221–2
Sub-Saharan Africa 130
Sunstein, C. R. 23–5
supply chain risk management, COVID-19 236–9
Sutcliffe, K. M. 50
Sweden 57, 167, 169, 199, 201, 203
swift role crafting 58–60
swift socialization 58
swift trust 61–3
swine flu 7
Switzerland 52, 207
syphilis 138, 140

Tam, Jonathan 268
team situation models (TSMs) 61
Thailand 217
thirteen pandemic risk leadership strategies and guidelines 263–6
Thompson, E. E. 141
Threat/Dread dimension 71, 76
This Time the Numbers Show We Can't Be Too Careful 27
tradeoffs 3, 6, 9–10, 12, 211

transactive memory systems 60–1
transboundary crises 49
transparency 7, 273–4
true positives 36
Trump, Donald 7, 49, 231
trust 6, 8, 9, 11, 12, 57, 62, 65, 84, 85, **87**, **88**, 164,
    165, 166–7, **168**, 170, 178, 183–4, 189–90, 197,
    201, 208, 223, 244, 274, 277–9; government 194;
    importance of 224; paradox of 195–6; problems
    of 225; public 196; social distancing 195;
    swift trust development 61; and uncertainty
    communication 196
Tucker-Lewis index (TLI) 122
Twitter 180, 191, 192–3, *193*; salience *192*

UK Biological Security Strategy, 2018 11
uncertainty 42–3; and contested knowledge 2;
    management theory 89; problem of 224
unfettered transparency 8
United Kingdom (UK) 6, 8, 12, 30, 40, 42, 53, 167,
    169, 170, 254, 261, 262, 276, 279, 281, 282
United States (US) 6, 8, 12, 23, 26, 39, 40, 45, 57, 76,
    167, 170, 217, 228, 242, 255

Vallance, Patrick 8
van der Linden, S. 163, 164
Van Maanen, John Eastin 57
Veterinary Services 143n1

vigilant role crafting 59
Vilhelmsson, Andreas 200
virtual evidence scenarios 43
Viva Italia party (part of the Government
    coalition) 180

Walker, B. 50
Weiboscope 216
Weick, K. E. 50
West African Health Organization (WAHO) 136, 137
West Nile virus 147, 148, 176, 184
Whitty, Chris 8, 268, 273
'Winter Willow' 266
Wolodarski, Peter 200
World Health Organization (WHO) 1, 6, 49, 77, 137,
    175, 178, 179, 181–3, 190, 215, 218, 220, 221, 243,
    252, 276, 277, 280, 281
World Risk Society 2, 201, 251
World Trade Center 26
Wuhan 1, 162–3, 175, 252

Xie, B. 164

Yang, J. Z. 117, 125

Zhuang, J. 117
Zika virus 48, 91, 96, 151
Zinman, J. 24